THE MANAGEMENT OF
IRISH INDUSTRY

This book reports the findings of a study carried out by the Irish Management Institute, during the period 1962-1966, into the needs and facilities for management education and training in Ireland.

The study consisted of a sample survey of 141 industrial firms and of a complete survey of educational institutions.

This report establishes, for the first time, the number of managers in Irish industry, their positions and levels, their academic background, their participation in management training, their age and nationality.

It forecasts the annual requirement for managers up to 1970, outlines their expressed training needs and describes the current standard of managerial practice in the fields of marketing, production, finance, personnel and general management.

Finally it describes in detail the existing institutions for both professional and management education and training, gives the opinions of managers about these facilities, and estimates their likely use of them.

On the basis of the facts outlined in this volume, the Consultative Board of the Irish Management Institute will make recommendations on a national policy for education and training for management.

These recommendations will issue as a separate publication.

The Management of Irish Industry

THE MANAGEMENT OF IRISH INDUSTRY

A Research Report by the Irish Management Institute

BREFFNI TOMLIN
Research Executive

HD
70
.I7 I7
1966

Designed by Bill Murphy MSIA

Printed in the Republic of Ireland
by Mount Salus Press Limited, Dublin 4

Foreword

Michael Rigby-Jones
Chairman
Irish Management Institute

*The Report of the Joint Committee on Education and Training for Management
was published in 1956. The Report of the Review Committee, successor to the Joint
Committee, was published in 1962. The Review Committee was representative of the
organisations in Ireland concerned with management education and training. Though
the Committee in its report made major recommendations to its constituent bodies,
it felt that the long term development of management education and training must
be based not on a consensus of opinion but on objective research into the educational
and training needs of Irish management.*

*This book is the result of a recommendation of the Review Committee. It marks a
significant development in the work of the Institute. It will be a basis for the
Institute's Consultative Board in formulating a co-ordinated policy for management
education and training in Ireland.*

*Since the book is the first study of its scope to be undertaken in any country it is our
hope that it will be read widely not only in Ireland but by all those concerned with the
development of the science and practice of management.*

*The Institute is grateful to the many managers and organisations who co-operated
so willingly to make the report possible. I should like to express to them our appreciation
and to thank in particular An Foras Talúntais for use of their computer and the
Central Statistics Office for providing us with essential lists of firms.*

*I wish to thank the Department of Industry and Commerce for financial help
with the project.*

*And I should like to thank Mr. Breffni Tomlin, the Institute's Research Executive,
who conducted the research and wrote this book.*

Dublin October 1966

Acknowledgements

In the course of this study over two hundred managers of industrial firms and officers of educational organisations were interviewed. I should like to thank them for the courtesy with which they received me and for their frankness and patience in answering my questions.

I wish to thank Dr. Max Adler, Director of Education of the College of Marketing and Mr. Dermot Harrington, Acting Head of the Statistical Department of An Foras Talúntais, for their assistance at two crucial stages of the project: the research and questionnaire design and the planning of the analysis. Mr. Alan Stuart of London University gave valuable guidance on some aspects of statistical testing. My thanks are due also to Miss Mary McCarthy, formerly of I.B.M. (Ireland) Ltd., who wrote the programmes for the analysis and supervised the processing of the data.

I should like to express my gratitude to the following authors and publishers for permission to reproduce material from their publications: Professor Raymond V. Lesikar, Professor Albert K. Wickesberg and the Small Business Administration, Washington D.C. (Education for Leadership in Small Business and Organizational Relationships in the Growing Small Manufacturing Firm); Professor M. Woitrin and l'Office Belge pour l'Accroissement de la Productivité, Brussels, (Les Dirigeants d'Entreprise de l'Economie Belge); Miss J. Woodward and the Oxford University Press, London, (Industrial Organisation: Theory and Practice).

Finally I should like to thank the Chairman and members of the Consultative Board and my colleagues on the staff of the Institute for their help in bringing this work to completion.

Breffni Tomlin.

TABLE OF CONTENTS

PART I

The Present Numerical Position

PART II

The Need for Education and Training

PART III

Facilities for Education and Training

PART IV

Technical Appendices

Glossary of Terms

Population

Research studies are often concerned with a totality of objects, in this case all the managers in Irish industry. Such a totality is referred to as a population or universe.

Sample

In many cases sufficient resources are not available to allow every member of the population to be studied. In such cases it is usual to select a section of the population in the expectation that conclusions arrived at by studying the section will hold true for the population in general. Such a selection from a population is called a sample.

Random Sampling

Unless all members of the population are exactly alike the process of sampling introduces some degree of uncertainty into conclusions about the population as a whole. It is the concern of statistical theory to measure this degree of uncertainty and to allow it to be reduced to tolerable limits. A fundamental requirement if this is to be done is that the sample be drawn at random, that is to say the members of the population to be included in the sample must be selected by chance, and each one must have an equal chance of being selected

Confidence Limits

Samples are drawn either to estimate some population value or to allow some hypothesis about the population to be tested. Wherever an estimate is made in any table in this book, it is usually accompanied by a range of variation showing the limits between which the true population figure almost certainly lies. These limits are called confidence limits.[1] The larger the sample the narrower the limits become but the greater becomes the cost of the survey. Sample design aims at achieving the best balance between precision and cost.

Where the whole population is studied, as in the top size-stratum in this survey, it is unnecessary either to attach confidence limits to estimates or to carry out tests of significance.

Statistical Significance

A hypothesis is put forward about the population and a sample drawn to see if there is any evidence that the hypothesis is true. Statistical tests exist to show whether the sample provides sufficient evidence to say that what is true of the sample is almost certainly true of the population. A hypothesis always involves differences between groups: if the test is positive the differences are said to be statistically significant.[2] This means that the sample results signified that the difference observed between groups in the sample existed also in the population. It does not mean that the differences in the population were large or of practical importance, merely that some difference existed.

As in the case of confidence limits, the larger the sample the more confident one may be that a given difference is significant but again the cost of a larger sample must be weighed against its greater power.

In this book quite substantial differences sometimes appear between sample members which a statistical test shows not to be significant. This lack of significance does not necessarily imply that no difference exists in the population; it may mean that the sample was too small to say with any certainty that a difference did exist.[3]

Technical Notes

1. Use of confidence limits depends on certain underlying assumptions about the nature of the population. These assumptions are not usually met by the data on managers. It is better to treat the ranges of variation shown in estimates made about managers as indications of the magnitude of sampling variability rather than as strict confidence limits.

2. The significance level used throughout is $p = 0.05$.

3. This would not arise if one specified in advance what size difference one wished to establish as significant and selected a sample sufficiently large to give a significant result if a difference of the desired size were found. This was not possible in the present survey because, being a pioneer study, the relative frequency in the population of characteristics to be used as a basis of classification was unknown. The results of the present study can be used to pre-plan future surveys so as to avoid "not proven" verdicts.

Introduction

This book gives the findings of a research project carried out by the Irish Management Institute. The project had two objectives. One was to provide the facts, based on a study of the needs and facilities for education and training for management in Ireland, which would enable the Consultative Board of the Irish Management Institute to make policy recommendations to the constituent bodies of the Board. The other was to provide information on which the Institute could act in planning its own training activities.

The introduction is in two sections. Section I gives a short description of the project and how it was carried out; section II is a description of Irish industry, its background, structure and size. Section I is essentially a summary for the general reader of material given in more complete form in the technical appendix at the back of this volume.

Section I. Objectives and Methodology of the Study.

Background to the Project

The Irish Management Institute was founded in 1952 with the objective of raising the standard of management in Ireland.

In 1956 a committee of the Institute, examining the facilities for management training in Ireland, recommended changes to the various bodies involved — universities and vocational education authorities — and further recommended that the Institute set up a small management development unit.

This was done and, in December 1960, a committee, representative of all interests, sat to review progress towards the implementation of the recommendations. This Review Committee issued a report in 1962 which, besides recommending that the Institute's training activities and staff be expanded, stated that a long-term national policy on education and training for management was necessary and that an investigation should be carried out to provide the facts on which this policy would be based.

It recommended that ". . . the investigation . . . consist of identifying the educational needs of management in Ireland, of studying the facilities for education for management and of preparing a long-term plan for management education for the country." [1]

When the Institute commenced its training activities a Consultative Board, representative of industry and educational bodies, was formed to advise on the training programme. As it was the only body on which the various interests dealing with management education formally met, its scope widened so that, instead of simply advising on the Institute's work, the Board now provides a forum for discussion on the work of all the bodies represented.

It was therefore decided that the Board should make recommendations, based on

---

1. Irish Management Institute. *Education and Training for Management*. Report of the Review Committee. Dublin: IMI, 1962 (page 8).

this investigation, for a national policy for education and training for management. This book is a statement of the facts about needs and facilities. The Board's recommendations based on these facts will issue as a separate volume.

Resources

It had originally been thought that the research project might cost £5,000 and take about two years to complete. The Department of Industry and Commerce gave a grant of £2,500 for the work. It was in the context of resources of this order of magnitude that the research design was evolved. In the event the project took four years to complete and cost about £14,000. A breakdown of the time-scale of the project and of the cost is given in technical appendix A.

The Research Problem

As stated by the Review Committee, the study had two foci — needs and facilities. The problem was to design a project to investigate both within the confines of the available resources of money, time and skill. Skill was an important element as the author, whose training was in economics, was the only one working on the project: the Institute had not at that time appointed specialist teaching staff, nor were there in the country any students of business studies at graduate level.

The question of needs had two aspects, one related to numbers of managers and one to the education and training needed to improve managerial performance.

On the quantitative side it was considered necessary to establish the present number of managers and various facts about them, such as their educational background and age, and also to estimate the future numerical requirements caused by growth, retirement, death and other losses. Because there were not sufficient published data it was decided to carry out a sample survey of Irish managers to collect the necessary information. The only feasible way to sample the population of Irish managers was to sample the firms for which they worked.[1] As resources were limited it was first decided to confine the sample to firms with over twenty employees, a preliminary survey having shown that this was a rough dividing line between firms with one manager and firms with more than one. A later decision was to limit the coverage to industry and to omit all other business activity, both to use the available resources to best advantage and because it proved impossible to construct a worthwhile sampling frame for non-industrial firms.

The sampled firms were to be visited so as to avoid the bias which arises in using postal questionnaires through returns being made by the more progressive firms and through faulty answering.

The evolution of a design to cover the quantitative side of management needs thus presented few difficulties in principle. Evolving a design to investigate management's training needs was not so simple. An obvious way was to ask managers what they considered their needs to be, and to ask for the opinion of those in a position to observe needs, for instance industrial consultants. It was decided that it was necessary but not sufficient to do both: not sufficient because managers might be unable to perceive their own needs or be unwilling to state them, and because consultants' clients might not be representative of industry as a whole.

The problem arose of finding a method of assessing more objectively the training needs of management, bearing in mind the author's background, the resources available and the fact that a decision had been made to conduct interviews in a large sample of

1. See glossary of terms for a definition of the terms 'population', 'sample', 'random sample'.

firms in order to collect numerical data. There is a detailed description in the technical appendix of all the approaches tried and rejected before it was decided that the only feasible way to obtain an objective addition to managers' opinions was to use the sample of firms being visited to estimate how far some of the more widely-applicable techniques of management now available were being used in Irish industry. It was felt that reasonably valid inductions could be made about the training needs of management by finding to what extent the present body of knowledge was being used in Irish firms.

The aspect of management investigated by this method was the use of improved techniques of decision-making. The whole area of interpersonal relations was omitted because of the difficulty of studying it and the lack of trained staff. This point is discussed in technical appendix A.

It had been hoped in the survey to get opinions from each manager in the firms visited, and also to interview managers in different functions. Testing proved this to be impossible with the available resources, particularly of time, as questionnaires were almost never completed if sent before, or left after, the firm was visited. It was also unusual to be able to arrange to have all the necessary executives available for interview on a given day. The interviews were therefore conducted with one individual, usually the chief executive, but sometimes another executive senior enough to be a satisfactory substitute for the purposes of the study. All opinions expressed are those of one executive in each firm, at or near chief executive level.

The other major focus of the project was on facilities. A decision was made to collect information from all concerned with providing education and training for professions relevant to management, as well as those providing management training *per se*. One of the many criteria for assessing the adequacy of these facilities (which the Institute's Consultative Board will have to do in framing its recommendations) is the opinions managers have about them. It was therefore decided to use the sample survey to collect the opinions of chief executives on existing facilities, and their preferences for, and likely use of, various suggested facilities.

The Research Design

The final design decided on was to conduct interviews with a sample of firms in transportable-goods industry employing over 20 people and, using a structured questionnaire (reproduced in technical appendix C), to obtain the following information from the chief executive of each firm visited:

1. The number of managers in the firm and a variety of facts concerning them such as their educational background, age, function and level in the firm, nationality and experience of management training.

2. The firm's requirement for managers arising out of growth, retirement, etc.

3. His opinions on his firm's training needs.

4. The use by the firm of various techniques of management.

5. His opinions on facilities, existing or projected, his preferences for and likely use of them.

Information would also be collected by visiting those responsible for providing professional and management education and training.

Various additions were contemplated but not carried out because of the time taken to complete the execution and analysis of the basic design.

Design of the Sample

It had originally been intended to cover in the study managers in all branches of economic activity outside agriculture. A breakdown by sector of the total working population is shown in table 1 below.

TABLE 1.   *Total at Work in 1961, by Sector of Economy.*

Sector of Economy		Total at Work	Total in Private Business Activity[1]	Number of Establishments with 20 or more Employees	Number Employed in Establishments >20
	Agriculture	376,272	—	—	—
	Fishing	2,460		n.a.	n.a.
Transportable goods — Mining, etc.		9,640	9,640		
Industry — Transportable goods — Manufacturing		179,436	179,436	1,299[2]	126,878[2]
Building and Construction		59,587	38,635	n.a.	n.a.
Service — Electricity, gas and water		10,172	9,651	n.a.	n.a.
	Commerce	143,195	143,195	679[3]	33,650[3]
	Insurance, Banking etc.	14,239	14,239	n.a.	n.a.
	Transport, Communications and Storage	54,167	35,637	n.a.	n.a.
	Public Administration & Defence	40,580	—	—	—
	Professions	85,952	19,951	n.a.	n.a.
	Personal Service	63,314	30,087	n.a.	n.a.
	Entertainment and Sport	10,986	10,986	n.a.	n.a.
	Other	2,539	—	—	—
	Total	1,052,539	491,457	—	—

n.a. means " not available ".

1.   Refers to economic activity outside agriculture, carried on by private firms or individuals, or by State-financed but autonomous enterprises. Excludes non-agricultural activity by central or local government.

2.   In 1958, by respondents to the Census of Industrial Production.

3.   In 1956, by respondents to the Census of Distribution.

Source: Col. 1 & 2.   *Census of Population* 1961. Dublin: The Stationery Office, 1964 (Vol. IV, tables 1 and 9).
         Col. 3 & 4.   *Irish Trade Journal and Statistical Bulletin.* Dublin: Central Statistics Office, Supplement to December 1962 issue.
         Census of Distribution 1956-1959. Dublin: The Stationery Office, 1962 (tables 6 and 59).

It can be seen that industry is the most important non-agricultural economic activity, though followed closely by commerce (retail and wholesale distribution plus a few other smaller activities). If only those working in firms with over 20 employees are included, industry's dominance becomes more marked. Tables AII and AIII of technical appendix A show that industry is scheduled to grow in relative importance with the passage of time. Within industry, the transportable goods sub-sector, i.e. mining and manufacture, is most important.

The Central Statistics Office conducts two censuses of business, the Census of Industrial Production, carried out continuously and covering roughly the industrial sector as shown in table 1, and the Census of Distribution last carried out in 1956 (another one is now being conducted) which covered roughly the same area as commerce in table 1. It was hoped that, as a result of these censuses, lists of firms would be available from which a sample could be drawn, excluding firms with less than 20 employees. The Central Statistics Office was unable to provide lists indicating size for firms in distribution, but was able to give a complete up-to-date listing of all establishments in transportable goods industry, showing the size-group in which they fell. An attempt was made by writing to trade associations to construct lists for distributive firms and others not covered by either census, but it proved impossible to do so. The decision was therefore made to confine the survey to firms employing 20 or more people in transportable goods industry in the Republic of Ireland. The sample was drawn from a list covering that population and provided by the Central Statistics Office in mid-1963. Firms in the Shannon industrial zone were deliberately excluded from the list sampled, as it was felt that they were untypical of industry in the rest of the country. At the time the list was constructed there were 12 such firms employing a total of 1,200 people. These numbers have since grown considerably.

Two main questions arise in designing a sample. They are: what sort of sample to use and what size sample is necessary? The laws of statistical theory enable the results of sample surveys to be interpreted with a known degree of confidence only if samples are drawn at random; there must be no deliberate selection of firms for inclusion or any other form of bias. But many sorts of random sample can be designed, some more efficient than others in that they give narrower confidence limits for estimates made on the basis of the sample.[1] When dealing with highly-variable data it is often better first to break the population into different sections, called strata, and to select a sample at random from each stratum. That was done in this study, the population being divided into three groups — firms employing at least 500 people, firms with 100 to 499 employees and firms with 20 to 99 employees.

It was decided that a total sample of about 150 firms would give an acceptable balance between cost and precision. So few firms employed over 500 people that it was decided to visit them all. One-fifth of the firms employing 100 to 499 people were selected, and one firm in twenty employing 20 to 99 people. The total number of such firms, the number sampled, and the number with which interviews were completed are shown in table 2 below. The reasons for selecting a sample of this size from each stratum and the sample design in general are discussed at greater length in technical appendix A. Stratifying the sample produced considerable gains in this case; the results obtained were four times as precise as would have been achieved with a sample of the same size which had not been stratified.

TABLE 2.   *Allocation of Firms to Strata.*

Size of Firm (No. of Employees)	Number of Firms	Allocation	Number Responding
20-99	946	47	46
100-499	256	51	48
500 or More	47	47	47
	1,249	145	141

1.   See glossary of terms for an explanation of the term 'confidence limits'.

The sample selected was tested to see how representative it was of industry as a whole. On every count — industrial classification, location, and membership of the Irish Management Institute — it reflected the population almost exactly, as tables A VIII to A X of technical appendix A demonstrate.

Collecting and Processing the Information.

Considerable care was taken in approaching firms, first writing and then telephoning to confirm each appointment. The result was almost 100 per cent response (see table 2).

Interviews were carried out during 1964 by the author, using a closely structured questionnaire designed to allow machine-processing of the results.

Because of the great volume of data, the large number of estimates to be made, and the number of tests to be performed, it was planned from the beginning that the data would be analysed by computer. The processing was carried out by the service bureau of I.B.M. Ireland Limited on a model 1401, and necessitated the writing of original programmes described briefly in the technical appendix. These programmes may be made available by the Irish Management Institute to other research institutions on request.

Layout of Book

The body of the book is in three parts. There is in addition a number of technical appendices in which there is an extended discussion of the design and analysis of the project.

Part I consists of chapters 1-9 and gives a detailed picture of the numerical situation at January 1st, 1964, the base date of the survey. Chapter 1 deals with the total number of managers, chapter 2 with their division by function, chapter 3 with level, and so on to chapter 7 dealing with nationality. Chapters 8 and 9 are concerned with inter-relationships between the characteristics discussed singly in chapters 2-7.

Part II deals with the needs of Irish firms. Chapter 10 discusses numerical needs due to growth, etc. Chapter 11 is concerned with what chief executives expressed as the training needs of their firms. Chapters 12-15 deal with the current standard of management practice in each of the areas of marketing, production, finance and personnel management and with the impact on it of the circumstances of the firm and of various methods of raising the standard of management. Chapter 16 summarises the position and attempts an international comparison.

Part III is about facilities. The existing facilities are outlined in chapter 17, and the opinions of the executives interviewed and firms' past practices with respect to facilities are given in chapter 18.

There is a summary of the main findings at the beginning of each chapter, and of detailed findings in each sub-section of a chapter.

Section 2.   A Description of Irish Industry

Industry in Ireland is small, new, highly diversified, not technologically advanced and largely concentrated in Dublin.

In late 1963 there were about 3,000 separate firms in transportable goods industry.[1]

---

1   A firm is defined as a separate legal entity, i.e. if there are several firms under common ownership, but each having a distinct legal identity, each is counted separately.

Of these, only 47 employed over 500 people, 256 employed between 100 and 500, while 946 employed between 20 and 100. The remaining 1,800 or so all employed less than 20.

Much of Irish industry is comparatively new, owing its inception to Government measures, either through protection in the 1930s and 1940s, or through the encouragement of foreign participation since the later 1950s. One hundred and forty-one firms were visited in the course of this survey and, as stated in section 1, they were very representative of Irish industry as a whole. Of the 47 firms employing over 500 people, 30 had been founded since 1930 and, of these, 27 had been set up as a direct result of protection or State encouragement. Twenty-five of the 48 firms employing between 100 and 500 people had also been started since 1930, as had 23 of the firms with less than 100 employees.

Of the remaining 63 firms which were longer-established, 12 had enjoyed some measure of protection. Of the other 51, thirty were food-processing companies.

The policy of industrialisation was therefore successful in diversifying a structure from one almost solely concerned with processing agricultural products to one in which most forms of industrial activity are represented. Food-processing remains the dominant industry and, although there has been a large measure of diversification, industry remains predominantly light. The complete absence of raw materials has meant that Ireland does not have the highly-developed chemical, metallurgical and metal fabricating industries of industrially more advanced countries. Table 3 shows that textiles, clothing and metal and engineering come next in importance to food. Most of the metal and engineering firms are light metal-fabricators or assemblers. Apart from having the greatest number of firms, these four industries have the greatest number of employees and, except for drink and tobacco, also lead in the size of their output.[1]

Table 3 shows that there is a considerable concentration of industry in the Dublin area. (For the purposes of this survey Dublin was defined as Dublin County plus anywhere outside Dublin County served by a scheduled city bus route. Cork was defined as Cork City plus surrounding villages within a ten-mile radius.) Textiles and food-processing are about the most widely-dispersed industries geographically, while textiles has the highest proportion of large units. In the 100 to 499 employee size-group there is a greater concentration of printing and engineering firms in Dublin than elsewhere. In the 20 to 99 employee group the largest industry in Dublin is clothing. This reflects Dublin's position as the capital and the centre of the fashion trade. Outside Dublin food-processing is dominant.

Firms with under 20 employees (not shown in table 3) are much more widely dispersed and over one-third of them, including a large number of small creameries, are engaged in food-processing.

While it is true that only about 10 per cent of Irish industrial companies employ over 100 people, and less than 2 per cent employ more than 500, this small number of companies employs the majority of workers in industry and accounts for the greater part of total industrial output, as table 4 shows.

---

1. A detailed analysis of Irish industry was published as a supplement to the December 1962 issue of the *Irish Trade Journal and Statistical Bulletin,* published by the Central Statistics Office. A commentary on the analysis by Mr. T. P. Linehan is available as a reprint from the 1961-'62 *Journal of the Statistical and Social Inquiry Society of Ireland.*

Table 3. The Number of Firms Engaged in Each Industry, by Size of Firm and Location of its Head Office.

Size of Firm (No. of employees)	Location of Head Office	MAIN INDUSTRY[1]											
		Extraction	Food	Drink & Tobacco	Textiles	Clothing & Footwear	Wood & Furniture	Paper & Printing	Chemicals	Glass & Clay	Metals & Engineering	Miscellaneous	Total
500 or more	Dublin	2	9	3	1	—	—	6	1	2	5	1	30
	Cork	—	—	—	2	—	—	—	—	—	3	—	5
	Limerick												
	Waterford												
	Dundalk												
	Drogheda	—	1	1	1	2	—	—	—	1	—	—	6
	Rest of Country	—	—	—	4	—	—	—	—	1	1	—	6
	TOTAL:	2	10	4	8	2	—	6	1	4	9	1	47
100–499	Dublin	—	21	7	18	25	6	13	5	6	21	2	124
	Cork	1	6	3	6	4	—	3	1	—	2	1	27
	Limerick												
	Waterford												
	Dundalk												
	Drogheda	—	8	—	3	10	1	1	1	—	4	—	28
	Rest of Country	5	19	4	19	14	—	2	2	1	7	4	77
	TOTAL:	6	54	14	46	53	7	19	9	7	34	7	256
20–99	Dublin	2	54	9	40	137	39	50	34	12	74	39	490
	Cork	1	17	3	4	12	12	2	4	2	9	2	68
	Limerick												
	Waterford												
	Dundalk												
	Drogheda	—	15	1	3	2	6	10	4	—	6	2	49
	Rest of Country	23	116	15	38	23	31	28	5	12	30	18	339
	TOTAL:	26	202	28	85	174	88	90	47	26	119	61	946

1 Several firms have factories producing goods in more than one industry. These firms were assigned to the industry in which the greatest number of their workers was employed.

Source: Compiled from lists supplied by the Central Statistics Office in 1963, and which formed the sampling frame for the present inquiry.

TABLE 4.   *Relative Importance of each Size-Group.*

Average No. of Persons Engaged per establishment	No. of Establish-ments	Gross Output	Materials used	Net Output	Wages and Salaries	Remainder of Net Output	Average No. of persons engaged
			Percentage				
Under 15	50.1	7.0	7.4	5.9	5.9	6.0	7.6
15-99	40.1	29.1	29.3	28.5	29.9	26.9	33.4
100-499	8.8	40.5	41.6	37.9	38.8	36.8	38.2
500 and over	1.0	23.4	21.7	27.7	25.4	30.3	20.9
TOTAL	100.0	100.0	100.0	100.0	100.0	100.0	100.0

Note that these figures relate to employment by *establishments*, i.e. individual factories, and not to *firms*, any of which may have several factories. If figures were shown for firms they would indicate that the relevant importance of large companies is even greater than table 4 suggests.

Source : T. P. Linehan, "The Structure of Irish Industry", *Journal of the Statistical and Social Inquiry Society of Ireland*, 1961/62, p. 222.

Between 1938 and 1958 the number of establishments with over 100 employees grew from 225 to 304 and their number of employees from 53,800 to 83,700, i.e. from 53 per cent of the industrial labour force to 59 per cent. There is some evidence from the present sample of 141 firms that this process of concentration is continuing, and that by 1964 as many as 66 per cent of all employees were in firms of 100 or more people. According to the sample, firms with over 500 employees then accounted for one-third of all employees, so that their relative importance has risen very considerably.

Table 5 shows that, although the size-structure of Irish industry does not differ greatly from that of other countries, there is still a long way to go before factories of over 1,000 people employ such a high proportion of the labour force as in other countries : Ireland still lacks the comparative handful of giant companies which dominate other economies.

It is possible as a result of the present survey to say something of the ownership, type of market served and type of production-process of Irish firms.

The executives interviewed were asked whether their firms were either family-owned or subsidiaries of foreign companies. On the basis of the replies the estimates shown in table 6 were made. It is probable that the newer foreign-owned companies established since the late 1950s are under-represented in the sample (firms in the Shannon industrial zone were deliberately excluded from the sampled population). In addition several firms had a close association with foreign companies, though not owned by them. The degree of foreign participation in Irish industry is therefore almost certainly underestimated in table 6.

Most Irish firms are family-owned, but the proportion decreases steadily with increasing size so that over 75 per cent of firms with more than 500 employees are public companies. The proportion of foreign-owned firms is low but, unlike family ownership, foreign ownership becomes more likely with increasing size.

TABLE 5.   *Size Structure of Manufacturing Industry in Some European Countries.*
(Establishments with 10 (*a*) or more persons engaged).

Note—The data on which this table is based have been derived from various year-books, official reports etc. and relate to 1958 except as follows:—U.K. 1954; Holland 1957; Italy 1951; Belgium 1947; Norway 1960.

Country	Number of persons engaged						
	(*a*) 10–50	50– 100	100– 200	200– 500	500– 1,000	1,000 and over	Total
	Number of Establishments						
Northern Ireland ...	610	235	168	135(*c*)	29(*c*)	16(*c*)	1,193
West Germany (*b*) ...	28,527	9,095	5,815	4,143	1,304	916	49,800
United Kingdom ...	31,558	10,826	7,162	5,076	1,534	1,054	57,210
Holland (*d*)	6,742	1,790	921	517	194	134	10,298
Italy	22,293	3,907	3,383		436	274	30,293
France	38,829	6,863	4,045	2,554	738	387	53,416
Sweden (*e*)	5,960	1,072	575	379	112	53	8,151
Ireland	1,350	291	161	112	26	5	1,945
Belgium (*e*)	8,849	1,363	812	511	123	50	11,708
Norway	4,123	614	290	173	65		5,265
	Percentage Distribution of Number of Establishments						
Northern Ireland ...	51.1	19.7	14.1	11.3(*c*)	2.4(*c*)	1.3(*c*)	100
West Germany (*b*) ...	57.3	18.3	11.7	8.3	2.6	1.8	100
United Kingdom ...	55.1	18.9	12.5	8.9	2.7	1.8	100
Holland (*d*)	65.5	17.4	8.9	5.0	1.9	1.3	100
Italy	73.6	12.9	11.2		1.4	0.9	100
France	72.7	12.8	7.6	4.8	1.4	0.7	100
Sweden (*e*)	73.1	13.2	7.1	4.7	1.4	0.7	100
Ireland	69.4	15.0	8.3	5.8	1.3	0.3	100
Belgium (*e*)	75.6	11.6	6.9	4.4	1.1	0.4	100
Norway	78.3	11.7	5.5	3.3	1.2		100
	Percentage Distribution of Number of Persons Engaged						
Northern Ireland ...	9.2	9.8	14.5	24.0(*c*)	11.4(*c*)	31.2(*c*)	100
West Germany (*b*) ...	10.4	9.5	12.1	19.2	13.4	35.3	100
United Kingdom ...	10.4	10.0	13.1	20.3	13.7	32.5	100
Holland (*d*)	14.7	11.2	12.1	15.0	12.4	34.7	100
Italy	20.8	11.8	30.1		13.0	24.4	100
France (*f*)	21.4	12.0	14.2	19.4	12.7	20.2	100
Sweden (*e*)	22.6	12.7	13.7	19.4	13.3	18.3	100
Ireland	23.1	15.2	16.0	23.9	13.4	8.4	100
Belgium (*e*)	25.7	13.3	15.9	21.8	11.7	11.5	100
Norway	30.5	15.2	14.1	18.8	21.4		100

(*a*) Eleven persons for Northern Ireland, United Kingdom, Italy, Sweden and France.
(*b*) Excluding Saarland and Berlin.
(*c*) Breakdown between three largest size groups is estimated.
(*d*) The unit is the enterprise, not the establishment.
(*e*) Classification is on the basis of number of wage-earners, and total shown is number of wage-earners (excluding proprietors and salaried).
(*f*) Estimated from number of establishments above and from average sizes in each class for other countries.

Source: T. P. Linehan, "The Structure of Irish Industry," *Journal of the Statistical and Social Inquiry Society of Ireland*, 1961/62, p. 245.

TABLE 6. *The Ownership of Irish Industry, by Size of Firm.*

Size of Firm (No. of Employees)	Estimated Percentage	
	Family-Owned	Foreign-Owned
500 or more	24.7	27.7
100-499	45.8	10.4
20-99	76.1	8.7
Overall	68.0	9.7

Firms were asked whether their goods were sold to domestic consumers or to industry, and whether they were sold locally only, regionally only, nationally, or exported. A firm was classified as exporting if any proportion of its output, however small, was regularly sold outside the Republic of Ireland. Table 7 was constructed from their replies. "Other" firms in table 7 are firms engaged exclusively in repair work or selling all their output to a parent company.

TABLE 7. *The Percentage of Irish Companies Serving Markets of Specified Type, by Size of Firm.*

Size of Firm (No. of Employees)	Type of Goods	Local	Regional	National	Export	Other	Total
500 or More	Consumer	—	4.3	6.4	48.9	—	59.6
	Industrial	—	—	2.1	31.9	2.1	36.1
	Other	—	—	—	—	4.3	4.3
	Total	—	4.3	8.5	80.8	6.4	100.0
100-499	Consumer	4.2	4.2	14.6	41.7	—	64.6
	Industrial	4.2	4.2	8.3	16.7	—	33.3
	Other	—	—	—	—	2.1	2.1
	Total	8.4	8.4	22.9	58.4	2.1	100.0
20-99	Consumer	10.9	6.5	26.1	21.7	2.2	67.5
	Industrial	4.3	2.1	8.7	15.2	2.2	32.5
	Other	—	—	—	—	—	—
	Total	15.2	8.6	34.8	36.9	4.4	100.0
Overall	Consumer	9.1	6.0	23.0	26.9	1.6	66.6
	Industrial	4.1	2.5	8.4	16.1	1.7	32.8
	Other	—	—	—	—	0.5	0.5
	Total	13.2	8.5	31.4	43.0	3.8	100.0

Percentages do not add to 100 *because of rounding*

In every size-group firms selling consumer-goods are in a majority. Most companies in every size-group sell at least nationally and often export: the proportion of firms exporting rises with size of firm, but a substantial proportion of firms with under 100 employees sell abroad. There appears to be a slight tendency among larger and smaller firms for manufacturers of industrial goods to be more likely to export than firms making consumer-goods, but among small firms the difference is not statistically significant[1].

Firms selling industrial goods were confined mainly to the extraction (i.e. mining, quarrying and peat-production), textiles, paper and printing, and metal and engineering industries. The industries with the highest proportion of exporters were food, textiles, clothing and metal and engineering.

The typical Irish firm therefore, is one selling consumer-goods on at least a national scale, and often exporting.

Firms were asked whether they manufactured by fabricating, i.e. making and assembling piece-parts, or by processing, or whether they simply assembled or packaged goods made elsewhere.[2]

They were also asked whether they mostly made goods to customers' specification or whether they had standard products and, if the latter, whether they made goods continuously or in batches. Their replies are analysed in table 8.

TABLE 8.   *Estimated Percentage of Irish Firms Manufacturing in Specified Ways, by Size of Firm.*

Size of Firm (No. of Employees)	Type of Manufacture	Type of Production					Total
		Order	Batch	Continuous	Repair	Other	
500 or more	Fabrication	4.3	14.9	2.1	—	—	21.3
	Processing	8.5	36.1	23.4	—	—	68.0
	Other	—	2.1	4.3	4.3	—	10.7
	Total	12.8	53.1	27.8	4.3	—	100.0
100-499	Fabrication	2.1	20.8	2.1	—	—	25.0
	Processing	2.1	35.4	27.1	2.1	—	66.7
	Other	—	2.1	2.1	—	4.2	8.4
	Total	4.2	58.3	31.3	2.1	4.2	100.0
20-99	Fabrication	6.5	28.3	2.2	—	—	37.0
	Processing	13.0	28.3	19.6	—	—	60.9
	Other	—	2.2	—	—	—	2.2
	Total	19.5	58.8	21.8	—	—	100.0
Overall	Fabrication	5.5	26.2	2.1	—	—	33.9
	Processing	10.6	30.0	21.2	0.4	—	62.3
	Other	—	2.1	0.6	0.2	0.8	3.7
	Total	16.1	58.3	23.9	0.6	0.8	100.0

Percentages do not add to 100 because of rounding

1 See glossary of terms for an explanation of 'statistical significance'.

2 In their book *Anatomy of Automation* (Englewood Cliffs, N.J. Prentice-Hall Inc., 1962) Amber & Amber define processing (page 32) as "manufacture by continuous means, or by a continuous series of operations, for a specific purpose . . . . The process industries are those that treat a more or less continuous product, not made up from individual parts, though various ingredients may be used."

Most firms in each size-group were engaged in processing. Fabrication is confined almost exclusively to the clothing, wood-working and metal and engineering industries. The high proportion of clothing firms in the 20 to 99 size-group explains its higher-than-average proportion of fabricating companies. The dominant type of production was batch production, but processing firms showed a greater tendency than fabricating firms to have achieved continuous production and also, surprisingly, to make to customers' specifications. This tendency for processing firms to make to specification was largely due to those firms in the textile and paper and printing industries.

To summarise the foregoing, the typical Irish company is small, family-owned, possibly founded since 1930, processing goods in batches for sale to consumers on a national scale, and quite likely to be exporting as well. The facts outlined in this section should be borne in mind when studying the behaviour of firms in Irish industry and when comparing it with industry in other countries. Comparison is often made unfairly between the behaviour of Irish companies and that of much larger firms abroad. It is a useful corrective to keep relative size in mind and to make comparisons only between firms of the same size in different countries[1].

---

1. But see the discussion following Linehan's paper referred to at table 6 above, in which it is suggested that productivity may be lower in Irish companies, size for size, than in companies abroad.

PART I

The Present Numerical Position

CHAPTER 1

The Number of Managers in Industry

The purpose of this chapter is to estimate the total number of managers in Irish industry[1], showing the number in each of three size-groups, in firms based in Dublin and outside Dublin, and in firms which are corporate members of the Irish Management Institute. The average number of managers per firm is also shown. In the second part of the chapter a study is made to see if the sample provides evidence that differences in the average number of managers per firm are associated with differences in the firm's size, location, membership of the Irish Management Institute, type of market served, type of manufacture, breadth or nationality of ownership. Because the number of separate industries is large relative to the size of the sample, it was not possible to investigate whether a firm's number of managers is associated with the industry in which it is engaged.

There is a comparison in chapter 10 between the average number of managers per firm in the Republic of Ireland and in some other countries.

Summary of Results

In the size-groups investigated there was a total of about 6,600 managers, the majority working for firms based in Dublin. About 40 per cent worked for corporate members of the Irish Management Institute. The average number of managers per firm differed widely from size-group to size-group. There is evidence that the average was also affected by the type of manufacture in which the firm engaged and possibly by whether or not it was family-owned, but there was no evidence that it was influenced by any other factor studied.

Understanding the Tables

So far as possible technical matters have been confined to appendices at the back of this volume, but two points which have an important bearing on every chapter in the book are discussed in the technical notes in page 2. The first note explains why differences arising out of size of firm are more likely to be proven significant than those arising out of other factors. The second note explains a discrepancy between figures in tables relating to estimates and those in tables relating to tests of significance.

From chapter 10 onwards, most tables show percentages of firms rather than of managers. These tables are of two kinds, some concerned with estimates and others with tests of hypotheses. For instance table 14. 2. 1. is concerned with the estimated proportion of firms using budgetary control, tables 14. 2. 2. to 14. 2. 7. with testing various hypotheses about the use of budgetary control. As explained in the glossary of terms, estimates are almost always accompanied by a range of variation within which the true result almost certainly lies. This range is usually indicated in the form x per cent $\pm$ y per cent, but sometimes for technical reasons is shown as x per cent (y per cent to z per cent).

For reasons explained in technical note 2 on the next page, tests are based on only 131 firms. The number of firms on which a test is based is also shown in each table.

Percentages shown in this book often do not total to 100 per cent. This is due to rounding-off by the computer.

In the course of the text the three size-strata are referred to sometimes as top,

---

[1] i.e. in transportable-goods industry, in firms employing 20 or more people, in the Republic of Ireland.

middle and bottom, sometimes as large, medium and small. These terms, refer respectively to the strata of firms with 500 or more, 100 to 499 and 20 to 99 employees.

Technical Notes:

1). The term "statistically significant" is explained in the glossary of terms where it is pointed out that, the greater the number of items in the sample, the greater is the possibility of establishing the significance of an observed difference. In what follows tests will often be carried out to establish the significance or otherwise of differences between many factors. For instance, in this chapter tests are carried out to see if the sample provides evidence that the average number of managers per firm differs with company size, or in family-owned as against non-family firms, or in firms serving a consumer market as against firms serving an industrial market, and so on. It is often the case that differences between the size-groups are established as significant, while those between some other factors are not. This can happen not only because the difference between the size-groups are larger than those between the other factors (although this is usually the case), but also because of the structure of the sample.

The total number of firms was broken into three size-groups, and different fractions were selected from each. Consequently, when testing for differences between factors other than size, e.g. between family and non-family firms, comparisons had to be made within each size-group in turn. That is, firms employing 500 or more were taken first and examined to see if there were significant differences between family and non-family firms; then firms with 100 to 499 employees were considered and finally firms with 20 to 99 employees. Thus the test was based on results for only 45 companies in the case of the larger firms, 44 in the medium-sized ones, and 42 in the smaller ones. (It was sometimes, but not always, possible to combine the results of the three separate tests.) When comparing the size-groups against one another, the comparison was based on results for 131 firms. Therefore an observed difference of given magnitude between size-groups had a greater probability of being shown to be significant than an observed difference of equal magnitude between any other factor, unless the results of the separate tests on the other factor could be combined. This must be borne in mind before concluding that size is the only influence, or the most important one.

2). The second point is the manner of dealing with the problem raised by firms which changed their size. Firms were selected from each of three size-groups on the basis of lists supplied in 1963. When the survey was carried out in 1964 it was found that some firms no longer belonged to the size-group from which they had been selected.

To estimate the total number of individuals in a stratum it is necessary to know the total number of firms, because totals are estimated by multiplying the number of individuals in the sample by the reciprocal of the sampling fraction. In the case of averages and proportions, to get from a stratified sample an estimate of the overall average or proportion, the individual strata estimates have to be weighted according to the total (not the sample) number of firms in the stratum, divided by the total number of firms overall. Since there was no way of knowing how these totals had changed between 1963 and 1964, the 1963 totals had to be used. To the extent that the weighting-factors are altered by this change, an element of bias is introduced into the estimates. (See appendix B, note 10.1 and addendum.)

In making estimates, whether of totals, averages or proportions, firms were regarded, for the reasons given above, as being still in their original groups. In carrying out tests the reasons mentioned did not hold. It was therefore possible to omit any firms which had changed size. It follows that the averages and proportions quoted in dealing with tests differ from those used in making estimates because of the exclusion of ten firms. For an example, compare the figures for arithmetic averages in table 1.2 with those in table 1.8.

Section 1. Estimates of Numbers

In this section the total number of managers and average number per firm, as at January 1st 1964, is estimated for each size-group, by location and corporate membership of the Irish Management Institute. For the purposes of this survey the following definition was adopted for the term "manager".

Definition of Manager

"A manager is anyone who works full-time in the firm and who *is held responsible for* a share in the managerial work of the company, that is making, implementing and evaluating decisions about the application of systems of resources to achieving goals. Those who duties are purely supervisory, whether in office or in works, are to be excluded".

The basic purpose of the definition was to include both those in line positions and those in staff positions. It was considered that the latter were members of the management team because of their contribution to the overall management of the firm, whether or not they had direct subordinates. It was thought possible that, particularly in small firms, there would be individuals with a considerable share in the decision process, who had no direct subordinates. A case in point is the accountant in such companies. Definitions which focused on an individual having subordinates were therefore avoided. Non-executive directors were excluded as they could not be regarded as whole-time managers. Supervisors were also excluded. On any definition supervisors perform managerial functions but, because a great deal of information was being sought about each manager, supervisors could not be included in the time available. A study on supervisors has been carried out by the Department of Industry and Commerce.

In practice the definition adopted was used as a guide. The problem was tackled by drawing an organisation-chart for each company, starting with the chief executive and finishing at the last level above supervisory. As the chart was being drawn, the executive being interviewed was asked whether all those who met'the definition were included, with special reference to any staff people who might have been overlooked.

Although the definition may appear to differ widely in principle from definitions which insist that a manager have subordinates, in practice the distinction counted for little as almost every staff executive included had someone working under him. In the following chapter a breakdown is given showing in detail the types of position included. Occasional difficulty was experienced in deciding on people whose duties were "purely supervisory". The criteria used in deciding whether to exclude individuals at this level were the degree of discretion they were expected to exercise about the work under their control, and their discretionary powers in respect of discipline and expenditure. Also excluded were purely professional workers, for instance, design engineers or research chemists. However, those held responsible for directing design or research activities were included.

Table 1.1 shows the number of managers in transportable goods industry in three

TABLE 1. 1.   *Estimated Total Number of Managers in Transportable Goods Industry, by Size of Firm and Location of its Head Office.*

Size of Firm (No. of Employees)	Dublin	Rest of Country	Total
500 or More	907	285	1,192
100-499	1,161±208	1,001±251	2,168±317
20-99	1,811±679	1,467±471	3,270±787
TOTAL	3,879±704	2,753±522	6,630±844

sizes of firm based in Dublin and the rest of the country[1]. Statistical points arising in calculating these figures are discussed in statistical note 1.1 of technical appendix B. The reason for calculating totals only for sizes, locations and membership of the Irish Management Institute is explained in statistical note 1.2.

From the table it can be seen that most managers work in small firms, and in firms based in Dublin. Firms employing under 20 people are not included, but a small preliminary survey of Institute members suggested an average figure of 1¼ managers per firm of this size. Since there were approximately 1,700[2] such firms in 1963, there were probably about 2,100 managers in the size-group, which would give an estimated total of about 8,700 managers in industry at January 1st 1964. As more very small firms are based outside Dublin than inside, the overall total number of managers is divided nearer to 50/50 between locations than table 1.1 shows.

In the following table several types of average are shown. Averages are usually quoted to show the typical position. The arithmetic average is not useful for this purpose: no firm employs 5.3 managers[3]. To describe the typical position the median or mode are more useful. Thus we may say from table 1.2 that the typical large firm in Dublin employs about 21 managers, the typical medium-sized firm outside Dublin employs about 6 managers, while the typical small firm employs about three[4].

TABLE 1.2.   *Estimated Average Number of Managers per Firm, by Size and Location of Firm.*

Size of Firm (No. of Employees)	Location of Head Office	Arithmetic Average	Median	Mode
500 or More	DUBLIN	30.23	22	21
	REST OF COUNTRY	16.76	16	11
	OVERALL	25.36	21	—
100-499	DUBLIN	9.29±1.67	8	8
	REST OF COUNTRY	7.58±1.90	6	6
	OVERALL	8.44±1.24	7.5	6
20-99	DUBLIN	3.70±1.38	3	4
	REST OF COUNTRY	3.22±1.03	3	2
	OVERALL	3.46±0.83	3	—
TOTAL	DUBLIN	6.01±1.09	—	—
	REST OF COUNTRY	4.55±0.86	—	—
	OVERALL	5.30±0.67	—	—

[1]Note that the estimated figures for Dublin when added to the estimated figures for the rest of the country do not add to the estimated totals in the extreme right-hand column. This will be true throughout. The reason is that the three sets of figures were calculated according to the formula mentioned in statistical note 1.1, and therefore the figure for total managers is not weighted to take account of the differing numbers of firms based inside and outside Dublin. Only if the sample had been stratified by location as well as by size would the sum of Dublin and the rest of the country have added to the total given. This is also true of the estimates for members and non-members of the Irish Management Institute.
[2]This figure does not include very small firms employing less than three people.
[3]The arithmetic average is the sum of the values for the objects under review divided by the number of objects: in this case the sum of the number of managers per firm divided by the number of firms. The median is the value lying half-way between the greatest and smallest values. The mode is the value which occurs most frequently.
[4]Note that neither large nor small firms have an overall mode, that is there is no one value which occurs more frequently than any other. This is one reason why the ranges of variation shown cannot strictly be regarded as confidence limits.

The arithmetic average is shown because, if the total number of firms is known, the product of the two figures gives the total number of managers. The total number of firms will be known relatively frequently from the Census of Industrial Production[1]. It can be seen that there are large differences between the average figures for each size-group, and smaller differences between averages for each location. These differences will be tested in the following section to see if they might have arisen by chance. The figures are accompanied by a range of variation, e.g. the average for small firms is 3.46±0.83, that is to say, it may lie anywhere between 2.63 and 4.29. It is probably safer to assume that the true average lies in the lower half of the range, because firms which had changed out of the group are included and because there is some evidence that the firms in the sample were larger than the average in that group. This is true also of the medium-sized firms. An overall average figure of 5.30 is quoted for firms with over 20 employees. If firms with under twenty employees are included, a total of approximately 3,000 firms employing an estimated 8,700 managers is arrived at, giving an overall average of about three managers per firm.

TABLE 1. 3.   *Estimated Total Number of Managers, by Size of Firm and Corporate Membership of the Irish Management Institute.*

Size of Firm (No. of Employees)	Corporate Members of I.M.I.	Not Corporate Members of I.M.I.	Total
500 or More	1132	60	1192
100–499	875±215	1283±232	2168±327
20–99	535±355	2599±593	3270±811
TOTAL	2543±438	3942±616	6630±844

Table 1.3 shows the number of managers employed by firms which are corporate members of the Irish Management Institute. About 38 per cent of managers overall are employed by member-firms, with the proportions varying widely between the different size-groups.

Table 1.4 shows various averages for members and non-members and it appears that member-firms employ on average more managers than non-members. This conclusion is subjected to a test in the next section.

TABLE 1. 4.   *Estimated Average Number of Managers per Firm, by Size of Firm and Corporate Membership of Irish Management Institute.*

Size of Firm (No. of Employees)	Membership Status of Firm	Arithmetic Average	Median	Mode
500 or More	MEMBER	26.95	21	19
	NON-MEMBER	12.00	11	—
100-499	MEMBER	10.06±2.47	8	—
	NON-MEMBER	7.55±1.37	6	6
20-99	MEMBER	5.25±3.48	3.5	—
	NON-MEMBER	3.08±0.70	3.0	—
OVERALL	MEMBER	11.01±1.89	—	—
	NON-MEMBER	3.87±0.60	—	—

[1]More correctly, it is the number of establishments which is known, but the number of firms does not differ greatly from the number of establishments.

The Number of Supervisors in Industry

Supervisors were excluded from the survey by definition. It was, however, thought desirable to get some general idea of their number without going into the detail asked for in the case of managers. Firms were asked for the number of supervisors employed and the number of employees other than managers and supervisors. Sometimes, particularly in larger firms, these figures were not easily available, and had to be estimated roughly by the chief executive. The figures quoted below are therefore tentative.

TABLE 1.5.   *Estimated Total of Supervisors and Total Employees[1], by Size of Firm.*

Size of Firm (No. of Employees)	Total Supervisors	Total Employees
500 or More	2,700	58,800
100–499	3,000	64,700
20–99	2,900	55,700
TOTAL	8,600	179,200[2]

[1]Total Employees = Managers + Supervisors + Other Employees.
[2]From this figure it is obvious that there is an upward bias in the sample within the 100 to 499 and 20 to 99 size-groups. The estimated total number of employees in transportable-goods industry on January 1st 1964 was 181,500 (see chapter 10 below), which would leave only 2,300 employees in firms with under 20 employees. This latter figure is too low by at least 12,000.

TABLE 1.6.   *Average Number of Managers, Supervisors and Other Employees per Firm, by Size of Firm (all firms).*

Size of Firm (No. of Employees)	Average Managers	Average Supervisors	Average Other Employees
500 or More	25.4	57.5	1,168
100–499	8.4	11.8	233
20–99	3.5	3.1	51
TOTAL	5.3	6.9	141

TABLE 1.7.   *Average Number of Managers, Supervisors and Other Employees per Firm, by Size of Firm (firms unchanged in size).*

Size of Firm (No. of Employees)	Average Managers	Average Supervisors	Average Other Employees
500 or More	26.1	57.5	1,204
100–499	8.4	11.8	234
20–99	3.1	3.1	48

Section 2. Tests of Association

In this section a variety of factors is considered to see if there is evidence that these factors have an effect on the average number of managers employed in a firm. Apparent differences have already been noted between firms in different size-groups and in different locations, and between members and non-members of the Irish Management Institute. These differences are examined here. It was thought that numbers might vary according to the type of ownership. It was thought also that the average might differ from industry to industry. Because the sample was too small it was not possible to test this hypothesis. However, an attempt was made to investigate the effect of environment and technology by examining the type of market served and the type of manufacturing activity engaged in. For an outline of the test procedure used, see statistical note 1.3 in technical appendix B.

Association between Size, Location and Average Number of Managers per Firm

The table which follows shows averages for each size-group and for each location. The differences between the size-groups are large, both for firms based in Dublin and for firms in the rest of the country.

TABLE 1.8.   *Average Number of Managers Employed per Firm in Sample Firms which Remained Unchanged in Size, by Size and Location of Firm.*

Size of Firm (No. of Employees)	Dublin	Rest of Country	Total
500 or More	31.7	16.76	26.07
100–499	9.0	7.77	8.38
20–99	2.9	3.27	3.10

In both cases they are very highly significant: there is less than one chance in a thousand that they could have arisen by chance due to sampling. Whatever other factor it is considered in conjunction with, size is always associated with a significant difference. It may therefore be said that it is well-established that size exerts an influence on the number of managers employed by a firm, and it will not be discussed further.

TABLE 1.8.a.   *Ratio of Managers to Other Employees[a] in Sample Firms which Remained Unchanged in Size, by Size and Location of Firm.*

Size of Firm (No. of Employees)	Dublin	Rest of Country	Total
500 or More	1:44.2	1:50.2	1:47.6
100–499	1:27.1	1:32.0	1:29.3
20–99	1:16.7	1:16.3	1:16.5

[a]i.e. supervisors and others. The same holds for tables 1.9a to 1.13a.

As regards location, in the larger firms those based in Dublin employ many more on average than those outside.[1] The differences in medium-sized and smaller firms are not great and testing showed that they might easily have arisen by chance. It might be objected that the differences in the larger firms are caused by differences in size: that the average Dublin firm in this group is larger than the average non-Dublin firm.

[1]Statistical Note: the variances do not differ significantly, except in the lower stratum. It would therefore not be worthwhile to stratify by location as well as by size to increase accuracy. The variances differ a great deal between size-groups.

This is true, but table 1.8a shows that such differences do not account for all the observed differences.

The table shows the ratio of managers to other employees. It can be seen that while, for large firms, the disparity between Dublin-based and other companies is now greatly reduced it is not entirely eliminated. (In the medium-sized firms it is actually increased, but the differences in averages have already been dismissed as possibly due to sampling fluctuation). However, when the industrial structure of the firms is considered the differences disappear. In fact when the original returns were examined most of the difference was seen to be caused by a handful of firms, the outlook of the chief executive, rather than location, being the dominant influence.

CONCLUSION. There is little or no evidence that the location of a firm as such influences the number of managers it employs, but its size exerts a considerable influence. The larger a firm the greater its number of managers, but the lower its ratio of managers to other employees.

Association between Membership of Irish Management Institute and Average Number of Managers per Firm.

The next table shows that for larger and medium-sized firms there are wide differences between member companies of the Irish Management Institute and non-members.

TABLE 1.9.   *Average Number of Managers Employed per Firm in Sample Firms which Remained Unchanged in Size, by Size of Firm and Corporate Membership of Irish Management Institute.*

Size of Firm (No. of Employees)	Corporate Membership Status	
	Member	Non-Member
500 or More	27.82	12.0
100–499	10.37	7.25
20–99	2.83	3.14

Both differences are real, but the difference in the smaller firms could have arisen by chance.

TABLE 1.9.a.   *Ratio of Managers to Other Employees in Sample Firms which Remained Unchanged in Size, by Size of Firm and Corporate Membership of Irish Management Institute.*

Size of Firm (No. of Employees)	Corporate Membership Status	
	Member	Non-Member
500 or More	1:46.3	1:71.8
100–499	1:25.3	1:32.6
20–99	1:21.7	1:15.6

The table above shows that the difference cannot be explained by the fact that member companies are larger than non-members. The conclusion is not of practical importance in the large firms, as all but a few belong to the Institute. In the medium size-group the exclusion of one member-firm with an extremely high number of managers brought the differences observed well within the range of sampling variation[1]. In this case it would be unwise to assume that firms which are members are likely —simply because they are members—to employ more managers than firms which are not.

CONCLUSION. *Membership of the Irish Management Institute is not, as such, associated in any practically important way with the average number of managers employed by a firm.*

Association Between Type of Market Served and Average Number of Managers per Firm
    It was decided to see whether the type of market served by a firm, that is whether its goods were for use by consumers or by industry, had any influence on its number of managers.

TABLE 1. 10.   *Average Number of Managers Employed per Firm in Sample Firms which Remained Unchanged in Size, by Size of Firm and Type of Market Served.*

Size of Firm (No. of Employees)	Type of Market	
	Consumer	Industrial
500 or More	26.19	25.89
100–499	8.31	8.53
20–99	3.11	3.07

This table shows that there is no difference between firms classified on this basis. Their ratios of managers to other employees (table 1.10a) are also virtually identical, except in the middle stratum.

TABLE 1. 10. a.   *Ratio of Managers to Other Employees in Sample Firms which Remained Unchanged in Size, by Size of Firm and Type of Market Served.*

Size of Firm (No. of Employees)	Type of Market	
	Consumer	Industrial
500 or More	1:47.8	1:47.3
100–499	1:27.0	1:33.8
20–99	1:16.5	1:16.4

CONCLUSION. *The type of market exerts no influence on a firm's number of managers, but it will be seen in the following chapter that it exerts a considerable influence on how these managers are assigned to different functions.*

[1]Statistical Note: the difference was only barely significant anyhow, and as the underlying distributions are not normal—that for members is very skewed—the result of the t-test in this case would not be reliable.

Association between Type of Manufacture and Average Number of Managers per Firm

While it was impossible to test whether a firm's industrial classification affected its number of managers, it was decided to attempt to take some account of the effect of differing technologies by seeing whether firms which manufactured by fabrication differed from those in processing industries.

TABLE 1. 11.   *Average Numbers of Managers Employed per Firm in Sample Firms which Remained Unchanged in Size, by Size of Firm and Type of Manufacture.*

Size of Firm (No. of Employees)	Type of Manufacture	
	Fabrication	Processing
500 or More	17.8	25.43
100–499	6.18	9.21
20–99	2.13	3.61

The table shows differences in every size-group between fabricating and processing companies, with process firms always employing a greater number of managers. In no case is it likely that these differences are chance ones. Neither can they be explained by differences in size: the next table shows that processing firms have a consistently more favourable ratio of managers to other employees.

TABLE 1. 11. a.   *Ratio of Managers to Other Employees in Sample Firms which Remained Unchanged in Size, by Size of Firm and Type of Manufacture.*

Size of Firm (No. of Employees)	Type of Manufacture	
	Fabrication	Processing
500 or More	1:56.6	1:45.9
100–499	1:34.5	1:28.2
20–99	1:20.5	1:15.1

Except in medium-sized firms the difference is not confined to any one type of manager, but extends over all functional areas. In the middle size-group the difference is mainly due to the fact that process firms employ more production managers than fabricating companies do.

CONCLUSION. *The type of manufacture in which a firm engages exercises a marked influence on the number of managers it employs. Firms in process industry employ more on average than firms manufacturing by fabrication.*

Association between Family Ownership and Average Number of Managers per Firm

It was thought that the number of managers employed might be influenced by whether or not a firm was family-owned.

TABLE 1. 12.   *Average Number of Managers Employed per Firm in Sample Firms which Remained Unchanged in Size, by Size of Firm and Breadth of Ownership.*

Size of Firm (No. of Employees)	Breadth of Ownership	
	Family	Non-Family
500 or More	29.09	25.09
100–499	8.75	8.08
20–99	2.79	4.22

Table 1.12 shows no very marked differences between firms on this score. Except in small firms the differences are not large. In small companies the difference is not statistically significant but is very nearly so. In this case it might be well not to reject the hypothesis that family ownership has an influence.

The differences in table 1.12 are not caused by size, as the next table shows, nor is there an association between ownership and any other factor which might account for the difference in the lowest stratum.

TABLE 1. 12. a.   *Ratio of Managers to Other Employees in Sample Firms which Remained Unchanged in Size, by Size of Firm and Breadth of Ownership.*

Size of Firm (No. of Employees)	Breadth of Ownership	
	Family	Non-Family
500 or More	1:48.2	1:47.3
100–499	1:27.8	1:30.8
20–99	1:17.5	1:13.9

This will not be the last time that the trend shown in table 1.12 will occur. It will often be seen that, among small companies, family businesses compare unfavourably with non-family firms, but that, among larger companies, the differences disappear.

CONCLUSION. *Except in small companies there is no evidence that ownership affects the issue, and even here the evidence is not strong.*

Association between Nationality of Ownership and Average Number of Managers per Firm

Finally, it was thought that Irish-owned companies might differ from firms with foreign parent companies.

TABLE 1. 13.   *Average Number of Managers Employed per Firm in Sample Firms which Remained Unchanged in Size, by Size of Firm and Nationality of Ownership.*

Size of Firm (No. of Employees)	Nationality of Ownership	
	Irish	Other
500 or More	27.69	22.08
100–499	8.33	8.80
20–99	3.07	3.50

Table 1.13 shows that they do not. The only difference of any size—that in large firms—is explained by the fact that Irish-owned companies in that group are larger than foreign-owned enterprises. The ratios of managers to other employees differ very little.

TABLE 1. 13. a.   *Ratio of Managers to Other Employees in Sample Firms which Remained Unchanged in Size, by Size of Firm and Nationality of Ownership.*

Size of Firm (No. of Employees)	Nationality of Ownership	
	Irish	Other
500 or More	1 : 48.0	1 : 46.1
100–499	1 : 29.6	1 : 27.1
20–99	1 : 16.3	1 : 19.0

CONCLUSION. The average number of managers employed by a firm is not associated with its nationality of ownership.

CHAPTER 2

The Assignment of Managers to Functional Areas

In chapter 1 estimates were made of the total number of managers and various hypotheses were tested about average numbers per firm. Having looked at the overall position, attention is now focused on the areas of responsibility of managers. The term "functional area" has been used to describe these broad divisions. In the interests of a more standardised terminology it might be more desirable to reserve the word "function" to describe those activities of managers which differentiate them from other workers, and to find some other term to describe the division into marketing, production, finance, etc. However, the use of the word "function" to describe this latter classification is fairly widespread and, as it is difficult to find another term which is not stilted or awkward, it was decided to use it here. In this chapter estimates are made of the totals, averages and percentages in each function, and tests are carried out to examine the association between a number of factors and the proportion in which managers are assigned to different functions.

Summary of Findings

Estimates are made in tables 2.1 to 2.5 of the total, average, and percentage of managers in each function in each of three size-groups, for firms based in Dublin and in the rest of the country, and for member-firms of the Irish Management Institute.

In section 2 of the chapter it is demonstrated that in firms with over 100 employees the greater proportion of managers is in the production area, with marketing and finance next and about equal to each other. In firms with less than 100 employees chief executives form the largest group, followed by production managers.

Of the factors considered, size of firm and type of market served are shown to be associated with differences in the assignment of executives to functions. There is no evidence that any other factor affects the situation.

Definitions

The divisions into which management responsibilities were divided were those of chief executive, marketing, production, finance, personnel, and other managers. 'Other managers' include those whose responsibilities did not allow them to be fitted into any of the major areas. In larger firms their responsibility was mainly general management, usually that of a branch or depot, but sometimes including those who, while not at chief executive level, nevertheless had broad responsibility. Among smaller firms, they tended mainly to be people whose area of responsibility was not defined.

The way in which this classification was arrived at was to ask, for each individual manager, the title of his job and that of his immediate superior. The interviewer assigned the individuals to functional areas on the basis of the definitions given below.

CHIEF EXECUTIVE: the executive ultimately responsible for the day-to-day running of the business.

MARKETING EXECUTIVES: executives engaged in activities related to the investigation of markets, promotion of sales, selling, warehousing and physical distribution of finished products.

PRODUCTION EXECUTIVES: those responsible for the fabrication, processing and assembly or packaging of products, together with the related activities of research, design, industrial engineering, production planning and control, stores (other than those of finished products), purchasing, inspection and quality control, maintenance and plant engineering.

FINANCE EXECUTIVES: those responsible for the production of financial and costing information. Also included is anyone responsible for legal and company-secretarial work or for office administration.

PERSONNEL EXECUTIVES: executives responsible for this function usually have a title such as personnel manager or industrial relations officer. Those responsible for training, welfare and the provision of services to employees are also included.

It will be seen from the above definitions that it was intended to introduce some degree of consistency into the classifications. Consequently, executives were not assigned to areas on the basis of the department in which they happened to be in their particular firm, but in accordance with the definitions given. For instance, executives in charge of purchasing sometimes reported to the chief executive, sometimes to the top financial executive. Nevertheless they were uniformly assigned to production as it seemed that in industry a properly planned purchasing system could issue only from production and inventory control decisions. This assignment of executives to areas was not arbitrary. A list of typical positions is given at the end of this chapter and it will be seen that most Irish companies are organised departmentally on the basis of a division into marketing, production, finance and, more rarely, personnel activities.

As in chapter 1, this chapter will be in two sections, in the first of which a variety of estimates is made and in the second some tests of hypotheses carried out.

Section 1. Estimates of Numbers

In this section of the chapter, estimates are made of the total number of managers in each functional area in different locations, in member-firms and non-members of the Irish Management Institute, and in different size-groups. The average number per firm in each area and the proportion of the total in each are also estimated.

The first figures of interest are the total numbers in each functional area, and they are shown, broken down by size and location of firm, in the following table.

TABLE 2. 1.   *Estimated Total Number of Managers in Each Functional Area, by Size and Location of Firm*

Size of Firm (No. of Employees)	Location of Head Office	Chief Executives	Marketing	Production	Finance	Personnel	Other
500 or More	DUBLIN	36	54	138	53	13	7
	REST OF COUNTRY	20	207	632	211	33	33
	TOTAL	56	153	494	158	40	26
100–499	DUBLIN	135±19	219±100	505±107	245±63	16±16	42±27
	REST OF COUNTRY	137±10	99±50	517±155	214±68	—	33±22
	TOTAL	273±22	321±115	1,023±180	460±90	16±16	75±34
20–99	DUBLIN	511±98	170±148	597±369	277±196	21±43	234±186
	REST OF COUNTRY	496±80	99±81	397±167	198±97	—	278±400
	TOTAL	1,008±121	267±160	987±383	473±206	21±40	514±435
TOTAL	DUBLIN	683±100	542±174	1,596±381	680±203	77±45	302±187
	REST OF COUNTRY	653±81	252±93	1,052±222	466±116	13	318±401
	TOTAL	1,337±123	796±195	2,642±420	1,144±223	90±43	622±436

TABLE 2.2. *Estimated Average Number of Managers per Firm in Each Functional Area, by Size and Location of Firm.*

Size of Firm (No. of Employees)	Location of Head Office	Chief Executive	Marketing	Production	Finance	Personnel	Other
500 or More	DUBLIN	1.20	5.10	16.47	5.27	1.33	0.87
	REST OF COUNTRY	1.18	3.18	8.12	3.12	0.76	0.41
	OVERALL	1.19	4.40	13.45	4.49	1.13	0.70
100-499	DUBLIN	1.08±0.15	1.75±0.80	4.04±0.86	1.96±0.51	0.12±0.13	0.33±0.21
	REST OF COUNTRY	1.04±0.08	0.75±0.38	3.92±0.38	1.62±0.51	—	0.25±0.17
	OVERALL	1.06±0.08	1.25±0.45	3.98±0.70	1.79±0.35	0.06±0.06	0.29±0.13
20-99	DUBLIN	1.04±0.20	0.35±0.30	1.22±0.75	0.56±0.40	0.04±0.09	0.48±0.38
	REST OF COUNTRY	1.09±0.18	0.22±0.18	0.87±0.37	0.43±0.21	—	0.61±0.88
	OVERALL	1.06±0.13	0.28±0.17	1.04±0.40	0.50±0.22	0.02±0.04	0.54±0.46
TOTAL	DUBLIN	1.06±0.15	0.84±0.27	2.47±0.59	1.05±0.32	0.12±0.07	0.47±0.29
	REST OF COUNTRY	1.08±0.13	0.42±0.15	1.74±0.37	0.77±0.19	0.02	0.52±0.66
	OVERALL	1.07±0.10	0.64±0.15	2.11±0.34	0.92±0.18	0.07±0.03	0.50±0.35

TABLE 2.3. *Estimated Percentage of Managers in Each Functional Area, by Size and Location of Firm.*

Size of Firm (No. of Employees)	Location of Head Office	Total Number of Managers	Chief Executive %	Marketing %	Production %	Finance %	Personnel %	Other %
500 or More	DUBLIN	907	4.0	16.9	54.5	17.4	4.4	2.9
	REST OF COUNTRY	285	7.0	18.9	48.4	18.6	4.6	2.5
	OVERALL	1,192	4.7	17.4	53.0	17.7	4.4	2.8
100–499	DUBLIN	1,161±208	11.7	18.8	43.5	21.1	1.3	3.6
	REST OF COUNTRY	1,001±251	13.7	9.9	51.6	21.4	—	3.3
	OVERALL	2,168±317	12.6	14.8	47.2	21.2	0.7	3.5
20–99	DUBLIN	1,811±679	28.2	9.4	32.9	15.3	1.2	12.9
	REST OF COUNTRY	1,467±471	33.8	6.8	27.0	13.5	—	18.9
	OVERALL	3,270±787	30.8	8.2	30.2	14.5	0.6	15.7
OVERALL	DUBLIN	3,879±704	17.6	14.2	41.1	17.5	2.0	7.8
	REST OF COUNTRY	2,753±522	23.7	9.2	38.2	16.9	4.8	11.5
	OVERALL	6,630±844	20.2	12.0	39.9	17.3	1.3	9.4

In table 2.1 there appear to be very many more production executives than of any other type, at least in the two larger size strata. The picture in the bottom stratum appears rather different with a greater tendency for chief executives to be the dominant class. The question of these differences is not taken up in this section, but left for investigation to section 2, as comment cannot usefully be made on them without first carrying out statistical tests. Continuing the analysis by size and location, the following tables show the proportion of executives in each area, and also the average number per firm.

The purpose of table 2.2 is to enable rough estimates to be made, in future, of the number of managers in each functional area as the number of firms in the country becomes available from the Census of Industrial Production. In statistical note 2.1 there is a short discussion of the sampling variability of the mean in table 2.2 and others of this type.

Table 2.3 is the first in which the estimated proportion of managers possessing a particular characteristic has been shown. The problem of associating confidence limits with such proportions is discussed in statistical note 2.2.

TABLE 2.4.   *Estimated Total Number of Managers in Each Functional Area, by Size of Firm and Corporate Membership of the Irish Management Institute.*

Size of Firm (No. of Employees)	Corporate Membership of I.M.I.	Chief Executive	Marketing	Production	Finance	Personnel	Other
500 or More	MEMBER	49	194	610	200	52	27
	NON-MEMBER	7	13	22	11	1	6
100–499	MEMBER	87± 14	113± 60	461±127	179± 68	10±13	26±18
	NON-MEMBER	186± 17	208±104	554±114	280± 60	5± 6	49±30
29–99	MEMBER	89± 25	76± 74	229±175	115± 89	13±25	13±25
	NON-MEMBER	933±126	155±109	666±259	311±150	—	533±480
TOTAL	MEMBER	225± 31	383± 98	1300±222	494±116	75±30	66±32
	NON-MEMBER	1126±124	377±145	1242±274	602±157	6±10	588±470

TABLE 2.5.   *Estimated Average Number of Managers per Firm in Each Functional Area, by Size of Firm and Corporate Membership of the Irish Management Institute.*

Size of Firm (No. of Employees)	Corporate Membership of I.M.I.	Chief Executive	Marketing	Production	Finance	Personnel	Other
500 or More	MEMBER	1.17	4.62	14.52	4.76	1.24	0.64
	NON-MEMBER	1.40	2.60	4.40	2.20	0.20	1.20
100-499	MEMBER	1.00±0.16	1.29±0.68	5.29±1.46	2.06±0.79	0.12±0.15	0.29±0.21
	NON-MEMBER	1.10±0.10	1.23±0.61	3.26±0.67	1.64±0.35	0.03±0.06	0.29±0.18
20-99	MEMBER	0.87±0.25	0.75±0.73	2.25±1.71	1.12±0.88	0.12±0.25	0.12±0.88
	NON-MEMBER	1.10±0.15	0.18±0.13	0.79±0.31	0.37±0.18	—	0.63±0.57
OVERALL	MEMBER	0.97±0.13	1.66±0.42	5.63±0.96	2.14±0.50	0.32±0.13	0.28±0.14
	NON-MEMBER	1.10±0.12	0.37±0.14	1.22±0.27	0.59±0.15	0.01±0.01	0.58±0.46

Having considered the analysis into functional areas by size and location of firm, estimates are now made of the numbers in each functional area in firms which were corporate members of the Irish Management Institute. Table 2.4 shows the position.

Again it is not intended here to comment on this table: comment must wait upon the execution of statistical tests, and is therefore deferred until section 2. In the case of membership, the average number per firm is shown in table 2.5.

Section 2. Tests of Association

Before discussing the hypotheses to be tested concerning the division of managers between functional areas, it should be emphasised once more that this part of the chapter is concerned with exploring associations and not with making estimates. The reader who wishes to get an estimate of the number or percentage of managers in a functional area should refer to section 1.

In chapter 1 questions of the type "is the average number of managers the same in every sort of firm?" were investigated. Such questions do not appear to be of interest in the present context. Each functional area could be taken in turn and such questions asked as "is the average number of production managers greater in some types of firm than in others?" But there is likely to be greater interest in the question of whether there are *relatively* more production managers present than absolutely more, for the latter might simply reflect the fact that there were more managers of every type. Concern then is with such questions as "does this sample provide evidence that the division of managers between functional areas is associated with the type of firm for which they work, or could the observed differences have arisen by chance?"

It seemed that the factors most likely to influence functional divisions were:
(i) size; (ii) type of market served: whether consumer or industrial; (iii) type of manufacture: whether fabrication, processing or some other type; (iv) type of production-organization: whether goods were made to order, or in batches or continuously; and, from the point of view of action on future training needs, the two further factors; (v) location; (vi) membership of Irish Management Institute.

The procedure followed in testing these factors is outlined in the technical note at the end of this chapter.

Differences between Functions

Before considering the effect of the various factors on the functions it must first be seen whether the differences observed between functional areas are real or caused by chance. As stated in the technical note, the question must be asked for each size-stratum in turn.

It may be stated that, for the top stratum, there are many more production managers than any other type, with marketing and finance about equal, and with a very low proportion of chief executives, personnel managers and others.

The overall percentages for the next size-group show that, again, the largest category is production, with the categories chief executive, marketing and finance not differing too widely from one another, and personnel and others very much the lowest. The observed differences are very highly significant: the probability is less than one in a thousand that they could have arisen by chance.

Moving to the lowest size-group again there are wide divergences between areas, but with a rather different pattern from the other sizes. Chief executives now form the largest group, followed by production, with finance and others following, marketing very low and personnel non existent. This is not an unexpected pattern: practically every firm whatever its size will have only one chief executive and, with the small number of managers in small firms, chief executives could be expected to form a large proportion of the total. Many small firms do not define the functions of managers too closely, consequently they have a high proportion of managers who are not designated to a particular function, who can only be called "others". With the growth of the firm the chief executive seems first to turn over responsibility for production to another executive (which accounts for the high proportion of production managers), retaining the administration of finance under his own control until a later stage and seemingly relinquishing contact with the firm's customers last of all. A formal personnel function does not appear at all in this size-group. The observed pattern is highly significant statistically, again beyond the 0.001 level.

Association between Size, Location and Functional Area
    The next problem is to consider the effects of size and location on the different functions, again looking first at the effect of location within each size-group in turn.

TABLE 2.6.   *Percentage of Managers in Each Functional Area, by Size and Location of Firm.*

Size of Firm (No. of Employees)	Location of Head Office	No. of Managers in Analysis	Chief Executives %	Marketing %	P'duction %	Finance %	Personnel %	Other %
500 or More	DUBLIN	887	3.84	17.03	54.57	17.37	4.51	2.71
	REST OF COUNTRY	285	7.02	18.95	48.43	18.60	4.57	2.46
	OVERALL	1172	4.61	17.50	53.08	17.67	4.53	2.65
100-499	DUBLIN	196	12.25	18.88	44.39	21.43	(a)	3.07
	REST OF COUNTRY	171	13.46	9.95	52.05	21.64	—	2.93
	OVERALL	369	12.74	14.64	47.70	21.41	0.55	2.99
20-99	DUBLIN	58	36.21	6.90	27.59	13.80	—	15.52
	REST OF COUNTRY	69	33.34	7.25	27.54	14.50	—	17.46
	OVERALL	127	34.65	7.09	27.56	14.18	—	16.54

(a) Personnel omitted because the number was too small to allow a test of significance. For this reason Dublin and Rest of Country total adds to only 367 instead of 369.

The top stratum of table 2.6 shows the following picture:

	%	%	%	%	%	%
Dublin	3.84	17.03	54.57	17.37	4.51	2.71
Rest of Country	7.02	18.95	48.43	18.60	4.57	2.46

    Inspection of this sub-table shows a striking similarity of pattern between Dublin and the rest of the country. It may quite confidently be said that in this size-group location has no influence on the functional organisation of companies.

Inspection of the other two groups shows that, in these also, the patterns are very similar, and a test confirms this conclusion.

There remains the possibility that location is related to some other factor which, if it had been considered, would have had the effect of showing location to be significant. As stated in the technical note above, this problem was tackled by carrying out tests to see if any such relationship existed. None was discovered, except that in the lowest size-group there appeared to be a relationship between location and type of manufacture, with a significantly higher proportion of fabrication shops in Dublin as against the rest of the country. This hardly affected the issue, and the main conclusion stands that there is no evidence of location having any effect.

It was remarked earlier that there appeared to be a rather different pattern of division over functions in the smallest size-group than in either of the others. This question of the effect of size is now taken up. Looking back at table 2.6 the overall percentages are as follows:

	%	%	%	%	%	%
500 or More	4.61	17.50	53.08	17.67	4.53	2.65
100-499	12.74	14.64	47.70	21.41	0.55	2.99
20-99	34.65	7.09	27.56	14.18	—	16.54

These patterns appear to differ, and this is confirmed by a test which shows that there is less than one chance in a thousand that the observed difference could be a chance one. There is a very striking difference between the proportion of chief executives in the biggest and smallest group, a very high proportion of executives with undefined functions in the smallest group, together with a much lower percentage of production managers and, in the middle size-group, an unexpectedly low proportion of personnel managers.

CONCLUSION. *The conclusion from table 2.6 is that location does not affect function, whereas size affects it very strikingly.*

Association between Membership of Irish Management Institute and Functional Area

The effect of membership of the Irish Management Institute is now considered. In this case the entire lowest size-group was omitted because the number of managers in member-firms was too small to test, and personnel management was left out of the 100 to 499 group for the reason stated in the footnote to table 2.7.

Taking the top size-group first, there appears to be a fair disparity in pattern between member-firms and non-members. The main differences are that non-members have a higher proportion of chief executives in conjunction with a lower proportion of production managers, while also having a higher percentage of people in the "other" category. The first two differences are a reflection of the fact that within the top size-group the non-member firms included are smaller than member-firms (12 managers per firm as against 37.8). Consequently, given that a firm rarely has more than one chief executive, non-members must have a higher percentage of chief executives. As firms grow, so

TABLE 2. 7. *Percentage of Managers in Each Functional Area, by Size of Firm and Corporate Membership of th[e] Irish Management Institute.*

Size of Firm (No. of Employees)	Corporate Membership of I.M.I.	No. of Managers in Analysis	Chief Executives %	Marketing %	P'duction %	Finance %	Personnel %	Other %
500 or More	MEMBER	1112	4.23	17.26	53.96	17.63	4.68	2.24
	NON-MEMBER	60	11.67	21.67	36.67	18.33	1.67	10.00
	OVERALL	1172	4.61	17.50	53.08	17.67	4.53	2.65
100-499	MEMBER	164	9.76	13.42	53.05	21.35	(a)	2.44
	NON-MEMBER	203	15.28	15.77	43.85	21.68	—	3.45
	OVERALL	369	12.74	14.64	47.70	21.41	0.55	2.99

(a) Personnel omitted for the same reason as in table 2.6, therefore intermediate totals do not add to overall total.

does their proportion of production executives. As a result, a smaller firm will be likely to have a lower proportion of production managers than a larger one. The relatively high percentage of "others" is accounted for by the fact that the largest of the non-member firms had a large number of decentralized branches, with a manager in charge of each. While there is evidence therefore of a difference in pattern in the top size-group, it may be accounted for largely by difference in average size within the group. Membership, as such, does not appear to have a very important effect.

In the medium size-group the observed differences could very easily have arisen by chance, being far from significant. On balance there is little overall evidence that membership of the Irish Management Institute affects division by functional areas. So far as the two size-groups considered are concerned, there is no evidence of any relationship between membership and any other factor which might cause this conclusion to be altered.

Taking size in conjunction with membership, there were not enough member-firms in the 29 to 99 group to perform a test. Taking non-member firms, however, there was again a very significant difference between size-groups, the pattern being similar to that found earlier. In fact, everywhere that size was considered in this chapter, in conjunction with any factor whatever, it was found to have an extremely significant effect. This effect has been discussed already and will not be discussed again.

CONCLUSION. *There is no evidence that membership of the Irish Management Institute is associated with the way in which managers are assigned to different functions.*

Association between Type of Market Served and Functional Area

The next factor considered is the type of market served by the firm.

Looking first at the top size-group there is a very striking difference: firms serving an industrial market have a much higher percentage of production managers *vis-à-vis* consumer-goods firms, and at the same time a considerably lower proportion of marketing managers. The other areas differ hardly at all.

TABLE 2. 8.   *Percentage of Managers in Each Functional Area, by Size of Firm and Type of Market.*

Size of Firm (No. of Employees)	Type of Market	No. of Managers in Analysis	Chief Executives %	Marketing %	P'duction %	Finance %	Personnel %	Other %
500 or More	CONSUMER	706	4.68	23.66	45.33	17.99	4.96	3.40
	INDUSTRIAL	466	4.51	8.16	64.81	17.17	3.87	1.51
	OVERALL	1172	4.61	17.50	53.08	17.67	4.53	2.65
100-499	CONSUMER	239	12.56	18.42	45.19	20.93	(a)	2.93
	INDUSTRIAL	128	13.29	7.82	53.13	22.66	—	3.13
	OVERALL	369	12.74	14.64	47.70	21.41	0.55	2.99
20-99	CONSUMER	85	35.30	4.71	25.89	10.59	—	23.53
	INDUSTRIAL	42	33.34	11.91	30.96	21.43	—	2.39
	OVERALL	127	34.65	7.09	27.56	14.18	—	16.54

(a) Personnel omitted for the same reason as in table 2.6, therefore intermediate totals do not add to overall total.

The next size group (100 to 499) appears to show a somewhat similar pattern, though not so markedly. In fact, when tested, the differences did not turn out to be significant. While it may be suspected that a difference exists and a good explanation found for it *a priori*, nevertheless the evidence in this case cannot be regarded as being sufficient to confirm this suspicion.

In the smallest group there is an entirely different pattern. Here consumer-goods firms have a very high percentage in the category "other", while industrial-goods firms have a very low percentage. The differences between the types are significant, one rather surprising difference being that industrial-goods firms appear to have a higher proportion of marketing managers. The explanation for the differences is not size, since both types of firm are almost exactly similar in this respect. It seems that, in this size-group, firms selling to industry are more likely than consumer-goods firms to have formally-assigned functions. Possibly a higher level of technical complexity makes it important to formalise functions at any earlier stage in their case.

CONCLUSION. *The conclusion is that the type of market served does markedly affect functional areas in both large and small firms, though not in the same way. It may be that it affects medium-sized firms in the same way as large ones, but the evidence is not sufficient to support such a statement. There is not enough evidence of a relationship between type of market and any other factor to cause this conclusion to be altered, though there is a suggestion that firms serving an industrial market are more likely than consumer goods firms to make to order.*

Association between Type of Manufacture and Functional Area

Contrary to usual practice table 2.9 is not in percentage form. The reason is that the manufacturing category "other" had to be omitted in order to meet the conditions of the statistical test. As a result the intermediate percentages would have differed very widely from the size-group total percentages. To avoid confusion in interpretation it was decided to print the original data.

TABLE 2. 9.   *Number of Managers in Each Functional Area, by Size of Firm and Type of Manufacture.*

Size of Firm (No. of Employees)	Type of Manufacture	Chief Executive (No.)	Marketing (No.)	P'duction (No.)	Finance (No.)	Personnel (No.)	Other (No.)	Total (No.)
500 or More	FABRICATION	11	33	93	31	8	2	178
	PROCESSING	39	153	366	141	35	28	762
	OTHER	4	19	163	35	10	1	232
	TOTAL	54	205	622	207	53	31	1172
100-499	FABRICATION	12	11	28	14	—	3	68
	PROCESSING	30	36	134	58	2	7	267
	OTHER	5	7	14	7	—	1	34
	TOTAL	47	54	176	79	2	11	369
20-99	FABRICATION	12	1	9	3	—	7	32
	PROCESSING	31	7	26	13	—	14	91
	OTHER	1	1	—	2	—	—	4
	TOTAL	44	9	35	18	—	21	127

It turned out that, considering only fabrication and processing, type of manufacture had no effect whatever on functional area, in any of the size-groups. All the tests failed to show significant differences.

CONCLUSION. *There is no evidence that type of manufacture is associated with division by function.*

Association between Type of Production and Functional Area
    Finally, type of production-organisation is considered. It had been hoped to consider make-to-order, batch, continuous and other types of production. There were not sufficient data for so fine a breakdown, and categories had to be combined. It was considered that there was likely to be a greater difference between firms making to order and firms which had achieved a level of standardisation sufficient to allow batch or continuous production. The classification decided on was therefore "make-to-order" and "other".

TABLE 2. 10.   *Percentage of Managers in Each Functional Area, by Size of Firm and Type of Production.*

Size of Firm (No. of Employees)	Type of Production	No. of Managers in Analysis	Chief Executives %	Marketing %	Production %	Finance %	Personnel %	Other %
500 or More	MAKE TO ORDER	78	8.97	7.69	58.97	17.95	2.56	3.8
	OTHER	1094	4.30	18.19	52.65	17.64	4.66	2.5
	OVERALL	1172	4.61	17.50	53.08	17.67	4.53	2.65
20-99	MAKE TO ORDER	29	34.49	3.45	37.94	17.25	—	6.90
	OTHER	98	34.70	8.17	24.49	13.27	—	19.39
	OVERALL	127	34.65	7.09	27.56	14.18	—	16.54

There were not sufficient make-to-order firms in the middle size-group to permit any tests and this group was omitted.

It might appear from table 2.10 that some differences were present, but in the 20 to 99 size-group the difference is not at all significant. Furthermore, it was mentioned earlier that there was a suggestion of a relationship between type of market and type of production-organisation, with firms making industrial goods appearing slightly more likely to make to order (though the relationship does not reach statistical significance). Therefore, whatever association there appears to be between type of production and function is probably caused by the slight relationship between type of production and type of market.

CONCLUSION. It cannot confidently be said that type of production-organisation affects division by function.

ADDENDUM TO CHAPTER 2

In chapter 1 it was shown that firms in process industry employ more managers on average than fabricating firms. In the present chapter the type of market served has been shown to have an effect on the way in which managers are allocated to broad functional areas but technology, as illustrated by type of manufacture and production, has not been shown to be so associated.

Woodward (1) has suggested, based on a study of large firms in South Essex, that technology and type of organisation are associated. The findings of the present chapter do not go counter to her suggestion. It is possible that, within the broad functional areas here used, technology has a considerable influence on the division into "staff" and "line", on the type of "staff" positions filled and the activities engaged in.

It is hoped at a later stage to subject the original data to a more detailed analysis to see how far they bear out Woodward's findings. For the present the following more detailed breakdown of functions is given, showing that firms are organised mainly on the basis of division into marketing, production and financial departments, that "staff" positions are a minority but that they increase in importance with size of firm. The figures shown are sample results only. To estimate roughly the position in industry as a whole, the figures for the 100 to 499 employee size-group should be multiplied by 6, and those for the 20 to 99 employee group multiplied by 23.

TABLE 2. 11. *No. of Individuals in Sample Firms in Each Sub-Division of a Major Function, by Size of Firm.*

SUB-DIVISION OF MAIN FUNCTIONS	Size of Firm (No. of Employees)		
	500 or More	100-499	20-99
CHIEF EXECUTIVE			
Executive Chairman	3	4	—
Managing Director	23	24	23
General Manager	14	11	1
Joint Managing Director or General Manager	14	8	20
TOTAL	54	47	44

TABLE 2. 11. (cont'd.) *No. of Individuals in Sample Firms in Each Sub-Division of a Major Function, by Size of Firm.*

SUB-DIVISION OF MAIN FUNCTIONS	Size of Firm (No. of Employees)					
	500+		100-499		20-99	
MARKETING						
Chief Marketing Manager	36		22		8	
Assistant Marketing Manager	21		8		—	
Sub-section Manager (e.g. brand manager)	77		9		—	
Field Sales Manager	8	142	3	42	—	8
Market Research	4		—		—	
Advertising	9		1		—	
Sales Promotion, Publicity, P.R.	10		—		—	
Merchandising	4		—		—	
Warehouse	10		2		—	
Transport	17		8		1	
Sales Office	8		1		—	
Other	1	63	—	12	—	1
TOTAL		205		54		9
PRODUCTION						
Chief Production Manager	50		36		18	
Assistant P.M.; Branch Factory Manager, etc.	172		48		11	
Dept. Managers	76	298	41	125	3	32
Research and Development	8		—		—	
Project and Development Engineers	14		—		—	
Design	9		4		—	
Drawing Office	2		1		—	
Production Engineers	17		2		—	
Work Study	29		3		—	
Production Planning & Control	25		4		1	
Stores and Stock Control	12		1		—	
Purchasing	28		8		—	
Quality Control	10		1		—	
Chemist or Lab. Head	22	176	13	37	—	1
Chief Engineer	24		4		—	1
Engineers on P. and E. maintenance and installation	98	122	7	11	—	
Technical Managers and Others		26		3		2
TOTAL		622		176		35

TABLE 2. 11. (cont'd.) *No. of Individuals in Sample Firms in Each Sub-Division of a Major Function, by Size of Firm.*

SUB-DIVISION OF MAIN FUNCTIONS	Size of Firm (No. of Employees)		
	500+	100-499	20-99
FINANCE			
Chief Financial Manager	27	12	5
Co. Secretary	31	31	11
Accountant, Assistant Secretary, Assistant Accountant	57	21	1
Financial Accountant	9	1	—
Cost Accountant	25	6	—
Management Accountant	6	2	—
O & M	3	—	—
Office Manager, Chief Clerk, etc.	24	5	1
Chief Cashier, Wages Office Manager, etc.	9	—	—
Credit Control	5	—	—
Internal Audit	4	1	—
Data Processing	5	—	—
Other	2	—	—
TOTAL	207	79	18
PERSONNEL			
Personnel Manager	15	2	—
Personnel Officer or Asst. P.M.	14	—	—
Industrial Relations Manager	4	—	—
Departmental P.O.	9	—	—
Training Officer	8	—	—
Others	3	—	—
TOTAL	53	2	—
OTHER			
General Management	9	2	2
Deputy M.D. or Asst. M.D.	3	2	3
Branch or Area G.M.	12	2	9
Other	7	5	7
TOTAL	31	11	21

Note on Test Procedure.

The test procedure now described has been used throughout the book. (The statistical test used was usually the chi-square test. The conditions under which this test may be used and the extent to which they were met by the data in this survey are discussed in statistical note 2.3 in the technical appendix, where is it explained that the usual form of the test had to be adjusted in chapters 2-9, in which attributes of managers are being investigated, to allow for the effect of cluster-sampling. From chapter 10 onwards it was often possible to use Fisher's Exact Probability Test where the theoretical conditions for using chi-square were not met. See statistical note 4.1).

Two main groups of questions arise in this book:

1). The distinguishing feature of the first group is that it is not concerned with examining associations, except between attributes of managers. It is concerned with such questions as: " Could observed differences between the proportions of managers in each function (or at each level, or qualified and not qualified etc.) have arisen by chance?" or from chapter 10 onwards with such questions as: "Could the observed difference between the proportion of firms using work study and the proportion of firms not using work study have arisen by chance?" A sub-group in chapter 8 and 9 are such questions as: " Is there evidence of an association between the functional area in which a manager works and his likelihood of being qualified ? "

Because of the structure of the sample a test of significance had to be carried out on each size-group in turn. Thus each question was answered separately in stratum 1 (in which observed differences were significant by definition), stratum 2 and stratum 3. If no significant differences were found it would have been desirable to combine the results of the separate chi-square tests so as to have an overall test based on larger numbers. As explained in statistical note 2.4 in the technical appendix, this was sometimes possible from chapter 10 onwards when dealing with attributes of firms but never in earlier chapters when dealing with attributes of managers.

2). The second group of questions is concerned with tests of association. In chapters 2-7 the associations are between attributes of firms and attributes of managers, e.g. " Is there evidence of an association between the type of market served by a firm and the way in which its managers are allocated to different functions ? " From chapter 12 onwards the associations are between attributes of firms only, e.g. "Is there evidence of an association between a firm's location and its use of budgetary control ? " It is usually required to investigate associations for a variety of factors. For instance in the present chapter associations are investigated between a firm's size, location, type of market, type of manufacture etc. and the way it allocates managers to functions.

The approach adopted was to take each factor for study in turn instead of attempting to study them all simultaneously. Thus, instead of a single table showing the data broken down by size of firm, then by location, then by type of market and so on, there were in the present chapter five separate tables, one showing the data broken down by size and location, the next by size and type of market and so on. As usual the factors other than size of firm had to be considered in conjunction with size because of the sample structure. Table 2.12 is typical of the tables in the book.

A possible theoretical objection to this practice of studying factors serially rather than simultaneously is discussed in statistical note 2.5 of the technical appendix. Two practical objections are considered here before going on to outline the test procedure followed.

The first objection is that the factors under study might be related. Imagine for instance that it was demonstrated that firms based in Dublin employed a higher proportion of academically-qualified managers than firms outside Dublin, and that it was desired to see whether firms serving a consumer market employed a higher proportion of qualified managers than firms selling to industry. Now, if it happened that most consumer-goods firms were in Dublin while a high proportion of industrial-goods firms were outside Dublin, an association might be found between type of market and proportion qualified which was entirely spurious and which would disappear if location were considered.

It was not feasible to overcome this objection by considering all factors simultaneously as there would not have been sufficient data to allow the necessary sub-division It was overcome by carrying out a series of tests to see if any of the factors whose effects were being studied were related. Where such relationships were found the fact is referred to in the text and its implications for the point under investigation are discussed.

There is thus no danger that a spurious relationship will be accepted.

The second objection is that a possible real relationship will be overlooked. Consider, for instance, the following table.

		X	Y	Total
Family-owned	Consumer-Market	10	0	10
	Industrial-Market	0	10	10
Not family-owned	Consumer-Market	0	10	10
	Industrial-Market	10	0	10

There is obviously a relationship between type of market and X, Y, but the relationship is different for family and non-family firms. Such interactions between factors are impossible to discover without obtaining cross-classifications of the type shown, as can be seen when the results of the table above are shown first for type of ownership alone and then for type of market alone.

	X	Y	Total		X	Y	Total
Family-owned	10	10	20	Consumer-Market	10	10	20
Not family-owned	10	10	20	Industrial-Market	10	10	20

This objection has not been overcome because the sample was too small to allow the necessary sub-division, particularly when considering attributes of firms.

The steps in the test procedure were as follows:

i. First, the factor other than size was examined by carrying out a test of association within each size-group in turn. If no significant differences were found it was sometimes possible, from chapter 12 onwards, to combine the results of separate chi-square tests on each stratum to get a more powerful overall test.

ii. Size was considered next. If the other factor did not show significant differences within a size-group, the overall results for every size-group were taken and tested against one another.

iii. Where the factor other than size did show significant differences within a size-group, step ii was not permissible. Suppose the factor under consideration was location and that in stratum 2 it was found that firms in Dublin differed significantly from those outside Dublin. Apart from the dubious meaning of an overall set of figures for that stratum, arrived at by combining two significantly different sets of figures, information would be lost by combining. In such a case the procedure was to consider, first, Dublin firms only and to compare the three size-groups in Dublin, then to take firms in the rest of the country and to compare the size-groups outside Dublin.

The test procedure outlined above, and the statistical tests used were always carried out on the data in numerical form — i.e. as shown in table 2.12. It was felt, however, that the tables would be more meaningful and the relationships to be explored more easily shown up if the tables were printed in percentage-form. This has been done throughout the book. In order that the reader will not be misled, the totals on which the percentages were based are also printed, usually in the left-hand column of each table. For the convenience of other research workers who might be willing to work to a significance-level other than that adopted in this study ($p=0.05$), all percentages are quoted correct to two places of decimals so that anyone who wishes to re-express the tables in numerical form can carry out the necessary calculations.

TABLE 2. 12.   *Number of Managers Included in Sample in Each Functional Area, by Size of Firm and Type of Market*

Size of Firm (No. of Employees)	Type of Market	Chief Executive	Marketing	Production	Finance	Personnel	Other	Total
500 or More	CONSUMER	33	167	320	127	35	24	706
	INDUSTRIAL	21	38	302	80	18	7	466
	TOTAL	54	205	622	207	53	31	1172
100-499	CONSUMER	30	44	108	50	2	7	241
	INDUSTRIAL	17	10	68	29	—	4	128
	TOTAL	47	54	176	79	2	11	369
20-99	CONSUMER	30	4	22	9	—	20	85
	INDUSTRIAL	14	5	13	9	—	1	42
	TOTAL	44	9	35	18	—	21	127

Reference:

1. J. Woodward *Industrial Organisation*: *Theory and Practice*. London: Oxford University Press, 1965.

CHAPTER 3
Assignment of Managers to Levels

In this chapter an attempt is made to assess the numbers at each level of management and to investigate the effect of a variety of factors upon the situation.

Summary of Findings.

The total, average per firm, and percentage of managers at each level is estimated in tables 3.1. to 3.5. It is shown that the proportions at each level differ. There is clear evidence that the proportions at each level are influenced by the size of the firm. It is not possible to say unequivocally whether membership of the Irish Management Institute or the breadth of ownership of the company has any effect. Location has none.

Discussion of Definitions.

It must be said at the outset that the problem of arriving at a satisfactory definition proved more difficult in the case of level than of any other attribute studied. The definitions finally settled on are not entirely satisfactory. They are, however, among the least ambiguous and serve as a fair general indication of the position.

It had been hoped to find a set of definitions which would be objective, consistent, criteria for assigning an individual to a given level without reference to the situation in the particular firm for which he worked. An extensive search of the literature failed to discover any such criteria.

Definitions.

The position of chief executive was taken as the reference point with respect to which other levels were fixed. (It was considered that the nature of the chief executive's work differed sufficiently in kind from that of the other executives for his position to be regarded as a separate level.)

TOP EXECUTIVE POSITIONS were taken to be those reporting directly to the chief executive for an important area of responsibility.

MIDDLE LEVEL was taken as those positions reporting to a top executive for an important segment of his area of responsibility and also those reporting to the chief executive for a circumscribed area.

JUNIOR MANAGEMENT were taken to be those above supervisory level and reporting to middle management, or to top management for a limited segment of a top manager's area.

Thus, no attempt was made to allow for variation in size of firm or any other factor. A man reporting to the chief executive of a very small company was regarded as in top management, just as was the manager responsible for many more employees and reporting to the chief executive of a large firm. Subjectivity was not completely eliminated as a decision had to be made on what constituted an important segment of an executive's responsibility. This was mainly done on the basis of the breadth of the the role. For instance, companies not employing a personnel manager might have a training manager reporting to the chief executive. Such a manager, while assigned to the general area of personnel, was not regarded as a top personnel executive because he was not responsible for the entire personnel function.

The definitions might prove unworkable for very large companies in which there are great numbers in middle management with a wide variety of sub-strata within this broad level but, in Ireland, where firms are small, they proved satisfactory.

Section 1. Estimates of Numbers

In the first of the tables below estimates are given of the number of executives at each level.

TABLE 3. 1.   *Estimated Number of Managers at Each Level, by Size and Location of Firm.*

Size of Firm (No. of Employees)	Location of Head Office	Chief Executives	Top Management	Middle Management	Junior Management
500 or More	DUBLIN	36	142	406	323
	REST OF COUNTRY	20	58	134	73
	TOTAL	56	200	540	396
100-499	DUBLIN	135±19	339±49	427±103	260±114
	REST OF COUNTRY	137±10	347±64	346±107	171±165
	TOTAL	273±22	685±78	776±145	434±193
20-99	DUBLIN	511±98	639±253	575±482	85±102
	REST OF COUNTRY	496±80	515±167	397±386	59±88
	TOTAL	1,008±121	1,152±288	967±590	144±129
TOTAL	DUBLIN	683±100	1,120±256	1,408±490	669±149
	REST OF COUNTRY	653±81	920±177	877±398	303±183
	TOTAL	1,337±123	2,037±297	2,283±607	974±230

TABLE 3. 2.   *Estimated Percentage of Managers at Each Level, by Size and Location of Firm.*

Size of Firm (No. of Employees)	Location of Head Office	Total No. of Managers	Percentage Chief Executives	Percentage Top Management	Percentage Middle Management	Percentage Junior Management
500 or More	DUBLIN	907	4.0	15.7	44.8	35.6
	REST OF COUNTRY	285	7.0	20.4	47.0	25.6
	OVERALL	1,192	4.7	16.8	45.3	33.2
100-499	DUBLIN	1,161±208	11.7	29.1	36.8	22.4
	REST OF COUNTRY	1,001±251	13.7	34.6	34.6	17.0
	OVERALL	2,168±317	12.6	31.6	35.8	20.0
20-99	DUBLIN	1,811±679	28.2	35.3	31.8	4.7
	REST OF COUNTRY	1,467±471	33.8	35.1	27.0	4.1
	OVERALL	3,270±787	30.8	35.2	29.6	4.4
OVERALL	DUBLIN	3,879±704	17.6	28.9	36.3	17.2
	REST OF COUNTRY	2,753±522	23.7	33.4	31.8	11.0
	OVERALL	6,630±844	20.2	30.7	34.4	14.7

Table 3.1. shows that the number of junior managers is less than that in middle management and, outside the top stratum, is also less than the number in top management. This is an indication of the small average size of firm and the consequent shallowness of their management structure.

TABLE 3.3.   *Estimated Average Number per Firm of Managers at Each Level, by Size and Location of Firm.*

Size of Firm (No. of Employees)	Location of Head Office	Chief Executive	Top Management	Middle Management	Junior Management
500 or More	DUBLIN	1.20	4.73	13.53	10.77
	REST OF COUNTRY	1.18	3.41	7.88	4.29
	OVERALL	1.19	4.25	11.49	8.43
100-499	DUBLIN	1.08±0.15	2.71±0.39	3.42±0.82	2.08±0.92
	REST OF COUNTRY	1.04±0.08	2.62±0.49	2.62±0.81	1.29±1.25
	OVERALL	1.06±0.08	2.67±0.30	3.02±0.56	1.69±0.75
20-99	DUBLIN	1.04±0.20	1.30±0.52	1.17±0.98	0.17±0.20
	REST OF COUNTRY	1.09±0.18	1.13±0.37	0.87±0.85	0.13±0.19
	OVERALL	1.06±0.13	1.22±0.30	1.02±0.62	0.15±0.14
OVERALL	DUBLIN	1.06±0.15	1.74±0.40	2.18±0.76	1.04±0.23
	REST OF COUNTRY	1.08±0.13	1.52±0.29	1.45±0.66	0.50±0.30
	OVERALL	1.07±0.10	1.63±0.24	1.83±0.49	0.78±0.18

Further comment on these tables is reserved for the next part of the chapter.

The estimated total and average number at each level is shown for member-firms of the Irish Management Institute in tables 3.4. and 3.5.

TABLE 3.4.   *Estimated Number of Managers at Each Level, by Size of Firm and Corporate Membership of Irish Management Institute.*

Size of Firm (No. of Employees)	Corporate Membership of I.M.I.	Chief Executive	Top Management	Middle Management	Junior Management
500 or More	MEMBER	49	182	509	392
	NON-MEMBER	7	18	31	4
100-499	MEMBER	87±14	230± 41	322± 80	235±155
	NON-MEMBER	186±17	455± 70	450±123	192±110
20-99	MEMBER	89±25	204± 86	217±259	25± 51
	NON-MEMBER	933±126	888±266	666±470	111±115
TOTAL	MEMBER	225±31	616±102	1048±301	653±165
	NON-MEMBER	1126±124	1362±267	1147±473	307±153

TABLE 3. 5.   *Estimated Average Number per Firm of Managers at Each Level, by Size of Firm and Corporate Membership of Irish Management Institute.*

Size of Firm (No. of Employees)	Corporate Membership of I.M.I.	Chief Executive	Top Management	Middle Management	Junior Management
500 or More	MEMBER	1.17	4.33	12.12	9.33
	NON-MEMBER	1.40	3.60	6.20	0.80
100-499	MEMBER	1.00±0.16	2.65±0.48	3.71±0.92	2.71±1.78
	NON-MEMBER	1.10±0.10	2.68±0.41	2.64±0.72	1.13±0.65
20-99	MEMBER	0.87±0.25	2.00±0.84	2.12±2.54	0.25±0.50
	NON-MEMBER	1.10±0.15	1.05±0.31	0.79±0.56	0.13±0.14
OVERALL	MEMBER	0.97±0.13	2.67±0.44	4.54±1.30	2.83±0.71
	NON-MEMBER	1.10±0.12	1.34±0.26	1.13±0.46	0.30±0.15

Section 2. Tests of Association

Before examining the effect of various factors on the way in which managers are divided between different levels, the differences observed between the proportions at each level must first be tested to see if they are statistically significant. Table 3.6 shows the following position:

Size of Firm (No. of Employees)	Chief Exec. %	Top Mgt. %	Middle Mgt. %	Junior Mgt. %
500 or more	4.61	16.56	45.40	33.45
100-499	12.74	31.98	36.32	18.96
20-99	34.65	37.01	28.35	

Taking the top stratum first there are very wide differences between the percentages at different levels. These are of course statistically significant by definition. The differences in the second size-group are significant beyond any doubt. In the third size-group the differences are small and are not statistically significant, that is, they might easily have arisen by chance. It could be argued that chief executives ought to be left out of this analysis on the basis that there is seldom more than one to each firm and that, therefore, at least in the two larger size-groups, it is only to be expected that there will be a much higher percentage at the other levels than at the level of chief executive. However, even if they are excluded there are still significant differences between the three remaining levels. In the bottom size-group above, junior and middle management were combined. If they are separated the following picture is seen.

Size of Firm (No. of Employees)	Chief Exec. %	Top Mgt. %	Middle Mgt. %	Junior Mgt. %
20-99	34.65	37.01	24.41	3.94

This difference now becomes highly significant showing that there is a very much lower number of junior managers in this size-group than of any other type, the other three levels being still reasonably similar.

CONCLUSION. *There are wide differences between the numbers at each level and it appears that the different size-groups show a different pattern.*

The effect of size and of three other factors is now examined. The factors, other than size, chosen for examination were: location, membership of the Irish Management Institute, and breadth of ownership.

Association between Size, Location and Level

In table 3.6. below there seems, in the top size-group, to be some association between the location of a firm and the proportion of managers at each level. There is no evidence of association in the other two groups. However, the difference in the

TABLE 3. 6. *Percentage of Managers at Each Level of Management, by Size and Location of Firm.*

Size of Firm (No. of Employees)	Location of Head Office	No. of Managers in Analysis	P'cent Chief Executives	P'cent in Top Mg'ment	P'cent in Middle Mg'ment	P'cent in Junior Mg'ment
500 or More	DUBLIN	887	3.84	15.34	44.88	35.97
	REST OF COUNTRY	285	7.02	20.36	47.02	25.62
	OVERALL	1172	4.61	16.56	45.40	33.45
100-499	DUBLIN	198	12.13	29.80	37.38	20.71
	REST OF COUNTRY	171	13.46	34.51	35.09	16.96
	OVERALL	369	12.74	31.98	36.32	18.98
20-99	DUBLIN	58	36.21	39.66	24.14(a)	
	REST OF COUNTRY	69	33.34	34.79	31.89(a)	
	OVERALL	127	34.65	37.01	28.35(a)	

(a) Junior and middle management were combined because there were too few in these categories to allow a test of significance.

top size-group may be explained by differences in size within the group — Dublin firms in this size-group are larger than those in the rest of the country. Location, then, does not appear to have any effect. Because of the apparent differences in the top size-group it is not possible to combine locations within size and to test the three size-groups against one another directly. Dublin firms were therefore taken first and the three size-groups compared, the procedure being repeated for the rest of the country. In each case testing showed that the differences were very highly significant. The same result was found any time that size was considered, irrespective of the other factor under review at the time. It may therefore be asserted confidently that size of firm has a considerable effect on the division of managers over different levels. This is what might be expected: small firms, having a small number of managers, will be most likely to have a high percentage of chief executives and also a high percentage of people reporting directly to the chief executive. As the firm grows in size both the number of managers and the number of levels of management increase. Consequently, more junior and middle managers appear.

CONCLUSION. *Size of firm, but not location, has an affect on the proportion of managers at each level. Higher proportions of middle and junior managers are present in larger firms.*

Association between Membership of the Irish Management Institute and Level
    The question is now raised whether there is any basis for the suggestion that membership of the Irish Management Institute affects the situation.

TABLE 3. 7.   *Percentage of Managers at Each Level of Management, by Size of Firm and Corporate Membership of Irish Management Institute.*

Size of Firm (No. of Employees)	Membership of I.M.I.	No. of Managers in Analysis	P'cent Chief Executives	P'cent in Top Mg'ment	P'cent in Middle Mg'ment	P'cent in Junior Mg'ment
500 or More	MEMBER	1112	4.23	15.83	45.06	34.90
	NON-MEMBER	60	11.67	30.01	51.67	6.67
	OVERALL	1172	4.61	16.56	45.40	33.45
100-499	MEMBER	166	9.64	26.51	37.37	26.51
	NON-MEMBER	203	15.28	36.46	35.47	12.81
	OVERALL	369	12.74	31.98	36.32	18.98
20-99	MEMBER	17	29.42	58.83	11.77(a)	
	NON-MEMBER	110	35.46	33.64	30.91(a)	
	OVERALL	127	34.65	37.01	28.35(a)	

(a) Middle and junior combined as in table 3.4.

    Taking the data in table 3.7 there are highly significant differences between member and non-member firms in the top two size strata and no significant difference in the bottom stratum. However, the difference may be accounted for by the fact that, within each of the size-groups, member firms employ, on average, a somewhat higher number of managers than do non-members. It is not possible to break the data down any further in order to eliminate the effect of these within-size-group differences, as the number of firms would be too small to allow the test of significance to be carried out.

CONCLUSION. *While there appears to be a difference between members and non-members, it is possible that this difference was caused, or at least magnified by differences in sizes of firm.*

Association between Family Ownership and Level
    Turning to family and non-family firms, the situation is shown in table 3.8.
    There is no evidence of difference between family and non-family firms in either of the top two strata. There is a significant difference in the bottom stratum. Here

again, however, the situation is complicated by the fact that, in this stratum, family firms normally employ a smaller number of managers than non-family firms. It cannot therefore be said unequivocally that family ownership is associated with the proportion at each level, even in the case of the smallest size group.

TABLE 3. 8. *Percentage of Managers at Each Level of Management by Size of Firm and Breadth of Ownership.*

Size of Firm (No. of Employees)	Breadth of Ownership	No. of Managers in Analysis	Per cent. Chief Executives	Per cent. in Top Mg'ment	Per cent. in Middle Mg'ment	Per cent. in Junior Mg'ment
500 or More	FAMILY	320	5.63	17.51	46.26	30.63
	NON-FAMILY	852	4.23	16.20	45.08	34.51
	OVERALL	1172	4.61	16.56	45.40	33.45
100-499	FAMILY	175	12.01	35.43	34.86	17.72
	NON-FAMILY	194	13.41	28.87	37.63	20.11
	OVERALL	369	12.74	31.98	36.32	18.98
20-99	FAMILY	89	40.45	38.21	21.35(a)	
	NON-FAMILY	38	21.06	34.22	44.74(a)	
	OVERALL	127	34.65	37.01	28.35(a)	

(a) Middle and junior combined as in table 3.4.

CONCLUSION. There is little evidence that family ownership as such affects the proportions at different levels.

There is no evidence that the three factors considered are associated with any other attribute of the firm in such a way as to cause a change in the conclusions arrived at above.

CHAPTER 4
Managers and Academic Qualifications

This chapter is concerned with a question very close to the core of the study: the academic qualification of managers in Irish industry. Because it is desired to examine this question in detail, the chapter is laid out somewhat differently from others. It falls into two main parts: part A which is concerned with estimates and inferences about the number of managers with any academic qualification, and part B which is concerned with the number having particular types of qualification. There is a comparison in chapter 10 of the proportion of executives with qualifications in the Republic of Ireland and in some other countries.

Summary of Findings: Part A

A little over 2,000 managers have an academic qualification, i.e., less than one manager in three, the proportion varying between the size-groups.

The nature and extent of variation between sizes depend on the other factors in conjunction with which size is considered.

There is little evidence that a firm's location or membership of the Irish Management Institute is associated, as such, with variation in its proportion of academically qualified managers.

There is some evidence that the type of market served and the technology of a firm are so associated, but in the case of type of market the difference may be caused by the fact that firms selling consumer goods employ a high proportion of marketing managers, and these tend not to have academic qualifications.

Small family-owned firms have a lower proportion of qualified executives than small public companies. Because of the small number involved, the evidence for asserting that foreign-owned companies employ a higher proportion of qualified managers than Irish-owned companies is not conclusive, although the proportions differ markedly among smaller and medium-sized firms.

Outside the largest firms, there is no difference in the proportions of qualified managers between firms which did and firms which did not use consultants.

Summary of Findings: Part B

The most frequently encountered qualifications are financial and secretarial professional qualifications, followed by university degrees in engineering, science and dairy science. Except for engineering, few other professional qualifications are common, while holders of university degrees in arts or commerce are rare, except in the 100 to 499 size-group.

The relative importance of the main qualifications varies from size-group to size-group. Accountants are most important numerically in every size of firm, engineers are more numerous than scientists in firms with over 500 employees, but the position is reversed in the 100 to 499 stratum. In firms of under 100 employees neither engineers nor natural scientists are frequent, but dairy scientists are almost as usual as accountants.

Large firms are comprehensive in their employment of qualified men, many of them employing engineers, scientists and accountants. Medium-sized firms with qualified men usually employ either an accountant alone or an accountant and a scientist.

Few small companies have qualified staff. Where a qualified man is employed he is most likely to be an accountant, particularly outside the dairying industry. In small firms, holders of qualifications other than accountancy, engineering, science or dairy science are mostly members of the owning family.

Definitions.

Managers who have a qualification are those who are university graduates or are members of a professional institute.[1] These terms are now defined.

UNIVERSITY GRADUATE: A university graduate is anyone who has been conferred with a degree by a recognised university, viz. the National University of Ireland, the University of Dublin, the Queen's University of Belfast, the Royal College of Surgeons in Ireland, or an equivalent institution abroad.

PROFESSIONAL QUALIFICATION: An executive is regarded as possessing a professional qualification if he is a member of an institute which requires that aspirants to membership shall follow a formal course of study culminating in an examination, and where such study imparts knowledge or skill which may be used in a variety of industries, i.e. it must not relate solely to the technology of a particular product or industry.

The emphasis in the definition of graduate is on the word "degree". People who attended university and were awarded diplomas as a result of following some course of study were not included among university graduates. In the case of professional qualifications, the accent is on the words "formal study" and "transferability" as it was felt that qualifications in the technology of a single product were better regarded as training rather than as professional education. It had originally been intended to include such technical training as a separate category but, in the general scaling down of the questionnaires which was necessary, it was decided to omit it.

In order to find out the qualification of the individual manager, the interviewee was asked whether the manager concerned had any sort of academic qualification and if so what it was. If the qualification conformed to any of the above definitions the appropriate area was marked. Within the broad classification into degree and professional qualification there were further sub-divisions. In the case of university degrees, these were commerce, arts, engineering, science and other. In the case of professional qualifications they were financial or secretarial, engineering or scientific, marketing, personnel and other. In the case of the longer-established and better known qualifications, no difficulty was experienced in deciding on their status and assigning them to a sub-division. Some less usual qualifications came up in the course of the study. They are discussed here.

Membership of the Irish Work Study Institute was not regarded as being a professional qualification as, on the base date of the survey—January 1st, 1964—it was not a condition of membership that a formal course of study be pursued, leading to examinations. Since carrying out this survey, the Institute has made such studies a condition for membership in future, and it may therefore be regarded in future surveys as constituting a professional qualification. Mining engineers, marine engineers and aeronautical engineers were all regarded as having professional qualifications, although it might seem at first glance that they are special to particular industries. It was found that this was not so: the general engineering content of these

---

[1] Such managers will usually be referred to in the text as "qualified managers". This is to avoid the lengthy phrase "academically-qualified managers". It does not of course imply that only they are qualified to manage a business.

qualifications is large and their holders are employed in a range of industries. Barristers-at-law who had not first taken a university degree in law were regarded not as university graduates but as professionally qualified and put into the category "other". The only other qualification encountered which gave rise to any question as regards its assignment to an area within the broad classification was the qualification in dairy science from University College, Cork. It was decided, as its subject matter was not confined exclusively to the natural sciences, that it would be better to include it in the category "other university degree".

PART A.   QUALIFICATIONS IN GENERAL

Section 1. Estimates of Numbers

In this section estimates are made of the total, proportion and average number per firm, of managers with and without academic qualification, by size of firm, location of firm and its membership of the Irish Management Institute.

TABLE 4. 1.   *Estimated Number and Percentage of Managers With and Without Qualifications, by Size and Location of Firm.*

Size of Firm (No. of Employees)	Location of Head Office	Total Number	Number With Qualification	Number Without Qualification	Percentage With Qualification	Percentage Without Qualification
500 or More	DUBLIN	907	407	500	44.9	55.1
	REST OF COUNTRY	285	108	177	37.9	62.1
	TOTAL	1,192	515	677	43.2	56.8
100–499	DUBLIN	1,161±208	380±145	781±129	32.7(a)	67.3
	REST OF COUNTRY	1,001±251	275±93	726±210	27.5	72.5
	TOTAL	2,168±317	659±171	1,510±236	30.4± 5.7	69.6
20–99	DUBLIN	1,811±679	469±481	1,342±313	25.9	74.1
	REST OF COUNTRY	1,467±471	377±299	1,090±237	25.7	74.3
	TOTAL	3,270±787	843±536	2,427±377	25.8±10.8	74.2
TOTAL	DUBLIN	3,879±704	1,256±498	2,623±334	32.4± 8.8	67.6
	REST OF COUNTRY	2,753±522	760±311	1,993±308	27.6± 7.1	72.4
	TOTAL	6,630±844	2,017±561	4,614±441	30.4± 5.8	69.6

(a) Confidence limits for proportions are shown in stratum 2 and 3 for the total only and not for each location. This is due to theoretical factors which are discussed in statistical note 2.2 in technical appendix B.

Table 4.1 shows the number and percentage of qualified and unqualified managers in each size of firm inside and outside of Dublin. The majority of managers in every size-group are not qualified. The overall proportion qualified is less than one in three, with no great differences between the two locations, but fairly marked differences between the sizes. These differences will be commented on in section 2 of this part.

Table 4.2 shows averages per firm, in order to assist in future estimates, while tables 4.3 and 4.4 show the position with respect to membership of the Irish Management Institute.

TABLE 4. 2. *Estimated Average Number per Firm of Managers With and Without Qualifications, by Size and Location of Firm.*

Size of Firm (No. of Employees)	Location of Head Office	Average per Firm with Qualification	Average per Firm Without Qualification
500 or More	DUBLIN	13.58	16.67
	REST OF COUNTRY	6.35	10.41
	OVERALL	10.96	14.40
100-499	DUBLIN	3.04±1.16	6.25±1.03
	REST OF COUNTRY	2.08±0.70	5.50±1.59
	OVERALL	2.56±0.66	5.87±0.92
20-99	DUBLIN	0.96±0.98	2.74±0.64
	REST OF COUNTRY	0.83±0.65	2.39±0.52
	OVERALL	0.89±0.57	2.56±0.40
OVERALL	DUBLIN	1.94±0.77	4.07±0.52
	REST OF COUNTRY	1.26±0.51	3.29±0.51
	OVERALL	1.61±0.45	3.69±0.35

TABLE 4. 3. *Estimated Number and Percentage of Managers, With and Without Qualifications, by Size of Firm and Corporate Membership of Irish Management Institute.*

Size of Firm (No. of Employees)	Corporate Membership of I.M.I.	Number With Qualification	Number Without Qualification	Percentage With Qualifiication	Percentage Without Qualification
500 or More	MEMBER	500	632	44.2	55.8
	NON-MEMBER	15	45	25.0	75.0
100-499	MEMBER	256± 78	619±187	29.2(a)	70.8
	NON-MEMBEBR	400±161	883±136	31.2± 8.5	68.8
20-99	MEMBER	217±267	319±118	40.5(a)	59.5
	NON-MEMBER	533±356	2,066±363	20.5±10.2	79.5
TOTAL	MEMBER	973±309	1,570±221	38.2± 5.9	61.8
	NON-MEMBER	948±378	2,993±376	24.2± 6.6	75.9

(a) Confidence limits not quoted for technical reasons. See statistical note 2.2.

TABLE 4. 4.   *Estimated Average per Firm of Managers With and Without Qualifications, by Size of Firm and Corporate Membership of Irish Management Institute.*

Size of Firm (No. of Employees)	Corporate Membership of I.M.I.	Average per Firm with Qualification	Average per Firm without Qualification
500 or More	MEMBER	11.90	15.05
	NON-MEMBER	3.00	9.00
100-499	MEMBER	2.94±0.89	7.12±2.15
	MON-MEMBER	2.35±0.95	5.19±0.80
20-99	MEMBER	2.12±2.62	3.12±1.15
	NON-MEMBER	0.63±0.42	2.45±0.43
OVERALL	MEMBER	4.21±1.34	6.80±0.96
	NON-MEMBER	0.93±0.37	2.94±0.37

In chapter 1 there is a technical note in which it is explained that in making estimates it was necessary to include in each stratum some firms which had left that size-group between the time the sample was chosen and the time the firm was visited. This has led, in the 20 to 99 employee size-group in tables 4.1 and 4.3, to quite a serious upward bias in the estimate of the proportion of qualified managers for firms in Dublin and for members of the Irish Management Institute, due to the inclusion of two firms which had grown beyond the 100 employee mark and which employed an extremely high proportion of qualified executives. The corresponding figures in tables 4.5 and 4.6 are probably better estimates of the true position.

Section 2.   Tests of Association

Because of the importance of academic qualifications it was decided to look for associations with a wide variety of factors. The factors considered in this context were (i) location, (ii) membership of the Irish Management Institute, (iii) type of market, (iv) type of manufacture, (v) type of production organisation, (vi) breadth of ownership, (vii) nationality of ownership, (viii) use of consultants.

In section 1 of this part there seemed to be differences between the proportions of managers qualified and unqualified and, before going on to consider the effect of the factors mentioned, it must first be seen whether the differences observed are statistically significant. The size-group totals in table 4.5 below are as follows:

Size of Firm (No. of Employees)	Percentage Qualified	Percentage Unqualified
500 or more	43.35	56.66
100-499	28·73	71.28
20-99	20.48	79.53

A statistical test showed each of these differences to be highly significant — in each case beyond the .001 level. This means that there is no possibility that even one-half of the managers in any size-group are qualified.

Association between Size, Location and Qualification.

The first question of interest was whether or not firms in Dublin employed a higher percentage of qualified managers than firms outside Dublin.

TABLE 4.5.   *Percentage of Managers Having Either a University Degree or a Professional Qualification, by Size and Location of Firm.*

Size of Firm (No. of Employees)	Location of Head Office	No. of Managers in Analysis	Percentage with Degree or Professional Qualification	Percentage with Neither
500 or More	DUBLIN	887	45.10	54.91
	REST OF COUNTRY	285	37.90	62.11
	OVERALL	1172	43.35	56.66
100-499	DUBLIN	198	29.30	70.71
	REST OF COUNTRY	171	28.08	71.93
	OVERALL	369	28.73	71.28
20-99	DUBLIN	58	13.80	86.21
	REST OF COUNTRY	69	26.09	73.92
	OVERALL	127	20.48	79.53

In the largest size-group there is, indeed, a difference between Dublin and non-Dublin firms with Dublin firms employing a higher proportion of qualified managers than firms outside. This may be caused by the fact that firms in Dublin are bigger on average than the others. In neither of the other strata is any significant difference present, i.e. the observed differences could have arisen by chance.

In the case of the bottom stratum, despite the fact that the evidence from the sample is not conclusive, it is likely *a priori* that firms outside Dublin employ a higher proportion of qualified managers than Dublin-based companies. The reason is that there are different types of industry in the two locations. In Dublin a high proportion of the firms in this size-group are engaged in the fashion clothing industry, in which there is not high stress on academic qualifications. In the rest of the country a high proportion of the firms are in the food industry, particularly the dairy industry, in which managers must, by law, have qualifications in dairy science.

Looking at size in the context of location it is not possible, because of the difference between locations in the top size-group, to combine them in order to test the size-group totals against one another. As usual in that situation, Dublin firms are taken first, then firms in the rest of the country, and within these classifications the three size-groups are tested. In both cases there are significant differences between the size-groups, this being most marked in the case of Dublin firms, where significance reaches the .001 level.   In the case of non-Dublin firms significance reaches the .05 level.   The fact that size has a much more marked effect in Dublin than outside is caused by the different types of industry in the two locations. In the large size-group there is, in Dublin, a high proportion of very large food-processing firms and also other high-technology industries.   In the rest of the country this is not so.   In the bottom size-stratum the position is practically reversed with Dublin having a high proportion of low-technology industry, viz. clothing, and firms outside Dublin having a high proportion of industry in which qualification is insisted upon. It is therefore reasonable to expect that there will be large differences between size-groups in Dublin but that, outside of Dublin, these differences will be less marked.

CONCLUSION.   The apparent differences between locations do not reach statistical significance except, by definition, in the top stratum.   The difference here may be caused by the fact that Dublin firms are bigger on average than others.   In the bottom stratum there may be differences caused by the different types of industry in the two places. Because of the differences in types of industry the effect of size is much more marked in Dublin than outside.

Association between Size, Membership of the Irish Management Institute, and Qualification.

The question of association between a firm's membership of the Irish Management Institute and the extent to which it employs qualified managers is now examined.

TABLE 4. 6.   *Percentage of Managers Having Either a Degree or Professional Qualification, by Size of Firm and Corporate Membership of the Irish Management Institute.*

Size of Firm (No. of Employees)	Corporate Membership of I.M.I.	No. of Managers in Analysis	Percentage with Degree or Professional Qualification	Percentage with Neither
500 or More	MEMBER	1112	44.34	55.67
	NON-MEMBER	60	25.01	75.01
	OVERALL	1172	43.35	56.66
100-499	MEMBER	166	29.52	70.49
	NON-MEMBER	203	28.08	71.93
	OVERALL	369	28.73	71.28
20-99	MEMBER	17	17.65	82.35
	NON-MEMBER	110	20.91	79.09
	OVERALL	127	20.48	79.53

In the 20 to 99 size-stratum and the 100 to 499 size-stratum there is no difference between members and non-members on this point.   It is only in the 500 or more employee group that a significant difference arises.   This may be caused by difference in size between members and non-members in this group and is not, anyhow, of practical importance. Looking at size in the context of membership it is not possible to combine members and non-members to test sizes. Neither is it possible, because of the low number of managers employed in member firms in the bottom stratum, to carry out a test of association on size within member firms. Taking non-member firms, there is no significant difference between the three size groups.

CONCLUSION. *A firm's membership of the Irish Management Institute is not associated in any practically important way with its proportion of qualified managers. Among firms which are not members there is no difference between the three size-groups, all of them employing a low percentage.*

Association Between Size, Type of Market and Qualification.

Looking at table 4.7 there appears to be a persistent tendency for firms serving an industrial market to employ a higher proportion of qualified managers than consumer-goods firms. Only in the case of the top stratum, however, is this difference established as statistically significant. In the case of the other two strata the differences might well have arisen by chance. Differences in organisation could account for at least some of these observed differences, as firms serving a consumer market have a high proportion of marketing managers. It is shown in chapter 8 that marketing executives are less likely than others to have academic qualifications. Looking at size in the context of type of market served, there are in both cases highly significant differences between the size-groups in their proportion of qualified managers.

TABLE 4. 7. *Percentage of Managers Having Either a University Degree or a Professional Qualification, by Size of Firm and Type of Market.*

Size of Firm (No. of Employees)	Type of Market	No. of Managers in Analysis	Percentage with Degree or Professional Qualification	Percentage with Neither
500 or More	CONSUMER	706	40.94	59.07
	INDUSTRIAL	466	47.00	53.01
	OVERALL	1172	43.35	56.66
100-499	CONSUMER	241	27.39	72.62
	INDUSTRIAL	128	31.26	68.76
	OVERALL	369	28.73	71.28
20-99	CONSUMER	85	17.65	82.36
	INDUSTRIAL	42	26.20	73.81
	OVERALL	127	20.48	79.53

CONCLUSION. *The difference between consumer-market and industrial-market firms is not significant outside the top size-group and, such as it is, may be caused by differences in organisation. There are differences between the size-groups in firms serving each type of market.*

Association between Size, Type of Manufacture and Qualification.
The effect of type of manufacture on proportion qualified is now considered.

TABLE 4. 8.   *Percentage of Managers Having Either a University Degree or a Professional Qualification, by Size of Firm and Type of Manufacture.*

Size of Firm (No. of Employees)	Type of Manufacture	No. of Managers in Analysis	Percentage with Degree or Professional Qualification	Percentage with Neither
500 or More	FABRICATION	178	40.45	59.56
	PROCESSING	762	43.65	56.36
	OTHER	232	44.59	55.41
	OVERALL	1172	43.35	56.66
100–499	FABRICATION	68	14.71	85.30
	PROCESSING	267	30.72	69.29
	OTHER	34	41.18	58.83
	OVERALL	369	28.73	71.28
20–99	FABRICATION	32	9.38	90.63
	PROCESSING	91	24.18	75.83
	OTHER	(a)	(a)	(a)
	OVERALL	(b)	(b)	(b)

(a) The category "other" refers mainly to firms engaged in extraction and in repair-work. There were too few such firms in the bottom stratum to include their managers in a test of significance.
(b) An overall percentage is not shown because the exclusion of the category "other" would cause it to differ from that already shown in earlier tables.

The top size-group shows little difference between types of manufacture; in the middle size-group there is a highly significant difference and in the bottom size-group the difference, though large, is not statistically significant. So marked are the differences in the two lower groups that it is very likely that in firms with under 500 employees an association does exist. Thus up to this point technology exerts an influence, the fabricating firms up to this level being, in the main, low-technology enterprises. Looking at size in the context of type of manufacture, there are very highly significant differences between the three size-groups in the case of both fabrication and processing firms. There are not enough firms in the "other" category to carry out a test.

CONCLUSION. It is likely that, up to 500 employees, firms in process industries employ a higher proportion of academically-qualified managers than the lower-technology fabricating firms. Beyond that point there is little difference. In both process and fabrication there are differences between the size-groups, in both cases the significant differences being between firms with over 500 employees and firms with less than 500. The differences between small and medium-sized firms are not great.

Association between Size, Type of Production Organisation and Qualification

It was considered that the type of production organisation in a firm might effect the extent to which it found it necessary to employ qualified managers, and that firms making specially to order might exhibit a different proportion from those firms which had reached some stage of standardisation.

TABLE 4. 9. *Percentage of Managers Having Either a University Degree or a Professional Qualification, by Size of Firm and Type of Production.*

Size of Firm (No. of Employees)	Type of Production	No. of Managers in Analysis	Percentage with Degree or Professional Qualification	Percentage with Neither
500 or More	MAKE TO ORDER	78	29.49	70.52
	OTHER	1094	44.34	55.67
	OVERALL	1172	43.35	56.66
100-499	MAKE TO ORDER	11	27.27	72.73
	OTHER	349	27.79	72.21
	OVERALL(a)	369	28.73	71.28
20-99	MAKE TO ORDER	29	10.35	89.66
	OTHER	98	23.47	76.54
	OVERALL	127	20.48	79.53

(a) The overall total does not add to the sum of the other two figures because some extractive firms were omitted.

So few firms outside the smallest size-group make to order that it is only in that group that the question is of practical importance. Even there the number is not large and, while the difference is in the direction expected, it is not statistically significant. Taking first make-to-order firms, there is no difference between the three size-groups — all employ a low proportion of academically-qualified executives. In the case of " other " firms the differences are significant, larger firms, as usual, employing a higher proportion of qualified managers than either of the other two size-groups.

CONCLUSION. Outside the smaller firms, few make to order. In the smallest group the difference between firms making to order is in the direction expected, but is not statistically significant. There is little difference between the size-groups in firms making to order, all of them employing a low proportion of qualified managers. In firms making standard products there are differences between firms with over 500 employees and firms with less than 500, but not between the other two groups.

Association between Size, Breadth of Ownership and Qualification.

Family businesses tend to be looked on as being more conservative than those with wider ownership and it therefore appeared worthwhile to look at the proportion of qualified managers employed by each type to discover if, in this respect, such a contention was borne out.

TABLE 4. 10.   *Percentage of Managers Having Either a University Degree or a Professional Qualification, by Size of Firm and Breadth of Ownership.*

Size of Firm (No. of Employees)	Breadth of Ownership	No. of Managers in Analysis	Percentage with Degree or Professional Qualification	Percentage with Neither
500 or More	FAMILY	320	39.38	60.63
	NON-FAMILY	852	44.84	55.17
	OVERALL	1172	43.35	56.66
100-499	FAMILY	175	29.15	70.86
	NON-FAMILY	194	28.36	71.65
	OVERALL	369	28.73	71.28
20-99	FAMILY	89	12.36	87.65
	NON-FAMILY	38	39.48	60.53
	OVERALL	127	20.48	79.53

In fact this table provides no evidence of difference between family and non-family firms in either of the two top size-strata. In the lowest size-group, however, there is a very striking difference, with non-family firms employing, as suspected, a significantly higher proportion of qualified managers than family firms. This may be explained to some extent by the fact that non-family firms in this size-group are larger on average than family firms. However, this does not seem a likely explanation of such a large difference. It is interesting that family-firms in this size-group employ a higher proportion of executives aged under 35 than non-family firms. In the two upper size-groups younger managers are more likely to be qualified than older executives (chapter 9). This is not true of the 20 to 99 employee group. Thus there is no tendency yet evident in small family-owned firms for the position with regard to employment of academically-qualified managers to improve automatically with time.

In the context of breadth of ownership, size is once again a significant factor. In the case of both family and non-family firms there are wide differences between the three size-groups. In the case of the non-family firms a rather unusual pattern is shown in table 4.10. In this case, the largest size-group employs as usual the highest proportion of qualified managers, but the smallest group appears to employ a higher proportion than the medium size-group. Further tests within this category showed, however, that the difference between medium-sized and small is not significant, and that the truly significant difference in this case arises between large and medium-sized firms.

CONCLUSION. *Family firms in the 20 to 99 employee group employ a lower proportion of academically qualified managers than other firms in that group, despite the fact that their managers are younger. Size has an affect both in family and non-family firms. In the latter case the significant difference is between large and medium-sized firms, with small companies employing a surprisingly high proportion of qualified managers.*

Association between Size, Nationality of Ownership and Qualification

Because few studies are available on which to base international comparisons, it was decided to see whether foreign-owned companies operating in Ireland employed a different proportion of academically-qualified executives to Irish companies.

TABLE 4. 11. *Percentage of Managers Having Either a University Degree or a Professional Qualification, by Size of Firm and Nationality of Ownership.*

Size of Firm (No. of Employees)	Nationality of Ownership	No. of Managers in Analysis	Percentage with Degree or Professional Qualification	Percentage with Neither
500 or More	IRISH	885	44.75	55.26
	OTHER	287	39.03	60.98
	OVERALL	1172	43.35	56.66
100-499	IRISH	325	27.08	72.93
	OTHER	44	40.91	59.10
	OVERALL	369	28.73	71.28
20-99	IRISH	120	19.17	80.83
	OTHER	7	42.86	57.14
	OVERALL	127	20.48	79.53

In the top stratum the difference is negligible. In the other two it is marked, but is not statistically significant because of the small number of managers employed by foreign-owned concerns. (In the bottom stratum Fisher's test was used: see statistical note 4.1 in technical appendix B.) It is likely that recently established foreign-owned companies are under-represented in the sample (see chapter 7). Because of this it would be unwise to reject completely the conclusion that foreign companies based in Ireland employ a higher proportion of qualified executives than Irish firms of the same size.

Size exerts no influence in foreign-owned firms: irrespective of size, about 40 per cent of their managers have qualifications. In Irish firms there are marked differences between the size groups.

CONCLUSION. *It is possible that foreign-owned companies in the small and medium size-groups employ a higher proportion of academically-qualified managers than Irish-owned companies, even though the differences observed in table 4.11. are not statistically significant. Size does not affect the extent to which foreign firms employ qualifed executives—in each size-group they employ about 40 per cent—but it does affect Irish firms.*

Association between Size, Use of Consultants and Qualification.

The final question looked at was whether or not firms which used the services of consultants employed a different percentage of qualified executives to firms which did not, to see whether consultants tended to be used to make up for any lack of expertise caused by a shortage of qualified staff, or tended to be used by firms already employing a high proportion of qualified executives, to supplement their expertise.

TABLE 4. 12.   *Percentage of Managers Having Either a University Degree or a Professional Qualification, by Size of Firm and its Use of Consultants.*

Size of Firm (No. of Employees)	Use by Firm of Consultants	No. of Managers in Analysis	Percentage with Degree or Professional Qualification	Percentage with Neither
500 or More	USED	936	45.09	54.92
	DID NOT USE	236	36.45	63.56
	OVERALL	1172	43.35	56.66
100-499	USED	160	26.26	73.76
	DID NOT USE	209	30.63	69.38
	OVERALL	369	28.73	71.28
20-99	USED	23	17.39	82.61
	DID NOT USE	104	21.15	78.85
	OVERALL	127	20.48	79.53

The answer shown by table 4.12 is that, in neither the bottom nor the middle stratum, is there any evidence of a difference, while in the top stratum firms which have used consultants employ a higher proportion of qualified managers than firms which have not. This leads to the conclusion that in large companies the more highly qualified a firm's management is the more likely it is to use the services available to supplement its own expertise.   Looking at size in this context, in the case of firms which used or did not use consultants there are significant differences between the size-groups, the differences being less marked among firms not using consultants.

CONCLUSION. In large firms, the more highly qualified a firm's management the more likely it is to use consultants. There is no such tendency in small or medium sized firms. Size of firm affects the situation both in firms which have and firms which have not used consultants.

PART B. INDIVIDUAL QUALIFICATIONS

The first part of this chapter was concerned with qualifications in general. This part deals with individual qualifications.

The number of holders of each qualification is estimated in table 4.13. The number of holders exceeds the number of qualified managers, as executives with more than one qualification are counted once for each qualification held. For instance, many of those with university degrees in engineering also hold professional qualifications in that subject. It should be emphasised that the figures in this part refer to the number of industrial managers with each type of qualification, and not to the total number of individual holders: many holders of these qualifications are in positions other than industrial management.

The method of estimation used for table 4.13 differs from that used elsewhere. As explained in chapter 1 it was necessary, when making estimates, to regard firms which had changed size before they were surveyed as being still in their original size-group, as otherwise the sampling fractions used would have been indeterminate. It was pointed out in part A of this chapter that this introduced serious bias into the estimated number of qualified managers in the smallest size-group, as two firms which had grown beyond 100 employees were particularly heavy employers of qualified executives. This would have been even more serious when considering particular types of qualification as one of the firms employed a high proportion of technical staff.

It was therefore decided to omit results from any firm which had changed size and to regard the resulting samples as constituting one-sixth of the total number of firms in the 100 to 499 group, and one-twenty-third of the total in the 20 to 99 group. The population totals were estimated by multiplying the sample results by 6 and by 23 respectively.

The top size-group was reduced to 45 firms, which is almost certainly too low: it is probable that some firms not sampled had grown to over 500 employees. To that extent the figures for the top group are underestimates but, as the concern in this part is with relative rather than with absolute numbers, this underestimation is not serious.

No estimates of sampling variability are attached to any of the estimates in this part for technical reasons, but it should not be forgotten that the estimates are subject to this uncertainty.[1]

TABLE 4.13. *Estimated Approximate Number of Managers with Each Type of University Degree or Professional Qualification, by Size of Firm.*

Type of Degree or Qualification	Size of Firm (No. of Employees)			
	500 or more	100-499	20-99	Total
University Degree				
Commerce	63	72	69	204
Arts	42	48	92	182
Engineering	144	90	23	257
Science	86	144	69	299
Other	26	12	230	268
Professional Qualifications				
Finance	152	228	207	587
Engineering	56	78	—	134
Marketing	8	12	—	20
Personnel	4	—	—	4
Other	8	42	46	96

See text above for an explanation of how these estimates were made.

1. As figures 4.1 to 4.4 show, the distributions of the qualifications are so far from normal that use of the t-distribution could not be justified.

It appears from table 4.13 that professional qualifications in finance are the leading qualification, followed by science, engineering and "other university degrees", mainly in dairy science. Dairy scientists are mainly concentrated in the smallest size-group and in the milk-processing industry. The relative importance of the different qualifications varies from size-group to size-group. In the top group university-trained engineers are almost as frequent as accountants[1]. In the 100 to 499 group accountants are by far the most important, followed by scientists. Professional engineers are almost as frequent as those trained at university. In the bottom group accountants and dairy scientists dominate, engineers being virtually non-existent.

These conclusions are tentative due to the double counting referred to earlier. Table 4.14 shows in detail the results for the sample, the categories now being mutually exclusive. Inspection of table 4.14 shows little change in the relative position of the individual qualifications. The only important change is that, in the largest size-group, the importance of qualifications in arts or commerce alone is diminished by separating those who are also qualified accountants while, in the middle group, those with professional engineering qualifications alone are less important numerically than university-trained engineers when the latter include those with both university and professional qualifications.

There seems little doubt from tables 4.13 and 4.14 that industry prefers people with specialist qualifications to those with a more general training. This conclusion is reinforced by figures 4.1 to 4.4 below which show the distribution of qualifications over firms.[2] These show that, as well as being the most numerous, accountants, engineers and scientists are the most widely dispersed, i.e. more firms employ executives with those qualifications than with any others.

It was seen in chapter 2 that, in firms of over 100 employees, positions in production management outnumber any other group. For that reason it is not surprising to find a relatively high number of managers with qualifications in engineering and science. It is interesting to note the pattern of employment. In small firms neither engineers nor scientists are numerous. Scientists are numerous in medium-sized companies, reflecting the fact that most industry in Ireland is process industry. University-trained engineers are not nearly so usual as scientists nor so widely employed. In firms of over 500 employees, engineers become more usual than scientists even though most firms in this size-group are also processing companies. This suggests that either engineers in process industry may largely be employed on engineering rather than line management work, their increased employment in large firms being due to the more complex and costly capital installation, or that the potential contribution of engineers is underestimated by medium-sized companies. Discussion of this question is postponed to chapter 8, as it involves the relationship between qualification and function which forms the subject of that chapter.

The greater numerical importance in managerial positions of university-trained engineers *vis-à-vis* those with a professional qualification is a reflection of the fact that by far the greatest proportion of engineers are trained at university. So many more qualify through university than otherwise, that the number of those in managerial positions with professional qualifications alone is surprisingly high.

1. To avoid the use of long phrases, executives with qualifications related to finance will be referred to as accountants, although many of them qualified as company secretaries.
2. To avoid confusion in interpretation, the distributions are of those holding each type of qualification only. Thus firms employing, for instance, an accountant with both a degree and a professional qualification are counted as having no one with a financial qualification only.

TABLE 4. 14. *Number of Managers in the Sample[1] with Each Type of Qualification Alone, by Size of Firm.*

Type of Qualification	Size of Firm (No. of Employees)					
University Degree Alone[2]	500 or more		100-499		20-99	
Commerce Alone	28		9		1	
Commerce and Arts	5		1		—	
Commerce and Engineering	4		—		—	
Commerce and Science	1		—		—	
Commerce and Other Degree	—	38	—	10	—	1
Arts Alone	23		3		2	
Arts and Engineering	—		—		—	
Arts and Science	—		—		—	
Arts and Other Degree	1	24	2	5	—	2
Engineering Alone	116		9		1	
Engineering and Science	3		—		—	
Engineering and Other Degree	—	119	—	9	—	1
Science Alone	77		21		3	
Science and Other Degree	1	78	—	21	—	3
Other Degree Alone	21	21	1	1	9	9
Professional Qualification Alone[3]						
Finance Alone	119		36		6	
Engineering & Science Alone	33		5		—	
Marketing Alone	7		2		—	
Personnel Alone	4		1		—	
Other Qualification Alone	7		6		1	
Degree & Professional Qualification						
Commerce and Finance	22		—		1	
Commerce, Arts and Finance	4		2		1	
Arts and Finance	7		—		1	
Arts and Other Qualification	1		—		—	
Arts, Engineering and Engineering	1		—		—	
Engineering and Engineering	17		5		—	
Engineering, Science and Eng.	2		1		—	
Engineering, Law and Engineering	1		—		—	
Science and Engineering & Science	2		2		—	
Agriculture and Marketing	1		—		—	
Law and Finance	1		—		—	
Law and Other	—		—		1	

1. Excluding firms which changed size. To estimate approximately the number of each type in the population, multiply the figures for the 100 to 499 size-group by 6 and those for the 20 to 99 group by 23.

2. No university graduate without a professional qualification had more than two degrees.

3. No one with professional qualifications alone had qualifications in more than one area.

Figure 4. 1.

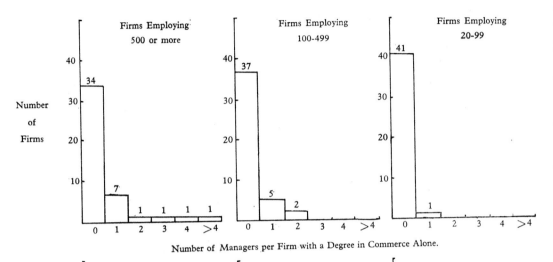

Number of Managers per Firm with a Degree in Commerce Alone.

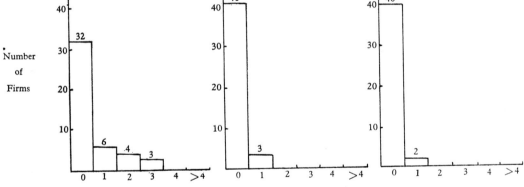

Number of Managers per Firm with a Degree in Arts Alone.

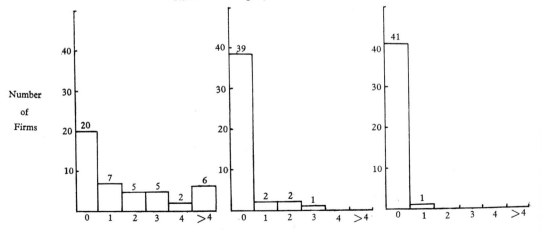

Number of Managers per Firm with a Degree in Engineering Alone.

Figure 4. 2.

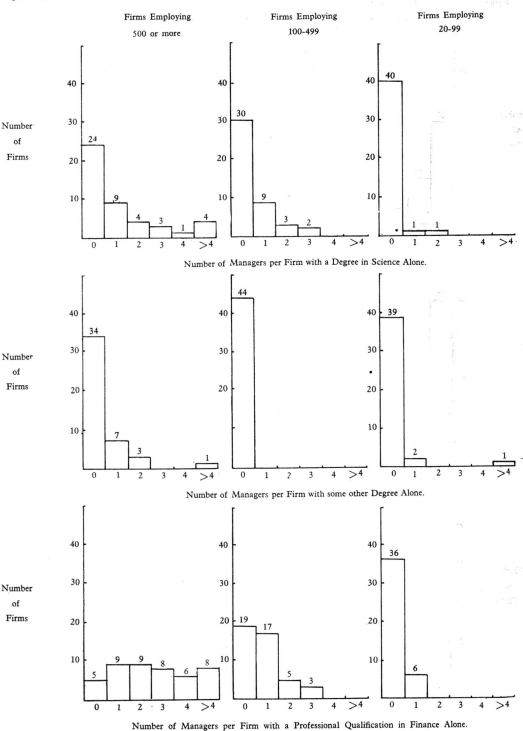

Firms Employing 500 or more

Firms Employing 100-499

Firms Employing 20-99

Number of Firms

Number of Managers per Firm with a Degree in Science Alone.

Number of Managers per Firm with some other Degree Alone.

Number of Managers per Firm with a Professional Qualification in Finance Alone.

Figure 4. 3.

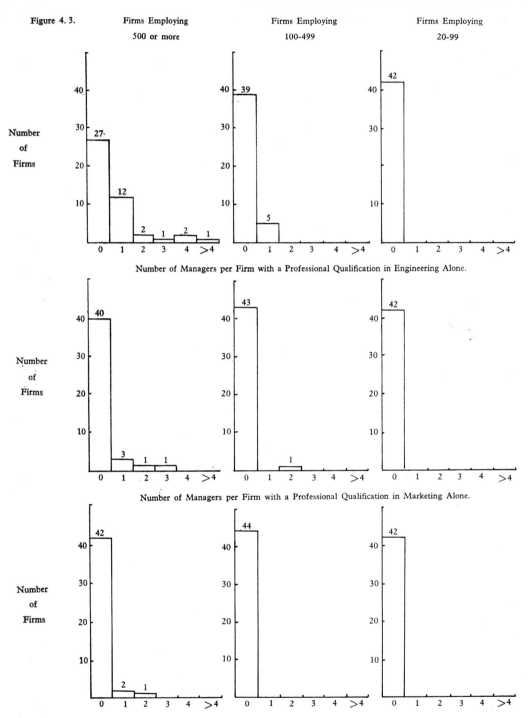

Number of Managers per Firm with a Professional Qualification in Engineering Alone.

Number of Managers per Firm with a Professional Qualification in Marketing Alone.

Number of Managers per Firm with a Professional Qualification in Personnel Management Alone.

Figure 4. 4.

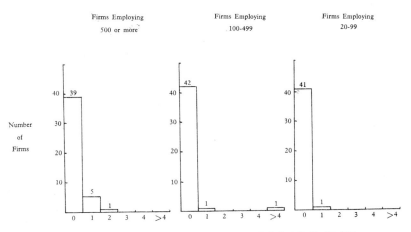

Number of Managers per Firm with some other Professional Qualification Alone.

The very large number of qualified accountants and the high proportion of finance executives who are qualified are a result of both supply and demand. To a certain extent the fact that finance has a higher proportion of qualified executives than any other function indicates that business attaches a greater importance to this area than to any other. But it also reflects the availability of qualified accountants. The fact that qualification in accountancy and secretarial work is through professional organisations, and by part-time study, and the fact that until comparatively recently these were almost the only bodies in any field offering a professional qualification, meant that people who had not the opportunity to go to university and wished to qualify themselves for advancement, largely studied accountancy. Consequently there was available a supply of qualified accountants.

The estimated number of men in executive positions who hold qualifications in marketing is low, but this situation could change quite rapidly, as there are now very large numbers of students taking a qualification (see chapter 17) and who will probably start to reach management level within a few years.

Employment of arts graduates is very limited. This is particularly true of economists, who are very rarely employed in industry. The scope for employing general arts graduates is small, because Irish companies are not of a size to have the type of general administrative position in which someone without specialist qualifications might be employed. It might have been expected that this difficulty would be less acute in the case of economists, but such is obviously not the case: industry does not appreciate the contribution which economists are trained to make.

The fact that commerce, the one university degree directly oriented toward business, is so poorly represented may appear surprising. (In fact it is even less widespread than table 4.14 shows. Of the 28 graduates in the 500 or over size-group who have a commerce degree only, 12 are employed in one large company. Of the 9 such graduates in the sample from the 100 to 499 group, 5 are employed by three companies in Cork city.) On reflection it is understandable enough. Production management, by its nature, is virtually closed to all but technical graduates. Finance is dominated by professional accountants, who have in their studies covered their subject at a much more advanced level than is aimed at in the commerce degree course. This leaves marketing and personnel management, neither of which is extensively treated in commerce courses. In any event the number of specialist personnel managers is limited, while firms do not place a high priority on employing qualified executives in marketing positions. There is, therefore, a limited number of posts in which a commerce degree alone equips a graduate to perform better than those with other qualifications. In fact the commerce degree is at present intended only as an introductory course, preferably to be followed in the case of those desiring a business career by taking a professional qualification. If its essentially preparatory nature were better understood, some of the dissatisfaction expressed by executives (chapter 18) might have been avoided.

It was decided to investigate to what extent firms employed executives with the three main types of qualification, to see whether firms in general tended to be limited or comprehensive in their employment of qualified staff. This was done by counting, in each size group the number of firms with no qualified staff, the number employing only an accountant (whether professionally qualified only, or combining a degree and qualification), only an engineer or only a scientist, the number of firms employing both engineers and accountants and so on. The results are shown in table 4.15. Note that the focus is on the three main types of qualification only: firms employing, for instance, both an accountant and an arts graduate, but no other qualified executive, would be counted in this table as "employing an accountant only", as otherwise the number of combinations possible would be too great. Firms employing neither an accountant, an engineer nor a scientist, but employing a manager with some other qualification are not included in the table. This explains why the total of firms does not add to the sample total. Firms changed in size are omitted from this table also.

Table 4.15 shows striking disparities between the three size-groups. Nearly all the large firms employ some qualified staff, and half of them employ engineers, scientists and qualified accountants or secretaries. One-fifth employ both engineers and accountants but no scientists, and another one-fifth employ only an accountant. It is true in all three size-groups that, where a firms employs only one type of qualified man, he is most likely to be an accountant.

Firms in the medium size-group are somewhat less likely than large ones to employ qualified staff, but the majority (over 80 per cent) do have someone qualified. They are less comprehensive in their employment of qualified men than larger firms: only 5 out of 44 employ engineers, scientists and accountants. (Engineers include both university-trained and professionally-qualified men.) Six out of 44 employ a scientist and an accountant, while 14 employ only an accountant.

Small firms are least likely to employ qualified executives: out of 42 firms, only 17 had any qualified staff. Only 10 of these employed either an engineer, a scientist or an accountant and, of these, 7 employed an accountant only.

Of the 45 large companies 26 employed a university-trained engineer, while 32 employed a qualified engineer of some sort. Twenty-four employed scientists, while 42 employed qualified accountants.

The sample included 44 medium-sized companies. Eight of these employed university-trained engineers: 13 employed a qualified engineer of some sort. Fifteen employed scientists and 27 employed a qualified accountant — 16 out of 22 firms in Dublin, but only 9 out of 22 outside Dublin.

There were 42 small firms, only one of which employed a qualified engineer. Two employed scientists, while 9 employed a qualified accountant — 2 in Dublin and 7 outside. Seven companies employed only executives with some qualification other than finance, engineering or science. Six of these were family firms. One employed a commerce graduate, a member of the family. One employed an arts graduate, also a family member. One employed a medical doctor and two a barrister, all of them family members. The other employed an arts graduate, not a family member, and a dentist who was. The non-family firm was a creamery, employing graduates in dairy science. Thus it is obvious that, in small companies, the only type of career managers with qualifications are accountants and dairy scientists. Almost all the other types of qualification are held by owners or by members of owning families.

TABLE 4.15.   *The Three Most Frequent Types of Qualification, Showing the Number of Firms Employing Managers with Each Type, by Size and Location of Firm.*

Type of Qualified Executive	Size of Firm (No. of employees)					
	500 or more		100-499		20-99	
	Dublin	Rest of Country	Dublin	Rest of Country	Dublin	Rest of Country
Engineer Alone						
University-trained	—	—	1	1	1	—
Other	—	—	—	2	—	—
Scientist Alone	—	—	—	2	—	—
Accountant Alone	3	6	8	6	1	6
Engineer & Scientist Alone	1	—	—	2	—	—
Engineer & Accountant Alone	6	3	1	1	—	—
Scientist & Accountant Alone	1	1	5	1	1	1
Engineer, Scientist & Accountant	16	6	3	2	—	—
No Qualified Executives	—	1	3	5	13	12

CHAPTER 5

Participation in Management Training

In a study concerned with the educational and training requirements of management, one of the most important questions is the extent to which managers have participated in management training courses. It had been hoped to go into some detail on this question and to ask for each individual the type and duration of course at which he had attended, as well as a variety of other questions on this subject. Testing showed, however, that unless all the information required was collected during the interview it was unlikely to be provided—test questionnaires sent for completion before the interview, or left after it, were very rarely filled in. It quickly became obvious in the course of further testing, especially in larger companies or where the manager had participated in training courses before joining the company, that while the chief executive invariably knew whether the individual concerned had ever attended a course or seminar, he rarely had details of the type or length of course and would not usually be able to get them without carrying out enquiries. If he was asked to do so during the interview goodwill tended to be lost and valuable time taken up, while if he was asked to send details afterwards the matter tended to be overlooked. Consequently, it was decided to ask simply whether each executive had ever attended any formal management training course or seminar however short, not counting any course of study already covered in chapter 4. There is no suggestion that only those are included who attended courses run by the Irish Management Institute.

Summary of Findings.

At January 1st 1964 firms in industry employed over 1,600 managers who had attended some training activity. This was just under one quarter of the total employed at that date.

The proportions varied a great deal between firms with over 500 employees and the rest: in fact almost half of all those who had participated were employed by the handful of firms employing 500 people or more.

Even in firms employing some managers with training there remained a high proportion of executives who had not participated in courses.

Neither location nor family ownership nor use of consultants was associated with a firm's proportion of qualified executives. Large and medium-sized firms which were members of the Irish Management Institute, and foreign-owned firms of every size, employed a higher proportion than other firms of executives with training.

There is some evidence that type of market and technology influenced the situation.

Use of training therefore appears to be, in part, a response to increasing complexity. Small size is an inhibiting factor on participation even in firms which are members of the Irish Management Institute: more inhibiting even than location. This barrier may not be insuperable as foreign-owned companies irrespective of size employ a high proportion of executives with training.

Section 1. Estimates of Numbers

The number of managers who had attended courses up to January 1st 1964 is shown in table 5.1.

Most of those who attended worked for firms based in Dublin, while almost half worked in firms employing 500 or more people. The proportions are shown in table

5.2., and show that there is little difference between firms in Dublin and outside, wide difference between firms with over 500 employees and the rest, and little differ-

TABLE 5. 1. *Estimated Number of Managers who Attended Management Training Courses, by Size and Location of Firm.*

Size of Firm (No. of Employees)	Location of Head Office	Attended Courses	Did Not Attend Courses
500 or More	DUBLIN	560	347
	REST OF COUNTRY	168	117
	TOTAL	728	464
100-499	DUBLIN	250±125	911±149
	REST OF COUNTRY	214±187	786±118
	TOTAL	466±215	1,703±190
20-99	DUBLIN	277±223	1,534±652
	REST OF COUNTRY	178±112	1,289±447
	TOTAL	452±236	2,817±752
TOTAL	DUBLIN	1,087±251	2,792±666
	REST OF COUNTRY	561±214	2,192±460
	TOTAL	1,646±315	4,984±774

TABLE 5. 2. *Estimated Percentage of Managers attending Management Training Courses, by Size and Location of Firm.*

Size of Firm (No. of Employees)	Location of Head Office	Total Number of Managers	Percentage Attended	Percentage Did Not Attend
500 or More	DUBLIN	907	61.7	38.3
	REST OF COUNTRY	285	58.9	41.1
	OVERALL	1,192	61.1	38.9
100–499	DUBLIN	1,161±208	21.5	78.5
	REST OF COUNTRY	1,001±251	21.4	78.6
	OVERALL	2,168±317	21.5±7.4	78.5
20–99	DUBLIN	1,811±679	15.3	84.7
	REST OF COUNTRY	1,467±471	12.2	87.8
	OVERALL	3,270±787	13.8±6.9	86.2
OVERALL	DUBLIN	3,879±704	28.0±5.8	72.0
	REST OF COUNTRY	2,753±522	20.4±6.1	79.6
	OVERALL	6,630±844	24.8±3.9	75.2

ence between small and medium-sized firms. (Inclusion of firms no longer in their original strata did not introduce as much bias into the estimates in this case as it did in chapter 4. This can be seen by comparing table 5.2. with table 5.6.).

The position with respect to membership of the Irish Management Institute is shown in tables 5.3 and 5.4.

TABLE 5. 3.   *Estimated Number of Managers who Attended Management Training Courses, by Size of Firm and Corporate Membership of Irish Management Institute.*

Size of Firm (No. of Employees)	Corporate Membership of I.M.I.	Attended Courses	Did Not Attend Courses
500 or More	MEMBER	721	411
	NON-MEMBER	7	53
100-499	MEMBER	256±164	619±106
	NON-MEMBER	203±135	1,080±165
20-99	MEMBER	89±97	446±350
	NON-MEMBER	333±199	2,265±567
TOTAL	MEMBER	1,066±190	1,476±406
	NON-MEMBER	543±232	3,399±574

TABLE 5. 4.   *Estimated Percentage of Managers attending Management Training Courses, by Size of Firm and Corporate Membership of Irish Management Institute.*

Size of Firm (No. of Employees)	Corporate Membership of I.M.I.	Total Number of Managers	Percentage Attended	Percentage Did Not Attend
500 or More	MEMBER	1,132	63.7	36.3
	NON-MEMBER	60	11.7	88.3
100–499	MEMBER	875±215	29.2	70.8
	NON-MEMBER	1,283±232	15.8±8.2	84.2
20–99	MEMBER	535±355	16.7	83.3
	NON-MEMBER	2,599±593	12.8±6.9	87.2
OVERALL	MEMBER	2,543±438	41.9±5.9	58.1
	NON-MEMBER	3,942±616	13.8±5.1	86.2

The proportion participating in training courses is markedly higher for members than for non-members except in small firms, where there is little difference. It is worth noting that in medium-sized companies about 40 per cent of those who participated in courses were not employed by member-companies, while in small companies the great majority of participants were employed by non-members.

It is interesting to look at the situation in firms which employed some executives who had participated in training activities.

TABLE 5. 5. *Number of Managers in the Sample Who Had Attended Courses, by Size of Firm and its Employment of Trained Managers (all sample firms included).*

Size of Firm (No. of (Employees)	Employment of Trained Management	Number of Trained Managers Employed	Number of Untrained Managers Employed
500 or More	Firms Employing No Trained Managers	—	47
	Firms Employing Some Trained Managers	727	417
	TOTAL	727	464
100-499	Firms Employing No Trained Managers	—	118
	Firms Employing Some Trained Managers	87	200
	TOTAL	87	318
20-99	Firms Employing No Trained Managers	—	93
	Firms Employing Some Trained Managers	22	43
	TOTAL	22	136

The figures in this table are actual figures for all the firms in the sample. Their totals therefore do not agree with figures in the tables following, which are for firms which remained in their original size-groups (see technical note in chapter 1).

In large firms the great majority of executives worked in companies employing some trained managers. (To avoid lengthy phrases the words "trained managers" will often be used to refer to an individual who has participated, however seldom, in any course however short.) There was still in such firms a substantial minority of executives yet to be reached by training.

In the middle size-group, also, a majority of executives worked for firms employing some trained men, but in this case most of the managers in such firms had not yet attended courses. In small companies only a minority of managers worked for firms with trained men, and here again most executives in such companies had not participated.

It is likely that the picture shown in tables 5.1. to 5.5. above has changed since the base-date of the survey, due to the expansion in the last two years in the activities of the Irish Management Institute. Nevertheless an analysis of Institute records shows that most small and medium-sized companies have still not participated in training. It is probably still true that there remains a substantial proportion of executives who never attended a course, even in firms with some trained men on their staff. This points to the haphazard nature of training activities at this level in most companies. It is very much the exception for individuals to participate in courses as part of a planned management development programme.

Section 2. Tests of Association

Because of the importance of this topic the same factors are examined as in chapter 4, that is, size, location, membership of the Irish Management Institute, market and technology, breadth and nationality of ownership, and use of consultants.

Association between Size, Location and Proportion with Training.
The picture shown in table 5.6 may appear surprising.

TABLE 5. 6.   *Percentage of Managers Who Had Attended Management Training Courses, by Size and Location of Firm.*

Size of Firm (No. of Employees)	Location of Head Office	No. of Managers in Analysis	Percentage with Training	Percentage without Training
500 or More	DUBLIN	887	61.90	38.11
	REST OF COUNTRY	285	58.95	41.06
	OVERALL	1172	61.18	38.83
100-499	DUBLIN	198	18.19	81.82
	REST OF COUNTRY	171	22.23	77.78
	OVERALL	369	20.06	79.95
20-99	DUBLIN	58	15.52	84.49
	REST OF COUNTRY	69	13.05	86.96
	OVERALL	127	14.18	85.83

It appears from the table, and this is confirmed by a statistical test, that there is virtually no difference between Dublin and non-Dublin firms in the extent to which they employ trained managers. In none of the strata were the small differences statistically significant. Some explanation for this may be found in the definition of location which, it will be remembered, was based on the location of the head office of the firm. Consequently, some firms having factories outside Dublin are located in Dublin for the purposes of the study. Nevertheless, these cases are few and the main conclusion stands. There is no evidence therefore, that a firm's being outside Dublin inhibits its employment of trained managers. It might, of course, be argued that such firms employ trained managers after they have received their training. The question of the effect of a firm's location on its use of courses is complicated and is taken up further in chapter 18.

Looking at size in this context, the differences between the size-groups are very highly significant. This, however, arises out of the difference between the top stratum and the other two: a further test shows that there is no significant difference between the middle and lower strata.

CONCLUSION. Location has no effect on the employment of trained managers, but firms employing over 500 people employ a significantly higher proportion of trained managers than either firms employing between 100 and 499 or between 20 and 99, with no evidence of any differences between the latter size-groups.

Association between Size, Membership of Irish Management Institute and Employment of Trained Management.

An obvious association to be investigated was that between membership of the Irish Management Institute and training.

TABLE 5.7.   *Percentage of Managers Who Had Attended Management Training Courses, by the Size of Firm and Corporate Membership of the Irish Management Institute.*

Size of Firm (No. of Employees)	Corporate Membership of I.M.I.	No. of Managers in Analysis	Percentage with Training	Percentage without Training
500 or More	MEMBER	1112	63.85	36.16
	NON-MEMBER	60	11.67	88.34
	OVERALL	1172	61.18	38.83
100-499	MEMBER	166	29.52	70.49
	NON-MEMBER	203	12.32	87.69
	OVERALL	369	20.06	79.95
20-99	MEMBER	17	17.65	82.35
	NON-MEMBER	110	13.64	86.36
	OVERALL	127	14.18	85.83

The differences between members and non-members in the two larger strata could not have arisen by chance but, in view of the fact that most firms in the top stratum are members, the difference in this case is of little practical importance. In the middle stratum, although member firms employ a significantly higher proportion of trained managers than non-members, that proportion is still quite low. Once the smallest stratum is reached there is no evidence of any difference: here even member firms employ trained men to a limited extent only.

Looking at size in the context of membership, there are highly significant differences between the size-groups. The difference is significant, however, only between the top stratum and the other two. There is no conclusive evidence that the middle stratum differs from the lower. The fact is that, even for member firms, it is only in large companies that a high proportion of managers are trained. In non-member firms there are no differences between the strata showing that, irrespective of size, non-member firms use training only to a very limited extent.

CONCLUSION. *In medium and large-sized companies membership of the Irish Management Institute is associated with employment of a greater proportion of managers with training. In small firms even members participate to a limited extent only.*

Association between Size, Type of Market and Training.

It was considered desirable to investigate the effect of some factors connected with the work situation of the firm to see if they affected its use of training, i.e. to see whether decisions to employ managers with training were a reaction to perceived needs, caused perhaps by increasing complexity. It was not possible in the time available to isolate many factors leading to complication in a firm's operations. It was, however, decided to look at the main divisions in marketing and production to see if they had any effect, taking first the principal division of marketing operations into firms serving a consumer market and firms serving an industrial market.

TABLE 5. 8.   *Percentage of Managers Who Had Attended Management Training Courses, by Size of Firm and Type of Market.*

Size of Firm (No. of Employees)	Type of Market	No. of Managers in Analysis	Percentage with Training	Percentage without Training
500 or More	CONSUMER	706	62.75	37.26
	INDUSTRIAL	466	58.71	41.29
	OVERALL	1172	61.18	38.83
100-499	CONSUMER	241	24.90	75.11
	INDUSTRIAL	128	10.94	89.07
	OVERALL	369	20.06	79.95
20-99	CONSUMER	85	15.30	84.71
	INDUSTRIAL	42	11.91	88.10
	OVERALL	127	14.18	85.83

There is only a small difference between consumer- and industrial-market firms in the top stratum. In the 100 to 499 size-group the difference is significant, in the bottom stratum it is not. The association between type of market and overall use of trained managers, though consistent, is not strong. It may well be however that, if different functional areas were looked at, the areas in which training was concentrated would be seen to differ. Looking at size in this context there are significant differences between the size-groups both in the case of consumer and industrial firms but, as usual, the differences are only between the top and the other two strata. In neither case is there evidence of difference between the middle and bottom size-groups.

CONCLUSION. There is a slight tendency for consumer-goods firms to be associated with a higher proportion of trained executives than firms selling to industry. In both cases large companies differ significantly from medium or small firms.

Association between Size, Type of Manufacture and Training.
The factors investigated in this and the following section both relate to production: first the fundamental division of firms into fabrication and processing firms, and next the division into firms which make to order and others.

There is a difference in the top size-group, fabricating firms employing a higher proportion than processing firms. The reverse seems true in the next group but the difference is not significant, nor is it significant in the bottom stratum.

TABLE 5.9.   *Percentage of Managers Who Had Attended Management Training Courses, by Size of Firm and Type of Manufacture.*

Size of Firm (No. of Employees)	Type of Manufacture	No. of Managers in Analysis	Percentage with Training	Percentage without Training
500 or More	FABRICATION	178	67.98	32.03
	PROCESSING	762	57.49	42.52
	OTHER	232	68.11	31.90
	OVERALL	1172	61.18	38.83
100-499	FABRICATION	68	11.77	88.24
	PROCESSING	267	22.10	77.91
	OTHER	34	20.59	79.42
	OVERALL	369	20.06	79.95
20-99	FABRICATION	32	18.75	81.25
	PROCESSING	91	13.19	86.81
	OTHER	(a)	(a)	(a)
	OVERALL	(b)	(b)	(b)

(a) Figures for " other " are omitted, for the reason given in footnote (a) to table 4.8.
(b) Overall percentages not quoted, for the reason given in footnote (b) to table 4.8.

To the extent to which it is reasonable to think that complexity increases more rapidly with increasing size in the case of fabrication than of processing, the pattern in table 5.9 lends a little weight to the suggestion that participation in training is a response to perceived needs arising from complexity, as the proportion of executives with training rises more rapidly with increasing size in the case of fabricating than it does in process firms. In the case of both fabricating and processing firms size has a marked influence with, as usual, significant difference between the largest size-group and the other two (it was not possible to carry out a test of signficance on "other" firms because of the low numbers in the bottom stratum).

CONCLUSION. *Outside the top size-group there is no evidence of differences between type of manufacture. In both fabricating and processing firms there are significant differences between the top and the other two size-strata.*

Association between Size, Type of Production Organisation and Training.
It was thought that firms making to order might differ in their proportion of trained executives from firms which had reached some degree of standardisation.
Table 5.10 appears to show that there is some evidence to support this hypothesis. However, only in the case of the bottom size-group is it possible to establish statistical significance. In the case of the top stratum the difference is small and not of practical importance. In the middle stratum there are so few firms making to order in the sample

TABLE 5.10   *Percentage of Managers Who Had Attended Management Training Courses, by Size of Firm and Type of Production.*

Size of Firm (No. of Employees)	Type of Production	No. of Managers in Analysis	Percentage with Training	Percentage without Training
500 or More	MAKE TO ORDER	78	58.98	41.03
	OTHER	1094	61.34	38.67
	OVERALL	1172	61.18	38.83
100-499	MAKE TO ORDER	11	—	100.00
	OTHER	349	20.92	79.08
	OVERALL (a)	369	20.06	79.95
20-99	MAKE TO ORDER	29	—	100.00
	OTHER	98	18.37	81.64
	OVERALL	127	14.18	85.83

(a) Extractive firms omitted, so intermediate figures do not add to total.

that it is not surprising that a test of significance (Fisher's) does not reach a significant level despite the size of the difference. Taking size in conjunction with this factor, there are significant differences between the size-groups, the difference in both cases being confined to that between the top stratum and the other two.

CONCLUSION. Firms making standard products employ a higher proportion of managers with training than firms making to order but, except in small companies, the difference is of no practical importance, because so few firms make to order. Size of firm is associated in both cases with differences in the proportion with training.

TABLE 5.11.   *Percentage of Managers Who Had Attended Management Training Courses, by Size of Firm and Breadth of Ownership.*

Size of Firm (No. of Employees)	Breadth of ownership	No. of Managers in Analysis	Percentage with Training	Percentage without Training
500 or More	FAMILY	320	53.44	46.57
	NON-FAMILY	852	64.09	35.92
	OVERALL	1172	61.18	38.83
100–499	FAMILY	175	20.58	79.43
	NON-FAMILY	194	19.59	80.42
	OVERALL	369	20.06	79.95
20–99	FAMILY	89	15.74	84.27
	NON-FAMILY	38	10.53	89.48
	OVERALL	127	14.18	85.83

Association between Size, Breadth of Ownership and Training.

The next question considered is whether the fact that a firm was family-owned exerted any influence on its proportion of trained managers.

In table 5.11. there are significant differences in the top stratum but not in either of the other two, with family firms in the top stratum employing a lower proportion of trained managers than non-family firms. Taking into consideration the fact that firms in the other strata greatly outnumber those in the top stratum, the conclusion is that, practically speaking, family ownership has little or no influence on use of training. In the case of both family and non-family firms size has a statistically significant influence.

CONCLUSION. There is no evidence, outside the top stratum, that family firms differ from public companies in their proportion of executives with training. Size has a significant influence in both cases.

Association between Size, Nationality of Ownership and Training.

As in the case of the proportion qualified it is desirable, because of the paucity of studies in other countries, to see whether there is any tendency for foreign-owned firms to employ relatively more or less trained managers than Irish-owned companies.

TABLE 5. 12.   *Percentage of Managers Who Had Attended Management Training Courses, by Size of Firm and Nationality of Ownership.*

Size of Firm (No. of Employees)	Nationality of Ownership	No. of Managers in Analysis	Percentage with Training	Percentage without Training
500 or More	IRISH	885	59.10	40.91
	OTHER	287	67.60	32.41
	OVERALL	1172	61.18	38.83
100-499	IRISH	325	17.83	82.16
	OTHER	44	36.37	63.64
	OVERALL	369	20.06	79.95
20-99	IRISH	120	12.50	87.50
	OTHER	7	42.86	57.14
	OVERALL	127	14.18	85.83

The conclusion from table 5.12 is that nationality of ownership does indeed influence the situation, with foreign-owned firms employing a higher proportion of trained managers than Irish. The differences reach significant levels only in the case of the two larger strata. In the case of the bottom stratum, considering the low number of managers employed in non-Irish companies, the difference is very nearly statistically significant. In general then, there are good grounds for asserting that foreign companies lay heavier stress on training than do Irish-owned firms.

In this context also, size is significant. In the case of Irish-owned companies the usual pattern is seen. In the case of foreign firms it is not possible to carry out a test because of the low number in the bottom stratum, but the differences observed are by no means so marked as in Irish-owned companies.

CONCLUSION. Even small foreign-owned concerns employ quite a high proportion of managers with training. Irish firms in general employ less men with training than do foreign-owned firms.

Association between Size, Use of Consultants and Training.

It seemed important in terms of the aims of the enquiry to look for associations between various ways of improving the standard of management. An association is looked for here between the use by a firm of consultants and its use of management training to see whether, in general, trained management is used in conjunction with consultants, or whether firms employing trained managers seem not to find any need to use the services of consultants.

TABLE 5. 13.   *Percentage of Managers Who Had Attended Management Training Courses, by Size of Firm and its Use of Consultants.*

Size of Firm (No. of Employees)	Use of Consultants	No. of Managers in Analysis	Percentage with Training	Percentage without Training
500 or More	USED	936	62.72	37.29
	DID NOT USE	236	55.09	44.92
	OVERALL	1172	61.18	38.83
100-499	USED	160	23.76	76.26
	DID NOT USE	209	17.23	82.78
	OVERALL	369	20.06	79.95
20-99	USED	23	13.04	86.96
	DID NOT USE	104	14.42	85.58
	OVERALL	127	14.18	85.83

Contrary to what might be expected there is evidence of an association only in the case of the top stratum. In neither of the other strata is there evidence that use of consultants is connected with employment of trained managers either one way or the other. In the case of the top stratum there is a difference, though a small one, showing that firms using consultants have a higher proportion of trained managers than firms which do not. Once again, in both cases, size exerts its usual influence.

CONCLUSION. There is no evidence that firms using the services of consultants are more likely in general to employ a higher proportion of managers with training than firms not using consultants. In both types of firm size influences the situation in the usual way.

CHAPTER 6

The Age Structure of Management

In this chapter the age structure of management is considered. When asked for the ages of managers the executives interviewed were sometimes unable to give exact replies, and sometimes did not have ages on record. Consequently they were able to give only approximate answers. For this reason it was decided to examine age structure by looking at the numbers and proportions in different age-groups rather than by comparing average ages[1]. Rough averages are shown in table 6.1. They are probably quite reliable as there is no reason to think that interviewees consistently under-estimated or over-estimated age.

TABLE 6. 1. *Approximate Average Ages of Managers, by Size and Location of Firm.*

Size of Firm (No. of Employees)	Location of Head Office		
	Dublin	Rest of Country	Overall
500 or More	43.6	41.9	43.2
100–499	43.0	43.3	43.2
20–99	42.1	42.1	42.1
OVERALL	42.7	42.5	42.7

There is obviously little difference between either locations or size-groups, all being close to the overall average age of 42.7 years.

Summary of Results.

Most managers are in the 35 to 50 age-group, with approximately equal numbers under 35 and over 50. Thus, unlike some European countries where particular age-cohorts were decimated by war, there are no gaps in the age groupings of Irish managers.

There is evidence that there is a higher proportion of older managers in large Dublin firms than in large firms elsewhere. Member-firms of the Irish Management Institute employ a higher proportion of younger managers than do non-members. The same is true for firms which have used the services of consultants.

Except in large firms there is no evidence that managers in family businesses are older than those in public companies. Irish firms do not differ from foreign-owned companies in this respect, neither does size of firm have any influence.

Age Groupings Chosen.

In deciding upon the age-groups into which the data ought to be broken, several factors had to be borne in mind. The first was that too fine a sub-division would reduce the numbers in each class to such an extent that it might not be possible to test any hypotheses about them. Secondly, it was desirable that the divisions decided upon should divide the life-span of managerial activity into almost equal parts. Finally it was desirable that the dividing lines should have some meaning in terms of a manager's career span. For these reasons it was decided that the number of classes should not

---

1 It is because of this doubt about the basic data that the technique of analysis of variance has not been used. See statistical note 6.1.

exceed three, and the decision to be taken was whether to use as dividing lines the years 40 and 55 or the years 35 and 50. The second basis of classification was decided on for

TABLE 6. 2. *Estimated Number and Percentage of Managers in Each Age-Group, by Size and Location of Firm.*

Size of Firm (No. of Employees)	Location of Head Office	Under 35	Number Aged 35-49	50 or Over	Percentage Aged		
					Under 35	35-49	50 or Over
500 or More	DUBLIN	194	432	281	21.4	47.6	31.0
	REST OF COUNTRY	79	146	60	27.7	51.2	21.1
	TOTAL	273	578	341	22.9	48.5	28.6
100–499	DUBLIN	281±128	568±143	312±67	24.2	48.9	26.9
	REST OF COUNTRY	247±110	445±157	308±64	24.7	44.5	30.8
	TOTAL	530±163	1,017±208	621±90	24.4	46.9	28.6
20–99	DUBLIN	575±407	767±403	469±211	31.8	42.4	25.9
	REST OF COUNTRY	357±173	773±249	337±240	24.3	52.7	23.0
	TOTAL	925±418	1,542±449	802±311	28.3	47.2	24.5
TOTAL	DUBLIN	1,050±423	1,767±423	1,062±220	27.1	45.6	27.4
	REST OF COUNTRY	683±201	1,365±288	705±247	24.8	49.6	25.6
	TOTAL	1,728±447	3,138±491	1,764±323	26.1	47.3	26.6

TABLE 6. 3. *Estimated Average Number per Firm of Managers in Each Age-Group, by Size and Location of Firm.*

Size of Firm (No. of Employees)	Location of Head Office	Aged Under 35	Aged 35-49	Aged 50 or over
500 or More	DUBLIN	6.47	14.40	9.37
	REST OF COUNTRY	4.65	8.59	3.53
	OVERALL	5.81	12.30	7.25
100-499	DUBLIN	2.25±1.02	4.54±1.15	2.50±0.54
	REST OF COUNTRY	1.87±0.83	3.37±1.19	2.33±0.49
	OVERALL	2.06±0.63	3.96±0.81	2.42±0.35
20-99	DUBLIN	1.17±0.83	1.56±0.82	0.96±0.43
	REST OF COUNTRY	0.78±0.38	1.70±0.54	0.74±0.53
	OVERALL	0.98±0.44	1.63±0.47	0.85±0.33
OVERALL	DUBLIN	1.63±0.66	2.74±0.65	1.65±0.34
	REST OF COUNTRY	1.13±0.33	2.26±0.48	1.16±0.41
	OVERALL	1.38±0.36	2.51±0.39	1.41±0.26

two reasons: first, because a comparable Belgian study had used this age grouping; second, because in the event of uncertainty about exact ages it seemed that managers would be less likely to err about age-groups if 35 and 50 were used. Furthermore, tendencies towards increasing frequency of academic qualifications were likely to be more marked in under-thirty-fives than even in under-forties, and hence comparisons likely to be more striking.

Section 1. Estimates of Numbers

Table 6.2 shows the total number and percentage of managers in each age-group. The distribution is almost symmetrical, with the greatest numbers in the middle age-group and almost equal numbers younger and older. Average numbers per firm in each age-group are shown in table 6.3. The position with regard to membership of the Irish Management Institute is shown in tables 6.4 and 6.5.

TABLE 6. 4. *Estimated Number and Percentage of Managers in Each Age-Group, by Size of Firm and Corporate Membership of Irish Management Institute.*

Size of Firm (No. of Employees)	Corporate Membership of I.M.I.	Under 35	Number Aged 35-49	50 or Over	Percentage Aged Under 35	35-49	50 or Over
500 or More	MEMBER	268	549	315	23.7	48.5	27.8
	NON-MEMBER	5	29	26	8.3	48.3	43.3
100–499	MEMBER	179±98	445±167	251±65	20.5	50.9	28.7
	NON-MEMBER	351±138	565±116	367±61	27.4	44.0	28.6
20–99	MEMBER	242±192	242±167	51±38	45.2	45.2	9.5
	NON-MEMBER	577±275	1,244±402	777±338	22.2	47.9	29.9
TOTAL	MEMBER	689±229	1,236±238	617±75	27.1	48.6	24.2
	NON-MEMBER	933±297	1,838±407	1,171±334	23.7	46.6	29.7

TABLE 6. 5. *Estimated Average Number per Firm of Managers in Each Age-Group, by Size of Firm and Corporate Membership of Irish Management Institute.*

Size of Firm (No. of Employees)	Corporate Membership of I.M.I.	Aged Under 35	Aged 35-49	Aged 50 or over
500 or More	MEMBER	6.38	13.07	7.50
	NON-MEMBER	1.00	5.80	5.20
100-499	MEMBER	2.06±1.13	5.12±1.92	2.88±0.74
	NON-MEMBER	2.06±0.81	3.32±0.68	2.16±0.36
20-99	MEMBER	2.37±1.88	2.37±1.64	0.50±0.38
	NON-MEMBER	0.68±0.33	1.47±0.47	0.92±0.40
OVERALL	MEMBER	2.98±0.99	5.35±1.03	2.67±0.32
	NON-MEMBER	0.92±0.29	1.80±0.40	1.14±0.33

Section 2. Tests of Association

Before exploring associations it should first be said that a test showed highly significant difference between age-groups; that is, there is no chance that there are equal numbers in each group. The factors whose effects on age are investigated are size, location, membership of the Irish Management Institute, breadth of ownership, nationality of ownership and use by the firm of management consultants.

Association between Size, Location and Age

Taking location first there is evidence, confirmed by a statistical test, that in the top size-group Dublin firms employ a higher percentage of older managers than firms outside Dublin. Testing in the other two size-groups shows no evidence of significant

TABLE 6. 6.   *Percentage of Managers in Each Age-Group, by Size and Location of Firm.*

Size of Firm (No. of Employees)	Location of Head Office	No. of Managers in Analysis	P'cent aged under 35	P'cent aged 35-49	P'cent aged 50 or Over
500 or More	DUBLIN	887	21.20	47.92	30.90
	REST OF COUNTRY	285	27.72	51.23	21.06
	OVERALL	1172	22.79	48.73	28.50
100-499	DUBLIN	198	21.22	51.02	27.78
	REST OF COUNTRY	171	25.15	45.03	29.83
	OVERALL	369	23.04	48.24	28.73
20-99	DUBLIN	58	24.14	43.11	32.76
	REST OF COUNTRY	69	26.09	53.63	20.29
	OVERALL	127	25.20	48.82	25.99

differences. This tendency in the largest size-group towards a higher number of older managers in Dublin may, to some extent, be caused by the fact that Dublin firms are somewhat larger than non-Dublin firms and that, consequently, having further to go along the ladder of advancement, a man may be older before reaching management level in Dublin than outside. On the other hand, on testing for differences between the three size-groups, it is found that neither in Dublin nor outside Dublin is there any evidence that the size of a firm affects the age distribution of its management.

CONCLUSION. Size is not associated with differences in age. Large firms in Dublin employ a higher proportion of executives over fifty, and a lower proportion under thirty-five, than large firms elsewhere.

Association between Size, Membership of the Irish Management Institute and Age.

Member firms in the top stratum employ a higher percentage of young managers than non-member firms.

TABLE 6. 7. *Percentage of Managers in Each Age-Group, by Size of Firm and Corporate Membership of the Irish Management Institute.*

Size of Firm (No. of Employees)	Corporate Membership of I.M.I.	No. of Managers in Analysis	P'cent aged under 35	P'cent aged 35-49	P'cent aged 50 or Over
500 or More	MEMBER	1112	23.57	48.75	27.70
	NON-MEMBER	60	8.34	48.34	43.34
	OVERALL	1172	22.79	48.73	28.50
100-499	MEMBER	166	20.49	51.81	27.72
	NON-MEMBER	203	25.13	45.33	29.56
	OVERALL	369	23.04	48.24	28.73
20-99	MEMBER	17	35.30	52.95	11.77
	NON-MEMBER	110	23.64	48.19	28.19
	OVERALL	127	25.20	48.82	25.99

In the middle size-group there is virtually no difference between them. In the bottom size-group, although there appears to be a difference, it was not possible to carry out a statistical test as there were not sufficient managers in member firms in the sample to allow it.

Looking at size in the context of membership it is not possible to carry out a test on member firms as there are not enough data to support one. Taking non-member firms, there is evidence that the larger companies employ a higher percentage of old managers than either the medium-sized or smaller firms.

CONCLUSION. *Large firms which are members of the Irish Management Institute employ a higher proportion of managers under 35 and a lower proportion of managers over 50, than large firms which are not members. Among firms which are not members, large companies employ a higher proportion of older managers than medium and small-sized firms.*

Association between Size, Breadth of Ownership and Age.

The next factor considered is breadth of ownership, to see whether there is any tendency for family firms to employ older or younger managers than non-family firms.

In the top size-group, family firms employ a higher percentage of older managers than non-family firms. There is no such evidence in the case of the medium or smaller size-groups. Taking size in conjunction with breadth of ownership there is no proof that in non-family firms size has any effect. There is, however, a significant difference between the size-groups in the case of family firms, mainly due to the high number of older managers in the larger firms.

CONCLUSION. *Large family businesses employ more older managers than large non-family businesses. The differences in the other size-groups are not statistically significant. Large family firms employ a higher proportion of older managers than either medium or small-sized family businesses.*

TABLE 6.8.   *Percentage of Managers in Each Age-Group, by Size of Firm and Breadth of Ownership.*

Size of Firm (No. of Employees)	Breadth of Ownership	No. of Managers in Analysis	P'cent aged under 35	P'cent aged 35-49	P'cent aged 50 or Over
500 or More	FAMILY	320	18.13	45.94	35.94
	NON-FAMILY	852	24.54	49.77	25.91
	OVERALL	1172	22.79	48.73	28.50
100-499	FAMILY	175	26.29	45.72	28.01
	NON-FAMILY	194	20.11	50.52	29.39
	OVERALL	369	23.04	48.24	28.73
20-99	FAMILY	89	29.22	46.07	24.72
	NON-FAMILY	38	15.79	55.27	28.95
	OVERALL	127	25.20	48.82	25.99

Association between Size, Nationality of Ownership and Age.

Table 6.9 shows the situation with respect to nationality of ownership. It had been thought that foreign-owned companies might employ younger managers than Irish firms, and that this might explain some of the differences observed in the proportions with academic qualifications and management training.

TABLE 6.9.   *Percentage of Managers in Each Age-Group, by Size of Firm and Nationality of Ownership.*

Size of Firm (No. of Employees)	Nationality of Ownership	No. of Managers in Analysis	P'cent aged under 35	P'cent aged 35-49	P'cent aged 50 or Over
500 or More	IRISH	885	21.93	49.38	28.71
	OTHER	287	25.44	46.69	27.88
	OVERALL	1172	22.79	48.73	28.50
100-499	IRISH	325	22.77	48.01	29.24
	OTHER	44	25.01	50.01	25.01
	OVERALL	369	23.04	48.24	28.73
20-99	IRISH	120	25.84	48.34	25.84
	OTHER	7	14.29	57.14	28.58
	OVERALL	127	25.20	48.82	25.99

There is no evidence in table 6.9. to support the suggestion of an association — the statistical test carried out did not reach a significant level — neither does size have any effect when taken in conjunction with nationality of ownership.

CONCLUSION. There is no evidence that the nationality of ownership of the firm is associated with differences in the age structure of its management.

Association between Size, Use of Consultants and Age.

The final question considered was whether there was any association between the use by a firm of the services of management consultants and the age of its management, as it was thought that firms with younger management might be more inclined to use consultants.

TABLE 6. 10.   *Percentage of Managers in Each Age-Group, by Size of Firm and its Use of Consultants.*

Size of Firm (No. of Employees)	Use of Consultants	No. of Managers in Analysis	P'cent aged under 35	P'cent aged 35-49	P'cent aged 50 or Over
500 or More	USED	936	24.36	49.15	26.50
	DID NOT USE	236	16.53	47.04	36.45
	OVERALL	1172	22.79	48.73	28.50
100-499	USED	160	25.63	45.01	29.38
	DID NOT USE	209	21.06	50.72	28.23
	OVERALL	369	23.04	48.24	28.73
20-99	USED	23	34.79	47.83	17.40
	DID NOT USE	104	23.08	49.04	27.89
	OVERALL	127	25.20	48.82	25.99

The table provides some backing for this suggestion.   In the top size-group those firms using consultants have a higher proportion of younger managers than those not using them.   There is no such association in the case of the middle-size stratum and while in the bottom stratum there does appear to be a suggestion of an association in the direction expected, it is not supported by a test, which failed to reach a significant level. Looking at size in this context, tests show that it has no influence on the situation.

CONCLUSION. There is some evidence that firms using the services of consultants have younger managers than those which do not.

CHAPTER 7

The Nationality of Managers

A factor worth considering was the nationality of managers in Ireland, not merely to assess the overall numbers, but to explore possible inter-relationships with functional areas and levels and also with type of firm, to see if foreign managers were concentrated in particular functional areas (this would be one indication of a deficiency in some Irish training or educational facility), or at particular levels or in particular types of company. The question of inter-relationship between nationality, areas, levels and other attributes of the manager is postponed until chapter 9. For the present the problem is to make simple estimates of the numbers of foreign managers and to study the effect on the position of various characteristics of the firms employing them. At this stage it should be pointed out that, as explained in the technical appendix, firms in the industrial estate at Shannon Free Airport were excluded from the population from which this sample was drawn. It may also be that firms founded in other parts of the country with foreign participation have grown at a rate more rapid than average, and that consequently the importance of such firms is understated in the survey. It would be better to regard the following estimates as the number of foreigners employed in longer-established companies, rather than those set up following the adoption by the Government of a policy of encouraging outside investment.

Summary of Findings.

Only about 10 per cent of managers were born outside Ireland.

Large firms outside Dublin employ a higher proportion of foreign-born executives than either large firms in Dublin or other firms outside Dublin, mainly because some of them introduced technologies new to the country and had to draw their production management from abroad. Membership of the Irish Management Institute is not associated with the proportion of foreign-born executives in a firm except in the top size stratum. It is true only in the top stratum that foreign-owned companies employ a higher proportion of foreign-born managers than Irish companies.

Definition.

When someone is described as being Irish, it is usually meant that he was either born in Ireland and spent the greater part of his life here, or was born outside Ireland but lived here from an early age, having adopted the norms of the community. However, from the point of view of a study concerned with training and educational requirements, it seemed best not to consider anyone born outside the country as Irish unless he had lived here from a sufficiently early age to have been educated in this country. In the event, as it was the aim to keep definitions as simple as possible, it was decided to define a person's nationality on the basis of his country of birth. Consequently, anyone born outside Ireland was regarded, irrespective of his present citizenship, as either British or "other". It was realised that this definition would not allow for "accidents of birth" as a result of which persons living all their lives in Ireland, but born while their parents were temporarily abroad, would be regarded as foreign. It was thought likely that the number of such cases would be very small. In fact, in the entire survey covering over 1,700 managers, the number of such people did not reach double figures.

TABLE 7. 1. *Estimated Number of Managers of Each Nationality, by Size and Location of Firm.*

Size of Firm (No. of Employees)	Location of Head Office	Irish-born	British	Other
500 or More	DUBLIN	810	85	12
	REST OF COUNTRY	232	40	13
	TOTAL	1,042	125	25
100-499	DUBLIN	1,016±212	125±58	21±18
	REST OF COUNTRY	896±223	88±44	16±23
	TOTAL	1,917±299	214±71	37±28
20-99	DUBLIN	1,534±541	170±193	107±139
	REST OF COUNTRY	1,388±469	79±94	—
	TOTAL	2,920±685	247±204	103±132
TOTAL	DUBLIN	3,360±573	380±200	139±140
	REST OF COUNTRY	2,516±510	207±102	29±23
	TOTAL	5,879±743	586±215	165±135

TABLE 7. 2. *Estimated Percentage of Foreign-Born Managers, by Size of Firm.*

Size of Firm (No. of Employees)			
500 or More	100-499	20-99	Total
12.6	11.6±3.5	10.7±5.9	11.4±3.2

TABLE 7. 3. *Estimated Number of Managers of Each Nationality, by Size of Firm, and Corporate Membership of Irish Management Institute.*

Size of Firm (No. of Employees)	Corporate Membership of I.M.I.	Irish-born	British	Other
500 or More	MEMBER	994	119	19
	NON-MEMBER	48	6	6
100-499	MEMBER	788±201	72± 40	15±15
	NON-MEMBER	1119±220	143± 63	22±24
20-99	MEMBER	433±251	64±101	38±76
	NON-MEMBER	2399±617	155±142	44±63
TOTAL	MEMBER	2216±329	254±118	73±86
	NON-MEMBER	3565±636	304±151	72±65

Section 1. Estimates of Numbers

The first concern is to estimate the total number of managers by broad nationality grouping. Tables 7.1 and 7.2 show, by size and location of firm, the total and percentage in each group.

The total number of managers of each nationality is shown in table 7.3 analysed by size of firm and corporate membership of the Irish Management Institute.

The number of managers born outside Ireland is small — only about 10 per cent of the total — and most of them are British.

Section 2. Tests of Association

It was seen in section 1 that there are very large differences between the percentages of managers who are Irish and foreign-born. The confidence limits show, and the statistical test confirms, that there is no possibility that these differences could have arisen by chance.

It is interesting, however, to take only those firms which employ some foreign managers and to see how the percentage of Irish compares with the percentage of foreign-born managers in those firms. In the two larger size-strata this makes practically no difference. In the bottom stratum a different picture appears. Almost 36 per cent of the managers are foreign-born in the sample of small firms employing foreign managers. Owing to the sampling variation inherent in this estimate, it could be that in such firms as many as half of their managers were born abroad.

The effect of size, location, membership of the Irish Management Institute and nationality of ownership on the extent to which a firm employs foreign managers is now examined.

Association between Size, Location and Employment of Foreign-born Managers.

The position is shown in table 7.4. In the top stratum there is an association between location and employment of foreign managers, non-Dublin firms employing a higher percentage than Dublin firms.

This is somewhat surprising, and is mainly caused by the fact that in this stratum a high percentage of firms outside Dublin introduced technologies new to the country and consequently had to draw much of their production management from abroad. There is no difference in the middle stratum, while it was not possible to carry out a statistical test on the bottom stratum because the number of foreign-born managers was too small.

Because of the difference between locations in the top stratum it is not possible to combine the two so as to carry out an overall test on the size-groups. Dublin firms are therefore taken first, then non-Dublin firms, and the sizes compared within these locations. There is no evidence that there is any difference between the sizes so far as Dublin firms are concerned.

In the case of non-Dublin firms there is a significant difference, with the largest size-group employing the highest percentage of foreigners and the smallest size-group employing the lowest percentage.

CONCLUSION. Large firms outside Dublin employ a higher proportion of foreign-born executives than large firms in Dublin, and a higher proportion than small firms outside Dublin

TABLE 7. 4.   *Percentage of Managers of Each Nationality, by Size and Location of Firm.*

Size of Firm (No. of Employees)	Location of Head Office	No. of Managers in Analysis	Percentage Irish-born	Percentage Other
500 or More	DUBLIN	887	89.63	10.38
	REST OF COUNTRY	285	81.41	18.60
	OVERALL	1172	87.63	12.38
100–499	DUBLIN	198	85.86	14.15
	REST OF COUNTRY	171	88.89	11.12
	OVERALL	369	87.27	12.74
20–99	DUBLIN	58	89.66	10.34
	REST OF COUNTRY	69	94.20	5.80
	OVERALL	127	92.05	7.95

Association between Size, Membership of the Irish Management Institute, and Employment of Foreign-born Managers.

Going on to study the effect of membership of the Irish Management Institute, the position is shown in table 7.5.

TABLE 7. 5.   *Percentage of Managers of Each Nationality, by Size of Firm and Corporate Membership of the Irish Management Institute.*

Size of Firm (No. of Employees)	Corporate Membership of I.M.I.	No. of Managers in Analysis	Percentage Irish-born	Percentage Other
500 or More	MEMBER	1112	88.04	11.97
	NON-MEMBER	60	80.00	20.00
	OVERALL	1172	87.63	12.38
100-499	MEMBER	166	89.76	10.25
	NON-MEMBER	203	85.23	14.78
	OVERALL	396	87.27	12.74
20-99	MEMBER	17	94.12	5.88
	NON-MEMBER	110	**91.82**	8.18
	OVERALL	127	92.05	7.95

In each size-group there appears to be a slight tendency for non-members to employ a higher percentage of foreign-born managers than members but, except in the top stratum, this difference is not statistically significant. Neither is there any difference between the size-groups.

CONCLUSION. Membership of the Irish Management Institute is not associated in a practically important way with employment of foreign-born executives.

Association between Size, Nationality of Ownership and Employment of Foreign-born Managers.

It might have been expected that foreign-owned companies would employ a higher proportion of foreign-born executives than Irish firms.

TABLE 7. 6.   *Percentage of Managers of Each Nationality, by Size of Firm and Nationality of Ownership.*

Size of Firm (No. of Employees)	Nationality of Ownership	No. of Managers in Analysis	Percentage Irish-born	Percentage Other
500 or More	IRISH	885	89.50	10.51
	OTHER	287	81.89	18.12
	OVERALL	1172	87.63	12.38
100-499	IRISH	325	87.08	12.93
	OTHER	44	88.64	11.37
	OVERALL	369	87.27	12.74
20-99	IRISH	120	92.50	7.50
	OTHER	7	85.71	14.29
	OVERALL	127	92.05	7.95

Table 7.6 shows that this is not so except in the top size-group, and even here the difference is not great.   There is no difference between the size-groups, either in Irish or in foreign companies.

CONCLUSION. The nationality of ownership of a firm is not associated with the nationality of its managers.

CHAPTER 8

Relationship between Function and Other Attributes of Managers

An examination was made in chapters 2 to 7 of a variety of characteristics possessed by managers and of associations between these characteristics and a variety of attributes possessed by the firms for which the managers worked. In the two following chapters inter-relationships between the characteristics of managers are considered. The general plan has been to take these characteristics in the same order in which they were examined in chapters 2 to 7, exploring in turn the relationship between each characteristic and the remainder. Because of the importance of relationships involving functional areas a whole chapter is devoted to them. (All the other relationships are dealt with in chapter 9.)

The present chapter is divided into five sections, one for each relationship between function and another characteristic. Chapter 9 is in five parts, each part being divided into sections. It was decided to form a single chapter with five parts rather than to have five separate chapters, because there is a diminishing number of relationships in each part. Within each section, estimates are made and tests of significance carried out.

It will be noticed that, in general, only two-way classifications are examined. For instance, the relationship between function and qualification is explored but not the relationship between function, qualification and level. Neither is any association examined between attributes of firms and inter-relationships between attributes of their managers. For instance, no attempt is made to look for an association between the type of market served by a firm and the proportion of its managers in each function who possess an academic qualification. The reasons are that such tables are complex, there are seldom enough data available outside the top stratum to allow such fine breakdowns, and the testing of hypotheses about these breakdowns is difficult.[1]

There are, however, occasions on which it is necessary to have at least three-way classifications. These occur when it is suspected that three factors influence one another mutually. An example is the relationship between function, qualification and age. It is found that some functions have a higher proportion than others of managers with academic qualifications. They also have younger managers. But younger managers are more likely than older ones to have qualifications. To be certain therefore that the higher proportion of qualified managers in some areas is not simply a reflection of their greater youth, it is necessary to look at the situation in each age-group in turn. Where such involved relationships were found to exist, three-way breakdowns were obtained to see whether the conclusion arrived at in the original two-way classification still stood. The results are referred to in the text but, because of their complexity, the tables are not reproduced.

Summary of Results of Section 1: Relationship between Function and Level.

At every level, more managers work in the area of production than in any other. The majority of middle and junior managers are in production, in every size of firm.

Because there are more managers in production than in any other area and, because

---

1 Snedecor (1) gives a method of dealing with tests of hypotheses in three-way classifications, by analysis of variance on transformed proportions. It is not clear how the results of the analysis may be interpreted when, as in the present case, different proportions are sampled from separate strata of a finite population.

the number of top level jobs is restricted by definition, there is a significantly lower proportion of executives at top level in production than in the other functions.

Summary of Results of Section 2: Relationship between Function and Qualification.
The greatest number of qualified managers is in production, but the highest proportion qualified is in finance. The lowest proportion qualified is in marketing. All areas except marketing show a decided trend towards having a higher proportion of qualified managers in the younger age-groups. The position with regard to marketing could change quickly because of the very large number of people now studying for professional qualifications in marketing.

University degrees are more common than professional qualifications except in the area of finance, where the great majority of qualified executives have professional qualifications.

Very few economists are employed in industry. The high proportion of arts men who are chief executives is largely explained by the fact that they are either non-Irish nationals employed by foreign-owned companies, or are members of the owning family.

Most executives seem to spend their working lives in the areas to which their basic degrees relate: there is little transfer between areas and, because of the small size of Irish businesses, there are few high-level general administrative positions. These facts are worth considering in discussing the type of education and training to be provided for management.

Practically all the scientists employed in medium-sized companies are engaged on laboratory work. The proportion of line production executives with qualifications is very small in such firms. In large companies most scientists are in line production management. The proportion of engineers on engineering work is greater in large than in medium-sized firms, but there are considerable numbers also in line management.

The trend towards greater qualification in younger age-groups is marked in every area except marketing. There does not so far seem to be a marked trend towards particular types of qualification except in finance where there is a tendency, at least in large companies, for young executives to have taken a university degree and a professional qualification rather than a professional qualification alone.

Summary of Results of Section 3: Relationship between Function and Management Training.
More production managers than any other type have attended training courses. There is not a great difference between the proportions attending from each area. The position will have changed, perhaps considerably, since the survey was carried out because of the expansion in the activities of the Irish Management Institute.

Summary of Results of Section 4: Relationship between Function and Age.
In firms with over 100 employees, chief executives are older, and managers in finance younger, than managers in other areas. In firms employing under 100 people, marketing and finance executives are younger than others.

Summary of Results of Section 5: Relationship between Function and Nationality.
The highest proportion of foreign managers are either chief executives or in production management. In the latter case this is largely because they were brought in for their technical know-how, and it may be that the proportion will diminish in time. The chief executives are largely either men who came to Ireland to start their own businesses, or are employed by foreign-owned companies.

Section 1: Relationship between Function and Level

Management training courses are commonly aimed at particular functional areas and at particular levels of management within each area. It is therefore important when planning courses to know how many individuals there are by area and level. Estimates are made separately for locations and for member-firms of the Irish Management Institute in tables 8.1.1. and 8.1.2. in the following pages. Chief executives are omitted from these tables as their position was taken to constitute both an area and a level. Their number has already been estimated in chapter 2.

Since the primary interest in the tables is in establishing numbers it is difficult to see any relationships. It can be seen, however, that there is a greater number of production managers at every level than of any other sort, the predominance being more marked at middle and junior level. In fact, the majority of all middle and junior managers are concentrated in production.

Because there are more production managers than any other type, while the number of top positions is by definition limited, it is to be expected that there will be a lower proportion of production executives at top level than of any other type. The percentages are shown in table 8.1.3. (As usual when a test of significance is to be carried out on a table, the table is based on the returns for only those 131 firms which had not changed their size before the survey was carried out.) It can be seen that the expectation is borne out. The proportion at top level is markedly lower for production in the top stratum, where the observed difference is significant by definition. It is marked and statistically significant in the middle stratum. Because of the small number of managers in smaller firms a test would not have been theoretically valid. However, the difference is in the expected direction and, in view of the results in the other two strata, can probably be regarded as real.

Section 2. The Relationship between Function and Qualification

The purpose of this section is first to establish the number and proportion of executives in each function who possess an academic (i.e. university or professional) qualification and to establish whether or not there are significant differences between the proportions qualified in each area. Particular types of qualification are then examined, their frequency in each area and the implications arising from the facts established.

The number and proportion qualified are shown in detail in tables 8.2.1. to 8.2.4., distinguishing, first, firms based in Dublin from those in the rest of the country and, then, firms which were corporate members of the Irish Management Institute from those which were not. Without first carrying out a statistical test it is impossible to comment very much on the tables. The proportions qualified in the finance area differ between firms in Dublin and those outside Dublin: in the medium size-group firms in Dublin have a very much higher proportion of qualified executives in the finance area than in any other, and also a greater proportion qualified than firms outside Dublin. The reverse is true in the 20 to 99 group. The relationship in the 100 to 499 group may reflect greater availability of qualified accountants in Dublin, though this would seem to be contradicted by the high proportion qualified outside Dublin in the 20 to 99 group. These latter figures are however subject to wide sampling variability.

Member-firms have a higher proportion of qualified men than non-members in practically every function.

The next step is to see whether the differences observed between the proportions qualified in each area are statistically significant. Again testing was carried out on results for only 131 firms: these results are shown in table 8.2.5.

TABLE 8. 1. 1.   *Estimated Number of Managers at Each Level in Each Functional Area, by Size and Location of Firm.*

Size of Firm (No. of Employees)	Location	Level of Management	Marketing	Production	Finance	Personnel	Other
500 or More	DUBLIN	Top	27	58	32	8	17
		Middle	76	245	62	17	6
		Junior	50	191	64	15	3
	REST OF COUNTRY	Top	14	20	18	4	2
		Middle	30	72	22	6	4
		Junior	10	46	13	3	1
	TOTAL	Top	41	78	50	12	19
		Middle	106	317	84	23	10
		Junior	60	237	77	18	4
100-499	DUBLIN	Top	73± 28	125± 20	109± 25	—	31± 25
		Middle	83± 46	219± 69	99± 37	16±16	11± 13
		Junior	62± 54	161± 88	36± 33	—	—
	REST OF COUNTRY	Top	55± 25	154± 38	115± 17	—	22± 19
		Middle	27± 21	247± 72	60± 36	—	11± 14
		Junior	16± 23	115±109	38± 38	—	—
	TOTAL	Top	128± 37	278± 41	225± 30	—	54± 31
		Middle	112± 52	466± 96	161± 51	16±16	21± 19
		Junior	80± 59	278±134	75± 48	—	—
20-99	DUBLIN	Top	107± 87	192±121	149± 97	—	192±184
		Middle	64± 95	383±318	85± 80	21±43	21± 43
		Junior	—	21± 43	43± 86	—	21± 43
	REST OF COUNTRY	Top	59± 66	198± 97	178± 96	—	79± 74
		Middle	20± 40	159±110	20± 40	—	198±361
		Junior	20± 40	40± 80	—	—	—
	TOTAL	Top	165±105	391±148	329±132	—	267±189
		Middle	82± 97	535±320	103± 86	21±40	226±366
		Junior	21± 40	62± 89	41± 81	—	21± 40
TOTAL	DUBLIN	Top	207± 91	375±122	291±100	8	240±186
		Middle	223±103	847±324	246± 87	54±45	38± 45
		Junior	112± 54	374± 96	143± 91	15	24± 43
	REST OF COUNTRY	Top	128± 70	372±103	312± 97	4	103± 76
		Middle	77± 44	478±128	102± 53	6	213±361
		Junior	46± 45	201±132	51± 38	3	1
	TOTAL	Top	334±111	747±153	604±135	12	340±191
		Middle	301±109	1318±333	347± 99	60±43	258±366
		Junior	161± 71	577±160	193± 93	18	25± 40

TABLE 8. 1. 2. *Estimated Number of Managers at Each Level in Each Functional Area, by Size of Firm and Corporate Membership of Irish Management Institute.*

Size of Firm (No. of Employees)	Corporate Membership of I.M.I.	Level of Management	Marketing	Production	Finance	Personnel	Other
500 or More	MEMBER	Top	37	70	46	12	17
		Middle	98	304	77	22	8
		Junior	59	236	77	18	2
	NON-MEMBER	Top	4	8	4	—	2
		Middle	8	13	7	1	2
		Junior	1	1	—	—	2
100-499	MEMBER	Top	41± 20	97± 24	77± 19	—	15± 15
		Middle	46± 34	194± 58	61± 33	10±13	10± 13
		Junior	26± 23	169±113	41± 34	—	—
	NON-MEMBER	Top	88± 33	181± 36	148± 24	—	38± 28
		Middle	66± 41	269± 78	99± 41	5±10	11± 14
		Junior	55± 58	104± 62	33± 34	—	—
20-99	MEMBER	Top	38± 37	89± 46	76± 33	—	—
		Middle	38± 53	140±153	13± 25	13±25	13± 25
		Junior	—	—	51± 66	—	—
	NON-MEMBER	Top	111± 95	267±131	222±124	—	289±207
		Middle	22± 45	333±219	89± 86	—	222±406
		Junior	22± 45	67±100	—	—	22± 45
TOTAL	MEMBER	Top	116± 45	256± 55	199± 40	—	32± 16
		Middle	182± 66	639±179	151± 42	45±30	31± 30
		Junior	85± 24	405±116	169± 73	18	2
	NON-MEMBER	Top	203± 98	455±132	374±123	—	329±204
		Middle	96± 59	615±226	195± 93	7±10	235±397
		Junior	78± 71	172±113	33± 34	—	24± 44

TABLE 8. 1. 3. *Managers in Each Functional Area, Showing the Percentage at Each Level, by Size of Firm.*

Size of Firm (No. of Employees)	Level	Marketing	Production	Finance	Personnel	Other
500 or More	Number of Managers in Analysis	205	622	207	53	31
	Percentage at Top Level	19.52	12.06	23.19	22.65	61.30
	Percentage at Middle Level	51.22	50.49	39.62	43.40	25.81
	Percentage at Junior Level	29.27	37.46	37.20	33.97	12.91
100-499	Number of Managers in Analysis	54	176	79	2(a)	11(a)
	Percentage at Top Level	40.75	27.85	50.64	—	63.64
	Percentage at Middle Level	35.19	46.03	35.45	100.00	36.36
	Percentage at Junior Level	24.08	26.14	13.93	—	—
20-99	Number of Managers in Analysis	9	35	18	—	21
	Percentage at Top Level	77.78	42.86	77.78	—	52.38
	Percentage at Middle Level	11.11	48.57	22.22	—	42.86
	Percentage at Junior Level	11.11	8.57	—	—	4.76

(a) Omitted from the statistical test as the numbers were too small (see statistical note 2.3).

TABLE 8.2.1. *Estimated Number of Qualified and Unqualified Managers in Each Functional Area, By Size and Location of Firm.*

Size of Firm (No. of Employed)	Location of Head Office	Qualification Status	Chief Executive	Marketing	Production	Finance	Personnel	Other
500 or More	DUBLIN	Qualified	21	35	221	101	16	13
		Unqualified	15	118	273	57	24	13
	REST OF COUNTRY	Qualified	9	13	41	39	4	2
		Unqualified	11	41	97	14	9	5
	TOTAL	Qualified	30	48	262	140	20	15
		Unqualified	26	159	370	71	33	18
100-499	DUBLIN	Qualified	36±22	47±37	104±59	167±55	10±13	16±16
		Unqualified	99±28	172±94	401±69	78±46	5±10	26±20
	REST OF COUNTRY	Qualified	33±22	11±14	148±90	71±33	—	11±14
		Unqualified	104±26	88±51	368±143	143±57	—	22±19
	TOTAL	Qualified	70±30	59±40	252±102	241±69	10±13	27±21
		Unqualified	203±37	262±107	771±150	220±72	5±10	48±27
20-99	DUBLIN	Qualified	107±87	43±60	170±303	107±107	21±43	21±43
		Unqualified	405±102	128±142	426±267	170±134	—	213±18
	REST OF COUNTRY	Qualified	29±66	20±40	20±40	119±86	—	159±24.
		Unqualified	436±91	79±79	379±160	79±79	—	119±16.
	TOTAL	Qualified	165±105	62±68	185±286	226±131	21±40	185±24.
		Unqualified	843±132	206±152	802±294	247±146	—	329±24.
TOTAL	DUBLIN	Qualified	164±89	124±68	496±307	374±119	48±45	50±45
		Unqualified	519±105	418±167	1,100±274	306±140	29±10	252±18
	REST OF COUNTRY	Qualified	101±69	44±42	209±97	229±91	4	172±24
		Unqualified	552±94	208±88	842±209	236±92	9	146±16
	TOTAL	Qualified	264±109	169±79	699±303	607±147	51±42	227±25.
		Unqualified	1,073±137	627±184	1,943±328	537±162	38±10	395±24.

TABLE 8.2.2. *Estimated Percentage of Managers in Each Functional Area Who are Qualified, by Size and Location of Firm.*

Size of Firm (No. of Employees)	Location of Head Office	Chief Executive % Qualified	Marketing % Qualified	Production % Qualified	Finance % Qualified	Personnel % Qualified	Other % Qualified
500 or More	DUBLIN	58.3	22.9	44.7	63.9	40.0	50.0
	REST OF COUNTRY	45.0	24.1	29.7	73.6	30.8	28.6
	OVERALL	53.6	23.2	41.5	66.4	37.7	45.5
100-499	DUBLIN	26.7	21.4	20.6	68.1	66.7	38.1
	REST OF COUNTRY	24.0	11.1	28.7	33.3	—	33.3
	OVERALL	25.5±11.0	18.3±11.4	24.6± 8.2	52.3±11.6	66.7±48.6	36.0±21.
20-99	DUBLIN	20.8	25.0	28.6	38.5	100.0	9.0
	REST OF COUNTRY	12.0	20.0	5.0	60.0	—	57.1
	OVERALL	16.3± 9.6	23.1±24.1	18.8±24.3	47.8±19.2	100.0	36.0±24.
OVERALL	DUBLIN	23.9±12.9	23.0±12.4	31.1±15.0	55.1±12.5	61.9±10.3	16.6±14.
	REST OF COUNTRY	15.5±10.4	17.4±18.1	19.9± 8.3	49.2±14.4	30.8	54.0±14.
	OVERALL	19.7± 7.1	21.2± 9.3	26.5± 9.8	53.0± 9.4	57.4± 8.9	36.5±21.

TABLE 8.2.3. *Estimated Number of Qualified and Unqualified Managers in Each Functional Area, by Size of Firm and Corporate Membership of Irish Management Institute.*

Size of Firm (No. of employees)	Corporate Membership of I.M.I.	Qualification Status	Chief Executive	Marketing	Production	Finance	Personnel	Other
00 or More	MEMBER	Qualified	27	48	259	133	20	13
		Unqualified	22	146	351	67	32	14
	NON-MEMBER	Qualified	3	—	3	7	0	2
		Unqualified	4	13	19	4	1	4
00-499	MEMBER	Qualified	26± 18	26± 23	108± 43	82± 29	5± 9	10± 13
		Unqualified	61± 18	87± 54	353±116	97± 57	5± 9	15± 15
	NON-MEMBER	Qualified	44± 25	33± 34	143± 98	159± 66	6±10	16± 17
		Unqualified	143± 33	175± 98	411± 83	121± 45	—	33± 23
0-99	MEMBER	Qualified	13± 25	13± 25	89±178	76± 51	13±25	13± 25
		Unqualified	76± 33	64± 76	140±115	38± 53	—	—
	NON-MEMBER	Qualified	155±109	44± 63	44± 63	111± 95	—	178±275
		Unqualified	777±135	111± 95	622±256	200±136	—	355±263
TOTAL	MEMBER	Qualified	65± 32	86± 35	456±203	291± 62	38±30	36± 30
		Unqualified	160± 40	297± 96	844±164	202± 79	37±10	29± 16
	NON-MEMBER	Qualified	202±109	77± 69	190±113	277±112	6±10	196±270
		Unqualified	924±135	300±132	1052±261	325±139	1	392±258

TABLE 8.2.4. *Estimated Percentage of Managers in Each Functional Area Who are Qualified, by Size of Firm and Corporate Membership of Irish Management Institute.*

Size of Firm (No. of employees)	Corporate Membership of I.M.I.	Chief Executive % Qualified	Marketing % Qualified	Production % Qualified	Finance % Qualified	Personnel % Qualified	Other % Qualified
00 or More	MEMBER	55.1	24.7	42.5	66.5	38.5	48.1
	NON-MEMBER	42.9	—	13.6	63.6	—	33.3
00-499	MEMBER (a)	29.9	23.0	23.3	45.7	50.0	40.0
	NON-MEMBER	23.5±12.3	15.8±14.7	25.7± 9.0	56.9±25.9	100.0	33.3±41.2
0-99	MEMBER (a)	14.6	16.7	38.9	66.7	100.0	100.0
	NON-MEMBER	16.7±11.6	28.6±39.2	6.7± 9.4	35.7±34.9	—	33.3±55.1
OVERALL	MEMBER	29.3±12.9	22.6± 8.4	35.1±14.5	59.1±19.8	51.4± 8.8	56.0±24.8
	NON-MEMBER	18.0± 9.3	20.5±18.5	15.3± 9.3	46.1±22.1	71.4	33.0±51.7

(a) No confidence limits shown because the number of firms was too small (see statistical note 2.2).

It was stated in chapter 4 that the inclusion in the bottom stratum of firms which had subsequently left it led to a strong upward bias in the estimate of the proportion qualified in that size-group. Comparison of the bottom stratum of table 8.2.5. with that of 8.2.2. shows that the exclusion of these larger firms reduces considerably the proportion qualified in production management but has little effect on the others.

TABLE 8.2.5. *Managers in Functional Areas, Showing the Percentage Qualified and Unqualified, by Size of Firm.*

Size of Firm (No. of Employees)	Qualification Status	Chief Executive	Marketing	Production	Finance	Personnel	Other
	Number of Managers in Analysis	54	05	622	207	53	31
500 or More	Percentage Qualified	53.71	23.42	41.81	66.19	37.74	45.17
	Percentage Unqualified	46.30	76.59	58.20	33.82	62.27	54.84
	Number of Managers in Analysis	47	54	176	79	2 (a)	11 (a)
100-499	Percentage Qualified	25.54	14.82	24.44	49.37	50.00	27.27
	Percentage Unqualified	74.47	85.19	75.57	50.64	50.00	72.73
	Number of Managers in Analysis	44	9	35	18	—	21
20-99	Percentage Qualified	15.91	22.22	5.71	44.44	—	33.33
	Percentage Unqualified	84.10	77.78	94.29	55.56	—	66.67

(a) Omitted from the statistical test because the numbers were too small.

In the group of firms employing 500 or more people there are striking differences between the areas, with marketing having by far the lowest proportion qualified and finance having the highest. In the medium size-group the same pattern is repeated. A statistical test, from which personnel managers were omitted because they were too few, showed that there was less than one chance in a thousand that the observed differences could have arisen by chance. The significant difference is between marketing and finance; the other areas differ from one another hardly at all. In the bottom stratum production appears lowest and finance highest, but it was impossible to carry out a test on all the areas. It was decided to compare chief executives with the remainder but this showed no significant difference. It may be concluded that, in firms with over 100 employees, finance executives are most likely to be qualified, marketing least likely and the remainder about equal. The pattern is roughly similar in firms with under 100 employees, but the sample is too small to be confident that the observed difference is real.

It will be seen in section 4 below that there is a relationship between function and age, with finance executives being younger than others. Because it was later discovered that younger managers are more likely to be qualified than older ones it was necessary to have a further breakdown by age to ensure that the conclusion above still stood. It was found that, in every age-group, finance had the highest proportion qualified, and marketing the lowest. Furthermore, marketing has lost ground. It is the one area which does not, so far, show a tendency for younger managers to be more qualified than older ones.

It should be pointed out that this position may change rapidly, due to the large numbers of people not yet in managerial positions who are studying for professional qualifications in marketing (see chapter 17).

The question is now taken up of the inter-relationship between functional areas and particular types of qualification. Taking first the broad division of qualified executives into those with university degrees alone, those with professional qualifications alone, and those with both, the position is shown in table 8.2.6.

In almost every area in each size-group the majority have a university degree alone. The exception is finance where the great majority have a professional qualification alone.

TABLE 8.2.6. *Qualified Managers in Functional Areas, Showing the Percentage with Each Type of Qualification, by Size of Firm.*

Size of Firm (No. of Employees)	Type of Qualification	Chief Executive	Marketing	Production	Finance	Personnel	Other
500 or More	Number of Qualified Managers in Analysis	29	48	260	137	20	14
	Percentage with a University Degree Only	62.07	50.01	76.16	12.41	65.00	57.15
	Percentage with a Professional Qualification Only	20.69	41.67	16.54	66.43	35.00	35.72
	Percentage with Both	17.25	8.34	7.31	21.17	—	7.15
100–499	Number of Qualified Managers in Analysis	12	8	43	39	1	3
	Percentage with a University Degree Only	83.33	75.00	58.14	10.26	—	66.67
	Percentage with a Professional Qualification Only	—	25.00	30.23	84.62	100.00	—
	Percentage with Both	16.67	—	11.63	5.12	—	33.33
20–99	Number of Qualified Managers in Analysis	7	2	2	8	—	7
	Percentage with a University Degree Only	57.14	100.00	100.00	12.50	—	100.00
	Percentage with a Professional Qualification Only	28.57	—	—	62.50	—	—
	Percentage with Both	14.29	—	—	25.00	—	—

In the top size-group there is also a higher proportion of executives in finance with both degrees and professional qualifications. The fact has already been referred to in chapter 4 that engineers and scientists are largely university-trained, while accountants and company secretaries have traditionally qualified through professional institutes.

Table 8.2.7. shows how those with university degrees alone are divided between functions. These figures relate only to sample firms unchanged in size at the date of the survey. For an approximate estimate of the number in each area, with each type of degree, in industry as a whole, the figures in the top stratum should be taken as they stand, those in the middle stratum multiplied by about 6, and those in the bottom stratum by about 23[1]. The same holds for tables 8.2.8. and 8.2.9.

TABLE 8.2.7. *Managers with University Degrees Only, Showing the Number in the Sample in Each Functional Area with Each Type of Degree, by Size of Firm.*

Size of Firm (No. of Employees)	Type of Degree	Chief Executive	Marketing	Production	Finance	Personnel	Other	Total
500 or More	COMMERCE	1	8	5	12	3	—	29
	ARTS	6	3	8	3	7	1	28
	ENGINEERING	5	2	107	—	1	2	117
	SCIENCE	3	6	67	1	—	4	81
	OTHER	3	5	11	1	2	1	23
	TOTAL	18	24	198	17	13	8	278
100–499	COMMERCE	2	3	1	3	—	—	9
	ARTS	2	1	—	1	—	—	4
	ENGINEERING	1	—	8	—	—	—	9
	SCIENCE	4	1	16	—	—	1	22
	OTHER	1	1	—	—	—	1	3
	TOTAL	10	6	25	4	—	2	47
20–99	COMMERCE	—	—	—	1	—	—	1
	ARTS	2	—	—	—	—	—	2
	ENGINEERING	—	1	—	—	—	—	1
	SCIENCE	—	—	2	—	—	1	3
	OTHER	2	1	—	—	—	6	9
	TOTAL	4	2	2	1	—	7	16

The striking fact emerging from this table is the extent to which executives are concentrated in the areas to which their basic degrees relate, practically all the engineers and scientists working in production management. Those with degrees in arts or commerce are not so concentrated. The high proportion of arts graduates who are chief executives is worth noting. In almost every case they are either non-Irish nationals employed by

1 The figures in tables 8.2.7 to 8.2.9 were arrived at by a computer count rather than by hand. To cut down complications it was necessary to specify counts starting with "other", then science, engineering etc. Thus, scientists with engineering qualifications are counted only as scientists. The figures in tables 8.2.7 to 8.2.9 therefore differ slightly from those in part B of chapter 4.

foreign companies or are members of the owning family. It is not the case that they reached higher positions in direct competition with holders of other degrees, due to whatever advantage is conferred by a liberal arts background. In passing, the very small number of economists employed in marketing may be noted.

TABLE 8.2.8. *Managers with Professional Qualifications Only, Showing the Number in the Sample with Each Type of Professional Qualification in Each Functional Area, by Size of Firm.*

Size of Firm (No. of Employees)	Type of Professional Qualification	Chief Executive	Marketing	Production	Finance	Personnel	Other	Total
500 or More	FINANCE	3	12	6	91	3	4	119
	ENGINEERING, ETC.	1	1	33	—	—	—	35
	MARKETING	2	5	—	—	—	—	7
	PERSONNEL	—	—	—	—	4	—	4
	OTHER	—	2	4	—	—	1	7
	TOTAL	6	20	43	91	7	5	172
100–499	FINANCE	—	—	2	33	—	—	35
	ENGINEERING, ETC.	—	—	5	—	—	—	5
	MARKETING	—	2	—	—	—	—	2
	PERSONNEL	—	—	—	—	1	—	1
	OTHER	—	—	6	—	—	—	6
	TOTAL	—	2	13	33	1	—	49
20–99	FINANCE	1	—	—	5	—	—	6
	ENGINEERING, ETC.	—	—	—	—	—	—	—
	MARKETING	—	—	—	—	—	—	—
	PERSONNEL	—	—	—	—	—	—	—
	OTHER	1	—	—	—	—	—	1
	TOTAL	2	—	—	5	—	—	7

Concentration in particular areas was obvious among holders of university degrees. As table 8.2.8. shows, it is even more marked among executives with professional qualifications. Almost every one of them worked in the area to which his qualification was directly relevant. (Note that, at least in large firms, a greater number of qualified marketing executives have qualifications in accountancy than in any other subject, including marketing.)

Finally, examination of those with both degrees and professional qualifications shows the same picture.

It was pointed out in chapter 4 that, in medium-sized businesses, the number of scientists was greater than the number of engineers, whereas in large companies the reverse was true.

Two possible explanations were put forward. The first was that engineers were employed mainly on engineering work rather than in production management and that smaller companies, therefore, whose capital installation was not so extensive or complex,

TABLE 8.2.9. *Managers with Both University Degrees and Professional Qualifications, Showing the Number of Each Type in the Sample in Each Functional Area, by Size of Firm.*

Size of Firm (No. of Employees)	Type of Combined Qualification	Chief Executive	Marketing	Production	Finance	Personnel	Other	Total
500 or More	B.COMM. & FINANCE	1	2	—	23	—	—	26
	B.COMM. & OTHER	—	—	—	—	—	—	—
	ANY OTHER COMBINATION	4	2	19	6	—	1	32
	TOTAL	5	4	19	29	—	1	58
100–499	B.COMM. & FINANCE	—	—	—	2	—	—	2
	B.COMM. & OTHER	—	—	—	—	—	—	—
	ANY OTHER COMBINATION	2	—	5	—	—	1	8
	TOTAL	2	—	5	2	—	1	10
20–99	B.COMM. & FINANCE	—	—	—	2	—	—	2
	B.COMM. & OTHER	—	—	—	—	—	—	—
	ANY OTHER COMBINATION	1	—	—	—	—	—	1
	TOTAL	1	—	—	2	—	—	3

would find less use for graduate engineers than would large firms. The second possible explanation was that the value of engineers was underestimated by companies in the medium-size range. (It will be remembered that small firms employ neither engineers nor scientists to any extent.) A third explanation would be the industrial structure of the groups.

Although the proportion of food processing firms is the same in both size groups, the sample from the 100-499 group includes too many such firms to be truly representative. Since food processing companies are likely to employ scientists, it is possible that this over-representation of the industry accounts for the high proportion of scientists in the 100 to 499 employee stratum.

In an addendum to chapter 2, table 2.11 shows a detailed breakdown of the types of managerial positions in industry. The positions in the general area of production management are broken down into four groups, the first consisting of those in direct line management, the second showing those in staff positions. The third includes those on engineering and maintenance work, and the fourth consists of those called technical advisers. The occupiers of these positions were analysed into those with no qualifications and those with qualifications in engineering, science and other areas.

The results of the analysis were interesting. In the 100 to 499 group there was a total of 135 production executives in line positions. Only one-sixth of them had any sort of qualification. Of the 21 qualified, 8 were graduate engineers and another one was a professional engineer. Five of those 9 engineers were employed by only 2 firms. There were 5 scientists and 6 executives with other qualifications. Four of the latter were employed by a single company. It can therefore be said that, apart from a very small proportion of companies, the overwhelming majority of executives in line production positions have no academic qualifications.

The position is the same for staff positions, with the exception of those in charge of laboratories. There were 37 staff positions, of which 13 were as chemists. Only 4 of those in staff positions, other than as laboratory heads, had qualifications, but of the 13 chemists 11 were qualified and all those qualified were graduate scientists.

Only 3 of those on engineering and maintenance work were qualified, and all were engineers.

It appears that, apart from the specialised work of chemists, virtually no one, either in line or in staff positions is qualified academically. Almost all the scientists employed work as chemists, few being in line management, whereas most of the engineers are line managers.

The position is a little different in firms employing over 500 people. Almost one-third of production executives in line positions are qualified. For top production managers the proportion is even higher — almost half.

With the exception of chemists the same is true of staff executives: about one-third have qualifications.

There are considerable differences between the proportions qualified in different staff positions. About two-thirds of all laboratory heads are qualified. Most executives in research and development, in project or development engineering, and in production engineering have qualifications. Almost half the work study managers, designers and quality controllers are qualified, and about one-third of the production planners. On the other hand most stores or stock controllers and most purchasing managers have no formal qualifications.

Over half of all those on engineering work have qualifications, and almost exactly half of all technical advisers.

It must, however, be said that the bulk of the qualified production engineers, and a good proportion of the qualified general engineering executives, were employed by one large company.

Taking the two most frequent qualifications—engineering and science—it was found that in the group of firms employing over 500 people about half the scientists and half the engineers were line managers. Most of the scientists not in line management were chemists in charge of laboratories. The remainder were mainly in research and development, quality control or technical positions. The engineers not in line management were mostly in plant engineering or in project or development engineering.

It therefore appears that neither of the first two possible explanations put forward to explain the situation referred to in chapter 4 is adequate.

It is true that scientists predominate over engineers in the middle stratum, but this is caused mainly by the fact that the sample included a high proportion of food processing companies, most of which employed qualified chemists. So far as line positions went, neither engineers nor scientists were common, but such qualified men as occupied such positions were most likely to be engineers.

In large companies there are about equal numbers of scientists in line and in staff positions. The number of engineers in line positions about matches the number in staff and engineering.

Thus it is true that, as firms increase in size, the expansion in the proportion of engineers is most marked in engineering jobs. It is, however, not true that scientists lose ground proportionately in line positions. On the contrary, as firms increase in size the openings in line management become greater for scientists who, in smaller firms, are confined mainly to laboratory work.

The fact that the proportion of scientists on staff work falls as the size of firms increases may appear surprising, but this reflects the fact that the amount of research and development work by large companies based in Ireland is limited. Given that a good proportion of such companies are owned by foreign parent companies, this lack of new-product orientation is not surprising, as most of these companies confine their manufacture to products developed in other countries by their parent firms.

The situation revealed by tables 8.2.7. to 8.2.9. has implications for recommendations on management education and training. Most managers are general managers to some extent, in that they must make decisions about the groups under their control, decisions which involve people and money. To function effectively as a member of a management team a manager must be able to understand the terminology and see the point of view of specialists in areas other than his own. A limited number of individuals reach top positions in which it is necessary to understand not only other areas within their own firms, but the operation of external environmental forces acting on the firm as a whole. It is further necessary for individuals to be so educated that they have the capacity to assimilate developments as yet unforeseen. All those points are valid arguments against rigid specialisation in training. Yet so long as business remains predominantly small and organised departmentally along the lines indicated in chapter 2, and so long as individuals continue to spend most of their working lives in one or other of those areas, it would appear to be a legitimate aim of training to provide a thorough working knowledge of the area of specialisation to which the trainee is addressing himself. It is essential that the claims of generality and professional competence in a specialism be reconciled, rather than that one should prevail at the expense of the other.

The final question examined in this chapter is whether there are discernible trends towards particular types of qualification. It will be seen in chapter 9 that there is a definite tendency for younger people to be more qualified in general. The question of particular types of qualification is examined here rather than in chapter 9; owing to the large number of combinations possible, there would not have been enough data to examine each separately. Each functional area was therefore taken in turn and, within each area, a breakdown was obtained of managers in different age-groups into those with university degrees, only, those with professional qualifications only, and those with both. It was felt, because of the close identification of qualifications with functions, that this would give at least an indication of any trends emerging.

Even this restricted breakdown gave numbers too small for testing. Observations were therefore confined to the top stratum, in which differences are significant by definition. The only marked tendency was in the case of finance. Here, executives aged under thirty-five were much more likely than older managers to combine degrees with professional qualifications, the combination invariably being a B.Comm. and a qualification in accountancy. In fact, in the top size-group, about one young finance executive out of every three qualified had this combination.

TABLE 8. 3. 1. *Estimated Number of Managers in Each Functional Area who Attended Management Training Courses, by Size and Location of Firm.*

Size of Firm (No. of Employees)	Location of Head Office	Attendance at Courses	Chief Executive	Marketing	Production	Finance	Personnel	Other
00 or More	DUBLIN	Attended	20	104	286	107	32	11
		Did Not Attend	16	49	208	51	8	15
	REST OF COUNTRY	Attended	10	33	75	36	12	2
		Did Not Attend	10	21	63	17	1	5
	TOTAL	Attended	30	137	361	143	44	13
		Did Not Attend	26	70	271	68	9	20
00-499	DUBLIN	Attended	16±16	78±56	94±49	47±31	5±10	10±13
		Did Not Attend	120±26	141±73	411±94	198±59	10±13	31±25
	REST OF COUNTRY	Attended	16±17	27±26	115±98	55±73	—	—
		Did Not Attend	121±21	71±33	401±92	159±33	—	33±22
	TOTAL	Attended	32±22	107±62	209±103	102±74	5±10	11±14
		Did Not Attend	241±32	214±81	814±127	359±68	11±14	64±33
0-99	DUBLIN	Attended	64±71	43±60	107±107	21±43	21±43	21±43
		Did Not Attend	447±123	128±142	490±347	256±196	—	213±185
	REST OF COUNTRY	Attended	99±81	20±40	20±40	20±40	—	20±40
		Did Not Attend	397±120	79±74	377±170	178±96	—	258±401
	TOTAL	Attended	165±105	62±68	123±110	41±56	21±40	41±56
		Did Not Attend	843±166	206±152	864±364	432±206	—	473±435
TOTAL	DUBLIN	Attended	100±77	225±79	486±116	175±56	59±44	43±45
		Did Not Attend	583±126	317±157	1109±358	505±203	18±13	259±187
	REST OF COUNTRY	Attended	126±82	80±46	210±104	111±81	12	22±40
		Did Not Attend	528±122	172±80	841±190	355±100	1	296±401
	TOTAL	Attended	227±107	306±91	693±150	286±92	70±41	65±60
		Did Not Attend	1110±168	490±171	1949±384	859±216	20±14	557±436

TABLE 8.3.2. *Estimated Percentage of Managers in Each Functional Area who Attended Management Training Courses, by Size and Location of Firm.*

Size of Firm (No. of Employees)	Location of Head Office	Chief Executive % Attended	Marketing % Attended	Production % Attended	Finance % Attended	Personnel % Attended	Other % Attended
500 or More	DUBLIN	55.6	68.0	57.9	67.7	80.0	42.3
	REST OF COUNTRY	50.0	61.1	54.3	67.8	92.3	28.6
	OVERALL	53.6	66.2	57.1	67.8	83.0	39.4
100-499	DUBLIN	11.8	35.7	18.6	19.1	33.3	25.0
	REST OF COUNTRY	11.7	27.6	22.3	25.6	—	—
	OVERALL	11.8± 8.2	33.3±15.5	20.4± 7.8	22.1±13.3	33.3±48.6	14.7±16.9
20-99	DUBLIN	12.5	25.0	17.9	7.6	1C0.0	9.0
	REST OF COUNTRY	20.0	20.0	5.0	10.0	—	7.1
	OVERALL	16.3±10.4	23.1±24.1	12.5±10.4	8.7±11.8	100.0	8.0±12.
OVERALL	DUBLIN	14.6±10.8	41.5±13.0	30.5± 6.9	25.7± 7.4	75.8±10.3	14.1±14.
	REST OF COUNTRY	19.2±13.0	31.8±16.7	20.0± 9.4	23.7±16.6	92.3	6.8±14.
	OVERALL	16.9± 8.5	38.4±10.3	26.2± 5.3	25.0± 6.7	78.1± 8.9	10.5±10.

TABLE 8.3.3. *Estimated Number of Managers in Each Functional Area who Attended Management Training Courses, by Size of Firm and Corporate Membership of Irish Management Institute.*

Size of Firm (No. of Employees)	Corporate Membership of I.M.I.	Attendances at Courses	Chief Executive	Marketing	Production	Finance	Personnel	Other
500 or More	MEMBER	Attended	30	137	357	141	43	13
		Did Not Attend	19	57	253	59	9	14
	NON-MEMBER	Attended	—	—	4	2	1	—
		Did Not Attend	7	13	18	9	—	6
100-499	MEMBER	Attended	10±13	36±28	128±85	77±66	—	5±9
		Did Not Attend	77±19	77±46	333±80	102±40	10±13	20±17
	NON-MEMBER	Attended	22±19	71±59	77±51	22±24	5±10	5±10
		Did Not Attend	165±28	137±71	477±99	258±57	—	44±29
20-99	MEMBER	Attended	38±37	13±25	13±25	13±25	13±25	—
		Did Not Attend	51±38	64±76	217±165	102±94	—	13±25
	NON-MEMBER	Attended	111±95	44±63	111±115	22±45	—	44±63
		Did Not Attend	822±164	111±95	555±244	289±148	—	489±48.
TOTAL	MEMBER	Attended	78±43	186±38	498±90	231±71	56±29	18±10
		Did Not Attend	147±45	198±93	803±197	263±110	19±13	47±22
	NON-MEMBER	Attended	133±95	116±83	192±122	46±49	6±10	50±62
		Did Not Attend	993±162	261±115	1050±255	555±154	—	539±47(

Section 3: The Relationship between Function and Attendance at Management Training Courses

An important aim of the survey was to establish the extent to which executives had already participated in management training, by whatever institution it was carried out. The overall situation was shown in chapter 5. In this section participation is shown by function, analysed according to size, location and corporate membership of the Irish Management Institute. Because the figures refer to January 1964 they have probably changed quite considerably due to the expansion since that date in the activities of the Irish Management Institute.

TABLE 8. 3. 4. *Estimated Percentage of Managers in Each Functional Area who Attended Management Training Courses, by Size of Firm and Corporate Membership of Irish Management Institute.*

Size of Firm (No. of Employees)	Corporate Membership of I.M.I.	Chief Executive % Attended	Marketing % Attended	Production % Attended	Finance % Attended	Personnel % Attended	Other % Attended
500 or More	MEMBER	61.2	70.6	58.5	70.5	82.7	48.1
	NON-MEMBER	—	—	18.2	18.2	100.0	0.
100 499	MEMBER	11.5	31.8	27.8	42.9	0.	20.0
	NON-MEMBER	11.8±10.0	34.2±18.0	34.9± 7.6	7.8± 7.8	100.0	10.2±19.2
20-99	MEMBER	42.9	16.7	5.6	11.3	100.0	0.
	NON-MEMBER	11.9± 9.8	28.6±33.1	16.7±15.3	7.1±13.5	—	8.3±12.9
OVERALL	MEMBER	34.7±16.2	48.5± 8.9	38.3± 4.7	46.8±10.4	75.7	28.0±13.1
	NON-MEMBER	11.8± 9.3	30.6±17.1	15.5± 9.2	7.6± 8.4	85.7	8.4±10.6

Table 8.3.2. shows that location does not appear to have a great deal of influence on the functional areas in which training is most widespread. In table 8.3.3. it can be seen that, in firms with over 100 employees, the majority of participants in management training in almost every function were employed by member-firms of the Irish Management Institute. Member-firms in the medium size-group appear in table 8.3.4. to have laid greater stress on finance than non-member firms, where marketing showed the highest rate of participation. In small firms, chief executives from member-firms had the highest rate of participation in training.

To establish the significance of the difference observed between the different functions a statistical test was carried out on the data used for table 8.3.5. (Comparison of table 8.3.5. with 8.3.2. shows that the inclusion in the latter of firms changed in size did not lead to a large upward bias in any area, as it did in the case of qualifications.) In the top size-group personnel executives were most likely to have attended courses, followed by executives in marketing and finance. In the middle group marketing and finance were to the fore, and in the bottom size-group marketing led clearly. However in neither case did the test reach a significant level, that is to say, the differences could have arisen by chance. The table does not therefore provide strong evidence that functional areas differ much in the extent to which their executives had attended training courses.

TABLE 8.3.5.   *Managers in Each Functional Area, Showing the Percentage who Attended Management Train-*
                ing Courses, by Size of Firm.

Size of Firm (No. of Employees)	Attendance at Courses	Chief Executive	Marketing	Production	Finance	Personnel	Other
	NO. OF MANAGERS IN ANALYSIS	54	205	622	207	53	31
500 or More	Percentage ATTENDED	53.71	66.35	57.24	67.64	83.02	38.71
	Percentage DID NOT	46.30	33.66	42.77	32.37	16.99	61.30
	NO. OF MANAGERS IN ANALYSIS	47	54	176	79	2 (a)	11 (a)
100–499	Percentage ATTENDED	10.64	27.78	19.32	24.06	—	9.10
	Percentage DID NOT	89.37	72.23	80.69	75.95	100.00	90.91
	NO. OF MANAGERS IN ANALYSIS	44	9	35	18	—	21
20–99	Percentage ATTENDED	15.91	33.33	14.29	5.55	—	9.52
	Percentage DID NOT	84.10	66.67	85.71	94.45	—	90.48

(a) Omitted from the statistical test because the numbers were too small.

Section 4: The Relationship between Functional Area and Age

An estimate of the number of managers in each age-group is shown broken down by function and size of firm in table 8.4.1. In almost every area the majority of managers are in the 35 to 49 age group.

TABLE 8.4.1.   *Estimated Number of Managers in Each Age-Group in Each Functional Area, by Size of Firm.*

Size of Firm (No. of Employees)	Age-Group	Chief Executive	Marketing	Production	Finance	Personnel	Other
500 or More	Under 35	—	48	151	61	9	4
	35-49	20	100	306	110	30	12
	50 or Over	36	59	175	40	14	17
100-499	Under 35	5±10	64±33	268±97	177±77	5±10	11±14
	35-49	75±35	150±64	557±142	198±58	11±14	27±21
	50 or Over	193±39	107±41	198±52	86±36	—	37±29
20-99	Under 35	123±96	144±118	329±199	185±128	21±42	123±141
	35-49	555±153	123±96	411±270	226±135	—	226±216
	50 or Over	329±136	—	247±151	62±70	—	165±181
TOTAL	Under 35	129±94	256±119	748±214	423±144	35±41	138±137
	35-49	650±152	373±111	1,274±294	534±141	41±14	265±211
	50 or Over	558±137	166±48	620±154	187±76	14	219±178

Because the data are in numerical form it is difficult to see any relationship which may exist. They are therefore shown in percentage form in table 8.4.2. on which a statistical test was carried out.

TABLE 8.4.2.   *Managers in Functional Areas, showing the Percentage in Each Age-Group, by Size of Firm.*

Size of Firm (No. of Employees)	Age-Grouping	Chief Executive	Marketing	Production	Finance	Personnel	Other
500 or More	Number of Managers in Analysis	54	205	622	207	53	31
	Percentage Aged Under 35	—	23.42	23.80	28.99	16.99	6.46
	Percentage Aged 35-49	37.04	48.30	48.72	51.70	56.61	38.71
	Percentage Aged 50 or Over	62.97	28.30	27.50	19.33	26.42	54.84
100–499	Number of Managers in Analysis	47	54	176	79	2(a)	11
	Percentage Aged Under 35	2.13	20.38	24.44	35.45	—	18.19
	Percentage Aged 35-49	27.66	46.30	56.26	44.31	100.00	36.37
	Percentage Aged 50 or Over	70.22	33.34	19.32	20.26	—	45.46
20–99	Number of Managers in Analysis	44	9(a)	35	18	—	21
	Percentage Aged Under 35	13.64	44.44	28.58	33.33	—	28.58
	Percentage Aged 35-49	56.82	55.56	40.01	50.01	—	42.86
	Percentage Aged 50 or Over	29.55	—	31.43	16.67	—	28.58

(a) Omitted from the statistical test as the numbers were too small.

Table 8.4.2. shows that the functions differ quite considerably in the ages of their managers. In the top group chief executives and "others" are older than the rest, finance executives younger, while marketing and production are remarkably similar. This picture is repeated in the middle size-group, though in this case marketing executives are somewhat older than those in production. The differences observed could not have arisen by chance. In the bottom stratum the differences observed, though much the same as in the other strata, are based on small numbers and could have arisen by chance.

Section 5: The Relationship between Functional Area and Nationality

Questions were asked on the nationality of managers primarily so that this cross-classification could be obtained. It was thought that concentration of foreign-born executives in a particular function would indicate that some sort of ability in that function, not necessarily managerial, was lacking in Ireland. Estimates of the number and proportion of managers born abroad are given in tables 8.5.1. and 8.5.2.

TABLE 8.5.1. *Estimated Number of Irish and Foreign Managers in Each Functional Area, by Size of Firm.*

Size of Firm (No. of Employees)	Nationality of Manager	Chief Executive	Marketing	Production	Finance	Personnel	Other
500 or More	IRISH	36	188	535	206	49	28
	OTHER	20	19	97	5	4	5
	TOTAL	56	207	632	211	53	33
100-499	IRISH	220±35	305±110	857±171	450±94	16±17	70±34
	OTHER	54±32	16±17	166±60	11±20	—	5±10
	TOTAL	273±22	321±115	1,023±180	460±90	16±16	75±34
20-99	IRISH	905±157	267±165	823±324	411±165	21±42	494±448
	OTHER	103±89	—	165±149	62±92	—	21±42
	TOTAL	1,008±121	267±160	987±383	473±206	21±40	514±435
TOTAL	IRISH	1,160±156	761±191	2,214±353	1,067±183	86±43	591±436
	OTHER	176±91	35±16	428±155	77±91	4	31±41
	TOTAL	1,337±123	796±195	2,642±420	1,144±223	90±43	622±436

TABLE 8.5.2. *Estimated Percentage of Managers in Each Functional Area who are Foreign-born, by Size of Firm.*

Size of Firm (No. of Employees)	Nationality of Manager	Chief Executive	Marketing	Production	Finance	Personnel	Other
500 or More	Percentage FOREIGN-BORN	35.7	9.2	15.3	2.4	7.5	15.2
100–499	Percentage FOREIGN-BORN	19.8±10.8	5.0± 4.3	16.2± 5.1	2.4± 4.1	0.	6.7±12.3
20–99	Percentage FOREIGN-BORN	10.2± 8.4	0.	16.7±11.6	13.0±15.3	0.	4.0± 8.2
OVERALL	Percentage FOREIGN-BORN	13.2± 7.1	4.4± 1.54	16.2± 4.8	6.8± 6.4	4.4	4.9± 7.5

It appears from table 8.5.2. that the highest concentration is among chief executives and production managers. A test of significance was carried out on the data used to form table 8.5.3. below. (Note how the exclusion from that table of firms which had changed their size has reduced the proportion of foreign-born finance executives in the bottom size-group.) The test showed that the differences observed were very highly significant.

No test was possible on the 20 to 99 size-group because of the small number of foreign-born managers.

The foreign-born chief executives are mostly either employed by foreign-owned companies or came to Ireland and started their own businesses, largely because of their technical know-how. The same is true of the executives in production. Most of them were brought in at an early stage of our industrial development because of their technical skill. In many cases they are in the 50 years or over age-group, and when they retire will be replaced by Irish executives.

TABLE 8.5.3.   *Managers in each Functional Area, showing the Percentage of each Nationality, by Size of Firm.*

Size of Firm (No. of Employees)	Nationality of Manager	Chief Executive	Marketing	Production	Finance	Personnel	Other
500 or More	NO. OF MANAGERS IN ANALYSIS	54	205	622	207	53	31
	Percentage IRISH-BORN	64.82	90.74	84.73	98.07	92.46	87.10
	Percentage OTHER	35.19	9.27	15.28	1.94	7.55	12.91
100–499	NO. OF MANAGERS IN ANALYSIS	47	54	176	79	2 (a)	11 (a)
	Percentage IRISH-BORN	78.73	94.45	82.39	97.47	100.00	90.91
	Percentage OTHER	21.28	5.56	17.62	2.54	—	9.09
20–99	NO. OF MANAGERS IN ANALYSIS	39	9	35	18	—	21
	Percentage IRISH-BORN	88.64	100.00	88.57	94.45	—	100.00
	Percentage OTHER	11.36	—	11.43	5.55	—	—

(a) Omitted from the statistical test because the numbers were too small.

Reference:

(1) G. W. Snedecor. *Statistical Methods.* 5th edn. Ames, Iowa: The Iowa State University Press, 1956 (p. 231).

CHAPTER 9

Further Inter-relationships between Characteristics of Managers

This chapter is in five parts. Part A is concerned with relationships between level and other attributes, part B with those between qualification and attributes not already dealt with, part C with those between management training and others, part D with age and nationality, while part E summarises the findings related to nationality.

Summary of Main Findings of Part A.
SECTION A1. This section deals with the relationship between level and qualification. It is found that, in every age group, those who possess an academic qualification are nearer to the top than those who do not. This tendency is more marked among older than among younger managers. This might suggest that those with qualifications pull farther ahead as they grow older. It might also suggest that competition is becoming stronger: when those with qualifications were in a minority they were quite likely to be promoted, whereas now that most younger managers in large firms are qualified a substantial proportion of them will never reach top level.

SECTION A2. This section deals with the relationship between level and management training. Generally speaking the greatest number of managers participating in training come from middle and junior management. The proportions from the different levels do not vary much in the top size-group. In the middle size-group chief executives, even from member-firms, do not attend to any great extent, whereas in small companies, particularly those outside Dublin and those which are members of the Irish Management Institute, there is a slight tendency for chief executives to have attended to a greater extent than others.

Even in firms which employ managers with training there is no evidence of an association between training and level; even if there were it would be dangerous to assume a cause-effect relationship.

SECTION A3. Relationship between level and age. There are no obvious gaps in age at any level: the number aged under 50 appears adequate to replace those over 50 as they retire. There is no conclusive evidence that promotion within management comes automatically with age, as there are quite large numbers of executives aged over 50 still in junior positions.

SECTION A4. Relationship between level and nationality. Foreign-born managers form over 20 per cent of the top echelons in firms with over 500 employees. They are not so important proportionally in firms employing less than that number. Irrespective of age, foreign-born managers reach higher levels than Irish managers even in Irish-owned companies. This tendency is more marked in foreign-owned firms. Part of the explanation for the high proportion at senior level in Irish-owned, small firms is that some of these firms are owned and are still being run by men born abroad but now domiciled in Ireland.

Summary of Main Findings of Part B.

SECTION B1. Relationship between qualification and training. A large number of managers even in large companies have neither an academic qualification nor any training in management. There is no evidence that training is used exclusively either to supplement or to substitute for academic qualifications. It is used to the same extent by those with and by those without qualifications.

SECTION B2. Relationship between qualification and age. In firms with over 100 employees there is a definite tendency for younger managers, particularly those aged under 35, to be more likely than those in older age-groups to have an academic qualification. In firms with under 100 employees there is no evidence that those under 35 are more likely to be qualified than those aged 35 to 49. That is to say, there is no evidence that the proportion of qualified executives in small firms is rising automatically with the passage of time.

SECTION B3. Relationship between qualification and nationality. Irish-born managers, especially in the older age-groups, appear slightly more likely to have a qualification than managers born in Britain. The difference is not large nor, outside the top group, is it statistically significant.

Summary of Main Findings of Part C.

SECTION C1. Relationship between training and age. There is a marked tendency for younger managers to be more likely than older ones to have attended management training courses. Except in small firms which are members of the Irish Management Institute, those aged 50 or more are least likely to have attended.

SECTION C2. Relationship between training and nationality. Outside the top size-group there is no evidence that Irish-born executives are more or less likely than foreign-born managers of the same age to have participated in training courses. In firms with 500 or more employees, Irish-born executives are more likely than foreign-born managers to have attended, in every age-group. This shows again the largely technical orientation of foreign-born executives working in Ireland.

Summary of Main Findings of Part D.

SECTION D1. Relationship between age and nationality. Foreign-born managers are, on average, older than Irish managers. It is likely that, in longer-established companies, the proportion of foreign managers will decrease in time, these managers being replaced as they retire by Irish executives.

Summary of Main Findings of Part E.

This part summarises the findings of previous sections on the question of nationality.

PART A.   LEVEL AND OTHER CHARACTERISTICS

In chapter 8, the relationship between level and function was examined. It was found that the lowest proportion of top managers was in production. The relationship between level and the remaining attributes of managers is dealt with in this part.

Section A.1. Level and Qualification.

In designing courses aimed at different levels of management it is important to know

TABLE 9a. 1. 1.   *Estimated Number of Qualified and Unqualified Managers at Each Level, by Size and Locati. of Firm.*

Size of Firm (No. of Employees)	Location of Head Office	Qualification Status	Chief Executive	Top Management	Middle Management	Junior Manageme
500 or More	DUBLIN	Qualified	21	86	190	110
		Unqualified	15	56	216	213
	REST OF COUNTRY	Qualified	9	32	46	21
		Unqualified	11	26	88	52
	TOTAL	Qualified	30	118	236	131
		Unqualified	26	82	304	265
100-499	DUBLIN	Qualified	36± 22	156± 40	135± 64	52± 61
		Unqualified	99± 23	182± 40	292± 79	208± 80
	REST OF COUNTRY	Qualified	33± 22	115± 48	104± 70	22± 24
		Unqualified	104± 26	231± 62	242± 77	148±143
	TOTAL	Qualified	70± 30	273± 61	241± 91	75± 65
		Unqualified	203± 37	412± 70	535±107	359±157
20-99	DUBLIN	Qualified	107± 87	149±131	213±352	—
		Unqualified	405±102	490±216	362±228	85±102
	REST OF COUNTRY	Qualified	59± 66	178± 96	139±124	—
		Unqualified	436± 91	337±132	258±191	59± 88
	TOTAL	Qualified	165±105	329±155	350±389	—
		Unqualified	843±132	823±242	617±284	144±129
TOTAL	DUBLIN	Qualified	164± 89	391±136	538±357	162± 61
		Unqualified	519±105	728±219	870±238	507±126
	REST OF COUNTRY	Qualified	101± 69	326±105	289±221	43± 24
		Unqualified	552± 94	594±144	588±203	260±165
	TOTAL	Qualified	264±109	720±166	827±399	206± 65
		Unqualified	1073±137	1317±251	1456±302	768±201

something of the likely background of the participants. For this reason estimates are made in this section and in the following section of the extent to which managers at every level have academic qualifications or have attended management training courses.

Table 9a.1.2 shows that, in large firms both in Dublin and outside, chief executives and top managers are more likely than others to have a qualification. In firms with under 500 employees the emphasis shifts to top and middle management, particularly in small firms outside Dublin, and even more so in firms which are members of the Irish Management Institute. A statistical test confirmed that in firms with over 100 employees top managers are most likely to be qualified.

Any two-way relationship can be looked at from two angles. In tables 9a.1.2. and 9a.1.4. the concern was to express the number of qualified managers at each level as a proportion of the total at each level. Perhaps a more interesting way to look at the situation is to express the number of qualified managers at each level as a proportion of the total number of qualified managers, and to do the same for unqualified managers.

TABLE 9a. 1. 2.   *Estimated Percentage of Managers at Each Level who are Qualified, by Size and Location of Firm.*

Size of Firm (No. of Employees)	Location of Head Office	Chief Executive % Qualified	Top Management % Qualified	Middle Management % Qualified	Junior Management % Qualified
500 or More	DUBLIN	58.3	60.6	46.8	34.1
	REST OF COUNTRY	45.0	55.2	34.3	28.8
	OVERALL	53.6	59.0	43.7	33.1
100–499	DUBLIN	26.9	46.2	31.7	20.0
	REST OF COUNTRY	24.0	33.3	30.2	12.9
	OVERALL	25.5±11.0	39.8± 7.4	31.0± 8.8	17.3±11.0
20–99	DUBLIN	20.8	23.3	37.0	—
	REST OF COUNTRY	12.0	34.6	35.0	—
	OVERALL	16.3± 9.6	28.6±12.7	36.2±38.0	—
OVERALL	DUBLIN	23.9±12.9	35.0± 6.7	38.2±14.5	24.2± 6.5
	REST OF COUNTRY	15.5±10.4	35.4± 9.2	33.0±11.4	14.2± 3.6
	OVERALL	19.7± 7.1	35.3± 7.5	36.2±16.6	21.2± 4.9

TABLE 9a. 1. 3.   *Estimated Number of Qualified and Unqualified Managers at Each Level, by Size of Firm and Corporate Membership of Irish Management Institute.*

Size of Firm (No. of Employees)	Corporate Membership of I.M.I.	Qualification Status	Chief Executive	Top Management	Middle Management	Junior Management
500 or More	MEMBER	Qualified	27	112	230	131
		Unqualified	22	70	279	261
	NON-MEMBER	Qualified	3	6	6	0
		Unqualified	4	12	25	4
100–499	MEMBER	Qualified	26± 18	113± 39	82± 40	36± 28
		Unqualified	61± 18	118± 46	241± 69	200±132
	NON-MEMBER	Qualified	44± 25	159± 49	159± 87	38± 62
		Unqualified	143± 33	296± 55	291± 80	154± 76
20–99	MEMBER	Qualified	13± 25	76± 51	127±202	—
		Unqualified	76± 33	127± 51	89± 81	25± 51
	NON-MEMBER	Qualified	155±109	222±140	155±240	—
		Unqualified	777±135	666±251	511±285	111±115
OVERALL	MEMBER	Qualified	65± 32	301± 66	439±229	167± 29
		Unqualified	160± 40	315± 69	609±108	486±142
	NON-MEMBER	Qualified	202±109	387±144	321±248	38± 61
		Unqualified	924±135	974±250	826±288	269±133

TABLE 9a. 1. 4.   *Estimated Percentage of Managers at each Level who are Qualified, by Size and Corporate Membership of Irish Management Institute.*

Size of Firm (No. of Employees)	Corporate Membership of I.M.I.	Chief Executive % Qualified	Top Management % Qualified	Middle Management % Qualified	Junior Management % Qualified
500 or More	MEMBER	55.1	61.5	45.2	33.4
	NON-MEMBER	42.9	33.3	19.4	—
100–499	MEMBER	29.4	48.9	25.4	15.2
	NON-MEMBER	23.5±13.5	34.9± 8.0	35.4±12.7	19.8±12.0
20–99	MEMBER	14.6	37.5	58.8	—
	NON-MEMBER	16.7±10.6	25.0±13.9	23.3±21.8	—
OVERALL	MEMBER	29.3±12.9	48.8± 7.4	41.9± 7.0	25.5± 2.3
	NON-MEMBER	18.0± 9.3	28.4± 9.7	27.9±13.7	12.4±15.3

TABLE 9a. 1. 5.   *Managers Qualified and Unqualified, Showing the Percentage at Each Level, by Size of Firm, for Firms Employing Qualified Managers.*

Size of Firm (No. of Employees)	Level	Qualified	Unqualified
500 or More	NUMBER OF MANAGERS IN ANALYSIS	508	659
	Percentage CHIEF EXECUTIVES	5.71	3.65
	Percentage in TOP MANAGEMENT	22.84	11.54
	Percentage in MIDDLE MANAGEMENT	45.48	45.38
	Percentage in JUNIOR MANAGEMENT	25.99	39.46
	TOTAL	100.00	100.00
100–499	NUMBER OF MANAGERS IN ANALYSIS	106	228
	Percentage CHIEF EXECUTIVES	11.33	11.41
	Percentage in TOP MANAGEMENT	43.40	25.01
	Percentage in MIDDLE MANAGEMENT	37.74	37.72
	Percentage in JUNIOR MANAGEMENT	7.55	25.88
	TOTAL	100.00	100.00
20–99	NUMBER OF MANAGERS IN ANALYSIS	26	47
	Percentage CHIEF EXECUTIVES	26.93	27.66
	Percentage in TOP MANAGEMENT	46.16	29.77
	Percentage in MIDDLE MANAGEMENT	26.93	34.04
	Percentage in JUNIOR MANAGEMENT	—	8.51
	TOTAL	100.00	100.00

In this way the question is raised "does it pay to be qualified?" i.e. is the proportion of qualified managers at top level higher than the proportion of non-qualified executives? To get an unequivocal answer it was decided to make the comparison only among firms which employed some qualified managers (all firms employed some managers with no academic qualifications), as only in such firms were qualified and non-qualified executives in direct competition for advancement.

Table 9a.1.5. shows that it does indeed pay to be qualified. In firms of every size, managers with an academic qualification reach higher levels than those without. A statistical test showed that the differences observed in the top and middle size-groups could not have arisen by chance. Those in the bottom group, while in the same direction as the other two, were not statistically significant, i.e. it could be, if the whole population of small firms were examined instead of only a sample, that no difference would be found in the levels attained by qualified and unqualified executives.

TABLE 9a. 2. 1.   *Estimated Number of Managers at Each Level who have Attended or Not Attended Management Training Courses, by Size and Location of Firm.*

Size of Firm (No. of Employees)	Location of Head Office	Attendance At Courses	Chief Executive	Top Management	Middle Management	Junior Management
500 or More	DUBLIN	Attended	20	85	247	208
		Did Not Attend	16	57	159	115
	REST OF COUNTRY	Attended	10	39	78	41
		Did Not Attend	10	19	56	32
	TOTAL	Attended	30	124	325	249
		Did Not Attend	26	76	215	147
100-499	DUBLIN	Attended	16 ± 16	94 ± 43	99 ± 64	42 ± 33
		Did Not Attend	120 ± 26	245 ± 47	328 ± 84	219 ± 97
	REST OF COUNTRY	Attended	16 ± 17	38 ± 38	88 ± 63	71 ± 96
		Did Not Attend	121 ± 21	308 ± 68	258 ± 91	99 ± 75
	TOTAL	Attended	32 ± 22	134 ± 53	187 ± 86	112 ± 96
		Did Not Attend	241 ± 32	551 ± 80	589 ± 121	321 ± 124
20-99	DUBLIN	Attended	64 ± 71	85 ± 80	128 ± 128	—
		Did Not Attend	447 ± 123	554 ± 244	447 ± 449	85 ± 102
	REST OF COUNTRY	Attended	99 ± 81	79 ± 74	—	—
		Did Not Attend	397 ± 120	436 ± 169	397 ± 386	59 ± 88
	TOTAL	Attended	165 ± 105	165 ± 105	123 ± 124	—
		Did Not Attend	843 ± 166	987 ± 283	843 ± 566	144 ± 129
TOTAL	DUBLIN	Attended	100 ± 77	264 ± 89	474 ± 141	250 ± 33
		Did Not Attend	583 ± 126	856 ± 247	935 ± 455	419 ± 137
	REST OF COUNTRY	Attended	126 ± 82	157 ± 82	166 ± 63	112 ± 96
		Did Not Attend	528 ± 122	763 ± 180	711 ± 394	190 ± 112
	TOTAL	Attended	227 ± 107	422 ± 119	636 ± 150	361 ± 96
		Did Not Attend	1110 ± 168	1615 ± 293	1647 ± 578	612 ± 176

Taking age into consideration does not alter this conclusion. In every age-group qualified men are farther ahead. This superiority is more marked in the older age groups. Because few managers aged under 35, whether qualified or not, had yet reached top positions this was not unexpected. It may show that as qualified men grow older they pull farther ahead of those without qualifications. It may also show that competition is becoming more severe: that when qualified men were comparatively scarce their chances of being promoted were assured, but now that most executives aged under 35 in larger companies have qualifications a high proportion of them will never reach top level.

It is not possible to say what sort of qualification has in the past given the best chance of reaching the top in industry. The greatest number of executives is in production and, since the number of top positions is limited by definition, it follows that one's chances of reaching top level are more limited in that area than in any other. Since executives have tended to stay in the areas to which their degrees are most directly relevant, it also follows that individual engineers and scientists, while having had the best chance of getting into industry, also had the least chance of rising to the top. This had nothing to do with their qualifications or abilities as such, but was simply a function of the size and organisation of Irish firms.

Section A.2.   Level and Attendance at Management Training Courses

In tables 9a.2.1. to 9a.2.4. estimates are made of the number and percentage of managers at each level of management who, at the base-date of the survey, had ever attended a management training course. Table 9a.2.2. shows that in firms with 500 or more employees most managers at every level had participated, with little or no differ-

TABLE 9a. 2. 2.   *Estimated Percentage of Managers at Each Level who have Attended Management Training Courses, by Size and Location of Firm.*

Size of Firm (No. of Employees)	Location of Head Office	Chief Executive % Attended	Top Management % Attended	Middle Management % Attended	Junior Management % Attended
500 or More	DUBLIN	55.6	59.9	60.8	64.4
	REST OF COUNTRY	50.0	67.2	58.2	56.2
	OVERALL	53.6	62.0	60.2	62.9
100–499	DUBLIN	11.8	27.7	23.2	16.0
	REST OF COUNTRY	11.7	11.1	25.4	41.9
	OVERALL	11.8± 8.2	19.5± 8.2	24.1±11.2	25.9±24.1
20.99	DUBLIN	12.5	13.3	22.2	—
	REST OF COUNTRY	20.0	15.4	—	—
	OVERALL	16.3±10.0	14.3± 9.4	12.8±14.3	—
OVERALL	DUBLIN	14.6±10.8	23.6± 8.2	33.6±12.0	37.3± 5.5
	REST OF COUNTRY	19.2±13.0	17.0± 9.6	18.9± 6.1	37.2±38.9
	OVERALL	16.9± 8.5	20.7± 5.9	27.9± 7.1	37.1±10.9

TABLE 9a. 2. 3. *Estimated Number of Managers at Each Level who have Attended or Not Attended Management Training Courses, by Size of Firm and Corporate Membership of Irish Management Institute.*

Size of Firm (No. of Employees)	Corporate Membership of I.M.I.	Attendance At Courses	Chief Executive	Top Management	Middle Management	Junior Management
500 or More	MEMBER	Attended	30	122	320	249
		Did Not Attend	19	60	189	143
	NON-MEMBER	Attended	—	2	5	—
		Did Not Attend	7	16	26	4
100-499	MEMBER	Attended	10 ± 13	61 ± 36	107 ± 60	77 ± 87
		Did Not Attend	77 ± 19	169 ± 45	215 ± 67	159 ± 90
	NON-MEMBER	Attended	22 ± 19	71 ± 46	77 ± 61	33 ± 34
		Did Not Attend	165 ± 28	384 ± 69	373 ± 107	159 ± 85
50-99	MEMBER	Attended	38 ± 37	25 ± 33	25 ± 51	—
		Did Not Attend	51 ± 38	178 ± 74	191 ± 247	25 ± 51
	NON-MEMBER	Attended	111 ± 95	133 ± 103	89 ± 108	—
		Did Not Attend	822 ± 164	755 ± 272	577 ± 457	111 ± 115
TOTAL	MEMBER	Did Not Attend	78 ± 43	209 ± 49	453 ± 79	326 ± 90
		Attended	147 ± 45	407 ± 91	595 ± 285	327 ± 103
	NON-MEMBER	Attended	133 ± 95	207 ± 109	171 ± 119	33 ± 34
		Did Not Attend	993 ± 162	1155 ± 273	976 ± 457	274 ± 138

TABLE 9a. 2. 4. *Estimated Percentage of Managers at Each Level who have Attended Management Training Courses, by Size of Firm and Corporate Membership of the Irish Management Institute.*

Size of Firm (No. of Employees)	Corporate Membership of I.M.I.	Chief Executive % Attended	Top Management % Attended	Middle Management % Attended	Junior Management % Attended
500 or More	MEMBER	61.2	67.0	62.9	63.5
	NON-MEMBER	0	11.1	16.1	—
100–499	MEMBER	11.5	26.7	33.3	32.6
	NON-MEMBER	11.8 ± 10.0	15.7 ± 9.0	17.1 ± 11.2	17.1 ± 10.8
OVERALL	MEMBER	42.9	12.4	11.6	—
	NON-MEMBER	11.9 ± 9.8	15.0 ± 11.2	13.3 ± 15.7	—
TOTAL	MEMBER	34.7 ± 16.2	33.9 ± 7.1	43.2 ± 6.2	49.9 ± 7.5
	NON-MEMBER	11.8 ± 9.3	15.2 ± 7.7	14.9 ± 9.9	10.7 ± 6.8

ence between firms in Dublin and outside. In the 100 to 499 group, Dublin-based companies appeared to favour top and middle management to a greater extent than firms in
the rest of the country, who leaned more towards participation by junior managers. The
position is reversed in the 20-99 group. Large firms which were members of the Irish
Management Institute showed (table 9a.2.4.) much the same rate of participation by
all levels. In the 100 to 499 group they tended to emphasise participation by lower levels
to a greater extent than non-members, whose proportion with training was uniformly
low. In small firms, chief executives of member-firms were most likely to have attended,
with little difference between members and others with respect to lower levels. The
position will have changed, perhaps considerably, since 1964.

It is sometimes said that management training courses fail to attract top managers.
It was decided to see whether the sample provided any evidence to support this statement, by carrying out a test to see whether the proportions with training differed from
level to level. The comparison was made only for firms employing some managers with
training, as others were not being reached at all. Almost 96 per cent of the managers in
the top stratum worked for such firms, over 70 per cent of executives in the middle

TABLE 9a. 2. 5.   *Managers at Each Level, Showing the Percentage With and Without Training,
by Size of Firm, for Firms Employing Trained Managers.*

Size of Firm (No. of Employees)	Training Status	Chief Executive	Top Management	Middle Management	Junior Management
	NO. OF MANAGERS IN ANALYSIS	49	179	509	388
500 or More	Percentage WITH TRAINING	59.19	67.04	62.87	63.92
	Percentage WITHOUT TRAINING	40.82	32.97	37.14	36.09
	TOTAL	100.00	100.00	100.00	100.00
	NO. OF MANAGERS IN ANALYSIS	29	74	95	61
100–499	Percentage WITH TRAINING	17.25	29.73	39.19	24.33
	Percentage WITHOUT TRAINING	82.76	70.28	69.48	70.50
	TOTAL	100.00	100.00	100.00	100.00
	NO. OF MANAGERS IN ANALYSIS	17	19	18	2
20–99	Percentage WITH TRAINING	41.18	36.85	22.23	—
	Percentage WITHOUT TRAINING	58.83	63.16	77.78	100.00
	TOTAL	100.00	100.00	100.00	100.00

stratum, and about 44 per cent of those in the bottom group. These figures show how haphazard participation in courses is: although over 70 per cent of managers in the middle group worked in firms which employed some executive with training, less than half the executives in those firms had ever attended courses.

Table 9a.2.5 shows the position. There are no very marked differences in the top size-group. The middle group seems to show chief executives as least likely to attend, while the bottom group seems to show the reverse, but in neither case are the differences between the levels statistically significant. There is therefore no evidence that those at higher level are less likely than others to have attended courses. This does not completely answer the question as it is possible that those now at top level had attended courses while still at lower levels, and also that their attendance is less frequent. The striking fact emerging from table 9a.2.5 is not that of any difference between levels, but the low rate of participation by executives at every level, even in firms which had some executive with training.

There is no evidence of an association between level and training which would suggest that it pays to be trained. Those with training do not show a higher proportion at upper levels than those without. Such an association, if it did exist, would not imply that training was cause and that level was effect: it might have been that managers were selected to be sent on courses because they had reached a higher level or looked like doing so. In the case of the association between qualification and training it was possible to suggest a cause-effect relationship because qualifications are normally taken before reaching management level.

TABLE 9a. 3. 1.   *Estimated Number of Managers in Each Age-Group at Each Level, by Size of Firm.*

Size of Firm (No. of Employees)	Age-Group	Chief Executive	Top Management	Middle Management	Junior Management
500 or More	Under 35	—	15	128	130
	35-49	20	93	277	188
	50 or Over	36	92	135	78
100-499	Under 35	5 ± 10	112 ± 47	252 ± 80	161 ± 91
	35-49	75 ± 35	311 ± 68	396 ± 105	236 ± 134
	50 or Over	193 ± 39	262 ± 61	128 ± 55	372 ± 25
20-99	Under 35	123 ± 96	329 ± 208	432 ± 302	41 ± 58
	35-49	555 ± 153	514 ± 212	391 ± 283	82 ± 116
	50 or Over	329 ± 136	308 ± 146	144 ± 188	21 ± 42
TOTAL	Under 35	129 ± 94	456 ± 207	812 ± 302	332 ± 104
	35-49	650 ± 152	918 ± 215	$1,064\pm291$	506 ± 170
	50 or Over	558 ± 137	663 ± 153	407 ± 190	136 ± 47

Section A.3. Relationship between Level and Age.

The number of managers at each level in each age-group is shown in table 9a.3.1. There do not appear to be noticeable gaps at any level. In every case there appears to be an adequate number of younger executives to replace those aged 50 years or over, as they retire.

It looks from table 9a.3.1. as if there is a relationship between age and level, with those at higher levels being older than those below them. This appears even more clearly in table 9a.3.2. which shows the position in percentage form (but excluding firms which changed their size before the survey). In firms with over 100 employees, chief executives

TABLE 9a. 3. 2.   *Managers at Each Level, Showing the Percentage in Each Age Group, by Size of Firm.*

Size of Firm (No. of Employees)	Age-Group	Chief Executive	Top Management	Middle Management	Junior Management
500 or More	NO. OF MANAGERS IN ANALYSIS	54	194	532	392
	Percentage UNDER 35	—	7.74	23.31	32.66
	Percentage 35-49	37.04	46.91	51.51	47.45
	Percentage 50 OR OVER	62.97	45.37	25.19	19.90
	TOTAL	100.00	100.00	100.00	100.00
100–499	NO. OF MANAGERS IN ANALYSIS	47	118	134	70
	Percentage UNDER 35	2.13	16.11	32.09	31.43
	Percentage 35-49	27.66	45.77	51.50	60.01
	Percentage 50 OR OVER	70.22	38.14	16.42	8.58
	TOTAL	100.00	100.00	100.00	100.00
20–99	NO. OF MANAGERS IN ANALYSIS	44	47	31(a)	5
	Percentage UNDER 35	13.64	25.54	38.71	40.00
	Percentage 35-49	56.82	46.81	41.94	40.00
	Percentage 50 OR OVER	29.55	27.66	19.36	20.00
	TOTAL	100.00	100.00	100.00	100.00

(a) Middle and junior management were combined when testing, as the numbers would otherwise have been too small.

and top managers are significantly older than those in middle and junior management. In the bottom size-group the relationship is not so marked and could have arisen by chance. In this group even executives aged under 35 tend to have reached a fairly high level. This follows inevitably on the definition of level, given that small firms have a low average number of managers.

It is interesting to look at the relationship in the other way and to see what level has been reached by managers in each age-group. This could show whether or not increasing age automatically brings promotion. Evidence for this would be provided if it were found that older managers were concentrated at higher levels with few in junior management while younger managers were mostly at junior level with few in top management.

Table 9a.3.3 shows that, at least in large and small firms, there is little suggestion that age is the criterion for promotion. In large firms a substantial proportion of executives aged over 50 are still in junior management,[1] while in small companies even quite

1 It could of course be that these were men who were promoted to managerial positions only after passing 50 and that, if only those who had become managers at an earlier age were considered, it would be found that few were still at lower levels.

young managers are at high levels. There is a suggestion of "automatic promotion" in the middle size-group but, taken overall, there is little evidence that it is the norm.

TABLE 9a. 3. 3.   *Managers in Each Age-Group, Showing the Percentage at Each Level, by Size of Firm.*

Size of Firm (No. of Employees)	Level	Aged Under 35	Aged 35-49	Aged 50 or More
	NO. OF MANAGERS IN ANALYSIS	267	571	334
500 or More	Percentage CHIEF EXECUTIVES	—	3.51	10.18
	Percentage in TOP MANAGEMENT	5.62	15.94	26.35
	Percentage in MIDDLE MANAGEMENT	46.45	47.99	40.12
	Percentage in JUNIOR MANAGEMENT	47.95	32.58	23.36
	TOTAL	100.00	100.00	100.00
	NO. OF MANAGERS IN ANALYSIS	85	178	106
100–499	Percentage CHIEF EXECUTIVES	1.18	7.31	31.14
	Percentage in TOP MANAGEMENT	22.36	30.34	42.46
	Percentage in MIDDLE MANAGEMENT	50.59	38.77	23.60
	Percentage in JUNIOR MANAGEMENT	25.89	23.60	5.67
	TOTAL	100.00	100.00	100.00
	NO. OF MANAGERS IN ANALYSIS	32	62	33
20–99	Percentage CHIEF EXECUTIVES	18.75	40.32	39.39
	Percentage in TOP MANAGEMENT	37.50	35.48	39.39
	Percentage in MIDDLE MANAGEMENT	37.50	20.97	18.18
	Percentage in JUNIOR MANAGEMENT	6.25	3.23	3.03
	TOTAL	100.00	100.00	100.00

Section A.4.   Relationship between Level and Nationality

Tables 9a.4.1 and 9a.4.2 show the number and proportion of foreign-born executives at each level of management. While neither the overall number or proportion is great it can be seen that over 20 per cent of the top managers of firms with 500 or more employees were born abroad. Table 9a.4.2 shows the proportion of each nationality who have reached each level. It suggests that foreign-born managers reach higher levels than those born in Ireland.

This suggestion is weakened but not eliminated when age is taken into account. (It was necessary to consider age because foreign-born executives are older than those born in Ireland and more likely for that reason alone to be at higher levels). It was therefore decided to examine the question further and to see to what extent foreign-born managers advanced further than Irish-born executives, looking first at Irish-owned firms employing some non-Irish managers, and then at foreign-owned firms.

TABLE 9a. 4. 1.   *Estimated Number of Irish and Foreign Managers at Each Level, by Size of Firm.*

Size of Firm (No. of Employees)	Nationality of Manager	Chief Executive	Top Management	Middle Management	Junior Management
500 or More	IRISH	36	167	466	373
	OTHER	20	33	74	23
	TOTAL	56	200	540	396
100–499	IRISH	219±35	589±83	691±140	418±194
	OTHER	54±32	96±37	85±41	16±22
	TOTAL	273±22	685±78	776±145	434±193
20-99	IRISH	905±157	1,069±295	843±543	103±107
	OTHER	103±89	82±80	124±128	41±83
	TOTAL	1,008±121	1,152±288	967±590	144±129
TOTAL	IRISH	1,160±156	1,825±297	2,000±543	894±214
	OTHER	176±91	212±85	283±130	80±83
	TOTAL	1,337±123	2,037±297	2,283±607	974±230

TABLE 9a. 4. 2.   *Estimated Percentage of Irish and Foreign Managers at Each Level, by Size of Firm.*

Size of Firm (No. of Employees)	Nationality of Manager	Chief Executive %	Top Management %	Middle Management %	Junior Management %	Total
500 or More	IRISH	3.5	16.0	44.7	35.8	100.0
	OTHER	13.4	22.0	49.4	15.4	100.0
100-499	IRISH	11.5± 2.4	30.7± 4.9	36.0± 4.9	21.8± 6.9	100.0
	OTHER	21.5± 9.0	38.1± 9.6	34.0±10.9	6.4± 8.0	100.0
20-99	IRISH	31.0± 7.6	36.6± 8.2	28.9±12.2	3.5± 3.5	100.0
	OTHER	29.4±23.5	23.4±19.2	35.5±33.1	11.7±24.3	100.0
OVERALL	IRISH	19.8± 3.1	31.0± 5.0	34.0± 6.6	15.2± 2.1	100.0
	OTHER	23.6±11.4	28.0± 9.8	37.8±16.4	10.7±11.8	100.0

Table 9a.4.3 shows that even in Irish-owned companies executives born abroad are at higher levels than managers born in Ireland. This is not unreasonable: a company is unlikely to take the trouble to bring an executive from abroad to fill a low-level position. The differences in the two larger size-groups are statistically significant, but it was not possible to carry out a test on the bottom stratum because so few managers

TABLE 9a. 4. 3. *Managers of Each Nationality, Showing the Percentage at Each Level, by Size of Firm, for Irish-owned Firms Employing Non-Irish Managers.*

Size of Firm (No. of Employees)	Level	Irish-born	Other
	NO. OF MANAGERS IN ANALYSIS	719	93
500 or More	Percentage CHIEF EXECUTIVES	3.20	9.68
	Percentage in TOP MANAGEMENT	15.44	20.44
	Percentage in MIDDLE MANAGEMENT	42.98	50.54
	Percentage in JUNIOR MANAGEMENT	38.39	19.36
	TOTAL	100.00	100.00
	NO. OF MANAGERS IN ANALYSIS	172	42
100–499	Percentage CHIEF EXECUTIVES	9.31	21.43
	Percentage in TOP MANAGEMENT	26.75	35.72
	Percentage in MIDDLE MANAGEMENT	38.38	35.72
	Percentage in JUNIOR MANAGEMENT	25.59	7.15
	TOTAL	100.00	100.00
	NO. OF MANAGERS IN ANALYSIS	10	9
20–99	Percentage CHIEF EXECUTIVES	30.00	55.55
	Percentage in TOP MANAGEMENT	40.00	22.22
	Percentage in MIDDLE MANAGEMENT	10.00	22.22
	Percentage in JUNIOR MANAGEMENT	20.00	—
	TOTAL	100.00	100.00

TABLE 9a. 4. 4. *Managers of Each Nationality, Showing the Percentage at Each Level, by Size of Firm, for Foreign-owned Firms Employing Non-Irish Managers.*

Size of Firm (No. of Employees)	Level	Irish-born	Other
	NO. OF MANAGERS IN ANALYSIS	235	52
500 or More	Percentage CHIEF EXECUTIVES	2.56	19.24
	Percentage in TOP MANAGEMENT	15.75	25.01
	Percentage in MIDDLE MANAGEMENT	49.79	48.08
	Percentage in JUNIOR MANAGEMENT	31.92	7.70
	TOTAL	100.00	100.00
	NO. OF MANAGERS IN ANALYSIS	24	5
100–499	Percentage CHIEF EXECUTIVES	8.33	20.00
	Percentage in TOP MANAGEMENT	25.00	60.00
	Percentage in MIDDLE MANAGEMENT	54.17	20.00
	Percentage in JUNIOR MANAGEMENT	12.50	—
	TOTAL	100.00	100.00

The 20-99 size-group is omitted because the numbers employed in foreign-owned firms are too small to justify inclusion.

were involved. The high proportion of foreign-born executives in this stratum is worth commenting on. For the most part these are men who came to Ireland and started their own businesses, or are members of those men's families.

It is interesting to note that in large foreign-owned companies, not only are foreign executives at a higher level than those born in Ireland, but this tendency for foreign executives to be higher is much more marked than in the case of Irish-owned companies employing executives born abroad. It was not possible to carry out a test on the 100-499 group because the numbers were too small.

PART B. QUALIFICATION AND OTHER CHARACTERISTICS

It was seen in chapter 8 that there were relationships between qualification and function, executives in finance being most likely to be qualified and those in marketing least

TABLE 9b. 1. 1.   *Estimated Attendance at Management Training Courses by Qualified and Unqualified Managers, by Size and Location of Firm.*

Size of Firm (No. of Employees)	Location of Head Office	Qualification Status	Attended Courses (No.)	Did not Attend Courses (No.)
500 or More	DUBLIN	Qualified	273	134
		Unqualified	287	213
	REST OF COUNTRY	Qualified	78	30
		Unqualified	90	87
	TOTAL	Qualified	351	164
		Unqualified	377	300
100-499	DUBLIN	Qualified	104 ± 62	276 ± 103
		Unqualified	146 ± 77	635 ± 121
	REST OF COUNTRY	Qualified	60 ± 42	214 ± 88
		Unqualified	154 ± 154	572 ± 82
	TOTAL	Qualified	166 ± 74	493 ± 131
		Unqualified	300 ± 163	1210 ± 145
20-99	DUBLIN	Qualified	43 ± 86	426 ± 472
		Unqualified	234 ± 175	1108 ± 319
	REST OF COUNTRY	Qualified	59 ± 66	318 ± 262
		Unqualified	119 ± 104	971 ± 261
	TOTAL	Qualified	103 ± 104	740 ± 510
		Unqualified	350 ± 196	2077 ± 394
TOTAL	DUBLIN	Qualified	420 ± 104	836 ± 481
		Unqualified	667 ± 188	1956 ± 337
	REST OF COUNTRY	Qualified	199 ± 77	562 ± 273
		Unqualified	362 ± 182	1630 ± 271
	TOTAL	Qualified	620 ± 126	1397 ± 525
		Unqualified	1026 ± 251	3587 ± 418

likely. It was found in part **A** of this chapter that qualification is related to level. executives having an academic qualification being likely to be at a higher level than those who do not. The remaining relationships involving qualification are dealt with in this part.

Section B.1.   Qualification and Attendance at Management Training Courses

The number of executives with and without academic qualifications who had attended management training courses is shown in tables 9b.1.1 to 9b.1.4. Table 9b.1.1 shows that for the country as a whole 620 managers, about 9 per cent of the total, had both qualifications and some training, while over 3,500, about 54 per cent of the total, had neither. The proportions varied a great deal between the size-groups. In firms with 500 or more employees about 30 per cent had both, while a little over 25 per cent had neither. In the 100 to 499 size-group the proportions were about 8 per cent and 56 per cent, and in the 20 to 99 stratum they were 3 per cent and 63 per cent respectively. In firms which were corporate members of the Irish Management Institute almost 25 per cent of executives overall had both qualifications and training, while something over 42 per cent had neither.

TABLE 9B. 1. 2.   *Estimated Percentage of Qualified and Unqualified Managers who have Attended Management Training Courses, by Size and Location of Firm.*

(No. of Employees) Size of Firm	Location	Qualified: % Attended	Unqualified: % Attended
500 or More	DUBLIN	67.1	57.4
	REST OF COUNTRY	72.2	50.8
	OVERALL	68.2	55.7
100-499	DUBLIN	27.4	18.7
	REST OF COUNTRY	22.0	21.2
	OVERALL	25.2± 8.0	19.9± 8.4
20-99	DUBLIN	9.1	17.5
	REST OF COUNTRY	15.8	10.9
	OVERALL	12.2±11.8	14.4± 8.0
OVERALL	DUBLIN	33.4± 7.2	25.5± 7.0
	REST OF COUNTRY	26.1± 8.1	18.2± 7.5
	OVERALL	30.7± 6.0	22.3± 5.5

The main question to be answered in this section is whether firms use management training to supplement qualifications or to make up for the lack of them. Tables 9b.1.2 and 9b.1.4 would suggest that in both locations, and in member-firms and non-member-firms, training is used to a somewhat greater extent by those with academic qualifications than by those without.

The question has meaning only for firms employing at least one manager with both academic qualifications and management training. Firms with some trained managers but no qualified managers must use training to make up for lack of qualifications, while the question does not arise at all for firms with no trained managers.

TABLE 9b. 1. 3. *Estimated Attendance at Management Training Courses by Qualified and Unqualified Managers, by Size of Firm and Corporate Membership of Irish Management Institute.*

Size of Firm (No. of Employees)	Corporate Membership of I.M.I.	Qualification Status	Attended Courses (No.)	Did Not Attend Courses (No.)
500 or More	MEMBER	Qualified	349	151
		Unqualified	372	260
	NON-MEMBER	Qualified	5	10
		Unqualified	5	40
100-499	MEMBER	Qualified	97±41	159±68
		Unqualified	159±139	461±78
	NON-MEMBER	Qualified	66±60	335±119
		Unqualificd	137±84	746±126
20-99	MEMBER	Qualified	25±51	191±267
		Unqualified	64±53	255±102
	NON-MEMBER	Qualified	67±76	466±314
		Unqualified	267±195	1,799±404
TOTAL	MEMBER	Qualified	472±767	501±307
		Unqualified	594±150	976±131
	NON-MEMBER	Qualified	134±93	814±326
		Unqualified	409±205	2,585±411

TABLE 9b. 1. 4.   *Estimated Percentage of Qualified and Unqualified Managers who Have Attended Management Training Courses, by Size of Firm and Corporate Membership of Irish Management Institute.*

Size of Firm (No. of Employees)	Corporate Membership of I.M.I.	Qualified % Attended	Unqualified % Attended
500 or More	MEMBER	69.8	58.9
	NON-MEMBER	33.3	11.1
100–499	MEMBER	38.0	25.6
	NON-MEMBER	16.5±10.2	15.6±8.2
20-99	MEMBER	11.6	20.0
	NON-MEMBER	12.5±15.1	12.9±9.0
OVERALL	MEMBER	48.5± 6.8	37.9±6.7
	NON-MEMBER	14.2± 9.9	13.7±6.7

TABLE 9b. 1. 5. *Qualified and Unqualified Managers, Showing the Percentage With and With-out Training, by Size of Firm, for Firms in the Sample Employing Both Trained and Qualified Managers.*

Size of Firm (No. of Employees)	Training Status	Qualified	Unqualified
	NO. OF MANAGERS IN ANALYSIS	499	626
500 or More	Percentage WITH TRAINING	69.94	58.79
	Percentage WITHOUT TRAINING	30.07	41.22
	TOTAL	100.00	100.00
	NO. OF MANAGERS IN ANALYSIS	75	163
100–499	Percentage WITH TRAINING	34.67	26.39
	Percentage WITHOUT TRAINING	65.34	73.62
	TOTAL	100.00	100.00
	NO. OF MANAGERS IN ANALYSIS	18	29
20–99	Percentage WITH TRAINING	16.67	34.49
	Percentage WITHOUT TRAINING	83.33	65.52
	TOTAL	100.00	100.00

Table 9b.1.5 shows that, in firms employing managers with both academic qualifications and academic training, there was little tendency for training to be used exclusively either as a substitute or as a supplement. It is used to much the same extent by both qualified and non-qualified executives. None of the differences in the table is statistically significant except that in the top size-group which is significant by definition but not very large. Ninety-six per cent of executives in the top stratum work for firms with both trained and qualified managers: over 64 per cent of executives in the middle stratum do so, and 37 per cent in the bottom stratum.

TABLE 9b. 1. 6. *Managers Employed by Firms in the Sample Employing no Qualified but Some Trained Managers, Showing the Numbers With and Without Training, by Size of Firm.*

Size of Firm (No. of Employees)	Number With Training	Number Without Training	Total
500 or More	—	—	—
100-499	5	17	22
20-99	5	4	9

Table 9b.1.6 shows the number of executives with management training working for firms in the sample which employed managers with training but none with academic qualifications. Their number is small: only about 6 per cent of executives in the sample

from the 100-499 size-group worked for such firms. In the 20-99 group the figure was 7 per cent.

TABLE 9b. 1. 7.   *Managers Employed by Firms in the Sample Employing Some Qualified but No Trained Managers, Showing the Numbers Qualified and Unqualified, by Size of Firm.*

Size of Firm (No. of Employees)	Number Qualified	Number Unqualified	Total	Percentage of Total in Sample
500 or More	9	33	42	3.6
100–499	31	65	96	26.0
20-99	8	18	26	20.5

Table 9b.1.7 shows the number of qualified managers employed by sample firms which had some qualified managers, but no trained managers. It shows that quite a large percentage of executives in the small and medium size-groups work for firms of that type.

TABLE 9b. 1.8.   *Number of Managers Employed by Firms in the Sample Employing Neither Trained nor Qualified Managers.*

Size of Firm (No. of Employees)	Number in Sample	Percentage of Total in Sample
500 or More	5	0.004
100-499	13	3.500
20-99	45	35.400

Finally table 9b.1.8 shows the number of executives working for firms which employ only executives with neither academic qualifications nor management training. Such firms employ only a tiny percentage of the total number of executives in firms with over 100 employees, but in firms with 20 to 99 employees over 35 per cent of all managers work in companies employing no one with qualifications or training.

Section B.2.   Relationship between Qualification and Age

The estimated number and percentage of executives in each age-group holding academic qualifications is shown in tables 9b.2.1 and 9b.2.2. It seems clear from the second of these tables that younger executives are more likely to have qualifications than either those in the 35 to 49 age-group or those aged 50 or more, the exception being in the case of small firms, where those aged under 35 appear no more likely to be qualified than those aged 35 to 49.

It is impossible to be certain of the reality of these differences without first carrying out a statistical test. As usual, when performing a test, firms which had changed their size before the survey date were excluded. Comparison of table 9b.2.3 with table 9b.2.2 shows that this makes little difference except in the smallest size-group, where the proportion of qualified executives aged under 35 is greatly reduced.

TABLE 9b. 2. 1.   *Estimated Number of Qualified and Unqualified Managers in Each Age-Group, by Size of Firm.*

Size of Firm (No. of Employees)	Qualification Status	Aged Under 35	Aged 35-49	Aged 50 or over
500 or More	QUALIFIED	166	244	105
	UNQUALIFIED	107	334	236
	TOTAL	273	578	341
100-499	QUALIFIED	230±101	289±106	139±61
	UNQUALIFIED	300±98	728±183	482±82
	TOTAL	530±163	1,017±208	621±90
20-99	QUALIFIED	267±270	494±284	82±80
	UNQUALIFIED	658±258	1,049±316	720±280
	TOTAL	925±418	1,542±449	802±311
TOTAL	QUALIFIED	664±279	1,027±293	326±97
	UNQUALIFIED	1,065±267	2,111±352	1,438±283
	TOTAL	1,728±447	3,138±491	1,764±323

TABLE 9b. 2. 2.   *Estimated Percentage of Managers in Each Age-Group Who are Qualified, by Size of Firm.*

Size of Firm (No. of Employees)	Qualification Status	Aged Under 35	Aged 35-49	Aged 50 or Over
500 or More	Percentage QUALIFIED	60.8	42.2	30.8
100–499	Percentage QUALIFIED	43.4± 9.8	28.4± 8.6	22.4± 8.2
20–99	Percentage QUALIFIED	28.9±18.8	32.0±12.3	10.3± 7.8
OVERALL	Percentage QUALIFIED	38.4±10.7	32.7± 6.9	18.5± 5.1

The difference in the top size-group is, of course, real. That in the middle size-group is also highly significant statistically, but here the accent on qualification came later than in the case of large companies, the growth in the proportion qualified taking place only among those under 35, whereas in the top group it was already obvious among those aged 35 to 49. In the bottom size-group those aged under 35 appear less likely to be qualified than those aged 35 to 49, but the differences in this group are just short of being significant. It is obvious that there is as yet no tendency in small businesses for the proportion of qualified executives to rise automatically with the passage of time.

The question of trends to particular types of qualification has already been dealt with in chapter 8.

TABLE 9b. 2. 3.   *Managers in Each Age-Group, Showing the Percentage Qualified and Un-*
qualified, by Size of Firm.

Size of Firm (No. of Employees)	Qualification Status	Aged Under 35	Aged 35-49	Aged 50 or More
500 or More	NO. OF MANAGERS IN ANALYSIS	267	571	334
	Percentage QUALIFIED	61.05	42.21	31.14
	Percentage UNQUALIFIED	38.96	57.80	68.87
	TOTAL	100.00	100.00	100.00
100–499	NO. OF MANAGERS IN ANALYSIS	85	178	106
	Percentage QUALIFIED	41.18	25.85	23.59
	Percentage UNQUALIFIED	58.83	74.16	76.42
	TOTAL	100.00	100.00	100.00
20–99	NO. OF MANAGERS IN ANALYSIS	32	62	33
	Percentage QUALIFIED	15.63	29.04	9.10
	Percentage UNQUALIFIED	84.38	70.97	90.91
	TOTAL	100.00	100.00	100.00

TABLE 9b. 3. 1.   *Estimated Number and Percentage of Managers of Each Nationality, Who*
are Qualified and Unqualified, by Size of Firm.

Size of Firm No. of Employees)	Qualification Status	Irish No.	Other No.	Irish %	Other %
500 or More	QUALIFIED	460	55	44.1	36.7
	UNQUALIFIED	582	95	55.9	63.3
	TOTAL	1,042	150	100.0	100.0
100-499	QUALIFIED	610±166	48± 34	31.8± 7.3	19.1±12.0
	UNQUALIFIED	1,306±221	203± 75	68.2(a)	80.9
	TOTAL	1,916±299	251	100.0	100.0
20-99	QUALIFIED	761±489	82±100	26.1±11.2	23.5±18.0
	UNQUALIFIED	2,159±379	267±175	73.9	76.5
	TOTAL	2,920±685	349	100.0	100.0
TOTAL	QUALIFIED	1,831±499	185±102	32.1± 5.8	24.6± 9.3
	UNQUALIFIED	4,048±423	566±184	68.9	75.4
	TOTAL	5,879±743	751	100.0	100.0

(a) No confidence limits were calculated for the percentages unqualified.

Section B.3. Relationship between Qualification and Nationality

It was decided to see whether executives born abroad were more likely to have academic qualifications than those born in Ireland. The purpose was not simply to see how the proportions compared but also to see whether the fact already noted that foreign-born executives had reached higher levels than Irish-born managers could be explained by their being more highly-qualified academically.

Table 9b.3.1 shows the estimated total and proportion of qualified executives of each nationality. If anything, a higher proportion of Irish-born executives had qualifications. A further breakdown by age showed this to be true of almost all age-groups, and particularly *vis-à-vis* managers born in Britain.

It was decided to put these differences to the test. Because the levels reached by each nationality had been compared using only firms employing some foreign-born managers, the present comparison was restricted to those firms also.

TABLE 9b. 3. 2. *Managers of each Nationality, Showing the Percentage Qualified and Unqualified, by Size of Firm, for Firms Employing Some Non-Irish Managers.*

Size of Firm (No. of Employees)	Qualification Status	Irish-born	Other
500 or More	NO. OF MANAGERS IN ANALYSIS	954	145
	Percentage QUALIFIED	44.13	37.25
	Percentage UNQUALIFIED	55.88	62.76
	TOTAL	100.00	100.00
100–499	NO. OF MANAGERS IN ANALYSIS	196	47
	Percentage QUALIFIED	29.60	19.15
	Percentage UNQUALIFIED	70.41	80.86
	TOTAL	100.00	100.00
20–99	NO. OF MANAGERS IN ANALYSIS	12	10
	Percentage QUALIFIED	33.33	20.00
	Percentage UNQUALIFIED	66.67	80.00
	TOTAL	100.00	100.00

The figures in table 9b.3.2 show Irish-born executives still ahead but the differences, when tested, were found not to be statistically significant. The test was repeated on all firms with the same result. There is therefore no real evidence outside the top stratum to show that Irish-born executives are more or less likely to have academic qualifications than those working in Ireland but born abroad.

PART C. MANAGEMENT TRAINING AND OTHER CHARACTERISTICS

The relationship of training with function, level and qualification has already been examined. It was found that all functions and levels have participated in training to much the same extent, and that training courses are used about equally by both qualified and non-qualified executives. The relationship of training with age and nationality is examined in this part.

Section C.1. The Relationship between Training and Age

Estimates are made of the number and proportion of executives with training, in each age-group, for firms based in Dublin and outside, and for firms which are corporate members of the Irish Management Institute. These estimates are shown in detail as they could have implications for the size of the market which exists for management training. If it were found that few older managers had attended courses while most younger ones had done so, then obviously either an effort would have to be made to attract older managers or the fact would have to be recognised that the market was effectively restricted to younger managers who already had some training.

TABLE 9c. 1. 1.   *Estimated Number of Managers in Each Age-Group, Who Have and Have Not Attended Management Training Courses, by Size and Location of Firm.*

Size of Firm (No. of Employees)	Location of Head Office	Attendance at Courses	Aged Under 35	Aged 35-49	Aged 50 or Over
500 or More	DUBLIN	Attended	133	296	131
		Did Not Attend	61	136	150
	REST OF COUNTRY	Attended	55	91	22
		Did Not Attend	24	55	38
	TOTAL	Attended	188	387	153
		Did Not Attend	85	191	188
100–499	DUBLIN	Attended	89± 55	104± 55	57± 42
		Did Not Attend	193± 82	464±123	255± 69
	REST OF COUNTRY	Attended	82± 78	110±105	22± 19
		Did Not Attend	165± 67	335± 85	286± 57
	TOTAL	Attended	171± 91	214±112	80± 46
		Did Not Attend	359±103	803±151	541± 87
20–99	DUBLIN	Attended	128±142	128±156	21± 43
		Did Not Attend	447±352	639±409	447±215
	REST OF COUNTRY	Attended	59± 88	99± 81	20± 40
		Did Not Attend	297±170	674±245	317±204
	TOTAL	Attended	185±159	226±165	41± 56
		Did Not Attend	740±369	1,316±422	761±286
TOTAL	DUBLIN	Attended	349±151	528±163	210± 58
		Did Not Attend	701±360	1,239±387	853±224
	REST OF COUNTRY	Attended	197±115	300±129	64± 44
		Did Not Attend	486±180	1,065±257	641±211
	TOTAL	Attended	544±182	827±198	274± 72
		Did Not Attend	1,184±382	2,310±446	1,490±298

TABLE 9c. 1. 2.   *Estimated Percentage of Managers in Each Age-Group Who Have Attended Management Training Courses, by Size and Location of Firm.*

Size of Firm (No. of Employees)	Location of Head Office	Aged Under 35 % Attended	Aged 35-49 % Attended	Aged 50 or Over % Attended
500 or More	DUBLIN	68.6	68.5	46.4
	REST OF COUNTRY	69.6	62.3	36.7
	OVERALL	68.9	67.0	44.9
100–499	DUBLIN	31.5	18.3	18.3
	REST OF COUNTRY	33.3	24.7	7.1
	OVERALL	32.3±13.5	21.1±10.6	12.9±6.9
20–99	DUBLIN	22.2	16.7	4.5
	REST OF COUNTRY	16.7	12.8	5.9
	OVERALL	20.0±14.7	14.7±10.4	5.1±8.0
OVERALL	DUBLIN	33.3± 9.5	29.9± 8.3	19.6±5.4
	REST OF COUNTRY	28.8±15.9	22.0± 9.9	9.0±5.1
	OVERALL	31.5± 9.4	26.4± 6.4	15.5±4.6

TABLE 9c. 1. 3.   *Estimated Number of Managers in Each Age-Group Who Have and Have Not Attended Management Training Courses, by Size of Firm and Corporate Membership of the Irish Management Institute.*

Size of Firm (No. of Employees)	Corporate Membership of I.M.I.	Attendance at Courses	Aged Under 35	Aged 35-49	Aged 50 or More
500 or More	MEMBER	Attended	185	383	153
		Did Not Attend	83	166	162
	NON-MEMBER	Attended	3	4	0
		Did Not Attend	2	25	26
100-499	MEMBER	Attended	92± 70	128± 97	36± 32
		Did Not Attend	87± 45	317±118	215± 60
	NON-MEMBER	Attended	77± 61	82± 53	44± 36
		Did Not Attend	274± 96	483±100	323± 65
20-99	MEMBER	Attended	51± 91	25± 39	13± 30
		Did Not Attend	191±200	217±210	38± 44
	NON-MEMBER	Attended	111±115	200±176	22± 45
		Did Not Attend	466±256	1,044±350	755±308
TOTAL	MEMBER	Attended	328±104	536±102	202± 40
		Did Not Attend	361±194	700±221	415± 70
	NON-MEMBER	Attended	191±126	286±179	66± 56
		Did Not Attend	742±265	1,552±354	1,105±307

TABLE 9c. 1. 4.   *Estimated Percentage of Managers in each Age-Group Who Have Attended Management Training Courses, by Size of Firm and Corporate Member-ship of the Irish Management Institute.*

Size of Firm (No. of Employment)	Corporate Membership of I.M.I.	Aged Under 35 % Attended	Aged 35-49 % Attended	Aged 50 or Over % Attended
500 or More	MEMBER	69.0	69.8	48.6
	NON-MEMBER	60.0	13.8	—
100–499	MEMBER	51.4	28.7	14.3
	NON-MEMBER	21.9±10.8	14.6±7.8	11.9±9.2
20–99	MEMBER	21.1	10.5	25.0
	NON-MEMBER	19.2±17.6	16.1±11.8	2.9±4.7
OVERALL	MEMBER	47.6±10.2	43.4± 5.5	32.7±5.8
	NON-MEMBER	20.4±11.8	15.6± 9.0	5.7±5.0

TABLE 9c. 1. 5.   *Managers in each Age-Group, showing the Percentage With and Without Training, by Size of Firm, in Firms Which Employ Trained Managers.*

Size of Firm (No. of Employees)	Training Status	Aged Under 35	Aged 35-49	Aged 50 or Over
500 or More	NO. OF MANAGERS IN ANALYSIS	265	548	311
	Percentage WITH TRAINING	70.19	69.71	47.91
	Percentage WITHOUT TRAINING	29.82	30.30	52.10
	TOTAL	100.00	100.00	100.00
100–499	NO. OF MANAGERS IN ANALYSIS	66	130	64
	Percentage WITH TRAINING	40.91	26.93	18.76
	Percentage WITHOUT TRAINING	59.10	73.08	81.26
	TOTAL	100.00	100.00	100.00
20–99	NO. OF MANAGERS IN ANALYSIS	19	25	12
	Percentage WITH TRAINING	31.58	44.01	8.34
	Percentage WITHOUT TRAINING	68.43	56.01	91.67
	TOTAL	100.00	100.00	100.00

Tables 9c.1.2 and 9c.1.4 show that, at the time of the survey, the position was not quite so extreme. There was a tendency for younger managers to have participated to a greater extent than older ones, particularly among medium-sized member-firms, but in large companies a high proportion of executives aged over 50 had been reached by training, while a high proportion of younger executives in medium and small sized firms had yet to be reached.

It was necessary to test the significance of the observed differences, and it was decided that the comparison would be more meaningful if made only among firms which employed some managers with training, to see what the position was in firms which actually used courses.

Table 9c.1.5. shows a definite tendency for younger executives to be more likely to have attended courses. (Note how the proportion attending training courses is increased in the bottom stratum by concentrating on firms with some trained men). In small and medium-sized companies the proportion of participants aged over 50 is so low that it may be that the market is effectively confined to younger men. The differences observed are highly significant in the top and middle size-groups, and very nearly significant in the bottom group.

Section C.2.   The Relationship between Training and Nationality

This section is devoted to the question of a possible association between nationality and management training, to see whether the fact that foreign managers are at a higher level could be explained by their being more likely to have formal training in management.

The number and proportion of Irish and foreign-born executives who had participated in training courses is shown in table 9c.2.1.

TABLE 9c. 2. 1.   *Estimated Number and Percentage of Irish and Foreign Managers who Have and Have Not attended Management Training Courses, by Size of Firm.*

Size of Firm (No. of Employees)	Nationality of Manager	Attended Training Courses No.	Did Not Attend Training Courses No.	Attended Training Courses %
500 or More	IRISH	654	388	62.8
	OTHER	74	76	49.3
100–499	IRISH	418±208	1,499±178	21.8± 7.6
	OTHER	48± 31	203± 74	19.1±10.3
20–99	IRISH	432±243	2,488±687	14.8± 7.8
	OTHER	21± 42	329±232	6.0±10.3
TOTAL	IRISH	1,503±307	4,376±687	25.6± 5.3
	OTHER	143± 50	608±236	19.0± 6.3

In fact it seems that Irish-born executives have the advantage, at least in large companies. A further breakdown (not shown) was obtained by age, because it was seen above that younger managers are more likely to be trained, and it is found in part D below that foreign-born managers are older than those born in Ireland. The small differences in firms with less than 500 employees disappeared completely when this was done but, in firms with over 500 employees, Irish-born executives in every age group were more likely to be trained than those born abroad.

It was decided to carry out a statistical test, confining it to firms employing some foreign managers, because levels were compared only for those companies.

TABLE 9c. 2. 2.   *Managers, Irish-born and Other, Showing the Percentage With and Without Training, by Size of Firm, for Firms Employing Non-Irish Managers.*

Size of Firm (No. of Employees)	Training Status	Irish-born	Other
	NO. OF MANAGERS IN ANALYSIS	954	145
500 or More	Percentage WITH TRAINING	64.16	49.66
	Percentage WITHOUT TRAINING	35.85	50.35
	TOTAL	100.00	100.00
	NO. OF MANAGERS IN ANALYSIS	196	47
100–499	Percentage WITH TRAINING	23.47	19.15
	Percentage WITHOUT TRAINING	76.54	80.86
	TOTAL	100.00	100.00
	NO. OF MANAGERS IN ANALYSIS	12	10
20–99	Percentage WITH TRAINING	25.00	10.00
	Percentage WITHOUT TRAINING	75.00	90.00
	TOTAL	100.00	100.00

The test showed that the differences observed in firms with under 500 employees could easily have arisen by chance. It cannot therefore be said that foreign-born executives reached higher levels because they had more formal training in management than executives born in Ireland.

PART D. AGE AND OTHER CHARACTERISTICS

It was seen in chapter 8 that age and function are associated, chief executives being older than others and finance executives younger. In part A of this chapter it was seen that managers at higher levels are older than those in more junior positions. Parts B and C showed that younger managers were more likely than older executives to have academic qualifications and management training. In this part the one remaining relationship, that between age and nationality, is examined.

Section D.1. The Relationship between Age and Nationality

The number and proportion of executives of each nationality in each age-group is shown in tables 9d.1.1 and 9d.1.2. The main interest in this section is to see whether foreign managers are older than Irish as, if this were so, it might be inferred that the proportion of foreign-born executives could be expected in later years to fall off as they retired.

This inference might be dangerous as it is possible, especially among foreign-owned companies, that foreign-born executives as they retire are replaced from abroad by other executives who are already middle-aged. If this were so it would not be correct to assume that the proportion of executives born abroad would fall with the

TABLE 9d. 1. 1. *Estimated Total Number of Irish and Foreign-born Managers in Each Age-group, by Size of Firm.*

Size of Firm (No. of Employees)	Nationality of Manager	Aged Under 35	Aged 25-49	Aged 50 or Over
500 or More	IRISH	251	510	281
	OTHER	22	68	60
100-499	IRISH	503±157	910±185	503± 81
	OTHER	27± 25	107± 46	118± 48
20-99	IRISH	864±378	1,337±385	720±312
	OTHER	62± 68	206±172	82± 78
TOTAL	IRISH	1,618±407	2,757±425	1,504±322
	OTHER	110± 72	381±178	260± 91

TABLE 9d. 1. 2. *Estimated Percentage of Managers in Each Age-group who are Foreign-born.*

Size of Firm (No. of Employees)	Aged Under 35 % Foreign-born	Aged 35-49 % Foreign-born	Aged 50 or Over % Foreign-born
500 or More	8.1	11.8	17.6
100-499	5.1±4.3	10.5±3.5	19.0±6.8
20-99	6.7±5.7	13.3±9.4	10.3±9.8
OVERALL	6.4±3.8	12.1±4.8	14.8±5.0

passage of time. Furthermore, it must be remembered that the sample of firms is representative only of longer-established foreign companies. Many foreign-owned firms have started operations in this country over the last ten years, and others will do so in future, bringing with them some executives from abroad.

A statistical test was carried out on the data in table 9d.1.3. Except in the bottom size-group the differences were highly significant. There were too few foreign-born managers in the bottom group to allow a test to be carried out. It may be said with considerable confidence that the proportion of executives born outside Ireland diminishes in the lower age-groups. The impression gained by the auther when conducting the interviews was that most foreign executives were brought in for their technical skill and that, when they retire, they will in general be replaced by Irish nationals at present working under them.

PART E. NATIONALITY AND OTHER CHARACTERISTICS

All the relationships involving nationality have already been examined. It remains only to summarise them.

Foreign-born executives are mostly either chief executives or production managers. They have reached higher levels in their companies than Irish-born executives of the same age. This is sometimes because they started these companies themselves, while in foreign-owned companies it may reflect past policy. It cannot be explained by the fact that they are more likely than Irish-born managers to have academic qualifications or management training—if anything they are less likely. For the most part their employment reflects an earlier lack of technical know-how in Irish industry which made it necessary to get executives with such knowledge from abroad.

TABLE 9d. 1. 3.   *Managers of Each Nationality, Showing the Percentage in Each Age-Group, by Size of Firm.*

Size of Firm (No. of Employees)	Age-Group	Irish-born	Other
	NO. OF MANAGERS IN ANALYSIS	1027	145
500 or More	Percentage AGED UNDER 35	24.06	13.80
	Percentage AGED 35-49	48.98	46.90
	Percentage AGED 50 OR OVER	26.98	39.32
	TOTAL	100.00	100.00
	NO. OF MANAGERS IN ANALYSIS	322	47
100–499	Percentage AGED UNDER 35	24.85	10.64
	Percentage AGED 35-49	49.07	42.56
	Percentage AGED 50 OR OVER	26.09	46.81
	TOTAL	100.00	100.00
	NO. OF MANAGERS IN ANALYSIS	117	10
20–99	Percentage AGED UNDER 35	26.50	10.00
	Percentage AGED 35-49	48.72	50.00
	Percentage AGED 50 OR OVER	24.79	40.00
	TOTAL	100.00	100.00

PART II

The Need for Education and Training

Introduction

The purpose of this part of the report is to assess the needs, quantitative and qualitative, for education and training for industrial management.

Chapter 10 deals with the number and type of additional managers required between 1964, the base date of the survey, and the year 1970.

Chapter 11 is an analysis of the replies given by interviewees when asked what they considered to be the most important area of management training for their firms, and includes a comparison of their replies with the results of studies carried out in Belgium and in the United States.

Chapters 12 to 15 are taken up with an attempt to infer something of firms' management training needs by examining the extent to which certain activities and techniques of management are carried out by companies in the Republic of Ireland, and the extent to which use of those techniques is associated with use of various methods of raising the standard of management.

Chapter 16 summarises some of the findings of chapters 12 to 15, and includes an attempt to compare the findings of these chapters with those of studies abroad.

Before the survey began many different methods of assessing the training needs of managers were considered — methods which might be more objective than the opinions of managers themselves. These considerations are discussed at length in the technical appendix.

It is explained that interpersonal relations in industry were not examined because of the impossibility of studying a sample sufficiently large to allow valid generalisation.

At some future time this gap in the research design will need to be filled by making a study of the human side of enterprise. Meanwhile it can be said that, if effective interpersonal behaviour is the norm of Irish business, this is not due to any familiarity with the findings of research. The degree of knowledge of the tools of decision-making is limited, and there is no reason to think that knowledge of other areas is more widespread.

The questions selected cover some basic activities and techniques of planning and control. Many factors in a firm's situation influence the extent to which it is necessary or feasible to engage in a given activity or to use a given technique. It had initially been hoped to examine comprehensively the extent to which firms operated in conditions in which the techniques chosen might be expected to apply. Because this comprehensive approach led to the draft questionnaires being too long either to administer or to analyse, it was decided to select for investigation a few methods of wide applicability, while at the same time making some effort to assess the existence of the necessary conditions, by examining the data for associations between the use of techniques, the type of market served by the company, and its type of production process.

It is true that there is accumulating, through the efforts of research workers in the human sciences, a body of evidence suggesting that much of the emphasis placed by management on measurement and control was based on a view of man at work as a machine analogue responding to simple inputs of reward or punishment, and that behaviour based on this view led to consequences which were deleterious psychologically and socially to employees, and a hindrance to the achievement of the greater efficiency which was its aim.

It is not necessary to agree with the more extreme proponents of this view to admit that the damaging side-effects of unduly restrictive control are well-documented. On the other hand it cannot be denied that the use of techniques of measurement, planning and control has led to demonstrable increases in productivity. It is the purpose for which measurement and controls are used, and the spirit in which they are implemented, that is crucial rather than the techniques themselves.

The selection of the method of approach and of the particular questions asked does not, therefore, imply a commitment to forms of management practice founded on the premise that man is basically an unreliable machine.

It is felt that the replies to the questions asked give a fair indication of the current level of management practice and ability.

This is felt to be so, not merely on the basis of the extent to which techniques are used, but because of the reasons for not using them.

It was hardly ever the case that firms had weighed carefully the benefits of using some technique which they were capable of operating, and had decided against it.

In general, wherever a technique was not used, those interviewed would not, unaided, have been able to implement it. Whether or not the techniques chosen are always appropriate, the fact that they are not used reflects unfamiliarity with them rather than a decision that they do not suit, and the replies to the questions asked indicate the general level of ability to use the techniques in question.

Because there are extensive investigations of associations in the following chapters, a word must be added on their interpretation. The fact that two things are associated does not mean that one is cause and the other effect. It may be that they are mutually related to some other causal agent. For instance the fact that attendance at management training courses is associated with greater likelihood of a given technique being used does not necessarily imply that the former was the cause of the latter. It may be that attendance at courses and use of techniques are both symptoms of a progressive outlook on the part of a firm's management.

Conversely the absence of an association does not mean that the factor under study had no effect. If, for instance, it is found that firms attending training courses are no more likely than others to use a given technique it does not follow that attendance at courses had no effect. It might well be that none of the firms attending courses had used the technique before attending but that some had started to use it after doing so.

Thus, care must be taken in interpreting associations. Nevertheless it would be surprising if a factor having an effect on a situation did not show some association with it, and for that reason tests of associations have been carried out.

CHAPTER 10

Future Numerical Requirements

The purpose of this chapter is to assess the number of managers which it will be necessary to provide by 1970. The different elements of demand are first discussed. The period 1964-67 is considered, then the period 1967-70 and, finally, some implications of the demand situation are examined.

Summary of Main Findings.

It is estimated that over the years 1964-67 the annual requirement for managers in industry will have been about 325, or just under 5 per cent of the existing stock. This is roughly the same rate of requirement as in 1960-64.

The greatest absolute requirement is expected in firms employing 20 to 99 people. More managers are required in the field of production than in any other, but the fastest percentage rate of growth is expected to be in marketing. Apart from large companies, it was thought that executives would be recruited mainly from outside the firm: this is especially true of top management.

Over the period 1967-70 it is estimated that the annual requirement will be around 4.3 per cent per annum of the stock, of which 2.7 per cent will be caused by growth, about 1 per cent by deaths and about 0.6 per cent by retirement.

Firms mostly specified that those selected would be expected to have had previous managerial experience. Unless such positions are filled by immigration this will lead only to increased competition for managers without the desired objective being attained. The small size of the requirement relative to the total stock makes it unlikely that firms, especially small and medium-sized companies, will consider it worthwhile to start executive development programmes solely to meet their need for additional managers. It may be that more could be done to keep track of potential managers who emigrate, especially those with qualifications, so that their return might later be facilitated.

The Elements of Demand.

The first question to be raised is the meaning of numerical requirement, that is, to ask how a demand for managers arises. Briefly it arises because of shortages or changes: shortages because, judged by some criterion, the present number is inadequate to cater for firms' present needs; changes because firms grow, managers retire, die or are severed from the system by emigration, demotion or termination of employment.

If all these elements were recognised and projected an estimate could be made of total future requirements. But this would not be enough to know what sort of managers were required. It would be necessary, in addition, to know the flows taking place within the system.

For example, suppose a firm decides to appoint an additional top marketing manager. It is decided to fill the position by promoting a middle marketing manager and his position is filled, in turn, by transferring a junior finance executive. The position to be filled from outside the system is that of junior finance executive, although the additional position created was that of top marketing manager. The picture is further complicated if the junior finance position is filled by getting from another firm someone already in a managerial position, thus giving rise to a further series of shifts.

To arrive at a complete specification of future requirements it would be necessary not only to know the positions in which growth, retirements, death and severance would take place, but also the series of flows within the system arising out of those events. The number of positions of each type necessitated by growth would be estimated and from it subtracted the number of positions to be filled by those already in managerial positions, giving the number to be found outside the system. The promotions and transfers caused by positions being filled from inside management would then be followed through until it was discovered at what point and to what extent[1] this replacement demand caused a requirement for additional managers. Replacement demand would then be added to growth demand to get total demand arising from growth. The same procedure would have to be followed for retirement, death and severance. Finally, demand arising from shortages (which would become effective demand only if shortages were recognised and acted upon) would be added to give overall future demand.

It can be seen that the system is not simple. Many of the quantities, especially the flows, may not be foreseeable and satisfactory forecasts will not be made until a great deal more data are accumulated through continuing studies in this field.

In this study the only feasible way to estimate demand was to carry out a survey of firms' intentions. The other methods: use of judgment, time-series projection or use of a mathematical model, require either long familiarity with the stratum or historical data. Because this was the first such study no past data were available. The firms surveyed were asked questions 1-17 of the questionnaire, and it is on their replies that this chapter is mainly based.

Before considering the replies to the survey the question of shortages is taken up.

Shortages.

One of the sources of potential demand mentioned above is shortages, that is, the extent to which the present number of managers is inadequate for present requirements.

To make a decision on this point there must be a criterion of adequacy. There is no theoretical ratio of managers to other employees which can be applied. A possible measure would be to see how many would be needed to bring all firms up to the level of the best, but this raises problems in defining "best".

A natural procedure would be to compare the average number of managers per firm with that in other countries. A similar study was carried out in Belgium (1) and a comparison with that study is shown in table 10.1.

Columns 1 and 2 show the average number of managers in comparably sized firms in Ireland (year 1964) and in Belgium (year 1957). In every case the Belgian figure exceeds the Irish. Columns 3 and 4 show the ratio of managers to other employees. This again favours Belgium, showing that the difference is not due to Belgian firms being bigger within each size-group than Irish firms.

The figures do not show conclusively that Irish firms lag behind. In the first place, both sets are based on samples so that, at least up to 1,000 employees, the differences may be within the range of sampling variation. Secondly, the Belgian study was based on returns to a postal questionnaire and may therefore be biased. While the definition of manager was substantially the same in both studies, that in Belgium included all research workers as managers, whereas in Ireland only those directing or solely responsible for research were so considered. This may account for some of the difference be-

---

1 because it might be decided not to replace some of those promoted or transferred.

TABLE 10. 1.   *Average Number of Managers per Firm, and Ratio Managers/Other Employees, in Belgian and Irish Management Institute Studies, by Size of Firm.*

| Size of Firm (No. of Employees) | Managers per Firm | | Ratio Managers to Other Employees | |
	Belgium (1957)	Ireland (1964)	Belgium (1957)	Ireland (1964)
50-100	5.0	4.1	1:15.0	1:18.3
100-500	10.0	8.4	1:24.0	1:27.3
500-1,000	23.7	19.8	1:28.5	1:39.9
1,000-2,000	42.9	25.8	1:31.9	1:56.5
2,000 and over	128.9	60.0	1:30.2	1:57.6

tween firms with over 1,000 employees. Finally, the industrial structure of Belgium differs greatly from that of Ireland, Belgium having many high-technology industries such as metallurgy, chemicals, etc., largely lacking here. It may be that if all these factors were allowed for there would be little difference between the two countries.

Some studies have been carried out in other countries, but none of them gives figures so directly comparable as those for Belgium.

A German study (2) shows the ratio of managers to total employees for four levels of management. The study covers economic activities other than industry, which the present study does not. The lowest management group in the study includes supervisors, and may therefore be excluded for comparative purposes. It can be deduced from table 3 of reference (2) that the ratio of managers to total employees is about 1:16 for firms with under 500 employees, 1:38 for firms with 500 to 999 employees, and about 1:37.7 for firms with 1,000 to 4,999 employees. Compared with these figures Irish firms with under 500 employees and over 1,000 employees have much less favourable ratios. Again it must be borne in mind that the German figures include non-industrial firms, that the industrial structure of Germany differs from that of Ireland, that the average size of firm in those size-groups is not given and that the figures are subject to bias (because the questionnaire was posted) and to wide sampling variation.

A study (3) was carried out in the region served by the University of Aix-Marseille. It covered activities other than industry, but it is possible to arrive at an overall ratio of managers to total employees by abstracting figures for industry only. It is not possible to deduce the ratios for different size-groups in industry. The returns are based on a sample of 107 industrial firms of which 30 employed under 100 people, 63 employed 100 to 499 and 24 employed 500 or more. The ratio of managers (cadres) to total employees in the sample was 1:22.2. The overall weighted ratio obtained in the present study was 1:20.7.

Woodward (4) has described the results of a research project carried out in the South Essex region. The project covered practically all the firms in that region employing over 100 employees. Most of those firms were in high-technology industries such as chemicals, electronics and motors. This must be borne in mind when comparing the results with those obtained in Ireland.

On page 27 of reference (4) there is a figure illustrating the ratio of managers and supervisors to other staff. This is based on returns from 95 firms. Unfortunately, no details are given of the size-breakdown of the respondents, nor are the ratios shown separately for different size-groups. Of the 110 firms in the project, 73 employed from 100 to 499 people, while 37 employed 500 or more. In the Irish Management Institute survey 78 firms with over 100 employees gave details of their number of supervisors as well as of their managers. Of the 78 firms, 40 employed 100 to 499 people while 38 employed 500 or more. Thus it might be expected that the results for the sample of Irish firms with 100 or more employees would appear less favourable owing to the higher proportion of larger firms: larger firms have a greater number of non-supervisory staff per manager than smaller firms.

The figures below show that this was not the case. If anything, Irish firms have a higher number of managers and supervisors, relative to other employees, than the firms in Woodward's study.

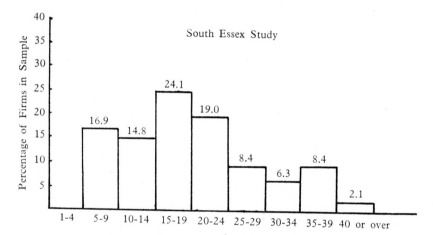

Fig. 10. 1.   Ratio of non-Supervisory Staff to Managers and Supervisors.

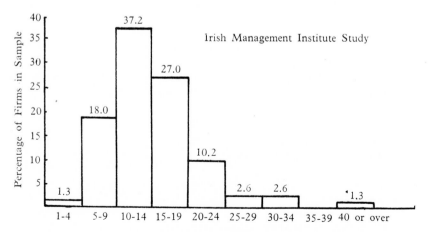

Fig. 10. 2.   Ratio of non-Supervisory Staff to Managers and Supervisors.

The average ratio of non-supervisory staff to managers and supervisors in the present study is 7.7:1 for firms with 20 to 99 employees, 11.6:1 for the 100 to 499 employee group and 14.4:1 for the 500 or over group. Comparison with the ratios for selected firms shown on page 57 of (4) confirms that Irish firms do not compare unfavourably.

The result of the international comparisons made is inconclusive. Another measure of adequacy would be to ask the chief executives interviewed whether they considered their numbers sufficient, indicating the type of insufficiency where necessary. This possibility was overlooked. However, instead of asking in the next section for requirements due to growth, executives were asked what additional managerial positions they expected to create. Their estimates therefore incorporate not only growth but any shortages recognised and to be remedied.

Because it is difficult to get a satisfactory criterion of adequacy, and because of the inconclusive result of the international comparisons made, shortages will not be considered further and the estimates to be made of future requirements will not include demand arising from this source except insofar as it is contained in "additions".

It should not be forgotten that implications regarding numerical requirements may arise out of consideration of later findings on the level of management practice. It may be that to raise the standard of practice it will be necessary for firms to employ executive-level staff in addition to those already employed. For instance, if it is considered desirable that firms should use costing and budgetary control systems, it may be necessary for them to employ additional accountants to instal and operate them. This would constitute a further element of demand to be added to the estimates derived below.

Another possible stimulus to demand would be a decision to raise the proportion of executives with academic qualifications to a level other than that at present, for instance to the level prevailing in other countries. It is not likely that demand from such a source would manifest itself in practice. However desirable it might be considered to raise the proportion qualified, this will probably happen only by employing qualified rather than non-qualified executives as part of the normal process of growth and replacement considered below. An effort deliberately to raise the proportion rapidly could only become effective if firms were to recruit qualified staff to an extent beyond that necessitated by growth or replacement, which might not be economic, or if they were to remove their present staff and replace them with academically qualified men.

Nevertheless, the question of whether or not Irish industry falls behind industry in other countries in employing managers with academic qualifications is relevant. There is an addendum to this chapter in which a comparison is made between the position as shown by the present study and that found in studies in Belgium and in Britain.

Section 1.   Demand in the Years 1964-67

This section is concerned with showing the likely demand in different sizes of firm for managers in each functional area and at each level, between January 1st, 1964, and January 1st, 1967. The estimates of demand are based on replies to questions asked in the survey of 141 firms. No attempt has been made to provide estimates for different industries or locations, as the sample was too small.

The elements of demand mentioned above are growth, replacement due to retirement, death or severance, and flows caused by promotion or transfer. Each firm was asked about additional positions (i.e. growth plus recognised shortages) created since

January 1st, 1964, or expected before December 31st, 1966, and about retirements between those dates. Each was also asked to what extent positions would be filled by promotion within the firm's management and what shifts would follow from these promotions. Deaths during 1963 were asked for, but not by functional area, so they are not included here. No questions were asked about severance, i.e. emigration, demotion or dismissal, as it was felt that these were largely unforeseeable while, if they were foreseen, chief executives would not wish to divulge information about them. The following estimates do not therefore include replacement demand arising from death or severance.

TABLE 10. 2.　*Estimated Total Requirement of Executives 1964-67, by Functional Area and Size of Firm. Showing the Expected Source of Recruitment.*

Size of Firm (No. of Employees)	Source of Recruitment	Chief Executive	Market-ing	Produc-tion	Finance	Person-nel	Other	Total
500 or More	INSIDE THE FIRM	—	32	37	7	1	3	80
	OUTSIDE THE FIRM	—	7	30	8	1	6	52
	TOTAL	—	39	67	15	2	9	132
100-499	INSIDE THE FIRM	—	16	32	11	—	—	59±49
	OUTSIDE THE FIRM	5	48	118	32	—	5	208±71
	TOTAL	5	64	150	43	—	5	268±83
20-99	INSIDE THE FIRM	—	41	41	21	—	—	103±86
	OUTSIDE THE FIRM	—	165	165	144	—	—	473±269
	TOTAL	—	206	206	165	—	—	576±297
TOTAL	INSIDE THE FIRM	—	89	110	39	1	3	242±98
	OUTSIDE THE FIRM	5	220	313	184	1	11	734±277
	TOTAL	5	309	423	223	2	14	976±308

Before commenting on the figures in the table above, their reliability must first be examined. They are open to four objections.

1) Sampling variability. Because they are based on a sample only, the figures are uncertain. In the extreme right-hand column an indication of sampling variation is given[1]. It is considerable.

2) Inherent uncertainty. Because the figures are based only on businessmen's estimates of the future they are necessarily uncertain. Estimated retirement is probably accurate, estimated additions less so. Executives were asked for their estimates of growth only up to the end of 1966 because it was not thought that realistic estimates could be made for more than three years ahead.

1 The figures cannot be taken as strict confidence limits because the underlying distribution is not normal. The true confidence interval would be even wider than the figures shown.

3) Addition. It is not sufficient to add each firm's estimates of the promotions it will make and the flows which will result inside the firm in order to get an estimate of final demand for the system, because this ignores flows between firms. As may be seen from table 10.2 a large number of managers will have to be sought outside firms. Insofar as firms specify previous managerial experience and insofar as the positions are not filled by immigration, this will lead to managers shifting between firms, giving rise to a further series of transfers, the result of which may be that final demand in each area will be for numbers different from those shown in table 10.2.

4) Weighting. The estimates were made by multiplying the sample numbers by the reciprocal of the sampling fractions, giving a total for the population of firms sampled. This population is based on lists given in late 1963. There is therefore no allowance for the fact that new firms will have come into operation between then and 1967. The estimates, to this extent, understate the likely demand.

From these considerations it is obvious that the figures quoted in table 10.2 must be treated with caution.

The first thing to be said is that the requirement is not very large. A total of 976 over three years, or 325 a year, means an annual requirement of under 5 per cent of the total stock. (6,630 in 1964).

The largest absolute requirement is likely to arise among small firms. The differences between the size-groups are wide: the average for large firms is about one manager per year, for medium sized firms about one manager each three years and for smaller firms about one every nine years.

Large companies are in rather a strong position. They expect to find the majority of their new executives among their own non-managerial staff. Medium and smaller firms predominantly will have to look outside their staff for managers.

The greatest absolute demand will be for production managers, which is to be expected in view of the fact that they are the largest constituent in the existing stock (see chapter 2). The greatest relative demand will be for marketing executives as may be seen more clearly in table 10.6.

Generally speaking, there is no difference between the sources of recruitment for the different areas. The one exception is in the case of large companies, where a markedly higher proportion of marketing executives than of any other type will be found inside the firm.

It may be that this demonstrates that large companies have nurtured carefully their potential marketing talent. It seems more likely that the tradition is being carried on of promoting salesmen not qualified academically which has resulted in marketing having a lower proportion of academically-qualified executives than any other area. This may be because top managers do not see a need for any preparation other than experience, or because there are not enough qualified men of an age to be promoted to managerial positions.

TABLE 10.3.   *Estimated Total Requirement of Executives 1964-67, by Level of Management and Size of Firm, Showing the Expected Source of Recruitment.*

Size of Firm (No. of Employees)	Source of Recruitment	Chief Executive	Level of Management			
			Top	Middle	Junior	Total
500 or More	INSIDE THE FIRM	—	1	38	41	80
	OUTSIDE THE FIRM	—	11	20	21	52
	TOTAL	—	12	58	62	132
100-499	INSIDE THE FIRM	—	—	27	32	59±49
	OUTSIDE THE FIRM	5	64	112	27	208±71
	TOTAL	5	64	139	59	268±83
20-99	INSIDE THE FIRM	—	41	41	21	103±86
	OUTSIDE THE FIRM	—	309	165	—	474±269
	TOTAL	—	350	206	21	576±297
TOTAL	INSIDE THE FIRM	—	42	106	94	242±98
	OUTSIDE THE FIRM	5	384	297	48	734±277
	TOTAL	5	426	403	142	976±308

This table shows the requirement for managers of each level and their likely source of recruitment. Large firms will look mainly for middle and junior managers, medium-sized firms mainly for middle management and small firms for top and middle management (see chapter 3 for definitions). In each size group the further up the hierarchy the position is, the less likely that firms will be able to fill it from among their non-managerial staff. This is not unexpected: someone not already a manager is unlikely to be promoted to top management. However, the total number of top management vacancies arising due to additions and retirement was checked and it was seen that few of them will be filled even by promoting an existing manager. Demand for top managers will therefore typically be met by looking outside the firm.

Because firms usually specify previous managerial experience when looking for top managers (table 10.14), everyone will be trying to recruit from every-one else — a sort of managerial " beggar-my-neighbour " — unless the vacancies are filled by immigration. This may not be bad for the individual manager, as it increases the prospect of mobility. It does suggest, however, that firms might pay more attention to planning management development so as to have a source of recruitment. It is probably unrealistic to expect smaller firms to be able to develop their talent in this way, particularly when the appointments to be made are in an area in which the firm has not previously had a manager, e.g. marketing. This would suggest that more might be done to keep track of potential managers going abroad, particularly graduates, so as to have a further pool on which to draw.

TABLE 10.4   *Requirement of Executives 1964-67 by Firms in the Sample, by Level of Management, Functional Area and Size of Firm.*

Size of Firm (No. employees)	Level of Manage-ment	Marketing	Production	Finance	Personnel	Other	Total
500 or More	Top	3	5	1	1	2	12
	Middle	19	24	10	1	4	58
	Junior	17	38	4	—	3	62
	TOTAL	39	67	15	2	9	132
100–499	Top	3	5	3	—	1	12
	Middle	6	16	4	—	—	26
	Junior	3	7	1	—	—	11
	TOTAL	12	28	8	—	1	49
20–99	Top	8	5	4	—	—	17
	Middle	2	4	4	—	—	10
	Junior	—	1	—	—	—	1
	TOTAL	10	10	8	—	—	28

The firms in the sample were examined to see if there was any difference between the functional areas in the level of management for which it would be necessary to recruit. Table 10.4 shows no major differences except a tendency in larger firms for production to have a higher proportion of junior managers. This is to be expected because of the greater depth of management in that area.

To check the reliability of chief executives' forward estimates, they were asked what had happened over the four years from the beginning of the decade, i.e. from January 1st, 1960, to December 31st, 1964. In tables 10.5 and 10.6 actual net additions over the period January 1960 to December 1964 are compared with expected net additions over the period January 1964 to December 1966. (Net additions means the total of additional positions created minus former positions abolished. The total number of managers in one year plus net additions equals the total number in the following year).

The figures in table 10.5. probably underestimate growth because the sample results were grossed-up to the 1963 population of firms, whereas in 1960 there were probably fewer firms in operation. Quite large sampling variability can be seen to be present. The table shows that in the main the fastest growing of the numerically more important areas was marketing.

Net additions in the years 1964-67 are shown in table 10.6.

TABLE 10.5   *Estimated Number of Managers Employed in 1960 and 1964, with Estimated Numerical and Percenta Change, by Functional Area and by Size of Firm.*

Size of Firm (No. employees)	Date & Change	Chief Exec.	Marketing	Production	Finance	Personnel	Other	Total
500 or More	1964	56	207	632	211	53	33	1192
	1960	52	170	547	184	41	25	1019
	Numerical Change	4	37	85	27	12	8	173
	Percentage Change	7.69	21.76	15.53	14.67	29.27	32.0	16.98
100–499	1964	273	321	1023	460	16	75	2168
	1960	273	235	895	385	11	64	1863
	Numerical Change	0±14	86±81	128±67	75±46	5±10	11±14	305±14
	Percentage Change	—	36.60	14.30	19.48	45.45	17.19	16.37
20–99	1964	1008	267	987	473	21	514	3270
	1960	967	226	781	452	21	514	2962
	Numerical Change	41±56	41±56	206±191	21±91	—	—	308±27
	Percentage Change	4.24	18.14	26.38	4.65	—	—	10.40
OVERALL	1964	1337	796	2642	1144	90	622	6630
	1960	1292	632	2223	1021	73	603	5844
	Numerical Change	45±58	164±98	419±201	123±101	17±10	19±59	786±30
	Percentage Change	3.48	25.95	18.85	12.05	23.29	3.15	13.45

The figures in table 10.6 have the same drawbacks in grossing-up and sampling variability (not indicated but just as large) as table 10.5. Further, they do not allow for abolition of jobs through death or severance. When compared with table 10.5, and allowing for the fact that they relate to a three-year rather than a four-year period, they appear quite consistent with previous experience. They would appear even more consistent if one large firm with a very rapid growth-rate in 1960-64 were omitted. It seems that executives expected growth to continue at much the same rate and in much the same areas as in the immediate past. Smaller firms expected a faster rate, with very marked growth in marketing and finance, but these figures are subject to wide sampling variability.

It may be that the difficulties of the past few years as compared with 1960-64 have upset their intentions, but the correspondence between intentions and earlier reality gives some confidence in the realism of chief executives' forward estimates.

It was mentioned above that, in large companies, a big percentage of total growth in 1960-64 was accounted for by one firm. The question of spread of change (i.e. growth or contraction) was taken up to see whether change was confined to a small number of firms or more widely dispersed.

ABLE 10.6. *Estimated Number of Managers Employed in 1964, and Estimated Number Expected in 1967, with Estimated Numerical and Percentage Change, by Functional Area and by Size of Firm.*

Size of Firm (No. employees)	Date & Change	Chief Exec.	Marketing	Production	Finance	Personnel	Other	Total
)0 or More	1967	55	237	678	220	55	44	1289
	1964	56	207	632	211	53	33	1192
	Numerical Change	minus 1	30	46	9	2	11	97
	Percentage Change	,, 1.76	14.49	7.28	4.27	3.77	33.33	8.14
)0–499	1967	273	370	1140	487	16	80	2366
	1964	273	321	1023	460	16	75	2168
	Numerical Change	—	49	117	27	—	5	198
	Percentage Change	—	15.26	11.44	5.87	—	6.67	9.13
)–99	1967	987	473	1193	638	21	514	3825
	1964	1008	267	987	473	21	514	3270
	Numerical Change	minus 21	206	206	165	—	—	555
	Percentage Change	,, 2.08	77.15	20.87	34.88	—	—	16.97
VERALL	1967	1315	1081	3019	1346	92	634	7481
	1964	1337	796	2642	1144	90	622	6630
	Numerical Change	minus 22	285	369	201	2	16	851
	Percentage Change	,, 1.65	35.80	13.98	17.57	2.22	1.93	12.84

TABLE 10.7. *Percentage of Firms Having Some Numerical Change in Managerial Positions between 1960 and 1964, by Size of Firm.*

	SIZE OF FIRM (No. of employees)			
	20-99	100-499	500 or More	TOTAL
PERCENTAGE CHANGED	32.6	45.8	68.1	36.7

A majority of large companies reported some change, about half the middle size group and about one-third of the smaller firms.

Growth expectations in 1964-67 were then analysed and from table 10.8 it can be seen that there is a remarkable consistency between the proportions in that table and those in table 10.7.

Finally, the experience of change in 1960-64 was compared with expectations for 1964-67 to see if only the same firms which had previously changed were expecting to grow. It can be seen from table 10.9 that there is no difference in expectation between those which had and had not changed. That is to say, those firms which changed in 1960-64 are not widening the gap between themselves and the firms which had not

TABLE 10. 8.   *Percentage of Firms Expecting Some Numerical Change in Managerial Positions between Jan. 1st 1964 and Jan. 1st 1967, by Size of Firm.*

| | SIZE OF FIRM (No. of employees) | | | |
	20-99	100-499	500 or More	TOTAL
EXPECTING CHANGE	32.6	50.0	61.7	37.3
EXPECTING NO CHANGE	50.0	37.5	27.7	46.6
UNCERTAIN	17.4	12.5	10.6	16.1

TABLE 10. 9.   *Comparison between Expectations of Firms Which Changed and Firms Which Did Not Change 1960-64.*

| Size of Firm (No. employees) | Changes 1960-64 | Expectation of Additions 1964-67 | | | |
		Additions	No Additions	Undecided	Total Firms
500 or More	Additions	20	9	3	32
	No Additions	9	4	2	15
	TOTAL	29	13	5	47
100–499	Additions	11	7	4	22
	No Additions	13	11	2	26
	TOTAL	24	18	6	48
20–99	Additions	4	9	2	15
	No Additions	11	14	6	31
	TOTAL	15	23	8	46

changed, but neither is the gap being narrowed. It is interesting to note that whereas almost all large firms will have experienced some change between 1960 and 1967, about a quarter of the medium group, and one-third of the smallest group will not.

Firms in Dublin were compared with those outside to see if there was any difference in the proportion changing or expecting change. None was found. No other factor was examined: the only one of importance might have been industry, but the sample was too small to allow it to be studied.

The main conclusions from the study of demand over the period 1964-67 are that it was expected to grow at much the same rate as in 1960-64. The greatest absolute demand would be among small firms and for production managers. The greatest relative demand would be in marketing. Except for the largest firms executives would have to be recruited mainly from outside the firm, and this is especially true of top management. Growth was more widely dispersed among larger than among smaller companies and the overall growth rate was not expected to be great.

Section 2.   Demand in the Years 1967-70

In the last section an attempt was made, using a survey of firms' intentions, to forecast in detail the demand for executives over the period January 1st, 1964 to December 31st, 1966. In this section an attempt will be made to cover the period January 1st, 1967, to December 31st, 1969.

It is not possible to attempt a forecast in detail, showing demand in different areas and at different levels, because it was not considered that executives would be able to forecast their detailed requirements for more than three years ahead and because there are not sufficient historical data to use any other forecasting method. The attempt will be made only to forecast total demand. For this reason it will not be necessary to consider flows in the system which result in final demand manifesting itself in some area other than that in which the initial need arose.

Method Used.

Total requirement is made up of:

Gross Additions plus Replaced Retirements plus Replaced Deaths plus Replaced Severance minus Unreplaced Promotions and Transfers .... (1)

This is identical with:

Net Additions plus Total Retirements plus Total Deaths plus Total Severance ...... (2)

where Net Additions = Gross Additions minus Unreplaced Retirements minus Unreplaced Deaths minus Unreplaced Severance minus Unreplaced Promotion and Transfer, i.e. = total number of managers at time $t + \triangle$ minus total number of managers at time t.

In projecting future demand the elements either of 1 or of 2 could be projected and summed to give total demand. It was preferred to use 2 because the elements were simpler to measure and because it was felt that the aggregate "net additions" would be more stable than the smaller quantities "replaced retirement" etc.

Because no questions were asked about severance in the survey no attempt can be made to include it. The forecast will therefore be based on an attempt to project net additions, deaths and retirements over the period January 1st, 1967 to December 31st, 1969, adding the separate projections to get the total requirement.

Total Deaths.

The firms surveyed were asked how many executives had died during the year 1963. The estimated total number of deaths in industry is shown in table 10.10.

TABLE 10. 10   *Estimated Percentage of Firms in Which an Executive Died, and Estimated Number of Executives Who Died, in 1963, by Size of Firm.*

Size of Firm (No. employees)	Percentage of Firms	Estimated Number of Executives
500 or More	25.5	10
100–499	2.1(0.0—11.1)	5±10
20–99	6.5(1.3—17.9)	62±68
OVERALL	6.3±5.4	77±69

See statistical note 10.1 for an explanation of the confidence limits on percentages in the table above.

Subject to the wide sampling variation shown, the estimated total is 77 which, over a three-year period, would give a total of about 230.

There is no reason to believe that the number of deaths will change from the 1963 figure. Any additional firms coming into business are unlikely to have executives of an age with a high death-rate. The growth in the number of managers has also taken place largely among the younger age-group. Therefore the population of managers in the age-group likely to have a high death-rate is unlikely to increase, at least up to 1970.

The estimated total of managers at January 1st, 1964, was 6,630, while at January 1st, 1960, it was 5,844 (see table 10.5). The average number of managers during 1963 was therefore about 6,500[1]. Expressing total deaths as a percentage of total managers, a death rate of about 1.2 per cent per annum is arrived at. Because the total number of managers is rising while the total number in the older age-group is probably fairly static, it is unlikely that this rate will increase and it might even fall to about 1 per cent per annum in the years 1967-70.

Total Retirements.

Firms were asked how many executives were expected to retire over the three years from the beginning of 1964 to the end of 1966. Total retirements are shown in table 10.11 estimated on the basis of their replies.

TABLE 10. 11. *Estimated Number of Executives Retiring, 1964-67, by Functional Area and Size of Firm.*

Size of Firm (No. employees)	Chief Exec.	Marketing	Production	Finance	Personnel	Other	Total
500 or More	1	8	19	5	—	2	35
100–499	11	16	27	16	—	—	70±36
20–99	21	—	—	—	—	—	21±40
TOTAL	32	24	46	21	—	2	125±53

The total is 125, giving an average of about 40 a year. Because retirement is a relatively certain matter in larger firms, which contribute most to the expected total, this figure should be reliable.

For the same reason as in the case of deaths it is unlikely that the annual number of retirements will increase, while the annual percentage may even fall. Taking the average number of managers over the period 1964-1967 as about 7,000[2], an annual number of 40 retirements gives an annual percentage of 0.55 per cent.

TABLE 10. 12. *Percentage of Firms with a Fixed Retirement Age, by Size of Firm.*

	SIZE OF FIRM (No. of Employees)		
	20-99	100-499	500 or More
PERCENTAGE FIXED	10.9	37.5	68.1

Tables 10.12 and 10.13 show the differences in retirement policy between the size-groups.

1. Roughly $6,630 - \left(\dfrac{6,630-5,844}{8} \right)$. Division is by 8 because mid-1963 is $\frac{7}{8}$ of the distance between January 1st, 1960, and January 1st, 1964.

2. Roughly $6,630 + \left(\dfrac{7,481-6,630}{2} \right)$ See table 10.6.

Table 10.12. shows how unusual it is for small companies to have a fixed retirement age. Even in the medium-sized companies a minority have a definite ruling on the point. A number of companies have pension-schemes under which executives have the option of retiring at 65, without retirement being mandatory.

TABLE 10. 13.   *Percentage of Firms Expecting an Executive to Retire between 1964 and 1967, by Size of Firm.*

	SIZE OF FIRM (No. of Employees)		
	20-99	100-499	500 or More
PERCENTAGE EXPECTING	2.2	23.4	54.3

Table 10.13. on expectations of retirement reinforces the estimates in table 10.12.

Net Additions.

An attempt will be made to forecast net additions using two methods: 1) projecting the number of managers as estimated from the sample, 2) applying an estimated ratio of managers to total employees to a projection of total industrial employment in 1970, as given in the Second Programme for Economic Expansion.

In tables 10.5 and 10.6 there are figures for net additions in 1960-64 and chief executives' estimates of net additions in 1964-67. It was mentioned earlier that the totals were estimated by weighting the sample figures up to the total number of firms in 1963. The result is that growth in 1960-64 and 1964-67 is underestimated because there were probably less firms in 1960 than in 1963 and there will probably be more in 1967, so that the weighting factor applied to the 1960 data is too large, and that applied to the 1967 data is too small. As against this the figure for net additions in 1964-67 does not include an allowance for unreplaced deaths and severance, to that extent overestimating true net additions and counterbalancing the underestimation due to weighting.

1). PROJECTION.   Projections are made by fitting a curve to a series of values collected at equidistant points in time past, and extending the curve into the future. It is usually desirable to have a large number of values, that is, the series should extend over a large number of intervals: years, months or whatever. No such series exists for numbers of managers. There is only a figure for 1964, a figure for 1960 which is probably a slight overestimate, and an estimate of what the figure might be in 1967.

Apart from the question of the propriety of using a forward estimate as part of a time series, the values are not equidistant in time. It would not be possible therefore to fit curves by statistical methods, even if an estimate could be made of the shape of the curve. It is possible only to fit a variety of simple curves which depend on different assumptions about the rate of growth in numbers and which result in widely-differing estimates of numbers in 1970. The curves which might be fitted are:

1.   A straight line through 1960 and 1964. This assumes that the rate of growth will not change, but will be the same as in the period 1960-64. It gives an estimate of 7,800 managers in 1970. It is probable that this is an underestimate, in view of expectations about the period 1964-67, which would result in a figure of 7,481 in 1967, leaving a growth of only 319 in the remaining period.

2.   A parabola through the three points 1960, 1964 and 1967. This assumes that

the rate of growth will increase by a constant amount over the decade 1960-1970. It gives an estimate of 8,400 managers in 1970. This may be an overestimate, as there is no reason to believe that the rate of growth will continue to increase.

3.   A straight line through 1964 and 1967. This assumes that the rate of growth will not change but will be the same as for the period 1964-67. It gives an estimate of 8,300 managers in 1970.

4.   A straight line through 1960 and 1967. Assumes the rate of growth will not change but will be the same as the average for the period 1960-67. It gives an estimate of about 8,170 managers in 1970.

5.   A straight line fitted by eye to the years 1960, 1964 and 1967. Assumes the rate of growth will not change, being the same as the average for 1960-67, but takes account of the different rates between 1964-1967. It gives an estimate of 8,120 for 1970.

2). USE OF RATIO. A forecast of average employment in transportable goods industry during 1970 is available from the Second Programme for Economic Expansion. By estimating a figure for January 1st, 1970, and dividing it by the ratio of total employees to managers, an estimate can be made of the number of managers at the beginning of 1970.

An attempt must first be made to estimate the likely ratio of total employees to managers at the beginning of 1970. First, the ratio must be established for the year 1964. One problem is to estimate the number of managers in firms employing less than twenty people. There are approximately 1,700 such enterprises. A small survey of Irish Management Institute members, carried out before the main survey, gave an average number of about $1\frac{1}{4}$ managers per firm of that size. This means that there were about 2,100 managers in the group at the beginning of 1964. Added to the total in firms with over twenty employees (6,630) this would give a total number of managers on January 1st, 1964, of 8,730.

The following table shows employment in the years 1959-66 and projected to 1970. Assuming that employment on January 1st of any year is midway between the figures given for that year and the preceding year, total employment on January 1st, 1964, was 181,500. This gives a ratio of total employees to managers of $\dfrac{181{,}500}{8{,}730}$ or 20.7:1.

TABLE 10. 14.   *Average Yearly Employment in Transportable Goods Industry.*

Year	Employment (000)
1959	153.1
1960	160.7
1961	168.2
1962	173.5
1963	178.7
1964[1]	184.3
1965[1]	186.4
1966[1]	188.0
....	....
1970[2]	215.4

1 Estimated.
2 Revised projection.

Source: Central Statistics Office. *Statistical Abstract* 1962. Dublin: the Stationery Office. (Table 115.)
National Industrial Economic Council. *Report on Review of Industrial Progress.* Dublin: the Stationery Office, 1965. (Appendix C.)

Is there any reason to believe that this ratio will be the same in 1970? There is evidence from the sample to show that total employment, and therefore total managers, in the under-20 size-group has not changed very much[1]. Suppose the number of managers in 1960 was 2,000. Added to the estimated over-20 total of 5,844 this gives a total of 7,844 managers. Taking employment in January 1st, 1960, as 156,000 (same assumption as for 1964 above) gives a ratio of 20:1. Assuming that the number of managers grew as expected in 1964-67, the ratio at the beginning of 1967 would be a little under 20:1. It can be seen that the ratio is stable. It would seem reasonable to take a ratio of about 20.5:1 for 1970, as the ratio of less than 20:1 in 1967 is probably too low due to the slow growth of total employment in the years 1964-67.

If the target for 1970 is to be met, employment in each of the years 1967 to 1970 will have to rise by an average of about 7,000, i.e. by about 3,500 each half-year. This would give a total employed on January 1st, 1970, of about 212,000. A ratio of 20.5:1 applied to a total of 212,000 employees gives a total number of managers of 10,340. If it is taken that the number employed in firms under 20 will have grown from 2,100 to about 2,250, the total number of managers in firms employing over 20 employees will be about 8,100.

A number of methods have now been used to project net additions to 1970. They give a total number of managers varying between 7,800 and 8,400. It does not seem unreasonable to take 8,100 as the estimate, as the assumptions underlying the projections giving results around this figure seem valid.

A total of 8,100 would give a net addition between January 1st, 1967, and January 1st, 1970, of 619 managers, or a growth rate of 2.7 per cent per annum. This would represent a falling-off from the expected net addition in 1964-67 which was 851, i.e. 4.1 per cent per annum. It may be that the difficulties of the years since 1964 have slowed down the rate of growth in numbers of managers just as they have slowed the

---

1. Firms in the sample were asked how many people they employed *in toto*. Weighting up their replies would give estimates of 60,000, 63,000 and 51,000 for the groups 500 plus, 100-499 and 20-99 respectively. This would leave hardly any employed in the under 20 group (because total employment=181,500). There is evidence that the samples in the 20-99 and 100-499 groups were biased towards the larger firms within each group. When cumulative percentages of total employees in each size-group are plotted against the size-group limits on double probability-paper the resulting graph often follows a straight line. This is true of Belgium in 1957 and of Ireland 1958. Taking the total employment as 181,500 and employment in the 500 plus group as 60,000, various combinations were tried for the under 20-99 and 100-499 groups. The following employment totals give a reasonable fit to a straight line and do not seem incompatible with what is known of the total number of firms.

Size of Firm (No. empls.)	Estimated Total Employees at Jan. 1, '64	Size of Firm (No. empls.)	Actual Total Employees in 1958
Under 20	15,500	Under 15	9.800 (abt. 14,000 udr. 20)
20-99	46,000	15-99	42,700 (,, 38,500 in 20-99)
100-499	60,000	100-499	52,000
500 or more	60,000	500 or more	37,900
Total	181,500	Total	142,400

Comparisons with the actual figures for 1958 show little change in total employment in the under 20 group, and a considerable rise in the 500 plus group, showing the increasing importance of large firms. Figures for 1958 are taken from a paper read to the Social and Statistical Inquiry Society of Ireland on May 18, 1962, by Mr. T. P. Lenihan of the Central Statistics Office.

rate of growth in total employment. In that case the figure for 1967 may not be reached. This will mean that the ground lost must be made up in 1967-70, thus increasing the requirement over that period.

If it is assumed that the total number of managers in firms employing 20 or more people will be 8,100 on January 1st, 1970, the growth between January 1st, 1964, and that date will be almost 1,500 and the rate of growth will be 3.4 per cent per annum, compared with 3.2 per cent in 1960-64. Over the decade 1960-70, growth will be 2,256, which is 38.6 per cent or 3.33 per cent per annum.

Total Requirement.

In earlier sections the requirement arising from deaths was estimated at about 230 over a three-year period, i.e. about 1 per cent per annum. Retirements are expected to give rise to a requirement of about 125 over a 3-year period, or about 0.6 per cent per annum. Added to a requirement of 619 additions (2.7 per cent per annum), these figures give a total of 974 managers over the three years, or about 4.3 per cent of the total stock per annum. (This is almost exactly equal to the estimated requirement of 976 in 1964-67—see table 10.2). Over the decade 1960-70 the rate of net additions is over 3 per cent, giving a total annual requirement of about 5 per cent of the existing stock.

Section 3: Required Background for Executives

In the section on the period 1964-67 it was seen that, of the total requirement of 976 in the period 1964-67, about three in every four of the number required would have to be found outside the firm's own staff. Chief executives were asked what background they would specify when recruiting.

TABLE 10. 15. *Desired Background of Executives to be Recruited Outside the Firm* 1964-67, *by Size of Firm.*

Size of Firm (No. employees)	Degrees or Professional Qualifications	Percentage of Those to be Recruited Having:				
		Previous Managerial Experience	Both	Neither	Uncertain	Total
500 or More	28.8	19.2	40.4	1.9	9.6	100.00
100-499	13.2	34.2	36.8	2.6	13.2	100.00
20-99	26.2	30.4	4.3	8.7	30.4	100.00

Table 10.15 shows that, at least in larger firms and to a considerable extent in smaller companies, firms will be looking for men with previous managerial experience, sometimes with academic qualifications as well.

Firms were also asked (Qs. 14 & 15 of questionnaire) whether they had actually experienced difficulty in getting suitable men. Their replies are shown in tables 10.16 and 10.17. Although the numbers involved are not large there seems to be fairly wide-

TABLE 10.16 *Percentage of Firms Reporting Inability to Recruit Executives with Background Desired, between 1961 and 1964, by Size of Firm.*

	SIZE OF FIRM (No. of employees)		
	20.99	100-499	500 or More
PERCENTAGE REPORTING	19.6	41.7	48.9

TABLE 10. 17.   *Estimated Number of Positions for which Executives with the Desired Background Were Not Available, by Functional Area and Size of Firm.*

Size of Firm (No. employees)	Chief Exec.	Marketing	Production	Finance	Personnel	Other	Total
500 or More	1	4	30	2	1	2	40
100-499	5	10	86	—	—	10	112±39
20-99	—	—	165	41	—	—	206±128
TOTAL	6	14	280	43	1	13	358±133

spread experience of shortages, particularly in larger firms. The greatest scarcity, both numerically and proportionally, is of production executives and the most frequent reason given was that it was difficult to find men with the desired experience or the required blend of experience and academic or technical qualifications.

To see if there was a pool of unused talent from which the scarcity might be supplied, firms were asked (Q.16) whether they employed any academically-qualified people in non-professional or non-managerial positions.

TABLE 10. 18.   *Percentage of Firms Employing Academically Qualified People in non-Professional and non-Managerial Positions, by Size of Firm.*

	SIZE OF FIRM (No. employees)			
	20-99	100-499	500 or More	Total
Percentage EMPLOYING	2.2(0.0—11.6)	8.3(2.3—20.0)	26.7	4.4±4.4

TABLE 10. 19.   *Estimated Number of Academically-Qualified People in non-Professional and non-Managerial Positions, by Type of Qualification and Size of Firm.*

Size of Firm (No. employees)	Commerce	Arts	Engineering	Science	Other	Total
500 or More	21	5	—	1	40	67
100-499	—	11	—	21	16	48
20-99	—	—	—	41	—	41
TOTAL	21	16	—	63	56	156

It is probable that the larger firms understated the extent to which people are doing work for which they are over-qualified. Nevertheless it can be seen that, at least within transportable goods industry, there is not a considerable pool of talent to be tapped.

The implications of the foregoing are clear. Unless positions are filled by immigration, the search for additional managers with previous experience cannot succeed and will lead only to firms competing for one another's managers. However desirable from the individual's point of view, this cannot solve the overall problem. Firms will have to settle for inexperienced people who, in the absence of management development schemes, may not be prepared for work in managerial positions.

The fact that the number required is small relative to the existing stock means that firms are unlikely to regard the facts outlined above as sufficient in themselves to warrant formal development programmes. This is particularly true of smaller companies. Nevertheless it is obvious that if a sufficient number of managers of the type industry requires is to become available, either firms must engage in development work or some means must be instituted of keeping track of qualified people going abroad, so that firms can be put in touch with men who have the required experience.

ADDENDUM TO CHAPTER 10

A study carried out in Belgium was referred to above, and the limitations involved in making comparisons with conditions in Ireland were pointed out. The figures in table 10.20 below show the percentage of academically-qualified managers in the Belgian study and in the present study.

TABLE 10. 20. *Percentage of Managers with Academic Qualifications in Belgium and in Ireland, by Size of Firm.*

	50-99	100-199	200-499	500-999	1000-1999	2000 or More
Belgium (1957)	40.3	48.9	46.9	56.1	55.6	72.4
Ireland (1964)	22.6	27.0	28.7	36.7	44.0	54.5

The definition of qualifications is identical in both studies. The Irish figures are for firms still in the size-groups indicated, i.e., which had not changed size between the selection of the sample and the survey date.
Source: (1) page 85.

It is probable that the different industrial structure of the two counties contributes something to the differences observed. It was pointed out that there are more high-technology industries in Belgium than in Ireland. The only industry for which it was possible to make a comparison between the two countries was the textile industry. In both Ireland and Belgium the proportion of qualified executives in this industry was low.

A study was carried out by Clark (5) on firms in the Manchester area employing over 600 people. It was found that over 53 per cent of the executives in private industry had either university degrees or professional qualifications. A further 8.2 per cent had Higher National Certificates or Diplomas, and another 14.5 per cent had followed some courses of study after leaving school, but without qualifying formally. The percentage of managers qualified in firms in Ireland employing 500 or more people is 43.2 per cent which is below the figures quoted by Clark.

Although the proportion of qualified executives is lower in Ireland than in Manchester, the proportion attending management training courses outside their own firm is considerably higher: over 60 per cent as against under 25 per cent.

REFERENCES:
(1) Woitrin et alia. *Les Dirigeants d'Entreprise de l'Economie Belge.* Brussels: Office Belge pour l'Accroissement de la Productivité, 1960.
(2) S. Fassbender. *Die Weiterbildung betrieblicher Führungskräfte in Deutschland.* Frankfurt: Rationalisierungs-Kuratorium der Deutschen Wirtschaft, 1966.
(3) Association de l'Institut d'Administration des Entreprises de l'Université d'Aix Marseille, *Bulletin No. 5.* Mars: the Association, 1966.
(4) J. Woodward. *Industrial Organization: Theory and Practice.* London: Oxford University Press, 1965.
(5) D. G. Clark. *The Industrial Manager.* London: Business Publications Ltd., 1966.

CHAPTER 11

The Expressed Needs of Management

In the technical appendix there is a discussion on the most difficult problem in this survey — that of making an assessment of the educational and training needs of management — and on the design decided upon to deal with this problem. This chapter is concerned with one aspect of that design: the expressed needs of managers.

It may be as well to touch briefly on the problem and on the research design finally used. The reason it was felt necessary not to rely solely on the opinions expressed by managers was that it was felt that in many cases managers would not be able to formulate clearly and accurately the real basis of their problems and the consequent priority of their needs. (It was possible that, in addition to being unable correctly to perceive their needs, some managers might suppress some of those needs which they did perceive, or be deliberately misleading about them. It is the author's opinion, having administered the questionnaires, that this did not take place.) In order to achieve an assessment which would be more objective it was decided to focus, not on the problems of management, but on the techniques used in various areas to cope with problems.

There were two reasons for this: in the first place, even when it was decided to use firms rather than individual managers as the unit for study, it seemed that the difficulties of probing to find the real problems of the firms selected would prove impossible to overcome in the space of time available. It is probably only rarely, as most consultants would bear out from their experience, that the problems stated by management are the real problems to be faced. Even in very small firms the task of discovering the real problems is often protracted and is not something which can be accomplished in an interview lasting a couple of hours. Secondly, there would arise the difficulty of providing evidence that the problems had been correctly assessed. In the consultant/client relationship, agreement can generally be reached as to what the problems are and, because the only people involved are those between whom agreement has been reached, action can proceed.

In a survey such as this, however, in which the people who will take the action are not those who have agreed about the nature of the problems, the position is different. It would not be enough for a research worker to come back from his field interviews and say "I have conducted interviews with a large number of people. As a result of these interviews I have identified the following areas as being problem ones, and the interviewees agree with me". Those to whom he was reporting would rightly demand evidence to show that his conclusions were correct. Such evidence would be difficult to present in manageable form and, even with unlimited resources, it might well be that it would require information which firms were unwilling to give. It was therefore decided to concentrate instead on finding to what extent firms were using the techniques developed in the existing body of knowledge about management, as this would provide clear-cut and easily demonstrable evidence of their degree of advancement.

Having decided against any form of extended depth interview because of the limitation of resources, including anyone trained in such interview techniques, a decision had to be made on the best way of collecting information from managers on such of their perceived needs as they were willing to express. Three questions had to be answered:

(1) whose opinions should be sought? (2) what questions should they be asked? (3) how should those questions be asked?

As regards (1), it had been hoped to obtain opinions from every manager in the sample by sending in advance of every visit a questionnaire to be filled in. Testing showed that it would not be feasible to carry out this intention. It had then been hoped that at least the executives responsible for each of the major functional areas would be interviewed. Again, however, this was found to be impossible in the available time, and it was finally decided that interviews would be held with the chief executive only. Consequently the opinions gathered in this survey are those of a single individual, usually the chief executive, about the management training needs of his firm.

Taking (3) next, there are two basic ways in which questions on this subject can be asked. The first is to ask the question and to leave the respondent free to express his own opinions when answering; the other is to present the respondent with a set of choices which he can mark or rank in order and add to if he wishes.

There are advantages and disadvantages in both approaches: the latter has the advantage that it lends itself to processing and statistical manipulation and also that, if properly constructed, it provides an indication of the order of preferences. It suffers from the disadvantage that it may suggest to the individual some answers which he might not, himself, have considered. The advantages and disadvantages of the first method are the reverse of those of the second, and there is the added disadvantage that the respondents may forget to mention some perceived need. On balance the first method was considered preferable, mainly because it seemed that there would be some difficulty in constructing a satisfactory list of choices which would be comprehensive enough to be useful and, at the same time, brief enough to allow a genuine ranking to be made. It was felt, also, that the response of such a wide sample to an open-ended question would provide valuable guidance to the construction of such a check-list for future surveys.

As regards question (2), it was decided simply to ask what the interviewee considered to be the most important areas that management training could cover for his firm (question 35 of questionnaire). It was felt that to pursue such matters as the objectives of managers in attending courses, and how far these objectives were met, would involve too much time, and that the motives, aspirations, attitudes, and satisfactions of users of courses were sufficiently broad to require a separate study of their own.

This chapter, then, covers the training needs of the firms surveyed as seen by their chief executives. (Before going on to consider the findings, it must be pointed out that it is not possible in this chapter to test the significance of any differences between responses. The reason is discussed in statistical note 11.1.)

Summary of Findings
The broad conclusion is that there are interesting differences between the size-groups in the emphasis placed on particular needs. Executives' assessment of their firms' needs is not unreasonable, but may not be sufficiently comprehensive. It would be unwise to disregard the desire of small businesses for courses designed for their particular industry. Finally, so far as discriminating between the four functional areas goes, firms seem to underestimate the extent of their requirements in those techniques of management relevant to the personnel function. This function does not refer to the general question of dealing with people, but to the specialised activities usually looked after by a personnel department, e.g., manpower planning, selection and training, job evaluation, pay structure, labour negotiations, and so on. The findings of a Belgian and an American study are in broad agreement with the findings of this survey.

Discussion.

The responses of the interviewees to question 34 were sorted into broad categories and their frequency is shown in the following table.

TABLE 11.1. *Number of Responses Falling in Each Category, by Size of Firm.*

	Response - Category	Size of Firm (No. of Employees)		
		500 or More	100-499	20-99
1.	Production	9	14	12
2.	Marketing	11	10	11
3.	Finance	10	13	7
4.	Personnel	3	2	—
5.	Interpersonal Relations	15	6	5
6.	Organisation	2	—	—
7.	Communications	5	1	—
8.	Behavioural Change	2	4	—
9.	Broadening for Specialists	13	—	—
10.	All Aspects Weak	1	8	8
11.	Special Courses for Own Industry	—	—	8
12.	Supervisory Training	4	5	1
13.	Other Suggestions	9	2	2
	Total Suggestions	84	65	54
	Total Firms Answering	42	34	32
	Total Firms in Sample	47	48	46
	Average Replies per Respondent	2	1.9	1.7

It is interesting to look at those firms which did not reply positively to the question, the total number of these being 33. Three of the companies felt that management training would be of little use to them because of the particular circumstances in which they worked, and the circumstances they outlined seemed to the interviewer to justify this conclusion. Six firms felt that management training as such was worthless and did not believe in the idea of management as a subject for learning. Ten firms did not reply specifically, because they were unable to formulate their needs in any way. While not opposed to the idea of management training, they were so little aware of it as a concept that they could not indicate their requirements. Eight other companies whose managers were obviously well aware of modern management thinking did not feel that they could be specific about their requirements. Their awareness of modern thinking was obvious from their replies to later questions and also from the fact that most of them were members of the Irish Management Institute and had often attended courses. The remainder had no obvious reason for not replying.

It was thought that the level of advancement of a firm would affect both the quantity and quality of its replies. As regards quantity the affect might be in either direction: more advanced firms, owing to their greater level of awareness, might be able to specify more areas as requiring attention, or because of their already advanced level might need to specify fewer. Size might also have been expected to affect the situation, but again in indeterminate direction: increasing size perhaps leading to more problem areas, but less ability to recognise such problems because of the size of the organisation. In fact, however, size does not appear to have exerted much influence, as can be seen from the last line of table 11.1, where the average number of replies is much the same in each size of firm. Neither does an inspection of the replies by individual firms reveal any tendency for advanced companies to mention either more or less areas than other firms. The question of the quality of their perceptions is taken up later.

There are some interesting relationships in table 11.1 which, because of the fine breakdown used, may be somewhat obscured. The response categories are amalgamated into a broader classification in table 11.2 below. It should be remembered that, in table 11.1, the heading "personnel" refers to techniques of management appropriate to a personnel department, and not to the general question of dealing with other people, which is covered under the heading "interpersonal relations". In the broader breakdown categories 1 to 4 above are grouped into a new class called "functional area techniques". A second broad class called "interactional aspects" includes classes 5, 6, 7 & 9 above. This is because the replies in those categories seemed to deal mainly with factors affecting the interaction between people. The only query that might arise in this regard is in assigning "broadening for specialists" to this category. It was considered that when executives talked of the necessity for courses to broaden the outlook of people in specialist functions they had in mind the improvement, not simply of their present performance or of their promotability, but of their ability to understand the problems of, and to deal with, other people.

TABLE 11. 2.   *Percentages of Replies Falling in Broad Categories, by Size of Firm.*

	Response - Category	Size of Firm (No. of Employees)		
		500 or More	100-499	20-99
1.	Functional Area Techniques	39.0	60.0	56.0
2.	Interactional Aspects	42.0	10.0	9.0
3.	Overall Weakness	1.0	12.0	15.0
4.	Special Courses for Own Industry	—	—	15.0
5.	Other	18.0	17.0	6.0
		100.0	100.0	100.0

Totals do not add to 100.0, because of rounding-off.

The differences between the responses of the three sizes of firm are now very striking, with larger firms placing a lesser emphasis on techniques in the functional areas and a very much greater emphasis on problems arising out of interactions between people. Among medium sized and smaller companies, as well as a greater emphasis on improved techniques, there was a greater tendency to reply that every aspect of the business could benefit from attention. A fact well worth noticing is that in the smallest size group quite a few firms specified that training would be most useful if geared to the requirements of their own particular industry.

This desire of managers of small businesses for instruction related to their particular industry is sometimes an irritant to those engaged in management training, since the implication is that management is not a systematic body of knowledge which may be learned and applied. Because the objections often arise from lack of knowledge of modern management thinking and are frequently without foundation, there is sometimes a tendency to imply that small-business managers are wrong to insist on the unique nature of their needs.

This does not take into account the real reasons for the importance to the small-business man of courses directly related to his own industry. In the first place the average small firm employs very few managers and it is probably true that most of their time and attention is focused on the technical, rather than on the managerial aspects of their work. Because of their dual roles as managers and technicians and because of the limited time at their disposal, they feel that managerial and technical training ought to go hand in hand. It will be seen later that many of them express the opinion that potential managers ought to undergo a course of combined technical and management training, usually adding that such persons would be preferred to university graduates. Their concern with the technical side of their job did not seem unreasonable to the author as, especially among very small businesses, their success may at present be a function of knowledge of, or skill in, a particular process or activity, or at serving a particular market, rather than of the sophistication of their management. Whatever about the rights and wrong of their position it does seem that programmes aimed at small business are likely to meet with greater response if channelled through their particular industry, or at least through broadly similar industries, as in this case there would be less resistance to be overcome.

On the question of the quality of the replies, that is, the degree to which the needs expressed by the manager correlate with the firm's real requirements, it is not possible to say a great deal. Looking back at table 11.2, however, they seem broadly in accordance with what might be expected. Larger firms point to the importance of problems associated with the growth and formalisation of organisations, while the smaller ones point to techniques in specific functional areas as being of greater importance. It will appear in the following chapters that this accords quite well with the level of techniques in the functional areas: in larger firms the use of the elementary techniques investigated tends to be widespread, whereas in smaller firms this is not so. The only reservation that the author would have is that firms might not have been comprehensive enough in stating their weaknesses. It will be seen again in the following chapters that firms tend, on the whole, to be weak in every aspect of management technique and that therefore category 3 in table 11.2 above might well be increased. Finally, it should not be assumed that techniques in production, marketing and so on are unimportant to large firms. The replies indicate that these areas do not, in the opinion of chief executives, constitute so great a problem as interpersonal relations. To some extent this reflects a lack of awareness of more advanced techniques, but in the main it is probably the ability of large firms to employ specialists in these areas which leads to their not being seen as a major problem.

Category 1 of table 11.2 was broken down into each of the four main areas. The number of respondents mentioning each area as a percentage of the number of responses mentioning functional area techniques is shown in table 11.3. There is not a great deal of difference between the three size-groups in their responses. In chapters 12 to 15 it is very difficult to differentiate between the functional areas and to say that firms tend to be weaker in one than in another. It is not therefore possible to say to what extent executives were correct in their assessment of which functional areas could benefit most from training. It will, however, be seen that use of techniques of personnel management is not common and that firms are probably less advanced in this

TABLE 11.3.   *Percentage of Replies Relating to Functional Area Falling in Each Area, by Size of Firm.*

Functional Area	Size of Firm (No. of Employees)		
	500 or More	100-499	20-99
Marketing	33.0	26.0	37.0
Production	27.0	36.0	40.0
Finance	30.0	33.0	23.0
Personnel	10.0	5.0	—
	100.0	100.0	100.0

respect than in any other area. The low percentage of replies mentioning this area may indicate either that firms were not aware of their deficiencies or that they did not consider these techniques to be very important.

It may be interesting before leaving the subject of businessmen's perception of their needs to look at the results of some studies in other countries.

In an addendum to this chapter there is reproduced a summary of a report on a project carried out by Louisiana State University into the opinions of small-business managers in the area, under a grant given by the U.S. Small Business Administration. (Small business is defined in the U.S. as a business with up to 500 employees). The general tenor of the replies is very much in accordance with the feelings of small-business managers in Ireland: particularly the accent on subjects with a practical orientation. The similarity would probably be even more marked if the Louisiana study had included a higher proportion of manufacturing firms. The fact that the businessmen in the Louisiana study placed a higher emphasis on interpersonal relations and a lower emphasis on functional techniques than managers of comparably-sized businesses in Ireland may also be caused by the inclusion of non-manufacturing firms in the former study.

A study by Fassbender has already been referred to in chapter 10 (reference 2). Most of the firms responding employed over 500 employees. The subjects most often mentioned by these large companies were the ability to handle men, a broader outlook not only on the firm but on industry as a whole, and facility in self-expression and communication. This orientation on the part of large firms in Germany ties in well with that of large firms in Ireland.

The Belgian study referred to in chapter 10 includes a section on the perceived needs of businessmen in Belgium. The chief executives of the firms to which questionnaires were posted were asked to assign marks out of twenty to each of eight areas of training, first to indicate the importance of the topics to themselves and then their importance to the other managers in the company. The eight areas were as follows (unless they are self explanatory the study gives a note showing what they were intended to cover).

1). FORMATION GENERALE. Courses on general background, i.e. not directly professional. Encompasses general cultural background, objective of enterprises, evolution of technology, institutions, social and political ideas and so on.

2). ECONOMIE. Economics: national and international, national accounts, managerial economics, operations research, etc.

3). PSYCHOLOGIE, SOCIOLOGIE, RELATIONS HUMAINES, ORGANISATION DU PERSONNEL.

4). DIRECTION DES ENTREPRISES. Definition of objectives, choice and implementation of policies, definition of functions, control, conduct of meetings, use of time, etc.

5). ORGANISATION DE LA PRODUCTION. Rationalisation, production planning and control, work simplification, time and motion study, etc.

6). GESTION COMMERCIALE. Marketing: market research, sales and distribution policy, etc.

7). GESTION FINANCIERE ET COMPTABLE. Finance and accounting: pricing, budgetary control and costing, financial structure, methods of financing operations, etc.

8). RELATIONS AVEC LES ORGANISATIONS PROFESSIONNELLES PATRONALES.

The scores given to the various areas were analysed in two ways.[1] The order in which the different areas were ranked and the scores given to each are shown in table 11.4.

TABLE 11.4. *Arithmetic Average of Scores Assigned by Belgian Businessmen to each of Eight Suggested Subjects.*

CHIEF EXECUTIVES		TOP AND MIDDLE MANAGEMENT	
Subject	Average Score	Subject	Average Score
1. Direction of Firms	17.5	1. Production	17.1
2. General Background	16.4	2. Psychology & Human Relations	16.4
3. Psychology & Human Relations	16.1	3. Marketing	14.1
4. Finance	16.1	4. General Background	14.0
5. Marketing	15.4	5. Finance	13.7
6. Economics	15.2	6. Direction of Firms	13.7
7. Production	15.1	7. Economics	11.7
8. Relations with Professional Organisations	13.2	8. Relations with Professional Organisations	9.2
OVERALL AVERAGE	15.6	OVERALL AVERAGE	13.7

Source: Woitrin et al., *Les Dirigeants d'Entreprises de l'Economie Belge.* Brussels: Office Belge pour l'Accroissement de la Productivitè, 1960, (page 259).

The findings of the analysis were as follows:

1. The chief executives seemed to consider training in general more important for themselves than for other managers.[2]

2. There was greater differentiation between the importance given to the subjects in the case of middle managers than chief executives. Chief executives agreed less about which areas were important to middle management than about the areas which were important to themselves.

3. Chief executives regarded overall direction of firms and general education as most important for themselves. There was considerable agreement on this point.

4. Economics, production and relations with professional bodies scored worst. There was a large measure of agreement about this.

5. Psychology and human relations scored high, but there was considerable disagreement between executives as to its importance. This was largely caused by differences between sizes of firm. Large firms laid particular stress on this subject. Small firms laid stress on production and on marketing, while medium-sized companies regarded finance as important.

---

1 by analysis of variance and by ranking.
2 Author's note: this may be because the chief executives did not consider the eight subjects given as being important to other managers. There are further technical objections to this conclusion which leave it open to doubt.

6.   As regards middle and top management, chief executives were in close agreement that production and human relations were the most important fields. Large companies put more emphasis on human relations, small companies on production.

7.   There was considerable disagreement about the relative position of marketing. Small firms laid considerable stress on it, but the importance assigned to it diminished as firms grew in size.

8.   The importance of production for top and middle management was general. It was not confined only to firms having a high proportion of technical staff.

The authors conclude that the expressed needs of chief executives about their own training correspond closely to the orientation of university training centres, but that the expressed need for more specific, technique-oriented courses, particularly on production, runs counter to the thinking of the training centres. They point out that the growing intellectual content of courses on production systems, particularly the development of aids such as operational research, may help to bridge this divergence in outlook. They point out further that while economics is given a low score by chief executives this is not borne out by the behaviour of firms: training courses on economics tend to meet a high demand.

The results of Belgian research are also in agreement with those of the Irish project. The methods used in all the studies were simple. The perceived needs of managers were not investigated in real depth, but the degree of unanimity in the findings is interesting, even on the superficial level of perception at which the questions were asked.

ADDENDUM TO CHAPTER 11

EXCERPTS FROM SURVEY IN LOUISIANA

The following is a summary of the main findings of the study referred to in page 160.

In the survey of 161 small-business executives in the State of Louisiana[1], it was found that the typical executive of a small business must be prepared to cope with a great variety of functions.

Eighty-four per cent of the businessmen felt that at least half of the curriculum of a college-level business school should consist of practical courses.

Among the interviewees, 91 per cent of those who held university or college degrees in business, 31 per cent of the holders of liberal arts degrees, and 56 per cent of the holders of other non-business degrees felt that their education was adequate for a career in small business management.

In rating individual subjects as "essential", "desirable but not essential", or "not desirable", practical courses ranked higher generally than liberal-arts courses. Liberal-arts studies with immediate practical application—such as speech and English composition—ranked higher than those with less obvious practical value.

---

1. *Education for Leadership in Small Business*: Prepared for the State of Louisiana Department of Commerce and Industry by Raymond V. Lesikar, Professor of Management and Marketing, Louisiana State University, Baton Rouge, Louisiana.

The majority of 161 small-business executives who took part in the survey expressed a decided preference for a practical collegiate business curriculum. Many of these businessmen acknowledged the need to include in the curriculum such courses as psychology, mathematics, and a foreign langauge. They believed, however, that the emphasis in the business curriculum should be on practical subjects—courses that will prepare new graduates to assume specific duties in the business organisation immediately. Such courses as accounting, business-letter writing, and salesmanship ranked high in their thinking.

The investigation sought to learn (1) what small-business executives do on their jobs and (2) what they think is the best kind of education for their work.

Three major areas of consideration were probed:

First, the functions performed by executives in small businesses were analysed.

Second, the reactions of the Louisiana executives to the general nature of education for business were studied.

Finally, an analysis was made of the businessmen's opinions about conventional business and non-business courses of the type offered in business schools.

Management in the Small Business

One of the basic facts brought out by the study was that the typical executive of a small business must be prepared to cope with a great variety of functions. These functions are of such diversity that they are not easily separated into logical classifications. However, two basic functional areas were revealed.

Policy Determination   Ninety per cent of the executives interviewed said that they participated in some way in policy determination for their companies.

Effective policy determination often means the difference between the success and failure of the small business. It is greatly dependent on the ability of the executive to think creatively in establishing the objectives of the company and in planning the means by which those objectives will be attained.

Thus, the findings of the study indicate that the business-education curriculum must provide opportunity for the student to develop the ability to think creatively in dynamic business situations. Required courses in logic and philosophy might well be considered. Or present courses in the conventional business areas could put more emphasis on problem solving as it must be carried on in realistic business situations.

Human Relations   The second basic functional area brought out by the study was that of human relations. Eighty-seven per cent of the executives contacted stated that they directly supervised personnel. More than 80 per cent reported direct participation in handling customer adjustments; 79 per cent, in evaluating personnel; 79 per cent, in handling employee grievances; 77 per cent, in handling problems concerned with motivating employees.

The implication here is that the student who expects to work in small business must have access to courses in human relations, the behavioural sciences, and communications.

Other Functions   The following tabulation indicates the relative importance of various areas of business activity based on the percentage of the executives interviewed who contribute to, or carry out, functions in these areas:

Activities	Per cent of executives	Activities	Per cent of executives
Determining policy	90	Checking production performance	64
Supervising personnel	87	Credits and collections	63
Handling adjustments	81	Establishing production standards	57
Evaluating personnel	79	Budgeting	54
Handling grievances	79	Inventory control	51
Motivating personnel	77	Accounting	50
Pricing	73	Production planning	49
Forecasting	73	Research	47
Financing operations	71	Work methods	46
Product improvement	69	Display	35
Purchasing	67	Transportation and delivery	30
Hiring-firing	66	Conducting labour relations	26
Advertising	65	Manufacturing	15
Training	64		

Liberal Arts vs. Business Courses

The second major field of inquiry in the study was what basic curriculum should be used in meeting the needs of small business. The question here concerns the balance that should exist between the so-called liberal-arts studies and the practical studies. (For the purpose of the inquiry, "practical studies" were defined broadly as the subjects offered in the college business school. All other subjects were classified as "liberal".)

The majority of business teachers and businessmen probably favour some balance between the liberal-arts and the practical extremes. It is in determining just what this balance should be that opinions differ most sharply.

In contrast to the recorded opinions of leaders of the larger firms in the U.S., leaders in the small businesses participating in this study favoured a very practical type of business education. Almost half (48 per cent) of the 161 executives favoured a curriculum that is "mostly practical, some liberal". A second large group (28 per cent) favoured about half liberal-arts and half practical studies, and about 8 per cent thought the business curriculum should be "entirely practical".

In other words, 84 per cent of those interviewed felt that at least half of the curriculum should be made up of practical courses. Only 16 per cent favoured a larger proportion of liberal-arts than practical studies.

Moreover, of the businessmen interviewed who held degrees in business, 91 per cent felt that their education was adequate for careers in small-business management. All in this group who felt that their education had not been adequate said that their training should have been more practical.

Only 31 per cent of the holders of liberal-arts degrees and 56 per cent of the holders of other non-business degrees thought their education had given them adequate preparation for careers in business. Most (83 per cent) of the executives who did not have degrees of any kind felt that their education was inadequate.

The Value of Specific Courses

A final major area of inquiry in the study was the analysis of individual parts of the overall framework of business education. This area involved the businessmen's opinions of the contribution of specific courses to a career in small-business management.

Business Courses Many of the courses traditionally offered in business schools were looked upon favourably by a substantial majority of the executives interviewed. The following table shows a number of these course and the percentage of the businessmen rating them as essential or desirable.

Course	Per cent	Course	Per cent
Accounting (basic)	98.1	Office management	73.6
Business letter writing	95.6	Business report writing	71.7
Economics (basic)	93.8	Statistics	69.2
Business law	89.9	Retailing	67.9
Management (personnel)	89.3	Accounting (advanced)	63.5
Salesmanship	88.7	Insurance	62.3
Credit management	86.2	Wholesaling	61.6
Advertising	83.6	Investments	58.5
Corporation finance	80.5	Marketing research	54.1
Sales Management	79.9	Economics (advanced)	51.6
Money and banking	79.2	Labour (collective bargaining)	50.9
Marketing (basic)	78.6	Management (industrial)	39.6
Small-business management	78.6	Real estate	36.5

Liberal-Arts Courses

The practical nature of most of the courses listed above reveals further the tendency of small-business executives to prefer a practical business curriculum. At the same time, however, the interviewees recognised some basic courses that are taught outside the business school as essential in the business curriculum.

Eleven basic course areas that would fall within the classification of liberal-arts courses (as defined in this study) were designated by a majority of the executives as essential or desirable. The percentages of the executives so classifying them are shown in the following table:

Course	Per cent	Course	Per cent
Speech	88.8	Science	64.0
English composition	82.6	English literature	61.5
Psychology	82.0	Mathematics	60.2
Government	72.0	Sociology	59.6
Foreign language	65.2	Philosophy	58.4
History	64.0		

It is apparent that small-business executives acknowledge the need for including some liberal-arts courses in the business curriculum. Even here, however, courses with immediate practical application have a higher rating than courses that tend towards the cultural. For example, speech and English composition were rated as essential or desirable by a considerably higher percentage of the respondents than English literature.

CHAPTER 12

Marketing Management

The purpose of this chapter is to assess the need for activities aimed at improving the standard of marketing management, by examining the current level of management practice in that field. The original intention was to divide the marketing area into the activities of collection of marketing information, product planning and development, selection and management of channels of distribution, pricing, sales promotion, management of marketing forces, packaging and physical distribution and, then, to study each of them so as to pinpoint needs more closely. A wide variety of factors affect the degree to which firms engage in these activities, and the likely degree of advancement of their practices. For instance, the marketing pressure on a company manufacturing high-volume perishable goods on specialised and costly capital equipment is very different in degree and in kind to that on a firm manufacturing a low volume of products for a restricted industrial market. On the question of product planning and development, many companies in Ireland are simply manufacturing agents for products developed by parent companies abroad. For each activity, it had been intended to ask questions which would allow for the circumstances affecting the pattern and complexity of marketing practice. It was thought that the answers to these questions would provide the basis for a classification of firms in which it would be possible to recognise companies with broadly similar marketing activities and problems, to assign them to their relevant categories, and to make estimates of the numbers in each category in the population. Such a classification would be useful from the viewpoint of planning training activities, as it would give a good idea of the type and number of firms to which particular courses would apply. It had been hoped to do the same also for each of the other functional areas.

The length and complexity of the resulting questionnaires meant that they could not have been administered or analysed with the resources available. To reduce the questionnaires to manageable size it was decided to select a half-dozen or so questions in each area, which would give an indication of the general level of advancement of management practice in that function. As it was no longer possible to consider in any depth the circumstances of the individual firm, the questions selected had to be so basic as to apply on the widest scale.

In general it was decided to select questions relating to routines of measurement and information for decision-making. This led to asking firms what information they had about their sales, about their potential markets and about the future; what means they had used to collect this information and to what extent they planned their marketing operations. In addition a question was asked on sales training: it was felt that routines of information would be likely to exist either in all areas or in none, and in order to be able to discriminate between the level of advancement in different areas it was decided to ask a question not relating to such routines. The questions asked about marketing can be found in the questionnaire reproduced in technical appendix C (Q.45-59).

To provide a framework against which the replies to the questions can be judged the following tables are shown.

TABLE 12.0.1.   *Percentage of Firms Serving Each Type of Market, by Size of Firm.*

Size of Firm (No. of Employees)	Consumer Market	Industrial Market	Other Type
500 or More	59.6	36.2	4.3
100-499	64.6	33.3	2.1
20-99	67.4	32.6	—

TABLE 12.0.2.   *Percentage of Firms Serving Each Breadth and Type of Market, by Size of Firm.*

Size of Firm (No. of Employees)	Type of Market	Parent Company	Local	Regional	National	Export	Total
				Breadth of Market			
500 or More	CONSUMER		—	4.3	6.4	48.9	59.6
	INDUSTRIAL	2.1	—	—	2.1	31.1	36.2
	OTHER	4.3	—	—	—	—	4.3
	OVERALL	6.4	—	4.3	8.5	80.9	100.0
100-499	CONSUMER	—	4.2	4.2	14.6	41.7	64.6
	INDUSTRIAL	—	4.2	4.2	8.3	16.6	33.3
	OTHER	2.1	—	—	—	—	2.1
	OVERALL	2.1	8.3	8.3	22.9	58.3	100.0
20-99	CONSUMER	2.2	10.9	6.5	26.1	21.7	67.4
	INDUSTRIAL	2.2	4.3	2.2	8.7	15.3	32.6
	OTHER	—	—	—	—	—	—
	OVERALL	4.3	15.2	8.7	34.8	37.0	100.0

TABLE 12.0.3.   *Methods Used by Firms to Place Production Orders, by Size of Firm.*

Size of Firm (No. of Employees)	Number of Replies	Orders in Hand (No.)	Stocks Replacement (No.)	Sales Estimate (No.)	Other Methods (No.)	Combination of Methods (No.)
				Production Against		
500 or More	47	10	3	12	4	18
100-499	46	13	5	13	8	7
20-99	45	20	5	5	6	9

Most firms serve a consumer-market and most of them, even the smallest, sell on a national scale or even export. Anything from two-thirds to three-quarters of the firms in each size-group engage in processing rather than in fabrication. A high percentage of firms in the 20 to 99 employee group make against orders in hand. This does not mean that they design products specially to order: in most cases firms have standard designs and make up a batch whenever they have accumulated sufficient orders to make what they consider an economic run. Many small firms in Dublin are in the clothing industry. They show their range of designs at the beginning of the fashion year, book their orders and make against orders in hand.

The appropriateness and possibility of a system of marketing management based on looking forward, on collection of information from inside and outside the firm, and on detailed planning of sales, was not obvious to many such small firms. Many had rudimentary costing systems, while others stated that official statistics did not contain the information they wanted in sufficient detail and that they could not afford market research surveys.

Nevertheless, the questions selected and the answers given serve to indicate adequately the level of marketing management in the country.

Although it was thought that the questions asked related to activities which should be carried on by every type of firm, it was decided to see to what extent the sort of market served was associated with these activities. As most firms served a national market it was impossible to discriminate on the basis of breadth of market. It was decided, therefore, that consideration of the effect of market type would be confined to making contrasts between firms serving consumer markets and those selling to industry.

It was also decided to see whether use of any of the means of improving the standard of management practice was associated with the use of marketing techniques. The principal means of raising the standard are: use of training courses, employment of qualified staff and use of management consultants. Firms whose top marketing executive had ever attended a management training course were contrasted with firms whose executive had not; those whose executive had a university degree or professional qualification were contrasted with those whose executive had not; those which had used consultants were contrasted with those which had not and, finally, those which had ever participated in Irish Management Institute courses were contrasted with those which had not.

The last two contrasts were not really satisfactory, because firms rarely used consultants specifically for marketing assignments, and firms sending participants to Irish Management Institute courses had not necessarily sent them to marketing courses. The contrasts were made because it was thought that such firms might be expected to be more advanced in general than others. Not all those marketing executives with management training had attended courses at the Irish Management Institute. This explains why training and participation in Irish Management Institute courses were considered separately. Six firms were excluded from the analysis of marketing practice because they did not engage in any marketing activities. These firms were either manufacturing or repair establishments whose output was specified for them by a parent company and bought exclusively by that parent.

Summary of Findings.

As measured by the replies to the questions asked, the standard of marketing management is low. The percentage of firms with high scores is small, except in the group with 500 employees or more. The figures are not unexpected in the case of small firms, but companies in the 100 to 499 employee range score surprisingly poorly.

Apart from size the one factor examined which is associated consistently with higher scores is the attendance by the marketing executive at courses of training in management. Firms whose marketing executive had attended courses scored higher than those whose executive had not participated in training activities.

Section 1: Sales Analysis

The most basic marketing information a firm can have is an analysis of its total sales figures. Firms were therefore asked (question 47 of questionnaire) what routine breakdowns of their sales figures were made.

TABLE 12. 1. 1.   *Estimated Percentage of Firms Getting a Breakdown of their Total Sales Figures, by Size of Firm.*

Size of Firm (No. of Employees)	Total Firms Included	Percentage Getting Some Breakdown	Percentage Getting No Breakdown
500 or More	43	100.00	—
100–499	47	87.2 (74.3—95.2)	12.8
20–99	44	77.3 ±12.3	22.7
OVERALL		80.2 ± 9.5	19.8

TABLE 12. 1. 2.   *Estimated Percentage of Firms Getting Sales Breakdown by Various Factors, by Size of Firm.*

Size of Firm (No. of Employees)	Total Firms Included	Percentage Getting a Breakdown by				
		Product-Line	Salesman	Region	Type of Outlet	Some Other Factor
500 or More	43	97.7	60.5	65.1	32.6	16.3
100-499	47	78.7±5.4	61.7±12.8	40.4±12.9	17.0(7.7—30.8)	12.8(4.8—25.7)
20-99	44	68.2±6.8	36.4±14.1	15.9(6.7—30)	6.8(1.4—18.7)	13.6(5.1—27.4)
OVERALL		71.5±10.6	42.5±11.0	22.8±8.6	9.9±6.0	13.6±7.8

TABLE 12. 1. 3.   *Number of Factors by Which Firms Get a Breakdown of their Sales Figures, by Size of Firm.*

Size of Firm (No. of Employees)	Total Firms Included	Percentage With No Breakdown	Percentage Getting Breakdown by				
			1 Factor	2 Factors	3 Factors	4 Factors	5 Factors
500 or More	43	—	7.0	34.9	37.2	20.9	—
100-499	47	12.8	19.1	17.0	46.8	4.3	—
20-99	44	22.7	29.5	34.1	11.4	2.3	—
OVERALL		19.8	26.6	30.6	19.6	3.4	—

Table 12.1.1 shows that, irrespective of size, firms invariably get some breakdown of their total sales. The factors by which firms made their analysis are shown in table 12.1.2.

By far the most usual factor is product line. The figures for analysis by individual salesmen may appear low. However, many firms, especially in the medium-sized and smaller range, employ not more than one salesman. In their case the question of analysis by this factor does not arise. Analysis by type of outlet is rare.

Table 12.1.3. shows the number of factors by which firms analyse their total sales. Most companies of any size maintain a quite comprehensive set of figures.

Section 2: Analysis of Sales Costs

Another basic piece of information available from internal records and essential to market planning is the contribution made to profit or to overhead by various products, regions, types of outlet and so on.   The question was therefore put to firms whether they got figures regularly to show the margin earned over cost by different product-lines, salesmen or other factors. The replies to this question are shown in table 12.2.1.

CONCLUSION: *Small firms rarely have figures to show where the contributions are made to profit or overhead: even for firms with 100 to 499 employees the proportion is not high. Firms based in Dublin seem to be likely to obtain analyses at an earlier stage than firms outside Dublin. There are good grounds for thinking that the employment by a firm of a marketing executive who attended a management training course is associated with a greater likelihood that the firm will have a sales-cost analysis. There is insufficient evidence to say that there is an association of any practical importance with any of the other factors considered.*

TABLE 12. 2. 1.   *Estimated Percentage of Firms Analysing their Sales Costs, by Size of Firm.*

Size of Firm (No. of Employees)	Total Firms Included	Percentage Analysing Sales Costs	Percentage Not Analysing Sales Costs
500 or More	42	81.0	19.0
100–499	47	42.6 ± 13.0	57.4
20–99	44	13.6 (5.1—27.4)	86.4
OVERALL		22.1 ± 8.1	77.9

Because of the fact that firms were asked if breakdowns were received by any factor, and not simply by product-line or even by salesmen, it would not be valid to say that the very low percentages observed are caused by firms having only one product or one salesman. Even allowing for this possibility the percentages remain low.

This question was chosen for further investigation.   Associations are considered between sales-cost analysis and size, location, a variety of factors associated with the improvement of management and, finally, the type of market served by the company.

TABLE 12. 2. 2.   *Percentage of Firms Analysing their Sales Costs, by Size and Location of Firm.*

Size of Firm (No. of Employees)	Location of Head Office	Total Firms Included	Percentage Analysing Sales Costs	Percentage Not Analysing Sales Costs
500 or More	DUBLIN	25	84.00	16.00
	REST OF COUNTRY	15	80.00	20.00
	OVERALL	40	82.50	17.50
100-499	DUBLIN	21	61.91	38.10
	REST OF COUNTRY	22	22.73	77.28
	OVERALL	43	41.87	58.14
29-99	DUBLIN	20	5.00	95.00
	REST OF COUNTRY	21	23.81	76.20
	OVERALL	41	14.63	85.37

Table 12.2.2 shows the percentages of firms, in different locations and size-groups, which analyse sales costs. In the largest size-stratum firms based in Dublin are no more likely to analyse their costs than firms outside Dublin. In the middle group Dublin-based firms are significantly more likely to obtain an analysis, while in the smallest size-group the difference is not significant. There is no association between location and any other factor which would explain the difference in the middle group: cross-classifications showed that Dublin firms were not more likely to be consumer-goods firms or to employ more highly qualified marketing managers or to use consultants or management training courses.

There are very highly significant differences between the size-groups both in Dublin and outside. On closer investigation it was found that, in Dublin, the significance arises only from differences between the bottom group and the other two: there is no evidence of significant differences between the middle and top groups. In the case of non-Dublin firms the significant differences arise only between the top and the other two groups: there is no evidence of significant difference between the middle and bottom groups. This would suggest that change comes at an earlier stage in Dublin than in the provinces, Dublin firms becoming more likely to have sales-cost analyses as they go over the 100-employee mark, while non-Dublin firms do not appear to change very much until they employ more than 500.

The next factor considered is whether there is an association between a firm's employing a marketing executive who attended management training courses and its likelihood of having sales-cost analysis.

So few firms with less than 100 employees had a marketing manager that it was not possible to compare trained with untrained in that group. It is therefore omitted from the table. Replies are classified on the basis of whether a firm employed no marketing executive, a marketing executive with no management training, or an executive with training. Because of the small numbers involved it was not possible to test all three,

TABLE 12. 2. 3. *Percentage of Firms Analysing their Sales Costs, by Size of Firm and Training of their Marketing Executive.*

Size of Firm (No. of Employees)	Training of Responsible Exec.	Total Firms Included	Percentage Analysing Sales Costs	Percentage Not Analysing Sales Costs
500 or More	TRAINED	27	92.59	7.41
	UNTRAINED	9	55.56	44.44
	NO EXECUTIVE	4	75.00	25.00
	OVERALL	40	82.50	17.50
100-499	TRAINED	7	85.71	14.29
	UNTRAINED	17	41.18	58.82
	NO EXECUTIVE	19	26.32	73.68
	OVERALL	43	41.87	58.14

and comparisons were therefore made only between firms employing trained and untrained executives. There are wide differences between the firms: training appearing to be associated positively with a higher likelihood of analysis of costs. However, in the 100 to 499 size-group the difference is just short of a significant level (that in the top size-group is, of course, significant by definition). Considering the small number of firms involved there may be a case for the presumption that an association does exist. No tests could be carried out to measure the effect of size in this context, but inspection of the table shows that the biggest difference between the size-groups is for firms which do not employ any marketing executive. Thus it is the high proportion of firms in the 100 to 499 group not employing a marketing executive which is responsible for the poor score of the group.

The effect which the employment by a firm of a qualified as distinct from an unqualified marketing manager might have is now examined. ("Qualified" has its usual meaning of someone who has either any university degree or any professional qualification, not necessarily in marketing).

TABLE 12. 2. 4. *Percentage of Firms Analysing their Sales Costs, by Size of Firm, and Qualification of their Marketing Executive.*

Size of Firm (No. of Employees)	Qualification of Responsible Exec.	Total Firms Included	Percentage Analysing Sales Costs	Percentage Not Analysing Sales Costs
500 or More	QUALIFIED	12	100.00	—
	UNQUALIFIED	24	75.00	25.00
	NO EXECUTIVE	4	75.00	25.00
	OVERALL	40	82.50	17.50
100-499	QUALIFIED	6	50.00	50.00
	UNQUALIFIED	18	55.56	44.44
	NO EXECUTIVE	19	26.32	73.68
	OVERALL	43	41.87	58.14

In this case also, the bottom size-stratum is omitted because there were not sufficient qualified marketing managers either to carry out any test or to quote meaningful percentages. It is obvious from looking at the table that there is little difference between firms employing qualified and unqualified men.

It seemed possible that the use of business consultants would be associated with a higher general level of technique.

TABLE 12.2.5. *Percentage of Firms Analysing their Sales Costs, by Size of Firm, and Use of Consultants.*

Size of Firm (No. of Employees)	Use of Consultants	Total Firms Included	Percentage Analysing Sales Costs	Percentage Not Analysing Sales Costs
500 or More	USED	31	87.10	12.90
	DID NOT USE	9	66.67	33.33
	OVERALL	40	82.50	17.50
100-499	USED	17	41.18	58.82
	DID NOT USE	26	42.31	57.69
	OVERALL	43	41.87	58.14
20-99	USED	7	14.29	85.71
	DID NOT USE	34	14.71	85.29
	OVERALL	41	14.63	85.37

However, so far as sales-cost analysis goes, this does not appear to be the position except in the top stratum, because consultants are used by smaller firms more for production and financial than for marketing techniques. It was not possible to look at the effect of size in the context of use of consultants because of the small number not using them in the top size-group, and the small number using them in the bottom group.

The possibility of an association between sales-cost analysis and use by the firm of Irish Management Institute courses is considered next. It was not possible to specify the content of the courses, i.e. to look for an association between sales-cost breakdown and attendance at courses specifically on marketing techniques.

While there does seem to be a persistent tendency in each of the strata for firms using courses to be more likely than others to obtain sales-cost analyses, the observed differences are not statistically significant, and it cannot therefore be said that there is conclusive evidence that an association exists. In fact, it would be very difficult to establish significance in this case because of the very low number of firms using courses in the smallest size-group. The fact that so few firms in the top size-group have not used courses means that the difference there is not of practical importance since attendance at courses, even if followed directly by improvement in practice, could influence only two firms to analyse their costs.

Finally, the possibility of association between type of market and breakdown of costs is considered.

TABLE 12. 2. 6. *Percentage of Firms Analysing their Sales Costs, by Size of Firm and Use of Irish Management Institute Courses.*

Size of Firm (No. of Employees)	Use by Firm of I.M.I. Courses	Total Firms Included	Percentage Analysing Sales Costs	Percentage Not Analysing Sales Costs
500 or More	USED	36	86.11	13.89
	DID NOT USE	4	50.00	50.00
	OVERALL	40	82.50	17.50
100-499	USED	10	60.00	40.00
	DID NOT USE	33	36.36	63.64
	OVERALL	43	41.87	58.14
20-99	USED	6	33.33	66.67
	DID NOT USE	35	11.43	88.57
	OVERALL	41	14.63	85.37

TABLE 12. 2. 7. *Percentage of Firms Analysing their Sales Costs, by Size of Firm and Type of Market Served.*

Size of Firm (No. of Employees)	Type of Market	Total Firms Included	Percentage Analysing Sales Costs	Percentage Not Analysing Sales Costs
500 or More	CONSUMER	25	88.00	12.00
	INDUSTRIAL	15	73.34	26.67
	OVERALL	40	82.50	17.50
100-499	CONSUMER	29	48.28	51.73
	INDUSTRIAL	14	28.58	71.43
	OVERALL	43	41.87	58.14
20-99	CONSUMER	28	10.72	89.29
	INDUSTRIAL	13	23.08	76.93
	OVERALL	41	14.63	85.37

In none of the strata is there a significant difference between firms serving consumer markets and those firms serving industrial markets. It is interesting that in the bottom stratum industrial-goods firms seem somewhat more likely than consumer-goods firms to analyse their costs in this way, even though the difference is not significant. It was mentioned in chapter 2 that industrial-goods firms tended to be more likely than consumer-goods firms in this size-group to formalise the responsibilities of their executives. It will be interesting to see if this tendency towards a more highly organised approach persists. There would be good reason, *a priori*, to expect this to be so, as small firms serving industrial markets seem to be faced with greater technical complexity than consumer-goods firms.

In the context of type of market served, there are significant differences between the size-groups in the case of both consumer and industrial-goods firms. However, whereas consumer-goods companies show differences between each group, there is little difference between small and medium-sized industrial-goods firms.

Section 3: Formal Market Studies

The next question asked was whether a formal study had ever been made to discover the total size of the firm's market. It was made clear that what was in mind was not necessarily a field survey, but simply whether any systematic attempt had been made, using any source whatever, to assess total market size. Firms were later asked what means had been used to carry out this exercise and their replies are analysed in section 6.

CONCLUSION: Apart from firms with over 500 employees, few companies had ever made a formal study of their market. Firms employing a marketing executive who has management training are more likely to have studied their market than firms whose executive has not attended training courses. Firms with over 100 employees and serving a consumer market are more likely than those of the same size serving an industrial market to have carried out formal studies. There is not sufficient evidence to say that there is an association with any other factor.

TABLE 12. 3. 1.   *Estimated Percentage of Firms Making a Formal Investigation of Their Market, by Size of Firm.*

Size of Firm (No. of Employees)	Total Firms Included	Percentage Making A Formal Market Study	Percentage Not Making A Formal Market Study
500 or More	44	79.5	20.5
100–499	47	31.9 ± 12.3	68.1
20–99	44	15.9 (6.7—30.0)	84.1
OVERALL		21.6 ± 8.5	78.4

Some firms felt that there was no need to make such investigations, sometimes because their share of the total was so small that they considered any action on their part would have only a marginal effect, and that consequently there was no need for them to concern themselves too much with overall market size. Others felt that such a study was unnecessary because their market consisted of a small number of buyers whose requirements they knew from long experience.

An unexpected feature of table 12.3.1 is the low percentage of firms employing over 100 people which have made formal market studies.

Because of the importance to the marketing function of such a study, it was decided in this case also to explore any possible associations.

TABLE 12. 3. 2. *Percentage of Firms Making a Formal Market Study, by Size and Location of Firm.*

Size of Firm (No. of Employees)	Location of Head Office	Total Firms Included	Percentage Making A Formal Market Study	Percentage Not Making A Formal Market Study
500 or More	DUBLIN	26	84.62	15.39
	REST OF COUNTRY	16	81.25	18.75
	OVERALL	42	83.33	16.67
100-499	DUBLIN	21	38.10	61.91
	REST OF COUNTRY	22	27.28	72.73
	OVERALL	43	32.56	67.44
20-99	DUBLIN	20	15.00	85.00
	REST OF COUNTRY	21	19.05	80.96
	OVERALL	41	17.07	82.93

Table 12.3.2 shows virtually no difference between locations, but wide differences between the size-groups. A test confirmed this and showed also that there were significant differences only between the top size-group and the other two, i.e., there is insufficient evidence to show that any difference exists between the middle and lowest size-groups. Thus, it is only when a firm reaches 500 or more employees that it becomes likely to carry out formal studies of its market.

The training and qualification of the marketing executive are next examined.

TABLE 12. 3. 3. *Percentage of Firms Making a Formal Market Study, by Size of Firm and Training of Marketing Executive.*

Size of Firm (No. of Employees)	Training of Responsible Exec.	Total Firms Included	Percentage Making A Formal Market Study	Percentage Not Making A Formal Market Study
500 or More	TRAINED	28	96.43	3.57
	UNTRAINED	9	66.67	33.33
	NO EXECUTIVE	5	40.00	60.00
	OVERALL	42	83.33	16.67
100-499	TRAINED	7	71.43	28.57
	UNTRAINED	17	35.29	64.71
	NO EXECUTIVE	19	15.80	84.20
	OVERALL	43	32.56	67.44

Large firms employing a marketing manager with management training are more likely to have studied their market than are other firms. The same appears true of firms with 100 to 499 employees but here the difference is not significant, though very marked.

TABLE 12. 3. 4.   *Percentage of Firms Making a Formal Market Study, by Size of Firm and Qualification of Marketing Executive.*

Size of Firm (No. of Employees)	Qualification of Responsible Exec.	Total Firms Included	Percentage Making A Formal Study	Percentage Not Making A Formal Study
500 or More	QUALIFIED	12	100.00	—
	UNQUALIFIED	25	84.00	16.00
	NO EXECUTIVE	5	40.00	60.00
	OVERALL	42	83.33	16.67
100-499	QUALIFIED	6	50.00	50.00
	UNQUALIFIED	18	44.44	55.56
	NO EXECUTIVE	19	15.80	84.20
	OVERALL	43	32.56	67.44

TABLE 12. 3. 5.   *Percentage of Firms Making a Formal Market Study, by Size of Firm and Use of Consultants.*

Size of Firm (No. of Employees)	Use of Consultants	Total Firms Included	Percentage Making A Formal Study	Percentage Not Making A Formal Study
500 or More	USED	32	84.37	15.63
	DID NOT USE	10	80.00	20.00
	OVERALL	42	83.33	16.67
100–499	USED	17	35.29	64.71
	DID NOT USE	26	30.77	69.23
	OVERALL	43	32.56	67.44
20–99	USED	7	28.57	71.43
	DID NOT USE	34	14.71	85.29
	OVERALL	41	17.07	82.93

Again the small number of executives with training makes significance hard to establish. Qualification appears to be a good deal less strongly associated with market studies than training, and the differences between qualified and unqualified could easily have arisen by chance.

Table 12.3.5 shows that there is very little difference in this respect between firms using and not using consultants. There appear to be somewhat wider differences in the two smaller size strata between firms using and not using Irish Management Institute courses, but in neither case are the observed differences significant. There is therefore no conclusive evidence that use of consultants or attendance at courses affected the position.

The last attribute considered is the type of market served by the firm.

TABLE 12. 3. 6.   *Percentage of Firms Making a Formal Market Study, by Size of Firm and Use of Irish Management Institute Courses.*

Size of Firm (No. of Employees)	Use By Firm Of I.M.I. Courses	Total Firms Included	Percentage Making A Formal Study	Percentage Not Making A Formal Study
500 or More	USED	37	83.78	16.22
	DID NOT USE	5	80.00	20.00
	OVERALL	42	83.33	16.67
100-499	USED	10	50.00	50.00
	DID NOT USE	33	27.27	72.73
	OVERALL	43	32.56	67.44
20-99	USED	6	33.33	66.67
	DID NOT USE	35	14.29	85.41
	OVERALL	41	17.07	82.93

TABLE 12. 3. 7.   *Percentage of Firms Making a Formal Market Study, by Size of Firm and Type of Market.*

Size of Firm (No. of Employees)	Type of Market	Total Firms Included	Percentage Making A Formal Study	Percentage Not Making A Formal Study
500 or More	CONSUMER	27	96.30	3.70
	INDUSTRIAL	15	60.00	40.00
	OVERALL	42	83.33	16.67
100-499	CONSUMER	29	41.38	58.63
	INDUSTRIAL	14	14.29	85.71
	OVERALL	43	32.56	67.44
20-99	CONSUMER	28	14.29	85.72
	INDUSTRIAL	13	23.08	76.92
	OVERALL	41	17.07	82.93

It appears from table 12.3.7 that, in the top two strata, consumer-goods firms are more likely than firms selling to industry to study their market. The difference is not quite significant in the case of the middle size-group. In the lowest size-group the position appears to be reversed but again the difference is not significant.

Section 4: Study of Market Characteristics

On the subject of market investigation firms were further asked whether they had ever attempted to study different market segments (question 51) or whether they had ever attempted to study other characteristics of their market—for instance, its economic or social class-structure, age-structure, motivation and so on. The results are shown in the following tables.

TABLE 12. 4. 1.   *Estimated Percentage of Firms Carrying Out a Formal Study of Market-Segmentation, by Size of Firm.*

Size of Firm (No. of Employees)	Total Firms Included	Percentage Segmenting Market	Percentage Not Segmenting Market
500 or More	44	47.7	52.3
100-499	47	14.9(6.2—28.3)	85.1
20-99	44	4.5(0.5—15.5)	95.5
OVERALL		7.9±4.9	92.1

TABLE 12. 4. 2.   *Estimated Percentage of Firms Investigating any Further Aspects of Their Market, by Size of Firm.*

Size of Firm (No. of Employees)	Total Firms Included	Percentage Studying Further Aspects	Percentage Not Studying Further Aspects
500 or More	44	34.1	65.9
100-499	47	2.1(0—11.3)	97.9
20-99	44	—	100.00
OVERALL		1.7±0.8	98.3

The tables show that, so far as a study in depth is concerned, firms are not active. Detailed studies of market characteristics are almost non-existent in firms of less than 500 employees, and even in firms with over 500 employees the percentage carrying out such studies is not large.

TABLE 12. 5. 1.   *Estimated Use of Various Study Methods, by Firms Which Studied Their Market Formally, by Size of Firm.*

Size of Firm (No. of Employees)	Total Firms Included	Percentage Using Desk Research Only	Percentage Using Field Surveys Only	Percentage Using Both
500 or More	35	34.3	14.3	51.4
100-499	15	60.0	13.3	26.7
20-99	7	100.0	—	—
OVERALL		89.3	3.3	7.4

Section 5: Methods of Market Research

The firms which stated that they had made formal studies of their market were then asked what methods they had used to do so (question 54 of questionnaire) and the results are analysed in table 12.5.1.

From this table it can be seen that the activities of small and medium-sized companies are mostly confined to desk research. It seems that only about a quarter of the firms conducting market investigations in the middle size-group and only about half of those in the top group can be said to maintain a comprehensive on-going research activity, with their own internal studies being supplemented where necessary by field surveys.

Section 6: Use of Field Surveys

Firms were asked whether they had used market research surveys for any purpose, as distinct from their use to assess total market or other market characteristics. An example of such use would be the investigation of channels of distribution. Table 12.6.1 shows the results.

TABLE 12. 6. 1.   *Estimated Percentage of Firms Ever Using Market Research Surveys for Any Purpose, by Size of Firm.*

Size of Firm (No. of Employees)	Total Firms Included	Percentage Ever Using Surveys	Percentage Never Using Surveys
500 or More	44	59.0	41.0
100-499	47	19.1(9.1—33.3)	80.9
20-99	44	—	100.00
OVERALL		6.2 ± 2.1	93.8

Only about one firm in sixteen had ever used a field survey, with the proportions going from virtually none in the bottom stratum to about one-fifth in the middle stratum and about three-fifths in the top group. This question was also selected for further study.

CONCLUSION: The only firms using market research surveys to any extent were those with over 500 employees. There are grounds for thinking that firms with 100 or more employees whose marketing executive attended courses are more likely to have carried out surveys than firms whose executive is not trained. Firms which used consultants are more likely to have conducted surveys than firms which did not. In companies with 500 or more employees firms serving a consumer market are more likely to have conducted surveys than firms serving an industrial market, and firms whose executive is qualified are more likely to have done so than are those with an unqualified executive.

Location, as table 12.6.2 shows, does not appear to be very strongly associated with use of surveys. (The 20 to 99 employee size-group is omitted from all the tests in this section because none of the firms in it had used surveys).

TABLE 12. 6. 2.   *Percentage of Firms Using Market Research Surveys, by Size and Location of Firm.*

Size of Firm (No. of Employees)	Location of Head Office	Total Firms Included	Percentage Ever Using Surveys	Percentage Never Using Surveys
500 or More	DUBLIN	26	69.23	30.77
	REST OF COUNTRY	16	50.00	50.00
	OVERALL	42	61.91	38.10
100-499	DUBLIN	21	14.29	85.72
	REST OF COUNTRY	22	22.73	77.27
	OVERALL	43	18.61	81.40

TABLE 12. 6. 3.   *Percentage of Firms Using Market Research Surveys, by Size of Firm and Training of Marketing Executive.*

Size of Firm (No. of Employees)	Training of Responsible Exec.	Total Firms Included	Percentage Ever Using Surveys	Percentage Never Using Surveys
500 or More	TRAINED	28	71.43	28.57
	UNTRAINED	9	55.55	44.45
	NO EXECUTIVE	5	20.00	80.00
	OVERALL	42	61.91	38.10
100-499	TRAINED	7	57.14	42.86
	UNTRAINED	17	17.65	82.35
	NO EXECUTIVE	19	5.26	94.74
	OVERALL	43	18.61	81.40

TABLE 12. 6. 4.   *Percentage of Firms Ever Using Market Research Surveys, by Size of Firm and Qualification of Marketing Executive.*

Size of Firm (No. of Employees)	Qualification of Responsible Exec.	Total Firms Included	Percentage Ever Using Surveys	Percentage Never Using Surveys
500 or More	QUALIFIED	12	83.33	16.67
	UNQUALIFIED	25	60.00	40.00
	NO EXECUTIVE	5	20.00	80.00
	OVERALL	42	61.91	38.10
100-499	QUALIFIED	6	16.67	83.33
	UNQUALIFIED	18	33.33	66.67
	NO EXECUTIVE	19	5.26	94.74
	OVERALL	43	18.61	81.40

Testing confirms this suggestion. There is a highly significant association between size and use of surveys, with larger firms being a great deal more likely than either medium or small-sized firms to have had field investigations carried out. There is no significant difference between medium and small firms.

Large firms with a trained marketing executive are more likely to have carried out surveys than are other large companies. This may also be true of firms in the 100 to 499 group: the difference is not established as significant, but approaches close enough to it to cause suspension of judgement rather than rejection of the possibility of an association. Qualification, as table 12.6.4 shows, does not appear to be associated, except in the top group, with a higher likelihood of carrying out surveys.

Use of consultants and of Irish Management Institute courses are now considered as factors possibly associated with the conduct of field surveys.

TABLE 12. 6. 5.   *Percentage of Firms Using Market Research Surveys, by Size of Firm and Use of Consultants.*

Size of Firm (No. of Employees)	Use of Consultants	Total Firms Included	Percentage Ever Using Surveys	Percentage Never Using Surveys
500 or More	USED	32	65.62	34.38
	DID NOT USE	10	50.00	50.00
	OVERALL	42	61.91	38.10
100-499	USED	17	35.29	64.71
	DID NOT USE	26	7.69	92.31
	OVERALL	43	18.61	81.40

TABLE 12. 6. 6.   *Percentage of Firms Using Market Research Surveys, by Size of Firm and Use of Irish Management Institute Courses.*

Size of Firm (No. of Employees)	Use By Firm Of I.M.I. Courses	Total Firms Included	Percentage Ever Using Surveys	Percentage Never Using Surveys
500 or More	USED	37	62.16	37.84
	DID NOT USE	5	60.00	40.00
	OVERALL	42	61.91	38.10
100-499	USED	10	30.00	70.00
	DID NOT USE	33	15.15	84.85
	OVERALL	43	18.61	81.40

So far as use of consultants goes, there is little difference between firms in the top stratum, but a marked difference in the middle size-group, firms using consultants being much more likely to have carried out surveys than firms not using consultants. A statistical test did not quite reach significance in this case, but approached extremely close to it. This would, as usual, make us slow to reject the possibility that an association does exist. So far as use of courses goes, table 12.6.6 shows only quite small differences between firms attending and not attending, and the observed differences are not at all significant statistically.

The final association considered is that between type of market served and use of surveys. It seems from table 12.6.7 that in the largest size-group consumer-goods firms are a great deal more likely than others to have carried out surveys. In the 100 to 499 employee stratum there is little difference.

TABLE 12. 6. 7. *Percentage of Firms Using Market Research Surveys, by Size of Firm and Type of Market Served.*

Size of Firm (No. of Employees)	Type of Market	Total Firms Included	Percentage Ever Using Surveys	Percentage Never Using Surveys
500 or More	CONSUMER	27	77.78	22.23
	INDUSTRIAL	15	33.34	66.67
	OVERALL	42	61.91	38.10
100-499	CONSUMER	29	20.69	79.32
	INDUSTRIAL	14	14.29	85.71
	OVERALL	43	18.61	81.40

Section 7: Long-Range Plans

The next question asked (question 56a) was whether firms had made forecasts of their total market and market share for more than one year ahead. The replies are shown in table 12.7.1.

CONCLUSION: *Few firms have forecast the development of their market for more than one year ahead. The methods used are unsophisticated. Large firms are more likely to forecast than medium-sized companies, which are in turn more likely to forecast than small firms. There is some evidence that employment of an executive with training is associated with greater likelihood of making forecasts. Large firms whose executive is qualified are more likely to forecast than those whose executive is not qualified.*

Only about one firm in eight had made market forecasts, the proportion going from about one in fourteen of the smallest size-group to approximately one in four in the middle group, to about three in five in the top stratum. Because it was considered a very good index of marketing consciousness, and of management consciousness in general in the firm, this question was also selected for more extended study. Before going on to look at the various associations to be considered, table 12.7.2 shows the methods used by the companies which stated that they engaged in some sort of forward market-estimation.

The methods used are fairly unsophisticated: only six firms claimed to have used modern techniques of mathematics and statistics, the rest building up their estimates

TABLE 12. 7. 1.   *Estimated Percentage of Firms Making Long-Range Market Forecasts, by Size of Firm.*

Size of Firm (No. of Employees)	Total Firms Included	Percentage Making Forecasts	Percentage Not Making Forecasts
500 or More	44	61.4	38.6
100-499	47	23.4±11.1	74.6
20-99	44	6.8(1.4—18.7)	93.2
OVERALL		12.3±6.1	87.7

TABLE 12. 7. 2.   *Methods Used by Firms to Make Long-Range Market Forecasts, by Size of Firm.*

Size of Firm (No. of Employees)	Total Firms Included	Mathematical Model Or Statistical Projection	Number Using Estimate From Published Data	Experience and Internal Reports	Other Methods
500 or More	27	6	5	13	3
100-499	11	—	2	4	5
20-99	3	—	—	—	3

TABLE 12. 7. 3.   *Percentage of Firms Making Long-Range Market Forecasts, by Size and Location of Firm.*

Size of Firm (No. of Employees)	Location of Head Office	Total Firms Included	Percentage Making Forecasts	Percentage Not Making Forecasts
500 or More	DUBLIN	26	65.39	34.62
	REST OF COUNTRY	16	62.50	37.50
	OVERALL	42	64.29	35.72
100-499	DUBLIN	21	19.05	80.96
	REST OF COUNTRY	22	27.28	72.73
	OVERALL	43	23.26	76.65
20-99	DUBLIN	20	5.00	95.00
	REST OF COUNTRY	21	4.77	95.24
	OVERALL	41	4.88	95.13

mainly on the basis of judgment and feel of the trade. The category "other methods" included in the table relates, in the main, to cases where firms had their future market mapped out for them in the context of adaptation to freer trade, the exercise having been carried out either by their industry's adaptation council or by the Industrial Re-organisation Branch of the Department of Industry and Commerce. Thus the number of firms which engage on their own account in any form of systematic long-range market planning is very limited indeed.

The first association considered is that between location and forward planning.

There is virtually no difference between the location of a firm and its likelihood of making long-range market forecasts. There are marked differences between the three size-groups. These differences are highly significant statistically, with the top size-group being very much more likely to make forecasts than the medium group, which in turn is significantly more likely to do so than the smallest group.

The position in regard to training and qualification is shown in tables 12.7.4 and 12.7.5.

TABLE 12. 7. 4.   *Percentage of Firms Making Long-range Market Forecasts, by Size of Firm and Training of Marketing Executive.*

Size of Firm (No. of Employees)	Training of Responsible Exec.	Total Firms Included	Percentage Making Forecasts	Percentage Not Making Forecasts
500 or More	TRAINED	28	75.00	25.00
	UNTRAINED	9	44.44	55.56
	NO EXECUTIVE	5	40.00	60.00
	OVERALL	42	64.29	35.72
100-499	TRAINED	7	57.15	42.85
	UNTRAINED	17	23.53	76.47
	NO EXECUTIVE	19	10.53	89.47
	OVERALL	43	23.26	76.65

TABLE 12. 7. 5.   *Percentage of Firms Making Long-range Market Forecasts, by Size of Firm and Qualification of Marketing Executive.*

Size of Firm (No. of Employees)	Qualification of Responsible Exec.	Total Firms Included	Percentage Making Forecasts	Percentage Not Making Forecasts
500 or More	QUALIFIED	12	83.33	16.67
	UNQUALIFIED	25	60.00	40.00
	NO EXECUTIVE	5	40.00	60.00
	OVERALL	42	64.29	35.72
100-499	QUALIFIED	6	—	100.00
	UNQUALIFIED	18	44.44	55.56
	NO EXECUTIVE	19	10.53	89.47
	OVERALL	43	23.26	76.65

TABLE 12. 7. 6.　*Percentage of Firms Making Long-range Market Forecasts, by Size of Firm and Use of Consultants.*

Size of Firm (No. of Employees)	Use of Consultants	Total Firms Included	Percentage Making Forecasts	Percentage Not Making Forecasts
500 or More	USED	32	68.75	31.25
	DID NOT USE	10	50.00	50.00
	OVERALL	42	64.29	35.72
100-499	USED	17	23.53	76.47
	DID NOT USE	26	23.08	76.92
	OVERALL	43	23.26	76.65
20-99	USED	7	14.29	85.71
	DID NOT USE	34	2.94	97.06
	OVERALL	41	4.88	95.13

TABLE 12. 7. 7.　*Percentage of Firms Making Long-range Market Forecasts, by Size of Firm and Use of Irish Management Institute Courses.*

Size of Firm (No. of Employees)	Use By Firm Of I.M.I. Courses	Total Firms Included	Percentage Making Forecasts	Percentage Not Making Forecasts
500 or More	USED	37	67.56	32.44
	DID NOT USE	5	40.00	60.00
	OVERALL	42	64.29	35.72
100–499	USED	10	30.00	70.00
	DID NOT USE	33	21.22	78.79
	OVERALL	43	23.36	76.65
20-99	USED	6	—	100.00
	DID NOT USE	35	5.72	94.29
	OVERALL	41	4.88	95.13

　　Table 12.7.4. shows higher percentages in both size-strata for firms employing a trained executive, but in the 100 to 499 employee group the differences are not statistically significant. In table 12.7.5. there is no evidence that employment of an academically-qualified executive is positively associated with making long-range forecasts. In the middle size-group it can be seen, not for the first time, that firms employing unqualified managers appear rather more advanced than firms employing qualified managers. This difference is not significant statistically, i.e. it could have arisen by chance, which is not surprising in view of the small numbers of managers involved. It is, however, fairly close to being significant and is large enough to raise the question

especially when this tendency has been noticed before, whether there may not, in this size-group, be a negative association between the employment of a qualified marketing executive and the use of marketing techniques. If so, it is surprising, because some of the managers involved had qualifications in marketing or university degrees in commerce, which might have been thought directly relevant to this field.

In the top size-group in tables 12.7.6 and 12.7.7, both use of consultants and use of courses appear to be associated with a higher likelihood of making long-range forecasts. However, because of the small numbers of firms which did not use consultants and did not attend courses, these differences are not of practical importance. In neither of the other strata are there any significant differences between firms.

Finally, the association is investigated between the type of market served by a firm and its likelihood of making of forecasts (table 12.7.8).

TABLE 12. 7. 8.   *Percentage of Firms Making Long-range Market Forecasts, by Size of Firm and Type of Market.*

Size of Firm (No. of Employees)	Type of Market	Total Firms Included	Percentage Making Forecasts	Percentage Not Making Forecasts
500 or More	CONSUMER	27	62.97	37.04
	INDUSTRIAL	15	66.67	33.33
	OVERALL	42	64.29	35.72
100-499	CONSUMER	29	31.04	68.97
	INDUSTRIAL	14	7.14	92.86
	OVERALL	43	23.26	76.65
20-99	CONSUMER	28	—	100.00
	INDUSTRIAL	13	15.38	84.62
	OVERALL	41	4.88	95.13

In the top stratum the difference is not appreciable. In the middle stratum consumer-goods firms appear more likely than others to make such forecasts, but the difference is not statistically significant. In the bottom stratum the difference is not significant either but, as this is not the first time that a tendency was noticed for industrial goods-firms to appear more likely to use a technique or to be more formally organised than consumer-goods firms in this stratum, the cumulative effect of these admittedly non-significant differences is now striking.

Section 8: Annual Sales Plans

Firms were asked to what extent they made formal annual sales plans, and also about the detail into which these plans were broken down, in order to see if they could be regarded as truly operational statements of intention rather than hopes or estimates.

Table 12.8.1 shows that while firms are more likely to make annual plans than to have made long-range forecasts or formal studies of their markets, the overall proportion

TABLE 12. 8. 1.   *Estimated Percentage of Firms Making an Annual Sales Plan, by Size of Firm.*

Size of Firm (No. of Employees)	Total Firms Included	Percentage Making Annual Plan	Percentage Not Making Annual Plan
500 or More	44	77.3	22.7
100-499	47	59.6±12.9	40.4
20-99	44	34.9±14.2	65.1
OVERALL		41.6±11.1	58.4

—about 40 per cent—is still rather low, even allowing for the fact that the smallest size-group included a fair number of fashion clothing firms which considered it impossible to make concrete plans at all. A cross-classification was obtained of the firms making sales plans with those which had carried out market studies and the result is shown in table 12.8.2.

TABLE 12. 8. 2.   *Estimated Percentage of Firms Making an Annual Sales Plan and Formal Market Studies, by Size of Firm.*

Size of Firm (No. of Employees)	Total Firms Included	Percentage Making Studies and Plans	Percentage Not Making Studies and Plans
500 or More	44	66.0	34.0
100-499	47	25.5±11.5	74.5
20-99	43	9.3(2.6—22.1)	90.7
OVERALL		14.8±7.0	85.2

TABLE 12. 8. 3.   *Estimated Percentage of Firms Breaking Down their Plan by Various Factors.*

Size of Firm (No. of Employees)	Total Firms Included	By Product	Percentage Breaking Down By Salesman	By Region	By Any Other Factor
500 or More	44	72.7	43.2	34.1	9.1
100–499	47	53.2±13.1	31.9±12.3	6.8(1.4-18.7)	—
20–99	44	27.3±13.1	13.6(5.1-27.4)	4.5(0.5-15.5)	4.5(0.5-15.5)
OVERALL		34.3±10.3	18.5±8.0	6.2±5.1	3.8±4.6

The overall proportion of firms making a plan based on a formal study of the market, however superficial, is only about one in seven, while even for medium-sized firms the proportion does not rise much above one in four. Firms were then asked by what factors the plan was broken down and the results are shown in table 12.8.3.

It is most usual to plan the sales of each product, then to plan sales by each salesman, then sales in each region. Table 12.8.3 does not require much comment except perhaps to point out the rather low percentage of firms which break their plans down to individual salesman level, even allowing for the fact that some firms employed no salesmen. It might have been expected that, as the implementation of plans rests largely on salesmen, it would usually have been made clear to them just what their contribution to achieving the plan was to be.

That this does not often appear to be the case may reflect either a resistance by salesmen to anything suggestive of targets being held over them, or alternatively that firms' commitment to an aggressive marketing approach is less than wholehearted, even among those firms which go so far as to attempt to construct an annual plan.

Looking next at the number of factors by which the plan is broken down, it can be seen (table 12.8.4) that for the smaller and medium-sized firms it is most usual to have a breakdown by only one factor.

TABLE 12. 8. 4.   *Number of Factors by Which Firms Making Annual Sales Plans Break Them Down, by Size of Firm.*

Size of Firm (No. of Employees)	Total Firms Included	Percentage Breaking Down By			
		1 Factor	2 Factors	3 Factors	4 Factors
500 or More	34	29.4	38.2	29.4	2.9
100-499	28	53.6	28.6	17.9	—
20-99	15	60.0	33.3	6.7	—
OVERALL		57.5	32.5	9.8	0.1

This may again give rise to the query: to what extent plans, when made, are statements of intention, and to what extent they are merely guide lines or hopes.

Section 9: Sales Training

Finally, firms were asked to what extent they gave sales training to their salesmen.

The question of sales training did not arise in some cases, because firms employed no salesman. The percentage of such firms is shown in column 2 of table 12.9.1. About half the firms in the country give no form of sales training, though for the top size-group this proportion falls to about a quarter. Only about 10 per cent of firms give training in sales techniques, though the proportion, at over 40 per cent, is very much higher in the top size-group. The remaining firms, while making some effort, confine their training to giving information about the products sold or about the company. In many cases, this lack of training is due rather to lack of facilities than to unwillingness, as many executives expressed themselves dissatisfied with the existing facilities for sales training, and said that they would be extremely interested in having proper facilities provided.

TABLE 12.9.1.   *Estimated Percentage of Firms Giving Sales-Technique or Other Sales Training to Their Salesmen, by Size of Firm.*

Size of Firm (No. of Employees)	Total Firms Included	Percentage To Which Question Did Not Apply	Percentage Giving No Training	Percentage Giving Training Including Selling Techniques	Percentage Giving Training Excluding Selling Techniques
500 or More	47	17.0	25.5	44.7	12.8
100-499	48	13.0	54.3	17.4	15.2
20-99	46	39.1	50.0	6.5	4.3
OVERALL		32.9	50.0	10.2	6.9

Section 10: Overall Scores on Marketing

It was decided to summarise the results of this chapter by assigning to firms a rough score indicating their level of advancement in marketing management. Firms were given

TABLE 12.10.1.   *Estimated Percentage of Firms Achieving Specified Scores on Use of Marketing Techniques, by Size of Firm.*

Size of Firm (No. of Employees)	Total Firms Included	0	Percentage Scoring 1 or 2	3 or 4	5	Not Applicable
500 or More	47	4.3	14.9	29.8	44.7	6.4
100–499	48	29.2	37.5	22.9	8.3	2.1
20–99	46	54.3	30.4	10.9	—	4.3
OVERALL		47.3	31.3	14.1	3.4	4.0

TABLE 12.10.2.   *Percentage of Firms Achieving Specified Scores on Use of Marketing Techniques, by Size of Firm and Training of Marketing Executive.*

Size of Firm (No. of Employees)	Training of Responsible Executives	Total Firms Included	Percentage Scoring 2 or Less	3 or More
500 or More	TRAINED	28	3.57	96.43
	UNTRAINED	9	44.45	55.55
100-499	TRAINED	7	14.29	85.71
	UNTRAINED	17	76.47	23.53

one point each for having an analysis of their sales-costs, for carrying out a formal market-study, for basing it either on official statistics or on a field survey, for making long-range market forecasts and for making annual sales plans. A total of five marks was possible. The results are shown in table 12.10.1.

There are highly significant differences between the three size-groups. The firms with over 500 employees score significantly more highly than firms in the middle size-group which in turn score more highly than firms with 20 to 99 employees.

Associations were looked for between scores on marketing management and all the factors examined earlier. In no case was there evidence of an association except where firms employed a marketing executive with management training.

Firms employing an executive with training were very significantly more likely to score higher than firms whose marketing executive had not attended a course.

CHAPTER 13

Production Management

Production management embraces a wide variety of activities: factory layout; product design; variety control; production engineering; planning and control of inventory, purchasing and production; control of quality. The complexity of production management varies widely between firms of different types. At one extreme is the large-scale batch engineering works making many products incorporating perhaps hundreds of parts, many of them going through the works simultaneously and competing for capacity on general-purpose machines. Such a firm is faced with complex problems of layout, machine capacity assessment and production scheduling, for some of which optimal solutions have not yet been derived by even so powerful a technique as operations research. At the other extreme there is, for instance, the small creamery processing a single raw material on special-purpose machinery, producing a single end-product, with the raw material arriving daily and in quantities over which the creamery manager has no control. In such a case, production planning and control problems can hardly be said to exist at all.

In the general scaling-down of the questionnaires which testing showed to be necessary, it became impossible to cover all the activities mentioned and the conditions governing their complexity. As in the case of marketing some simple techniques of general applicability were selected to give an appreciation of the standard of production management. It was decided to see whether an association existed between the use of these techniques, a variety of methods of raising the standard of management and some factors which would have implications for the provision of facilities. These factors were substantially the same as those investigated in the chapter on marketing.

The structure of Irish industry was discussed in the introduction to this volume. It was seen that most firms are engaged in processing rather than in fabrication, and that batch-production predominates. Table 12.0.3 showed that, outside the largest companies, a high proportion of firms made against orders in hand, usually waiting until sufficient orders had been accumulated to make what they considered an economic batch. A number of firms were put down as using "other methods". Many of these were firms in the food industry with little or no control over the availability of their raw material, which was highly perishable. These firms simply took what material they could get and processed it immediately.

Given the foregoing facts, it is not to be expected that sophisticated systems of production management would be the norm. It will be seen that even the simple techniques asked about are not widely used. Because the techniques selected were so simple it was decided to ask a question which would discriminate firms on a higher level. Although there is considerable controversy about the merits of the mathematical "economic batch quantity" system of production ordering it was decided to ask to what extent firms used it. Not a single firm did so, but relied on their own judgment and experience to decide what constituted a worthwhile run. Furthermore none of them had considered and rejected it on theoretical grounds: they were simply not familiar with it. Since the survey was carried out some of the larger firms in the country have started to use this method, but on the replies to this question alone it seems reasonable to infer that use of advanced techniques is not widespread.

Summary of Findings.

As judged by the use of the techniques selected, the standard of production management is low. Firms with over 500 employees are more advanced than firms in either of the other size-groups: there is little evidence that medium-sized firms are more advanced than small ones. Fabrication firms may be slightly more likely to use machine load records and work study, processing firms more likely to score well on quality control, but these apparent tendencies are slight and could be caused by sampling fluctuations. One or other of the means of raising the standard of management is usually associated with greater likelihood of using a technique. The tendency is rarely very marked, and the different methods are so closely interrelated in the case of production management that it is often impossible with the given sample size to disentangle their individual effects.

Section 1: Works Documentation

The first question was asked to find whether firms kept basic works documentation: works orders, material requisitions and stock records.

TABLE 13. 1. 1.   *Estimated Percentage of Firms Having Specified Works Documentation, by Size of Firm.*

Size of Firm (No. of Employees)	Total Firms Included	Percentage With			Percentage With None
		1	2	3	
500 or More	47	8.5	4.3	74.4	12.8
100–499	48	6.2	12.5	52.1	29.2
20–99	46	13.0	2.2	41.3	43.5
OVERALL		11.5	4.4	44.8	39.4

Table 13.1.1 shows that firms usually have either all or none of these documents. Once the firm gets to any size, the tendency is to have all of them, though the fact that almost 30 per cent of firms in the middle size-group have none is rather surprising. In the smallest group over 40 per cent of the firms still rely on verbal instructions for ordering and on visual observation of the stock position.

Section 2: Production Control Departments

The next question asked was whether there existed in the firm a production planning and control department, i.e. one or more individuals responsible for this activity.

TABLE 13. 2. 1.   *Estimated Percentage of Firms Having a Production Planning and Control Department, by Size of Firm.*

Size of Firm (No. of Employees)	Total Firms Included	Percentage With Department	Percentage Without Department
500 or More	47	57.4	42.6
100-499	48	18.8(8.9—32.7)	81.2
20-99	46	4.3(0.5—14.8)	95.7
OVERALL		9.3±4.9	90.7

Only about one-tenth of the firms in the country had such a department, with the proportions going from about one in twenty-five in the smallest group, to about one in five in the middle stratum, and three in five in the top stratum.

Section 3: Machine Load Records

The low figures for production planning departments shown in table 13.2.1 were not unexpected, especially in the smallest size-group, where firms would hardly be large enough to have formalised this activity. Comparison of load and capacity is the primary planning activity which must be carried out irrespective of industry, type of manufacturing process or of any other variable affecting production. Without some mechanism for making this comparison, formal production planning can scarcely take place. Firms were therefore asked whether they kept machine-loading records. It was emphasised when asking this question (question 69a) that what was in mind was not necessarily complicated proprietary charts or planning boards, but simply any means whatever of recording on a formal, routine basis, the work loads on different centres.

CONCLUSION. Use of the basic production planning aid of machine-load records is very restricted except for firms employing 500 or more people. With regard to possible associations with the factors considered, there is no evidence that in firms of under 500 employees such associations exist. A possible exception is training which may, in the 100 to 499 employee group, interact with qualification to produce an association. In the top stratum there is no evidence that location affects the situation. There is some evidence that type of manufacture does so, and also that a complex of factors indicating the general level of management awareness in the company is associated with the keeping of records. These factors are use of consultants, attendance at courses, and employment of trained and qualified production executives. Because of the inter-relationship of many of these factors and the small number of firms in the size-group it is not possible to isolate their individual effect if any.

TABLE 13. 3. 1.   *Estimated Percentage of Firms Keeping Machine-Loading Records, by Size of Firm.*

Size of Firm (No. of Employees)	Total Firms Included	Percentage Keeping Records	Percentage Not Keeping Records
500 or More	47	60.9	39.1
100-499	48	14.6(6.1—27.8)	85.4
20-99	46	6.5(1.3—17.9)	93.5
OVERALL		10.2±5.7	89.8

It is obvious from this table that formalised production planning is not widespread. Many firms, especially those in the smaller group, consider it either unnecessary or impossible to plan production. Some of them are very simple firms with a short production cycle on simple process machinery, dealing only with a small volume of production with which the manager is in intimate daily contact. Nevertheless, the fact that, in the whole country, only about one firm in ten employs such an elementary tool of planning must be regarded as evidence that the management of production, as distinct from its technical aspects, is not at a very high level. This seems especially true in the case of the middle stratum, where only about one firm in seven keeps any form of record. Because of the importance of this question it was selected for more lengthy examination to see if any attributes of the firm affected the position shown in table 13.3.1. The first factor considered was location.

TABLE 13.3.2.   *Percentage of Firms Keeping Machine-Loading Records, by Size and Location of Firm.*

Size of Firm (No. of Employees)	Location of Head Office	Total Firms Included	Percentage Keeping Records	Percentage Not Keeping Records
500 or More	DUBLIN	27	55.56	44.45
	REST OF COUNTRY	17	70.59	29.42
	OVERALL	44	61.37	38.64
100-499	DUBLIN	22	9.10	90.90
	REST OF COUNTRY	22	18.19	81.82
	OVERALL	44	13.64	86.37
20-99	DUBLIN	20	5.00	95.00
	REST OF COUNTRY	22	4.55	95.46
	OVERALL	42	4.77	95.24

Location does not appear to be associated very strongly with the use of load records: the difference between locations in the table above are not statistically significant. The difference between size-groups are very highly significant, but this significance arises only from the difference between the top and the other two strata. The difference between the middle and bottom strata is not shown to be significant by the data.

The possibility of an association between the training or qualification of the production executive and the use of load records is examined next.

TABLE 13.3.3.   *Percentage of Firms Keeping Machine-Loading Records, by Size of Firm and Training of Production Executive.*

Size of Firm (No. of Employees)	Training of Responsible Exec.	Total Firms Included	Percentage Keeping Records	Percentage Not Keeping Records
500 or More	TRAINED	27	74.08	25.93
	UNTRAINED	16	43.76	56.26
100-499	TRAINED	8	12.50	87.50
	UNTRAINED	33	12.12	87.88

TABLE 13. 3. 4. *Percentage of Firms Keeping Machine-Loading Records, by Size of Firm and Qualification of Production Executive.*

Size of Firm (No. of Employees)	Qualification of Responsible Exec.	Total Firms Included	Percentage Keeping Records	Percentage Not Keeping Records
500 or More	QUALIFIED	18	77.78	22.22
	UNQUALIFIED	25	52.01	48.01
100–499	QUALIFIED	13	7.78	92.22
	UNQUALIFIED	28	14.29	85.72

Because of the very small number of trained and qualified executives in the bottom size-group it was omitted from these tables. In the middle size-group employment of a chief production executive with academic qualifications does not appear to be associated positively with the keeping of records. Neither does employment of an executive with management training. However, there is a slight association between qualification and training of production managers in this size-group, qualified managers being somewhat more likely to be trained than those unqualified. The fact that qualified managers in this group in the sample were less likely than unqualified managers to be associated with the keeping of records while, on the other hand, trained and untrained managers were virtually identical in this regard, suggests that training had some effect. There is probably an interaction, with employment of managers who have both training and qualifications being associated with a greater likelihood of using load records. The sample numbers are not large enough to explore this interaction and certainly not large enough to test its significance.

TABLE 13. 3. 5. *Percentage of Firms Keeping Machine-Loading Records, by Size of Firm and Use of Consultants.*

Size of Firm (No. of Employees)	Use of Consultants	Total Firms Included	Percentage Keeping Records	Percentage Not Keeping Records
500 or More	USED	33	66.67	33.33
	DID NOT USE	11	45.45	54.55
	OVERALL	44	61.37	38.64
100–499	USED	17	17.65	82.35
	DID NOT USE	27	11.11	88.89
	OVERALL	44	13.64	86.37
20–99	USED	7	—	100.00
	DID NOT USE	35	5.71	94.29
	OVERALL	42	4.77	95.24

So far as the top stratum goes there appear to be differences between qualified and unqualified as well as between trained and untrained managers. However, in this size-group there is a very marked association between the training and qualifications of the production executive, with qualified managers being much more likely to be trained than unqualified managers. Again, because of the low numbers involved, a two-way classi-fication would hardly be feasible and certainly not amenable to testing. For this reason, it cannot be said for certain whether qualification as such, or training as such, is associated positively with the likelihood of keeping load records.

The association with use of consultants and with attendance at Irish Management Institute courses is examined in tables 13.3.5 and 13.3.6.

TABLE 13. 3. 6.   *Percentage of Firms Keeping Machine-Loading Records, by Size of Firm and Use of Irish Management Institute Courses.*

Size of Firm (No. of Employees)	Use By Firm Of I.M.I. Courses	Total Firms Included	Percentage Keeping Records	Percentage Not Keeping Records
500 or More	USED	39	62.50	37.50
	DID NOT USE	5	40.00	60.00
	OVERALL	44	61.37	38.64
100-499	USED	10	20.00	80.00
	DID NOT USE	34	11.76	88.24
	OVERALL	44	13.64	86.37
20-99	USED	7	—	100.00
	DID NOT USE	35	5.71	94.29
	OVERALL	42	4.77	95.24

In the two bottom strata there is hardly any difference between firms using and not using consultants or between firms attending and not attending courses. None of the differences shown is significant. In the top group, there does appear to be an association between keeping records and both use of consultants and attendance at courses. However, in view of the small number of firms which has not used consultants and not attended courses, the difference is not of much practical importance and, in any event, both use of consultants and attendance at courses are associated with employment of a qualified production manager. Firms employing qualified executives are, in this size-group, more likely to have used consultants and to have attended courses than firms without a qualified executive in charge of production. It is therefore not possible to say positively that an association exists with either of these factors, even in the top stratum.

Finally, the question is considered of an association between type of manufacture and keeping machine loadings. As well as dividing firms into those manufacturing by fabrication and processing, it had been hoped to consider the effect of job, batch or con-tinuous production, but the number of jobbing shops was too small for such a fine breakdown.

TABLE 13. 3. 7.   *Percentage of Firms Keeping Machine-Loading Records, by Size of Firm and Type of Manufacture.*

Size of Firm (No. of Employees)	Type of Manufacture	Total Firms Included	Percentage Keeping Records	Percentage Not Keeping Records
500 or More	FABRICATION	10	80.00	20.00
	PROCESSING	29	55.18	44.83
100-499	FABRICATION	11	17.27	82.73
	PROCESSING	29	13.80	86.21
20-99	FABRICATION	15	—	100.00
	PROCESSING	26	7.70	92.31

The differences in the two bottom strata of table 13.3.7 are not significant. In the top stratum there is a greater tendency for fabrication firms to be associated with the keeping of records than for firms in process industry. Fabrication companies are less likely than processing concerns to employ a qualified production executive, and it was seen that there is some suggestion that employment of a qualified executive leads to a higher use of records. There seems therefore to be grounds for believing that, among these larger firms, type of manufacture has an effect. This might have been expected, as production problems are likely to be more complex for large firms making piece parts than for large processing firms.

Section 4: Standard Times and Methods

A further element in production planning is the existence of reliable estimates of the times taken for various operations. The most sophisticated measurement is the assignment of standard methods and times either based on actual studies or built up from synthetic data.

Firms were therefore asked whether they used work studied standard times or methods. Their replies are shown in table 13.4.1.

TABLE 13. 4. 1.   *Estimated Percentage of Firms Using Standard Times or Methods Based on Work Study, by Size of Firm.*

Size of Firm (No. of Employees)	Total Firms Included	Percentage Using Work Study Standards	Percentage Not Using Work Study Standards
500 or More	47	61.7	38.3
100-499	48	18.8(8.9—32.7)	81.2
20-99	46	6.5(1.3—17.9)	93.5
OVERALL		11.1 ± 5.8	88.9

About one in nine firms do so with, as might be expected, a very low proportion in the smallest group, a low proportion in the middle group, but over 60 per cent of the firms with over 500 employees. In case this might be regarded as too advanced a system for the smaller firm, the firms were asked whether or not they had ever used work study for any purpose, not necessarily for standard times or methods but for layout, materials handling and so on. Their replies are dealt with in the following section.

Section 5: Work Study

Because of its basic nature as a universally applicable technique, work study was selected for detailed examination. Table 13.5.1 shows the overall picture.

TABLE 13.5.1.   *Estimated Percentage of Firms Ever Using Work Study for any Purpose, by Size of Firm.*

Size of Firm (No. of Employees)	Total Firms Included	Percentage Using Work Study	Percentage Not Using Work Study
500 or More	47	78.7	21.3
100-499	48	35.4 ± 12.4	64.6
20-99	46	15.2(6.3—28.9)	84.7
OVERALL		21.8 ± 8.2	78.2

CONCLUSION. *Use of work study is unexpectedly limited, particularly in medium-sized companies. Many firms seem to consider that it is not worth using where the process dictates times and methods, in fact the accent seems to be less on improving methods than on timing, usually in conjunction with incentive payments. Use of consultants is the only factor associated with increased likelihood of using work study.*

In view of its basic nature and versatility it is surprising to find that only about one firm in five has ever used work study for any purpose. Most surprising in this respect is the low proportion of medium-sized firms which has ever done so. Many small-business men consider their workshops so simple or their methods so established that work study could be of little benefit to them.

Others fear the idea of expanding their output and their activities generally in case they should get out of their depth. Many are quite happy to remain small as they fear that they have neither the financial resources nor the ability to adopt a more adventurous policy. It is therefore perhaps only to be expected that, among small-business men, even so proven a tool as work study does not come in for extensive application.

However, it might have been thought that, by the time a firm had passed the 100-employee mark, it would have gone sufficiently far along the path of growth for earlier fears to have been allayed and for use of work study to have become the norm rather than the exception. This position does not appear to be reached until much nearer the 500-employee dividing line.

The first factor whose association with work study is investigated is, as usual, location.

TABLE 13. 5. 2.   *Percentage of Firms Ever Using Work Study, by Size and Location of Firm.*

Size of Firm (No. of Employees)	Location of Head Office	Total Firms Included	Percentage Ever Using Work Study	Percentage Never Using Work Study
500 or More	DUBLIN	28	82.15	17.86
	REST OF COUNTRY	17	76.48	23.53
	OVERALL	45	80.00	20.00
100-499	DUBLIN	22	31.82	68.19
	REST OF COUNTRY	22	36.37	63.64
	OVERALL	44	34.10	65.90
20-99	DUBLIN	20	10.00	90.00
	REST OF COUNTRY	22	18.19	81.82
	OVERALL	42	14.29	85.71

Table 13.5.2 shows that there are practically no differences between the locations. Between the size-groups, however, there is a very highly significant difference, with the largest group very much more likely than either of the others to have used work study. The difference between the two smallest groups is not quite significant.

Qualification and training of the production executive are considered next.

TABLE 13. 5. 3.   *Percentage of Firms Ever Using Work Study, by Size of Firm and Training of Production Executive.*

Size of Firm (No. of Employees)	Training of Responsible Exec.	Total Firms Included	Percentage Ever Using Work Study	Percentage Never Using Work Study
500 or More	TRAINED	27	85.19	14.81
	UNTRAINED	17	70.59	29.42
100-499	TRAINED	8	37.50	62.50
	UNTRAINED	33	33.34	66.67

TABLE 13. 5. 4.   *Percentage of Firms Ever Using Work Study, by Size of Firm and Qualification of Production Executive.*

Size of Firm (No. of Employees)	Qualification of Responsible Exec.	Total Firms Included	Percentage Ever Using Work Study	Percentage Never Using Work Study
500 or More	QUALIFIED	19	84.21	15.79
	UNQUALIFIED	25	76.01	24.01
100-499	QUALIFIED	13	7.69	92.31
	UNQUALIFIED	28	46.43	53.58

There does not seem to be much ground for inferring that training and use of work study are very strongly associated.[1] On looking at qualification it can be seen that in the 100 to 499 stratum firms whose production executive is not qualified are, surprisingly, much more likely to have used work study than firms employing a qualified executive, and this difference is statistically significant. It is difficult to explain this difference, as qualification is not associated with any other factor in such a way as to have caused it: firms employing a qualified production executive are, in this stratum, slightly more likely to have used consultants, but use of consultants is positively, and not negatively, associated with use of work study. The firms concerned were mainly in process industry and many of them were quite advanced in their use of techniques in other areas. The answer seems to be that work study is mainly used for timing, usually in connection with the introduction of incentive schemes. Where times are largely process-determined, firms do not seem to see much advantage in work study. (It must be said, however, that methods are also dictated to a certain extent by the process, and it may be that in such cases the area of application of work study is too restricted to make it worthwhile. Yet the fact that the use of work study to improve methods is not so widespread as its use to establish times may strike the observer as being indicative of an attitude towards human motivation which accords with the postulates of McGregor's "Theory X".) In the top stratum the difference between qualified and unqualified and between trained and untrained is not large and since these factors are associated with each other it is not possible to say which, if any, is associated with using work study.

The position regarding use of consultants and attendance at courses is shown in tables 13.5.5 and 13.5.6.

TABLE 13.5.5.   *Percentage of Firms Ever Using Work Study, by Size of Firm and Use of Consultants.*

Size of Firm (No. of Employees)	Use of Consultants	Total Firms Included	Percentage Ever Using Work Study	Percentage Never Using Work Study
500 or More	USED	34	79.41	20.59
	DID NOT USE	11	81.82	18.18
	OVERALL	45	80.00	20.00
100-499	USED	17	52.95	47.06
	DID NOT USE	27	22.22	77.78
	OVERALL	44	34.10	65.90
20-99	USED	7	42.86	57.14
	DID NOT USE	35	8.58	91.43
	OVERALL	42	14.29	85.71

---

1 The bottom stratum was omitted from table 13.5.3. There was a considerable difference between firms with trained and firms with untrained production executives. However, the number of firms with a trained executive was so small that the difference was not signficant. The result for the stratum is not shown because it was thought that a percentage based on such a small number of firms was not reliable enough to be worth showing.

TABLE 13. 5. 6. *Percentage of Firms Ever Using Work Study, by Size of Firm and Use of Irish Management Institute Courses.*

Size of Firm (No. of Employees)	Use By Firm Of I.M.I. Courses	Total Firms Included	Percentage Ever Using Work Study	Percentage Never Using Work Study
500 or More	USED	40	85.00	15.00
	DID NOT USE	5	40.00	60.00
	OVERALL	45	80.00	20.00
100-499	USED	10	30.00	70.00
	DID NOT USE	34	35.29	64.71
	OVERALL	44	34.10	65.90
20-99	USED	7	28.57	71.43
	DID NOT USE	35	11.43	88.57
	OVERALL	42	14.29	85.71

In the two lower strata use of consultants appears to be associated with a higher likelihood of using work study. Neither of the observed differences reach significant levels, although both are very close to them. In view of the small numbers involved, especially in the bottom stratum, it is best to suspend judgment on this factor rather than to say that no association exists.[1] In the top stratum there is no difference. In the case of use of courses, the differences in the two lower strata are not very large and are not at all significant. In the top stratum the difference, while large, is not of much practical importance because of the very small number of firms which did not use courses.

Finally, type of manufacture is considered and the position is shown in table 13.5.7.

TABLE 13. 5. 7. *Percentage of Firms Ever Using Work Study, by Size of Firm and Type of Manufacture.*

Size of Firm (No. of Employees)	Type of Manufacture	Total Firms Included	Percentage Ever Using Work Study	Percentage Never Using Work Study
500 or More	FABRICATION	10	90.00	10.00
	PROCESSING	32	73.34	26.67
100-499	FABRICATION	11	45.46	54.55
	PROCESSING	29	34.49	65.52
20-99	FABRICATION	15	20.00	80.00
	PROCESSING	28	11.54	88.47

1 For theoretical reasons (see statistical note 2.3) the chi-square test cannot be performed on the bottom stratum. It is therefore not possible to combine the results of two chi-square tests. If the conditions were ignored and the test carried out the results of the two tests would sum to a highly significant value (see statistical note 2.4).

In all three strata, fabrication firms appear slightly more likely to use work study, but in no case is the difference very marked nor does it reach significant level.

Section 6: Quality Control

The last production activity considered is the manner in which firms control the quality of their products. This is a problem arising universally irrespective of any characteristics of the firm. The questions asked (question 72 of questionnaire) relate to the inspection of articles, and asked whether inspection is routine; whether it is based on specified standards; whether it is carried on right through the manufacturing process or only on finished goods; and what system is followed, whether statistical sample, 100 per cent inspection, or some more haphazard approach. Quality control is, of course, a more positive matter than simply inspecting. In addition, both the ability and the necessity to inspect vary from firm to firm: food processing firms, for instance, must conform to standards of quality and purity laid down by statute and they mostly employ trained chemists for this purpose. In other cases, quality is not so important, and standards of quality are difficult to specify in advance. Nevertheless, it was felt that the questions asked would give a good indication of the quality-consciousness of management.

CONCLUSION. While there is evidence of a fair amount of concern to achieve good quality, the methods used, especially among the medium-sized and smaller firms, could be more rigorous and skilful. The main factors which appear to be associated with high scores on the use of inspection methods are size (but only among small firms in Dublin), attendance at Irish Management Institute courses and, possibly, type of industry.

TABLE 13. 6. 1.   *Estimated Percentage of Firms Using Various Procedures of Quality Control, by Size of Firm.*

Size of Firm (No. of Employees)	Total Firms Included	Percentage making Routine Inspections	Percentage having Specified Standards	Percentage Inspecting Only at Finish	Right Through Process	Percentage Inspecting 100%	Statistical Sample	Other
500 or More	47	93.5	70.2	34.0	57.4	19.1	44.7	27.7
100–499	48	81.2(8.9—32.7)	56.2±12.9	27.1	54.2	31.2	20.8	29.2
20-99	46	71.7±13.0	37.0±13.9	39.1	32.6	34.8	10.9	26.1
TOTAL		74.5±10.0	42.2±10.8	38.0	36.5	33.5	14.2	26.8

Table 13.6.1 shows the extent to which firms carried out various inspection activities. Almost all of them had some sort of routine inspection. Not so many, however, had specified standards against which to judge the quality of the inspected article—only about two-fifths of the companies all told. Only about one-third of the firms carried out inspection right through the process, the remainder waiting to do so until the articles were finished. Among small and medium-sized firms it was most usual to attempt 100 per cent inspection or to follow some haphazard selection system. It is only among the larger firms that statistical sampling becomes anyway common. In most cases this was confined to processing firms employing trained chemists who drew off samples at various stages of the process. The practice of a strict system of statistical

quality control was not widespread. In order to give some picture of the overall standard of quality control, firms were given one mark for each positive reply: one for routine inspection, one for having specified standards, one for inspection right through the process as distinct from inspection at the finish only, and one for either 100 per cent inspection or statistical sampling.   Thus, the maximum score was four. Associations between quality control and a variety of factors were studied by comparing the scores received.   The percentages achieving each score are shown in table 13.6.2.

TABLE 13. 6. 2.   *Estimated Percentage of Firms Achieving Specified Scores on Quality Control, by Size of Firm.*

Size of Firm (No. of Employees)	Total Firms Included	Percentage Scoring				
		0	1	2	3	4
500 or More	47	8.5	12.8	10.6	25.6	42.6
100–499	48	18.7	8.3	18.7	20.8	33.3
20–99	46	28.3	4.3	34.8	13.0	19.6
OVERALL		25.6	5.5	30.6	15.1	23.3

There are very wide differences between the size-groups. In the top group over two-thirds of the firms scored three or four, that is, they might be regarded as having a reasonably comprehensive system of quality control. In the middle group just over half scored three or four, while in the bottom group the figure was just under one-third.

TABLE 13. 6. 3.   *Percentage of Firms Achieving Specified Scores on Quality Control, by Size and Location of Firm.*

Size of Firm (No. of Employees)	Location of Head Office	Total Firms Included	Percentage Scoring	
			0, 1 or 2	3 or 4
500 or More	DUBLIN	28	32.15	67.86
	REST OF COUNTRY	17	23.53	76.48
	OVERALL	45	28.89	71.12
100-499	DUBLIN	22	40.91	59.10
	REST OF COUNTRY	22	50.00	50.00
	OVERALL	44	45.46	54.55
20-99	DUBLIN	20	80.00	20.00
	REST OF COUNTRY	22	54.55	45.46
	OVERALL	42	66.67	33.34

For the purpose of this analysis the scores were grouped as (0, 1 or 2) and (3 or 4). There would not have been enough firms to carry out tests on each score by itself, and it was thought that the most meaningful breakdown would be between those firms scoring 2 or less (these might be regarded as less thorough), and those firms scoring 3 or 4.

The first factor examined is location, the position being shown in table 13.6.3.

There is not much difference between the locations in either of the two top strata. In the case of the bottom stratum, firms outside Dublin scored better than firms in Dublin. This is explained by the make-up of industry in the two locations. In Dublin, there are many small clothing firms where inspection tends to be by examining each garment as it is packed for delivery. Consequently neither specified standards nor inspection through the process is usual. Outside Dublin, there is a much higher proportion of process industry, particularly food processing, in which specified standards are laid down by law. Consequently these firms are more likely than firms in other industries to get high scores for quality.

As regards size, there are significant differences between the scores of the different size-groups in Dublin. Outside Dublin the difference is not significant. The significant difference in Dublin is confined to that between the bottom and the other strata. In other words the poorest performers are small firms located in Dublin.

The training and qualification of the production executive is considered in tables 13.6.4 and 13.6.5.

TABLE 13.6.4.   *Percentage of Firms Achieving Specified Scores on Quality Control, by Size of Firm and Training of Production Executive.*

Size of Firm (No. of Employees)	Training of Responsible Exec.	Total Firms Included	Percentage Scoring 0, 1 or 2	3 or 4
500 or More	TRAINED	27	33.33	66.67
	UNTRAINED	17	23.53	76.48
100-499	TRAINED	8	50.00	50.00
	UNTRAINED	33	42.43	57.58

TABLE 13.6.5.   *Percentage of Firms Achieving Specified Scores on Quality Control, by Size of Firm and Qualification of Production Executive.*

Size of Firm (No. of Employees)	Qualification of Responsible Exec.	Total Firms Included	Percentage Scoring 0, 1 or 2	3 or 4
500 or More	QUALIFIED	19	31.58	68.42
	UNQUALIFIED	25	28.01	72.01
100-499	QUALIFIED	13	53.85	46.15
	UNQUALIFIED	28	42.86	57.15

These tables show that there are no very marked differences either on the score of training or qualification, and the differences, such as they are, are not statistically significant.

TABLE 13. 6. 6.   *Percentage of Firms Achieving Specified Scores on Quality Control, by Size of Firm and Use of Consultants.*

Size of Firm (No. of Employees)	Use of Consultants	Total Firms Included	Percentage 0, 1 or 2	Scoring 3 or 4
500 or More	USED	34	29.41	70.59
	DID NOT USE	11	27.28	72.73
	OVERALL	45	28.89	71.12
100-499	USED	17	29.42	70.59
	DID NOT USE	27	55.56	44.45
	OVERALL	44	45.46	54.55
20-99	USED	7	71.43	28.57
	DID NOT USE	35	65.72	34.29
	OVERALL	42	66.67	33.34

TABLE 13. 6. 7.   *Percentage of Firms Achieving Specified Scores on Quality Control, by Size of Firm and Use of Irish Management Institute Courses.*

Size of Firm (No. of Employees)	Use By Firm Of I.M.I. Courses	Total Firms Included	Percentage 0, 1 or 2	Scoring 3 or 4
500 or More	USED	40	22.50	77.50
	DID NOT USE	5	80.00	20.00
	OVERALL	45	28.89	71.12
100-499	USED	10	30.00	70.00
	DID NOT USE	34	50.00	50.00
	OVERALL	44	45.46	54.55
20-99	USED	7	—	100.00
	DID NOT USE	35	80.00	20.00
	OVERALL	42	66.67	33.34

It can be seen in table 13.6.6 that use of consultants does not, except in the middle size-group, appear to exercise a very large effect, and even here the difference is not significant. Table 13.6.7 shows that, in every size-group, there is a tendency for firms which sent participants to courses to score higher on quality control. This difference is highly significant in both the top and bottom strata. However, in the top stratum, the difference is not very important practically, because of the very small numbers of firms not attending.

There is practically no difference among the larger firms between fabrication and process industry as table 13.6.8 shows. In the bottom stratum, firms in process industry

TABLE 13. 6. 8.   *Percentage of Firms Achieving Specified Scores on Quality Control, by Size of Firm and Type of Manufacture.*

Size of Firm (No. of Employees)	Type of Manufacture	Total Firms Included	Percentage 0, 1 or 2	Scoring 3 or 4
500 or More	FABRICATION	10	30.00	70.00
	PROCESSING	30	30.00	70.00
100-499	FABRICATION	11	36.36	63.64
	PROCESSING	29	41.38	58.63
20-99	FABRICATION	15	80.00	20.00
	PROCESSING	26	57.70	42.31

appear more likely to score well, but the difference does not reach a significant level. It cannot therefore be said that there is conclusive evidence of a difference in this size-group, though good reason could be found *a priori* for such a difference.

Section 7:   Overall Scores on Use of Production Management Techniques

To summarise the position regarding the general level of production management techniques, firms were assigned one mark if they kept machine-load records, one mark if they used work study, and one mark for scoring 3 or 4 on quality control—a possible total of 3 marks. The scores are shown in table 13.7.1.

TABLE 13. 7. 1.   *Estimated Percentage of Firms Achieving Specified Scores on the Use of Production Techniques, by Size of Firm.*

Size of Firm (No. of Employees)	Total Firms Included	Estimated Percentage Scoring			
		0	1	2	3
500 or More	47	10.6	10.6	38.3	40.4
100–499	48	31.2	41.7	18.7	8.3
20–99	46	56.5	32.6	10.9	—
OVERALL		49.6	33.6	13.5	3.2

As measured by the use of the techniques mentioned, the level of production management is low. Most medium-sized companies scored 1 or less, while over half the small firms scored zero. The difference between the small and medium-sized companies is not significant, that is to say, there is no evidence that medium-sized firms are any better in this respect than small ones. Large firms score significantly better than the others.

Firms employing a production executive with training, firms using consultants and firms attending Irish Management Institute courses tended to score best, but the differences were not statistically significant outside the top stratum, and not of practical importance within that stratum.

CHAPTER 14

Financial Management

Some elements of financial and costing information and control are examined in this chapter. The questions asked relate to the use of formal cost accounting systems, of budgetary control and standard costs, to the availability of accounts and other financial information, and to capital forecasting. It might be argued that budgetary control and standard costing are complicated systems not suitable to, or feasible for, smaller firms, especially those not employing a qualified accountant. In spite of this objection they were included. It was felt that their inclusion was justified by the importance of distinguishing between financial record and financial control. Management must not only be aware of its costs and its financial position: it should take positive steps to plan and to control them. Unless some standard is set and performance appraised against this standard the functions of planning and control are not being carried out. Some less complex system than budgetary control and standard costing may well suffice, for instance the system of higher control. Firms were originally asked whether they used this method, but it quickly became obvious that the term was not familiar, nor the method practised. In fact, when the questionnaires were being tested it was generally found that, where neither budgetary control nor standard costing was practised, no method of setting formal standards and controlling against them was used. For the most part then, the questions asked provide a good index of the degree of advancement of financial management.

Summary of Findings.

Quite a high proportion of firms claimed to have formal cost accounts, but their claims may be exaggerated. Use of budgetary control and standard costs is not widespread. A fair proportion of firms make formal forecasts of their capital requirements: smaller and medium-sized companies do not make them for very far ahead, and rarely base them on forecasts of the development of their market. Only a low proportion of firms got high overall scores on use of techniques of financial planning and control.

Large firms score better than either medium- or small-sized companies. There is some evidence that firms in Dublin tend to be more advanced than those outside. One or other of the means of raising the standard of management is usually associated with greater use of a given technique. It is worth mentioning that, while use of consultants is associated with greater likelihood of having formal cost systems, it is not associated with use of standard costing. This suggests that consultants considered standard costing too complex for immediate introduction in small companies. This is not surprising as over half the firms with 20 to 99 employees had no full-time manager in charge of finance, while over half the firms which had an executive employed one with no formal qualifications.

Section 1: Formal Cost Accounts

The first question asked was whether or not the firm had a formal system of cost accounts and what factors might be associated with its reply.

CONCLUSION. While a fair proportion of firms claim to use cost accounts the claims may be overstated. It is possible that firms in the 100 to 499 employee range are more likely to have formal cost accounts if they are situated in Dublin. The likelihood of having costing systems increases with size of firm. Small firms using consultants are more likely to keep cost accounts than other small firms. None of the other factors considered is associated in a practically-important way with keeping accounts.

TABLE 14. 1. 1.   *Estimated Percentage of Firms Having Formal Systems of Cost Accounts, by Size of Firm.*

Size of Firm (No. of Employees)	Total Firms Included	Percentage Having Formal Costing-Systems	Percentage Not Having Formal Costing-Systems
500 or More	47	91.5	8.5
100-499	48	58.3±12.8	41.7
20-99	46	34.8±13.7	65.2
OVERALL		41.8±10.7	58.2

Taking industry as a whole, only about two firms out of every five would claim to have such a system, the proportion growing as the size of firm increases, from about one-third of the companies employing under 100, to about three-fifths of those in the middle group, to nine-tenths of those in the top stratum. As a check on these figures, a cross-classification was obtained between firms answering that they had formal costing systems and those which said that they analysed their sales to show the margin earned over cost by individual product lines.

TABLE 14.1. 2.   *Estimated Percentage of Firms Having Formal Costing Systems Which Also Analyse their Sales Costs by Product Line, by Size of Firm.*

Size of Firm (No. of Employees)	Total Firms Included	Percentage Analysing Sales-Costs	Percentage Not Analysing Sales-Costs
500 or More	43	76.7	23.3
100-499	28	67.9(47.6—84.1)	32.1
20-99	16	31.3(11.0—58.6)	68.7
OVERALL		40.5	59.5

The results show that, of those firms saying they had a formal system, only 40 per cent obtained figures showing contributions by individual lines. Whatever the explanation for this fact it certainly shows that the figures in table 14.1.1. are the upper limit for the proportion of firms keeping formal cost accounts.

The question of possession of cost systems was selected for examination to find if it was associated with any factors having implications for measures to improve the standard of practice.

TABLE 14. 1. 3.   *Percentage of Firms Having Formal Cost Systems, by Size and Location of Firm.*

Size of Firm (No. of Employees)	Location of Head Office	Total Firms Included	Percentage With Cost Systems	Percentage Without Cost Systems
500 or more	DUBLIN	28	89.29	10.72
	REST OF COUNTRY	17	100.00	—
	OVERALL	45	93.34	6 67
100-499	DUBLIN	22	68.19	31.81
	REST OF COUNTRY	22	50.00	50.00
	OVERALL	44	59.10	40.90
20-99	DUBLIN	20	20.00	80.00
	REST OF COUNTRY	22	45.46	54.54
	OVERALL	42	33.33	66.67

This table shows no consistent tendency for one or other location to be associated with keeping cost accounts, none of the differences in the table being statistically significant. However, in the middle size-group, many of the firms outside Dublin which claimed to have formal accounts did not analyse the margin over cost by their different products. It may therefore be that, in that size-group, keeping formal accounts is more widespread in Dublin[1].

There are highly significant differences between the size groups. In Dublin the differences are significant between all three. Outside Dublin they are significant only between the top and the other two strata, that is the figure for the smallest size-group is so close to that for the middle group that the difference might easily have arisen by chance.

Firms outside Dublin, already quite advanced in the 20 to 99 group, do not improve greatly until they reach 500 employees. Dublin firms are backward in respect of costing in the group with under 100 employees, possibly because of the high proportion of fashion-clothing firms, but they change markedly once they pass 100 workers.

The next two factors considered are the training and qualifications of the executive responsible for the financial function. Because so few firms in the bottom stratum em-

TABLE 14. 1. 4.   *Percentage of Firms Having Formal Cost Systems, by Size of Firm and Training of Financial Executive.*

Size of Firm (No. of Employees)	Training of Responsible Exec	Total Firms Included	Percentage With Cost Systems	Percentage Without Cost Systems
500 or More	TRAINED	30	96.67	3.33
	UNTRAINED	13	84.62	15.39
100-499	TRAINED	7	85.71	14.29
	UNTRAINED	35	57.15	42.86

1 It will be remembered that Dublin firms in that group are more likely than non-Dublin companies to employ a qualified accountant (chapter 8).

TABLE 14. 1. 5.   *Percentage of Firms Having Formal Cost Systems, by Size of Firm and Qualification of Financial Executive.*

Size of Firm (No. of Employees)	Qualification of Responsible Exec.	Total Firms Included	Percentage With Cost Systems	Percentage Without Cost Systems
500 or More	QUALIFIED	38	94.74	5.26
	UNQUALIFIED	5	80.00	20.00
100-499	QUALIFIED	26	69.24	30.77
	UNQUALIFIED	16	50.00	50.00

ployed an executive with either management training or formal qualifications, the stratum is omitted from tables 14.1.4. and 14.1.5. Table 14.1.4. shows that, so far as the top stratum is concerned, there is not a very appreciable difference between firms employing trained and untrained executives. In the 100 to 499 employee size group there is a wide difference, but it is not statistically significant. In the case of qualification, the difference in the top stratum of table 14.1.5. is not of much practical importance, as most firms employ a qualified manager. In the medium size group the difference is not very wide and could be a chance one.

The position regarding use of consultants and attendance at courses is shown in tables 14.1.6. and 14.1.7.[1]

TABLE 14. 1. 6.   *Percentage of Firms Having Formal Cost Systems, by Size of Firm and Use of Consultants.*

Size of Firm (No. of Employees)	Use of Consultants	Total Firms Included	Percentage With Cost Systems	Percentage With No Cost Systems
500 or More	USED	34	94.12	5.88
	DID NOT USE	11	90.91	9.10
	OVERALL	45	93.34	6.67
100-499	USED	17	64.71	35.29
	DID NOT USE	27	55.56	44.45
	OVERALL	44	59.10	40.90
20-99	USED	7	71.43	28.57
	DID NOT USE	35	25.72	74.29
	OVERALL	42	33.33	66.67

Use of consultants does not seem, in the two larger strata, to be associated with having cost systems. In the case of the bottom stratum, however, the difference is very marked. While it is not statistically significant (because of the very low number of firms using consultants) it is sufficiently near a significant level to cause us not to reject

1 As usual, there is no implication that consultants were employed specifically on assignments in the finance area, or that the courses to which firms sent participants were related to finance.

TABLE 14. 1. 7. *Percentage of Firms Having Formal Cost Systems, by Size of Firm and Use of Irish Management Institute Courses.*

Size of Firm (No. of Employees)	Use by Firm of I.M.I. Courses	Total Firms Included	Percentage With Cost Systems	Percentage Without Cost Systems
500 or More	USED	40	97.50	2.50
	DID NOT USE	5	60.00	40.00
	OVERALL	45	93.34	6.67
100-499	USED	10	70.00	30.00
	DID NOT USE	34	55.88	44.12
	OVERALL	44	59.10	40.90
20-99	USED	7	42.86	57.14
	DID NOT USE	35	31.43	68.57
	OVERALL	42	33.33	66.67

altogether the possibility that the difference observed is real. Use of courses (table 14.1.7) does not appear to make a very appreciable difference except in the case of the largest size-group, where the difference is of little practical consequence in view of the fact that only five firms have not attended courses.

It had been considered that the type of production organisation in the firm might have an effect on the keeping of cost accounts, with firms not making standard products finding it more difficult than others to keep accounts. However, because of the small number of firms in this category, it was not possible to compare job, batch and continuous production. It was decided then to see whether the type of manufacture, that is whether the firm was a fabricating or processing establishment, affected the situation. In fact, table 14.1.8. shows that the differences are very slight, and none of them reach a significant level.

TABLE 14. 1. 8. *Percentage of Firms Having Formal Cost Systems, by Size of Firm and Type of Manufacture.*

Size of Firm (No. of Employees)	Type of Manufacture	Total Firms Included	Percentage With Cost Systems	Percentage Without Cost Systems
500 or More	FABRICATION	10	90.00	10.00
	PROCESSING	30	93.34	6.67
100-499	FABRICATION	11	63.63	36.37
	PROCESSING	29	58.63	41.37
20-99	FABRICATION	15	26.67	73.33
	PROCESSING	26	38.47	61.54

Section 2: Budgetary Control

This section covers the extent of the use of the system of budgetary control and also the extent to which its use is affected by the factors already considered in relation to the keeping of cost accounts.

CONCLUSION. Most firms with over 500 employees use budgetary control: most others do not. In the 100 to 499 employee stratum, firms based in Dublin are more likely to use this system than firms outside: its use is very restricted outside Dublin until firms reach 500 employees. It is possible that firms employing a finance executive with management training, and firms which sent participants to Irish Management Institute courses, are more likely to have budgetary control, but the evidence for these associations is not conclusive.

TABLE 14. 2. 1.　*Estimated Percentage of Firms Using Budgetary Control, by Size of Firm.*

Size of Firm (No. of Employees)	Total Firms Included	Percentage Using Budgetary Control	Percentage Not Using Budgetary Control
500 or More	47	72.3	27.7
100-499	48	33.3±12.3	66.7
20-99	46	13.0(4.9—26.2)	87.0
OVERALL		19.4±7.8	80.6

This table shows the estimated percentage of firms using budgetary control and it can be seen from it that approximately one firm in five does so, the percentage increasing with size of firm, so that almost three-quarters of the firms with over 500 employees use this system.

TABLE 14. 2. 2.　*Percentage of Firms Using Budgetary Control, by Size and Location of Firm.*

Size of Firm (No. of Employees)	Location of Head Office	Total Firms Included	Percentage Using Budgetary Control	Percentage Not Using Budgetary Control
500 or More	DUBLIN	28	75.00	25.00
	REST OF COUNTRY	17	76.48	23.53
	OVERALL	45	75.56	24.45
100-499	DUBLIN	22	50.00	50.00
	REST OF COUNTRY	22	18.19	81.81
	OVERALL	44	34.10	65.91
20-99	DUBLIN	20	10.00	90.00
	REST OF COUNTRY	22	9.10	90.90
	OVERALL	42	9.53	90.48

The differences between locations are negligible in the top and bottom strata. In the middle stratum, however, the difference is marked and significant. It seems that firms in

Dublin are, in this size group, more likely than others to use the system. There is no association between location and any other factor which would cause amendment of this conclusion. Firms outside Dublin are much less likely than firms in Dublin to employ a qualified finance executive, but even those non-Dublin firms whose executive was qualified did not use budgetary control to any extent. The differences between size groups are marked and are highly significant, both in Dublin and outside. However, outside Dublin the significant difference arises only after 100 to 499 size group is passed: there is no evidence of any difference between this and the smaller group, whereas in Dublin the difference is significant only between the bottom group and the other two. This suggests that a change in the use of budgetary control comes at an earlier stage in Dublin than outside.

Training and qualification of the responsible executive are the next factors considered and the associations are shown in the tables below.

TABLE 14. 2. 3.   *Percentage of Firms Using Budgetary Control, by Size of Firm and Training of Finance Executive.*

Size of Firm (No of Employees)	Training of Responsible Exec	Total Firms Included	Percentage Using Budgetary Control	Percentage Not Using Budgetary Control
500 or More	TRAINED	30	76.67	23.33
	UNTRAINED	13	76.93	23.08
100-499	TRAINED	7	57.14	42.86
	UNTRAINED	35	31.43	68.58

TABLE 14. 2. 4.   *Percentage of Firms Using Budgetary Control by Size of Firm and Qualification of Finance Executive.*

Size of Firm (No. of Employees)	Qualification of Responsible Exec.	Total Firms Included	Percentage Using Budgetary Control	Percentage Not Using Budgetary Control
500 or More	QUALIFIED	38	78.95	21.05
	UNQUALIFIED	5	60.00	40.00
100-499	QUALIFIED	26	38.46	61.54
	UNQUALIFIED	16	31.25	78.75

The only marked difference is in the 100 to 499 group, between firms whose executive is trained and other firms. Even this difference is not quite significant. There is no evidence, therefore, that use of budgetary control is associated with either of these factors. Having seen that neither training nor qualification are associated with use of budgetary control, the possibility of an association with use of consultants, or attendance at Irish Management Institute courses is examined.

The differences between firms on the basis of use of consultants are not striking as may be seen in table 14.2.5, and in every case they might easily have arisen due to sampling fluctuations. With regard to attendance at courses the differences, except in

TABLE 14. 2. 5.   *Percentage of Firms Using Budgetary Control, by Size of Firm and Use of Consultants.*

Size of Firm (No. of Employees)	Use of Consultants	Total Firms Included	Percentage Using Budgetary Control	Percentage Not Using Budgetary Control
500 or More	USED	34	76.47	23.53
	DID NOT USE	11	72.73	37.26
	OVERALL	45	75.56	24.45
100-499	USED	17	41.18	58.82
	DID NOT USE	27	29.63	70.38
	OVERALL	44	34.10	65.91
20-99	USED	7	14.29	85.71
	DID NOT USE	35	8.58	91.43
	OVERALL	42	9.53	90.48

TABLE 14. 2. 6.   *Percentage of Firms Using Budgetary Control, by Size of Firm and Use of Irish Management Institute Courses.*

Size of Firm (No. of Employees)	Use by Firm of I.M.I. Courses	Total Firms Included	Percentage Using Budgetary Control	Percentage Not Using Budgetary Control
500 or More	USED	40	77.50	22.50
	DID NOT USE	5	60.00	40.00
	OVERALL	45	75.56	24.45
100–499	USED	10	60.00	40.00
	DID NOT USE	34	26.47	73.53
	OVERALL	44	34.10	65.91
20–99	USED	7	14.29	85.71
	DID NOT USE	35	8.57	91.43
	OVERALL	42	9.53	90.48

the middle stratum, are not particularly marked either. Even in the middle stratum the difference is not statistically significant, though approaching it quite closely. There is therefore not sufficient evidence to say that attendance at courses is associated positively with use of budgetary control.[1]

---

1 For theoretical reasons it is not permissible to combine the results of any of the separate tests on table 14.2.6. If the theoretical conditions were relaxed the combination of the results of a test on stratum 1 with one on stratum 2 would give a significant result. That is to say, there would be sufficient evidence to conclude that, in firms with 100 or more employees, attendance at courses is associated positively with greater likelihood of using budgetary control.

TABLE 14.2.7.   *Percentage of Firms Using Budgetary Control, by Size of Firm and Type of Manufacture.*

Size of Firm (No. of Employees)	Type of Manufacture	Total Firms Included	Percentage Using Budgetary Control	Percentage Not Using Budgetary Control
500 or More	FABRICATION	10	70.00	30.00
	PROCESSING	30	73.34	26.67
100-499	FABRICATION	11	27.27	72.73
	PROCESSING	29	34.49	65.52
20-99	FABRICATION	15	6.67	93.33
	PROCESSING	26	11.54	88.47

Finally, it can be seen in table 14.2.7 that there is no evidence of any association between type of manufacture and budgetary control, the differences being very narrow and not at all significant.

Section 3: Standard Costs.

The next question put was whether or not the firm used the system of standard costing. It was stated earlier that smaller firms would perhaps find this system unduly complicated and this is borne out by the evidence of table 14.3.1. below.

CONCLUSION. *Apart from those with 500 or more employees, very few firms use a standard costing system. Those smaller firms which claim to use it rarely base their standards on work-studied standard times or methods. Firms with over 100 employees which employ a finance executive with management training, or which have used consultants, are more likely than other firms of similar size to use standard costs.*

TABLE 14.3.1.   *Estimated Percentage of Firms Using Standard Costs, by Size of Firm.*

Size of Firm (No. of Employees)	Total Firms Included	Percentage Using Standard Costs	Percentage Not Using Standard Costs
500 or More	47	59.6	40.4
100-499	48	23.8 ± 9.7	76.2
20-99	46	6.5(1.3—17.9)	93.5
OVERALL		12.1 ± 5.7	87.9

Approximately one firm in eight stated that it used standard cost systems, the proportion being very much lower for firms with less than 100 employees, rising to about one-quarter for the medium size-group and almost three-fifths for the largest group. It was thought that it would be interesting to obtain a cross classification of the results of the answers to this question with the replies received when firms were asked whether they used standard times or methods in production. The results of this cross-classification are shown in table 14.3.2.

TABLE 14. 3. 2.   *Estimated Percentage of Firms Using Standard Costs and Standard Times or Methods, by Size of Firm.*

Size of Firm (No. of Employees)	Total Firms Included	Percentage Using Standard Costs and Times	Percentage Not Using Standard Costs and Times
500 or More	47	51.1	48.9
100-499	48	12.5 (4.7—25.2)	87.5
20-99	46	2.2 (0—11.6)	97.8
OVERALL		5.2±3.5	94.8

The effect is not very marked in the case of the top stratum — most of the firms using standard costs also use standard times. In the case of the middle and lower strata, however, only about one-half and one-third respectively of firms saying they had standard costs had also standard times. Some of this difference is probably accounted for by processing firms in which times are largely machine paced, being governed by the nature of the process itself. However, it does seem likely that in other cases the standards upon which costs are based are more in the nature of averages or estimates, than the relatively objective standards arrived at by work study.

The following table shows the position with respect to use of standard costs in Dublin and the rest of the country.

TABLE 14. 3. 3.   *Percentage of Firms Using Standard Costs, by Size and Location of Firm.*

Size of Firm (No. of Employees)	Location of Head Office	Total Firms Included	Percentage Using Standard Costs	Percentage Not Using Standard Costs
500 or More	DUBLIN	28	50.00	50.00
	REST OF COUNTRY	17	82.36	17.65
	OVERALL	45	62.23	37.78
100-499	DUBLIN	22	40.91	59.10
	REST OF COUNTRY	22	22.73	77.28
	OVERALL	44	31.82	68.18
20-99	DUBLIN	20	—	100.00
	REST OF COUNTRY	22	9.10	90.91
	OVERALL	42	4.77	95.24

There is no uniform tendency for one or other location to be associated with this technique. In fact, while firms in the 500 or over size stratum outside Dublin are more likely to use it, the position appears to be reversed in the 100 to 499 group. This latter difference is not significant although it approaches significance quite closely. As it was noted before that Dublin firms in this size-group are more likely to use budgetary control it seems possible that the use of both systems (which often go together) is genuinely more widespread in medium sized firms in Dublin than in firms of the same size in the provinces.[1] Regarding size, it is useful to look at the position for the two locations separately. On doing so, somewhat different patterns are found between them. In Dublin the significant difference arises between the bottom and the other two strata, whereas in the rest of the country it arises only between the top and the other two. It seems clear from this that use of the system comes at an earlier stage in Dublin than is the case outside Dublin, that beyond this stage increasing size does not bring very much change in Dublin, but that it brings considerable change outside.

TABLE 14. 3. 4.   *Percentage of Firms Using Standard Costs, by Size of Firm and Training of Finance Executive.*

Size of Firm (No. of Employees)	Training of Responsible Exec	Total Firms Included	Percentage Using Standard Costs	Percentage Not Using Standard Costs
500 or More	TRAINED	30	70.00	30.00
	UNTRAINED	13	46.16	53.85
100-499	TRAINED	7	71.43	28.57
	UNTRAINED	35	25.72	74.29

TABLE 14. 3. 5.   *Percentage of Firms Using Standard Costs, by Size of Firm and Qualification of Finance Executive.*

Size of Firm (No. of Employees)	Qualification of Responsible Exec.	Total Firms Included	Percentage Using Standard Costs	Percentage Not Using Standard Costs
500 or More	QUALIFIED	38	65.79	34.21
	UNQUALIFIED	5	40.00	60.00
100-499	QUALIFIED	26	38.47	61.54
	UNQUALIFIED	16	25.00	75.00

Table 14.3.4. shows that there are very marked differences between firms on the basis of the training of their finance executive. In both strata training is strongly associated in a positive way with use of standard costs (the difference in the middle stratum is not quite significant, but very close to it, while a combination of the results of the individual tests, though hardly permissible theoretically, gives a very significant result). Qualification also shows an association but, in the middle size-group, this association is a great deal less marked than in the case of training and is not, in fact, anywhere near a significant level. In the top size-group the difference is large but, because of the very small number of firms not employing a qualifid manager, it is not of much consequence.

---

1 Surprisingly, some firms outside Dublin which did not use budgetary control claimed to use standard costs.

There is a clear association in firms with over 100 employees between employment of consultants and use of standard costs. It is likely that in this area firms found it necessary to supplement their own expertise by using that of consultants. There is no association in the case of firms with under 100 employees, even though use of consultants is associated with keeping formal cost accounts. This may indicate that consultants considered standard costing too advanced a system to install without first putting in conventional systems of historical costing.

TABLE 14. 3. 6.   *Percentage of Firms Using Standard Costs, by Size of Firm and Use of Consultants.*

Size of Firm (No. of Employees)	Use of Consultants	Total Firms Included	Percentage Using Standard Costs	Percentage Not Using Standard Costs
500 or More	USED	34	70.59	29.41
	DID NOT USE	11	36.36	63.63
	OVERALL	45	62.23	37.78
100-499	USED	17	41.18	58.83
	DID NOT USE	27	25.93	74.08
	OVERALL	44	31.82	68.18
20-99	USED	7	14.29	85.71
	DID NOT USE	35	2.86	97.14
	OVERALL	42	4.77	95.24

TABLE 14. 3. 7.   *Percentage of Firms Using Standard Costs, by Size of Firm and Use of Irish Management Institute Courses.*

Size of Firm (No. of Employees)	Use by Firm of I.M.I. Courses	Total Firms Included	Percentage Using Standard Costs	Percentage Not Using Standard Costs
500 or More	USED	40	65.00	35.00
	DID NOT USE	5	40.00	60.00
	OVERALL	45	62.23	37.78
100-499	USED	10	40.00	60.00
	DID NOT USE	34	29.41	70.59
	OVERALL	44	31.82	68.18
20-99	USED	7	14.29	85.71
	DID NOT USE	35	2.86	97.14
	OVERALL	42	4.77	95.24

The differences in table 14.3.7 are not very large and none of them is significant. The widest difference, that in the top size-group, is not of much practical importance because of the limited number of firms which never attended courses.

Lastly, type of manufacture is considered and table 14.3.8. below shows that this has virtually no influence on the position. Although process firms are slightly more likely to use this technique, the differences are trifling and are not statistically significant.

TABLE 14. 3. 8.   *Percentage of Firms Using Standard Costs, by Size of Firm and Type of Manufacture.*

Size of Firm (No. of Employees)	Type of Manufacture	Total Firms Included	Percentage Using Standard Costs	Percentage Not Using Standard Costs
500 or More	FABRICATION	10	60.00	40.00
	PROCESSING	30	64.34	36.67
100-499	FABRICATION	11	27.27	72.73
	PROCESSING	29	31.04	68.97
20-99	FABRICATION	15	—	100.00
	PROCESSING	26	7.70	92.31

Section 4: Trading and Profit and Loss Accounts

In order to get some idea of the closeness with which financial affairs were watched, those companies not using budgetary control were asked how often they made out trading and profit and loss accounts. Their replies are shown in the table 14.4.1.

TABLE 14. 4. 1.   *Frequency of Availability of Trading and Profit-and-Loss Accounts in Firms Not Using Budgetary Control, by Size of Firm.*

Size of Firm (No. of Employees)	Total Firms Included	Percentage Getting Accounts		
		Monthly Or More Often	Half-Yearly Or More Often	Annually Only
500 or More	13	46.2	53.8	—
100-499	32	9.4	46.9	43.7
20-99	40	10.0	30.0	60.0

There is a tendency among larger firms to have accounts available quite frequently. A good proportion of medium-sized firms have them available monthly, quarterly or half-yearly, but something over 40 per cent receive them annually only. Among firms in the smallest group it is most usual to make out these accounts only each year, although 40 per cent receive them half-yearly or more often. The fact that such a high proportion of firms in the smallest group uses neither budgetary control nor standard costs, nor receives trading or profit and loss accounts sufficiently often to use them as a control document, is certainly not an indication of any lack of concern among small-business men about the financial aspects of their business. This can be seen in the replies to the next question, which is dealt with below. It is rather a reflection of lack of ability to compile accounts regularly and, particularly, to deal with troublesome items such as valuation of stocks and work in progress. The next question asked was what costing and financial information, other than trading and profit and loss accounts, was available to firms not using budgetary control, and how often. The frequency of availability is shown in table 14.4.2. below. As regards content it is almost impossible to summarise the wide variety of replies to this question: they ranged from very comprehensive monthly historical costings and financial analyses to rough checks every so often on the firm's liquidity position. A very rough summary is attempted in table 14.4.3. below.

TABLE 14. 4. 2.   *Frequency of Availability of Financial or Costing Information Other than Trading and Profit-and-Loss Accounts in Firms Not Using Budgetary Control, by Size of Firm.*

Size of Firm (No. of Employees)	Total Firms Included	Percentage Getting Other Information			
		Monthly Or More Often	1 Month To 1 Year	As Jobs Completed	Never
500 or More	13	100.00	—	—	—
100-499	32	62.5	6.2	—	31.2
20-99	40	55.0	7.5	10.0	27.5

TABLE 14. 4. 3.   *Type of Financial or Cost Information Other Than Trading or Profit-and-Loss Accounts Available to Firms Not Having Budgetary Control, by Size of Firm.*

Size of Firm (No. of Employees)	Number of Firms			
	Having Routine Cost Accounts or Reports	Having Routine Financial Accounts or Reports	Making Routine Checks on Cost or Financial Position	Making Occasional Checks on Their Position
500 or More	8	4	—	—
100-499	10	11	3	4
20-99	10	15	10	8

Table 14.4.2. shows that most companies make a check on some aspect of their financial or cost position monthly or more often.

Section 5:   Capital Forecasts

Finally, firms were asked whether they made formal estimates of their future capital requirements.

CONCLUSION. Quite a high proportion of firms make attempts to forecast their capital requirements but, apart from firms with over 500 employees, the forecasts do not extend very far forward and are rarely based on formal forecasts of the future development of the firm's market. Large firms are more likely to make capital forecasts than medium-sized firms, which are in turn more likely to forecast than small companies.

The most marked association is between forecasts and type of manufacture: processing firms with under 500 employees are much more likely to make forecasts than fabricating firms of the same size, possibly because their machinery is more complex and specialised.

As may be seen from table 14.5.1. it is fairly common for firms to make capital forecasts once they pass the 100 employee mark. Only about a quarter of those employing less than 100 employees make such estimates.

TABLE 14. 5. 1.   *Estimated Percentage of Firms Forecasting their Capital Requirements, by Size of Firm.*

Size of Firm (No. of Employees)	Total Firms Included	Percentage Making Capital Forecasts	Percentage Not Making Capital Forecasts
500 or More	47	76.6	23.4
100-499	48	50.0±13.0	50.0
20-99	46	26.1±12.6	73.9
OVERALL		32.9±9.9	67.1

As a check on the basis of these forecasts a cross classification was obtained of the replies to this question by those to the question dealing with estimation of future market trends. The results of this classification are shown in table 14.5.2.

TABLE 14. 5. 2.   *Estimated Percentage of Firms Making Both Sales and Capital Forecasts, by Size of Firm.*

Size of Firm (No. of Employees)	Total Firms Included	Percentage Making Sales and Capital Forecasts	Percentage Not Making Sales and Capital Forecasts
500 or More	44	56.8	43.2
100-499	47	14.9(6.2—28.3)	85.1
20-99	44	2.3(0—11.6)	97.7
OVERALL		6.9±3.8	93.1

This table shows that the capital forecasts are, in most cases, fairly rough and ready, at least in the case of medium and smaller firms where they are rarely based on any sort of estimate of future market demand. Among the largest firms, however, capital forecasts are usually based on future sales estimates. Capital forecasting in these firms tends to be for quite a long period ahead as may be seen in the next table which shows the length of the period to which capital forecasts apply.

Most of the firms in the top stratum forecast their requirements for over two years ahead, with one-third of them going to five years or longer. Among the medium sized

TABLE 14. 5. 3.   *Estimated Percentage of Firms Making Capital Forecasts for Various Periods Ahead, by Size of Firm.*

Size of Firm (No. of Employees)	Total Firms Included	Percentage Forecasting Ahead			
		1 Year Or Less	1-5 Years	5 Years Or More	Not At All
500 or More	47	8.5	34.0	34.0	23.4
100-499	48	22.9	20.8	6.2	50.0
20-99	46	13.0	6.5	6.5	73.9
OVERALL		14.9	10.5	7.5	67.1

firms it is the exception for plans to extend for five or more years, while among the smallest size group one-half of those making forecasts do so for periods of less than a year. The fact that so many firms forecast their requirements for less than a year affects the position in table 14.5.2 since, in the question on sales forecasting, firms were specifically asked to what extent they made estimates for more than one year ahead. However, even if those firms whose capital projections do not extend for more than a year are excluded, it is obvious that most of those firms in the two smaller groups which project their capital requirements for more than a year still do not do so on the basis of estimates of market trends.

Because of the importance of estimation of future capital requirements in the total planning of the firm it was also selected for investigating associations.

TABLE 14. 5. 4.   *Percentage of Firms Making Capital Forecasts, by Size and Location of Firm.*

Size of Firm (No. of Employees)	Location of Head Office	Total Firms Included	Percentage Making Capital Forecasts	Percentage Not Making Capital Forecasts
500 or More	DUBLIN	28	78.58	21.43
	REST OF COUNTRY	17	82.36	17.65
	OVERALL	45	80.00	20.00
100-499	DUBLIN	22	50.00	50.00
	REST OF COUNTRY	22	50.00	50.00
	OVERALL	44	50.00	50.00
20-99	DUBLIN	20	25.00	75.00
	REST OF COUNTRY	22	22.73	77.28
	OVERALL	42	23.81	76.20

The table shows almost no difference in this respect between locations, but in each case fairly marked differences between the size-groups, with the differences being highly significant in both cases.

Employment of a finance executive with management training or formal qualifications is considered next.

TABLE 14. 5. 5. *Percentage of Firms Making Capital Forecasts, by Size of Firm and Training of Finance Executive.*

Size of Firm (No. of Employees)	Training of Responsible Exec	Total Firms Included	Percentage Making Capital Forecasts	Percentage Not Making Capital Forecasts
500 or More	TRAINED	30	83.33	16.67
	UNTRAINED	13	76.93	23.08
100-499	TRAINED	7	85.71	14.29
	UNTRAINED	35	45.72	54.29

TABLE 14. 5. 6. *Percentage of Firms Making Capital Forecasts, by Size of Firm and Qualification of Finance Executive.*

Size of Firm (No. of Employees)	Qualification of Responsible Exec.	Total Firms Included	Percentage Making Capital Forecasts	Percentage Not Making Capital Forecasts
500 or More	QUALIFIED	38	86.84	13.16
	UNQUALIFIED	5	40.00	60.00
100-499	QUALIFIED	26	53.85	46.15
	UNQUALIFIED	16	50.00	50.00

TABLE 14. 5. 7. *Percentage of Firms Making Capital Forecasts, by Size of Firm and Use of Consultants.*

Size of Firm (No. of Employees)	Use of Consultants	Total Firms Included	Percentage Making Capital Forecasts	Percentage Not Making Capital Forecasts
500 or More	USED	34	79.42	20.58
	DID NOT USE	11	81.82	18.19
	OVERALL	45	80.00	20.00
100-499	USED	17	64.71	35.29
	DID NOT USE	27	40.75	59.26
	OVERALL	44	50.00	50.00
20-99	USED	7	—	100.00
	DID NOT USE	35	28.58	71.43
	OVERALL	42	23.81	76.20

Training does not, in the largest size-group, exercise a very marked effect. In the 100 to 499 employee stratum the difference is wide, but not quite significant. Again, however, it might be better to reserve judgment on this point as the test result is quite near significance. Table 14.5.6. shows that in the 100 to 499 group there is no association between qualification and capital forecasting. The difference in the top group is marked but is not of practical consequence.

Neither use of consultants nor attendance at Irish Management Institute courses is very markedly associated with capital forecasting, as tables 14.5.7 and 14.5.8 show.

TABLE 14.5.8.   *Percentage of Firms Making Capital Forecasts, by Size of Firm and Use of Irish Management Institute Courses.*

Size of Firm (No. of Employees)	Use by Firm of I.M.I. Courses	Total Firms Included	Percentage Making Capital Forecasts	Percentage Not Making Capital Forecasts
500 or More	USED	40	82.50	17.50
	DID NOT USE	5	60.00	40.00
	OVERALL	45	80.00	20.00
100-499	USED	10	60.00	40.00
	DID NOT USE	34	47.06	52.94
	OVERALL	44	50.00	50.00
20-99	USED	7	42.86	57.14
	DID NOT USE	35	20.00	80.00
	OVERALL	42	23.81	76.20

In the case of use of consultants the difference in the middle size-group is quite wide but not significant, while in the bottom size-group the association is in the reverse direction, but again is not significant. Taking use of courses, the association is in the same direction in each of the three strata, but it does not reach statistical significance, even if the three tests on the individual strata are combined.

TABLE 14.5.9.   *Percentage of Firms Making Capital Forecasts, by Size of Firm and Type of Manufacture.*

Size of Firm (No. of Employees)	Type of Manufacture	Total Firms Included	Percentage Making Capital Forecasts	Percentage Not Making Capital Forecasts
500 or More	FABRICATION	10	90.00	10.00
	PROCESSING	30	73.34	26.67
100-499	FABRICATION	11	18.19	81.82
	PROCESSING	29	58.63	41.38
20-99	FABRICATION	15	6.67	93.33
	PROCESSING	26	34.62	65.39

Finally, type of manufacture is investigated. In the two lower strata there is a very marked tendency for process firms to be more likely to make capital forecasts than fabrication firms. In neither case does the difference quite reach significant level, but approaches very closely to it. When the results are combined the differences become highly significant. This might reasonably be explained by the fact that, for smaller firms, machinery for processing is likely to be more complex and costly than that used in fabrication and that, consequently, capital forecasting becomes a matter of greater importance.

Section 6: Overall Scores on Financial Planning and Control Techniques

To summarise the overall position regarding use of techniques of financial planning and control, firms were assigned one point each for using budgetary control, for having a system of standard costs and for making forecasts of their capital requirements. The scores are shown in table 14.6.1.

TABLE 14. 6. 1.   *Estimated Percentage of Firms Achieving Specified Scores on Use of Financial Techniques, by Size of Firm.*

Size of Firm (No. of Employees)	Total Firms Included	0	Percentage Scoring 1	2	3
500 or More	47	10.6	19.1	21.3	48.9
100–499	48	43.7	22.9	12.5	20.8
20–99	46	73.9	15.2	6.5	4.3
OVERALL		65.3	16.9	8.3	9.4

Most large firms score well — significantly better than medium-sized companies, which in turn score better than small firms. There is not enough evidence to say that any of the factors considered in this chapter is associated with greater likelihood of achieving a high score. The only consistent association is with employment of an executive with training, but even this is not significant.

CHAPTER 15

Personnel and General Management

This chapter is in two parts. The first part deals with some aspects of the personnel function, the second with some questions relating to the overall direction of the firm.

This is not an attempt at a comprehensive assessment of personnel management. It should be emphasised again that the design was not intended to cover the broader question of interpersonal relations in the firm or its style of management generally, due to the difficulties discussed in the technical appendix under the heading "research design". It had been hoped to examine those areas which could be considered the responsibility of a specialised personnel department. The questions related to selection, training, promotion policies, pay and job evaluation, working conditions, welfare and other benefits. As in the case of the other areas, there are conditions affecting the extent to which these activities are possible, or necessary, in a firm. The existence of a multiplicity of types of worker, possibly attached to different unions, makes questions of pay and job evaluation more complex. Again, the frequency with which the firm recruits, and the general availability of people in the locality, will have an affect on its methods of selection. When it became necessary to scale down the questionnaire, only a very few questions could be selected for consideration.

The basic task of the personnel department is to give assistance in having available, and keeping, an adequate supply of workers capable of doing the work of the firm. It was decided to choose a few questions to indicate the skill with which firms set about ensuring a supply of workers. They would be asked to what extent they forecast their manpower requirements, what methods of selection they used, how committed they were to formal training, and to what extent they appraised the performance of their employees. The question of welfare, physical conditions and remuneration was ignored, as too many questions would have been necessary to cover these areas adequately.

It was considered that the basic element of a chief executive's job is to look to the future and to direct his company accordingly. The questions asked in the area of general management therefore relate to long-range market forecasts, capital forecasts, organisational planning, management development and planning for succession.

Summary of Findings of Part A

Manpower forecasts, use of selection techniques, comprehensive training and employee appraisal are very limited even in firms employing 500 people or more. So limited are they that it is possible to examine associations only in the case of these large firms. Firms employing a specialist personnel executive are more likely than others to plan their manpower requirements and to use techniques of selection other than interview. (There are too few personnel executives to differentiate between them on the basis of training or qualification). Attendance at Irish Management Institute courses is also associated with greater use of techniques, but the number of firms not attending courses is so limited that the association is not of practical importance.

Analysis of overall scores shows that firms with over 500 employees score higher than others. In the 500 or over stratum, firms employing a personnel executive, firms attending Irish Management Institute courses and firms located outside Dublin score better. There is no evidence of an association with the use of consultants: several very progressive companies had not felt it necessary to use outside consultants.

Summary of Findings of Part B

It was seen in chapters 12 and 14 that long-range market forecasts are rarely made, capital forecasts being more frequent. Use of tools of organisational planning is limited and not comprehensive. Very few firms have management development programmes. Overall scores on general management are low: large firms score better than either medium-sized or small companies.

Employment of a chief executive with management training is generally associated with greater likelihood that a given technique will be used. Use of consultants is associated in small firms with greater likelihood of use being made of methods of organisational planning, while in large firms attendance at Irish Management Institute courses is associated with having management development programmes. There are no other significant associations.

PART A. PERSONNEL MANAGEMENT

Section 1: Manpower Forecasts

The first question considered (question 78 of the questionnaire) is whether the firms surveyed had made any attempt to estimate their future manpower requirements, this being the basic information required for planning in the personnel function.

CONCLUSION. Manpower forecasting is not widespread or comprehensive, but is likely to come in for more interest in future as educational opportunities become greater and the demand for labour grows. The firms most likely at present to make manpower forecasts are large companies, particularly those employing a specialist personnel executive.

TABLE 15. 1. 1. *Estimated Proportion of Firms Making Manpower Forecasts, by Size of Firm.*

Size of Firm (No. of Employees)	Total Firms Included	Percentage Making Manpower Forecasts	Percentage Not Making Manpower Forecasts
500 or More	47	31.9	68.1
100-499	48	6.2(1.3—17.2)	93.7
20-99	46	6.5(1.3—17.9)	93.5
OVERALL		7.4±5.5	92.6

The figures in the table above show a very low degree of activity in this field. This is perhaps not surprising, especially in smaller firms, in view of the fact that in Ireland there has traditionally been a surplus of labour relative to the requirements of industry. Because labour was quite freely available, managements saw no reason to make advance plans. However, quite a few of the firms visited said that they were becoming more concerned with this aspect as the supply of labour became tighter. In fact, many firms reported shortages beginning to arise, and evidence of bottle-necks in some areas. The recently instituted Department of Labour should be very helpful to industry in dealing with this matter, and can count on a greater awareness of the problem now than would have been met with some years ago. Firms were also asked how far ahead their estimates extended and it can be seen from the following table that firms which made estimates usually did so for only a limited future period.

TABLE 15. 1. 2.   *Estimated Percentage of Firms Making Manpower Forecasts for Specified Periods Ahead, by Size of Firm.*

Size of Firm (No. of Employees)	Total Firms Included	Percentage Forecasting Ahead For			Not At All
		1 Year or Less	1-5 Years	5 or More Years	
500 or More	46	13.0	10.9	6.5	69.6
100-499	48	4.2	2.1	—	93.7
20-99	46	6.5	—	—	93.5
OVERALL		6.3	0.8	0.2	92.6

In the case of only one or two firms was there a comprehensive and detailed long-term estimate made in the context of extensive future planning and arising out of the intention to implement formal sales and capital programmes. This question was selected for an examination of the possibility of associations, though in view of the very low extent to which the activity is carried on it was not expected that any associations would be very marked.

TABLE 15. 1. 3.   *Percentage of Firms Making Manpower Forecasts, by Size and Location of Firm.*

Size of Firm (No. of Employees)	Location of Head Office	Total Firms Included	Percentage Making Forecasts	Percentage Not Making Forecasts
500 or More	DUBLIN	28	32.14	67.86
	REST OF COUNTRY	17	35.29	64.71
	OVERALL	45	33.33	66.67
100-499	DUBLIN	22	9.09	90.91
	REST OF COUNTRY	22	18.18	81.82
	OVERALL	44	6.82	93.19
20-99	DUBLIN	20	—	100.00
	REST OF COUNTRY	22	9.09	90.91
	OVERALL	42	4.77	95.24

Location, as table 15.1.3 shows, exercises virtually no effect. Size is associated with making forecasts, but the significant difference arises only between the top and the other two size-groups, i.e. there is no evidence of any difference between the middle and bottom strata. An association with the training and qualification of the responsible executive is usually considered after location. In this case, however, there were so few personnel executives that it was not possible to differentiate between them even in the top size-group. Outside of this size-group it was not possible to make any comparisons at all. It was decided that the most meaningful comparison was between firms employing a personnel executive and firms not doing so, and the division is shown for the top size-group in table 15.1.4.

TABLE 15. 1. 4. *Percentage of Firms Making Manpower Forecasts, by Size of Firm and Employment of a Personnel Executive.*

Size of Firm (No. of Employees)	Employment of Personnel Executive	Total Firms Included	Percentage Making Manpower Forecasts	Percentage Not Making Manpower Forecasts
500 or More	PERSONNEL EXEC.	28	42.86	57.15
	NO PERSONNEL EXEC.	17	17.65	82.36
	OVERALL	45	33.33	66.67

There is quite a marked positive association between employment of a personnel executive and the making of forecasts. Use of consultants and attendance at Irish Management Institute courses is examined in tables 15.1.5. and 15.1.6.

TABLE 15. 1. 5. *Percentage of Firms Making Manpower Forecasts, by Size of Firm and Use of Consultants.*

Size of Firm (No. of Employees)	Use of Consultants	Total Firms Included	Percentage Making Manpower Forecasts	Percentage Not Making Manpower Forecasts
500 or More	USED	34	29.41	70.59
	DID NOT USE	11	45.45	54.55
	OVERALL	45	33.33	66.67
100-499	USED	17	5.88	94.12
	DID NOT USE	27	7.41	92.59
	OVERALL	44	6.82	93.19
20-99	USED	7	14.29	85.71
	DID NOT USE	35	2.86	97.14
	OVERALL	42	4.77	95.24

As can be seen from table 15.1.5. there is little or no association between employment of consultants and making forecasts. In fact, in the top size-group the association is negative. This is a reflection of the fact that some very progressive companies had not felt that they had anything to gain from the use of consultants' services. Attendance at courses seems in the two larger size-groups to have a slight positive association with manpower forecasting, but the association is not significant.

TABLE 15. 1. 6.   *Percentage of Firms Making Manpower Forecasts, by Size of Firm and Use of Irish Management Institute Courses.*

Size of Firm (No. of Employees)	Use by Firm of I.M.I. Courses	Total Firms Included	Percentage Making Forecasts	Percentage Not Making Forecasts
500 or More	USED	40	35.00	65.00
	DID NOT USE	5	20.00	80.00
	TOTAL	45	33.33	66.67
100–499	USED	10	30.00	70.00
	DID NOT USE	34	—	100.00
	TOTAL	44	6.82	93.18
20–99	USED	7	—	100.00
	DID NOT USE	35	5.71	94.29
	TOTAL	42	4.76	95.24

Section 2: Selection Techniques

After considering forecasting manpower requirements, it seemed logical next to look at the question of selection (question 61 of questionnaire). Firms were asked whether they had ever used any method of selection other than interview, for instance, aptitude tests, I.Q. tests, personality assessment and so on. Their replies are shown in table 15.2.1. below.

CONCLUSION. Use of techniques of selection is minimal. As in the case of forecasting, the firms most likely to use techniques are those with 500 employees or more particularly those employing a full-time personnel executive.

TABLE 15. 2. 1.   *Estimated Percentage of Firms Using Any Selection Method Other Than Interview, by Size of Firm.*

Size of Firm (No. of Employees)	Total Firms Included	Percentage Using Selection Techniques	Percentage Not Using Selection Techniques
500 or More	47	29.8	70.2
100–499	48	6.2(1.3—17.2)	93.8
20-99	46	—	100.0
OVERALL		2.4±0.6	97.6

The use of such techniques of selection is minimal as the above table shows. Even among firms employing 500 or more people the proportion is less than one-in-three, while below that point their use is almost non-existent. This is, perhaps, another reflection of the traditional easy availability of labour in Ireland, though some firms stated that it was a function of scarcity rather than of abundance, saying that in some cases they had to take what they could get, while in others the general level of applicants was so low that those suitable stood out very obviously from the remainder. This latter observation may, however, be more a reflection of lack of interviewing skills by which the interviewees' abilities would be brought out and assessed.

The question of association between location and other factors and the use of selection techniques is now considered although, except in the top size-group, these associations cannot be very marked because of the general low level of use.

TABLE 15. 2. 2. *Percentage of Firms Using Selection Methods Other Than Interview, by Size and Location of Firm.*

Size of Firm (No. of Employees)	Location of Head Office	Total Firms Included	Percentage Using Selection Techniques	Percentage Not Using Selection Techniques
500 or More	DUBLIN	28	28.57	71.43
	REST OF COUNTRY	17	35.29	64.71
	OVERALL	45	31.12	68.89
100-499	DUBLIN	22	4.55	95.46
	REST OF COUNTRY	22	4.55	95.46
	OVERALL	44	4.55	95.46

It can be seen from table 15.2.2. that location shows no association but that there is a very significant difference in this regard between the two size-groups.

TABLE 15. 2. 3. *Percentage of Firms Using Selection Methods Other Than Interview, by Size of Firm and its Employment of a Personnel Executive.*

Size of Firm (No. of Employees)	Employment of Personnel Executive	Total Firms Included	Percentage Using Selection Techniques	Percentage Not Using Selection Techniques
500 or More	PERSONNEL EXEC.	28	39.29	60.72
	NO PERSONNEL EXEC.	17	17.65	82.36
	OVERALL	45	31.12	68.89

Table 15.2.3. shows that there is a fairly marked positive association between em-employment of a personnel executive and use of selection techniques.

The next factors considered are use of consultants and attendance at Irish Management Institute courses, the position in respect of which is shown in tables 15.2.4 and 15.2.5.

From table 15.2.4. it is obvious that use of consultants shows little or no association, while from the second it can be seen that attendance at courses is of little practical consequence either, the use of techniques being confined mostly to the larger size-group in which almost all the firms have sent people on courses at one time or another.

TABLE 15.2.4.   *Percentage of Firms Using Selection Methods Other Than Interview, by Size of Firm and Use of Consultants.*

Size of Firm (No. of Employees)	Use of Consultants	Total Firms Included	Percentage Using Selection Techniques	Percentage Not Using Selection Techniques
500 or More	USED	34	32.35	67.65
	DID NOT USE	11	27.27	72.73
	OVERALL	45	31.12	68.89
100-499	USED	17	11.76	88.24
	DID NOT USE	27	—	100.00
	OVERALL	44	4.55	95.46

TABLE 15.2.5.   *Percentage of Firms Using Selection Methods Other Than Interview, by Size of Firm and Use of Irish Management Institute Courses.*

Size of Firm (No. of Employees)	Use by Firm of I.M.I. Courses	Total Firms Included	Percentage Using Selection Techniques	Percentage Not Using Selection Techniques
500 or More	USED	40	35.00	65.00
	DID NOT USE	5	—	100.00
	OVERALL	45	31.12	68.89
100-499	USED	10	—	100.00
	DID NOT USE	34	5.88	94.12
	OVERALL	44	4.55	95.46

Section 3: Training

Having considered manpower forecasting and selection, the next activity investigated was training (question 60 of questionnaire). In this question, firms were asked whether they had any formal training arrangements for all employees. It was emphasised that the stress in this question was on the word "all". This was done because, for many types of employee, there are either statutory or traditional schemes of apprenticeship, as a result of which almost any firm would be expected to participate in some form of training irrespective of its commitment to the activity. It was decided to ask whether all employees were covered, as it was felt that only those firms which had made arrangements for all could be said to be truly committed to the improvement of performance through training. The definition was rigorous and its result was to understate quite heavily the degree to which firms participate in some form of training arrangements for their production workers. In most cases it is to these workers that training is confined, and many firms show a very high degree of willingness to have people trained technically. They obviously do not consider it so important to extend this concern to office workers, sales staff or other employees, as table 15.3.1. shows.

TABLE 15. 3. 1. *Estimated Percentage of Firms Having Formal Training Schemes for All Types of Employee, by Size of Firm.*

Size of Firm (No. of Employees)	Total Firms Included	Percentage With Training Scheme	Percentage Without Training Scheme
500 or More	47	25.5	74.5
100-499	48	2.1(0—11.1)	97.9
20-99	46	—	100.0
OVERALL		1.4±0.8	98.6

It is clear from this table that the idea of comprehensive training as a means of raising the total performance of the firm is not yet fully accepted.

Section 4: Appraisal

Firms were finally asked (question 62) whether they regularly appraised the performance of their employees. It was made clear to them that this did not imply the use of appraisal interviews or of counselling (which has come under a good deal of attack recently) but simply whether, at any intervals, the performance of employees was formally reviewed.

TABLE 15. 4. 1. *Estimated Percentage of Firms Regularly Appraising Employees, by Size of Firm.*

Size of Firm (No. of Employees)	Total Firms Included	Percentage Appraising	Percentage Not Appraising
500 or More	47	21.3	78.7
100-499	48	—	100.0
20-99	46	2.2(0—11.6)	97.8
OVERALL	141	2.4±3.2	97.6

This practice is very much the exception rather than the rule, being almost unknown until a firm reaches 500 or more employees and, even then, not being very common. This lack of formal review among smaller firms was not unexpected, as managers feel that they are in such close daily contact with their workers that it is not necessary. Also, in many such firms, the majority of workers are paid at negotiated rates over which their managers have no control. Consequently, there is no impetus towards review of performance as a factor in considering wage adjustments.

Section 5: Overall Scores on Personnel Management

Firms were given one mark each for making formal manpower forecasts, using techniques of selection and having comprehensive plans for training.

TABLE 15. 5. 1.   *Estimated Percentage of Firms Achieving Specified Scores on Personnel Management Practices, by Size of Firm.*

Size of Firm (No. of Employees)	Total Firms Included	0	Percentage Scoring 1	2	3
500 or More	47	55.3	19.1	10.6	14.9
100-499	48	87.5	10.4	2.1	—
20-99	46	93.5	6.5	—	—
OVERALL		90.8	7.8	0.8	0.6

A majority of firms did not score even one mark. Those with over 500 employees scored better than the rest but, even of these, 75 per cent scored only one point or less. Because so few firms with under 500 employees scored anything but zero it was impossible to look for associations in their case. In the case of firms with over 500 employees, those with a specialist personnel executive, those which had sent participants to Irish Management Institute courses and those located outside Dublin, scored better than the rest.

PART B.   GENERAL MANAGEMENT

Having considered each of the principal functional areas in turn, it seemed appropriate to look at the overall direction of the company, which is the responsibility of the chief executive. Some important concerns of the chief executive are planning the future direction of the company, devising an appropriate organisation structure, developing his subordinate managers and providing for succession. These activities are considered in turn.

Section 6:   Long-Range Market Forecasts
The basic element in forward planning is an assessment of the future market. This question was considered at length in chapter 12, but it is taken up again in this context to see if it was associated with attributes of the chief executive.

TABLE 15. 6. 1.   *Percentage of Firms Making Long-range Market Forecasts, by Size of Firm and Training of Chief Executive.*

Size of Firm (No. of Employees)	Training of Chief Executive	Total Firms Included	Percentage Making Forecasts	Percentage Not Making Forecasts
500 or More	TRAINED	27	77.78	22.22
	UNTRAINED	14	42.86	57.15
100-499	TRAINED	6	—	100.00
	UNTRAINED	36	27.78	72.23
20-99	TRAINED	6	—	100.00
	UNTRAINED	32	3.13	96.88

TABLE 15. 6. 2. *Percentage of Firms Making Long-range Market Forecasts, by Size of Firm and Qualification of Chief Executive.*

Size of Firm (No. of Employees)	Qualification of Chief Executive	Total Firms Included	Percentage Making Forecasts	Percentage Not Making Forecasts
500 or More	QUALIFIED	21	66.67	33.33
	UNQUALIFIED	20	65.00	35.00
100-499	QUALIFIED	12	33.33	66.67
	UNQUALIFIED	30	20.00	80.00
20-99	QUALIFIED	7	—	100.00
	UNQUALIFIED	31	3.23	96.78

Tables 15.6.1. and 15.6.2. show the position with respect to participation in management training and possession of academic qualifications. In the first it can be seen that there is a marked tendency in the top size-group for training to be associated positively with the making of forecasts. This positive association is not repeated in either of the other size-groups, in which the differences appear to be in the opposite direction without, however, being statistically significant. As regards possession of qualifications, this does not appear to exercise a very considerable effect as all the differences observed might easily have arisen by chance.

Section 7: Capital Forecasts

Another vital area for the chief executive is the future financial health of his organisation. Capital forecasting was, therefore, looked at again to see if training or qualification of chief executives is associated with it.

TABLE 15. 7. 1. *Percentage of Firms Making Capital Forecasts, by Size of Firm and Training of Chief Executive.*

Size of Firm (No. of Employees)	Training of Chief Executive	Total Firms Included	Percentage Making Capital Forecasts	Percentage Not Making Capital Forecasts
500 or More	TRAINED	27	81.48	18.52
	UNTRAINED	15	80.00	20.00
100-499	TRAINED	6	33.33	66.67
	UNTRAINED	37	54.06	45.95
20-99	TRAINED	7	71.43	28.57
	UNTRAINED	32	15.63	84.38

In the bottom stratum there is a very marked tendency for firms employing a chief executive with management training to be more likely to make forecasts than firms whose chief executive had not attended training courses. This difference is highly significant statistically. From table 15.7.2. it is obvious that possession of qualifications does not much alter the situation.

TABLE 15. 7. 2.   *Percentage of Firms Making Capital Forecasts, by Size of Firm and Qualification of Chief Executive.*

Size of Firm (No. of Employees)	Qualification of Chief Executive	Total Firms Included	Percentage Making Capital Forecasts	Percentage Not Making Capital Forecasts
500 or More	QUALIFIED	22	86.36	13.64
	UNQUALIFIED	20	75.00	25.00
100-499	QUALIFIED	12	58.34	41.67
	UNQUALIFIED	31	48.39	51.62
20-99	QUALIFIED	7	14.29	85.71
	UNQUALIFIED	32	28.13	71.88

Section 8: Organisational Planning

As both market and capital forecasts had already been treated in detail earlier in the survey, the first question selected for lengthier examination was the use by the firm of tools of organisational planning. In question 81 of the questionnaire firms were asked whether they had ever used organisation charts, statements of executive responsibility, statements of company objectives or statements of company policy. Their replies are shown in the table 15.8.1.

CONCLUSION. Use of tools of organisational planning is neither widespread nor comprehensive. As expected, large firms are more likely to use them than either small or medium-sized companies. Small firms which had employed consultants are more likely than other small firms to have statements of responsibility and policy, possibly introduced in conjunction with systems of costing and control.

TABLE 15. 8. 1.   *Estimated Percentage of Firms Using Specified Methods of Organisational Planning.*

Size of Firm (No. of Employees)	Total Firms Included	Organisation Charts	Percentage Using Statements of Executive Responsibility	Statements of Company Objectives	Statements of Company Policy
500 or More	47	51.1	46.8	14.9	25.5
100-499	48	18.8(8.9-32.7)	12.5(4.7-25.2)	4.2(0.5-14.2)	6.2(1.3-17.2)
20-99	46	2.2(0-11.6)	8.7(2.4-20.8)	2.2(0-11.6)	4.3(0.5-14.8)
OVERALL		7.4±3.8	10.9±6.4	3.1±3.3	5.5±4.6

The use of the tools mentioned is not very common. In the smallest size-group it is very rare indeed, as might have been expected, the necessity for formal organisation not usually being obvious when the number of employees is low. This can be seen from the fact that organisation charts are the least used aid in the case of the smallest size-group, whereas in the other two they are more often used than any of the others, showing that in the smallest group the number of people is usually so low that it is not necessary to formalise the organisation in this way. Table 15.8.2. shows the number of these tools used by firms.

TABLE 15.8.2. *Number of Organisational Planning Methods Used, by Size of Firm.*

Size of Firm (No. of Employees)	Total Firms Included	None	Percentage Using			
			One	Two	Three	All Four
300 or More	47	42.6	8.5	29.8	8.5	10.6
100-499	48	72.9	16.7	8.3	—	2.1
20-99	46	89.1	8.7	—	—	2.2
OVERALL		84.0	10.3	2.8	0.3	2.5

It is unusual for firms' practices to be any way comprehensive, very few of them using anything other than organisation charts and statements of responsibility. It was decided to investigate associations between a variety of factors and the use of organisational planning methods, the firms replying to this question being divided into those which used no methods and those which used some. The first factor considered is location.

TABLE 15.8.3. *Percentage of Firms Using Organisational Planning Methods, by Size and Location of Firm.*

Size of Firm (No. of Employees)	Location of Head Office	Total Firms Included	Percentage Using Some Methods	Percentage Using No Methods
500 or More	DUBLIN	28	60.72	39.29
	REST OF COUNTRY	17	52.95	47.06
	OVERALL	45	57.78	42.23
100-499	DUBLIN	22	27.28	72.73
	REST OF COUNTRY	22	27.28	72.73
	OVERALL	44	27.28	72.73
20-99	DUBLIN	20	15.00	85.00
	REST OF COUNTRY	22	4.55	95.45
	OVERALL	42	9.53	90.48

It is obvious that location is not associated with planning but that size is. The differences between the size-groups are highly significant, both overall and in each location, with increasing size leading to greater likelihood of some degree of organisational planning.

TABLE 15. 8. 4.   *Percentage of Firms Using Organisational Planning Methods, by Size of Firm and Training of Chief Executive.*

Size of Firm (No. of Employees)	Training of Chief Executive	Total Firms Included	Percentage Using Some Method	Percentage Using No Method
500 or More	TRAINED	27	59.26	40.75
	UNTRAINED	15	46.67	53.34
100-499	TRAINED	6	16.67	83.33
	UNTRAINED	37	27.03	72.98
20-99	TRAINED	7	28.57	71.43
	UNTRAINED	32	6.26	93.76

TABLE 15. 8. 5.   *Percentage of Firms Using Organisational Planning Methods, by Size of Firm and Qualification of Chief Executive.*

Size of Firm (No. of Employees)	Qualification of Chief Executive	Total Firms Included	Percentage Using Some Methods	Percentage Using No Methods
500 or More	QUALIFIED	22	40.90	59.10
	UNQUALIFIED	20	70.00	30.00
100-499	QUALIFIED	12	41.67	58.23
	UNQUALIFIED	31	19.36	80.65
20-99	QUALIFIED	7	28.57	71.43
	UNQUALIFIED	32	6.26	93.76

The association between training and organisational planning is neither very marked nor consistent, and in no case is it of statistical significance. Neither is qualification consistently associated positively with this activity. The differences shown in the two strata with under 500 employees in table 15.8.5. are not significant. The direction of the difference in the top size-group is rather surprising. The difference is, in fact, largely a function of size and nationality of ownership. Almost all foreign-owned companies with over 500 employees have used some methods of planning most likely because the large international organisations by which they are owned do so as a matter of course. Irish companies are not very likely to do so until they have passed 1,000 employees.

As usual, after considering the attributes of the responsible executive, associations are investigated with use of consultants and attendance at Irish Management Institute courses.

Use of consultants appears to make very little difference in the case of either of the two larger size-groups. In the case of the bottom stratum it shows a very marked association which is highly significant statistically. This might be expected where consultants are used for the installation of financial control methods, as these require clear-cut assignment of budget responsibilities. Attendance at courses, on the other hand, makes no difference of any consequence to the likelihood that a firm will use planning methods.

TABLE 15. 8. 6. *Percentage of Firms Using Organisational Planning Methods, by Size of Firm and Use of Consultants.*

Size of Firm (No. of Employees)	Use of Consultants	Total Firms Included	Percentage Using Some Methods	Percentage Using No Methods
500 or More	USED	34	58.82	41.18
	DID NOT USE	11	54.55	45.45
	OVERALL	45	57.78	42.23
100-499	USED	17	35.29	64.71
	DID NOT USE	27	22.22	77.78
	OVERALL	44	27.28	72.73
20-99	USED	7	42.86	57.14
	DID NOT USE	35	2.86	97.14
	OVERALL	42	9.53	90.48

TABLE 15. 8. 7. *Percentage of Firms Using Organisational Planning Methods, by Size of Firm and Use of Irish Management Institute Courses.*

Size of Firm (No. of Employees)	Use by Firm of I.M.I. Courses	Total Firms Included	Percentage Using Some Methods	Pecentage Using No Methods
500 or More	USED	40	60.00	40.00
	DID NOT USE	5	40.00	60.00
	OVERALL	45	57.78	42.23
100-499	USED	10	30.00	70.00
	DID NOT USE	34	26.47	73.53
	OVERALL	44	27.28	72.73
20-99	USED	7	—	100.00
	DID NOT USE	35	11.43	88.57
	OVERALL	42	9.53	90.48

Section 9: Provision of Information

Firms were asked (question 79) whether they made information available to executives on the progress of their departments, as it was considered that this was the most elementary step in helping their development. The replies given by those firms to which the question was applicable are shown in table 15.9.1. The question did not apply to some firms in the smallest size-group, sometimes because there were no managers other than the chief executive, and sometimes because no attempt had been made to assign particular areas as the responsibility of each executive.

TABLE 15. 9. 1.   *Estimated Percentage of Firms Organised Departmentally Having Departmental Reports Available to Responsible Executives.*

Size of Firm (No. of Employees)	Total Firms Included	Percentage Having Reports Available	Percentage Not Having Reports Available
500 or More	47	87.2	12.8
100-499	46	54.3	45.7
20-99	27	37.0	63.0
OVERALL		42.5	57.5

Among the largest firms, managers almost invariably receive some information about their department on a formal basis. This is true in only about half the firms in the middle size-group and only about one-third in the smallest. It would be wrong, in the case of the smallest size-group, to attribute this fact completely to an unwillingness on the part of the chief executive to give information, although this was undoubtedly true in some cases, and even pursued as a deliberate policy. It is probably more often due to the fact that members of the management team are in close daily contact with one another, the amount of formal information is limited, and such information as there is circulates freely among the executives.

Section 10:   Management Development Programmes

A question of vital concern in the survey was to see to what extent firms had formal management development programmes (question 25). It was emphasised that what was in mind was not the occasional or haphazard use of training courses, but a formulated policy of improvement. It was considered that such a policy ought to exist in any firm, however small, which had given serious thought to the problem. Table 15.10.1 shows the position.

TABLE 15. 10. 1.   *Estimated Proportion of Firms Having a Formal Management Development Programme, by Size of Firm.*

Size of Firm (No. of Employees)	Total Firms Included	Percentage Having Formal Programme	Percentage Not Having a Formal Programme
500 or More	47	40.4	59.6
100-499	48	8.3(2.3—20.0)	91.7
20-99	46	—	100.0
OVERALL		3.2±1.5	96.7

CONCLUSION. Very few firms outside the largest size-group have a formal programme of management development. The likelihood that a firm will have a programme is greater among large firms whose chief executive has himself attended a management training course and also among large firms which have sent participants to Irish Management Institute courses. Less than half the large firms sending participants had a formal programme.

It can be seen from this table that much remains to be done before formal management development becomes the norm. The existence of deliberate policies is virtually unknown until 500 or more people are employed by the firm and, even among firms as large as this, only about two in five are committed to any policy, however superficial. Because of its importance, this question was also selected for more extensive discussion. Location, as table 15.10.2 shows, is not associated with the existence of such policies.

TABLE 15.10.2. *Percentage of Firms Having a Formal Management Development Programme, by Size and Location of Firm.*

Size of Firm (No. of Employees)	Location of Head Office	Total Firms Included	Percentage Having a Formal Programme	Percentage Not Having a Formal Programme
500 or More	DUBLIN	28	39.29	60.72
	REST OF COUNTRY	17	47.06	52.95
	OVERALL	45	42.23	57.78
100-499	DUBLIN	22	4.55	95.45
	REST OF COUNTRY	22	13.63	86.37
	OVERALL	44	9.10	90.91

Size, however, is associated, but only after the 500 employee mark is passed.

An analysis by training and qualification of the chief executive is shown in tables 15.10.3 and 15.10.4.

TABLE 15.10.3. *Percentage of Firms Having a Formal Management Development Programme, by Size of Firm and Training of Chief Executive.*

Size of Firm (No. of Employees)	Training of Chief Executive	Total Firms Included	Percentage Having a Formal Programme	Percentage Not Having a Formal Programme
500 or More	TRAINED	27	55.55	44.45
	UNTRAINED	15	20.00	80.00
100-499	TRAINED	6	—	100.00
	UNTRAINED	36	11.11	88.89

Among the largest firms those employing chief executives with training are markedly more likely than others to have a formal programme. The possession by the chief executive of academic qualifications is associated hardly at all with the existence of a management development scheme.

TABLE 15. 10. 4. *Percentage of Firms Having a Formal Management Development Programme, by Size of Firm and Qualification of Chief Executive.*

Size of Firm (No. of Employees)	Qualification of Chief Exec.	Total Firms Included	Percentage Having a Formal Programme	Percentage Not Having a Formal Programme
500 or More	QUALIFIED	22	45.45	54.55
	UNQUALIFIED	20	40.00	60.00
100–499	QUALIFIED	12	16.67	83.33
	UNQUALIFIED	31	6.45	93.55

The next factors considered are the use of consultants and attendance at courses. It might be expected, *a priori,* that firms attending courses would be more likely than others to have a formal development programme.

TABLE 15. 10. 5. *Percentage of Firms Having a Formal Management Development Programme, by Size of Firm and Use of Consultants.*

Size of Firm (No. of Employees)	Use of Consultants	Total Firms Included	Percentage Having a Formal Programme	Percentage Not Having a Formal Programme
500 or More	USED	34	44.12	55.88
	DID NOT USE	11	36.36	63.64
	OVERALL	45	42.23	57.78
100-499	USED	17	11.76	88.24
	DID NOT USE	27	7.41	92.59
	OVERALL	44	9.10	90.91

TABLE 15. 10. 6. *Percentage of Firms Having a Formal Management Development Programme, by Size of Firm and Use of Irish Management Institute Courses.*

Size of Firm (No. of Employees)	Use by Firm of I.M.I. Courses	Total Firms Included	Percentage Having a Formal Programme	Percentage Not Having a Formal Programme
500 or More	USED	40	45.00	55.00
	DID NOT USE	5	20.00	80.00
	OVERALL	45	42.22	57.78
100-499	USED	10	20.00	80.00
	DID NOT USE	34	5.88	94.12
	OVERALL	44	9.09	**90.91**

Use of consultants, as can be seen from the first of these tables, is associated **hardly** at all, even in the top size-group, with the existence of a policy. On the other hand, **use** of courses shows a fairly marked association among larger firms, and a smaller one among medium-sized companies, where the observed difference is not significant statistically. It should be noted from this table that, in the case of both large and medium-sized companies, the majority of firms using courses did not have a formal programme, i.e., attendance at courses was *ad hoc* rather than planned.

Section 11: Succession

Finally, the question is considered of whether firms have available a successor to their chief executive (question 26). The question asked was whether, if the chief executive were to leave the company, an adequate replacement could be found for him from

TABLE 15. 11. 1. *Estimated Percentage of Firms Having a Successor Available for the Chief Executive, by Size of Firm.*

Size of Firm (No. of Employees)	Total Firms Included	Percentage With Successor	Percentage With No Successor	Percentage Not Replying
500 or More	47	61.7	31.9	6.4
100–499	48	41.7	41.7	16.7
20–99	46	43.5	52.2	**4.3**
OVERALL		43.8	49.3	7.0

within. Some interviewees preferred not to commit themselves on this point. Those who did reply were evenly divided between having and not having a successor, except in the case of firms with 500 or more employees, where twice as many said they had as gave a negative reply. Some of the interviewees were youngish men in family businesses who expected to be succeeded by some other member of the family, sometimes still being educated and sometimes in the company, but not yet, in the opinion of the interviewee, sufficiently experienced to be an adequate successor. It was noticeable, however, that this question caused some discomfort and, although it is numbered 26 in the questionnaire, was generally left until the end. Many of the executives interviewed said that this was the first time that they had ever been forced to think about the question and that it was not too pleasant a surprise to them to discover, on reflection, what the position was. The fact that as many as half of the executives interviewed felt that they had no readily available successor, and that very few companies had a formal policy of management development, is indicative that the provision of our future business leaders is still, to a great extent, left to chance.

Section 12: Overall Scores on General Management

Firms were given one mark each for making forecasts of the development of their market, for making forecasts of their capital requirements, for having a management development programme and for using any tool of organisational planning.

Companies with 500 or more employees tended to score rather well, those with under 500 scored badly. There was no difference between those with under 100 employees and those with 100 to 499 employees. There was a slight tendency for large firms whose chief executive had attended training courses to do better than those whose chief executive had not. None of the other factors considered was associated with higher scores.

TABLE 15. 12. 1.   *Estimated Percentage of Firms Achieving Specified Scores on General Management, by Size of Firm.*

Size of Firm (No. of Employees)	Total Firms Included	Percentage Scoring				
		0	1	2	3	4
500 or More	47	14.9	14.9	14.9	40.4	14.9
100–499	48	41.7	39.6	8.3	8.3	2.1
20–99	46	69.6	23.9	4.3	2.2	—
OVERALL		61.8	26.8	5.6	4.9	1.0

CHAPTER 16

An Overview of the Use of Management Techniques

In the first section of this chapter the findings of earlier chapters on the use of techniques or activities of management are summarised. An attempt is made in the second section to compare the position in Ireland with that abroad.

Summary of Findings

Scores were assigned to firms on the basis of their use of management techniques. High scores were achieved only by large companies. Foreign-owned companies showed some tendency to score higher than Irish-owned firms. Firms employing managers with training, and firms which had used the services of consultants, also tended to score better than others.

There was considerable similarity between the groups in the order of likelihood of using different techniques. This agreement was particularly marked between medium-sized and small firms. In general the most likely activities or techniques related to the past or to the present rather than to the future.

This bears out the author's general impression that few firms had considered carefully where they wished to go and formulated a set of plans to bring themselves to that position.

Because no comparable studies are available, it is not possible satisfactorily to compare the situation in Ireland with that abroad, but such slight evidence as there is suggests that Irish firms are less advanced than comparably sized firms in other countries.

Section 1: Overall Use of Techniques

At the end of each of the four preceding chapters the overall use of techniques in each particular area was summarised by giving to each firm a score based on its replies to some selected questions. A similar rough scoring system is used here to summarise the overall position.

In the area of marketing, one point was given for having sales cost analysis, another for formal study of the market, another if the study was based either on official statistics or field surveys, another for making long-range forecasts and a fifth point for making annual sales plans.

In production, a point was given for keeping machine-load records, for having used work study at any time and for achieving a high score on quality control activities.

In the finance area a point was given for using budgetary control, for using standard costs and for making capital forecasts.

In the area of personnel management and general management a point each was given for use of selection techniques, for having a comprehensive training scheme, for having a management development programme, for making manpower forecasts and for having statements of executive responsibility.

The scoring system is rough: equal weight is given to each technique, there are not equal numbers of techniques for each area (hence firms oriented to marketing have a better chance of achieving high scores than production-oriented firms) and not all the techniques are equally relevant to firms of different sizes. It is felt nevertheless that the scores give a useful overview of the current state of management practice in that area of management to which they refer.

TABLE 16. 1.   *Percentage of Firms Achieving Specified Scores on Overall Use of Management Techniques, by Size of Firm.*

Size of Firm (No. of Employees)	Total Firms Included[1]	Zero	Percentage Scoring		
			1-5	6-11	12-16
500 or more	42	2.4	11.9	45.2	40.5
100 — 499	43	9.3	51.2	37.2	2.3
20 — 99	41	39.0	53.7	7.3	—

[1]Firms which had changed size-groups, and firms making or repairing exclusively for a parent company, were excluded from this analysis.

Table 16.1 shows the percentage of firms of different size achieving specified ranges of scores. It confirms the broad picture seen in earlier chapters, that large companies employ the techniques mentioned to a considerable extent, that small companies employ them hardly at all, and that medium-sized firms employ them to a lesser extent than expected. The differences between the size-groups are statistically significant.

A wide variety of factors was examined to see whether they were associated with the scores achieved. A firm's location was not associated with its scores, nor was the type of market it served nor its type of production. Except in the top size-group, where most firms are members, firms which were members of the Irish Management Institute did not score higher than those which were not. In the group of small firms, public companies seemed less likely to score zero than family businesses, but the difference was not quite significant. Medium-sized and large family businesses scored just as well as public companies. Large foreign-owned companies were more likely to score between twelve and sixteen points than large Irish-owned firms. In the medium size-group foreign-owned firms were less likely than Irish-owned firms to score zero, while the only foreign-owned small firm achieved a high score.

Firms which employed some managers with academic qualifications showed a slight, but not significant, tendency to score higher than others

Large companies which had, in the past, sent participants to Irish Management Institute courses scored higher than large firms which had not, but this difference is of little practical importance since most large firms have attended courses. Small firms which participated were less likely than others to score zero, but the difference was just short of significance.

TABLE 16. 2.   *Percentage of Firms Achieving Specified Scores on Overall Use of Management Techniques, by Size of Firm and its Use of Management Consultants.*

Size of Firm (No. of Employees)	Use of Consultants	Total Firms Included	Zero	Percentage Scoring		
				1-5	6-11	12-16
500 or More	USED	32	—	12.5	47.0	40.5
	DID NOT USE	10	10.0	10.0	40.0	40.0
100–499	USED	17	—	35.4	58.8	5.9
	DID NOT USE	26	15.4	61.6	23.0	—
20–99	USED	7	14.3	71.4	14.3	—
	DID NOT USE	34	44.1	50.0	5.9	—

Table 16.2 shows the difference between firms which had used consultants and those which had not. Several very progressive large companies had not used consultants, some of them being branches of large international companies which provided internal consultancy and training. Thus, even companies not using consultants scored well in the top stratum. In the medium size-group, firms which had used consultants were markedly more likely to achieve high scores than firms which had not. The difference observed is statistically significant. Small companies using consultants appear less likely than others to score zero, but the difference is not statistically significant. This is not surprising in view of the small number using consultants.

TABLE 16. 3. *Percentage of Firms Achieving Specified Scores on Overall Use of Management Techniques, by Size of Firm, and its Employment of Some Managers with Management Training.*

Size of Firm (No. of Employees)	Employment of Trained Managers	Total Firms Included	Percentage Scoring			
			Zero	1-5	6-11	12-16
500 or More	EMPLOYS	38	—	10.5	44.7	44.7
	DOES NOT	4	25.0	25.0	50.0	—
100–499	EMPLOYS	28	3.6	46.4	46.4	3.6
	DOES NOT	15	20.0	60.0	20.0	—
20–99	EMPLOYS	13	15.4	69.2	15.4	—
	DOES NOT	28	50.0	46.4	3.6	—

The difference between firms employing some managers with training and firms not doing so is shown in table 16.3. In every size-group firms employing some trained managers scored better. So few firms in the top stratum do not employ some trained managers that the difference is of little practical consequence. In both middle and lower strata the differences observed are not statistically significant, though the tendency for small companies employing trained men to be less likely than other small firms to score zero approaches closely to significance.

The findings of the previous chapters are summarised in a different way in tables 16.4 and 16.5. Table 16.4 shows which factors in a firm's situation have been shown to be associated with the use of specific techniques. A tick indicates that, in some stratum at least, evidence was found of an association. A question mark indicates that test results approached so closely to significance as to cause judgement to be suspended rather than to cause the conclusion that no evidence of association existed.

Table 16.4 demonstrates again the overwhelming influence of size. The other factors most likely to be associated with use of techniques are whether or not the executive in charge of the appropriate area had attended management training courses, and whether or not the firm had ever used the services of consultants.

Table 16.5 shows the percentage of firms in each size-group using specified techniques. In every case there is a progressive increase in likelihood as firms increase in size.

What emerges even more strikingly is that, for each size-group, the ten techniques most likely to be used are the same. The agreement in order between small firms and medium-sized firms is particularly marked, demonstrating once again that medium-sized companies resemble small firms rather than large.

It is interesting that, with the exception of making capital forecasts and, to a lesser extent, making annual sales plans and using budgetary control, the most likely activities or techniques relate to analysing the past or to dealing with the present. There is little emphasis on the future. This is also reflected by the fact that few Irish companies have any research and development activity. The number making an effort to develop new products is very low.

This is not surprising in a country where industry is, as was seen in the introduction, mostly new, small and, until recently, concerned with serving a limited home market which was highly protected.

TABLE 16. 4.   *Summary of Associations Between Specified Factors and the Use of Specified Techniques.*

Technique or Activity	Size of Firm	Location of Firm	Type of Market or Production	Employment of Trained Executive	Employment of Qualified Executive	Past Use of IMI courses	Past Use of Consultants
Sales-Cost Analysis	✓	✓		✓		?	
Market Study	✓		?	✓		?	
Field Surveys	✓		✓	✓			✓
Long-range Market Forecasts	✓			?	? (a)		
Machine-Load Records	✓		?	?		?	?
Work Study	✓				✓ (a)		✓
Quality Control	✓	✓	?			✓	?
Cost Accounts	✓	?		?			✓
Budgetary Control	✓	✓				?	
Standard Costs	✓	?		✓			?
Capital Forecasts	✓		✓	?			
Manpower Forecasts	✓		(b)	✓(c)			
Selection Techniques	✓		(b)	✓(c)		?	
Organisational Planning Methods	✓		(b)				✓
Management Development Programme	✓		(b)	✓		?	

(a) The association is negative, firms with a qualified executive in charge being less likely than others to use the technique in question.

(b) No attempt was made to examine an association between type of market or production and any of these techniques or activities.

(c) Because so few firms employed a personnel executive the association examined was between firms with and without a personnel executive, not between firms whose personnel executive had training and those whose executive had not.

Few of those interviewed gave the impression that they had considered carefully where they wished their company to go, that they had a well-considered set of plans

TABLE 16. 5.   *Summary of the Percentages of Firms Using Specified Techniques of Management, by Size of Firm.*

Technique	Size of Firm (No. of Employees)			
	500 or more	100-499	20-99	Overall
Sales Analysis	100.0 (1)	87.2 (1)	77.3 (1)	80.2 (1)
Sale-cost Analysis	81.0 (4)	42.6 (7)	13.6 (9)	22.1 (7)
Study of Total Market	79.5 (5)	31.9 (10)	15.9 (7)	21.6 (9)
Study of Market Segments	47.7	14.9	4.5	7.9
Study of Other Market Characteristics	34.1	2.1	—	1.7
Use of Field Research	59.0	19.1	—	6.2
Long-range Market Forecasts	61.4	23.4	6.8	12.3
Annual Sales Plans	77.3 (7)	59.6 (3)	34.9 (3)	41.6 (4)
Training in Sales Techniques	44.7	17.4	6.5	10.2
Works Documentation	87.2 (3)	70.8 (2)	54.5 (2)	60.6 (2)
Machine-load Records	60.9	14.6	6.5	10.2
Standard Times and Methods	61.7	18.8	6.5	11.1
Work Study for Any Purpose	78.7 (6)	35.4 (8)	15.2 (8)	21.8 (8)
High Scores for Formal Quality Control	68.2 (10)	54.1 (5)	32.6 (5)	38.4 (5)
Formal Cost Accounts	91.5 (2)	58.3 (4)	34.8 (4)	41.8 (3)
Budgetary Control	72.3 (9)	33.3 (9)	13.0 (10)	19.4(10)
Standard Costs	59.6	23.8	6.5	12.1
Capital Forecasts	76.6 (8)	50.0 (6)	26.1 (6)	32.9 (6)
Manpower Forecasts	31.9	6.2	6.5	7.4
Selection Techniques	29.8	6.2	—	2.4
Comprehensive Training	25.5	2.1	—	1.4
Organisational Planning Methods	57.4	27.1	10.9	16.0
Management Development Programme	40.4	8.3	—	3.2

to bring the company to that position, or that they had an adequate system of information either to evaluate their goals or to indicate whether or not these were likely to be achieved.

The overall findings of the project have been confirmed by the Advisory Service of the Irish National Productivity Committee and by the members of the Management Consultants Association.

Since its inception the Advisory Service has carried out assignments in over 100 firms. The four member-firms of the Management Consultants Association carried out between them the following number of industrial assignments in the years 1961 to 1965[1]: Production—164, Marketing—59, Accounting—56, Personnel and Organisation—60 and General Management—34.

An accurate figure cannot be given for the number of clients served as it is possible

---

1. They also carried out assignments for non-industrial firms.

that several consultants carried out assignments for the same client. Adding the total of each consultant's clients gives 219 firms, of which 66 employed 20 to 99, 106 employed 100 to 499, and 47 employed 500 or more. Compared with the total number of firms in each group, the usual picture emerges of a progressive decline in the percentage as firms become smaller. In larger firms consultants tend to have carried out assignments in more than one area. In small companies assignments were usually limited. One would not, therefore, necessarily expect in such firms to find use of consultants to be associated with a generally higher level of use of techniques but rather with use of some specific techniques. This is what was found in practice.

Section 2:   An International Comparison

Having seen the situation in Ireland with regard to use of management techniques the question arises as to how Ireland compares in this respect with other countries.

Unfortunately it is not possible to answer this question adequately because, so far as it has been possible to trace, no studies comparable with the present one have yet been completed. Inquiries were made, without success, of the European Association of Management Training Centres, of the Small Business Administration in the United States and of centres in France, Greece, Germany, Italy and the Scandinavian countries.

The only comparable completed study was a survey carried out, under a Small Business Administration grant, by the University of Minnesota (1) The study investigated the extent to which, in that state, firms with under 500 employees had various internal departments and used various outside advisory agencies.

Figures are given in reference (2) and by Fassbender (3) which suggest that, in some respects, Irish firms may fall behind comparably sized firms in Germany. Reference (2) gives the percentage of firms in Germany using work study as 97 per cent of firms with over 250 employees and 85 per cent of firms with under 100 employees. If these figures are accurate they indicate that Irish firms are a long way behind in the use of this tool of management. Fassbender quotes the percentage of firms using organisation charts and statements of executive responsibility, and regularly appraising executive performance. In every size-group the German percentages are significantly higher than the Irish.

It should, however, be pointed out that Fassbender's figures are based on a postal questionnaire which was returned by only a small percentage of the firms to which it was sent. They are therefore likely to be biased upward.

There are differences too between the University of Minnesota study and the present one, and they must be borne in mind when comparing the results.

The first difference is that the U.S. study relates only to firms in the State of Minnesota employing less than 500 people and is not to be taken as a general indication of the position in the United States, whereas the present study is based on a stratified random sample drawn from all manufacturing firms in the Republic of Ireland employing between 20 and 500 employees, and may therefore be regarded as representative of the position in this country. The second point refers to the nature of the two samples. The Minnesota study includes firms with 3 to 500 employees, whereas the present one includes only firms employing 20 to 500 people[1]. Next, whereas the sample for Ireland is a strictly random one, that of the Minnesota study is not, and therefore the sampling variability of its

---

1 But statistical tests are carried out below only on firms with over 25 employees (see table 16.8).

estimates is not known, as a consequence of which comparisons cannot strictly be made. In the next place, the percentages quoted for Ireland are unbiased estimates of the true population percentage because, when being calculated, they were weighted to take into consideration the fact that different sampling fractions were selected from the two major size-strata. In the Minnesota study, however, the sample was not stratified, and is biased towards the larger-sized small companies in that state. This bias has not been corrected in making estimates. As a result of this fact, it is probable that the over-all percentages quoted in the Minnesota study overstate the degree to which internal units and external agencies are used in that state. As against this, the fact that that study includes firms employing less than 20, whereas the present one does not, acts in the direction of reducing the percentages in Minnesota *vis-à-vis* those in Ireland. Finally, the industrial classification of the firms differs in the two studies, and it is hard to say what the effect of this might be[1].

Internal Units

The first table shows the percentage of firms in the two studies having specified internal units.

TABLE 16. 6.   *Percentage of Firms in U.S. Study and in Irish Management Institute Study Having Specified Types of Department.*

Department	U.S[a]. %	Ireland %
Production	66.0± 9.2	64.9±11.3
Sales	45.3± 9.7	28.0± 9.8
Purchasing	29.2± 8.7	4.1± 3.8
Quality Control	20.7± 7.9	11.3± 6.2
Product Research and Development	15.1± 7.0	4.1± 3.8
Credits	12.2± 6.4	—
Personnel	7.5± 5.1	2.7± 3.5
Production Planning and Control	4.7	6.3± 5.0
Industrial Engineering	3.8	4.1± 3.8
Market Research	2.8	—

a. State of Minnesota. Confidence limits were not given in the original study.

TABLE 16. 7.   *Percentage of Firms in U.S. Study and in Irish Management Institute Study Having Specified Numbers of Departments.*

Number of Departments	U.S. %	Ireland %
0	29.3	31.7
1	18.9	33.8
2	13.2	19.1
3	17.0	8.2
4	8.5	5.0
5	8.5	2.2
Over 5	4.6	—

1 All extraction firms were removed from the sample for Ireland before making comparisons, which are therefore between strictly manufacturing firms in the two places.

Table 16.6 shows that practically every internal department mentioned is less likely to exist in firms in Ireland than in firms in Minnesota. Confidence limits have been associated with the U.S. figures although this is not done in the orginial study: they are approximate only and not really justified theoretically.

In table 16.7 it can be seen that firms in Ireland appear to have a smaller number of units per firm than those in the U.S. study. Almost two-thirds have either none of the internal units specified or only one, whereas the comparable figure for Minnesota is less than one-half. It should be pointed out that firms in Ireland have units other than those specified. For instance, over 50 per cent have an internal unit dealing with finance. Finance was excluded from the Minnesota study, as it was being made the object of another investigation. Consequently, comparisons are made only between units common to the two studies. With the exception of finance which, as we have seen, is important in Ireland, inclusion of other units would not make much difference to the situation, as they are not frequent. Because there is no reason to believe that internal financial units are less common in Minnesota than in Ireland, the fact that comparisons are confined to units included in both studies should not adversely effect the position in Ireland *vis-à-vis* that in Minnesota.

Table 16.8 shows the percentage of firms in each of the major size-groupings in the U.S. and Irish studies having the specified numbers of internal units.

TABLE 16. 8.   *Percentage of Firms Having Specified Numbers of Internal Units, by Size of Firm, in U.S. and Irish Management Institute Study.*

Size of Firm (No. of Employees)	Country of Study	0	1	Number of Units per Firm 2	3	4	5	Over 5	Total Firms
25-99	U.S.	19.4	19.4	22.2	2.5	11.1	2.8	—	36
	Ireland	36.0	41.0	18.0	5.0	—	—	—	39
100-499	U.S.	—	9.6	6.5	25.8	16.2	22.5	16.2	31
	Ireland	2.4	19.5	34.0	24.4	17.0	2.4	—	41

It was not possible to use a finer size-breakdown because there were not enough firms in either study to make meaningful comparisons within finer groupings. The use of the broader breakdowns does not mean that the data are not comparable as, within each of the broad classifications, the firms in both studies are roughly comparable in size. In order to carry out a statistical test of the differences between the firms in the two studies, the breakdown in the number of units per firm had to be re-grouped as, if the breakdown in table 16.8 above were used, the numbers involved would have been too small to allow a test to be made. The data were therefore broken into only two sections, the division in the case of firms employing 20 to 100 people being into firms having 0, 1 or 2 units and firms having 3 or more units.

This re-grouping was made by moving back from the extreme right-hand column, i.e. from firms having more than five units, until a breakdown was found with sufficient firms in each group to permit the conditions of the chi-square test to be met[1]. The test

[1]The chi-square test was used, though the fact that the U.S. study did not use a strictly random sample limits the validity of using any test.

shows highly significant differences between the two countries, with Irish firms likely to have less internal units than those in the U.S. study. The same procedure was followed to arrive at a new classification in the case of firms employing 100 to 500 people and resulted in using the classes 0 to 4 units and 5 or more units. In this case also the difference was highly significant and in the same direction, i.e., Irish firms had a lower number of units than firms in Minnesota. In case these divisions seemed arbitrary, various others were tried but made no difference to the result. Wherever a test was allowable it resulted in the same conclusion.

The conclusion is that, if the number of internal units in a firm may be taken as an index of the degree of advancement of its management, then, size-for-size, firms in Ireland are not so advanced as those in Minnesota. As there is no reason to believe that firms in Minnesota are more advanced than those in the rest of the United States, the conclusion might be extended to saying that Irish firms of a given size are less advanced than American firms of the same size, but there is, of course, no firm evidence of this.

Tables 16.9 and 16.10 show the proportions of firms in comparable size-groups in the two locations having each of the specified internal departments.

TABLE 16.9.   *Percentage of Firms Having Specified Types of Department, by Size of Firm, in U.S. Study.*

Size of Firm (No. of Employees)	Production	Sales	Purchasing	Quality Control	Product R. & D.	Credits	Personnel	Production P. & C.	Ind. Engineering	Market Research
25–49	62.5	18.7	6.25	6.25	6.25	6.25	—	—	—	—
50–74	91.7	83.3	25.0	41.7	25.0	—	—	8.3	—	8.3
75–99	75.0	62.5	37.5	25.0	37.5	12.5	—	—	—	—
Overall 25–99	75.0	50.0	19.4	22.2	19.4	5.5	—	2.8	—	2.8
100–199	100.0	64.3	50.0	21.4	14.3	35.7	—	—	—	—
200–299	87.5	100.0	87.5	62.5	25.0	37.5	25.0	12.5	12.5	12.5
300–399	66.7	100.0	100.0	33.3	33.3	66.7	33.3	33.3	66.7	—
400–499	100.0	100.0	83.3	83.3	50.0	16.7	83.3	33.3	16.7	16.7
Overall 100–499	93.5	83.9	71.0	45.2	25.8	35.5	25.8	12.9	12.9	6.5

Use of Outside Agencies.

In the United States study the intention was to arrive at estimates of the use of business consultants by small firms. As it was found difficult to define the term "consultant", firms were asked instead what type of outside agencies they used. The position with regard to the main outside agencies common to both studies is shown in table 16.11.

It should be mentioned that some agencies mentioned in the U.S. study are excluded. They are personnel, industrial relations and executive development. They were omitted because their use seemed to be ambiguous: personnel, for instance, related mainly to agencies consulted when hiring new employees, while labour-relations and negotiations related mainly to the use of industry associations which were relied on to

TABLE 16. 10. *Percentage of Firms Having Specified Types of Department, by Size of Firm, in I.M.I. Study.*

Size of Firm (No. of Employees)	Production	Sales	Purchasing	Quality Control	Product R. & D.	Credits	Personnel	Production P. & C.	Ind. Engineering	Market Research	Total Number of Firms in Sample
25-49	44.4	22.2	—	5.6	—	—	—	—	—	—	18
50-74	58.3	25.0	—	—	—	—	—	—	—	—	12
75-99	88.9	22.2	—	—	—	—	—	—	11.1	—	9
Overall 25-99	59.0	23.1	—	2.6	—	—	—	—	2.6	—	39
100-199	91.7	33.3	—	16.7	—	—	8.3	8.3	8.3	—	12
200-299	100.0	50.0	16.7	50.0	5.6	5.6	—	22.2	11.1	—	18
300-399	100.0	71.4	—	14.3	57.1	—	14.3	14.3	14.3	—	7
400-499	100.0	100.0	50.0	25.0	—	—	—	—	25.0	—	4
Overall 100-499	97.6	53.7	12.2	31.7	12.2	2.4	4.9	14.6	12.2	—	41

TABLE 16. 11. *Percentage of Firms in U.S. and Irish Management Institute Studies Using Specified Types of Outside Agency.*

Type of Service	U.S.[1]	Ireland
	%	%
Auditing	90.5	100.0
Legal	82.8	100.0
Advertising	50.0±9.7	34.4±10.8
Accounting	29.2±8.8	14.5± 8.0
Market Research	17.9±7.5	2.4± 1.8
Industrial Design	9.4±5.6	5.5± 4.0
Staff Training	8.5±	3.9± 4.7
Organisational Planning	7.5±	3.4± 4.6
Product Research	5.7±	—

[1]State of Minnesota. Confidence limits not shown in original study.

conduct wage negotiations with trade unions. The percentages quoted in the table above are subject to the limitations discussed in relation to table 16.6 Auditing and legal services, though hardly considered as consultancy, are widely used both in Ireland and in Minnesota. For the remaining services Irish firms are, in almost every case, less likely to use the service in question than firms in the U.S. study. An obvious type of service not mentioned in the Minnesota survey is use of consultants for advice on production methods. About 10 per cent of firms in Ireland employing under 500 employees stated that they had used consultants for that purpose. It is interesting to note from table 16.11 that, while Irish firms invariably use agencies to a lesser extent, the relative use of the different types of agency in the two places is very similar, with use of advertising agencies being most likely followed by use of advice on accounting problems, and with the other services being used very little in either place.

Table 16.12 shows the number of outside services used by firms. As in the case of internal units, firms in Ireland tend to use them to a lesser extent. Table 16.13 shows the position for the major size-groups.

TABLE 16. 12. *Percentage of Firms in U.S. and Irish Management Institute Study Using Specified Numbers of Outside Agencies.*

Number of Services	U.S.	Ireland
	%	%
0	2.0	—
1	3.9	0.475
2	10.7	50.3
3	26.5	36.7
4	26.5	8.5
5	14.2	3.6
Over 5	17.2	0.475

TABLE 16. 13. *Percentage of Firms Using Specified Numbers of External Services, by Size of Firm, in U.S. and Irish Management Institute Study.*

Size of Firm (No. of Employees)	Country of Study	Number of Services per Firm						
		0.	1.	2.	3.	4.	5.	Over 5
25–99	U.S.	—	—	8.3	27.8	27.8	25.0	11.1
	Ireland	—	—	51.3	38.5	7.7	2.6	—
100–499	U.S.	—	—	3.2	19.4	25.8	12.9	38.7
	Ireland	—	—	34.1	36.6	17.1	9.6	2.5

TABLE 16. 14. *Percentage of Firms Using Specified Types of Outside Agency, by Size of Firm, in U.S. Study.*

Size of Firm (No. of Employees)	Audit	Legal	Personnel	Advertising	Accounting	Market Research	Ind. Design	Training	Org. Planning	Product Research
25-49	93.8	81.3	62.5	37.5	12.5	6.2	12.5	—	—	12.5
50-74	100.0	91.7	91.7	50.0	33.3	25.0	8.3	8.3	—	—
75-99	75.0	100.0	25.0	50.0	37.5	25.0	—	—	25.0	—
Overall 25-99	91.7	88.9	63.9	44.4	25.0	16.7	8.3	2.7	5.5	5.5
100-199	92.9	85.7	64.3	78.6	14.3	14.3	7.1	21.4	7.1	—
200-299	87.5	100.0	37.5	50.0	25.0	62.5	37.5	25.0	25.0	—
300-399	100.0	66.7	66.7	66.7	—	33.3	—	—	33.3	—
400-499	100.0	83.3	83.3	100.0	50.0	33.3	16.7	50.0	33.3	16.7
Overall 100-499	93.5	87.1	61.3	74.2	22.6	32.3	16.1	25.8	19.4	3.2

In order to make a statistical test possible the number of agencies was re-grouped into broader classes using the same method as for internal units. In the case of firms with less than 100 employees this led to use of the classes 0 to 4, 5 and over; in the case of firms with 100 to 500 employees it led to the classes 0 to 5 and over 5. In both cases statistical tests showed highly significant differences, with firms in Ireland using less external services than firms in Minnesota. Using different groupings did not change this conclusion: wherever a test was valid, the same significant differences were found irrespective of where the dividing line came.

Tables 16.14 and 16.15 show the use of agencies by firms in each size-group in the two locations.

TABLE 16. 15.   *Percentage of Firms Using Each Type of Outside Agency, by Size of Firm, in I.M.I. Study.*

Size of Firm (No. of Employees)	Audit	Legal	Personnel	Advertising	Accounting	Market Research	Ind. Design	Training	Org. Planning	Product Research
25-49	100.0	100.0	—	27.8	5.6	—	—	—	5.6	—
50-74	100.0	100.0	—	41.7	25.0	—	8.3	16.7	8.3	—
75-99	100.0	100.0	—	33.3	11.1	—	—	—	—	—
Overall 25-99	100.0	100.0	—	33.3	12.8	—	2.6	5.1	5.1	—
100-199	100.0	100.0	—	41.7	16.7	8.3	16.6	16.6	—	—
200-299	100.0	100.0	5.6	55.5	33.3	5.6	22.2	—	—	5.6
300-399	100.0	100.0	—	57.1	14.3	28.6	14.3	—	—	—
400-499	100.0	100.0	—	50.0	—	25.0	25.0	—	—	—
Overall 100-499	100.0	100.0	2.6	51.2	22.0	12.2	19.5	2.6	—	2.6

This examination of the use of external agencies reinforces the conclusion arrived at earlier, that firms in Ireland are less advanced in their management practices than comparably sized firms in the State of Minnesota, and possibly in the United States generally.

References.

1. A. K. Wickesberg, *Organizational Relationships in the Growing Small Manufacturing Firm.* Minneapolis: University of Minnesota, 1961.

2. Irish National Productivity Committee. *Work Study Practices in Ireland.* Dublin: INPC, 1964, p. 2.

3. S. Fassbender. *Die Weiterbildung betrieblicher Führungskräfte in Deutschland.* Frankfurt: Rationalisierungs-Kuratorium der Deutschen Wirtschaft, 1966, p. 25, 26.

PART III

Facilities for Education and Training

CHAPTER 17

Facilities for Education and Training

This chapter describes the institutional facilities in Ireland for education and training for management. It does not include training done by firms themselves. The next chapter shows that such training is limited.

Because of the importance of basic academic qualifications, a description is given of all university degrees and professional qualifications which, as a result of the findings of chapters four and eight, are seen to be relevant to industrial management. The chapter is not therefore concerned only with educational activities directed solely towards business. In addition to degree and professional courses, some relevant non-degree courses are also considered: these mostly lead to diplomas or certificates. Apart from such diploma or certificate courses, the only arrangements discussed in parts A and B of this chapter are full degree or professional qualifications.

This discussion relates to the Republic of Ireland only[1], and to the facilities available or stated to be projected in mid-1966. Projected facilities refer to facilities which authorities were firmly committed to bringing into being.

While every effort was made to include all relevant bodies, it is possible that some have been overlooked, particularly in fields such as accountancy where there is a multiplicity of professional institutes, many based in Britain, for whose examinations student candidates can study by correspondence. It is not claimed that the list of bodies discussed is comprehensive.

The chapter is in four parts. The first deals briefly with the educational system in general, the second with university education, the third with non-university professional education, and the fourth with non-university training for management.

PART A.   THE EDUCATIONAL SYSTEM

The following short description of the existing system of education is based on the report *Investment in Education* (see footnote to table 17.1.). It is followed by an outline of projected changes.

The system in Ireland is State-aided rather than State-operated. The State insists that children be educated between the ages of six and fourteen years. The State gives financial assistance to national schools, lays down curricula and holds examinations, but does not own or administer schools. The management of primary schools is denominational. There are also some fee-paying private schools which the State does not assist financially, but for which it does lay down curricula. Beyond stipulating that education extend to age fourteen, the State does not prescribe: it is not necessary that any certificate examinations be taken, though in practice most children attempt the Primary Certificate examination.[2]

In the year 1962/63, about 55,000 pupils left national schools, and about 2,000 left private schools. The latter mostly went to secondary school, usually that to which their

---

1. Except for a description of the facilities for management studies at the Queen's University of Belfast.
2. Pupils reaching sixth standard must be entered for the examination, but about 14 per cent of those leaving full-time education from national school do not attempt it, presumably because they have not reached sixth standard even at fourteen years of age, and even though it is possible to enter national school some years before the statutory age for commencing education.

primary school was attached. Of those who left national school, 17,500 left full-time education altogether and only 28 per cent of these had passed their Primary Certificate examination. The remaining 37,500 went on to further education, 13,600 to vocational schools, the remainder mostly to secondary schools.

Thus, second-level schooling is in two streams. Secondary schools are all privately-owned and are mostly denominational. Most receive financial assistance from the State, both on capital and on revenue account. These schools must follow a curriculum pre-scribed by the Department of Education. A few receive no aid: these are free to follow any curriculum. Teachers must be university graduates (though not necessarily in the subjects they teach), and must have training in educational methods. Fees are charged at all secondary schools. Within the secondary school level, there are two cycles. The first culminates, after about three years, in the Intermediate Certificate examination, the second, after a further two years, in the Leaving Certificate. Neither examination is compulsory, nor is it necessary to have passed the Intermediate Certificate before going on to study for the Leaving Certificate. In general, children are not accepted into a secondary school without either passing the Primary Certificate or the school's entrance examination.

About 25,000 entered secondary schools in 1962/63. In that year, about 6,500 left before attempting the Intermediate Certificate examination. A further 1,800 left after taking the examination. This was about 10 per cent of the total who took it. Most of those who stayed in full-time education went on to the Leaving Certificate cycle, and few dropped out before attempting the examination. Some of the drop-outs and leavers from the junior cycle transferred to vocational schools.[1] In general, therefore, most of those who enter secondary school go on to attempt their Leaving Certificate unless they drop out before Intermediate Certificate level. This is particularly true of boys, especially those who get an honours Intermediate Certificate.

The other major stream of national school leavers, apart from those who leave school altogether, is into vocational schools. Vocational schools are non-denominational and are administered by local vocational education committees. Each committee has a full-time chief executive officer who acts as director of education. The committees are financed by State grant and local rates. Moderate fees are charged to pupils. The majority of whole-time teachers are either university graduates or are trained by the Department of Education.

Students may not enter vocational schools before the age of 12 years and must have completed sixth standard in the primary school. There is no stipulation as to qualifica-tion, and about 25 per cent of those who entered vocational schools in 1962/63 had no form of certificate, even Primary Certificate.

The basic full-time course in vocational schools is a " continuation " course leading to examinations for what is called the Group Certificate. The course lasts for two years and, unlike the great majority of secondary school courses, includes training in manual skills. Boys take woodwork, metalwork and mechanical drawing, as well as mathematics and other subjects. About one-third of the time is spent on manual subjects. These are not technician-level courses nor apprentice-training courses. Students also take Irish, English and a science subject (general, rural or domestic).

About 16,000 entered full-time vocational education in 1962/63, 13,600 from national school and 2,000 who transferred from secondary school. Only about 8,000 sat

---

1 Drop-outs are those who leave a cycle before taking an examination, leavers are those who leave after taking an examination.

the Group Certificate examination, and of these about 2,400 failed[1]. Over 8,000 left without taking the Group Certificate, only a little over 1,000 of whom had a Group Certificate from a previous year. Many of those who left probably did so on reaching the statutory school-leaving age of 14 years. Of approximately 6,000 who passed the Group Certificate almost 70 per cent left full-time education, most of the remainder staying on in vocational school to pursue either (a) a third-year wholetime continuation course leading to O level G.C.E. standard of the United Kingdom, (b) a two-year junior technician course in one of a variety of specialties, or (c) a revision course for the Group Certificate in order to obtain passes in additional subjects or to reach honours standard. Girls may stay on to complete a secretarial course. Virtually no one transfers from a vocational school to a secondary school.

Vocational school leavers at Group Certificate level can go on to apprenticeship or technical training. The latter is mainly confined to Dublin, Cork, Limerick and Waterford and is done mainly at night. Students who hold the Group Certificate and wish to proceed to higher education do so by means of "bridge" courses available on a wholetime or part-time basis in Dublin and in a small number of other centres and leading to the Leaving Certificate, Matriculation or G.C.E. Training at technological and professional level is done only at the Colleges of Technology in Dublin and to a lesser extent in Cork, and at the Colleges of Commerce in Dublin, Cork and Limerick. Entrance to courses at this level is confined mainly to those with Leaving Certificate or an equivalent standard.

Full-time higher education is given at universities, colleges of technology and colleges of commerce. Many study part-time for degrees or diplomas at universities, and for professional qualifications either at colleges of technology or commerce, or through correspondence courses.

Of the boys who attempted the Leaving Certificate in 1963, 43 per cent went straight to further full-time education, 26.4 per cent to university. Of those who obtained honours in the examination 58.2 per cent went on to full-time education, 42.9 per cent to university[2]. A further 8.2 per cent went to religious life, leaving only 33.5 per cent of honours boys, about 500 all told, who left full-time education. Some of these would undoubtedly go on later either to full-time or to part-time higher education[3].

Not all those with Leaving Certificate are automatically eligible for entrance to university. Some, particularly those with passes only, have taken combinations of subjects which do not exempt them from matriculation and consequently must take a separate examination. Furthermore, universities are beginning to insist on a minimum number of honours in the examination, while potential engineers must either have honours mathematics or pass a qualifying examination.

Universities are autonomous institutions, charging fees and receiving State subvention as required. There is a limited number of competitive scholarships awarded by local authorities to those whose parents' income does not exceed a stated level.

There are two universities in the Republic of Ireland: the National University of

---

1. In 1964-65, over 33,000 pupils entered vocational schools. Over 14,000 sat the Group Certificate examination, and of these a little over 5,000 failed.
2. To pass the Leaving Certificate it is necessary to pass in Irish and in four other subjects: to get honours a mark of 60 per cent must be obtained on honours papers in three of five subjects. There is no specialisation in secondary schools.
3. Table 6.35 page 169 and chart 6.7 page 172 of (1), shows that participation in post-primary education, entrance to secondary, as distinct from vocational, school and, most markedly, entrance to university, are all closely related to parents' social class.

Ireland and the University of Dublin.[1] In Northern Ireland there is one university, the Queen's University of Belfast, and a university college, Magee College, in Derry, which provides courses acceptable to the University of Dublin as exempting from some of its examinations (but not from its degree examinations).

The National University has three constituent colleges: University College, Dublin, University College, Cork, and University College, Galway. Maynooth College is a recognised college of the National University, but not a constituent college. It has, until this year, been confined to students for the Roman Catholic priesthood and will not be discussed further. The University of Dublin has one constituent college, Trinity College, Dublin.

In addition to universities, full-time and part-time third level courses are provided at the Colleges of Technology at Bolton Street and Kevin Street in Dublin and at the Crawford Municipal Technical Institute in Cork, at the College of Commerce at Rathmines in Dublin and at the Schools of Commerce at Cork and Limerick.

The number of full-time third level students outside university is small relative to the number at university: about 600 as against over 13,000 in 1964. Over 9,000 of the latter were in the National University.[2] Table 17.1 shows the number of entrants to each faculty in 1963 and the proportion of entrants who had honours Leaving Certificates. It can be seen that entry standards vary widely, though it is possible that a number of those who enter faculties with low honours rates could have achieved honours if this had been a condition of entry.

TABLE 17.1.   *Male Entrants (Irish) Year 1963, to the Colleges of the National University by Faculty, Showing the Percentage with Honours Leaving Certificate.*

Faculty	University College Dublin		University College Cork		University College Galway	
	No.	% Honours	No.	% Honours	No.	% Honours
Agriculture	69	30	19	24	27	44
Architecture	26	26	—	—	—	—
Arts (inc. Music)	248	48	94	42	94	45
Commerce[a]	149	25	48	29	36	36
Dairy Science	—	—	19	41	—	—
Engineering	132	85	50	80	42	80
Law	47	20	5	—*	—	—*
Medicine (inc. Dentistry)	134	29	50	25	37	31
Pharmacy	14	27	—	—	—	—
Science	160	62	64	71	52	45
Social Science	8	—*	—	—	—	—
Veterinary Medicine	77	14	—	—	—	—
Total	1,064	43	349	47	260	47

a   Including Arts and Commerce.
*   Small numbers.
Source: *Investment in Education.* Dublin: The Stationery Office, 1966, p. 128.
         Investment in Education Annexes and Appendices. Dublin: The Stationery Office, 1966, p. 369.

1 The Royal Colleges of Physicians and Surgeons in Ireland also confer degrees, but only in medicine.
2 It is the policy of the University of Dublin to limit the number of students at Trinity College to 3,000. The number of entrants to different departments is limited accordingly.

Little information is available on the destinations, immediate and ultimate, of university and other third-level graduates, and such information is collected only informally.

Projected Changes

Major changes in the system are proposed. It is intended by 1970 to raise the minimum school-leaving age to 15 years. The other changes relate mainly to opening up opportunities for further education to those entering the vocational education stream and, in general, to reducing separation, physical and curricular, between vocational and secondary streams.

Perhaps the most far-reaching change in its implications, though not in its extent, is that the State is building a limited number of comprehensive schools which will be State-administered. These schools will provide, under one roof, complete vocational and secondary education.

The syllabus of the Intermediate Certificate examination has been widened to include a greater range of manual subjects. From now on, all schools, both vocational and secondary, will work towards the Intermediate Certificate examination, taking a common core of subjects. Vocational schools will probably accent manual subjects to a greater extent in selecting their optional subjects, secondary schools will lean more to grammar-type optionals.

The Group Certificate examination is being retained at least for an interim period, but syllabi have been revised to bring them into alignment with courses for the Intermediate Certificate so that vocational school pupils remaining on for a third wholetime year may more easily proceed to the Intermediate Certificate examination. The retention of the Group Certificate enables pupils who are more than twelve years old leaving primary school to obtain a post-primary examination qualification before reaching the new statutory school-leaving age of fifteen.

The Minister for Education in May, 1963, announced his intention to establish a Technical Leaving Certificate and to arrange the provision of technical colleges with regional status in which the courses for the Certificate would be provided. The aim is to enable vocational school students — and secondary school students with practical aptitudes — who had completed the revised Intermediate Certificate course, to achieve a technical education standard comparable in esteem to that available in secondary schools. The Certificate would enable students to proceed to a professional qualification at a university or a college of technology or commerce, or to train as high level technicians or junior managers. The Certificate courses will cater for two broad streams — one technical, the other commercial. Other streams may develop, for instance, in home economics and in agricultural science. The Technical Leaving Certificate courses will be provided in the new regional colleges. Courses will eventually be organised in the larger urban centres and in at least one school in each county.

Pupils not within easy reach of the colleges will be provided with residential or travel scholarships, on a competitive basis.

In addition to courses for the Technical Leaving Certificate the regional colleges will provide a full range of apprentice, technician and special training.[1] They will also

---

1. Apprenticeship training is being increasingly formalised and extended through the efforts of An Cheard-Comhairle (the National Apprenticeship Board).

include commercial subjects. Courses will not be provided at full technological level unless local demand warrants them.

The net result of the proposed changes[1] will not only be to raise the general level of technical training and to increase the opportunities for those not entering the secondary school stream, it will also reduce the educational gap between managers and others in industry, where it is at present probably more marked than in any other economic activity.[2] This is one facet of a social revolution affecting the environment in which the managers of to-morrow will work, and having implications for the education and training of future executives.

PART B.   UNIVERSITY EDUCATION

This section will describe degrees relevant to industrial management. In addition to business studies and economics, those subjects are considered in which contributions are being made to the advancement of thinking on management. Also considered are degrees which the survey has established as being widely held in Irish industry.

Degree-level courses are discussed first. There is a short description at the end of each section describing courses leading to diplomas or certificates.

The National University has three constituent colleges, each offering a wide selection of courses. The colleges are organised internally by faculty. In general the faculties of arts and of science in each college have separate pass and honours courses, while the faculties of commerce and of engineering do not. In these faculties, honours are given on the results of a common examination. Degrees are conferred, not by the colleges, but by the National University.

The University of Dublin has only one constituent college. Trinity College, Dublin, is organised not by faculty but by school. Courses in the School of General Studies lead to a pass degree of B.A., taken in three subjects. Courses in the Honor Schools in Arts lead to an honours degree, B.A. (Mod.). Natural sciences are included in the Honor Schools in Arts. In addition to these, there are the professional schools of engineering, business and social studies, medicine, law, etc.

The total enrolment by faculty is shown for the colleges of the National University in table 17.2. Table 17.3. shows the number of degrees conferred at University College, Dublin, over the 5 years 1960-61 to 1964-65.

Degree-level courses are typically full-time. The only colleges now offering degree courses by evening study are University College, Dublin, and University College, Cork.

---

1.   Further proposed changes have been announced (Sept. 1966). Education will be free up to Intermediate Certificate level, unless a school wishes to opt out of the scheme. This will apply to all post-primary schools, whether secondary, vocational or comprehensive. More financial assistance will be made available for students wishing to go on to Leaving Certificate or to university.

2.   In the Civil Service, local authorities, banking and insurance, and other occupations, entry to many grades is dependent on reaching a certain level of education. Graduates are employed only to a limited extent, except in technical grades. Because many entrants to lower grades have more than the required standard of education, there is little difference between their educational level and that of many in higher grades and thus, inferentially, between their social background. In building and construction, and probably also in most retail distribution, those in charge are largely of the same background as those working for them. Industry, on the other hand, has a fair proportion of qualified men among its managers, and at the same time probably employs a large number of other staff from the vocational education stream, and others who never got even that far.

TABLE 17.2.   *Total Enrolment[1] in the Colleges of the National University by Faculty, Year 1964-65.*

	University College Dublin	University College Cork[2]	University College Galway
Arts	2,852	956	848
Commerce	902	218	230
Dairy Science	—	136	—
Engineering	518	218	134
Science	861	308	276
Agriculture	314	53	64
Architecture	146	—	—
Dentistry	127	52	—
Law	146	15	1
Medicine	992	201	355
Veterinary Medicine	292	—	—
TOTAL	7,150	2,157	1,908

1. Students following degree, diploma or certificate courses only. Occasional students excluded.
2. Includes evening students for degrees, but not diplomas. Excludes pre-medical and pre-dental students, as they were not differentiated in the source quoted.
Source: University College, Dublin. *Report of the President* 1964-65. Dublin: Browne and Nolan Ltd., 1965 (p. 83).
University College, Cork. *Report of the President* 1964-65 (p. 7).
University College, Galway. Information supplied by the College.

TABLE 17.3.   *Number of Degrees Discussed Below Conferred at University College Dublin in the Years* 1960-61 *to* 1964-65.

Degree or Diploma	1960-61	1961-62	1962-63	1963-64	1964-65
B.A.	287	381	360	423	547
M.A.	38	27	29	22	37
Ph.D.[1]	7	16	15	8	16
B.Comm.	114	69	100	116	152
D.P.A.	28	33	32	30	33
M.Comm. or M.Econ.Sc.	5	9	6	8	3
D.Econ.Sc.	—	1	1	—	—
B.E.	99	81	69	72	102
M.E.	1	1	—	—	4
M.Eng.Sc.	—	1	2	2	4
B.Sc.	94	118	119	125	175
M.Sc.	9	10	12	7	7
D.Sc.	—	—	1	2	—
Dipl. in Psychology	—	5	11	4	9
M.Psych.Sc.	—	—	—	2	6
B.Soc.Sc.	10	21	38	42	36

1. This degree may be conferred in the Faculties of Science and Commerce as well as in the Faculty of Arts. Some of those shown in the table are from the Faculty of Science.
Source: University College, Dublin. *Report of the President* 1964-65. Dublin: Browne and Nolan Ltd., 1965 (p. 103).

Courses leading to the B.Sc. degree of London University are conducted on both a full-time and part-time basis at the College of Technology, Kevin Street, Dublin.

Degrees are discussed below in alphabetical order, and the universities in alphabetical order also. Management education in the Queen's University of Belfast is discussed in page 275.

Degrees in Business Studies and Commerce

Degree courses in business studies are offered by Trinity College Dublin, and in commerce by all the constituent colleges of the National University of Ireland. Courses are at both undergraduate and graduate level, and will be discussed in that order. There is a course available at graduate level in the Queen's University of Belfast. This will also be discussed.

1   *Courses at undergraduate level.*

Trinity College, Dublin. The Schools of Commerce, Social Studies and Public Administration were succeeded in 1962 by the School of Business and Social Studies. The School has two departments: Business Studies and Social Studies. Associated with the school, though under a separate board of directors, is the Administrative Research Bureau, financed independently of the university by income from contract research and by financial support from business.

The course leading to the degree, Bachelor of Business Studies, lasts for four years, in each of which there are three seven-week terms. The subjects taken are as follows, (the number of hours lecturing per week has not yet been decided for the 1966-67 session).

FIRST YEAR. Economics I; economic geography; economic history; elements of law; elements of science — class; scientific method and elementary statistics.

SECOND YEAR. Accountancy I; administration I; economics II; law relating to business; political institutions; psychology; science and technology — class.

THIRD YEAR. Accountancy II; administration II; current affairs — seminar; economics III; employment relations; law relating to business; public finance.

FOURTH YEAR. Accountancy III; administration III; current affairs — seminar; economics IV; government in the economy.

There are also two hours of case studies per week, a seminar on administration and on current economic affairs, a business game, and lectures on data processing, elements of science and technology and the law of negotiable instruments.

In addition to taking courses, students must obtain approved business experience during the vacation following their second year. The optional courses on law, if taken, qualify successful students for exemption from the first two parts of the examinations of the Association of Certified and Corporate Accountants and from the first three parts of the examinations of the Institute of Chartered Accountants in Ireland, otherwise successful candidates will be exempt from only the first two parts.

The full-time staff members of the Department of Business Studies number four. There are two lecturers in management, a lecturer in accountancy, and a junior lecturer in economics. There are in addition three part-time lecturers attached solely to the department: a lecturer in administration, a lecturer in marketing and a lecturer in psychology. Staff members from other schools lecture as required, for instance in law, economics, science, etc. Occasional lecturers from outside the University and College staff are also used.

The first graduates received their degrees in 1966.

University College, Cork. The course at University College, Cork, leading to the degree B.Comm. now lasts for four years. It previously lasted for three years. The courses leading to the B.Comm. degree have been re-structured in all constituent colleges of the National University following discussions with the accountancy profession. As part of this re-structuring, it was decided in University College, Cork, to extend the degree course to four years and to divide it into two streams. Because there was no separate honours course in economics in University College, Cork, the B.Comm. degree attracted students who might otherwise have specialised in economics. Traditionally, many graduates went to work in local government and to teaching. Another group went into business or to study for accountancy qualifications. For this reason it was decided to divide the course into two streams, one oriented to economics and public administration and the other to accountancy and commercial law.

The degree is not intended to be terminal in the sense of producing graduates equipped to work immediately at a professional level. The intention is to provide an introductory training in a broad range of disciplines relevant to an administrative career, on which graduates can later build by specialising through study for membership of a professional institute.

For students entering the Faculty of Commerce in 1965 or later, the course is as shown below.

FIRST YEAR. Introductory accountancy (3); introductory law (2); mathematics (3); modern history (3); a modern language (2), which may be Irish or English. All five subjects are examined. (Hours per week are shown in parentheses for the first two years. The timetable for the third and fourth years has not been decided, and the figures for first and second year are provisional.)

After the first year two separate courses may be followed.

SECOND YEAR. Course I: Accountancy (4); law (4); statistics (3); applied psychology (3).
Course II: Economics (4); social philosophy (4); statistics (3); applied psychology (3).

THIRD YEAR. Course I: Accountancy; law; economics; sociology; public administration.
Course II: Law; economics; sociology; public administration.

FOURTH YEAR. Course I: Accountancy; law; economics; sociology.
Course II: Economics; sociology; public administration.

While subjects are common to both courses each common subject is treated in greater detail in the course in which it forms a major subject.

The previous three-year course included in the first year the subject economics, but not modern history nor a modern language. In both the second and third years the subjects were economics; accountancy and business administration; law; and public administration or sociology in alternate years. Thus a one-year course in two new subjects, statistics and applied psychology, has been added and, to course II, the subject social philosophy. There have been extensive additions to the courses in accountancy and law, and changes in the courses in economics, sociology and public administration.

University College, Cork, also provides an evening course for the degree B.Comm. Under the old regulations, this course covered the same subjects as the day course, but lasted for four, as against three, years. Now that the day course has been restructured to last for four years, the future of the evening course is uncertain.

There are three full-time staff members whose principal attachment is to the Faculty of Commerce, a professor of economics and two demonstrators. There is also a visiting lecturer in economics. There are four part-time staff members: a lecturer, an assistant, and a demonstrator in accountancy, as well as a part-time lecturer in public administration. The lectures in applied psychology, languages, law, mathematics, sociology and statistics are given by staff attached principally to other faculties.

University College, Dublin. University College, Dublin, also provides evening as well as day courses for a degree in commerce. From 1966 on, the evening course will last for four years as against three years for the day course, to allow more time for reading and for tutorials. The content of the courses is the same.

The degree was instituted in the early part of this century to provide the higher commercial training which would be needed in the event of some measure of national independence being granted. In fact the degree was never used solely by those intending to take up a business career directly on completing their studies. Until the last few years a considerable proportion of students intended to be teachers: it is not a condition of entry to the degree that a candidate should have matriculated in Latin, whereas this was formerly a condition in the Faculty of Arts. Many such candidates, especially girls, now prefer to take a degree in social science, so that both the number and proportion of girls taking the degree has fallen considerably during the 1960s.

Another group of candidates intend to go on to take professional qualifications in accountancy. Their number will probably increase now that the course has been restructured to allow so many remissions in the examinations of the Institute of Chartered Accountants and of the Association of Certified and Corporate Accountants.

Night students are mostly already in business, many in State service or in semi-State concerns.

As in the case of University College, Cork, the present aim of the degree is to provide a broad basis for later specialisation by professional study.

It was stated above that the course has been revised following discussions with the accountancy profession. The subjects of the new course are as follows, with the number of hours' lecturing per week shown in parentheses.

FIRST YEAR. Political economy (3); accountancy (2); mathematics (3); history or geography or a modern language which may be English or Irish (3).

SECOND YEAR. Political economy (3); economic history (1); accountancy (3); mercantile and executorship law (2); business administration (1); statistics (2).

THIRD YEAR. Political economy, including banking and finance (3); national economics (2); accountancy (3); company law (2); taxation or public administration (1); business administration (3).

There are no changes in the subjects taken in the first year, but there have been additions to the accountancy course. In the second year, national economics has been dropped, statistics, formerly a third-year subject, has been moved back to second year by dropping the second-year course on statistical mathematics, and there have been additions to the courses in accountancy, mercantile law and business administration.

Statistics has been dropped from the third year, company law and secretarial practice has been added, as have optional lectures in taxation. Additions have been made to the course in accountancy.

In addition to these changes, some minor subjects have been dropped over the last few years, to allow a greater concentration on the major subjects now on the curriculum. It is hoped to arrange a special course of lectures on political economy for students of commerce. Those studying commerce at present take their lectures on political economy in common with those taking a B.A. degree in economics.

There is a very close connection between the Faculty of Commerce and the Department of Economics. By spending an extra year it is possible for day students to take the degree B.A. in economics as well as the B.Comm. degree, and most of the full-time staff are common to both degrees.

The full-time staff listed for the session 1966-67 numbers 16: a professor, two associate professors, three college[1] lecturers and three assistants, all in economics; a professor and a college lecturer in accountancy; an associate professor and three college lecturers in business administration, and a lecturer in statistics.

There are in addition nine part-time lecturers for degree courses, six for the Diploma in Public Administration, and a further eight for the Certificate in Accountancy.

The economics staff also teach the B.A. degree course in economics. The business administration staff teach undergraduates in commerce and graduates preparing for the degree of Master of Business Administration. They also teach management subjects to students taking the degrees M.Econ.Sc., B.E. and B.Agr.Sc.

University College, Galway. There is a three-year course at University College, Galway, which leads to the degree B.Comm.

An examination is taken at the end of the first academic year. In the second year, students are required to take University examinations in four subsidiary subjects: a modern language, commercial law, economic geography and the Irish economy, such subjects forming part of the degree examination.

Economics and commerce, which includes accountancy, constitute the primary subjects and these are taken at the degree examination at the end of the third year.

The subjects taken in the B.Comm. course are as follows, and the number of lecturers per week in parentheses:

FIRST YEAR. Economics (2); British and continental economic history (1); commercial technique (1); accountancy (1); mathematics for commerce (1); a modern language (3); a second modern language or a science subject (3).

SECOND YEAR. Economics (2); economic geography (2); organisation of industry and commerce—two terms of two lectures per week on industrial organisation, one term of

---

1. College lecturers are appcinted by University College. They do not have the rank of statutory lecturers, who are appointed by the National University.

two lectures per week on business administration; a modern language (3); accounting (2); the Irish economy (2); commercial law (1).

THIRD YEAR. Economics, which comprises history of economic theory (2), economics of transport (2) and elementary statistics (2); organisation of industry and commerce—one term of two lectures per week on industrial relations, two terms of two lectures per week on banking and currency, three terms of two lectures per week on accountancy; industrial and commercial law (1); economic growth and development—three terms of two lectures per week.

All lectures are given through Irish except those on industrial and commercial law, mathematics for commerce and modern languages.

About 60 per cent of those taking the B.Comm. degree are girls, many of whom go on to teach in vocational and secondary schools.

There are two full-time staff members attached to the Faculty of Commerce: a professor of economics, commerce and accountancy and a lecturer in applied economics. Since 1965/66, there is also one full-time assistant in commerce and economic history and one part-time assistant in accountancy. Both are temporary appointments. It is intended to create two statutory lecturerships, one in accountancy and one in commerce and economics.

2. Courses at graduate level.

In the colleges of the National University, graduates in commerce can go on to take either the degree M.Comm. or M.Econ.Sc., these degrees being confined to those whose primary degree was in commerce. The degree M.Econ.Sc. is open also to those with a B.A. degree in economics. The University of Dublin has no higher degree confined to graduates in business studies. In addition to these confined degrees, University College, Dublin, and Trinity College, Dublin, offer courses leading to the degree Master of Business Administration and Master in Administrative Studies respectively. These degrees are open to graduates of all faculties. There is a graduate-level course at the Queen's University of Belfast which is also open to all faculties and which leads to the Diploma in Business Administration.

The older, confined degrees are discussed first, before considering the more newly-instituted courses.

University College, Cork. Anyone who has held a B.Comm. degree, whether pass or honours, for nine terms, can enter for the degree M.Comm. The candidate must submit a dissertation, take an examination, written and oral, in accountancy or business administration or public administration and in some other subject, and must have acceptable professional experience. Candidates with an honours B.Comm. or who have published work, or who have held exceptional responsibility, may be exempted from all or part of the written examination.

No lectures are given to candidates attempting the M.Comm. degree, and candidates are few.

The degree M.Econ.Sc. can be taken by anyone who has at least a second-class honours degree in commerce or in arts, or who has passed a qualifying examination. The degree can be taken after one year, by pursuing a post-graduate course, and by examination and essay, or by dissertation and examination. Alternatively, it can be taken after two years, without lectures, by examination and dissertation. It will not in future be open to anyone taking the B.Comm. degree by following course I.

The degrees Ph.D. and D.Econ.Sc. are also open to graduates in commerce. The degree Ph.D. is given on the basis of a dissertation on research carried out under the direction of the professor or other staff member. The dissertation must be worthy of publication, and the candidate may be examined orally on the subject of his dissertation.

The degree D.Econ.Sc. is awarded for original published work. The candidate may be asked in addition to pass an examination, but this may be dispensed with.

Teaching at graduate level is done by the same staff as at undergraduate level and is done by tutorials rather than by formal lectures.

University College, Dublin. A holder of the degree B.Comm. can obtain the degree M.Comm. nine terms later, by submitting a dissertation, presenting evidence of professional experience, and by carrying out any other exercises which may be prescribed.

Holders of the degree B.Comm. or B.A. in economics can take the degree M.Econ.Sc. either by thesis or by examination. Only those with a first-class honours B.Comm. can attempt it by thesis (which must be prepared under the supervision of the professor and on whose subject-matter the candidate may be examined).

The degree may be taken by examination by holders of a B.Comm. degree with second-class honours. Candidates must study, for three terms, any two of the following subjects: management accounting; business administration or public administration; marketing; industrial relations; business finance; economics of transport; and any one of the following group: econometrics; agricultural economics; development of economic thought; banking, currency and international payments; price theory; economic growth; economics of education; or any other approved subject. Not all of the subjects mentioned are available, their availability depending on that of lecturers.

In some subjects informal meetings rather than formal lectures are held, to guide students in covering the course.

The degrees Ph.D. and D.Econ.Sc. may be granted under the same conditions as in University College, Cork.

University College, Galway. Bachelors of Commerce can take the degree M.Comm. nine terms after their primary degree, by passing the prescribed examination and either presenting a dissertation or complying with such other conditions as may be laid down.

The examination is in four parts: commerce (including organisation); economics (including finance); accountancy (including law) and an essay. The papers covering these subjects respectively are set in business organisation; the evolution of the money market; advanced accounts; and an essay.

Candidates holding the B.Comm. degree with first-class honours can claim exemption from any two of the subjects mentioned.

Bachelors of Commerce can take the degree M.Econ.Sc. two years after their primary degree by submitting a dissertation and taking an examination equivalent to that for the degree M.A.

The same conditions hold for the degrees Ph.D. and D.Econ.Sc. as in University College, Cork.

In 1964, courses more directly related to an executive career were instituted at graduate level in both University College, Dublin, and Trinity College, Dublin.

The main difference between the courses is that the course in University College is a two year part-time course, confined to holders of a university degree who have business experience, whereas that at Trinity College is a one year, full-time course, open both to immediate post-graduate students and to executives who do not have formal qualifications. The latter students, if successful, are awarded a diploma, not a degree.

Trinity College, Dublin. While the course leading to the degree Master in Administrative Studies (M.S.A.) is open to graduates and to professionally qualified men, those whose studies covered a range substantially similar to that of the course are not encouraged to take it, and may be refused admission. For instance applications from graduates in business studies, commerce and economics are not favoured if, by granting them admission, chemists, engineers, lawyers, etc., would be displaced.

The aims of the course, the subjects studied, and the method of teaching are set out as follows in the prospectus:

In essence, the course presents the areas of knowledge and related techniques common to the fields elsewhere of business and public administration. For this reason it is called a course in administration.

Whatever the differences in kinds of undertaking and whatever the differences in title of those who work in them, there is a common aim — productive activity; there is a common need — for analytical skill; and there is a common pressure — to make decisions. On these common grounds, the course aims to equip students with:

(1) an understanding of the social, political and economic forces supporting, and constraining, productive activity;

(2) an appreciation of the analytical techniques and occupational skills needed to assess the value and limitations of specialist assistance;

(3) a balanced judgment when, as is usual in making decisions, conflicting interests have to be weighed.

Because needs in, and knowledge of, business and administration change, there is not a fixed syllabus from one year to the next. Instead, each year's studies will be concentrated in the directions which are currently regarded as most useful or urgent.

The fields within which the studies will be conducted are: 1) Administrative theory and practice including human behaviour, employment relations, organisation and the sociology of work. 2) Economics including bases and structure of industry, international business, money and national income. 3) Environment of business including financial institutions, government, law and trade unions. 4) Operations analysis including financial administration, information systems, operations research and work study. 5) Quantitative methods including accounting, data processing, decision theory, managerial economics, programming and statistics.

The course begins with lectures and classes in such underlying disciplines as accounting, economics and statistics. The instruction moves on to the environment of business produced by governmental, legal and social institutions and by economic, geographic and technological considerations. In the last part of the course more of the instruction is through seminars and group discussions to integrate the earlier studies and to foster and develop in the student a capacity for reasoning about business and administration, so that he can apply his knowledge and achieve a fruitful and socially useful career.

Every student works on a project assignment which is written up in the long vacation following the third term. Students who have not had substantial employment experience will work on a business project. Students with substantial employment experience will work on an academic project.

The projects are organised through the Administrative Research Bureau which is run in conjunction with the Department of Business Studies.

The number of hours' class-work per week devoted to each subject are: administrative theory and practice (4); economics (4); environment of business (2); operations analysis (6); quantitative methods (3).

With the exception of the lecturer on quantitative methods, an additional lecturer attached principally to the Department of Economics, the staff is as described for the undergraduate course in business studies.

University College, Dublin. The structure and conditions for entry to the course leading to the degree Master of Business Administration (M.B.A.) have been described above. Classwork for the degree is from 4.30 p.m. to 7.30 p.m., four evenings per week, for two years. Candidates awarded honours at the B.Comm. degree examination may be exempted from part or from all of the first year course. Enrolment is limited to 20 in any one year.

The subjects covered are (the number of hours' lecturing per year are shown in parentheses):

FIRST YEAR. Principles of finance (32); production analysis (32); principles of marketing (32); industrial psychology and ergonomics (25); micro-economics ($37\frac{1}{2}$); business environment—legal framework ($37\frac{1}{2}$), economic history (15), world resources ($7\frac{1}{2}$); quantitative analysis—accounting ($52\frac{1}{2}$), applied statistics ($37\frac{1}{2}$).

SECOND YEAR. Business policy (32); management accounting (32); business administration (32); industrial relations (32); marketing policy (32); industrial management (32); financial analysis (32).

After taking their final examination in June, candidates must submit a dissertation on a research project before September 1st following. Otherwise they must sit for the examination again.

There are five staff members attached principally to the Department of Business Administration. They also lecture to undergraduates in commerce and in arts, and direct the studies of those taking the M.Econ.Sc. degree by examination. The staff consists of an associate professor of business administration, and a lecturer each in business administration, finance, marketing and production. Outside lecturers are used as required.

Queen's University, Belfast. A chair of management studies has recently been endowed at Queen's University. The department is part of the Faculty of Economics, the staff at present consisting of a professor of business economics, an industrial psychologist, an economist, a specialist in quantitative methods and a research associate.

As a first step in developing management studies, it was decided to institute a one year full-time course open to graduates or, exceptionally, to non-graduates: it leads to a diploma rather than a degree. Graduates need not have business experience, and may occasionally be exempted from up to two subjects. Students who fail the examination will not normally be permitted to sit for it again, as it is felt that group cohesion would otherwise be lost.

The aim of the course is to provide both a sound basic introduction to management and a foundation for further advanced studies.

Six subjects must be taken, in each of which there will be two lectures per week plus seminars and tutorials. (Instruction will include the use of case-studies and seminars as well as lectures.)

The subjects are economics, business economics, quantitative methods, management accounting and finance, human relations, organisation and administration. Students are also required to submit a report on a practical project undertaken during the year.

The course for the diploma will commence in 1966. It is hoped in 1967 to introduce a specialisation in administration into the primary degrees in the Faculty of Economics.

3   Diplomas and certificates.

University College, Dublin, and University College, Cork, are the only institutions offering diplomas or certificates for night-students. Trinity College, Dublin, discontinued night courses some years ago in order to concentrate on full-time courses.

University College, Cork. There was a three-year course leading to a diploma in commerce, but it is now being abandoned. A college diploma in commercial education exists for the training of Bachelors of Commerce who intend to teach.

The Department of Applied Psychology organises a twenty week, part-time management development course, certificated by the College. There are six hours of lectures per week. Apart from those given by the Professor of Applied Psychology, the lectures are mostly given by part-time or outside staff.

Those attending the course are mostly executives from the Cork area. There is an examination at the end of the course.

University College, Dublin. University College, Dublin, offers a two year part-time course leading to the Diploma in Public Administration, and a two year part-time course for students of accountancy, leading to the Certificate in Accountancy.

Students may enrol for the D.P.A. at eighteen years of age, whereas they may not enrol for the evening B.Comm. course until the age of twenty. By taking mathematics as an additional subject, successful D.P.A. students may claim exemptions from the first year of the commerce course, and from accountancy in the second year. Thus, school leavers may commence study immediately on leaving school, instead of waiting until they are 20 years old, and may then go on to finish their B.Comm. degree in a further three years.

Those who graduate first in commerce may go on to take the D.P.A. in one year. Arts graduates in economics must take two years, but may claim exemptions from some subjects.

The course for the Certificate in Accountancy is open to those who have passed their matriculation examination, to articled clerks, and to students studying for the examinations of a recognised body of accountants.

4.   Numbers of students and graduates.

The number of those examined, and the number passing the various examinations in business studies and commerce, of the universities in the Republic of Ireland are shown in table 17.4.

This ends the description of degrees in business studies and commerce. It will be the function of the Consultative Board of the Irish Management Institute to assess the adequacy of the facilities available. The opinions of the staff members interviewed are relevant.

It is almost universally the case that staff members consider the facilities inadequate. The most serious difficulty is felt to be in securing adequate numbers of staff, and adequate accommodation and administrative assistance for both staff and students. The number of students has expanded enormously in the last ten years: in many cases staff numbers have not increased anything like comparably.

TABLE 17.4.   *Number of Students Examined In[1] and Passing Examinations in Business Studies or Commerce in 1965, and the Number of Staff, by University.*

University and Degree	STAFF[2] Full-time Commerce	Part Time	First Sat	First Passed	Second Sat	Second Passed	Third Sat	Third Passed	Final Sat	Final Passed
B.B.S.[4]			46	35	36	35	31	25	—	—
Trinity College	4	3								
B.Comm.									33	31
M.S.A.									—	—
Univ. College, Cork.	3	4								
B.Comm.[5]			85	51	50	47			43	42
M.Comm									1	1
M.Econ.Sc.									2	2
Ph.D. or D.Econ.Sc.									—	—
Univ. College, Dublin.	16	9[6]								
B.Comm.			344	213	259	196			213	155
M.Comm.									—	—
M.B.A.[7]			15	15					—	—
M.Econ.Sc.									13	13
Ph.D. or D.Econ.Sc.									—	—
Dip.Pub.Adm.[8]			69	47					57	30
Univ. College, Galway.	4	—								
B.Comm.			88	61	61	49			70	68
M.Comm.									—	—
M.Econ.Sc.									—	—
Ph.D. or D.Econ.Sc.									—	—

1. In each year supplemental examinations are held for those who failed in the initial examination. In tables 17.4. to 17.10. the numbers who passed were arrived at by adding the number who passed either the initial or supplemental examination. The numbers who sat include only the number sitting the initial examination, on the assumption that those sitting the supplemental examination include only those who failed in the initial examination immediately preceding it. This is not necessarily true, but is a reasonable approximation.
2. In addition to full time staff attached to degrees in business, university staff from other faculties lecture to students in business. Some staff listed above lecture to students in other faculties. Part-time staff are lecturers who work outside the university and lecture on a part-time basis. See text for details.
3. All examinations in tables 17.4. to 17.10. are University examinations only: there are also College examinations, e.g. at the end of the second year in arts in the National University. Such examinations are not included.
4. In 1965 no students had reached the final year of the Bachelor of Business Studies degree.
5. Until 1966 the B.Comm. degree course in all colleges of the National University lasted for only three years. Therefore no results are shown in the column headed "Third Year".
6. Lecturing to degree or diploma students. There are other part-time staff members lecturing to students for the Certificate in Accountancy.
7. Commenced 1964. No final examination until 1966.
8. Two year course only.

Source: National University. *Calendar of the National University of Ireland 1965.*
      Trinity College. Information supplied by the University.

Insofar as teaching by the lecture method is concerned a worsening staff-student ratio is not crucial, although in some cases lecture rooms are now quite inadequate to accommodate the numbers of students attending. The poor ratio has meant that, at undergraduate level, forms of teaching other than lecturing are almost impossible. It has also led to difficulty in giving adequate attention to students taking continuation degrees, and to so much of the staffs' time being taken up with teaching duties that no time is left for research or for publication. The situation with regard to libraries, reading-rooms and equipment is also unsatisfactory.

The graduate courses in administration are in better case, as the intake is limited and the staff ratios favourable.

The situation as seen by the staff is no doubt repeated in other faculties and departments, as student numbers continue to grow. The expansion of the last ten years will, at least, be equalled in the next decade. If present standards are to be maintained, let alone improved, a considerable increase in expenditure may be called for.

Degree in Dairy Science

University College, Cork, has a Faculty of Dairy Science, in which there are courses leading to a degree or a diploma in dairy science. Holders of the degree or diploma are regarded by the State as qualified for the position of manager or assistant manager at a registered creamery or cream-separating station. For that reason, many holders of the degree or diploma are found in managerial positions in industries based on milk-processing, and the courses include lectures in dairy accounting and in economics.

The degree course lasts for four years, with examinations at the end of each year. Following each of the first three examinations students must spend six to eight weeks in training at the college's experimental creamery or at some other creamery or dairy factory.

The subjects studied in each year are:

FIRST YEAR. Chemistry; experimental physics; mathematical physics; mathematics.

SECOND YEAR. Chemistry; civil engineering; dairy engineering; dairy and food microbiology. All subjects are examined.

THIRD YEAR. Dairy and food microbiology; dairy engineering; dairy husbandry; dairy technology; dairy accounting and economics; dairy chemistry.

FOURTH YEAR. Dairy accounting and economics; dairy and food microbiology; dairy chemistry; dairy technology. Lectures must also be attended in sociology and in co-operative law.

The course for the diploma lasts for two years. The first year consists of twenty weeks' lectures in dairy accounting and economics, dairy and food microbiology, dairy chemistry, dairy engineering and dairy technology. After twenty weeks the first examination is taken, and followed by twenty weeks' apprenticeship divided between the experimental creamery and another creamery. The second year consists of twenty weeks' lectures, followed by an examination in dairy accounting and economics, dairy engineering, dairy husbandry and dairy technology.

The faculty has a full-time staff of thirteen. In the first two years of the degree course, most of the class-work is done by the science and engineering faculties.

The full-time staff includes a professor in dairy accounting and economics, and a statutory lecturer in economics.

The number of students who were examined and who passed in 1965 is shown in table 17.5.

The structure and content of the degree reflects the fact that, to a great extent, graduates are employed in small co-operative creameries. In many of these creameries the graduate is the sole executive. Consequently graduates must have an all-round competence in technology and in administration. If the industry evolves in such a way that mergers take place leading to large centralised creameries, a considerable increase may take place in the employment of specialist administrative staff. Such a development might lead to modification in the present degree and diploma courses.

TABLE 17.5.   *Number of Students Examined In and Passing Examinations in Dairy Science, Year 1965.*

Degree or Diploma	STAFF		EXAMINATIONS							
	Full-time Dairy Science[1]	Part Time	First Sat	Passed	Second Sat	Passed	Third Sat	Passed	Final Sat	Passed
B.Sc.	13[2]	—	23	17	19	19	15	10	7	7
M.Sc.									1	1
Diploma[3]			25	23					45	34

1. Some of these staff members lecture in other faculties also. Students of dairy science attend lectures in other facilities. One lectureship, at present vacant, will be filled in 1966.
2. Excluding demonstrators.
3. Two-year course only.

Source: *Calendar of the National University of Ireland* 1965.

Degrees in Economics

The only colleges offering courses leading to specialist degrees in economics are Trinity College, Dublin, and University College, Dublin. It is possible in University College, Cork, and in University College, Galway, to select economics as one major subject in an honours degree in arts, but in both cases the course was, until this year, the same as that followed by students taking the B.Comm. degree. The combinations available at University College, Cork, are economics with applied psychology, economics with sociology, and economics with statistics, mathematics being taken as a minor subject.

Trinity College, Dublin.

Economics may be taken as a subject by a student proceeding to a B.A. degree in the School of General Studies, but the principal course is that in the Honor School of Economics and Political Science, for the B.A.(Mod.) degree.

The course lasts for four years. The first two years are "designed to provide a general training in analytical and applied economics and cognate studies". In the last two years "a series of more advanced courses gives some opportunity for specialisation within the fields of statistics, mathematical economics, politics and business administration".

The subjects taken in each year are shown below, with the number of hours' lecturing per week shown in parentheses.

FIRST YEAR. Introduction to economics (3); mathematics for economists (1); elementary statistics (2); political institutions (2); economic history (2).

SECOND YEAR. Theories of value and distribution (2); the economy of Ireland (2); political institutions (2); statistical method and sources (2); economic history (2) or mathematics (2).

THIRD YEAR. Economics I (2); economics II (2); and two of the following in specified combinations — statistical theory and methods (2); econometrics I (2); mathematical economics I (2); development of political thought (2); international political institutions (2); organisation and management (2); industrial relations (2).

FOURTH YEAR. Economics III (2); economics IV (2); and any two of the following in specified combinations — applied statistics (2); econometrics II (2); mathematical economics II (2); contemporary political theories (2); comparative government (2); law relating to business (2); industrial economics (2). Students are also examined in some third year subjects in their degree examination.

There are no formal lectures for post-graduate students. Those who want to work for a higher degree may do so by submitting a thesis on work done under the general direction of the department staff.

The staff consists of three professors, one on secondment to a Government department, and one about to retire in 1966, five lecturers and one junior lecturer in economics, and a lecturer in statistics. A professor, lecturer and junior lecturer in political science lecture to students of economics as well as servicing the School of Business and Social Studies, and there is a junior lecturer in economics attached primarily to the Department of Business Studies.

University College, Dublin.

There is an honours degree course lasting for three years in University College, Dublin, leading to the degree B.A. Economics may also be chosen as a subject in a pass degree, whether taken by day or by evening attendance. The honours course can be followed only by day.

Students have a choice of two courses for the honours degree. The second course, recently introduced, allows a combination of mathematics and economics. The older course is described first. The courses described are for the year 1965-66.

Course IX A[1]. FIRST YEAR. Political economy; some other specified subject; Latin or Greek if not already taken; some other subject. Honours courses must be taken in the first two subjects, pass courses may be followed in the others. All subjects are examined.

SECOND YEAR. Political economy; national economics; politics.

THIRD YEAR. Political economy; national economics; politics; either jurisprudence and Roman law, or economic statistics. There is no University examination in the second year. Political economy and national economics are major subjects, the others minor. The course in economic statistics is the same as that taken heretofore in the third year of the B.Comm. degree course, and now taken in the second year.

Course IX B. FIRST YEAR. Political economy; mathematics; Latin or Greek; any other specified subject. The first two must be taken at honours level, the last two may be at pass level.

SECOND AND THIRD YEARS. Political economy; national economics; mathematics. All are major subjects.

It has not been possible to provide a special course in mathematics designed for economists. Students taking Group IX B must therefore follow exactly the same course as those specialising in mathematics for their degree. The difficulty of this combination deters most students, only about 10 per cent electing to take this option.

Economics can be taken as a major subject with history by those proceeding to a B.A. degree in history, and as a major subject by those proceeding to a B.A. in geography.

1. This is the official designation of the course.

At graduate level, holders of a B.A. degree in economics can proceed to the degrees M.Econ.Sc., Ph.D., and D.Econ.Sc. exactly as described in the case of those holding the B.Comm. degree. Instead of taking the degree M.Econ.Sc., holders of a B.A. may elect to go on to the degree M.A., either by thesis or by examination.

Theses must show evidence of original research on some subject approved by the professor. The examination for the degree M.A. may be taken after three terms, in any three of the following subjects: econometrics; agricultural economics; development of economic thought; banking, currency, and international payments; price theory; economic growth; economics of education; any other approved subject.

The staff of the Department of Economics consists of those economists already mentioned as teaching in the Faculty of Commerce.

The number of students taking and passing honours examinations in economics in 1965 in Trinity College, Dublin, and in University College, Dublin, is shown in table 17.6.

TABLE 17.6. *Number of Students Examined In and Passing Examinations in Economics, Year 1965, by University.*

University and Degree	STAFF Full-time Economics	Part Time	EXAMINATIONS First Sat	Passed	Second Sat	Passed	Third Sat	Passed	Final Sat	Passed
Trinity College, Dublin.	10	—								
B.A.(Mod.)			20	16	22	21	33	28	32	32
M.Litt.									1	1
Ph.D.									1	1
Univ. College, Dublin.	9[1]	—								
B.A.			n.a.	n.a.	—	—	—	—	56	46
M.A.									n.a.	n.a.
Ph.D.									—	—
D.Econ.Sc.									—	—

1. These staff members lecture also in the Faculty of Commerce.
Source: Information supplied by the universities.

Degrees in Engineering

Four-year courses leading to degrees in engineering are available at all university colleges in the Republic of Ireland, but a greater range of specialisms is available in Dublin than in either Cork or Galway. University College, Dublin, has degree-courses in agricultural, chemical, civil, electrical and mechanical engineering. Trinity College has courses in aerodynamics, civil, electronic, and in mechanical and production engineering. There are courses leading to degrees in civil and electrical engineering in University College, Cork, and in civil engineering alone in University College, Galway.

In the colleges of the National University students may be awarded the degree Master of Engineering Science on the completion of one year of research in the college. This may be done immediately after the primary degree. Trinity College, Dublin, has a Graduate School of Engineering Studies in which there is a one-year course leading to the degree M.Sc. or, in the case of non-graduates, to a diploma. At present only one course is offered in the school. The course is called "computer applications", and has a high management science content. In both the National University and the University of Dublin there are other post-graduate engineering degrees which may be taken only after experience.

Students of engineering will not be admitted to any of the undergraduate courses mentioned above unless they either pass a qualifying examination or reach honours standard in the Leaving Certificate examination in mathematics or in an equivalent examination. In Trinity College, students must also take a B.A. degree, and will be granted only a licence in engineering unless they pass the B.A. examination.

Apart from the specialisation in mechanical and production engineering in Trinity College, there is nothing approaching a specialisation in industrial engineering at any university in the Republic. The subject of industrial engineering is now coming in for a great deal of interest (see below under "professional qualifications—engineering"), and the introduction of lectures in industrial engineering, leading perhaps to a full specialisation, is favoured by the staff of both University College, Dublin, and University College, Cork.

It was mentioned above that there is a considerable management science content in the post-graduate course at Trinity College, Dublin. A set of options on computing, numerical analysis and statistics, and operations research, is being introduced into the second, third and fourth years respectively of the course for engineers at University College, Galway.

At University College, Cork, both civil engineers and electrical engineers are examined in their third year on a one-year course on numerical methods and computers. Final year electrical engineering students presenting for an honours degree select two subjects additional to the pass degree course. One of these may be the subject "digital computers".

All the colleges of the National University feature some management content in their final-year courses. In University College, Cork, there is a full paper on economics and management and on industrial administration in the degree examination for both civil and electrical engineers. This follows a course of lectures, for one hour each week. The content of the courses is as follows:

Economics and management; interest, present worth and depreciation calculations; analysis of capital projects; economy studies for retirement and replacement; benefit-cost analysis; allocation of cost in multi-purpose projects; operations research.

Growth of scientific management; functions and principles of management; organisation; production control—method study, work measure, and planned maintenance; management accounting; industrial relations; public relations; problems of the professional employee.

Industrial administration; Development of industrial organisation, financial calculations, budgets and control, costing, planned maintenance, elements of method study and work measurement, safety. Scientific management, functions, and principles, industrial relations, public relations.

For final-year students in all branches of engineering in University College, Dublin, there is a compulsory paper on engineering economics and professional practice based on a one lecture a week course on the following syllabus:

General principles of management; division of functions; works organisation; selection of a suitable site for a works; selection and training of operatives and staff; welfare; health and safety; statutory requirements for process industries; inspection and quality control; records of progress; standard specifications and codes of practice; purchasing and storekeeping; contracts, estimates and tenders; the engineer's duties and responsibilities.

There is an optional paper on industrial organisation in the degree examination for chemical, electrical and mechanical engineers. It is intended in the session 1966-67 to introduce a course of lectures for final year students by the Professor of Psychology. The course will focus on the nature of man-machine systems. The content of the present course in industrial organisation is as follows: types of ownership of industrial organisations; single ownership; partnership; limited liability; companies and public corporations; the law in regard to limited liability companies; public companies and the stock exchange; nationalised industries; trade associations; trading profit and loss accounts; balance sheets; capital structure of the firm; depreciation; elementary balance sheet analysis; income tax; insurance; hire purchase; the organisation of the personnel department.

TABLE 17.7. *Number of Students Examined In and Passing Examinations in Engineering, Year 1965, by University.*

University and Degree	STAFF[1] Full-time Engineering	Part Time	EXAMINATIONS First Sat Passed	Second Sat Passed	Third Sat Passed	Final Sat Passed
Trinity Coll., Dublin.	11	—				
B.A., B.A.I.						
Civil				n.a. 22	n.a. 16	n.a. 17
Mech. & Prod.			46 35	n.a. 11	,, 7	,, 14
Electronic				n.a. 7	,, 12	,, 6
Aerodynamics				— —	— —	— —
M.A.I.						n.a. n.a.
M.Sc.						n.a. n.a.
Univ. College, Cork.						
B.E.						
Civil	11	—	71 62	53 48	26 23	24 24
Electrical					24 22	14 14
M.E.						3 3
M.Eng.Sc.						4 4
Univ. College, Dublin.						
B.E.						
Agricultural	3	—		4 4	6 5	1 1
Chemical	4	—		15 14	13 12	15 15
Civil	8	—	160 123	50 42	29 28	21 18
Electrical	7	—		46 45	48 45	47 41
Mechanical	7	—		40 28	31 28	30 25
M.E.						2 2
M.Eng.Sc.						8 3
Univ. College, Galway.						
B.E.						
Civil	5	—	43 29	38 32	30 27	20 19
M.E.						2 2
M.Eng.Sc.						— —

1. Excluding demonstrators.
Source: National University. *Calendar of the National University of Ireland* 1965.
      Trinity College. Information supplied by the University.

A series of ten lectures on business administration is given to final-year students in University College, Galway.

All the staff members interviewed were of the opinion that, short of introducing a specialisation in industrial engineering, or extending the length of the courses, there was not room at undergraduate level for anything more in management studies than is being done at present. There was a fair degree of confidence that students would be prepared to take an immediate post-graduate course in business studies, as it was noticeable that a good proportion expressed interest in a managerial rather than a professional engineering career.

The number of students attempting each part of the different engineering degrees is shown in table 17.7.

Degrees in Natural Science:

In the constituent colleges of the National University there are courses in natural science leading to a general B.Sc. degree, or to an honours B.Sc. The former is a three-year course, the latter lasts for another year beyond the pass degree. In Trinity College natural sciences are taught in the Honor School in Arts, and the four-year course leads to the degree B.A.(Mod.).

TABLE 17.8.   *Number of Students Examined In and Passing Examinations in Natural Science, Year 1965, by University.*

University and Degree	STAFF[1] Full-time Science	Part Time	EXAMINATIONS First Sat	Passed	Second Sat	Passed	Third Sat	Passed	Final Sat	Passed
Trinity College, Dublin.	55[2]									
B.A. (Mod.)			84	68	82	70	47	47	54	53
M.Litt.									n.a.	n.a.
Ph.D.									n.a.	n.a.
Univ. College, Cork.	28[3]	—								
B.Sc. (Pass)[4]			95	73					45	40
B.Sc. (Hons.)							53	52	40	39
M.Sc.									16	15
Ph.D.[5]									n.a.	n.a.
Univ. College, Dublin.	83	2								
B.Sc. (Pass)			240	179					117	69
B.Sc. (Hons.)							63	60	81	80
M.Sc.									6	6
Ph.D.									n.a.	n.a.
Univ. College, Galway.	45	—								
B.Sc. (Pass)			107	71	52	39			44	20
B.Sc. (Hons.)							21	20	23	23
M.Sc.									9	5
Ph.D.									n.a.	n.a.

1. Excluding demonstrators, research associates and assistants, visiting professors. Excludes staff attached principally to faculties of medicine, except for biochemistry lecturers, who are included.
2. Including biochemistry, but not bacteriology.
3. Five lectureships were listed as vacant in University College, Cork.
4. In the Colleges of the National University the B.Sc. (Pass) course lasts for only three years. There is no University examination at the end of the second year except in University College, Galway. Some B.Sc. (Hons.) courses last for only three years, others for four.
5. The National University Calendar does not differentiate Ph.D. results, between faculties, therefore the number of those taking it in science cannot be shown.

Source: As in table 17.7.

Those taking the honours B.Sc. in University College, Cork, can select statistics and psychology with mathematics as a minor, or statistics and economics, with mathematics as a minor. First-year B.Sc. students at University College, Galway, can take economics as a subject in their examination. Apart from these options, all courses in each university are confined to natural science subjects.

There are no courses in business studies for students of science at any university except University College, Cork, where graduate students of the professor of chemistry receive, from the Professor of Applied Psychology, two hours lecturing per week in management.

All university staff interviewed were convinced that there was not room in the under-graduate curriculum to incorporate lectures in management, even if this were considered desirable. Furthermore, unlike engineers, they did not think that young scientists, par-ticularly those with honours degrees, would be prepared to study management at imme-diate post-graduate level. Staff felt that the orientation of the honours science graduate was towards a career as a professional scientist, and that it was only after several years that many realised that their career was, after all, likely to be in management. There are, however, large number of graduates with pass degrees in science who, at present, take up secondary school teaching. If the employment opportunity existed some of these might be willing to follow a career in industry.

The number of managers in industry with a degree in science is so large that the question of how best to make science graduates realise that they are quite likely to end up as managers, and how best to prepare them for such a career, deserves careful study.

The number of students examined and passed at each examination in 1965 is shown in table 17.8.

In addition to the university courses described above, it is possible to study for the B.Sc. degree of the University of London at the College of Technology, Kevin Street. Students may, if they wish, attend a full-time course as far as the Intermediate examina-tion and afterwards proceed by either part-release or evening courses to the full degree examination. Alternatively students may attend from the beginning by part-release or in the evening. The evening course lasts for at least seven years, the part-release course for six.

Degrees and Diplomas in Psychology:

Extensive courses in psychology are available at Trinity College, Dublin, University College, Cork, and University College, Dublin.

As part of the B.A. degree course in University College, Galway, students may select psychology as a sub-section of the group in philosophy. The course covers experimental and speculative psychology, but does not refer directly to industrial psychology.

Trinity College, Dublin.

There is an honours course in philosophy and psychology leading to the degree B.A. (Mod.). The course in philosophy covers ground in common with the honours course in mental and moral science. The subjects in the course on psychology are as follows:

FIRST YEAR. History of psychology, learning and symbolic processes I. There are laboratory classes on learning and remembering.

SECOND YEAR. Biological foundations I; psychological measurements I; perception. There are laboratory classes in sensation and perception, and in animal behaviour.

THIRD YEAR. Biological foundations II; psychological measurements II; intelligence and personality assessment; personality theory; development psychology. There are laboratory classes in psychology testing.

FOURTH YEAR. Psychological measurement II; abnormal psychology; learning and symbolic processes II; social psychology; special topics. There are laboratory classes in advanced experimental work and on research projects.

The course is staffed by a reader and three junior lecturers in psychology.

University College, Cork.

There is a professorship of applied psychology in the Faculty of Science and Arts. Students taking a B.A. or B.Sc. pass degree can select psychology as one of their three final subjects. Honours students, after their first year, now take psychology as a major subject with one other subject at pass level, such as economics, sociology or history. If they wish to make a career in psychology, they are normally expected to spend a fourth year (M.A.) in specialised work in the industrial, clinical or educational field.

The undergraduate course lasts three years and covers the following subjects:

FIRST YEAR. Individual psychology; social psychology; laboratory work (honours students only).

SECOND AND THIRD YEARS. Physiological and comparative psychology; child and adolescent psychology; educational and clinical psychology; psychology and industry; history of psychology; psychology and religion.

The honours course involves a more intensive treatment of the general course together with the following: statistical methods and mathematical psychology; practical work in testing, work study, human relations.

The full-time staff of the department now numbers three, as two lecturers have been appointed this year. There are six part-time staff.

In addition to the B.A. and B.Sc. course, the Department of Applied Psychology provides courses in management for graduate science students and from this year will also service B.Comm. undergraduates.

Finally, the department of applied psychology organises a twenty week, part-time management development course (120 hours) certificated by the College. Apart from the staff of the department, lecturers are U.C.C. professors and visiting speakers. The course covers work study, psychology of management, an integrated series of conferences on operator training, mathematics for management and an introduction to marketing. The participants are mainly executives from Cork city and county.

University College, Dublin.

The principal courses in psychology at University College, Dublin, are at graduate rather than under-graduate level. It is, however, possible to take psychology as a subject for a pass B.A. degree, as a subject in the philosophy group for a B.A. honours degree and as a subject for an honours or pass Bachelor of Social Science degree.

The basic course is a full-time two year course open only to graduates and leading to the Diploma in Psychology. Because the numbers have to be restricted, entrance is competitive, and those whose basic degree is in science, medicine and social science are preferred.

The subjects of the two year course are as follows: rational psychology, ethics, and principles of philosophy; general psychology, including the history of psychology; experimental psychology; psychometrics, testing, and guidance techniques; development of the normal personality; principles of abnormal psychology; social psychology; psychology and religion; psychophysiology; the exceptional child; delinquency; principles of psychosomatic medicine; principles of psycho-therapy; industrial psychology; clinical child psychology; neurological principles of behaviour; statistics; mental hygiene.

The course includes lectures, seminars, experimental work, clinical training, and training in research methods. Experimental work and testing techniques occupy about six hours weekly during the first year and about three days weekly during the second year.

Students who have taken the diploma can go on after a further year to the degree Master of Psychological Science. If they wish, they can specialise in industrial psychology. In practice, however, most of those taking the diploma or degree follow careers in mental health work; only seven of the thirty-two people who took the diploma before 1966 are working in industry, where opportunities and salaries are restricted.

The full-time staff consists of a professor, an assistant lecturer, and three assistants. There is one part-time staff member, and outside lecturers are brought in for special topics.

Table 17.9 shows the number of students who were examined and who passed degree or diploma examinations in psychology in 1965.

TABLE 17.9. *Number of Students Examined In and Passing Final Examinations[1] in Pyschology, Year 1965, by College*

University and Degree	Staff[2]			Final Examination	
	Full Time Psychology	Part Time		Sat	Passed
University College, Cork.	3	6			
B.A. or B.Sc.[3]				8	8
M.A.				3	3
University College, Dublin.	5	1			
Dipl. in Psychology				9	9
M.Psych.Sc.				6	6

1. The degree B.A. (Mod.) including psychology has only recently been started in Trinity College, Dublin, (see text). There will be no final examination students until 1968.
2. In 1965. There have since been additions.
3. These are students taking psychology as a subject in B.A. or B.Sc. degree examinations.
Source: As in table 17.7.

Degrees in Sociology

There are full degree courses in social science at Trinity College, Dublin, and at University College, Dublin. In these colleges, social science forms a separate department within the School of Business and Social Studies and the Faculty of Arts respectively. In University College, Cork, sociology is a department of the Faculty of Arts and, until 1965, was taken only as a subject for the B.A. degree. Since that year a course has been available leading to the degree B.Soc.Sc., still within the Faculty of Arts. In University College, Galway, sociology may be selected as a subject for a B.A. degree, either pass or honours.

Trinity College, Dublin.

The course leading to the degree Bachelor in Social Studies (B.S.S.) lasts for four years of full-time study, and comprises both academic study and practical training.

Honours are awarded on the result of the examinations—there are no separate pass and honours courses. There is also a two year full-time course leading to the Diploma in Social Studies.

The subjects of the degree course are:

FIRST YEAR. Social structure; political institutions; economics I; ethics; scientific method and elementary statistics. Practical work must be done with groups of children.

SECOND YEAR. Psychology I; economics II; social administration; medical studies I; history and philosophy of science.

There are non-examined courses in introductory science and a seminar on principles of social work. During the summer vacation supervised practical work must be done in a public authority, voluntary body, or other organisation engaged in social or personnel work.

THIRD YEAR. Psychology II; social administration II; medical studies II; law; political theory; and seminars in elementary casework. Practical work is done under the supervision of medical or other social workers. During the vacation each student spends at least eight weeks of full-time work under supervision in a public authority or voluntary body.

FOURTH YEAR. Social administration III; social psychology and two of the following: mental health; business administration; principles and methods of social surveys; criminology. There is a seminar in elementary casework. A programme of practical work is drawn up for each student in the light of his or her choice of subjects. In the final examination there is a *viva voce* examination in casework.

The course for the Diploma in Social Studies is:

FIRST YEAR. Social structure; psychology; social administration I; medical studies; and a non-examined course in introductory science. There is a seminar in principles of social work. Practical work must also be carried out during the year and, in the vacation, eight weeks supervised practical work is done in a local authority or voluntary body.

SECOND YEAR. Political institutions; social psychology; social administration II; medical studies II; law; seminar in elementary casework. Practical work is also done.

Examinations are set in each year in the subjects of the course. There is a *viva voce* examination in casework.

The staff attached to the department consists of a professor and a lecturer in political science, who also lecture in the Honor School of Economics and in the Department of Business Studies, a director of practical training and an assistant, a lecturer in social administration, and a part-time lecturer in child care.

University College, Cork.

Since 1965, there has been a three-year course in University College, Cork, leading to the degree Bachelor of Social Science (B.Soc.Sc.).

To be admitted to the course it is not necessary to have taken the subject Latin for matriculation, but it is necessary to have taken the subject mathematics.

The subjects of the first year are social philosophy, applied psychology, mathematics and either modern history or a modern language. In the second and third years the subjects are sociology (including social research and social work), social administration and public administration, together with statistics in the second year and economics in the third year. Students in their second and third years must also attend the lectures on child and adolescent psychology in the Department of Applied Psychology.

The B.Soc.Sc. degree is an honours degree, but candidates whose answering at the final examination does not qualify them for the award of an honours degree may be awarded a pass if sufficient merit is shown.

There are two full-time staff members whose principal concern is with the degree B.Soc.Sc. They are a lecturer and an assistant in sociology. There is also a demonstrator in sociology.

University College, Dublin.

There are three year full-time courses leading to either a pass or honours degree B.Soc.Sc. Those who obtain at least second-class honours, grade I, in the honours B.Soc.Sc. degree examination may, after a further year, attempt the degree M.Soc.Sc. by thesis. They will be able to do so by examination from October 1967 onwards. There is also a two year full-time course for the Diploma in Social Science. The number of entrants to both degree and diploma is deliberately limited: not more than 100 students were accepted for the first year degree-course in 1966-67.

After the first year, in which they take philosophy, political economy and two optional subjects, students have a wide choice of groups to choose from for their degree examination. Sociology is taken in all groups. Other possible subjects include psychology, national economics, social statistics and social administration.

The course in sociology includes a section on industrial psychology which covers the following topics: social structure of industrial undertakings, systems of control, the process of decision making, automation, leisure and free-time and industrial relations.

The full-time staff consists of a professor, a college lecturer, seven assistants in social science and four research assistants.

Table 17.10 shows the number of students who were examined in and who passed examinations in social science in 1965.

TABLE 17.10. *Number of Students Examined In and Passing Examinations in Social Science Year 1965.*

University Degree	STAFF[1]		EXAMINATIONS							
	Full-time Soc. Science	Part Time	First		Second		Third		Final	
			Sat	Passed	Sat	Passed	Sat	Passed	Sat	Passed
Trinity College, Dublin.	5	1								
B.S.S.[2]			13	13	14	14	11	11	—	—
Diploma[3]			8	7					13	13
University College, Dublin.	9[4]	—								
B.Soc.Sc. (Pass)									41	39
B.Soc.Sc. (Hons.)			103	84	35	34	12	12	13	13
M.Soc.Sc.										
Dipl.Soc.Sc.[3]			4	4					8	8

1. Trinity College — 1965. University College — 1966.
2. No students had reached the final examination in 1965: the degree was instituted only in 1962.
3. Two year course only.
4. Excluding research assistants.

Source: As in table 17.7.

PART C.   NON-UNIVERSITY PROFESSIONAL EDUCATION

There is a multiplicity of professional qualifications relevant to business. Traditionally, membership of professional institutes has been achieved by evening study, sometimes by correspondence courses, sometimes by attendance at colleges of commerce and technology. Many of the institutes for which Irish students study for membership are based primarily in Britain, in some cases with an Irish branch or centre.

The whole question of qualifying by evening study alone is being discussed widely at present, particularly in Britain. Many professions are examining their structure critically. The question must also be faced in Ireland, bearing in mind that conditions differ in many respects from societies with large populations concentrated in great urban areas.

Every effort was made to include all relevant bodies for whose examinations Irish students prepare. There is a large number of professional institutes, particularly those incorporated in Britain, for whose examinations students can prepare by correspondence courses. It is therefore not claimed that the list is comprehensive. There is a number of other institutes which were not considered directly relevant to a career in industrial management or which refer directly to a particular economic activity. Some of those are mentioned briefly under the heading "other professional qualifications".

Before going on to discuss the various professional bodies, the facilities available at colleges of commerce and technology are outlined.

Colleges of Commerce and Technology

In general, colleges of commerce and technology prepare their students for membership of professional bodies. They do not give degrees but some give diplomas at this level. In addition to training at professional and technological level, courses are provided at less advanced levels in commerce, trade, and technical occupations.

College of Commerce, Rathmines, Dublin.

Higher-level education is provided by the School of Professional Studies and the School of Management Studies.

The School of Professional Studies provides courses suitable for a wide range of professions. Lectures take place mostly in the evenings though day-release of employees for advanced level courses is expanding. The facilities in the School of Management Studies are described in the next part of this chapter.

There is available in the School of Professional Studies a two year, full-time course leading to a Diploma in Business Studies. The course is intended for those entering a family business or hoping to enter industry or commerce as junior executives or trainees.

In addition to taking the Diploma students may, during the course or at the end, enter for the examinations of various accounting and secretarial bodies viz., parts I-III of the examinations of the Institute of Cost and Works Accountants; the intermediate examinations of the various associations of financial accountants; the full intermediate examination and part I of the final examinations of various institutes of professional company secretaries. Holders of the Diploma are exempted from the first two of the three parts of the examinations for the Diploma in Marketing of the Institute of Marketing.

Entrants to the course must have passed the Leaving Certificate or equivalent examinations, including the subjects mathematics and English.

The subjects of the course and the number of lectures per week are as follows:

Subjects	First Year	Second Year
Accountancy	8	3
Costing	2	5
Auditing	—	1
Statistics	4	2
Economics	3	1
Taxation	—	1½
Marketing	2	2
Principles of Law	1	1
Mercantile and Industrial Law	1	2
Company Law	—	2
Company Administration	1	1
Management and Industrial Administration	3	1½
Sociology	1	1
Foreign Trade Practice	—	1
English (Vocabulary, Correspondence, Precis, Essay, Report Writing) ...	1	1½
Effective Speaking	1	1
French	1	1

School of Commerce, Cork.

The School of Commerce provides courses for all the examinations of secretarial bodies, and the Institute of Transport. Courses for the earlier examinations of several accounting bodies and of the Institute of Marketing are also available. Courses are arranged for later parts when demand warrants.

Professional courses for insurance personnel were provided in the past, but lapsed through lack of support. It is intended to re-establish these courses in 1966-67. An approach is to be made to the banks with a view to providing professional courses for their staffs.

The facilities for work study training and the training of supervisors are described in the next part of this chapter.

School of Commerce, Limerick.

The School of Management and Professional Studies in Limerick provides courses for the examinations of the Irish Supervisors Institute, the Certificate in Storekeeping of the Purchasing Officers Association, the Diploma in Foreign Trade of the Irish Exporters Association, the Diploma in Marketing of the Institute of Marketing (part I only), the Diploma in Local Administration of the Institute of Public Administration and the Diploma in Hospital Administration of the Institute of Hospital Administrators. Courses are also provided for the examinations of various institutes of secretaries (all parts), the Institute of Transport (all parts), the Institute of Chartered Accountants (parts II and III), and the Chartered Insurance Institute (parts I and II). There are also appreciatory courses in work study.

All the above courses are held in the evening. There is a full-time course for school leavers, which lasts for one year and covers the subjects accountancy and costing; business administration; principles of law; statistics; economics and English. At the end of the year students can enter for the examinations of the Institute of Cost and Works Accountants (part I) and for the intermediate examinations of secretarial bodies.

Schools of commerce outside Dublin find it difficult to offer a wide range of subjects. Firms are slow to support courses and, even when the number of students coming forward initially is sufficient to justify starting courses, the drop-out rate during the year is often so great as to reduce class numbers well below economic levels. Low and unpredictable demand means that part-time teachers are used to a considerable extent.

College of Technology, Bolton Street, Dublin.

The College is organised in three schools: the School of Architecture and Building, the School of Engineering and the School of Printing and Book Production. In each school there are day and evening classes at trade, technician and technological level.

The School of Printing provides part-time day and evening training for administrative staff as well as for technical staff. The course covers three years, the first two concerned mainly with costing and estimating, the third with administrative duties. Diplomas are presented to successful students.

The School of Architecture and Building provides whole-time, part-time day and evening courses, leading to the examinations of the Royal Institute of Architects in Ireland, the Royal Institution of Chartered Surveyors, the Institute of Quantity Surveyors, the Building Surveyors' Institute, the Incorporated Association of Architects and Surveyors, the Institute of Building and the Town Planning Institute.

In the School of Engineering there are whole-time, part-time and evening courses leading to diplomas and to the examinations of the Institution of Structural Engineers, the Institution of Mechanical Engineers, the Institution of Heating and Ventilating and Air Conditioning Engineers, the Institute of Marine Engineers, the Institute of the Motor Industry and the Royal Aeronautical Society. A course has lately been introduced leading to the examinations of the Institution of Production Engineers.

In some cases the College diploma examinations exempt students from the examinations of the professional institution. In others the institution examinations must be taken. In such cases the college diploma is granted only to those successful in the institution examination as well as in the College examination.

The courses followed will be described below when professional engineering qualifications are being outlined.

College of Technology, Kevin Street, Dublin.

In addition to courses leading to the B.Sc. degree of London University, the College of Technology at Kevin Street offers part-release, sandwich and evening courses for the examinations of the Institution of Electrical Engineers, evening courses for the Institution of Chemical Engineers, and part-release courses for graduateship of the Institute of Physics. The course in chemical engineering is run jointly with Bolton Street and is restricted to graduates in mechanical engineering and to those with equivalent qualifications.

Professional Qualifications in Accountancy

Qualification for a career in accountancy is through membership of a professional institute. Traditionally, study for membership has been by evening attendance at a college of commerce or by taking a correspondence course. In the Republic of Ireland, evening courses are available at the College of Commerce, Rathmines, and at the Schools of Commerce in Cork and Limerick. There is also a two year evening course in accountancy at University College, Dublin.

The accountancy profession in Britain and Ireland is, at the time of writing, being discussed by the major accounting bodies — the Institute of Chartered Accountants in England and Wales, the Institute of Chartered Accountants of Scotland, and the Institute of Chartered Accountants in Ireland; the Association of Certified and Corporate Accountants; the Institute of Cost and Works Accountants; and the Institute of Municipal Treasurers and Accountants.

According to a statement issued, the purpose of the discussion is to consider in what way in the public interest the profession can best be developed, and in particular:

(1) Whether there is scope for reducing the number of separate professional bodies and qualifications in England and Wales, Scotland and Ireland respectively.

(II) Whether changes should be made in the form, methods and standards of education, training and experience, bearing in mind the qualities now needed for the performance of the more advanced professional services whether in public practice, industry, commerce or public service.

(III) Whether in the future there should be two recognised levels of professional qualification related respectively to higher and lower standards of education, training and experience and, if so, what arrangements there should be to enable those qualified in the lower level to proceed to the higher level.

(IV) Whether a single professional designation can be adopted having regard to the fact that training will be in public practice, industry, commerce or public service.

If agreement is reached on these matters there may be changes in the structure of the accounting bodies described below.

The bodies involved in the discussion mentioned above are described first, followed by some other bodies in alphabetical order.[1]

Before going on to consider the individual qualifications, a joint scheme, recently introduced, is described.

Joint Diploma in Management Accounting Services.

In response to industry's demand for management accounting, the Institute of Chartered Accountants in England and Wales, the Institute of Chartered Accountants of Scotland, the Institute of Cost and Works Accountants and the Association of Certified and Corporate Accountants have participated in the development and introduction of a Joint Diploma in Management Accounting Services. The Institute of Chartered Accountants in Ireland has joined the scheme, now that the legislation necessary to amend its charter has been passed.

The diploma is a "post-graduate" qualification, open to members of the above organisations, who are at least 26 years old and who have at least two years' experience of management accountancy in industry or management consultancy. Those who obtain the diploma can add to their original designatory letters, the designation J.Dip.M.A.

The examination is in two parts. Part I is a written examination on the subjects management accounting; management principles and business administration; office machines and methods and data processing; analytical techniques[2]; general financial knowledge and investigations. Candidates for Part II must have at least five years' acceptable experience, must submit a thesis on a subject chosen from Part I, and must pass an oral examination on both thesis and experience.

---

1. Many of these bodies have subjects in common and suggest very similar reading lists. Furthermore, students studying at colleges of commerce attend lectures in common.
2. Mainly statistics.

The first examination for which members of the Institute of Chartered Accountants in Ireland are eligible to sit will be held in October 1967.

The Institute of Chartered Accountants in Ireland.

The Institute was founded in 1888, and has a membership of about 2,000, about two-thirds of whom are in industry or commerce, the remainder in public practice as accountants. On passing the Institute examinations students join the Institute as associates (A.C.A.), and may later be elected to fellowship (F.C.A.). The Institute is the largest body of accountants in Ireland. (See table 17.11.)

It is stated by the Institute that "the education of a chartered accountant is directed to preparing him for the responsible positions which exist in the professional and business world. The training is a broad one, intended to give the chartered accountant a thorough grasp of the principles of accountancy and a general knowledge of the special problems which may confront him in his career. It follows that after qualification it may be necessary or advisable to undertake further specialist study in subjects such as cost or management accountancy or taxation".

All students must serve a period as a clerk articled to an accountant in public practice. To be accepted for articles, a student must have passed the secondary school Leaving Certificate with honours in two subjects or an equivalent examination. Students who are not graduates of a university recognised by the Institute Council must serve a period of five years under articles and pass all five parts of the Institute's examinations.

It is hoped that in future the normal mode of entry into the profession will be by university. To encourage students to take a university degree, the period under articles is reduced to three years for those holding any degree, and graduates holding an approved degree are exempted from the first three parts of the Institute's examinations. Holders of non-approved degrees are exempted from Part I only.

The approved degrees are the Bachelor of Commerce degree of the National University, the Bachelor of Business Studies degree of the University of Dublin[1] and the Bachelor of Economic Science degree at Queen's University, Belfast, with passes in appropriate subjects.

The subjects for the Institute's examinations are:

PART I. Elementary book-keeping; arithmetic and algebra; commercial knowledge and precis writing.

PART II. Accounting, taxation, auditing.

PART III. Mercantile and executorship law; company law; economics.

PART IV. Advanced accounting; advanced accounting including partnership, executorship and trust accounts; taxation; cost accounting.

PART V. Advanced accounting, auditing and the general duties of professional accountants; cost and management accounting, investigations and valuations.

Courses covering the entire syllabus are available at the College of Commerce, Rathmines, or from correspondence colleges. Economics has been added as a subject, and there is now a greater management accounting content than in the past. It was, however, felt that there was room for a course on management accounting intermediate in standard between the basic qualification and the Joint Diploma. For this reason the Institute of

---

1. Provided optional courses in law are taken, otherwise holders of the B.B.S. degree are exempt from only the first two parts.

Chartered Accountants in England and Wales, Scotland and Ireland has introduced a Certificate in Management Information to encourage members to study in this field.

Candidates are eligible to sit for the examination two years after admission to membership, but there is no specific requirement as to practical experience. The course requires a two year period of part-time study and covers the following subjects: business organisation and administration; design of systems and data processing; analytical and statistical techniques for management information; financial management and the use of accounting information. The first examination for which students in Ireland will be eligible to sit will be held in October 1967.

The Association of Certified and Corporate Accountants.

The association is a body incorporated in Britain. There is an Irish branch which covers the Republic of Ireland.

Membership of the association is obtainable only by examination and experience. Members and fellows use the designatory letters A.A.C.C.A. and F.A.C.C.A. respectively. Graduates are those who, though passing the Association's examinations, do not qualify for membership because of age or lack of experience.

Before entering on a course of study, a candidate must be at least 16 years old and must either pass a preliminary examination or be exempted by having the Leaving Certificate or equivalent qualification.

The examination is in four parts and is held half-yearly. Parts I and II may be taken together. The subjects of the four parts are:

PART I. Book-keeping and accounts I; economics; business statistics; costing.

PART II. Mercantile law; taxation; auditing; book-keeping and accounts II.

PART III. Advanced accounting; executorship and bankruptcy; company law; business administration; advanced costing.

PART IV. Advanced accounting; taxation; auditing and investigations; management accounting; industry and finance.

Exemptions from Parts I and II are available to those holding degrees (mostly the degree B.Comm. or B.B.S.) and certain other accounting and secretarial qualifications. Courses covering the syllabus are available at Rathmines and, up to part II, at Cork.

It is not necessary that candidates be articled as clerks, and many students in Ireland work in industry, commerce and public bodies. It is, however, necessary that applicants for membership be engaged on work of a specifically accounting nature. If not, they will not be elected.

The number of members in the Irish branch is 300, of whom about 225 are in industry, the remaining 75 being in public practice.

The Institute of Cost and Works Accountants.

The Institute is incorporated in Britain. In the Republic of Ireland there is a Dublin and District branch and a Munster sub-branch.

Membership is by examination only, in addition to which candidates must have at least three years' comprehensive practical costing experience. Associates use the designatory letters A.C.W.A. Fellows, who may be elected to that rank after five years' experience at a high level, use the letters F.C.W.A. There was formerly a special examination for associates which also led to a fellowship, but this has now become the foundation of the Joint Diploma in Management Accounting Services.

Students will not be enrolled unless they are at least 16 years old and have at least the Intermediate Certificate examination. The examination is in five parts, which may be taken separately or two at a time. The subjects are:

PART I. Industrial administration — production, marketing, purchasing, research and development, personnel, secretarial and accounting; book-keeping; economics; statistics.

PART II. Cost accountancy — labour; cost accountancy — materials; cost-accountancy — overhead.

PART III. Office management; financial accountancy (two papers); industrial and commercial law.

PART IV. Advanced cost and management accountancy — general costing procedures, costing techniques, budgetary control and standard costing, marginal costing and break-even analysis, presentation and use.

PART V. Advanced accountancy and financial management; management principles and practice; company law; taxation.

Holders of degrees in commerce or in economics are exempted from Part I. Various other exemptions are available to holders of accounting and secretarial qualifications.

Courses covering the entire syllabus are available at Rathmines, and for part of the syllabus at the Schools of Commerce in Cork and Limerick.

There are 170 members of the Institute of Cost and Works Accountants in Ireland.

Association of International Accountants.

The Association is incorporated in Britain.

Membership of the Association is by examination only. Candidates for membership must have not less than five years' accountancy experience, and must be engaged on such work at the time of their application. The designatory letters used by associates are the letters A.A.I.A. Fellows use the designatory letters F.A.I.A. There is a further grade of membership, called licenciate, which is confined to those who have passed or have been exempted from the intermediate examination and are studying for the final, or to those who, having passed the final examination, have not sufficient experience to qualify for associateship.

To be enrolled as a student, a candidate must either pass a preliminary examination or have the Leaving Certificate examination or its equivalent.

The examination is in two parts, each of which is in two sections. A candidate may elect either to take both sections of a part together or to take them separately. The subjects of the examinations are as follows:

INTERMEDIATE, SECTION I. Book-keeping and accounts I; book-keeping and accounts II; auditing.

SECTION II. Mercantile law; company law; a choice of economics or secretarial practice or general commercial knowledge.

FINAL, SECTION I. Advanced book-keeping and accountancy I; advanced book-keeping and accountancy II; auditing and the duties of accountants and auditors; general financial knowledge.

SECTION II. Mercantile law; company law; cost accounts and systems of costing; income tax law and practice.

Exemption from the intermediate examination may be granted to anyone aged over 25 and with either three years' experience as an accountant in public practice, or seven years' experience working for an accountant or as an accountant in business organisations or the Civil Service. Anyone aged over 30 and with adequate education and experience may be exempted, as may anyone who has passed an examination deemed to be of equal standard to the intermediate examination.

Membership in the Republic of Ireland numbers 46. There are 78 students.

Institute of Company Accountants.

Founded in 1928, the Institute of Company Accountants is incorporated in Britain.

Its aims are " to advance the interests of accountants engaged in industry, to separate and to keep distinct the professions of company accountant and public accountant and auditor, and to confer on the company accountant a definite professional status indicated by qualifying letters and a professional designation". Public accountants and auditors are not admitted to membership.

For a limited future period, membership can be by election, but it is intended that ultimately it will be open only to those who have passed the examinations of the Institute.

To be eligible for associate membership it is necessary to be employed as the accountant or assistant accountant of an industrial or commercial organisation or of a public body, or to have passed the Institute's examinations. Associates use the designatory letters A.I.A.C. To be transferred to fellowship it is necessary to have been an associate member for at least five years and to be the accountant of a large organisation. Fellows use the letters F.I.A.C.

To be enrolled as a student, a candidate must either pass or be exempted from a preliminary examination. Exemption will be granted to holders of the Leaving Certificate.

The examinations of the Institute are in two parts: Intermediate and Final. The latter may be taken in two stages if desired. The subjects of the examination are: INTERMEDIATE. Book-keeping and accounts (general); book-keeping and accounting of companies, or co-operative societies, or municipal accounts or hospital accounts; economics; mercantile law; company law, or law of co-operative societies, or law of local government and municipalities, or law relating to gas or to water, or to electricity supply or to building societies.

FINAL. Company accounts or municipal accounts or accounts of co-operative societies; company law or law relating to gas, or to water, or to electricity supply or to building societies; mercantile law; preparing for audit and preparations of reports; costing or hospital accounts; income tax with special relation to companies, or law relating to co-operative societies or to local government and municipalities; economics; business statistics.

The first four subjects may be taken as part I of the final examination, the remainder as part II.

Exemption may be claimed, by subject, by holders of equivalent professional qualifications, but applicants may be asked to sit the final examination.

A centre was inaugurated in Ireland in June 1966, and steps are being taken to have courses provided at colleges and schools of commerce. Courses are at present available at the College of Commerce, Rathmines.

There are 45 Fellows of the Institute in Ireland, 102 Associates and 71 students.

Irish Society of Certified Public Accountants.

The Society was incorporated in Ireland in 1943. Its members are recognised by statute as qualified to act as auditors to a company registered under the Companies Acts.

Membership of the Society is by examination only. Candidates must in addition have not less than five years' accountancy experience and must be engaged on accounting work at the time of their application. Associates may use the designatory letters A.C.P.A. Fellows use the letters F.C.P.A.

To be enrolled candidates must have the Leaving Certificate or its equivalent.

The examination is in four parts, and a year must elapse between the passing of one examination and the sitting of the next. The subjects are:

PART I. Book-keeping; commerce; foreign trade, transport and marine insurance; commercial arithmetic.

PART II. Book-keeping and accounts; economics; auditing; costing I.

PART III. Advanced accountancy I; company law; law (including company and partnership law); costing II.

PART IV. Advanced accountancy II; management accounting and statistics; business administration and finance; auditing and investigations; income tax law and practice.

Members of the Institute of Chartered Accountants in Ireland, and of the Association of Certified and Corporate Accountants, may be granted exemption from all parts. Candidates who have passed parts of the examinations of those bodies may claim some exemptions. Holders of the B.Comm. degree, or the Diploma in Business Studies of the City of Dublin Vocational Education Committee may be exempted from parts I and II.

Courses covering the entire syllabus are provided at Rathmines.

Members of the Society number approximately 160. There are 90 students.

The Society of Commercial Accountants.

The Society, incorporated in the United Kingdom, is concerned primarily with management accounting. There are branches of the Society in Dublin and in Belfast.

Membership is by examination, and entitles members to use the designatory letters A.Comm.A. Students must be engaged in accounting or clerical work and can proceed to membership in two ways. The first involves taking the intermediate and final examinations. The second allows candidates to proceed directly to a final examination. To be eligible for the second mode of entry, candidates must have professional accounting or secretarial qualifications, or degrees in engineering or commerce, or have not less than seven years' experience in senior posts in accountancy or management.

The courses for examination by the first method are:

INTERMEDIATE. Book-keeping and accounts, taxation and elementary principles of financial control; general principles of law; economics; costing; general commercial knowledge.

FINAL, PART I. Accounting, financial control, taxation; advanced accounting; mechanised accounting; company law.

FINAL, PART II. Cost accounting and budgetary control; mercantile law; administration and management of companies; economics of industry and commerce.

Part I must be completed before taking Part II. The course for each part usually takes about one year to cover.

The subjects for examination by the second method are accounting and financial control; administration and management of companies; and either cost accounting and budgetary control or mechanised accounting. The papers are set at advanced level.

Courses covering the entire syllabus are available at Rathmines.

Membership of the Dublin branch is 114: 23 Fellows, 35 Associates and 56 students.

Society of Incorporated Cost Accountants.

The Society, incorporated in Ireland, was founded in 1963 " to provide for cost accountants an organisation particularly suited to Irish industrial and agricultural conditions ".

Membership is divided into Associates and Fellows — designating letters being A.I.C.A. and F.I.C.A., respectively.

Admission to Associate Membership is confined to those having not less than five years' costing experience, and who have passed the Society's examinations. Persons having wide costing experience may be exempted from the examination, in which case a thesis is required. Fellows must have a minimum of five years membership of the Society, or of a body of accountants, approved by the Society, and not less than five years' experience as a cost accountant.

To be registered as a student a candidate must have the Leaving Certificate or Matriculation, or four subjects at advanced level in the Department of Education's Technical Instruction Branch examinations, or some equivalent examinations.

The examinations are in three parts, and would normally take four years to complete. The subjects of the examinations are:

PART I. Book-keeping and accounts; commercial arithmetic; costing; economics, including industrial evolution.

PART II. Cost accountancy; industrial organisation and administration — buildings, production, marketing, personnel, administration; industrial law.

PART III. Management accountancy or local government finance; statistics; advanced cost accountancy.

Holders of professional, university or other approved qualifications may be granted partial or total exemptions from the examinations.

The Society has 20 members and 12 students.

Company Secretarial Qualifications

The three main professional bodies of company secretaries functioning in Ireland are discussed in alphabetical order.

Chartered Institute of Secretaries.

The Chartered Institute of Secretaries is a body incorporated in Britain, with a branch in the Republic of Ireland whose chairman is a member *ex officio* of the Institute Council.

The principal aim is "to provide examinations to test the capacity of potential administrators in the fields of commerce, industry and the public service."

Membership is conditional on passing the Institute's examinations and possessing appropriate experience. Associates use the designatory letters A.C.I.S. Fellows use the letters F.C.I.S. Licentiates form another grade, but are not members. They are candidates who have completed the examinations but not the necessary period of qualifying service.

To be registered as a student a candidate must have passed the Leaving Certificate or an equivalent examination subject to certain conditions, and must comply with certain other regulations.

The subjects of the examinations, which normally take about five years to complete, are:

INTERMEDIATE. Acountancy; economic theory; English; general principles of law.

FINAL, PART I. Economic policies and problems; mercantile law or law of local government; secretarial and administrative practice I.

FINAL, PART II. Advanced accountancy or local government accountancy; one of the following law subjects — company law, law of local government II, building society practice and law, law of electricity supply, co-operative law and administration, or law of gas supply; secretarial and administrative practice II or public administration I.

FINAL, PART III. Company secretarial practice, or public administration II, or public administration I if not already taken; meetings — law and procedure; secretarial practice (taxation) or secretarial and administrative practice III or secretarial practice (local government).

Holders of degrees in commerce, economics, law, arts or science, and of certain other qualifications, are exempted from the intermediate examination.

Courses covering the entire syllabus are available at Rathmines, Cork and Limerick.

The Institute had 204 members in the Republic of Ireland at the end of March, 1966.

Corporation of Secretaries.

The Corporation is incorporated in the United Kingdom.

Membership is by examination. Candidates for associateship, in addition to passing the examinations, must have at least three years' experience of working in an office. Associates use the designatory letters A.C.C.S. Fellows, who may be elected after three years' service as secretary to a company, as assistant secretary or in an equivalent position, use the letters F.C.C.S. Candidates who have passed their examination but are not qualified for membership in other respects can become licentiates.

To be admitted to studentship it is necessary to pass a preliminary examination or to be exempted by having an equivalent standard of education. The post-preliminary examination consists of an intermediate and final, the latter in three parts, no two of which may be taken simultaneously. Examinations are held half-yearly. It is possible in the final examination, instead of following the general secretarial syllabus described below, to specialise in the administration of local government, national health or further education establishments. The subjects taken are as follows:

INTERMEDIATE. Accountancy; economic theory; English; general principles of law.

FINAL, PART I. Mercantile law; advanced economics; secretarial practice I.

FINAL, PART II. Accountancy; either company law or a choice of law and practice of agriculture, building societies, co-operative societies, the coal industry, electricity industry, gas industry; secretarial practice II, or agricultural administration.

FINAL, PART III. Company secretarial practice or principles of insurance; meetings — law and procedure; business administration.

Holders of degrees in commerce, law, economics, arts or science, or of various professional qualifications, or of the advanced certificate of the Technical Instruction Branch of the Department of Education may be granted certain exemptions.

Courses covering the syllabus are available at Rathmines, Cork and Limerick.

Membership in the Republic of Ireland is 256.

Irish Institute of Secretaries.

The Irish Institute of Secretaries is incorporated in Ireland. It was founded 25 years ago to cater specially for the needs of secretaries working in Ireland.

Membership is now mostly conditional on passing the Institute's examinations.

Associate members use the designatory letters A.I.I.S., Fellows designate themselves F.I.I.S.

To register as a student it is necessary to have the Leaving Certificate. The course is basically for three years, but in practice usually takes four. The subjects are:

INTERMEDIATE. Secretarial and administrative practice; accountancy; economic theory; general principles of law.

FINAL, PART I. Law of and procedure at meetings; mercantile law; advanced accountancy and taxation; advanced economics.

FINAL, PART II. Secretarial and administrative practice; company law; management accounting.

Holders of degrees and professional qualifications can apply for exemption from certain subjects.

Courses for the Institute's examinations are available at Rathmines, Cork, Limerick and Galway.

The Institute has approximately 220 members.

Professional Qualifications in Engineering and Science

The engineering profession differs from the accountancy profession in that the majority of engineers qualify through university. Some engineering graduates go on to take out membership of a professional institution, others do not. A much smaller number of engineers qualify by becoming members of a professional institution without first going to university.

As in the accountancy profession, most of the institutions through which it is possible to qualify are based in Britain, and as in accountancy there are moves to unify the profession.

Thirteen separate institutions have come together to form the Council of Engineering Institutions. The Council has been granted a charter, and will in future be the sole examining body.

Agreement has been reached on an examination divided into two parts. Part II will be set at the level of a British university degree. Part I is a common examination in six subjects — properties of materials, thermodynamics, fluid mechanics, mechanics of machines, mathematics and electrical engineering.

The Part II examination will consist of one compulsory paper and five others, chosen from groups of subjects which are seen to meet the needs of all the Institutions at present. The compulsory paper covers the responsibilities of engineers — statutory, contractual, professional and managerial.

Progress has been made towards listing courses and degrees acceptable as exemptions from the CEI examinations. From this, Institutions will list those courses acceptable to them for entry into graduate membership.

Of the thirteen institutions, the following are active in Ireland: the Institution of Chemical Engineers, the Institution of Civil Engineers, the Institution of Electrical Engineers, the Institution of Mechanical Engineers, the Institution of Municipal Engineers, the Institution of Production Engineers, the Institution of Structural Engineers.

In addition to these British-based bodies, there is the Institution of Civil Engineers of Ireland. The Institution was founded in 1835 and operates under a charter granted in 1870.

Although it acts as an examining body, university-trained engineers with adequate experience may be elected to membership, and the bulk of its membership was elected.

It is the intention of the Institution to bring about in Ireland a rationalisation such as has come about in Britain, by becoming the one basic professional engineering body, with separate divisions catering for various specialisations.

In response to the request of the Government, the Institution is organising a conference on industrial engineering, to examine how best to bring about, in Ireland, the application of industrial engineering. A committee of the Institution is considering also the education and training of professional engineers and of engineering technicians.

The Institution of Civil Engineers in Ireland has a total membership of 1,076 of which 275 are members and 801 are associates. There are 8 graduates and 15 students.

Non-university courses in engineering.

Courses leading to diplomas and to the examinations of various professional institutions are provided at the Colleges of Technology at Bolton Street and Kevin Street in Dublin and at the Crawford Municipal Technical Institute in Cork.

The College of Technology at Kevin Street conducts full-time and part-time courses for the examinations of the Institution of Chemical Engineers and the Institution of Electrical Engineers. Both examinations are in technical subjects only: they do not include any management or business studies content, and are not, therefore, discussed further. Students taking the examinations of the Institution of Electrical Engineers do, however, have one lecture a week on industrial organisation, in their fourth year.

There are courses in the College of Technology at Bolton Street leading to the examinations of the Institutions of Mechanical Engineers, Production Engineers and Structural Engineers. There are also courses in heating and ventilating engineering and in civil engineering. Courses for the examinations of the Institution of Chemical Engineers were started at Crawford Municipal Technical Institute in 1965.

The examinations of the Institution of Mechanical Engineers are in three parts. In the second part, work study may be taken as an optional subject. The third part consists of two papers in industrial administration. The majority of candidates for membership of the Institution must take this examination, in many cases even those who already hold a university degree in engineering.

The first paper is on the historical development of industrial organisation (including some elementary law, economics and accounting). The second paper is on a subject called " modern ideas on scientific management ".

The course in the College of Technology, Bolton Street, leading to membership of the Institution of Production Engineers is the only course in the Republic of Ireland which has a large element of industrial engineering, apart from the option available at Trinity College, Dublin. However, graduates of University College, Dublin, in mechanical or electrical engineering, or of Trinity College, Dublin, in mechanical and production engineering, are exempted from all parts of the examination of the Institution of Production Engineers.

The course is run by the College, which awards a diploma. A pass in the diploma examination is accepted by the Institution of Production Engineers as exempting students from all its examinations. This is not the case as yet with the Institution of Mechanical Engineers: students must sit the Institution's examination.

There is an evening mechanical engineering course, and also a part-release course in the College of Technology, but the principal course is a four year full-time course leading to the College diploma.

Students of both mechanical engineering and production engineering take the first two years in common. They also take common subjects in third and fourth years, but take different sets of optional subjects depending on their specialisation.

To be accepted as a student it is necessary to have the Leaving Certificate with honours in English, mathematics, physics and/or applied mathematics and two other subjects. Candidates who have only a pass Leaving Certificate must spend a year taking a course leading to the G.C.E. "O" level examination in the subjects listed above.

Having been accepted, the first year of the course is a "pre-professional" year, spent bringing the students up to G.C.E. "A" level in relevant subjects. This is followed by three years of professional courses. It is interesting that the authorities regard those with honours Leaving Certificate in five subjects as being still so far below G.C.E. "A" level as to require a full year's study to catch up.

After the pre-professional year, students embark on the professional courses proper. The subject "engineering economics" is included in the first professional year. The subjects "engineering administration" and "mathematics and statistics" are included in the core of common subjects in the second and third years, each being taught for two hours a week.

The optional subjects in production engineering are as follows (hours per week in parentheses):

SECOND YEAR. Design for production (3); machine tool design (3); production processes (2); production engineering lab. (3).

THIRD YEAR. Production processes (2); machine tool design (3); design for production (3); production management (3); production engineering lab. (3).

Students must get adequate practical experience during the summer months and must, in their final year, carry out a "design and make" project.

The first class in production engineering will graduate in 1967. The College expects to cater for about 10 students a year in production engineering. There are no space or staff constraints on increasing this figure to 20: the principal constraint is finding students of the right calibre.

Non-university examinations in science.

The fact has already been referred to that courses are available at the College of Technology, Kevin Street, for the B.Sc. degree examination of the University of London. There is also a two year part-release course leading to the graduateship examination of the Institute of Physics, London.

Professional Qualifications in Marketing

The only body offering a professional qualification in the field of marketing is the Marketing Institute of Ireland. There are, however, two further schemes of instruction in operation which are relevant to marketing, and these schemes are described also.

The first is the course conducted under the auspices of the Irish Exporters Association and leading to the Association's Diploma in Foreign Trade. The second is the educational scheme administered by the Institute of Advertising Practitioners in Ireland, leading to the Diploma and Higher Diploma in Advertising.

Courses of instruction for all these qualifications are provided at the College of Commerce, Rathmines, where students of some of these bodies take some lectures in common.[1] It is possible to study at the School of Commerce in Cork for parts I and II of the Institute of Marketing's examinations, and at the School of Commerce at Limerick for part I only (parts II and III will be covered when sufficient students have worked through to this level).

Marketing Institute of Ireland.

The Marketing Institute of Ireland was formerly the Irish branch of the Institute of Marketing and Sales Management, based in Britain (and now known as the Institute of Marketing). The Irish Institute became an autonomous body in 1962.

The two bodies are still closely associated; in fact, students working towards membership of the Irish Institute still take the examinations of the British body, but the Marketing Institute of Ireland hopes to have its own examinations at a later date and to make a reciprocal arrangement regarding recognition.

It is possible to be elected to membership of the Marketing Institute of Ireland, but the aim is that the normal mode of entry in future will be by examination.

Facilities for study have been available in Ireland only since 1958. Student registration was initially small, but has grown so considerably that it was necessary to limit the numbers because the Rathmines College of Commerce could not accommodate all those who applied.

It had earlier been found that there was a considerable drop-out during the first year, principally by those whose basic educational qualifications were inadaquate. Consequently, while it is not a formal condition of registration that students should have passed the Leaving Certificate examination, in practice the necessity to select a limited number from the total of applicants means that anyone without an honours Leaving Certificate is now unlikely to be accepted as a student.

The Institute's examinations are in three parts. In the United Kingdom there are courses leading to the Higher National Certificate and Higher National Diploma in Business Studies, awarded by the Ministry of Education. Holders of the certificate or diploma are exempted from the first two parts of the Institute's examinations. It is expected that those in Britain who intend to qualify for membership of the Institute will, in future, first take the H.N.C. or H.N.D. and then proceed to the Part III examination.

To cater for areas where the H.N.C. or H.N.D. are not available, parts I and II of the Institute's examination will be replaced by a two year programme for a new certificate to be known as the Institute of Marketing Higher Certificate in Marketing. Those who take this qualification will then go on to do the part III examination.

The subjects of the Institute's present examinations are:

PART I. Marketing I; economics; economic geography; business history of the United Kingdom.

PART II. Marketing II; commercial law; applied statistics; accounting.

PART III. Marketing III; advertising; market research.

Exemptions may be granted in some subjects, but not in marketing, market research or advertising, to holders of appropriate university degrees or professional qualifications. However, although the Institute would very much like them to do so, it rarely happens in Ireland that university graduates subsequently study for the Institute's examinations,

---

1   The courses for the examinations of the Institute of Marketing are provided in the School of Management Studies. Most other professional-level courses are in the School of Professional Studies.

most students being those who did not get the opportunity of going to university, and who wish to take out a professional qualification. Holders of the Diploma in Business Studies of the City of Dublin Vocational Education Committee are exempt from Parts I and II.

Passing the final examination does not entitle a candidate to associateship. Successful candidates are awarded a diploma and may designate themselves as graduates They may not, however, become associate members until they have had adequate marketing experience. Full membership is restricted to those who decide the marketing policy of their company and have controlled a minimum of three salesmen for at least two years.

There are at present 305 members of the Irish Institute of Marketing, of whom 48 became members by examinations, the remainder having been elected to membership. Registered students number over 800.

Diploma in Foreign Trade.

The Irish Exporters Association operates an examination scheme leading to the Diploma in Foreign Trade, granted by the Association.

On passing the prescribed examination a certificate is issued. The diploma is awarded to candidates, holding the Certificate, who have had at least three years' approved experience.

To be accepted as a student it is necessary to hold the Intermediate Certificate of the Department of Education (Secondary Branch) or the General Commercial Certificate of the Department of Education (Technical Institution Branch) with passes in at least five subjects, or certificates with passes in at least five subjects in the Department's examination in commerce (intermediate stage).

The examinations are in three parts. Exemptions from the part I examination may be granted in whole or in part to anyone passing an examination equivalent to the intermediate examination of an approved accountancy or secretarial institute, or to holders of Advanced Grade certificates of the Department of Education or equivalent higher certificates, or to those aged over 25 who have approved experience. Holders of university degrees may also make a case for exemption.

The subjects for examination are:

PART I. Book-keeping; economics; English; commercial geography; commercial knowledge.

PART II. Foreign trade practice I; marketing I; economics of foreign trade; elements of mercantile law; either a modern continental language or book-keeping and accounts.

PART III. Foreign trade practice II; marketing II; legal aspects of foreign trade; management; either a modern continental language or statistics.

Besides the facilities for evening study in the College of Commerce at Rathmines, arrangements have been made to provide a correspondence course for students outside Dublin.

A total of 27 students have been awarded diplomas since the inception of the scheme in 1953.

Institute of Advertising Practitioners in Ireland.

The Institute is an Irish organisation and is the representative professional body of service advertising agencies in Ireland. The members of the Institute are divided into four categories as follows: (a) Practitioners in Advertising; (b) Fellows; (c) Ordinary Members; (d) Associate Members.

To be eligible for election in category (a), firms or corporations must be service advertising agencies who are equipped to deal with a national advertising campaign in Ireland and who, in order to preserve their independent judgment in professional matters, are not directly or indirectly controlled by any advertiser or group of advertisers whose advertising it handles or by concerns wholly or mainly interested in the sale of advertising media or services.

To be elected as an ordinary or associate member, the applicant must pass an examination or examinations (whether general or specialist) which shall be in the form or forms for the time being prescribed by the Council. At present the standard for admission is the Higher Diploma in Advertising.

The Institute administers, on behalf of the Joint Advertising Education Committee, a scheme of examinations leading to the Diploma in Advertising and to the Higher Diploma in Advertising. Courses are provided at the College of Commerce, Rathmines.

The course for the Diploma is taken in the evenings and lasts for two years. Instruction in some subjects is at the College of Technology, Bolton Street. The Higher Diploma course, also an evening course, lasts for a further year.

To be accepted as a student for the diploma it is necessary to be an employee of an advertising agency and to have passed the Leaving Certificate examination, or the Matriculation or some equivalent examination. To be accepted as a student for the Higher Diploma it is necessary to have at least three years' approved experience and to have passed or been exempted from the basic Diploma examination. To be granted exemption, one must make a case subject by subject: exemption is not granted automatically to holders of other qualifications.

The subjects for the Diploma, which was instituted in 1963, are:

Part I. English; copywriting; layout, exhibition and display; printing and reproduction; media.

Part II. Copywriting; layout, exhibition and display; printing and reproduction; the television commercial; media.

Candidates for the Higher Diploma, instituted in 1964, have a choice of six subjects in which to specialise. They are: marketing and statistics; market research and statistics; media planning and statistics; printing and reproduction; design; copy.

The Institute has 179 members.

Personnel Management

The only examining body in this field is the Institute of Personnel Management. The Institute is incorporated in Britain, and there is a branch functioning in the Republic of Ireland. The branch has its headquarters in Dublin, and a centre in Cork. It is hoped next year to have centres in Limerick, Shannon and Waterford.

There are two classes of membership, each divided into grades. The first class, corporate membership, is divided into members and associate members. The second class, non-corporate membership, is divided into graduate members, affiliate members and students.

Entry to corporate membership is open to individuals who have completed a recognised course of training or have passed the Institute's examination, and have at least five years' approved experience. It is open also to university graduates or their equivalent, who have at least seven years' experience. Alternatively, anyone over 35 years of age, holding a senior post in personnel management, and who has at least seven years' approved experience, may be elected to membership.

Courses are not yet available in Ireland for anyone wishing to study for the Institute's examinations, but it is hoped that a course will be provided at the College of Commerce, Rathmines, from 1967 onwards. The only way to study at present is to take a correspondence course.

To be accepted as a student it is necessary to have passed the G.C.E. examination in five subjects, two at advanced level, or to have passed an equivalent examination. Those without this standard will be accepted if they have experience of work in a personnel department.

The subjects of the examination, which is in one part only, are as follows:

1. Business economics and administration—the structure of the economy and the business environment, organisation of the firm, activities of the management.
2. Industrial psychology and sociology—the individual in society and industry, the formal structure of the enterprise, the informal structure of the enterprise, the interaction of formal and informal structures.
3. Personnel management—the personnel function, personnel practice, communications, the training function, industrial relations at the national level, methods of implementation. Having taken these compulsory subjects, the student may choose one of 4) or 5).
4. Industrial relations including legal aspects—trade unions and employers' organisations, industrial relations at the national level, industrial relations in the firm and the plant, legal aspects.
5. Education and training—the training function, application of psychological theory to training practice, external resources, internal resources, the main methods of instructions and their application at various levels.

Although there are not yet in Ireland any courses leading to the Institute's examinations, the Irish branch this year conducted a ten-week introductory course in conjunction with the Irish Management Institute. The course is intended for university graduates or others contemplating a career in personnel management, and will be continued each year.

The Republic of Ireland branch has 84 members: one fellow, 27 members, 15 associates, 2 graduates, 25 affiliates and 14 students.

Purchasing

The only body functioning in the field is the Purchasing Officers Association, which is based in Britain, but has a branch in Ireland.

There are two principal classes of membership: full membership and associate membership. There is in addition a class of graduate membership open to those who have passed the Association's examination, but are not otherwise qualified for membership.

To become a member it is necessary to have a specified period of approved experience and to have passed the Association's examinations, but exemption from the examination may be granted to anyone who has either comparable qualifications or long experience in purchasing and/or stores work. Such applicants may have to submit a treatise.

The examination is in two parts, intermediate and final. The Association does not itself examine candidates at the intermediate stage. Candidates must take the Ordinary and Higher National Certificate in Business Studies (in Britain) or the Graduate examinations of the British Institute of Management. Those passing either examination are allowed to proceed to the Association's final examination.

The relevant subjects of the British Institute of Management's examinations are: The evolution of modern industrial organisation and management; economic aspects of industry and commerce; financial and cost accounting; statistical method; office management.

The Association further specifies an English language qualification.

The subjects of the Purchasing Officers Association final diploma are: purchasing —principles and practice (two years); new materials; storage and control of stock; legal aspects of purchasing; transport aspects of purchasing.

Courses are available at the College of Commerce, Rathmines, for the graduate examinations of the British Institute of Management. As the Institute is now abandoning its role as an examining body, it is expected that permission will be given to the College of Commerce by the Purchasing Officers Association to set papers and conduct examinations which will be accepted as equivalent to the standard required by the Association for intermediate level. This matter is at present under further consideration.

Students taking final examinations must at present take correspondence courses, and this may continue to be the case.

It is not necessary to have passed the Leaving Certificate examination to be accepted as a student, but the authorities at the College of Commerce would normally regard it as essential.

The Purchasing Officers Association also grants a Certificate in Storekeeping to anyone completing a one year course in the subject "storage and control of stock" and "nature of management". A course is available for the Certificate at the School of Commerce in Limerick, and at the College of Commerce, Rathmines.

There are 103 members in the Irish branch of the Purchasing Officers Association —18 full members, 43 associates, 3 graduates, 38 students, one certified storekeeper.

Professional Qualifications in Statistics

It is possible to study for membership of the Institute of Statisticians, which is a body incorporated in Britain.

The Institute's examinations are in four parts. Those who pass part I, and who have been employed on statistical work, may describe themselves as Registered Statistical Assistants. Anyone who passes all the parts of the Institute's examination or possesses an approved university degree and who has at least one year's experience with statistics in a responsible position may become an associate, and use the designatory letters A.I.S. Fellows, who may be elected after at least five years' experience, may designate themselves F.I.S.

It is possible at present to pursue a course of study for part I of the Institute's examinations at the College of Commerce, Rathmines. Anyone wishing to study for the latter parts must do so by taking a correspondence course.

The subjects covered in the various parts are:

PART I. Elementary statistical methods; computation and presentation; and a choice of economic statistics, medical statistics and industrial statistics.

PART II. Mathematics and elements of statistical theory; applied statistics.

PART III. Statistical theory; statistical organisation—theory and practice.

PART IV. General applied statistics; logical background of statistics; and a choice of market and opinion research, industrial statistics, economic and social statistics, agricultural statistics, medical statistics, educational and psychological statistics, biometry.

Anyone possessing a relevant university degree or equivalent qualification will be considered for exemption from parts I and II of the examinations.

The syllabus for the examinations is at present being revised.

There are very few members or students of the Institute in the Republic of Ireland.

Professional Qualifications in Transport

The Institute of Transport is incorporated in Britain. There is an Irish branch of the Institute which acts as an independent examining body, but whose examinations are recognised by the parent body as equivalent to its own.

Membership of the Institute is normally by examination but may, in exceptional cases, be by election. Associate members, who may use the designatory letters A.M. Inst.T., must have passed the examinations and have at least five years' approved experience. Members must first be associate members and must hold and have held, for at least five years, a high position of responsibility in the field of transport. They use the designatory letters M.Inst.T. There are also graduate members and associates.

The Institute has two examinations, each in two parts. The first examination is the graduateship examination, the second the associate membership examination. The former must be passed before studying for the latter. It is possible to take each part of each examination either separately or together. Anyone aged over 35, who has at least five years' experience and who either holds an executive position or a professional qualification, may be allowed to submit a thesis in lieu of the examinations.

From 1966 onwards the subjects of the examinations are:

GRADUATESHIP PART I. Elements of transport; evolution of modern transport; English.
PART II. Economics; principles of law; geography.
ASSOCIATE MEMBERSHIP PART I. Transport finance and accounting; law of transport; elements of statistics.
PART II. Economics of transport; management with special reference to transport; transport operation.

To be accepted for studentship of the Institute it is necessary to have passed an examination equivalent to the G.C.E. at Ordinary level.

Exemption will be given from certain subjects to holders of relevant degrees or other qualifications.

There are courses for the Institute's examinations at the Colleges of Commerce in Rathmines, Cork and Limerick and at Waterford, Galway and Ennis.

There are 274 members of the Institute in the Republic of Ireland: 18 members, 103 associate members, 10 associates, 37 graduates and 106 students.

Professional Qualifications in Work Study

The Irish Work Study Institute acts as an examining body in the field of work study. The Institute developed from the Irish Work Study Society, and was incorporated in 1963.

There are two types of membership, each with several classes. The first type is corporate membership and includes fellows, members and associate members. These use the designatory letters F.I.W.S.I., M.I.W.S.I. and A.M.I.W.S.I, respectively. The second type of membership is non-corporate membership and is comprised of graduates, student practitioners and registered students. Non-corporate members may not use designatory letters.

To be eligible for membership it will in future be necessary to have passed the membership examination or to have been exempted from it, and to have had at least three years' experience.

Associates may be elected without passing examinations provided they have practised work study for five years and hold a responsible position. Graduates must have passed the examinations and have at least two years' experience.

Thus, while it is possible to pass the examinations without having practical experience of work study, it is not possible without experience to become a corporate member of the Institute.

The examinations of the Institute are in two parts. It is not necessary to attempt all subjects in a part at the one sitting: it is possible to attempt individual subjects. Students are free to prepare for the examinations by any method they please, but courses are available at the College of Commerce, Rathmines, and at the School of Commerce at Cork. The courses take place in the evening and last for two years.

To be eligible for registration as a student it is necessary to have passed in English and mathematics in the Leaving Certificate examination. The subjects for examination are:

PART I. Work study I; work study II; work study III; the human factor—the nature of man and work, general psychology, industrial psychology, working conditions, ergonomics.

PART II. Costing and cost control; industrial administration; advanced work study; and either production planning and control or work study in the clerical field.

Applications for exemption will be considered, by subject, from anyone who has passed an examination covering the syllabus of any subject.

Membership of the Institute numbers 155.

Other Professional Qualifications

There are many other qualifications of professional standing which are less relevant to industrial management than those considered above, or which are restricted in their coverage to a particular type of business.

Examples of institutes granting such qualifications are the Institute of Chartered Surveyors, the Institute of Builders, the Institute of Hospital Administrators, the Institute of Bankers, and the Chartered Insurance Institute.

The examinations of the latter Institute are directed mainly to subjects relevant to insurance, but include in their final part the subjects economics, insurance administration, and commercial and company law. The Institute has a considerable membership in Ireland.

The Institute of Bankers conducts examinations for the Banking Diploma, Foreign Exchange Diploma, and Trustee Diploma. The syllabus for the Banking Diploma is not confined exclusively to banking subjects but includes economics, accountancy and English. The Institute of Bankers also has a large membership.

Numbers Qualifying in 1965

Table 17.11 shows, for each of the professional qualifications discussed above, the number of members and the number of candidates who were examined in, and who passed, each stage of their examinations in the year 1965, the last year for which results are available from all the bodies. Some of those finishing final examinations will already have taken either university degrees or the examinations of other professional institu-

LE 17.11.   *Membership and Examination Figures[1] of Professional Bodies, Year 1965.*

essional Body[2]	MEMBERSHIP			EXAMINATIONS									
	Full	Other	Student	First Sat	Passed	Second Sat	Passed	Third Sat	Passed	Fourth Sat	Passed	Fifth Sat	Passed
ountancy													
ıst. of Chartered	1,342	—	565	n.a.[3]	201[4]	n.a.	190	n.a.	176	n.a.	125	n.a.	96
ssoc. of Cert. & Corp.	300	—	400	117	41	61	34	58	18	30	9		
ıst. of Cost & Works	170	—	800	n.a.[5]	72	n.a.	45	n.a.	42	n.a.	16	n.a.	8
ssoc. of Inter. Accts.	46	—	78	10	2	3	3						
ıst. of Company Accts.[6]	101	—	60	12	10								
rish Soc. of Cert. Pub. Accts.	160	—	90	30	12	10	5	8	5	7	6		
oc. of Comm. Accts.[7]	58	—	56	7	4	—	—	12	8				
oc. of Incorp. Cost Accts.[8]	20	—	12										
npany Secretarial													
Chartered Inst. of Secs.	207	—	345	55	18	54	24	18	7	34	15		
Corp. of Secs.	256	—	151	36	12	17	5	25	8	69	20		
rish Inst. of Secs.[9]	220	—	60	14	8	8	5	6	4				
ʃineering													
ınst. of Chemical Engs.[10]	13	17	7	13	n.a.								
ınst. of Civil Engs. of Ireland	1,078	8	15	6	3	5	1	19	18				
ınst. of Electrical Engs.	329	—	124	n.a.	n.a.	n.a.	n.a.	n.a.	n.a.				
ınst. of Mechanical Engs.	157	103	130	24	13	14	4	5	2				
ınst. of Municipal Engs.													
ınst. of Prod. Engs.[11]	22	11	5										
ınst. of Structural Engs.[12]	43	36	19										
rketing													
Marketing Inst. of Ireland	275	n.a.	829	78	28	30	12	33	12				
rish Exporters Assoc.	27	3	37	8	4	10	6	5	4				
ınst. of Advert. Practitioners	179	—	90	44	22	18	14	12	6				
t. of Personnel Mgt.	43	27	14	n.a.	n.a.								
rchasing Officers Assoc.	18	42	38	n.a.	n.a.	1	1						
t. of Statisticians													
t. of Transport[13]	121	47	106	26	21	23	12	10	7	12	11		
sh Work Study Inst.	155	3	190	44	21	4	4						

For the Republic of Ireland only unless indicated otherwise. See the text for details of examination structures.
See the text for the dates of foundation of some of these bodies.
Examinations are held twice yearly. Candidates who fail at one session can sit again at the next one. It would have been impossible in the time available to eliminate this double-counting.
All Ireland. Students numbers are divided roughly in one ratio 1.44 : 1 between the Republic and Northern Ireland, so it is likely that passes are divided in approximately the same ratio.
Not available in time.

ontd. on next page)

tions. It would not, therefore, be correct to regard the sum of those shown as qualifying in table 17.11 and those shown as taking university degrees in tables 17.4 to 17.10 as constituting the total output from the system of higher education. It was not possible to eliminate the double counting caused by people taking multiple qualifications.

PART D. MANAGEMENT TRAINING.

The higher educational qualifications relevant to a career in industrial management have been described at length. An adequate supply of people of the necessary educational level is essential in the long term if the standard of management is to be placed on a higher footing. Any body addressing itself to the task of evolving a comprehensive policy for education and training for management must examine the adequacy of the facilities for post-school-leaving education.

Having described the relevant educational qualifications, it remains only to describe the facilities available for management training.

The bodies discussed are the Colleges and Schools of Commerce, the College of Industrial Relations, the Institute of Public Administration, and the Irish Management Institute. Several other bodies provide advice and assistance which help to raise the standard of management and, as this is the aim of management training, these bodies are discussed briefly.

Management consultants have carried out assignments in many Irish companies. The advice they have given and the experience gained by managers in operating systems installed by consultants, has contributed substantially to raising the standard of management in Ireland. In addition to their consultancy activities, the larger consultant organisations have training establishments of their own in Britain, and participants have gone from Ireland to attend training courses at these centres.

The Irish National Productivity Committee is a Government-sponsored organisation, representative of both trade unions and employers, which has the objective of increasing productivity in Ireland. As part of its effort in this field it operates an advisory service for small and medium sized businesses, which are defined as businesses with up to 200 employees. The service investigates and analyses the problems of firms, and helps them to prepare an outline of the steps needed to overcome them. It does not itself engage in full-scale consultancy. The service now has a staff of ten advisers and, since its inception in 1964, has completed over 100 assignments.

The graduate-level degree and diploma courses in administration at Trinity College, Dublin, and at University College, Dublin, and the executive development course of the Department of Applied Psychology at University College, Cork, have already been

---

6. Students have only recently commenced sitting for these examinations. No one has yet reached the Final.
7. Results of third examination consist of those doing Final II and Direct Final.
8. No one has yet sat for the Society's examinations.
9. No one has yet reached Final Part II under the new examination scheme.
10. Course started in Ireland only in 1965. The first examination was in September 1966.
11. Exemption is given to those passing the Diploma examinations of the College of Technology, Bolton Street. No one has yet reached the final Diploma examination in production engineering.
12. It is not possible to give examination results for the Republic of Ireland, as many students from Ireland go to Britain to sit their examinations.
13. The first two examinations are for graduateship; the others for associate membership.
Source: Information provided by professional bodies.

described. In addition to these courses, the Department of Business Administration in University College, Dublin, has organised two courses for practising executives, given by staff of the Harvard Business School and of the University of Pennsylvania's Wharton School.

The Irish Supervisors' Institute must also be mentioned. The Institute was founded in 1962. Until 1964 it had been possible to study for foremanship examinations held by the British Institute of Management. When the British Institute of Management ceased to act as an examining body, the Irish Supervisors' Institute, in conjunction with the Irish Management Institute, drew up a syllabus for a course leading to a Certificate in Supervision, and arranged to have courses provided by vocational education committees at various centres throughout the country.

The Irish Supervisors' Institute acts as the examining body for the certificate examinations. The course lasts for two years, and the subjects are as follows, with the total number of hours lecturing showing in parentheses.

FIRST YEAR. Industrial history (27); English or Irish (27); work and role of the supervisor (27).

SECOND YEAR. Work and role of the supervisor II—leading, controlling, co-ordinating (27); work and role of the supervisor III (27); social ethics (12); industrial and commercial techniques—production and planning (27), estimating and costing (15).

Colleges of Commerce

There are management training facilities at the College of Commerce, Rathmines, and at the Schools of Commerce at Cork and Limerick.

College of Commerce, Rathmines: The College of Commerce is divided into a School of General Studies, a School of Professional Studies and a School of Management Studies.

While most courses leading to professional qualifications take place in the evening in the School of Professional Studies, there are evening courses also in the School of Management Studies, leading to the examinations of the Irish Work Study Institute, the Institute of Marketing, the Institute of Hospital Administrators, the Purchasing Officers Association, the Institute of Public Administration and the Irish Supervisors' Institute. These courses are taught mostly by part-time staff.

The School's activity by day is carried out by the full-time staff of its Work Study Centre and its Training Within Industry Centre.

There are four basic courses in the training-within-industry scheme: job relations, job instruction, job methods and job safety.

There is a work study training course which is in two parts. Part 1 gives basic training in work study and lasts for four weeks of full time instruction. Part II gives advanced work study training and lasts for six weeks. Two separate courses on method-time-measurement (M.T.M.), one lasting for one week, the other for three weeks, are being instituted this year together with a series of courses on quantitative techniques.

The other long training courses are in organisation and method and in production management. Both courses are full-time and last for four weeks.

In addition to this basic core of programmes, other courses are organised as the demand warrants. They relate mainly to work study, production management and quantitative methods, and range in length from two days to four weeks.

The number of participants at courses between 1961 and 1965 is shown in table 17.12.

TABLE 17.12.   *Number of Participants Attending Day Courses in the School of Management Studies Rathmines, 1961-1965, by Type of Course.*

	1961	1962	1963	1964	1965
Work Study					
Appreciation	39	53	77	33	—
Training	43	43	37	64	74
Training Within Industry					
Job Instruction	21	18	49	11	18
Job Methods	6	5	19	11	3
Job Relations	6	28	66	20	2
Job Safety	7	4	10	8	2
O. & M. Training	—	—	22	15	14
Other Courses	233	44	106	130	135

There are at present seven full-time staff members in the School of Management Studies.

A study team of the Irish National Productivity Committee has recommended that the facilities for training in work study be improved generally throughout the country. It recommended that there should be an increase in the accommodation, equipment and ancillary staff of the Work Study Centre at Rathmines, so that it would be capable of becoming the national work study training centre.

School of Commerce, Cork. The Municipal School of Commerce in Cork provides long-term evening courses leading to professional qualifications, and also provides work study and training-within-industry courses.

The evening courses, as in Dublin, are taught mostly by part-time staff, and cover the examination syllabi of the following bodies: Institute of Marketing (parts I and II only), Institute of Transport, Institute of Cost and Works Accountants (part I only), all institutes of company secretaries (all parts), some institutes of accountants (intermediate level only), Irish Supervisors' Institute and the Irish Work Study Institute.

There is difficulty in providing courses for later parts of many examinations because the number of students reaching these parts is too small to justify holding classes. This is particularly true of accountancy and marketing where students are often away from home on audits or selling.

It is the universal experience that the number of evening students reaching the later stages of examination shows a drastic reduction from the initial enrolment. In a large centre such as Dublin this relative drop still leaves the absolute number large enough to make the holding of classes economical. The fact that this is not also true of Cork, which is a large city by Irish standards, shows how difficult it is in this country to provide a full range of evening courses at local centres, taught by part-time, locally-based, staff.

As well as having evening professional courses, the school also conducts a part-release, comprehensive work study training course and operates a training-within-industry scheme for supervisors. These courses are conducted by a full-time staff member trained to instruct in both these subjects.

It is stated that industry's response to these training courses is disappointing. In 1965/66, for instance, only four people were being trained in work study.

School of Commerce, Limerick: There is a School of Management Studies in the School of Commerce in Limerick.

Apart from the courses conducted by the School of Management Studies, there are evening courses in the School of Commerce leading to the examinations of the following bodies: the Association of Certified and Corporate Accountants, the Institute of Chartered Accountants, the Institute of Cost and Works Accountants, the professional institutes of company secretaries, the Institute of Bankers, the Institute of Transport, the Chartered Insurance Institute. There is a course leading to the Diploma in Social Science of University College, Cork.

As well as evening professional courses, there are evening courses at non-professional level in various business subjects.

A full-time day course lasting for one year has been started. The subjects covered are accounting and costing, business administration, principles of law, statistics, economics and English. At the end of the year students take either the intermediate examination of any of the professional secretarial institutions, or part I of the examinations of the Institute of Cost and Works Accountants.

The School of Management Studies provides two types of course, both in the evening. The first type leads to the examinations of the Institute of Marketing, the Irish Exporters Association, the Irish Supervisors' Institute, the Institute of Public Administration, the Institute of Hospital Administrators, and the Purchasing Officers Association (Certificate in Storekeeping).

The second type of course does not lead to examinations. With the exception of a one year non-examination course for supervisors and potential supervisors, the courses are short. They include appreciation courses on work study and on organisation and method.

There is one full-time staff member of the School of Management Studies, who is trained to instruct in work study and on training-within-industry. The other members of the staff are part-time.

As in Cork, the response of industry to the facilities provided by the school is considered disappointing.

College of Industrial Relations

The College of Industrial Relations was formerly known as the Catholic Workers' College, and is a foundation of the Society of Jesus.

It differs both in its aims and in its methods from other organisations providing training for management. The broad aim of the College is to help in the development of sound relationships between men at work, by forming in managers, supervisors and workers an outlook or philosophy on dealing with others.

It therefore conducts courses for managers, supervisors and trade unionists. The courses, which are held separately for each group, take place on one evening each week and are spread over three or four years. Both supervisors and trade unionists may take examinations set by the College and, if successful, are awarded a diploma.

The stated purpose of the course on management and business relations is "to help employers, businessmen, managers and managerial personnel to develop a social philosophy founded on reason and Christian principles".

The subjects of the course are: Christian humanism; human relations in industry;

industrial organisations; social organisation; Irish industry—organisation and control; industrial case-studies; social ethics; productivity appraisal; social and industrial legislation; industrial relations code; Irish foreign trade.

Subjects were chosen which would lead to the broad objective of the course being achieved by forcing managers to question basic assumptions, by introducing them to findings of the human sciences, by enabling managers to realise their firms' dependence on institutions and structures outside their control, and by bringing home to them the interdependence of human and technical aspects of work, so that decisions will not be based on technical criteria, without consideration of their human implications.

The College does not set out to train managers in the use of techniques, but does include sufficient discussion of techniques to allow participants to understand the human issues at stake in their use.

The staff of the College is made up of seven members of the Society of Jesus. Laymen from outside the College lecture on its courses.

Attendance at the courses since their inception in 1951 is shown in table 17.13.

TABLE 17.13.   *Number of Participants Attending Courses at the Institute of Industrial Relations, 1951-1966, by Type of Course.*

Year	Trade Union		Supervisory		Management
	Men	Women	Men	Women	
'51-52	44	—	—	—	59
'52-53	39	—	—	—	51
'53-54	45	—	—	—	44
'54-55	161	—	—	—	70
'55-56	152	—	31	—	84
'56-57	237	66	58	—	111
'57-58	312	107	59	—	172
'58-59	411	101	93	—	156
'59-60	414	112	92	—	136
'60-61	475	108	124	—	136
'61-62	516	121	108	—	148
'62-63	609	167	134	31	197
'63-64	574	287	233	(s)	202
'64-65	517	310	173	(s)	146
'65-66	496	318	190	(s)	171

(s) Suspended temporarily.

Source: Information supplied by the College.

Institute of Public Administration

The Institute of Public Administration was founded in 1957 by a group of public servants working in the Civil Service, local government and the State-sponsored bodies. Its aim is " to promote the study and improve the standard of public administration, to develop the sense of vocation in public servants, and to foster mutual understanding between the public and public servants."

The Institute is a voluntary organisation with corporate and individual members. The individual members numbered 1,185 in the year 1964-65. Of this total, 612 were employed in the service of local government, 450 in the Civil Service and 117 in State-sponsored bodies. There were 6 other members.

The corporate members are departments of State, local government authorities and State-sponsored organisations.

Apart from its training activities, the Institute engages in consultancy in hospitals. It provides library facilities for its members, and has published a series of books on various aspects of public administration in Ireland, as well as publishing the quarterly journal *Administration* and the bi-monthly *Leargas*. It is currently developing activity in research.

The Institute engages in training under several different heads, and they are discussed in turn. One form of training, now discontinued, was an extended (five weeks) residential conference for senior public servants.

School of Public Administration: The School of Public Administration provides a one year programme of training for two groups of people. The first group consists of persons either in the public service or intending to join it. The second group consists of students from developing countries, particularly in Africa, who will be engaged in public service in their own country.

The courses followed by the two groups are substantially the same: the same subjects are studied, with emphasis being laid on conditions in Ireland or in developing countries, depending on the group.

In practice the Irish students are predominantly practising public servants rather than intending public servants. Public servants attending the course are released on full pay by their departments. The full cost of tuition for all students, and of maintenance scholarships paid to graduates, is met from a grant paid by the Department of Finance.

The course lasts for one academic year of full-time study. The main areas of study are public administration and economic and social development, and the subjects taken are:

PUBLIC ADMINISTRATION. Government; administrative theory and process; local government; comparative government.

ECONOMIC AND SOCIAL DEVELOPMENT. Economic expansion; social planning and welfare; development planning.

There are additional lectures on political theory, introductory economics, applied statistics, modern Irish history, international affairs, Irish and French language.

Students are attached for a short period to some public body, and also carry out a research project.

There are four full-time staff members of the School. They are supplemented by lecturers from other divisions of the Institute and from outside, mainly from university faculties.

Diploma in Administration. The Institute acts as an examining body in the field of public administration.

There is a three-year course leading to examinations for the Diploma in Administration. The successful candidates are awarded a diploma and are entitled to use the designatory letters D.A.

Courses of instruction are available at various vocational education institutions, and also through correspondence.

The Diploma comprises four groups of subjects: local administration, social administration, central administration and management. There is a common intermediate examination, after which students take a two-part final examination specialising in one of the four groups mentioned.

The subjects of the intermediate examination are: institutions of government; history and structure of public organisation; outlines of public finance; elements of law; statistical sources and methods; essay on a general aspect of administration.

In the final examination the subjects "principles of public administration" and "administration of public services" are common to all groups.

TABLE 17.14.   *Number of Students Examined In and Passing the Diploma Examinations of the Institute of Public Administration, Year 1965.*

Examination	Sat	Passed
Diploma in Local Administration.		
Final, Part II	23	23
Final, Part I	20	19
Intermediate	25	18
Diplomas in Central Administration.		
Final, Part II	10	9
Final, Part I	7	6
Intermediate	13	10

Source: Institute of Public Administration. *Eighth Annual Report* 1965. Dublin: the Institute, (p. 38).

TABLE 17.15.   *Number of Participants Attending Courses at the Institute of Public Administration, Years 1963-64 and 1964-65, by Type of Course.*

	1963/64	1964/65
Number of Courses	43 (52 course weeks)	48 (55 course weeks)
Number of Man Course Days	2590	3034
PARTICIPANTS:		
—Civil Service	66	142
—Local Service	404	390
—State-sponsored Bodies	138	131
—Voluntary Hospitals	23	13
—Overseas		
(i) Manchester University Groups	14	15
(ii) Zambians	38	22
		(10 from York University)
Others (1964/65 figure includes 37 R.I.P.A. members)	1	53
TOTAL	684	766

Some of the courses held were organised exclusively for certain sections of the public service. These were as follows:	ex- Number of Courses	Numbers Attending
—Civil Service	1	25
—Local Service	15	269
—State Sponsored Bodies	3	40

Source: Institute of Public Administration. *Eighth Annual Report* 1965. Dublin: the Institute, (p. 33).

Short Courses. The Institute also conducts a series of short courses lasting from two days to two weeks to help provide for the development and training of staffs of public bodies, to introduce them to new techniques, and to secure the practical application of those techniques and skills.

Participation in the Institute's courses is shown in table 17.15 above. The cost of attendance at courses is borne by the participants' employers. The State, apart from its direct grant for the School of Public Administration, also subvents the activities of the Institute by a composite corporate membership subscription in respect of all government departments.

The Irish Management Institute

The Irish Management Institute is the principal management training body in Ireland. The Institute was founded in 1952 to raise the standard of management in Ireland. It is a private body, owned by its members. Membership is of three kinds: corporate, consisting of firms; individual, consisting of individual practising managers; and associate, consisting of students of management who are not in management positions. There are at present 540 corporate members, 1,367 individual members and 135 associates. Membership is by election: the Institute is not an examining body.

The Institute is a constituent member of the European Association of Management Training Centres and is the Irish national member of the International Council for Scientific Management.

In its earlier years the work of the Institute was directed mainly to gaining acceptance of the idea that management was an activity fit for study and capable of being improved by training. A committee representative of educational bodies and of business recommended in 1956 that the Institute should itself conduct training courses, and recommended that a small management development unit be set up within the Institute to do so. A second representative committee recommended in 1962 that the Institute's training activities be expanded by the recruitment of specialist staff in the areas of marketing, production, finance and personnel management.

This was done, and the Institute now has five full-time specialist staff engaged in management training. Additional staff are being recruited to conduct a training programme especially for the distributive sector of the economy. Lecturers from outside the Institute are also used.

As well as providing a programme of training, the Institute provides an information and library service for its members, publishes the journal *Management* and other occasional publications.

Attendance at courses conducted by the Institute is not restricted to members, and the response by business to the courses has been considerable. There is, in the following chapter, a detailed analysis of participation in courses during the years 1961 to 1965, in which it is shown that the number of managers attending grew from 606 in 1961/62 to 1,872 in 1964/65.

As well as having courses intended for managers generally, the Institute also conducts courses for particular industry groups and internal training courses for individual firms.

State grants of up to half the cost of attending certain courses are available to manufacturing and distributive firms. The State also gives, on a year-to-year basis, a direct grant to the Institute.

CHAPTER 18

Attitudes of Managers to Existing Facilities.

In this chapter it is intended to examine the opinions of managers about facilities. The degree to which firms used facilities in the past is also examined.

The chapter is in two parts. Professional education is first considered, university degrees and other professional qualifications being investigated. In the second part various other aids to management are dealt with.

Summary of Findings

UNIVERSITY DEGREES. Most Irish companies have made little use of graduates in the past, and do not intend to recruit them direct from university in the future. There are differences between size-groups in this regard. Most executives interviewed were unfamiliar with degrees and were unable to comment on them. Comments on engineering and science graduates were mainly favourable, and stressed the need for such graduates to receive management training. Comments on commerce degrees were unfavourable and stressed lack of depth in the courses. Firms employed more engineers and scientists than any other type of graduate and intended in future to recruit more of them than of any other type.

Apart from large firms, few companies would be in a position to use either of the present graduate courses in business or administration at the university colleges in Dublin. Firms were, however, favourably disposed to the courses, and many indicated that they would send executives to a part-time course if managers without formal academic qualifications were accepted.

PROFESSIONAL QUALIFICATIONS. Few firms commented on professional qualifications. The need for greater emphasis on management accounting was stressed. Provision of courses at professional level on production management and a more professional approach to marketing were suggested. Interviewees were neutral about the mechanics of providing such qualifications, whether by university or by professional institute.

POST-EXPERIENCE TRAINING. There has been marked growth in the use of facilities. Size appears to be the main factor influencing participation. Attitudes are predominantly favourable, and reinforced by experience. There is room for further research on attitudes and expectations in this field. Firms located outside Dublin stated that they would be prepared to send many more executives to courses in local centres than in Dublin.

Executives' opinions of the likely numbers of managers they would send to courses agree reasonably well with the numbers actually sent, but a substantial number of small firms expressing willingness to attend have not in practice done so. A firm's size affects the extent to which it is likely to prefer full-time to part-time courses, and the length of time for which it is prepared to release staff. Previous experience of management training is also associated with higher preference for full-time courses, and with greater willingness to release for extended periods. Firms generally prefer shorter courses to longer courses and, while it is dangerous to rely on past attendance at courses as an indication of preferences, nevertheless the pattern of attendance reflects well the pattern of preferences expressed in chapter 11.

OTHER FACILITIES. A minority of firms employ consultants, with size again having a noticeable effect. Those employing consultants appear satisfied with their services.

PART I. PROFESSIONAL EDUCATION

University

The first question considered is the extent to which manufacturing firms employ university graduates in managerial positions, or have in the past recruited them for any purpose.

TABLE 18. 1. *Estimated Percentage of Firms Employing Managers with University Degrees, by Size of Firm.*

Size of Firm (No. of Employees)	Total Firm Included	Qualification Status	
		University Degree Alone	Degree Alone or with Profession
500 or More	47	83.0	87.2
100-499	48	60.4	60.4
20-99	46	26.1	32.6
OVERALL		35.3	40.4

Table 18.1. shows the position with regard to the employment of managers with a university degree alone. Virtually all large firms, a majority of medium-sized ones, but only about a quarter of firms with under 100 employees have any graduate executives. The situation is not greatly altered by including individuals who, in addition to a degree, possess a professional qualification.

Even fewer firms ever recruited graduates direct from university in the past, or intend to do so in the future. A majority of large firms recruit at least to some extent.

TABLE 18. 2. *Estimated Percentages of Firms Which Ever Recruited Graduates Direct from University, by Size of Firm.*

Size of Firm (No. of Employees)			
500 or More	100-499	20-99	TOTAL
60.0	20.8±10.6	6.5 (1.3 - 17.9)	11.7±5.7

TABL1 18. 3. *Estimated Percentage of Firms Intending to Recruit Graduates Direct from University in 1964-67, by Size of Firm.*

Size of Firm (No. of Employees)	Total Firms Included	Will Recruit	Will Not Recruit	Don't Know
500 or More	47	55.3	38.3	6.4
100-499	48	14.6	68.7	16.7
20-99	46	8.7	80.4	10.9
OVERALL		11.7	76.4	11.9

Firms in the medium group recruit very little but seem able to attract graduates later. Firms in the smallest group recruit hardly at all, and do not subsequently attract graduates in quantity, many of the graduates in small firms being family members.

Firms were asked how many graduates they thought they would recruit in the period January 1st, 1964, to January 1st, 1967. Their estimates are shown in table 18.4.

TABLE 18.4.   *Estimated Number of Graduates to be Recruited Direct from University in 1964-67, by Size of Firm.*

Size of Firm (No. of Employees)			
500 or More	100-499	20-99	TOTAL
125	59±42	82±78	266±88

Apart from the inevitable uncertainty in looking to the future, the estimates are subject to large sampling variation. They suggest a yearly intake of about 100 graduates. Without estimates of demand from other sectors it is impossible to say whether the supply of graduates is in excess, or in deficit, of the economy's requirements. The heavy rate of emigration in the past and the fact that few firms have reported shortages of managers arising from lack of academic qualifications (see table 18.5) suggest that the number of graduates is at least sufficient to cater for effective demand. This does not

TABLE 18.5.   *Estimated Percentage of Firms Reporting Shortage of Academically-qualified Managers, by Size of Firm.*

Size of Firm (No. of Employees)			
500 or More	100-499	20-99	TOTAL
14.9	4.2	4.3	4.8

TABLE 18.6.   *Comments of Executives on University Degrees, by Size of Firm.*

Size of Firm (No. of Employees)	Total Firms Included	Criticised Some Degree %	Criticised No Degree %	Don't Know %
500 or More	47	74.5	2.1	23.4
100-499	48	47.9	2.1	50.0
20-99	46	41.3	—	58.7
OVERALL		43.9	0.5	55.6

rule out the possibility of shortages of particular types or at particular levels, especially in a period of renewed economic growth. So far as industry is concerned, adequacy of supply may be a consequence of the small size of most firms and a past history of slow growth as a result of which managers either do not see a need for graduates or, because they have never worked with one, are unable to assess the contribution a graduate can make.

Lack of demand may also be a reflection on the adequacy of qualifications. It may be, if the training of graduates were altered, that demand for their services would increase. Certainly degrees are not without their critics. The managers interviewed in the survey were asked whether they thought various degrees might be improved (Q.19 of questionnaire). Many of them criticised one or other of them, as table 18.6 shows.

Their comments will be considered later when each degree is examined in turn.

Without some criterion it is impossible to say whether the behaviour of Irish firms towards employment of graduates is unusual.[1] The facts above, and the data in chapters 4, 8, 9 and 10, show that much remains to be done if it is considered desirable that graduates should move in quantity into management. Present arrangements do not appear sufficient.

Individual degrees are now considered. Table 18.7. shows the percentage of firms employing a manager with each type of degree alone, i.e. not also having a professional qualification. It was felt that this was the most meaningful comparison, as a firm employing, for instance, a B.Comm. or a B.A. who was also an accountant might be presumed to have recruited him as much for his accountancy qualification as for his degree.

TABLE 18. 7. *Estimated Proportion of Firms Employing Managers with Each Type of Degree Alone, by Size of Firm.*

Size of Firm (No. of Employees)	Total Firms	Commerce	Arts	Engineering	Science	Other
500 or More	47	25.5	29.8	53.2	44.7	23.4
100-499	48	16.7	6.2	12.5	31.2	2.1
20-99	46	4.3	4.3	4.3	6.5	6.5
OVERALL		7.6	5.6	7.8	13.0	6.2

Firms with less than 100 employees employ graduates hardly at all, irrespective of degree. The position would be even worse if two firms which had grown beyond the 100 employee mark were excluded. In the case of Dublin firms in this group, almost all the graduates were members of the owning family. This was not so outside Dublin.

Firms in the middle group are not heavy employers of graduates either. The accent is mainly on science graduates. This is because of the preponderence of food-processing firms: virtually every firm employing a scientist in management was in the food industry. Graduates in this group were professional managers rather than family members.

It is only in the largest firms that graduate managers become at all frequent. Engineering and science graduates are far more widespread than others: not only do more firms employ them but they employ more of them (see table 18.9.).

It was argued in chapter 4 that the more widespread employment of technical than of non-technical graduates is not only a reflection of greater opportunity arising from the greater number of positions in production management than in other areas, but of a

---

1. *The Directory of Opportunities for Graduates* (London: The Cornmarket Press, 1966) shows that most companies advertising in the directory for graduates of British universities, employed over 500 people: indeed most employed over 5,000 people.

preference in areas other than production for professional qualifications rather than degrees. If graduates who also possess professional qualifications are included in the comparison the advantage of technical degrees disappears. It has been argued that this is not the best comparison, but it does serve to indicate a preference among firms for professional competence in a particular field. In fact, by taking a further qualification, these graduates have become "technical", usually in finance.

TABLE 18. 8. *Estimated Proportion of Firms Employing Managers with Each Type of Degree, Alone or With Another Qualification, by Size of Firm.*

Size of Firm (No. of Employees)	Total Firms	Commerce	Arts	Engineering	Science	Other
500 or More	47	55.3	46.8	57.4	53.2	29.8
100-499	48	20.8	16.7	18.7	31.3	6.2
20-99	46	13.0	10.9	4.3	4.3	10.9

TABLE 18. 9. *Number of Managers in the Sample having Each Type of Degree, by Size of Firm. (Firms Unchanged in Size.)*

Size of Firm (No. of Employees)	Degree Status	Commerce	Arts	Engineering	Science	Other
500 or More	Alone	28	23	116	77	21
	With Another Degree	10	6	7	5	2
	With a Profession[1]	26	13	21	2	2
100-499	Alone	9	3	9	21	1
	With Another Degree	1	3	—	—	2
	With a Profession	2	2	6	2	—
20-99	Alone	1	2	1	3	9
	With Another Degree	—	—	—	—	—
	With a Profession	2	2	—	—	1

1. Some managers had multiple degrees, sometimes with a professional qualification. There is therefore some double counting. For a complete breakdown see table 4.14.

TABLE 18. 10. *Estimated Percentage of Firms Intending to Recruit Graduates of Each Type Direct from University in 1964-67, by Size of Firm.*

Size of Firm (No. of Employees)	Total Firms Included	Commerce	Engineering	Science	Other
500 or more	47	10.6	31.9	23.4	21.3
100-449	48	—	6.2	8.3	4.2
20-99	46	—	2.2	4.3	2.2
OVERALL		0.4	4.1	5.8	3.3

In addition to their employment of graduate managers, firms were asked how many graduates from each faculty they anticipated recruiting direct from university. Direct recruitment was anticipated to be limited, even among larger firms.

TABLE 18. 11.   *Estimated Number of Graduates of Each Type to be Recruited Direct from University in 1964-67, by Size of Firm.*

Size of Firm (No. of Employees)	Commerce	Engineering	Science	Other
500 or more	22	43	24	36
100-499	—	21	21	16
20-99	—	21	41	21
TOTAL	22	85	86	73

As pointed out above, the figures are unlikely to be reliable, but indicate orders of magnitude and preference. Again engineers and scientists are more widespread than other graduates, though numerically (table 18.11.) their advantage is not so marked, mainly because three very large companies expected to recruit relatively large numbers of people with degrees in arts, commerce and agriculture.

It is interesting in this context to look at the type of job for which graduates of each type were to be taken on (table 18.12). Scarcely any companies intended to employ people as management trainees or in research. The most usual work was technical or professional, i.e. work in which individuals would exercise skills imparted in their studies. In the main, it was engineers or scientists who were expected to engage in such work. A small number of companies intended to recruit individuals, mainly from the faculties of arts and commerce, for general administrative work in which they would not use specific skills acquired by study.

Finally, interviewees were asked (Q.19 of questionnaire) for comments on the various degrees, and these are shown in table 18.13.

It can be seen in table 18.13. that in most cases executives were unable to comment. This is not surprising in view of the restricted employment of graduates. Even where graduates were employed, often only one or two had a particular degree. In many such cases, interviewees felt unable to distinguish the degree from the man, and to comment on the merit of the qualification as distinct from that of the individual holding it.

The degrees evoking most comment were commerce and engineering in the top group, commerce and science in the middle group, and commerce in the bottom group. The nature of the comments varied considerably between degrees.

Commerce

As a degree in its own right as distinct from a preparation for subsequent study in accounting, commerce came in for more criticism than any other degree. Not alone did more managers criticise it, but the nature and tone of their criticism was more severe. In the top size-group 20 out of 47 firms offered some criticism. These interviewees were mainly concerned about lack of depth in the course — 12 of them commented directly on this. Typical comments were: "they should learn to do something well" . . . "they can't do anything well" . . . "there has been improvement, but they are not in the same class as engineers as management material." Most of the others thought there ought to be more contact with industry before the degree was granted—that the graduates ought to have more practical experience.

In the middle group, 13 out of 48 firms commented adversely. Again the criticism related almost exclusively to lack of depth and rigour, with further comments on the need for closer identification with business, allied to practical experience. While the nature of the comments did not differ from that of the larger firms, the tone tended to

TABLE 18. 12.   *Number of Firms in Sample Recruiting Graduates for Specified Positions in 1964-67, and Number of Graduates Involved, by Size of Firm.*

Size of Firm (No. of Employees)	Total Firms in Sample	Nature of Job	Commerce	Engin-eering	Science	Other	Total
		Mgt. Trainee	1 (2)[1]	3 (4)	1 (1)	2 (2)	5 (11)[2]
		Research	—	1 (2)	1 (2)	—	1 (4)
500 or more	47	Tech/Prof.	2 (6)	9 (33)	9 (21)	6 (15)	16 (75)
		Other	2 (14)	2 (4)	—	2 (19)	5 (37)
		TOTAL	5 (22)	15 (43)	11 (24)	10 (36)	(125)
		Mgt. Trainee	—	1 (2)	—	1 (1)	2 (3)
		Research	—	—	—	—	—
100-499	48	Tech/Prof.	—	1 (1)	2 (2)	1 (2)	3 (5)
		Other	—	1 (1)	2 (2)	—	2 (3)
		TOTAL	—	3 (4)	4 (4)	2 (3)	(11)
		Mgt. Trainee	—	—	—	—	—
		Research	—	—	—	—	—
20-99	46	Tech/Prof.	—	—	1 (1)	—	1 (1)
		Other	—	1 (1)	2 (2)	1 (1)	3 (3)
		TOTAL	—	1 (1)	3 (3)	1 (1)	(4)

1. The figures in parentheses show the number of graduates involved.
2. One firm intended to employ two trainees, but specified no degree.

TABLE 18. 13.   *Comments by Executives on Specified Degrees, by Size of Firm.*

Size of Firm (No. of employees)	Comment on Need for Improvement	Commerce (No.)	Economics (No.)	Engin-eering (No.)	Science (No.)	Other (No.)
	Some needed	20	3	16	9	—
500 or More	None needed	4	3	8	6	—
	Don't know	23	41	23	32	47
	Some needed	13	2	5	8	1
100-499	None needed	3	3	3	2	—
	Don't know	32	43	40	38	47
	Some needed	10	1	3	3	2
20-99	None needed	—	1	1	1	—
	Don't know	36	44	42	42	44

be more astringent, principally among accountants and those who themselves had degrees in commerce: . . . "no practical benefit to me at all" . . . "only book-keepers really— the whole thing needs severe up-grading".

In the bottom group there were 10 comments, half relating to lack of specialisation, the rest to the need for practical experience before graduation.

It may be of interest to see the background of the critics (table 18.14.). In view of the high proportion of accountants who were not also graduates, it is possible that the comments carry some emotional content.

TABLE 18.14. *Academic Background of Interviewees Expressing Need for Improvement in Degrees in Commerce, by Size of Firm.*

ACADEMIC BACKGROUND	Size of Firm (No. of Employees)		
	500 or more	100-499	20-99
Accountancy and not B. Comm.	8	5	3
Accountancy and B. Comm.	3	2	1
B. Comm. alone, or with other Degree	1	1	—
Other Degree or Qualification	3	1	2
No Degree or Qualification	5	4	4
TOTAL	20	13	10

In spite of any reservations about the nature or value of the comments, the combination of comment and behaviour with regard to employment and recruitment makes it difficult to avoid the conclusion that the prevailing attitude of industry to the degree is a mixture of unfamiliarity and dissatisfaction.

Economics

The outstanding fact about economists is that industry employs them hardly at all, and knows nothing of them. Out of 141 interviewees, 128 replied "don't know" when asked to comment.

Engineering

Next to commerce, most comments related to engineers and scientists. In the top group, 16 out of 47 firms expressed a need for improvement in the preparation of engineers. Of the 16 comments, 14 concerned the need for engineers to have training

TABLE 18.15. *Academic Background of Interviewees Expressing Need for Improvement in Degrees in Engineering, by Size of Firm.*

ACADEMIC BACKGROUND	Size of Firm (No. of Employees)		
	500 or more	100-499	20-99
Engineers	2	1	2
Scientists	2	—	—
Accountants	6	1	—
Other Qualified	2	—	—
No Degree or Qualification	4	3	1
TOTAL	16	5	3

in business. Most were favourable in tone and regarded engineers as good management material if their lack of preparation for business could be made good. Five comments related to deficiencies in ability to handle people, mainly because of dogmatism or insufficient allowance for unpredictability: ". . . they want things too cut-and-dried". Others related to the need for familiarisation with finance and costing and to the need to develop a managerial outlook: ". . . they want to be managers but to remain engineers as well".

In the two lower size-groups there were hardly any comments, and such comments as there were showed no consistent pattern. The background of the commentators is shown in table 18.15.

Science

Science came in for less comment among the larger companies. Comments were largely the same as for engineering, seven out of the nine who wanted some change stating that there was need for training in management. In the middle group, four of the eight who commented made this suggestion also. The other comments related mainly to a desire for speciaiisation in the technology of the particular industry in which the firm was engaged, mainly food processing. As in the case of engineers, the tone of the comments was mainly favourable. The background of the commentators is in table 18.16.

TABLE 18.16.   *Academic Background of Interviewees Expressing Need for Improvement in Degrees in Science, by Size of Firm.*

ACADEMIC BACKGROUND	Size of Firm (No. of Employees)		
	500 or more	100-499	20-99
Scientists	1	3	2
Engineers	—	1	—
Accountants	6	—	—
Other Qualified	—	—	—
No Degree or Qualification	2	4	1
TOTAL	9	8	3

Other Degrees

There were hardly any comments on other degrees. Some firms commented on graduates in general, the main criticism being that they needed greater familiarity with business before graduating. They suggested closier liaison between university staff and business.

Graduate Studies in Business and Administration

Before the survey was carried out, it was proposed by the two university colleges in Dublin to have courses at graduate level in business administration and in administrative science (see chapter 17). It was decided to attempt to estimate the likely response of firms by asking whether they would be prepared to send executives or potential executives to the courses, which type of structure they preferred, and how many people they would send. The firms which would not use the courses were asked for their reasons. The replies to these questions form the subject matter of this sub-section.

This is not an attempt to measure the total likely demand for university courses at graduate level. It is probable that much of the demand, especially as time goes on, will come not from firms but from individual executives or potential managers who wish to enhance their prospects of advancement.

Table 18.17. shows the extent to which firms said they would use either type of graduate course.

TABLE 18. 17. *Estimated Proportion of Firms Prepared to Send Participants to University Courses in Dublin, by Size of Firm.*

Size of Firm (No. of Employees)	Total Firms Included	Percentage Prepared to Use Courses	Percentage Not Prepared to Use Courses
500 or more	47	44.7	55.3
100-499	48	12.5 (4.7—25.2)	87.5
20-99	46	6.5 (1.3—17.9)	93.5
OVERALL		9.2±5.7	90.8

The picture is as might be expected. Large companies are reasonably willing to participate, small firms are to a great extent either unwilling or unable. Medium-sized firms are much more like small than large firms in this respect.

It might also be expected that locations would influence a firm's response, with firms outside Dublin being less able to send participants.

TABLE 18. 18. *Proportion of Firms Prepared to Use University Courses, by Size and Location of Firm.*

(No. of Employees) Size of Firm	Location of Head Office	Percentage Prepared to Use	Percentage Not Prepared to Use
500 or More	DUBLIN	57.15	42.85
	REST OF COUNTRY	23.53	76.47
	OVERALL	44.45	55.55
100-499	DUBLIN	18.18	81.82
	REST OF COUNTRY	9.09	90.91
	OVERALL	13.64	86.36
20-99	DUBLIN	5.00	95.00
	REST OF COUNTRY	4.54	95.45
	OVERALL	4.76	95.24

Table 18.18. suggests that, outside the group of firms with 500 or more employees, the difference is negligible, due to the low number of firms based in Dublin which would be prepared to use the courses. A statistical test confirms that the difference between locations is not significant. Table 18.18. shows that, outside Dublin, there is no difference between the three size-groups. The only firms which differ from the others are large firms located in Dublin.

A series of tests was carried out to see whether a firm's willingness to use the courses was associated with its past use of management training courses, its employment of trained or qualified executives, its membership of the Irish Management Institute, and whether or not it operated a management development scheme. It was found that, in the group of large companies, firms which had used courses, employed trained managers, or were members of the Institute, were all more willing than others to send participants to the graduate courses. In the medium size-group both members and firms employing trained managers were more willing than others, but not significantly so. None of the other factors showed any association. This was true of all factors so far as small companies were concerned.

The reasons given by firms not participating showed that companies were not so much unwilling to use the courses as unable.

Out of 47 companies with over 500 employees, 26 would not use courses. Of that 26, 9 said they would be willing to send executives to attend the part-time course if the conditions of entry were relaxed to allow those with no formal academic qualifications to enter. Several of the companies which expressed willingness to use this course said they would send more participants if this restriction were lifted. Almost all the 26 companies mentioned had no-one in a position to attend courses who was also qualified. Many felt that a man of proven ability but with no qualifications stood to gain more from attendance at a university than someone who had already been there.

Of the remaining 17 firms which would not use courses, 5 said they had only a small number of qualified staff, at senior level, who could not spare the time to attend a full-time course and, being outside Dublin, could not attend part-time unless the course were held on several days per week instead of for several hours per day. Two of the remaining 12 would be prepared to use a part-time course if it were available in Cork.

Thus only 10 out of 47 firms were not positively interested in university-level courses, and only 4 of these were opposed to them, one because they already encouraged and paid for their staff to take the B.Comm. degree at night and wished to continue doing so.

In the medium-sized companies, 42 out of 48 would not use either of the present courses. Seven of the 42 would use the part-time course if entry were relaxed, while a further 3 were waiting to see what the course was like in practice before making a decision. Two others could not spare the time of their qualified staff, but might be prepared to encourage attendance if it were completely outside working hours.

Of the remaining 30 firms, 14 outside Dublin stated that they were too small to send anyone to the full-time course, and were too far away to send anyone part-time. Three of these firms were in Cork, and would be willing to use a part-time course at University College, Cork.

The 16 firms left were mainly not opposed to the idea of university courses but either had no-one qualified for the part-time course or had so few qualified that their time could not be spared, and in addition displayed no particular interest in sending non-qualified staff. They were unwilling to release staff for a year to attend the full-time course.

Forty-three out of 46 small companies would not attend. Three of them would send non-qualified staff to the part-time course, if this were permitted. Eighteen of the remaining 40 were located outside Dublin and could not use a part-time course.

Even if this were changed to days per week, hardly any of the firms would be in a position to use it, because they had no qualified staff, and some would not use it even if the conditions of entry were relaxed. Two of the 3 small firms in Cork said they would like to use a part-time course at University College, Cork.

Twenty-two firms displayed no interest even in a part-time course open to non-qualified staff, though the chief executive of one of them intended to send his son, who had a degree.

The above comments show that there is more goodwill for the idea of courses at university level than table 18.17. indicates. This might be given practical expression by firms in Dublin, but executives outside Dublin are unlikely ever to be able to attend a part-time course and would find it difficult to use a full-time one.

The number of executives which firms estimated they would send to university courses is shown in table 18.19. The population totals were not estimated from the sample in the usual way. In making estimates in the usual way, firms which had changed size were regarded as being still in their original size-groups. This would have introduced a serious bias in the estimate for the bottom stratum where only three firms expressed willingness to use courses. One of these firms had since left the stratum and was willing to send as many participants as the other two.

It was therefore decided to use the same method of estimation as in chapter 4, part B, i.e. to exclude all firms which had changed size and to multiply the resulting sample number by 6 and 23 to get approximate estimates of participation for the 100 to 499 and 20 to 99 size groups respectively.[1]

Apart from the uncertainty in businessmen's estimates of future behaviour there is considerable sampling variation attached to the estimates given, but they do indicate the order of magnitude of the likely demand from firms for the courses as organised at present. To this should be added demand from executives themselves.

TABLE 18. 19. *Estimated Number of Managers Whom Firms Would Send to University Courses, by Size and Location of Firm.*

Size of Firm (No. of Employees)	Location of Firm		Total
	Dublin	Rest of Country	
500 or more	47	6	53
100-499	48	18	66
20-99	46	46	92
TOTAL	141	70	211

The greatest demand is likely to be from firms in Dublin employing over 100 people. The demand from small firms outside Dublin is restricted to those within driving distance and may even be overestimated.

Those firms willing to send executives to university courses were asked whether they preferred full-time or part-time courses, and how many men they would send to each type. Their replies are shown in tables 18.20. and 18.21., the method of estimation described above being used in the latter table.

The figures on which table 18.20. is based are very small: too small to allow any test of significance to be carried out. It would be dangerous to assume that the figures

1. The figures for the 500-and-over group were taken as they stood. As some firms had joined this group since the sample was drawn, the figures are probably an underestimate.

in the middle size-group indicate that the difference observed would exist in the population of firms as a whole. Those for the top group are significant by definition, while those in the bottom group seem reasonable *a priori*, small firms being more likely to use part-time than full-time courses.

TABLE 18. 20.   *Estimated Proportion of Firms Preferring Specified Types of University Courses.*

Size of Firm (No. of Employees)	Total Firms Included	Prefer Full-time	Prefer Part-time	No Preference
500 or more	21	42.9	47.6	9.5
100-499	7	57.1	28.6	14.3
20-99	3	—	100.0	—

TABLE 18. 21.   *Estimated Number of Managers Who Would be Sent by Firms Preferring Various Types of Courses, by Size of Firm.*

Size of Firm (No. of Employees)	Prefer Full-time	Prefer Part-time	No Preference
500 or more	15	33	5
100-499	36	12	18
20-99	—	92	—
TOTAL	51	137	23

A more relevant indication of preference is the number of executives who would be sent to courses. Table 18.21 shows that by this criterion the preference of both large and small firms is for a part-time course, and also shows that full-time courses are still preferred by medium-sized companies. That sampling variation is inherent in these figures must again be emphasised. The estimates are based on sample returns for 20, 5, and 2 firms, reading from large to small.

The figures in table 18.20. were examined to see whether there was evidence of association between a firm's preference for a particular type of course and its size, location, previous use of management training courses, employment of trained or qualified staff, membership of the Irish Management Institute, and its operation of a management development scheme.

It was not possible to carry out any statistical tests, as the number of firms was too small. Even examining the top size-group only, it was impossible in most to show an association, as all the large firms willing to use university courses employed trained and qualified staff, had previously used management-training courses, and were members of the Irish Management Institute. There was a slight tendency for large firms operating a management development scheme to favour full-time courses to a greater extent than those not operating a scheme, but this may have been because they were, on average, larger. Larger firms outside Dublin, and not within driving distance, obviously had no choice but to choose full-time courses, but some at least would prefer a part-time course if it were possible to attend one.

Professional Qualifications

The position with regard to employment of managers with professional qualifications differs little from that of university graduates.

TABLE 18. 22.   *Estimated Percentage of Firms Employing Managers with Professional Qualifications, by Size of Firm.*

Size of Firm (No. of employees)	Total Firms Included	Qualification Status	
		Professional Alone	Professional Alone or with Degree
500 or more	47	89.4	97.9
100-499	48	64.6	70.8
20-99	46	17.4	26.1
OVERALL		29.8	38.0

Almost all the larger firms, a majority of the medium-sized group and a small minority of the smallest firms employ someone with a professional qualification. When asked for their comments (Q.21 of questionnaire) fewer large firms commented than did so in the case of university degrees, but more small firms did so. Again, however, the proportion of firms commenting was low.

TABLE 18. 23.   *Estimated Percentage of Interviewees Criticising Some Professional Qualification, by Size of Firm.*

Size of Firm (No. of Employees)			
500 or more	100-499	20-99	TOTAL
38.3	25.0±11.3	19.6 (9.3-34.0)	21.4±8.9

TABLE 18. 24.   *Estimated Percentage of Firms Employing Managers With Each Type of Professional Qualification, by Size of Firm.*

Size of Firm (No. of Employees)	Qualification Status	Financial or Secretarial	Engineering or Science	Marketing	Personnel	Other
500 or more	Professional Alone	87.2	38.3	10.6	6.4	8.5
	Alone or with Degree	95.7	46.8	10.6	6.4	10.6
100-499	Professional Alone	60.4	6.2	4.2	2.1	4.2
	Alone or with Degree	64.6	18.7	4.2	2.1	4.2
20-99	Professional Alone	17.4	2.2	—	—	2.2
	Alone or with Degree	23.9	2.2	—	—	6.5
OVERALL	Professional Alone	28.9	4.4	1.3	0.7	2.8
	Alone or with Degree	35.0	7.3	1.3	0.7	6.2

Going on to consider individual qualifications, the position is shown in tables 18.24. and 18.25. They show the preponderence of accountants in this field. This is a reflection of the fact that training for a career in accountancy is through study for associateship of a professional institute, while training for engineering is mostly a university activity. Non-university courses leading to qualifications in professions other than accountancy are not so long-established in Ireland and, it is probably fair to say, do not yet enjoy the recognition attaching to the professional accounting bodies.

TABLE 18.25.   *Number of Managers in the Sample Having Each Type of Professional Qualification, by Size of Firm. (Firms Unchanged in Size.)*

Size of Firm (No. of Employees)	Qualification Status	Financial or Secretarial	Engineering or Science	Marketing	Personnel	Other
500 or More	Professional Alone	119	33	7	4	7
	Combined with Degree	33	23	1	—	1
100-499	Professional Alone	36	5	2	1	7
	Combined with Degree	2	8	—	—	—
20-99	Professional Alone	6	—	—	—	1
	Combined with Degree	2	—	—	—	1

Firms were not asked their future recruitment intentions, but were asked to comment on the need for alteration or introduction of professional qualifications. Table 18.26 shows the number of replies.

TABLE 18.26.   *Number of Interviewees Expressing Need for Improvement or Introduction of Professional Qualification, by Type of Qualification and Size of Firm.*

Size of Firm (No. of Employees)	No. of Interviewees	Accounting (No.)	Production (No.)	Marketing (No.)	Personnel (No.)
500 or more	47	8	5	13	2
100-499	48	4	10	4	1
20-99	46	3	2	2	—

Accounting

Almost all those who commented on accounting qualifications thought that accountants were technically competent in financial accounting. They considered that accountants should be better-equipped in the techniques of management accounting, and not only equipped with the techniques but given a stronger orientation towards a managerial outlook: seeing their activity as the provision of information for decision-making. The introduction of the Joint Diploma in Management Accounting Services was welcomed, but some fears were expressed that it might be at too remote a level and that a heavier emphasis should instead be placed on management accounting in pre-qualification training.[1] A few companies also mentioned the desirability of training in human relations, and some thought that the various institutes of accountants should insist on their students having a university degree. In general, accountants whose training

1. See chapter 17 for details of a scheme for a Certificate in Management Information which is at a less advanced level than the Joint Diploma.

emphasised costing and management accounting were preferred to those whose training emphasised the financial and legal aspects of the accountant's work.

Production

All those who commented favoured the introduction of facilities for study in production management. To most of them it was immaterial whether this was provided by means of a university degree or by the introduction of non-university facilities on the model of accountancy training.

Marketing

Among large firms this was the most frequently mentioned area. The general wish was for a more professional approach to marketing. Here again executives did not consider it important whether this was to be realised by means of a degree or a professional qualification, so long as the result was achieved.

Personnel

Hardly anyone mentioned personnel as an area for development. This ties in with the earlier findings on the general lack of formalisation of personnel management activities in companies, and may point to a certain lack of perception on the part of management at the time of the survey.

PART. II. OTHER FACILITIES
FOR IMPROVING THE STANDARD OF MANAGEMENT

Post-experience Training:

This section is concerned with the attitude to management training of the executives interviewed, the use firms have made of facilities, and the preferred location, structure and length of courses. The section is based on opinions given in the sample survey, and on an analysis of the records of the Irish Management Institute. Figures are given in chapter 17 for attendance at courses at the School of Management Studies at Rathmines College of Commerce, and at the College of Industrial Relations.

To start the section on attitudes to training (Q.25 of questionnaire), firms were asked whether or not they had a management development programme in operation. Table 18.27. shows that firms with under 500 employees almost never have. A fair proportion of those with over 500 employees said that they operated a programme, but as they were not questioned very closely on this point it may be that the picture is somewhat exaggerated and that some programmes are not so comprehensive as they might be.

TABLE 18. 27.   *Estimated Percentage of Firms Having a Formal Management Development Programme, by Size of Firm.*

Size of Firm (No. of Employees)			
500 or more	100-499	20-99	TOTAL
40.4	8.3 (2.3-20.0)	—	3.2±1.5

While few companies have a formal management development scheme, many employ at least one executive who has attended a management training course, as table 18.28 shows.

TABLE 18. 28.   *Estimated Percentage of Firms Employing a Manager Who Had Attended a Management Training Course, by Size of Firm.*

	Size of Firm (No. of Employees)		
500 or more	100-499	20-99	TOTAL
91.5	60.4	32.6	40.5

Virtually all large companies employ at least one executive with training, a majority of medium-sized firms, but only about one-third of small businesses.

Executives were asked whether they thought management training could help their firms. Table 18.29 shows that most were favourably disposed to training. It is the author's opinion that replies to this question reflected genuine opinions rather than a desire to be polite to an employee of the Irish Management Institute. At all stages of the interviews frankness was the norm and interviewees were particularly encouraged to be frank when answering this question.

TABLE 18. 29.   *Estimated Percentage of Executives' Opinions on the Utility of Management Training Courses by Size of Firm.*

Size of Firm (No. of Employees)	No. of Interviewees	Can Help	Cannot Help	Don't Know
500 or more	47	93.6	4.3	2.1
100-499	48	79.2	4.2	16.7
20-99	46	73.9	10.9	15.2
OVERALL		75.7	9.2	15.0

Although most firms thought that training could benefit them, not all were willing to release staff to attend training courses. This was particularly true of small companies though, even of them, a majority was willing to release staff, if necessary to Dublin.

TABLE 18. 30.   *Estimated Percentage of Firms Expressing Willingness to Release Managers to Attend Courses.*

Size of Firm (No. of Employees)	No. of Interviewees	No Release	Attitude to Release		Don't Know
			Local Only	Local or Dublin	
500 or more	47	8.5	2.1	89.4	—
100-499	48	16.7	16.7	56.2	10.4
20-99	46	32.6	8.7	54.3	4.3
OVERALL		28.4	10.1	56.1	5.4

The question of willingness to release was examined to see if any factors affected the situation. The lower proportion of small firms willing to release has been remarked on and the difference between the size-groups is highly significant statistically.

There was no tendency for non-Dublin firms to be more or less willing to release staff than those in Dublin, though there appears to be a slight tendency for smaller non-Dublin firms to prefer local courses to courses in Dublin, which is consonant with their past behaviour. There was a consistent tendency for firms which were members of the Irish Management Institute, or employed managers with training, or had previously used Irish Management Institute courses, to be more willing to release than those not familiar with training. Thus, experience appears to reinforce favourable predispositions.

The records of the Irish Management Institute were analysed to show the number of firms and individuals participating in courses. In order to compare participants with the total, table 18.31 shows the total number of firms in transportable goods industry (roughly equal to manufacturing industry) according to a list received in 1963 and used as the sampling frame for this research project.

TABLE 18.31. *Total Number of Firms in Late 1963 in Transportable Goods Industry, by Location and Size of Firm.*

Location of Head Office	Size of Firm (No. of Employees)		
	500 or more	100-499	20-99
Dublin	30	124	490
Other	17	132	456
TOTAL	47	256	946

The total number of firms sending participants to courses is shown in table 18.32. below. The growth in participation is marked, particularly in non-manufacturing firms. As this project is confined to manufacturing, attention will be confined to that section of the table.

TABLE 18.32. *Number of Firms Sending Participants to Irish Management Institute Courses, by Sector, Location and Size of Firm.*

Year	Location of Head Office	Manufacturing				Mfg. Total	Non-Mfg. Total
		500+	100-499	20-99	<20		
1961–62	DUBLIN	16	22	22	4	64	68
	OTHER	10	31	28	18	87	24
	TOTAL	26	53	50	22	151	92
1962–63	DUBLIN	23	33	22	6	84	68
	OTHER	8	20	14	6	48	31
	TOTAL	31	53	36	12	132	99
1963–64	DUBLIN	24	42	34	17	117	108
	OTHER	10	26	33	7	76	43
	TOTAL	34	68	67	24	193	151
1964–65	DUBLIN	27	43	48	27	145	249
	OTHER	12	50	44	14	120	149
	TOTAL	39	93	92	41	265	398

On comparing the analysis with the total number of firms in table 18.31. above, it is obvious that there are wide disparities in the coverage achieved in the different size-groups. This bears out the findings of the sample survey which showed a high proportion of large firms using training courses, tailing off to a very low proportion of smaller companies, with the medium-sized companies participating at a rate rather lower than might have been expected.

Location has not in the past affected the rate of participation. Just as high a proportion of non-Dublin firms as Dublin firms have sent people which, in view of the fact that most of the Institute's courses are held in Dublin, may appear surprising. The fact that inconvenience due to location does not deter firms from attending, while size does, reinforces the importance of size as a determining factor. Comparison of the number of individuals participating with the number of managers estimated from the survey shows Dublin firms with a slight advantage, i.e. they appear to send more participants than non-Dublin firms. This may be biased, and the "market share" is heavily biased upwards, by the inclusion of supervisors among participants while they were excluded from the estimates of managers.

TABLE 18.33.   *Estimated Total Number of Managers in Transportable Goods Industry, January 1, 1964.*

Location of Head Office	Size of Firm (No. of Employees)		
	500 or more	100-499	20-99
Dublin	907	1161	1811
Other	285	1001	1467
TOTAL	1192	2168	3270

TABLE 18.34   *Number of Individuals Attending Irish Management Institute Courses, by Sector, Location and Size of Firm.*

Year	Location of Head Office	Manufacturing				Mfg. Total	Non-Mfg. Total
		500+	100-499	20-99	<20		
1961–62	DUBLIN	117	34	27	5	183	127
	OTHER	33	76	46	21	176	120
	TOTAL	150	110	73	26	359	247
1962–63	DUBLIN	164	66	31	7	268	158
	OTHER	30	45	22	7	104	40
	TOTAL	194	111	53	14	372	198
1963–64	DUBLIN	177	98	87	22	384	211
	OTHER	27	44	49	8	128	51
	TOTAL	204	142	136	30	512	262
1964–65	DUBLIN	278	153	105	37	573	709
	OTHER	107	149	91	19	366	224
	TOTAL	385	302	196	56	939	933

While it is true that non-Dublin firms attend courses in Dublin, there is little doubt that the smaller ones would prefer courses nearer to them if possible. Table 18.35. shows participation by firms in courses at different locations. In the two years in which there

TABLE 18.35. *Number of Attendances at Irish Management Institute Courses in Different Locations, by Location and Size of Firm (Manufacturing Only).*

Year	Location of Course	Dublin Firms					Other Firms				
		500+	100-499	20-99	<20	Total	500+	100-499	20-99	<20	Total
1961–62	DUBLIN	82	35	24	3	144	20	37	18	2	77
	OTHER	40	2	2	—	44	13	43	50	16	122
	TOTAL	122	37	26	3	188	33	80	68	18	199
1962–63	DUBLIN	169	78	40	6	293	30	52	24	7	113
	OTHER	—	—	—	1	1	—	2	5	1	8
	TOTAL	169	78	40	7	294	30	54	29	8	121
1963–64	DUBLIN	181	99	101	22	403	20	34	49	5	108
	OTHER	8	2	—	—	10	1	11	6	3	21
	TOTAL	189	101	101	22	413	21	45	55	8	129
1964–65	DUBLIN	296	161	125	37	619	81	121	67	11	280
	OTHER	18	3	2	—	23	16	44	42	16	118
	TOTAL	314	164	127	37	642	97	165	109	27	398

TABLE 18.36. *Estimated Number of Individuals Whom Firms Would Send Annually to Courses in Each Location, by Size and Location of Firm.*

Size of Firm (No. of Employees)	Location of Head Office	Location of Courses		Total[1]
		Dublin	Rest of Country	
500 or more	DUBLIN	231	42	—
	REST OF COUNTRY	45	54	—
	TOTAL	276	96	269
100–499	DUBLIN	203±114	10± 19	
	REST OF COUNTRY	55± 33	279± 89	
	TOTAL	262±124	300±113	535±157
20–99	DUBLIN	383±152	—	—
	REST OF COUNTRY	278±134	654±223	—
	TOTAL	658±199	679±298	1,028±237
TOTAL	DUBLIN	818±185	52± 19	—
	REST OF COUNTRY	378±142	1,005±226	—
	TOTAL	1,196±232	1,074±317	1,833±299

1. The figures for Dublin and the rest of country do not add to the total. This is because individuals are often common to both, the same individual being likely to be sent both to Dublin and local courses.

was an appreciable number of courses outside Dublin it is very noticeable that non-Dublin companies with under 100 employees sent a higher proportion of their participants to courses outside Dublin than did companies with over 100 employees.

The firms in the sample were asked how many individuals they would be prepared to send to courses locally, in Dublin, and in total. It is interesting to compare the estimates of attendance derived from the opinions of interviewees with the actual attendance at courses. Before doing so, it should be pointed out that comparison of the figures for actual participation by firms, shown in table 18.32., with the estimated proportions of firms willing to release executives to attend courses, shown in table 18.30., demonstrates that, while almost all the over-500 companies who are willing to attend courses do in fact attend, the number of firms with under 100 employees which send participants to courses falls far short of the number which would be prepared to release executives (over 50 per cent of a total of almost 1,000 firms).

Tables 18.36 and 18.37 reinforce the conclusion drawn from table 18.35. Firms located outside Dublin, even large ones, expressed themselves as willing to send many more executives to courses held locally than to courses held in Dublin. Since members of the Irish Management Institute might be expected to be most likely to attend courses, their replies were analysed.

TABLE 18. 37.   *Estimated Number of Individuals Whom Firms Would Send Annually to Courses in Each Location, by Size of Firm and Corporate Membership of the Irish Management Institute.*

Size of Firm (No. of Employees)	Corporate Membership Status	Location of Courses	
		Dublin	Rest of Country
500 or more	MEMBER	272	90
	NON-MEMBER	4	6
100–499	MEMBER	118±97	118±68
	NON-MEMBER	143±80	181±95
20–99	MEMBER	89±46	127±92
	NON-MEMBER	555±206	511±285
TOTAL	MEMBER	479±107	335±118
	NON-MEMBER	702±215	698±292

Unfortunately a cross-classification between membership and location was not obtained, but table 18.37 shows that, outside the top size-group, members differ little from non-members. It seems likely, therefore, that even member-firms outside Dublin would prefer if possible to use local courses. This is not true of all firms: several firms mentioned that they preferred to send executives to Dublin as the executives felt that more status attached to going to Dublin to a course than to attending a course nearer home.

Since almost all courses conducted by the Irish Management Institute have been held in Dublin, the estimated number of executives to be sent to courses in Dublin is compared with the actual number attending courses in 1964-65. Firms with over 500 employees anticipated sending 276 executives, while 385 actually attended courses. Some of this discrepancy can be explained by the inclusion in the latter figure of supervisors, and also by the inclusion of all executives attending from two firms, most of whose activities lay outside the manufacturing sector, but whose executives could not be identified with a particular sector, and had therefore to be included *in toto*. It is likely also that interviewees' opinions were to a considerable extent based on past experience. The year 1964-65 was one of marked expansion in the number of courses provided by the Institute, as it was the first year in which its team of management specialists was fully operative. Consequently opinions formed in the light of previous experience probably underestimated the rate of participation when more extensive opportunities were offered.

In the group of firms employing 100 to 499 people, the projected average annual attendance was 383, while the actual attendance in 1964-65 was 302. As the number of firms actually sending executives fell short of the estimated number willing to release staff to courses in Dublin (92 firms as against approximately 144), the actual number of executives attending is even larger than expected, possibly due also to underestimation based on past experience.

Firms with 20 to 99 employees sent only 196 managers to courses, while the estimated number of participants from that group was 658. This is consistent with the finding that the number of firms participating was far short of the estimated number willing to participate. This is true both of firms in Dublin and in the rest of the country.

It may be concluded that, provided the range of choice open to them is not altered radically, the estimates of attendance made by firms which actually use management courses are close to the figures for actual attendance, but that large numbers of small firms which express willingness to attend courses have not done so. It should not be forgotten that courses are available also at the Colleges of Commerce at Rathmines, Cork, and Limerick, and that attendance at these institutions must be added to that at the Irish Management Institute. Unfortunately, there was no convenient way of analysing attendance at colleges of commerce by size of company, or to match their records with those of the Institute so as to avoid double-counting of firms and executives who had attended at more than one centre.

Before going on to discuss detailed preferences in course structure and timing, it may be mentioned that, in every size-group, firms which had in the past attended training courses were willing to send a higher average number of managers per year to further courses. The same was true of firms employing managers with some training, and true also of firms which were members of the Irish Management Inistitute.

Structure of Courses

Firms were asked whether they were willing to attend courses at all, even if held after business hours, and if so whether they preferred them to be full-time, part-time or spare-time. Their replies are shown in table 18.38.

TABLE 18. 38. *Preferred Structure of Management Training Courses, by Size of Firm.*

Size of Firm (No. of Employees)	Percentage Would Not Attend	Percentage No Preference	Full-Time	Percentage of Firms Preferring			
				Hours per Day	Days per Week	Week-end	Spare Time
500 or more	4.3	10.7	68.1	...4.3	6.4	2.1	4.3
100-499	16.7	10.4	39.6	6.2	14.6	—	12.5
20-99	19.6	10.9	21.7	4.3	19.6	2.2	21.7
OVERALL	18.4	10.8	27.1	4.7	18.0	1.7	19.2

The situation shown in the table is as expected. Most firms are willing to use some sort of course, but small companies are less willing than large. About 10 per cent had no preference. In firms with some preference there was a marked tendency for preference for full-time courses to decline with the size of the firm, and for the preference for part-time and spare-time activity to increase. Of the possible methods of part-release, release for some days per week was preferred to release for either hours per day or for extended week-ends.

The different preferences observed were analysed to see whether any characteristic of the firm was associated with a particular preference. Table 18.39 shows preferences analysed by size and location.

TABLE 18.39.   *Preferences for Course-Structure by Firms Prepared to Use Management Training Courses, by Size and Location of Firm (Firms Unchanged in Size).*

Size of Firm (No. of Employees)	Location of Head Office	Number of Firms Included	Percentage Preferring Full-Time or No Preference	Percentage Preferring Other Courses
500 or More	DUBLIN	28	82.15	17.85
	REST OF COUNTRY	15	80.00	20.00
	OVERALL	43	81.40	18.60
100–499	DUBLIN	17	70.59	29.41
	REST OF COUNTRY	20	50.00	50.00
	OVERALL	37	59.45	40.55
20–99	REST OF COUNTRY	13	23.08	76.92
	DUBLIN	20	50.00	50.00
	OVERALL	33	39.40	60.60

There is no consistent pattern in the differences between locations, and none of the differences are statistically significant (except the top one, by definition, but it is trivial). It is obvious that the differences between size-groups are much less marked in firms outside Dublin than in Dublin. When tested it turned out that the size differences outside Dublin were not statistically significant. There is therefore no evidence that firms outside Dublin differ much in their preferences, while in Dublin the difference is very marked between firms with under 100 employees and the rest.

Table 18.40 shows the preference of firms analysed into those which had previously attended management training courses and those which had not.

TABLE 18.40.   *Preferences for Course-Structure by Firms Prepared to Use Management Training Courses, by Size of Firm and Previous Use of Irish Management Institute Courses.*

Size of Firm (No. of Employees)	Previous Use of Courses	Number of Firms Included	Percentage Preferring Full-Time or No Preference	Percentage Preferring Other Courses
500 or More	USED	39	87.18	12.82
	DID NOT USE	4	25.00	75.00
100–499	USED	9	66.67	33.33
	DID NOT USE	28	57.14	42.86
20–99	USED	7	85.71	14.29
	DID NOT USE	26	26.92	73.08

In both top and bottom strata there are marked differences, with users greatly more likely than non-users to prefer full-time courses. The differences are significant. There is little difference, either for users or for non-users, between the size-groups: users of all sizes prefer full-time courses, non-users prefer part-time. The only significant difference is that small non-users are less likely than medium-sized non-users to prefer full-time courses. If association implied cause-and-effect, table 18.40. would appear to indicate that attendance at courses "converts" those small firms using them to a preference for full-time attendance. It is, however, possible that those who had already attended courses were more forward-looking than those who had not, and would have preferred full-time release independently of their previous attendance.

There was a general tendency for member-firms of the Irish Management Institute to prefer full-time courses to a greater degree than firms which were not members, but the preference was neither marked nor significant. Firms employing managers with training displayed the same tendency, and in this case the difference was significant only in the bottom stratum. Too few firms operated a management development scheme to discriminate between them and those which did not, except in the top stratum, where the difference was negligible.

It may be said that increasing size, and the firm's familiarity with training, indicate a greater likelihood that it will prefer full-time courses.

Length of Courses

The next question asked in the survey was what firms considered to be the longest consecutive period for which it was possible to release executives for attendance at courses. This question was asked only of firms prepared to use full-time courses. The number of such firms does not equal the number preferring full-time release: some firms preferring other than full-time courses were nevertheless prepared to use them.

TABLE 18. 41.　*Stated Maximum Length of Release by Firms Prepared to Use Full-Time Courses, by Size of Firm.*

Size of Firm (No. of Employees)	Number of Firms Included	Under 1 Week	Percentage of Firms Prepared to Release for					
			1 Week	1-2 Weeks	2 Weeks	2 Weeks -1 Month	1 Month	Over 1 Month
500 or more	39	5.3	15.8	—	28.9	13.2	7.9	28.9
100-499	32	34.4	18.7	—	12.5	9.4	6.2	18.7
20-99	17	29.4	47.1	5.9	—	—	5.9	11.8
OVERALL		29.5	40.1	4.5	3.7	2.4	6.0	13.8

Table 18.41. shows the replies, and seems to indicate that the larger a firm the longer the period for which it is prepared to release staff. Those firms no longer in their original size-groups were omitted and the remaining replies analysed and tested to see whether any characteristic of the firm other than size affected the length for which it would release staff. It was discovered that differences between sizes were the only ones which could be established as significant. In almost all the other cases — previous attendance at courses, membership of the Irish Management Institute and so on — it was impossible to discriminate, as almost all the firms willing to release staff possessed the characteristic under review. For instance almost every firm had previously used courses,

and it was therefore impossible, with the given number of replies, to distinguish between the length for which users and non-users would release.

The records of attendance at Irish Management Institute courses were analysed to see whether they provided corroboration of the greater willingness of larger firms to attend longer courses. Table 18.42 shows that up to two weeks there is a consistent tendency for larger firms to have sent a higher percentage of their participants to longer courses. The differences between the size-groups are, however, very slight — nothing like so marked as in the case of expressed preferences.

TABLE 18. 42.   *Percentage of Total Participants from Industry Attending Courses of Specified Length in the Years 1961-65, by Size of Firm.*

Size of Firm (No. of Employees)	2 Days or Less	3 Day- 1 Week	Length of Course				Total
			1 Week	2 Week (Day)	2 Week (Night)	3 Weeks	
500 or more	54.5	27.0	11.4	6.3	0.3	0.5	100.0
100-499	59.2	22.0	11.5	5.4	1.1	0.8	100.0
20-99	60.0	25.5	10.6	2.9	0.5	0.5	100.0
Under 20	61.5	26.2	10.8	0.8	—	0.8	100.0
OVERALL	58.0	25.0	11.2	4.9	0.44	0.46	100.0

Table 18.42 is useful from the point of view of indicating differences between size-groups, but not from the point of view of indicating general preference for courses of specified length. The fact that such a high proportion of total participants attended sessions lasting two days or less reflects the fact that more such sessions were made available. A better measure is the average number of participants per course at courses of each length. These figures are given in table 18.43. They show a fairly consistent tendency for shorter courses to attract a higher average number of participants from every size-group, but the trend is marked only in the case of firms with under 100 employees. They also show that on a given course, whatever its length, most of the par-

TABLE 18. 43.   *Average Number of Participants from Industry[1] per Course, attending Courses of Specified Length in the Years 1961-65 by Size of Firm.*

Size of Firm (No. of Employees)	Length of Course			
	Less Than 1 Week	1 Week	2 Weeks or More	Overall
500 or more	5.0	4.1	4.6	4.8
100-499	3.6	3.1	3.5	3.5
20-99	2.9	2.2	1.5	2.7
Under 20	0.7	0.5	0.1	0.6
OVERALL	12.2	9.9	9.7	11.7

1. Participants also attended from non-industrial firms. In 1961-62 there was a total of 251 attendances from non-industrial firms against 387 from industry. In 1962-63 the figures were 220 and 415 respectively, in 1963-64 they were 280 and 542, in 1964-65 they were 1,015 and 1,039.

ticipants will be from firms with over 100 employees. A better measure than average attendance would be the percentage of capacity filled, including cases of over-fill leading to a course being repeated. Details of total applicants had not been kept, so that this suggestion was impracticable.

It is dangerous to use past experience to infer absolute preferences rather than differences between the preferences of different groups, for the reason that response is conditioned by what is offered, and what is offered is not conditioned only by the market. It is particularly dangerous to make inferences about preferences for different subjects when other factors have not been considered.

For instance greater attendance at courses on finance reflects to a certain extent the fact that there were more days' activity in the finance area than in the other major functions. In case it should be argued that the fact that it was possible to have more days' activity in finance than in any other subject indicates a greater preference for that subject, it should be pointed out that the amount of activity was dependent on availability of staff and on the limitations of physical facilities, and that the response is dependent on the attractiveness of the courses—topics, lecturers, method of teaching, even on title — and on the market at which they are aimed. This last point raises the issue that the criterion should not be total attendance, but the share of the market obtained. Market share can be measured only if the segment of the market at which courses are aimed is clearly stated. Not all courses in finance, for instance, are aimed at accounting executives.

Unless a programme of courses is planned in such a way as to keep all conditions constant except that under investigation, or laid out as a statistically-designed experiment, and unless an unambiguous criterion of attractiveness is defined, it is impossible on the basis of actual attendance to make any but gross generalisations on the preference for courses of varying subject matter, length, teaching method and so on.

It is, however, possible to make broad generalisations at least about length. Experience has shown that, with the type of course offered in the past, it has been almost impossible to attract firms to send executives to courses lasting longer than two weeks. If those firms expressing willingness to release managers for more than one month are to be persuaded to do so in practice, a different type of course is obviously called for.

The percentage of total participants from each size-group attending courses on different subjects in the years 1961-65 is shown in table 18.44, and the number of courses relevant to industry in the years 1961-66 is shown, analysed by subject and duration, in table 18.45.[1]

Table 18.44 bears out the preferences expressed by interviewees as discussed in chapter 11 above. Firms with over 100 employees place a much higher emphasis than others on courses in personnel management and organisation, and a higher emphasis also on production and junior management — the latter because of their large numbers of junior managers and supervisors.

Firms with 100 to 499 employees placed a much greater emphasis on finance. This was true also of firms with 20 to 99 employees, which also emphasised marketing to a greater extent than the others. Junior management also received fair attention. The importance of junior management courses to these firms, and more especially to firms with under 20 employees, is caused by the fact that, being unable to attend longer general management courses, proprietors of small businesses came instead to shorter courses

---

1. There were also courses for retailers and builders, and special courses for particular groups and individual firms.

TABLE 18. 44.   *Percentage of Total Participants from Industry Attending Courses in Specified Subjects in the Years 1961-65, by Size of Firm.*

Subject Areas	Size of Firm (No. of Employees)			
	500 or more	100-499	20-99	Under 20
General Management	15.0	13.0	12.4	19.2
Junior Management	25.6	18.8	23.8	31.5
Marketing	11.4	14.2	16.4	10.0
Production and Management Science	16.0	13.8	12.4	10.8
Finance	15.8	22.0	21.8	16.9
Personnel and Organisation	13.0	8.1	3.8	6.1
Other	3.2	10.1	9.4	5.5
Total	100.0	100.0	100.0	100.0

TABLE 18. 45   *Number of Courses, Relevant to Industry, Held by the Irish Managament Institute in the Years 1961-66, Analysed by Subject-Area and Duration.*

Duration	General Management	Junior Management	Marketing	Production	Finance	Personnel	Total
1 Day	14	2	10	11	17	4	58
2 Day	8	26	26	18	33	10	121
3 Day	1	—	3	11	4	5	24
4 Day	1	—	—	2	—	2	5
4 Night	—	48	—	—	—	—	48
5 Night	—	—	1	—	—	—	1
1 Week	1	—	7	3	12	9	32
2 Week (Night)	—	—	1	—	—	—	1
2 Week (Day)	9	—	3	—	—	—	12
3 Week	2	—	—	—	—	—	2
Total	36	76	51	45	66	30	304
Days Activity[1]	162	150	143	103	155	92	805

1. 4 nights and 5 nights counted as two days. 2 weeks (night) counted as 5 days.

aimed at giving to junior managers and supervisors a general appreciation of management. Very small firms also emphasised finance as an area of importance.

Timing

Firms were asked which months suited them best for attending courses. In most cases they found it easier to indicate the few least suitable months, and their replies are shown on that basis in table 18.46.

Most companies with over 500 employees had no preference. Those which had a preference indicated that they least preferred the months June to September, and the

TABLE 18. 46.   *Least-Preferred Months for Courses, by Size of Firm.*

Size of Firm (No. of Employees)	Percentage Wouldn't Attend	Percentage No Preference	Percentage Not Prepared to Attend in											
			Jan/ Feb.	Mar.	April	May	June	July	Aug.	Sept.	Oct.	Nov.	Dec.
500 or more	4.3	55.3	11.1	6.7	15.6	22.2	31.1	37.5	35.6	31.1	26.7	26.7	31.1
100-499	16.7	27.1	27.5	22.5	32.5	40.0	45.0	45.0	55.0	52.5	50.0	45.0	40.0
20-99	19.6	17.4	29.7	40.5	51.4	51.4	59.5	62.2	70.3	62.2	54.1	43.2	43.2
OVERALL	18.4	20.8	28.6	35.6	46.1	47.9	55.4	57.7	65.8	59.0	52.2	43.0	42.1

month of December. The summer months were not popular with medium-sized companies, nor was autumn. Small firms also preferred the early months of the year, neither summer nor autumn being popular. The low preference for summer and early autumn is understandable as most companies have staff on holiday over this period. Late autumn and early winter are times of high activity in training, so their rather low preference among small and medium-sized firms is surprising. However, a high percentage of participation in the Irish Management Institute's courses is by large companies, with which the months of October and November are reasonably popular.

General Comments

Firms were asked (Q.39 of questionnaire) to comment on the activities of the Irish Management Institute under the headings shown in the next table, in which their general comments on the standard, form and structure of activities are examined.

TABLE 18. 47.   *Number of Firms Commenting on Activities of the Irish Management Institute, by Size of Firm.*

Area of Comment	Size of Firm (No. of Employees)		
	500 or more	100-499	20-99
Content of Courses	16	9	7
Location of Courses	8	11	16
Duration of Courses	13	6	8
Timing of Courses	1	—	1
Lecturers on Courses	7	3	—
Form of Activity	15	4	9
Other Aspects of Activities	9	9	5
General Comments	14	10	3
Total Firms Commenting	41	32	26
Total Firms in Sample	47	48	46

There was a general feeling that the content of courses ought to be related closely to the work of the participants. This was shown by a desire among larger companies to have the intake on courses stratified: to have courses aimed at a certain level of management and to have no one not of that level admitted. Among smaller companies there was some feeling that stratification ought to be on the basis of industry. In other words, those who commented were in favour of reasonably homogeneous groups of participants. This was about the only consistent comment on content. For the rest, the replies were characterised by an almost total lack of a common thread, every firm having some different comment to make.

There was quite widespread agreement on the desirability of short courses. Firms favoured splitting up longer courses so that participants could alternate between study and work. Smaller companies favoured the provision of advice or modified consultancy.

The comments on location for the most part came from firms outside Dublin, which would like to see more courses available locally. One or two firms mentioned in-firm training, possibly on a group basis to make it economical outside areas of industrial concentration. A very few mentioned that they were not in favour of residential courses.

Comments on lecturers came mostly from large companies. All those commenting emphasised the necessity for lecturers to have practical experience of managing. Some would prefer lecturers familiar with conditions in Ireland or with the problems of firms of similar size to those in Ireland.

The comments on the form of training activity were made mostly by large and by small firms. Several large firms thought that there should be fewer, more selective, courses. Most favoured a greater degree of participation. This took the form of suggestions that lecturers should visit firms to do in-firm training or to give advice, and that, in the actual training courses, whether central or in-firm, greater stress should be put on case-studies and discussions than on lectures. All the small companies commenting mentioned that they would like lecturers to visit them and to give advice on problems and methods, sometimes in conjunction with lectures at some convenient local centre.

With regard to general comments these, like the comments on course content, had no common theme.

Firms which were members of the Irish Management Institute but had not attended any of its courses were asked their reasons for not doing so. All were small or medium-sized companies, and most were outside Dublin. These firms all said that they had too few managers to spare the time necessary to go to Dublin to attend courses. The three member-firms with head-offices in Dublin and which had not attended courses were unusual: two had a monopoly in their line, and manufactured their products by a simple process in a number of small diversely-located plants. One sold most of its output under contract to a single company. These firms did not consider that they had much to gain from attending management training courses. The remaining firm was very specialised, being the only one in the country doing its particular type of work. The firm was interested only in courses related directly to its own type of work.

Spare-time Diploma

Finally, firms were asked whether they would be prepared to encourage their staff to use a spare-time course in management studies leading, perhaps, to a diploma. This question was asked because interviewees had suggested, when draft questionnaires were being tested, that a long spare-time course would be useful to smaller firms located away from concentrations of industry, but that potential executives would be unwilling to study unless their studies led to some sort of formal recognition. The replies to this question are analysed in this section.

TABLE 18.48. *Estimated Proportion of Firms Prepared to Encourage Use of a Spare-Time Diploma in Management Studies, by Size of Firm.*

Size of Firm (No. of Employees)	Number of Firms Included	Percentage Prepared	Percentage Not Prepared	Percentage Don't Know
500 or more	47	63.8	23.4	12.8
100-499	48	58.3	33.3	8.3
20-99	46	37.0	58.7	4.3
OVERALL		42.3	52.2	5.5

The picture shown in table 18.48. is surprising, as it might have been expected that small companies would have most to gain from such a course. The replies are analysed by location in table 18.49. (firms which changed size being excluded). It can now be seen that the low rate for small firms is caused by firms in Dublin not being prepared to encourage their staff. Firms outside Dublin are prepared to encourage staff to much the same extent, irrespective of size, and do not differ in this respect from Dublin firms with over 100 employees.

TABLE 18.49. *Proportion of Firms Prepared to Encourage Use of a Spare-Time Diploma in Management Studies, by Size and Location of Firm.*

Size of Firm (No. of Employees)	Location of Head Office	Percentage Prepared	Percentage Not Prepared or "Don't Know"
500 or More	DUBLIN	67.86	32.15
	REST OF COUNTRY	58.83	41.18
	OVERALL	64.45	35.55
100-499	DUBLIN	50.00	50.00
	REST OF COUNTRY	68.19	31.81
	OVERALL	59.10	40.91
20-99	DUBLIN	20.00	80.00
	REST OF COUNTRY	59.10	40.90
	OVERALL	40.48	59.53

Small firms which had previously attended training courses at the Irish Management Institute were markedly more willing to encourage use of a spare-time course than firms which had not previously attended. Both member-firms and firms employing some managers with training were also more willing.

Many of the firms not willing to encourage staff members to study in their spare time thought that the idea of a spare-time course was a good one, but said that they had no younger people of an educational standard to follow the course. This shows how thinly spread are human resources in small businesses.

The likely number of candidates which firms would encourage to take a course of spare-time study is estimated in table 18.50. It shows that, apart from the top stratum (in which most firms are based in Dublin), there is likely to be a much higher demand from firms outside Dublin than from firms in Dublin.

TABLE 18.50.   *Estimated Number of Individuals Whom Firms Would Encourage to Use a Spare-Time Diploma in Management Studies, by Size and Location of Firm.*

Size of Firm (No. of Employees)	Dublin	Rest of Country	Total
500 or more	104	54	158
100-499	161±75	335±159	493±171
20-99	149±145	397±186	555±242
TOTAL	415±150	786±238	1,206±294

TABLE 18.51.   *Estimated Number of Individuals Whom Firms Would Encourage to Use a Spare-Time Diploma in Management Studies, by Size of Firm and Corporate Membership of the Irish Management Institute.*

Size of Firm (No. of Employees)	Member	Non-Member
500 or more	154	4
100-499	235±120	252±122
20-99	76±64	466±247
TOTAL	466±136	723±267

Table 18.51 shows that, while demand from member-firms of the Irish Management Institute could be substantial, the greatest potential demand is likely to be from non-member companies, particularly small ones. It may be that, in practice, such firms would be less likely than member-companies to use courses if provided.

Other Facilities for Improving the Standard of Management

Since the survey was started, the Advisory Service of the Irish National Productivity Committee has been instituted to provide advice for smaller businesses. To date, over 100 assignments have been completed in small and medium-sized firms, which are defined by the service as firms with up to 200 employees.

Another method of improving managerial performance is the use of consultants. Firms were asked to what extent they employed consultants and adopted their advice (Q. 84 a & b).

TABLE 18.52.   *Estimated Percentage of Firms Using Consultants, by Size of Firm.*

Size of Firm (No. of Employees)	Total Firms in Sample	Estimated Population-Percentage Using Consultants
500 or more	47	74.5
100-499	48	37.5±12.6
20-99	46	15.2 (6.3-28.9)
TOTAL		22.0±8.2

The familiar pattern is repeated in this table. Most large firms have used consultants at some stage, a minority of medium-sized companies and very few small ones. The over-all percentage lies between 14 per cent and 30 per cent. According to the Department of Industry and Commerce, technical assistance grants for consultancy were paid to over 240 firms in the five years ended April, 1965. Most of the companies would be manufacturing companies employing over 20 people. Since the total of such firms is about 1,250, the proportion of those who received grants is about 20 per cent, which checks very well with the sample estimate.[1]

The association between several factors and the use of consultants was investigated. Size, as has been seen, exercises a marked effect, with statistically significant differences between all three groups. No association was found between a firm's use of consultants and its location, membership of the Irish Management Institute, attendance at courses, employment of trained managers, or employment of qualified managers.

Almost every company which employed consultants stated that it had adopted their recommendations. Whether or not firms succeeded completely in implementing recommendations is another matter, but at least they claim to have made the effort.

TABLE 18. 53   *Percentage of Firms Using Consultants Which Adopted Consultants' Recommendations.*

Size of Firm (No. of Employees)	Total Using Consultants	Percentage Adopting Recommendations
500 or more	35	82.8
100–499	18	83.3
20–99	7	100.0
TOTAL		95.9

The conclusion is that small firms use consultants very little, and that firms using consultants are satisfied with them.

---

1. Figures are given in chapter 16 above showing the number of clients served, and the number of assignments of different types completed, in the years 1961-1965, by members of the Management Consultants Association.

PART IV

Technical Appendices

APPENDIX A

Research Problem, Design and Execution

Background to the Project

The Irish Management Institute was founded in 1952 by a group of businessmen to raise the standard of management in Ireland.

In 1956 a committee of the Institute, examining the facilities for management training in Ireland, recommended changes to the various bodies involved—universities and vocational education authorities — and further recommended that the Institute set up a small management development unit.

This was done. In December 1960 a committee, representative of all interests, sat to review progress towards the implementation of the recommendations. This Review Committee issued a report in 1962 in which, besides recommending that the Institute's training activities and staff be expanded, it stated that a long-term national policy on education and training for management was necessary and that an investigation should be carried out to provide the facts on which this policy would be based.

It recommended[1] that ". . . the investigation . . . consist of identifying the educational needs of management in Ireland, of studying the facilities for education for management and of preparing a long-term plan for management education for the country ".

When the Institute commenced its training activities a Consultative Board, representative of industry and educational bodies, was formed to advise on the training programme. As this was the only body on which the various interests dealing with management education formally met together, its scope widened. Instead of simply advising on the Institute's work, the Board now provides a forum for discussion on the work of all the bodies represented.

It was therefore decided that the Board should make recommendations, based on this investigation, for a national policy for education and training for management.

Objectives of the Project

The project had two objectives. One was to provide the facts, based on a study of needs and facilities, which would enable the Consultative Board of the Institute to make policy recommendations to its constituent bodies. The other was to provide information on which the Institute could act in planning its own training activities, then (1962) being expanded through the recruitment of staff to specialise in production, marketing, finance and personnel management.

Resources

The Review Committee suggested that the Institute appoint a research officer to carry out the study. It was envisaged that the study would last about two years and cost about £5,000, which the Institute would provide. The Department of Industry and Commerce agreed to give £2,500 for the project. In the section below on cost it will be seen that the initial estimate was considerably exceeded.

---

1 Irish Management Institute. *Education and Training for Management: Report of the Review Committee.* Dublin: IMI, 1962 (Page 8).

The Research Problem: Need for Education and Training

Essentially the problem was to design a project to provide the information neces-sary within the resources of time, money and personnel.

As stated by the Review Committee, the study had two foci — needs and facilities. The design to study facilities presented no problems. It is outlined after the following examination of the problems involved in designing a study of needs.

The question of needs appeared to have two dimensions, one in terms of numbers of managers and one in terms of requirements to improve their performance. They are discussed below under the headings "quantitative needs" and "qualitative needs."

In what follows, a need is regarded as "a divergence between states, one present and the other future, desired or imperative ". If needs are to be measured one must be in a position to establish the present position, have a criterion of desirability and be able to recognise a divergence between the present and the desired state.

Quantitative Needs

To speak of quantitative needs it was required to make estimates of the present number of managers and of any attributes they possessed relevant to management train-ing; to compare these numbers with some desired standard; to estimate the future numbers required and to compare growth potential with growth required. Many attributes were considered relevant but, after testing initial draft questionnaires, they were reduced to functional area, level, professional education, management training, age and nationality of managers.

No published figures were available which would give this information: the only ones available are Census of Population figures showing the total number of individuals describing themselves as managers. Besides problems of definition, these figures do not give details of attributes.

It was therefore necessary, if quantitative data were required, to carry out a survey. The most convenient way to sample managers was to sample business firms and to ask questions about their managers. Because of the usual tendency to bias in postal questionnaires and the amount of detail required, it was considered that a postal questionnaire would be unsatisfactory. This was confirmed by a trial, using much shorter questionnaires, on firms which were members of the Irish Management Institute. It was decided that quantitative data were necessary and that, in order to collect them, a sample of firms would be drawn and visited to gather information on their managers, rate of growth, future supply and so on.

Here the first limitation on the scope of the project arose. It had been envisaged that the investigation would cover all sectors of the economy: industry, distribution, finance, public services. With resources limited to £5,000, two years and one research worker it was obvious that some limitation would have to be imposed. If a sample survey of the size necessary to cover all sectors were to be attempted by one individual, the time taken would be great. If the time were to be reduced by hiring interviewers of the required calibre the cost would be expanded.

As a preliminary survey of Irish Management Institute members showed that firms with 20 employees constituted a rough dividing line between firms with one, and firms with more than one manager, it was decided to confine the survey to firms employing at least 20 people.

The Central Statistics Office was then approached to see if lists of firms might be obtained. Full and up-to-date lists could be given only for transportable goods industry.

A list could be given also of distributive firms which, at the last Census of Distribution, had fifty or more employees.

It was then further decided to concentrate resources on covering one sector thoroughly. Because of its importance, its higher proportion of larger organisations, its greater interest in and support for management training activities, and the fact that full lists were available, the sector selected was transportable goods industry. It was decided also that when the study on industry was finished an attempt would be made, if possible, to survey other sectors. As the study of industry took so long to complete this was not done.

Qualitative Needs.

The problem of design on the quantitative side was simple. That on the qualitative side was not. This may not appear because of the way in which the whole research problem is here compartmented and discussed in sequence. It was not tackled in this orderly sequential way. Many methods of approach were considered more or less simultaneously, and it was only after considerable time that the following framework was evolved.

An obvious way to evaluate needs is to ask the opinions of the individuals postulated to have needs, or of others in a position to assess them. In this case it was decided to ask managers their opinions, and also to seek the opinions of management consultants who had been in a position to study them.

It was felt that this would not be sufficient. Consultants' clients might not have provided a representative sample of the population, as they might be expected to include a higher proportion of larger and more forward-looking firms. Managers' views about their own needs might have proved unreliable. Needs can be existent, perceived or expressed. It could have been that managers perceived needs which they would not express. Even more likely, especially perhaps among smaller firms not exposed to thinking on management, it was possible that managers would have existent needs which they did not perceive.

It was felt necessary to find some more objective means of discovering existent needs. Again, no published data were available, though the reports of the Government's Committee on Industrial Organisation, which were then (1962) beginning to appear, suggested by implication that the standard of management in the country was not high.

As the study was to provide facts for a national policy, consideration was given first to interpreting the need for management education in the broadest sense, as being concerned with the provision of an adequate supply of individuals capable of holding managerial positions. In other words, it was thought that the study might concern itself with the general suitability of Irishmen for management, and with what might be done to improve it if necessary.

It is accepted that in some societies cultural forces obstruct industrial development. Thought was given to the necessity of investigating the qualities of Irishmen as management material and of seeing whether any shortcomings might be explained in terms of social forces amenable to change.

Suggested criteria for evaluation of suitability were: 1) some ideal standard, 2) comparison with foreign managers, and 3) managers' own opinions. To our knowledge there is no scientifically-established set of qualities which make for managerial success. It was thought that, short of testing against an ideal list, a sample of the population might be tested for attitudes towards concepts such as authority, responsibility, etc. Using foreigners as a basis for comparison, the comparison might have been made by testing matched samples for attributes, by comparing performance or, less objectively, by asking the opinion of foreign managers with experience of working with Irishmen. Finally, Irish managers and others could be asked for their own opinions.

It was decided not to proceed with this line of approach because of the unsatisfactory nature of the criteria, the lack of trained workers to carry out tests, the expense of commissioning outside experts to do so and of testing a sample sufficiently large for valid inference.

In short, Irishmen may, for whatever reason, have qualities which make them good or bad material for management, but this study has nothing to say on the point.

Having rejected this approach, a different one was suggested. In an appendix[1] to the Report of the Review Committee which recommended the investigation, an outline was suggested of the form this might take. One suggestion was that managerial jobs in various sectors might be analysed to see what elements they contained.

Few studies have been made of what managers actually do and there is no doubt that, in evolving a scheme to train people for managerial jobs, a study of what those jobs are would be useful. Insofar as training is concerned with those not yet in managerial positions and who might therefore be presumed to possess little of the relevant knowledge, such an investigation of job-content would be almost sufficient. To assess the training needs of those already filling the jobs it would further be necessary to evaluate their performance: a man already performing a job optimally cannot need training for that job.

It was decided not to attempt a study of managers' jobs because of the lack of resources and trained workers. However one may attempt to circumvent it, for instance by using diaries, a study of managers at work involves observation. The difficulty of the length of time necessary for meaningful observation may be got over by activity sampling, but the process of observation itself is not simple and, unless an individual is trained in many backgrounds, may necessitate a team approach. One may look at behaviour, but to describe it, to categorise it, requires some frame of reference against which its significance may be judged. It is not unlikely that individuals trained in different disciplines would differ in their observations: behaviour significant to one observer might not appear so to another, and the same acts might be categorised in different ways. A single research worker, trained as an economist, could not do justice to such a task. A further difficulty was the size of the sample necessary for valid inference about different sizes and sectors of business, areas and levels of management. Such a study was far beyond the available resources.

A new suggestion was that, instead of studying job-content and measuring individuals' performance in their jobs, a sample of managers should be drawn, job-specifications written for their jobs, and the individuals measured against the specifications. Although this method was rejected it contributed a useful slant on the problem.

It was rejected because of lack of trained workers to develop specifications and test against them and because it seemed that it would be costly to examine a sufficiently large sample of individuals. A further objection was that by selecting individuals some areas of weakness in firms might be overlooked. It seemed possible that in some firms managerial tasks were being neglected, not being carried out by any individual, and that by focusing on individuals these tasks would be ignored. This argument, taken with the difficulty of studying individuals and with another fact, gave a new slant to thinking. The other fact was that, in considering the problems of sampling for quantitative data,

1 *ibid.*, page 41.

the primary sampling unit was to be the firm rather than the individual manager. These strands came together to suggest that, in investigating needs for management education and training, the firm might be a more easily studied unit than the individual.

Before going on to discuss this approach, a word should be said on a further viewpoint which should have had its genesis in the suggestion of testing against job-specifications. This viewpoint contributed much to the eventual design. In fact it was arrived at only after several attempts at the problem of evaluating firms' training needs, but it is discussed here as it is obvious that it would have arisen if the implications of testing individuals against job specifications had been worked out.

The viewpoint concerns the suitability of measures of performance as indicators of need for training. It is understandable that an attempt to investigate training needs should focus on performance: managers are concerned with performance and undergo training because they believe they can thereby improve it. But to pinpoint weaknesses, measures of performance would have to be complex and precise. It would not be sufficient to know that, measured by some criterion, an individual's overall performance was inadequate. Specific areas of inadequacy would have to be isolated if the sort of training required were to be known. Such measures of performance might be difficult to construct (if not impossible without an observational study of individuals' jobs) and to apply. Furthermore, performance depends on the total situation and not only on the individual's knowledge and skill, which are the elements on which training works. Consequently, a highly-skilled individual in a poor situation, or one in which he was prevented from bringing his skill to bear, might score very badly on a measure of performance which did not consider his work situation. Since training is concerned with knowledge and skill it seemed better, in assessing training needs, to investigate deficiencies in knowledge and skill rather than in performance, while realising that the justification for training is the belief that it can increase skill and thereby improve performance.

This re-orientation would have taken place sooner had the mechanics of testing against job specifications been thought of, as in such testing the focus would be on the qualifications, knowledge and skill of the individual rather than on measuring his performance.

After encountering difficulties in formulating a design to study individuals some thought was given to studying firms. It seemed a fair assumption that what happened in firms would reflect the standard of their management, assuming that nothing prevented managers from exercising their abilities.

At this stage attention was still on measures of performance as indicators of training needs. In fact it was the difficulty of finding satisfactory measures to indicate the standard of management in firms which led to the abandonment of this approach. It was thought conceivable that in a country like Ireland, which was (in 1962) highly protectionist, the more common measures of performance focusing on financial results might reflect elements in a firm's total situation other than the ability of its management, and the task of evolving measures which would discount the influence of such elements seemed likely to be formidable in the context of a project intended to last two years.

From this stage onward, attention was directed to the possibility of evaluating the training needs of a firm's management in terms other than performance.

If the focus was to be on the qualities a manager brought to his job, it seemed desirable to analyse these qualities. A tentative analysis was into *personal qualities*, some not amenable to change, e.g. intelligence, others formed by environmental forces, *technical knowledge* interpreted broadly as knowledge of the products, processes, procedures and environment of the organisation, and *managerial skill* of two kinds, one relating to the disciplines and techniques relevant to decision-making, the other related to decision-implementation.

It is not suggested that these are mutually exclusive—personal qualities will obviously impinge on skill in both making and implementing decisions—but it was thought that the division was useful in helping to formulate an attack on the problem.

For reasons discussed earlier—mainly lack of satisfactory criteria and methods of evaluation—it was decided not to attempt to assess deficiencies in personal qualities. Similarly, because of the number and variety of industries, any effort to measure technical competence was ruled out. It was decided to concentrate on management skills.

It was considered useful to regard managerial work as the processes involved in making, implementing and evaluating decisions about the allocation of resources in the pursuit of goals. While it was found useful to consider decision-making and implementation separately, this was not to suggest that they are separate activities carried out in isolation, or to postulate a form of managerial behaviour in which decisions are made by one individual who then manipulates others to implement them. It was simply a recognition that the job of making decisions and building decision systems could conceivably be carried on in isolation relying on skills and disciplines of a largely intellectual nature which may be imparted by a simple transfer of knowledge, whereas decision implementation implies interaction with others, usually including some emotional involvement and consequently calling for skills whose learning may also involve the emotions. From a research point of view the division seemed useful, as the interpersonal aspect might be expected to prove more difficult to study than the other.

The question then arose of how deficiencies in these sorts of management skills could be measured by focusing on the firm. Performance measurements, if sufficiently refined and comprehensive, might have indicated weaknesses but were rejected for the reasons given earlier. It was then thought that evidence of deficiencies might be provided by the occurrence of problems or occasions when actuality did not match expectations. Consideration was given to interviewing managers and probing their perceptions of problem areas to see how adequately perception matched reality, then choosing a sub-sample of firms to be studied in depth, using observational methods and interviews over some period of time. However, it was thought unlikely that this method would provide evidence on the problems—and thus, inferentially, on the training needs—of a number of firms sufficiently large for valid generalisation, without resources very much larger than those available.

A new and final slant was given to the method of approach by the realisation that, at a given point in time, a unit which was equipped with all that education and training could provide and which still faced difficulties, could not be helped by training until the body of knowledge on which that training was based was expanded. At that point a unit already in possession of the available complement of knowledge and skills could not be said to have further need of training as it then existed. It seemed that the problem might be approached from the supply rather than from the demand side, by finding to what extent firms possessed the available supply of disciplines and techniques of management. It was to be taken as desirable that firms should possess the available body of relevant knowledge, on the assumption that this would contribute to better performance. Need for training was to be measured by the extent to which they did not possess it, on the assumption that skill could be imparted by education and training. No attempt would be made to test the assumption of association between training, possession of skill and improved performance because of the difficulty of measuring performance, and because it was considered unnecessary to demonstrate that the development of managerial technique to even its present state has produced better performance, or to demonstrate that some skill can be imparted by education and training.

In taking the available body of knowledge as a standard it was recognised that it was not ideal to have, for a measuring rod, something subject to change and not proved internally consistent. The fact that it is subject to change lays it open to the objection that, in using it as a standard by which to judge needs, it is implied that firms should first equip themselves with the present body of knowledge. It is conceivable that new developments could make this outmoded and that it would be better for firms to move from their present state to some future state without first going through the process of assimilating the present body. This argument is not crucial. So long as it is borne in mind that the solution may not be to advocate such assimilation, it appears useful to establish what the present state of practice is. The fact that management knowledge is not a fully-developed, internally consistent datum presented difficulties which are discussed below.

The extent to which firms were in possession of the available knowledge could, it was thought, be discovered by the extent to which they used it. The assumption that use and possession of skill are coterminous needs elaboration. It is possible for firms to have individuals possessing skills but not allowed to practise them. Such a situation could not easily be uncovered, so it was decided to ignore this objection. Conversely it could happen that firms were using techniques installed by consultants but did not have the skill to continue doing so.

It was considered that the use by a firm of management techniques could be discovered by asking questions. Two objections could be raised here: first, that interviewees might claim to use techniques when they did not do so; second, that the skill with which techniques were used would not be assessed. It was felt that the first objection could be overcome by some probing at the interview and also by the use of cross-checks in the questionnaire.

Some of these objections work in opposite directions, but the expected net effect would probably be to overstate the degree of genuine use of technique and thus of skill. Having carried out the project it may be said that the replies reflect quite well the real level of expertise—managers were uniformly straightforward in their replies—and, in any event, the main conclusions would not be altered by some overstatement. When only 20 to 30 per cent of firms claim to use a certain technique the task of getting it used is already large, even though the true proportion may be lower.

It was proposed, then, to assess the need for management education and training by asking to what extent firms used relevant techniques of management. Since there may be some objection to this concentration on technique, it is discussed here in terms of the distinction proposed earlier between decision-making and implementation.

In every art or science training and skill manifest themselves in the use of a frame of reference and selection of a method of attack when faced with a problem. At the point where task and training meet, training brings technique to bear in carrying out the task. Techniques may be of a high or a low order of difficulty, involving simple instruction or many years' study of basic disciplines. Professional education and training may be said to be concerned with providing the background and tools which will allow technique to be brought to bear on tasks. When speaking of technique in this volume, what is meant is the use of professional skill when faced by a task, not technique as a set of procedures grafted on to inadequately prepared human material.

Much work on management has been concerned with tools for making decisions of higher quality. Most of these are techniques or routines of measurement, information and analysis. Their use has usually been attended by improved results (measured by some criteria) and the conditions in which their use is possible are usually rather easily recognisable. Hence the possibility, appropriateness, and extent of use of such techniques in a firm may be investigated by simple questioning.

On the other hand, the interpersonal aspect of managerial work is not easily examined. Humans are multi-dimensional beings—physical, psychical, social, cultural. Further, they possess capacity to adapt and to make decisions. The literature reporting work on this aspect of management shows no promise of a simple universally applicable set of rules or techniques whose appropriateness and use could be established by questioning. Undoubtedly rules must be formulated if management is to claim to be a science or even a developed art, but they are not likely to be simple. It is probable that appropriate actions will depend on the psychological make-up of the individuals concerned, on the social and cultural environment and on the pressures on the organisation. Because behavioural science research has not evolved specifications of conditions and of behaviour appropriate to them (although progress has been made), it was decided to omit this whole aspect of management from the study. To repeat, the entire area of interpersonal relations was excluded because, while the existence of a certain style could be established, the appropriateness of that style to the conditions of the firm could be investigated only with difficulty and expense, even if universally agreed criteria of appropriateness existed. This total omission is now regretted. A question-and-answer technique would have been adequate to establish the style of relations in a firm, attitudes towards other possible styles and knowledge of research and writings on the subject. Such answers, though not conclusive, would have been illuminating. However, it can be said that relations in Irish firms are, for the most part, not influenced by behavioural science findings. The standard of knowledge of decision-making techniques is limited, so there is little reason to believe that knowledge of behavioural science is widespread. If effective behaviour is the norm this is due to accident rather than to design, to commonsense rather than to science.

An attempt was to be made, then, to assess the need for management training by asking about the use of managerial techniques bearing on decision-making. Because businesses are still to a large extent organised in this way (and keeping in mind the viewpoint of the Irish Management Institute which intended to recruit staff to specialise in these areas) it was decided to examine needs under the headings marketing, production, finance and personnel (personnel was not taken as meaning interpersonal relations, but those activities usually regarded as within the province of a personnel department: selection, training, remuneration-structure, physical conditions, amenities and welfare).

Each of these areas was broken down into constituent parts in order further to pinpoint needs, e.g. marketing was subdivided into advertising, pricing, sales force management, physical distribution, etc. In each activity, relevant routines and techniques of measurement, information-collection and choice were specified. However, it was not considered sufficient to ask: "do you engage in activity x?", e.g. advertising, or "what factors did you consider when making decision y?", e.g. on pricing. Firms differ greatly in their complexity and therefore in the scope and intensity of their use of techniques. For instance, a small creamery has a daily milk delivery which it must take and which it processes on single-purpose machinery set up in line to produce a single product. A large batch-engineering works may have hundreds of parts going through its plant on multi-purpose machines with competition for capacity. The first firm can hardly be said to have a production planning and control problem at all, whereas in the second case the problems are so complex that even so powerful a decision tool as operations research harnessed to computers may be unable to provide an optimal solution.

If comprehensive questions were to be asked, the conditions governing the scope for use of techniques would have to be isolated and firms asked if these conditions existed before their use of technique could be judged. It was felt that such classification of conditions would be doubly useful, first in influencing conclusions about adequacy of technique, second from an operational viewpoint in establishing the likely market among practising managers for courses on specific activities. For instance, if it were discovered that most firms had very simple conditions governing production, courses on complex methods of production control would not be demanded by practising managers, though this would not be a reason for future production managers not to include it in their studies.

Comprehensive questionnaires were evolved dealing with the conditions for the use of, and the actual use of, routines and techniques in each area and activity. Because of the length of the questionnaires it would have been impossible to analyse each question separately. It was therefore hoped to obtain expert help to assess the answers and to assign a judgment or score to the total activity on the basis of the replies, and then to carry out a statistical analysis on the scores.

This intention broke down for two reasons. First, the questionnaires were too lengthy to administer to a single individual, and testing proved that it was rarely possible to contact all the necessary individuals on a single visit. Second, it became obvious that it would be impossible to get people with the time to evaluate the replies.

Testing showed that the interview operation would have to be complete in itself: nothing sent in advance or left behind was likely to be answered. Furthermore, interviews could be scheduled with only one individual if the time-span was not to get completely out of control. Finally, it was found that interviews should not last much longer than $1\frac{1}{2}$ hours.

These results meant that the questionnaire had to be scaled down drastically. It was decided in each of the areas of marketing, production and finance to choose a few questions on techniques of almost universal applicability as indicators of the level of sophistication of management. The questions related mainly to planning and control information routines. It was felt that these could give a fair indication of the level in each area, though they would be almost powerless to discriminate between areas, because planning and control tend to be integrated: either a firm plans and controls all areas or none. Some questions having nothing to do with planning and control were therefore put in to give some means of discrimination.

Personnel management was less satisfactory to handle because the activities falling in this area tend to be diffuse and, short of asking questions on each activity—which would leave the questionnaire almost as long as the original—would be difficult to cover. One or two questions were again selected, but it is felt that this area was not treated really satisfactorily.

Testing showed the final design to be feasible, and experience proved it adequate as an indicator of a firm's level of advancement.

Finally, it should be mentioned that firms function within a structure of size, capital, product and location. This structure may inhibit performance and negative efforts to improve through training: there may be little point in training an individual to be a better small-business manager if small businesses are disappearing. In 1962-63, when the project was designed, reports of the Committee on Industrial Organisation frequently suggested that firms should consider amalgamation to reap the benefit of economies of scale. Consideration was therefore given to the necessity for a study of the development of the structure of Irish industry. This was regarded as too ambitious, but in early questionnaires firms were asked of any contemplated changes in structure. Testing showed that it was too early for them to answer, as the idea was new and not always accepted. The questions were therefore dropped. In framing recommendations the present structure should not be regarded as immutable, but this may not be important as structural deficiencies may be symptoms rather than causes of poor management.

The Research Problem: Facilities for Education and Training

Decisions on the scope of the investigation on needs affected that on facilities. For instance, the decision not to investigate personal qualities meant that it was not considered necessary to study in detail the education of young people at school. The facilities to be investigated were therefore confined to post-school education and training, with school facilities to be examined only insofar as recommendations for post-school training would have implications for schools.

Adequacy of facilities also has both quantitative and qualitative aspects.

Quantitative.

Facilities had to be examined to see if they were adequate to produce the numbers required to meet needs, and also to see if they were adequate to cater for the numbers who would demand to use them. They were to be evaluated by visiting the institutions concerned to collect information on trends in student numbers, on physical equipment, numbers of staff and so on.

Qualitative.

A crucial factor is the quality of teaching provided. Important here are objectives, staff-student ratios, staff qualifications, curricula, etc. Indeed even quantitative adequacy cannot be evaluated without some qualitative criteria, e.g. as to desirable staff ratios.

Many standards of assessment could be used here: for instance, how far the present body of knowledge is made available, or how facilities compare with those abroad, or how they compare with managers' opinions, or with the opinions of those who have used them, or how far they cover the content of managerial jobs, or how likely they seem to remedy deficiencies shown up in the use of management techniques.

The process of assessment is inextricable from that of recommendation. It was considered to be the job of the Consultative Board to form judgements, and that this report should confine itself to providing facts on staff ratios, objectives of courses, details of curricula, etc. These were to be obtained by interviews with those providing the facilities. Further relevant information would be the opinions of managers on facilities, and their past and projected future use of facilities. These data were to be obtained by interviews when visiting firms, and by analysis of institutional records. No definite decision was taken on studying facilities available abroad or on obtaining the opinions of past users of facilities.

Research Design

The final design was to carry out interviews with the chief executives of a sample of industrial firms employing 20 or more people and, in the interview, to find:

1. The number of managers and their various attributes.
2. Numerical requirements due to shortages, growth, retirements, death.
3. Chief executives' opinions on their firms' training needs.
4. The extent to which firms used techniques of management.
5. Chief executives' opinions on, and estimates of likely use of, available and suggested future facilities.

In addition, the opinions of management consultants would be sought on needs, the internal records of training organisations analysed to show past use-pattern, and institutions visited for information on physical facilities, staff, objectives, curricula, student body, etc.

An open mind was kept on the possibility of supplementing this design by studying other sectors of the economy, by conducting a postal census, by observing a small sub-sample of firms, by studying facilities abroad and by conducting an opinion-survey among graduates, etc. However, the execution and analysis of the sample survey used so much time and resources that these supplementary sections were not carried out.

It was realised that, due to the successive limitations discussed above, the final design was not a complete fulfilment of the Review Committee's brief. The limitations were imposed by the desire to keep the project within the resources available, yet even the rather modest final design took four years and cost about £14,000 to complete— more than double the time and cost originally intended.

Population Sampled, Sampling Unit and Frame

Having decided on a sample survey, the population to be surveyed had to be defined and the survey method specified.

Population

The most comprehensive inquiry into occupational and industrial employment is the decennial Census of Population. When planning the project the results of the 1961 Census were not available, but as they have since been published the results are shown in table A.I.

In column 1 it can be seen that the total work force is slightly over one million. The Census of Population gives some data on the number of employers and managers but, apart from definitional problems, there are considerable problems in reconciling various figures.

It was decided to conserve resources and not to attempt to cover all branches of economic activity. The first decision was to exclude agriculture and all activities of central and local government, the latter because of the existence of the Institute of Public Administration. Column 2 of table A.I. shows that this division excluded over half the total work force.

As it was obvious that managers could be sampled effectively only by sampling firms, the Central Statistics Office was approached for lists of firms in all private economic activity. The Central Statistics Office conducts two censuses of business, the Census of Industrial Production which is carried out continually, and the Census of Distribution last carried out in 1956 (a fresh Census is being carried out in 1966). The former covers industry as defined in table A.I., but includes also laundries, which in the Census of Population are counted under "personal service" while it excludes those working in very small units of under 3 people. The Census of Distribution covers commerce as defined in table A.I., and also some activities included under "personal service" and "entertainment."

TABLE A. 1.   *Total at Work in 1961, by Sector of Economy.*

Sector of Economy			Total at Work	Total in Private Business Activity[1]	Number of Establishments with 20 or more employees	Number Employed in Establishments >20
Industry	Transportable goods	Agriculture	376,272	—	n.a.	
		Fishing	2,460		n.a.	
		Mining, etc.	9,640	9,640		
		Manufacturing	179,436	179,436	1,299[2]	126,878[2]
	Service	Building and Construction	59,587	38,635	n.a.	
		Electricity, gas and water	10,172	9,651	n.a.	
		Commerce	143,195	143,195	679[3]	33,650[3]
		Insurance, Banking etc.	14,239	14,239	n.a.	
		Transport, Communications and Storage	54,167	35,637	n.a.	
		Public Administration & Defence	40,580	—	—	
		Professions	85,952	19,951	n.a.	
		Personal Service	63,314	30,087	n.a.	
		Entertainment and Sport	10,986	10,986	n.a.	
		Other	2,539	—	—	
		Total	1,052,539	491,447		

n.a. means " not available ".
1.   Refers to economic activity outside agriculture, carried on by private firms or individuals, or by State-financed bu autonomous enterprises. Excludes non-agricultural activity by central or local government.
2.   In 1958, by respondents to the Census of Industrial Production.
3.   In 1956, by respondents to the Census of Distribution.
Source: Col. 1 & 2.   *Census of Population 1961*. Dublin: The Stationery Office, 1964, Vol. IV (tables 1 and 9)
       Col. 3 & 4.   *Irish Trade Journal and Statistics Bulletin*. Dublin: Central Statistics Office, Supplement t December 1962 issue.
       Census of Distribution 1956-1959. Dublin: The Stationery Office, 1962 (tables 6 and 59).

     The Central Statistics Office was not in a position to provide complete and up-to-date lists especially when it was decided, again in order to conserve resources, to exclude from the survey firms employing 20 or fewer people. As the Census of Distribution had not been analysed on punched-cards the task of identifying the firms employing 20 or more from over 30,000 original returns was too great. Fortunately an analysis had been made of firms in the transportable-goods section of the Census of Industrial Production. The service industry and building section had not been analysed: it was felt that the lists, particularly of building firms, were unsatisfactory, and again it would have been troublesome to refer back to the original returns.

     It was possible therefore to get complete lists of establishments employing over 20 people only for the transportable-goods section of industry.

     An attempt was made to construct lists for the other sectors, i.e. service industry, distribution, and the sectors in table A.I. not covered by either the Census of Industrial Production or the Census of Distribution. This was done by listing their activities, finding from trade directories any relevant trade associations, and writing to them. A list of activities and associations is given in appendix D. Most associations co-operated, but it was soon obvious that the coverage was inadequate and unrepresentative, being biased towards the larger firms.

The attempt was abandoned and the decision made to confine the inquiry to firms in transportable-goods industry employing 20 or more people. The present and projected importance of industry, particularly of establisments employing over 20 people, is shown in tables A.II. and A.III.

TABLE A. II.   *Output and Employment* 1960-1970, *by Sector of Economy.*

Sector of Economy	Sectoral Products in 1960 at 1960 current prices	Sectoral Products in 1970 at 1960 prices
	£m.	£m.
Agriculture, forestry, fishing	139.5	186.0
Industry	167.7	330.0
Other domestic	244.4	349.0
Net foreign income	33.7	18.0
G.N.P. at factor cost	585.3	883.0
	Employment in 1960 (000)	Employment in 1970 (000)
Agriculture	390	324
Industry	248	334
Other domestic	417	475
Total	1,055	1,133

Source: *Second Programme for Economic Expansion, Part II.* Dublin: The Stationery Office, 1963, pp. 298, 299.

TABLE A.III.   *Output in Industry and Commerce, by Size of Firm* (£000).

Sector	Total Net Output or Sales	Net Output or Sales by Establishments employing 20 or more
Manufacturing Industry	103,260[1]	94,396
Commerce:		
Retail Distribution	243,351[2]	54,946
Wholesale Distribution	225,837[2]	120,353

1. Net Output, year 1958, by respondents to Census of Industrial Production.
2. Sales, year 1956, by respondents to Census of Distribution.
Source: *Irish Trade Journal and Statistical Bulletin.* Dublin: Central Statistics Office, Supplement to December 1962 issue.
   Census of Distribution 1956-59. Dublin: The Stationery Office, 1962 (tables 6 and 59.)

Sampling Unit

The Central Statistics Office collects information in its business censuses from the individual *establishment,* that is, the individual factory or, if two industries are carried on under the one roof, part of a factory. A firm which has several factories or is in several industries appears several times in a list of establishments.

From the point of view of a sample enquiry into management, the establishment is not a convenient unit. Apart from its artificiality, serious problems of double-counting would arise in grossing-up due to the number of managers common to several establishments, e.g. office managers, sales managers, etc. A better unit is the firm or legal entity. Even this is not perfect because of the existence of groups of firms sharing common managers. It was felt that these would be insufficiently numerous to justify efforts to get the information necessary to group firms in this way.

The sampling unit adopted was the individual firm, i.e. organisation having a separate legal identity. Firms which were engaged in activities outside industry but which made returns to the Census of Industrial Production were included, but only that section making returns to the Census was investigated.

The Frame

The Central Statistics Office provided two basic lists. One was of *concerns* (i.e. firms) which employed 100 or more people. The other was a list of *establishments* (i.e. individual factories) marked to show those employing 20 or more people. Establishments with the same name were amalgamated to form a new list of firms. It is possible that some firms with several establishments each employing under 20 but totalling to over 20 were excluded, but this is unlikely to have been common. Strictly speaking the frame was a list of firms each of which had at least one establishment employing 20 or more people.

Firms in the Shannon industrial zone were excluded from this frame, as it was felt they would be untypical and would require a separate study. These firms were all established within the past few years in response to efforts by the Government to develop an industrial estate at Shannon which would generate freight-traffic through the airport. They are all subsidiaries of foreign companies making, for export, products new to this country.

The Central Statistics Office stratified their list of concerns into those employing 500 or more and those employing 100 to 499, and their list of establishments into those employing 20 or more, and those employing under 20. From these an alphabetical list of firms stratified into those employing 500 or more, 100 to 499, and 20 to 99 was prepared for sampling.

The list was provided in mid-1963, and was as complete as possible a coverage of firms employing 20 or more people. It was probably a little out of date by the time the fieldwork commenced in 1964—10 firms out of a total sample of 141 were found to have moved from their assigned size-groups—but unlikely to have altered so considerably as to invalidate the main estimates and conclusions.

Sample Design

In designing a sample investigation of a specified population, several decisions must be made. 1. What type of sample to use; 2. What size sample to draw; 3. If a stratified sample is to be used, how to divide the population into strata: (a) on what basis to stratify, (b) where to draw the dividing lines; and how to allocate the sample to the strata.

Type of Sample

It was decided to sample a population of firms to estimate the total number of managers, various attributes of managers and various attributes of firms. Nothing but a strictly probabilistic sample was considered.

TABLE A.IV. *Total and Average Employed, by Size of Establishment, in Manufacturing Industry.*

Size of Establishment	Number of Establishments		Total Employed		Average per Establishment.
Under 5	480		1,477		
5– 9	681		4,615		
10– 14	395		4,658		
15– 19	251	1,807	4,220	14,970	8.3
20– 29	321		7,756		
30– 49	383		14,746		
50– 99	291	995	20,624	43,126	43.3
100–199	161		21,732		
200–299	112	273	32,435	54,167	198.0
500 & over	31	31	29,585	29,585	954.4
TOTAL		3,106		141,848	45.6

Source: *Irish Trade Journal and Statistical Bulletin.* Dublin: Central Statistics Office. Supplement to December 1962 issue.

It is obvious from the table above that the material being sampled was highly variable, and that it might be expected that accuracy would be improved by stratification. It was therefore decided to use a stratified sample.

So far as attributes of managers were concerned, the sample was a stratified one-stage cluster sample, with complete enumeration of each cluster. So far as total managers and attributes of firms were concerned it was a stratified random sample.

Size of Sample

In every sample inquiry it is desired to minimise the uncertainty due to sampling, as measured by the standard errors of the statistics calculated, within the limits of available resources, i.e. to find an acceptable balance between precision, which is improved by an increase in sample size, and cost.

The size of sample is calculated by substituting in the appropriate confidence limit formulae a value of n (sample size) which will result in confidence limits of the width considered acceptable. As the variance of the characteristic under review is usually unknown it is necessary to substitute in the formula an estimate of the variance, which may be arrived at in a variety of ways (see Cochran (1)).

In the present survey it was decided that, as the interviewing was to be carried out by one individual, a sample of about 150 would balance the time available against the precision acceptable. This was estimated by assuming the proportion of firms possessing any attribute as 50 per cent and substituting this value in the formulae[1].

Inquiries were made about the possibility of obtaining help with the interviewing. As the questionnaires were long and complex and, while structured, might be expected to give rise to discussion on matters connected with all aspects of management, highly-

1 Because a proportion of 50 per cent gives wider confidence limits than any other. Therefore a sample giving acceptable limits for a proportion of 50 per cent will give acceptable limits for any other proportion.

skilled interviewers would have been necessary. Firms in industrial market research were approached. The cost of retaining them to cover a sample of the size necessary to effect a worthwhile improvement over one of 150 firms was too great in the context of the resources within which the project was being planned. In the context of the final cost of the project, the additional cost of the extra interviews would not have been so large proportionally and, if the final cost had been known at the time the decision on sample-size was taken, a larger sample might have been used, both to increase the precision of estimates and to increase the power of statistical tests, particularly in the lowest size stratum.

Method of Stratification.

BASIS OF STRATIFICATION. Obviously the best basis on which to stratify, insofar as it was wished to stratify by size of unit, would have been the number of managers per firm. As this was not known, the next best basis was the number of total employees per firm. It was decided not to stratify by size on the basis of turnover or capital employed as this information would not be provided. (Number of employees, turnover and capital are in any event closely related: there are few capital-intensive, low-employee firms in Ireland). It was also decided not to stratify on any basis other than size, e.g. by industry, as the sample was too small.

NUMBER AND LOCATION OF STRATA. The whole question of stratified sampling is discussed in Hansen, Hurwitz & Madow (2), chapter 5, section 6 to end. In section 11 some desirable rules are given for locating strata for an optimal allocation when stratifying by size.

In this case no such rules were followed. Because only a relatively small sample could be afforded, not more than three strata were feasible. These three would have to be selected from among those in table A.IV. It seemed reasonable on common-sense grounds to choose 100 and 500 employees as the dividing lines.

ALLOCATION OF SAMPLE TO STRATA. The final problem was the allocation of the sample of approximately 150 firms to the three selected strata. Supposing costs may be ignored and sampling is only to estimate a single characteristic, e.g. number of managers per firm, the allocation which will result in minimum variance, i.e. will give the narrowest confidence limits, occurs when the sample is divided over strata proportionately to the standard deviations of the characteristic in the separate strata. (For an illustration see Snedecor (3).) When the strata standard deviations are unknown each may be estimated in the same way as the overall standard deviation, as described in reference (1). However, it is often the case that the ratio of the standard deviations is approximately the same as the ratio of some other quantity. In this case it was assumed that the ratio of average number of employees per establishment (or total employees in the strata, which is the same thing) in table A.IV., would reflect the standard deviation of managers per firm, and it was decided to see what allocation this implied.

TABLE A.V.   *Trial Allocation of Firms to Strata, Proportional to Total Employees in Stratum.*

Size of Firm (No. of Employees)	Number of Firms	Total Employees in Stratum[1]	Allocation of Sample
20–99	946	43,126	51
100–499	256	54,167	64
500 or More	47	29,585	35
Total	1,249	126,878	150

1 From table A.IV. the figures given are approximate because they refer to employees in the stratum of *establishments* employing 20-99 etc., not *firms* employing 20-99, etc.

It was decided, in view of the small number of firms, that the 500 + stratum would have to be enumerated completely, and that the samples in the other strata should be reduced accordingly.

In fact sampling was not for one characteristic but for several, and among the most important requirements was to make comparisons between the size-strata. In that case it is desirable to have somewhat the same numbers in each stratum. It was noticed that taking the convenient sampling fractions of 1/5th and 1/20th from the 100 to 499 and 20 to 99 strata respectively would result in samples of 51 and 46. (These fractions would allow rapid preliminary calculations, but it should be mentioned that in the actual calculations the exact raising factor $\dfrac{N_h}{n_h}$ was used, where N_h=total firms in stratum, e.g. 946, n_h=number of respondents to survey in stratum). The actual allocation used and the response achieved is shown below.

TABLE A.VI. *Actual Allocation of Firms to Strata.*

Size of Firm (No. of Employees)	Number of Firms	Allocation.	Number Responding.
20–99	946	47	46
100–499	256	51	48
500 or More	47	47	**47**
	1,249	145	141

It is now known as a result of the survey that, insofar as the only concern was to estimate the average number of managers per firm, the actual allocation departed widely from the optimal (ignoring cost) as the following shows.

TABLE A.VII. *Optimal Allocation to Strata for Estimating the Average Number of Managers per Firm.*

Size of Firm (No. of Employees)	Number of Firms, N_h	Standard Deviation[1] σ_h	Allocation $n_h = n \times \dfrac{N_h \sigma_h}{\Sigma N_h \sigma_h}$
20–99	946	3.27	91
100–499	256	4.38	34
500 or More	47	18.19	25
	1,249		150

1 Calculated from those firms which had not changed size between the time lists were compiled and interviews were carried out.

In future surveys it would be desirable to expand the total sample size so as to increase the coverage of the 20 to 99 stratum, especially in view of the low average number of managers per firm. This means that, to include sufficient managers to improve the power of statistical tests, a sample of fair sized is called for.

In order to help in planning future surveys, especially if it is desired to locate the strata differently, a list is given in appendix E showing the number of employees and the number of managers in each sampled firm which had not changed size between the time the lists were compiled and the time the interviews were carried out. It is obvious that there is a considerable amount of rounding in the figures for total employees as given by the chief executives interviewed, but this does not invalidate their usefulness.

By using these data to provide estimates of strata variances, and by using information on proportions (to be found in the text) and on the cost of the present survey, it will be possible in future to plan more efficient surveys, not having to rely, as in the present case, on a rather arbitrary sample size allocated without much information. For a discussion see Cochran, chapter 5, sections 5.5, 5.9 and 5.12.

Cochran (4) shows how to calculate from a sample the gain due to stratification. Following his method it was found that an estimate of the sampling variance of the overall mean number of managers per firm in a simple random sample of size 141 was 0.4958. The variance using the stratified sample was 0.1160. Use of a stratified random sample therefore reduced the sampling variation to less than a quarter of what it would have been using a simple sample: in other words precision was increased more than four-fold.

Sample Selection and Coverage

Each stratum was sampled randomly. The firms in each stratum were listed alphabetically to provide a convenient permanent record and the required number of firms was selected, using an excerpt from the Rand Corporation's tables of random numbers, and rejecting any number which appeared more than once; i.e. the sampling was without replacement.

Randomness is no guarantee of representativeness. A sample selected at random may not reproduce relevant characteristics of the population. The sample was therefore compared with the population to see how well it reflected the distribution of factors which might be expected to influence management structure and practice. The factors were industrial classification, location, and membership of the Irish Management Institute.

It was not necessary to examine the 500+ stratum because the entire population was investigated. Neither was it necessary to consider size: all overall population estimates are sums of the separate strata estimates weighted by the reciprocals of the sampling fractions, so that little bias could arise on that score.[1]

Industry

Table A.VIII. shows the position. Firms were assigned to an industry on the basis of what was thought to be their main activity. The figures are therefore approximate.

Because of the condition on expected values the chi-square test for goodness of fit cannot be used (see statistical note 2.3 below), but it is obvious that the fit in the 20 to 99 group is near perfect. That in the 100 to 499 group is less perfect but is also good.

Location

Firms were assigned to locations on the basis of the location of their head office,

---

1 In fact, within each of the two lower strata, there is evidence that the sample had an upward bias. The firms in the sample appear to have been somewhat larger than the average for these strata.

defined as the place where their chief executive normally worked. Those with establishments in more than one location were telephoned to find at which place this was. The fit in the case of location is almost perfect.

TABLE A.VIII. *Comparison of Industrial Classification of Sample with Population, by Size of Firm.*

Industry	Number of Firms in Population Size		Expected Number in Sample[1] Size		Actual Number in Sample Size		Number of Respondents Size	
	20-99	100-499	20-99	100-499	20-99	100-499	20-99	100-499
Mining, Quarrying & Turf	26	6	1	1	0	3	0	3
Food	202	54	10	11	11	18	11	18
Drink & Tobacco	28	14	1	3	3	4	3	4
Textiles & Hosiery	85	46	4	9	2	5	2	5
Clothing & Footwear	174	53	9	11	8	8	8	7
Wood & Furniture	88	7	4	1	3	2	3	2
Paper & Printing	90	19	4	4	4	1	4	1
Chemicals, Fertilisers, etc.	47	9	2	2	1	1	1	1
Glass & Clay Products	26	7	1	1	2	1	2	1
Metals & Engineering	119	34	6	7	6	7	5	5
Miscellaneous	61	7	3	1	7	1	7	1
Total	946	256						

1 To nearest integral value, based on sampling fraction of 1/20 for 20-99, 1/5 for 100-499.

TABLE A. IX. *Comparison of Location of Sample with Population, by Size of Firm.*

	Size-Group 20-99		Size-Group 100-499	
	Dublin	Rest of Country	Dublin	Rest of Country
No. of Firms in Population	490	456	124	132
Expected Number in Sample	24	23	25	26
Actual Sample	24	23	26	25
Number of Respondents	23	23	24	24

Membership of Irish Management Institute

Table A.X. shows that the actual sample reflected very well the membership status of the population at the time the sample was drawn (late 1963).

TABLE A. X. *Comparison of Sample with Population for Membership of Irish Management Institute, by Size of Firm.*

	Size-Group 20-99		Size-Group 100-499	
	Member	Non-Member	Member	Non-Member
Number of Firms in Population	102	844	87	169
Expected Number in Sample	5	42	17	34
Actual Sample	6	41	20	31
Number of Respondents	6	40	18	30

On every relevant count the sample appears to have been very representative of the population as a whole.

Execution of the Survey

Design of Questionnaire.

The working-out of the research design has been described in considerable detail. During this process many questionnaires were tried out. The final questionnaire was designed and tested in September/October, 1963.

The final research and sample design were scrutinised by Dr. Max Adler, now Director of Studies at the College of Marketing, London, and formerly Adviser on Market Research to the board of the General Electric Company. The final questionnaire was designed with Dr. Adler's collaboration.

The questionnaire was in two parts. It was decided that questions would be asked about each manager in the firm, and that to tabulate the replies it would be necessary to assign a punched card to each individual. A pre-coded questionnaire was designed for this purpose.

Further information was to be obtained by interviewing each chief executive. Because it was obvious that the volume of information required and of statistical tests to be carried out could be handled only by computer, the questionnaire for this interview was closely structured and also pre-coded as far as possible. It was later decided that the processing would be handled somewhat differently from first intentions and the coding scheme had to be altered. The original codes have therefore been deleted from the questionnaire reproduced at the end of the volume.

Care was taken with the questionnaire to ensure that all the questions could be answered from memory without undue difficulty, given the small size of most firms. It was also designed so that topics followed one another naturally in conversation. As a result, questions which belong to one part of the analysis sometimes appear with questions belonging to another part. In broad outline, Q.1-17 refer to quantitative needs, Q.18-39 to facilities, Q.47-83 to use of techniques, the rest being mainly classificatory. Questions, however desirable, which were found to be potentially troublesome were omitted, which may account for the fact that out of 142 who agreed to be interviewed, only one person terminated an interview before completion.

Definitions.

Instead of gathering all definitions together, terms have been defined as they arose in the body of the text, mainly in the introduction and in part I.

Fieldwork.

Fieldwork commenced in January 1964, and January 1st, 1964 was taken as the base-date of the survey. Each selected firm was telephoned for the name of its chief executive and a letter was sent to him asking for his co-operation and suggesting a date for interview. The firm was later telephoned to confirm the suitability of the suggested date.

Interviews were scheduled to be completed at the rate of two per day, to allow for travel, and itineraries were constructed on that basis. Firms outside Dublin kept rigidly to appointments, so that interviews were completed as scheduled, with little need for call-backs. Dublin firms in the smallest size-group (20 to 99 employees) were rather difficult to complete, a reflection of the fact that many of them are one-man firms in which the chief executive is subject to many calls on his time.

As a result the fieldwork, though substantially finished, was incomplete even in

July of 1964, and some larger firms were not interviewed until as late as December of that year. The fieldwork was carried out by the author, so it was not necessary to brief and control field staff. The questionnaires were edited each day.

Data Processing

It had been decided from the start that processing would have to be by computer. It was carried out by the Service Bureau of I.B.M. (Ireland) Limited. The problems of processing will be discussed under the following headings: preparation of specifications; editing and coding; programming and running.

Preparation of Specifications

August and September, 1964, were spent in doing hand-tabulations on uncoded questions. Work then commenced on preparing specifications for programming in order to produce the information required, and on checking the validity of the statistical tests proposed. Because of the great volume of information, cross-classifications and tests, complete specifications were not finalised until May, 1965.

The main plan of the book was laid out, each question to be answered was considered, and the necessary count and test specified. Eventually it was worked out that, in addition to existing programmes, five main new procedures would have to be programmed to provide the required results.

The work of reducing the volume of data to a handful of procedures would not have been possible without the collaboration of Mr. Dermot Harrington, Acting Head of the Statistical Department of an Foras Taluntais (the Agricultural Institute). Mr. Harrington also scrutinised all the statistical tests proposed, laid them out for programming and wrote a programme to adjust the chi-square test for the effect of cluster-sampling (see statistical note 2.3).

Editing and Coding

Editing was done by the author as interviews were completed. The coding system originally devised had later to be abandoned and a new one substituted. The data on the questionnaires were then transferred to standard punching-sheets using the new code, and cards were punched.

Programming and Running

For one requirement—Fisher's test—a standard programme existed. For one other —comparing means of two strata—the requirement was infrequent and was done by hand. The remaining requirements had to be programmed specially. Details of the programmes, written in Fortran for running on a 1401 computer, can be obtained from I.B.M., but short notes are given here.

a). The first programme provided estimates of stratum and population means and totals, with the standard errors of the means and their associated effective degrees of freedom. Input was cards showing, for each firm, the number of individuals possessing the characteristic under review and obtained from the basic cards by a counting programme which also printed out individual values so that the shape of their distribution could be inspected.

b). The second programme was a variation of the counting programme referred to, which totalled the values so as to output tables showing the number of individuals in each cell. These tables formed the raw material for most of the tables in the book, and this was by far the most widely-used programme. The tables were of the form:

		Attribute A	Attribute B
500+	Classification x	n_{11}	n_{13}
	Classification y	n_{12}	n_{14}
	Total	$n_{11}+n_{12}$	$n_{13}+n_{14}$
100–499	Classification x	n_{21}	n_{23}
	Classification y	n_{22}	n_{24}
	Total	$n_{21}+n_{22}$	$n_{23}+n_{24}$
20–99	Classification x	n_{31}	n_{33}
	Classification y	n_{32}	n_{34}
	Total	$n_{31}+n_{32}$	$n_{33}+n_{34}$

c).   It would have been possible but too complicated to devise a programme combining (b) and the one now described. A table such as that shown can give rise to a variety of sub-tables on each of which it is required to carry out tests of significance (see chapter 2). Because it was usual to want to answer a variety of questions arising out of such tables, the output of (b) was inspected, the required sub-tables formed and, after a calculation to see if the restriction on expected values was met, the data from the sub-tables were punched onto cards for input into a procedure for carrying out chi-square tests. If the restrictions on expected values were not met and the data could be cast in a 2×2 table, cards were punched for input to a Fisher's test programme.

The programme for the chi-square test varied with the size of the table and incorporated continuity-corrections where necessary. It gave as output the original cell frequencies, the frequencies expressed as a percentage of both row and column totals, the cell expected values, the individual cell chi-square values, the overall chi-square value and the associated degrees of freedom.

d).   The fourth programme calculated strata and population proportions for attributes of firms, with their standard errors.

e).   The final programme calculated strata and population proportions for attributes of managers. Because managers were sampled in firms the sample in this case was a cluster-sample. The sample proportions were therefore ratio estimates, and the programme calculated the variance and standard error of the ratio estimate required.

Apart from the special programmes and the ones which were available, two further procedures were used. Where the proportion in (d) above did not meet the requirements for reference to the normal distribution, the Agricultural Institute allowed the use of its computer for a programme to calculate the binomial limits. A further programme was also necessary to adjust the chi-square test.

Programming commenced in June, 1965, starting with programme (b) as its output required inspection and manipulation to form the input to (c). The bulk of the processing was completed by mid-October.

Timing and Cost

To help in planning similar surveys the following details of timing and cost are given.

Time-Scale of the Project

The following is an indication of the time spent on different stages of the project.

May 1962-February 1963: Background reading, formulation of the problem, research design, drafting of questionnaires.

February-March 1963: Testing first draft of questionnaires.

April-December 1963: Re-drafting and coding questionnaires, design of sample, preparation of lists, preparation for fieldwork.

January 1964-July 1964: Fieldwork on needs.

August-September 1964: Planning and layout of analysis. Hand-tabulations.

October 1964-May 1965: Preparation of specifications, design of computer procedures, completion of fieldwork on needs.

June-October 1965: Programming of procedures and running the data.

September 1965-May 1966: Drafting of report, fieldwork on facilities.

May-September 1966: Re-drafting, proof-reading and printing.

Cost of the Project

The estimated cost of the project was broken down as follows, in round figures.

		£
Ancillary Expenses		
Duplicating, lists, books, postage, etc.	... ...	220
Professional advice, visits to research centres	... ...	520
Fieldwork	... ...	730
Other travel	... ...	200
Data Processing		£
Programming	... ...	915
Punching and running	... ...	1,300
		2,215
Printing Report ...	... ...	3,450
Salaries and Wages	... ...	6,500
Incidental Expenses	... ...	400
		£14,235

Estimated Time and Cost of Repeated Surveys

If it could be assumed that a half-dozen graduates from Master's programmes in business would be released for some months by their firms, the project could be repeated more quickly, but not much more cheaply. It is unlikely that exactly the same questions would be asked, and quite likely that some refinements would be introduced in sampling and testing, e.g. possible use of the same sample to achieve greater power to detect changes. Any such changes in design would increase the time and cost estimated below, which are based on the assumption that exactly the same questions would be asked and the same procedures followed. (The estimates also assume that prices will not change.) Advantage could be taken of the larger field-force to select a sample large enough to allow analysis by industry-groupings: a sample of about 360 might be sufficient.

The following are estimates of the time and cost of two sizes of sample, one of about 150 (present project) and one of about 360.

TIME	Small Sample	Large Sample
Preliminary work (compiling lists, writing specifications, training interviewers, planning fieldwork)	6 months	6 months
Fieldwork	1½ months	4 months
Processing (editing, hand-tabulations, input, running, forming tables)	6 months	8 months
Fieldwork on facilities	3 months	3 months

Writing	...	8 months	8 months
Proofing and printing	...	3 months	3 months
		27½ months	32 months

Cost (excluding salaries and wages of permanent staff)	Small Sample	Large Sample
	£	£
Fieldwork (salaries of seconded staff, travel and hotel expenses)	1,700	4,500
Processing	1,500	1,900
Printing	2,500	2,500
	5,700	8,900

When salaries are added to these figures they are not far below the cost of the present project.

References:

1.   W. G. Cochran. *Sampling Techniques,* 2nd edition New York: Wiley & Sons, 1963 (pp. 77-79).
2.   Hansen, Hurwitz & Madow. *Sample Survey Methods and Theory,* Vol. I. New York: Wiley & Sons, 1953.
3.   G. W. Snedecor. *Statistical Methods,* 2nd edition. Ames: Iowa State University Press, 1956 (p. 509).
4.   W. G. Cochran, ibid. (pp. 137-140).

APPENDIX B
Statistical Notes

Many points of interest arose in the statistical procedures of estimation and testing. They are discussed here to show how they were treated. The notes are numbered according to the chapters in which the points arose, and according to their order within the chapter.

Statistical Note 1.1.

It was desired to make, from a stratified sample, point estimates of each stratum mean and total, and of the overall population mean and total, and to associate with these estimates their confidence limits, using only sample data. Before confidence limits for means and totals can be calculated, the investigator must know the sampling distributions of means and total, and be in a position to determine their standard errors. When the standard errors have to be estimated from the data, means are referred to the t-distribution rather than the normal, and this involves the assumption of normality in the distribution of the variate whose mean is being calculated. It also involves the calculation of quantities called "degrees of freedom", for reference to tables of the t-distribution.

In the case of the individual strata means and totals, the procedure used was simple. Each stratum mean and total was calculated, together with their standard errors, using the usual formulae (see Yates (1)) incorporating the finite population correction-factor. (In the case of the top stratum the entire population in the stratum was measured, so that no sampling variation was present). The individual values were printed out, and their distribution inspected for normality. Reference was then made to the t-distribution with n_i-1 degrees of freedom, where n_i=number of units sampled from the stratum.

The overall population mean and total were also calculated, together with their standard errors. It is pointed out by Cochran (2) and by Sampford (3) that for reference to the t-distribution a quantity called the "effective degrees of freedom" must be estimated. The formula used was that given by Sampford, and is shown below.

In order to use the calculated standard errors to put confidence limits on point estimates there must be a sampling distribution to which to refer. In the case of the individual strata, reference was made to the t-distribution. There are some queries about the validity of referring an overall mean to that distribution.

The first question arises when a test of significance shows that the strata means differ from each other.

(a). What meaning in that case can be attached to an overall mean? To take the first example in the book, if the average number of managers per firm differs between the three size-groups, in what sense can there be an overall average? In that case, the null hypothesis tested results in the inference that the three strata samples represent samples from three different infinite populations. It was argued nonetheless, that it was known *a priori* that the sample was obtained from a single finite population which was stratified on the basis of size of firm. These strata were at choice: different strata might just as easily have been decided on. It was argued, therefore, that a single average applied to the overall total number of firms has meaning. It also has obvious utility: the total number of firms in industry is known relatively often from censuses, the total number in each size-stratum is known only infrequently. Anyone wishing to have a rough guide to the the total number of managers will wish to have an average by which to multiply the total number of firms.

(b). If the strata are found to differ significantly, in what sense can the overall mean be regarded as coming from a single distribution, in view of the inference arrived at? It was argued as above that the strata distribution arose out of a subdivision of an overall population distribution.

(c) The question then arises of the shape of the overall distribution whose existence was argued. Can it be regarded as normal? In general, there was a fair degree of skewness in the distributions in the present study, even in the individual strata. Because of this lack of normality, reference to the t-distribution is scarcely valid even for strata means and totals. The limits quoted are therefore to be taken rather as an indication of the degree of variability of the estimates of means and totals than as true confidence limits.

Estimated effective degrees of
freedom for the population total $\quad 1 \ / \ \sum_k \frac{1}{v_i} \left[\frac{V_i(\hat{Y}_i)}{V(Y)} \right]^2$

$V_i(\hat{Y}_i)$ = Variance of estimated total in the ith stratum
$V(\hat{Y})$ = Variance of estimated overall total
v_i = $n_i - 1$ = number of degrees of freedom in the ith stratum
n_i = number of sampling units from the ith stratum included in the sample
k = number of strata

Estimated effective degrees of freedom for the population mean are the same as for the population total.

Statistical Note 1.2.

In addition to estimates for size-groups, point and interval-estimates were made only for location and membership of the Irish Management Institute. They were not made for any other factor. The reason is that in the case of the two factors used, called "domains of study", the total number of firms in each domain was known. When the total number of firms in a domain is known, calculation of the mean and total and of their standard errors is a straight-forward extension of the procedure described in statistical note 1.1. When the number of firms is not known more complexity is introduced, and it did not seem that the importance of the other domains justified the cost of the calculations. The problem is discussed by Cochran (4) and Yates (5).

Statistical Note 1.3.

It was desired to investigate associations between a variety of factors and the average number of managers per firm. Consideration was first given to use of analysis of variance. It was decided not to use this method because it was considered unlikely that the assumptions underlying its use would be met. For instance, it did not seem likely that cell variances would be equal. Rather than having to cast around each time for a suitable transformation of the data which would permit the use of analysis of variance, the fact that sampling variation was present in only two strata suggested a different approach. (As the top stratum sample included the entire stratum population no sampling variation was present.)

The middle and bottom size-strata were taken and, within each, the other factors for study were taken in turn, each one as a dichotomy (e.g. Dublin/Other; Irish/Other; Consumer/Industrial) so that never more than two means were being compared. Any differences observed within the top size-group were, of course, statistically significant by definition. Where it was desired to see if the top group differed from the other two, the confidence limits put on the means of the other groups were examined to see whether they overlapped the mean of the top group.

The usual statistical test for the difference between two means, the t-test, rests on the assumption of normality and of equality of variances. Where variances are not equal, Welch's test for the difference between two means may be used. The data were rarely normally distributed. The other assumption, that of equality of variances, was tested for each time. The statistical procedure used on the middle and bottom groups was, therefore, as follows, taking location as an illustration.

i. Within the middle size-group the ratio of the variances of Dublin/non-Dublin firms was computed, and referred as $\dfrac{\text{larger variance}}{\text{smaller variance}}$ to the F-distribution in a two-tailed test (i.e. to get the 5 per cent probability-level, reference was made to the $2\frac{1}{2}$ per cent level, because the null hypothesis did not specify direction of difference). In the calculation of the variances, finite correction factors were omitted (Yates (6)).

ii. Where the variances did not differ significantly, the ordinary t-test for the difference between two means was carried out.

iii. Where the variances did differ significantly, a modified form of Welch's test was used.

iv. Where no differences were found between factors within a stratum, either as to means or variances, the factors were combined and an overall stratum mean and variance calculated. The two strata means were then compared, using the procedure outlined in i-iii above.

v. Where factors within a stratum were found to differ with respect either to their means or variances no overall stratum mean could be calculated. Hence the size-strata were compared within the other factor under review, e.g. first Dublin firms were taken and the two size-strata compared within Dublin, then non-Dublin firms were taken and the size-strata compared within them. The test procedure was as in i-iii above.

The statistical procedure of steps i-iii is not recommended by Snedecor (7) who points out that the combination of two tests, the first of H_o: $\sigma_1 = \sigma_2$ and then of H_o: $\mu_1 = \mu_2$ affects the final test in some unknown complicated way. It was, however, used because the alternative suggested by him did not seem likely to make much difference to the result, while it would have involved a good deal of time in inspecting the data.

A further objection to the test procedure is that the use of the same data to test a series of hypotheses in turn without first carrying out an overall test of significance might lead to "capitalisation on chance". This objection was rejected because it appeared that the hypotheses being tested were quite independent of one another, and hence that testing in series rather than simultaneously could not affect the probability levels of the tests.

Finally, the fact that the data were not normally distributed means that the results of the t-test are approximate only.

Welch's Test: The form of Welch's test used was to refer the statistic

$$t = \frac{\bar{x}_1 - \bar{x}_2}{\sqrt{\dfrac{s_1^2}{n_1} + \dfrac{s_2^2}{n_2}}} \quad \text{to the t-distribution}$$

$$\text{with degrees of freedom} = \frac{\left(\dfrac{s_1^2}{n_1} + \dfrac{s_2^2}{n_2} \right)^2}{\dfrac{1}{n_1+1}\left(\dfrac{s_1^2}{n_1} \right)^2 + \dfrac{1}{n_2+1}\left(\dfrac{s_2^2}{n_2} \right)^2} - 2$$

$$\bar{x}_1 = \text{mean of factor } 1 = \frac{\Sigma x_{1i}}{n_1}$$

$$\bar{x}_2 = \text{mean of factor } 2 = \frac{\Sigma x_{2i}}{n_2}$$

$$s_1^2 = \text{estimate of variance of factor } 1 = \frac{1}{n_1-1}\, \underset{i}{\Sigma}\, (x_{1i} - \bar{x}_1)^2$$

$$s_2^2 = \text{estimate of variance of factor } 2 = \frac{1}{n_2-1}\, \Sigma\, (x_{2i} - \bar{x}_2)^2$$

n_1 = number in sample of factor 1

n_2 = number in sample of factor 2.

Statistical Note 2.1.

The standard errors of means and totals in this case were calculated using the same formula as in chapter 1. It might have seemed preferable, in view of the fact that more than one mean was involved, to have carried out an analysis of variance and used the appropriate mean square to estimate the variance required. However, as already pointed out, the data never seemed likely to meet the major conditions for analysis of variance, and the number of calculations to be performed in the book ruled out the possibility of looking for suitable transformations. It was therefore decided to adhere to the simpler procedure.

Statistical Note 2.2:

It should be noted that in dealing with attributes of managers the sample was a stratified single-stage cluster sample. The sampling unit was the firm, not the manager. When dealing with estimates of the proportion of individual managers possessing a certain attribute the managers were clustered within a set of firms selected at random, from a population stratified by size. Consequently the estimates were essentially ratio-estimates. This meant that the usual binomial sampling variance did not apply, and that the variance of the ratio-estimate had to be used. This gives approximate confidence limits only, as the sample estimate of the population proportion is subject to bias, the variance of the ratio-estimate is known only approximately and its sample estimate is also subject to bias. The computational formulae are given below and are essentially those given by Yates (8).

Cochran provides guidance on the distribution of the ratio-estimate. He states (9) that for N (sample size) greater than 30, the estimate may be regarded as being approximately normally distributed, and that the approximate variance may be regarded as close to the true (unknown) variance. A further restriction is that the co-efficients of variation of both x and y, as defined below, are less than 10 per cent. He therefore suggests reference to the normal distribution. This was done whenever N exceeded 30.

In referring the overall proportion to its distribution the same questions arose as in the case of the mean (see statistical note 1.1) and the same arguments were used to justify the procedure.

COMPUTATIONAL FORMULAE:

$$\text{Stratum proportion} = R_h = \frac{\sum_{i=1}^{n_h} y_{hi}}{\sum_{i=1}^{n_h} x_{hi}}$$

$x_i \ldots \ldots_{n_h}$ are the n_h values showing the total number of managers in each of the n_h firms from the hth stratum, included in the sample.

$y_i \ldots \ldots_{n_h}$ are the n_h values showing the number of managers having the attribute under review in each of the n_h firms, i.e., each y is a sub-set of the corresponding x.

$$\text{Population proportion} = \bar{R} = \frac{\sum_{h=1}^{k} \bar{R}_h X_h}{X}$$

X_h = estimated number of managers in the hth stratum of the population.
X = estimated number of managers in the population overall.
Variance of stratum proportion

$$= \frac{1}{\left[\sum_{i=1}^{n_h} x_{hi}\right]^2} \cdot \frac{N_h - n_h}{N_h} \cdot n_h \cdot \frac{1}{n_h - 1} \left[\sum_{i=1}^{n_h} y_{hi}^2 - 2\bar{R}_h \sum_{i=1}^{n_h} x_{hi} y_{hi} + \bar{R}_h^2 \sum_{i=1}^{n_h} x_{hi}^2\right] = V(\bar{R}_h)$$

Standard error of stratum proportion $= \sqrt{\overline{V(R_h)}}$

Variance of population proportion $\quad = \quad \sum_{h=1}^{k} \frac{X_h^2}{X^2} V(\bar{R}_h) = V(\bar{R})$

Standard error of population proportion $= \sqrt{\overline{V(\bar{R})}}$

Note that X_h and X are not known *a priori* but are estimated from the sample. This means that the overall ratio-estimate above, while looking like a separate estimate, is in fact equivalent to a combined estimate.

Statistical Note 2.3:

In using the chi-square test to test the differences between proportions certain conditions must be met. The principal conditions are discussed here, together with the extent to which they were met by the data.

1. *Independence:* The chi-square test and any other statistical test rests on the basic assumption that a selection procedure has been followed which renders the observations in the sample independent of one another. That is to say, the selection of one individual must not affect the probability of inclusion of any other.

This condition is met by a simple random sample. The question arises whether it is met when dealing with observations of manager attributes, in which case the sample is a cluster-sample. (In this note only tests within a stratum are considered. The question of an overall test on the results for the three strata is discussed in note 2.4 following.) It might be thought that lack of independence would arise because of a systematic tendency for managers in a firm to resemble one another with respect to the attribute in question, e g., for most of them to be qualified or very few qualified. In the case of qualification, and more especially in the case of training, there is some force in this objection.

It was nevertheless argued that the observations were independent, i.e., that while P (=proportion possessing the attribute) varied from firm to firm it did so randomly around the firm-mean-proportion. The reason was that in most cases the suggestion of non-independence was too slight to warrant the consequence of being unable to carry out any test.

2. *Expected Values:* It is a condition of the test that the quantities calculated and called the cell expected values should not be too small. The interpretation of "small" varies between authorities. The conditions observed in the study are those quoted by Siegel (10). These vary with the type of table—whether it is $1 \times C$, 2×2, $R \times C$, etc. The main condition is that no more than 20 per cent of the cells should have expected values of less than 5.

The reason for this condition is based on the theoretical nature of the test. We shall say something of this here, as the discussion of the next condition involves it also.

Suppose there is a set k of classes into which an observation may fall. The probability of falling in a cell is p and f, the number of observations in the cell in a sample of size n, follows the binomial distribution. Therefore it has a mean np, a variance npq and, provided n is large enough, the binomial distribution of f can be approximated by the normal distribution. (It is generally accepted that "large enough" means that np should be 5 or greater—hence the condition). $\frac{f-np}{\sqrt{npq}}$ is a standard normal variate, and $\Sigma \frac{(f-np)^2}{npq}$ is a sum of squares of standard normal variates. Such a sum follows the chi-square distribution. Therefore $\Sigma \frac{(f-np)^2}{np}$ has approximately the chi-square distribution. Now p, the probability of being in a certain cell, is unknown. But, given the null hypothesis, it can be estimated. The null hypothesis is that $p_{ij} = p_i.p_{.j}$. Therefore $\Sigma \frac{(f-np_i.p_{.j})^2}{np_i.p_{.j}}$ is distributed approximately as chi-square. $p_i.$ is estimated by $\frac{n_i.}{n}$ where $n_i. =$ row total, n = grand total. $p_{.j}$ is estimated by $\frac{n_{.j}}{n}$ where $n_{.j} =$ column total.

These estimates are maximum-likelihood estimates, and an important theorem states that, so long as the unknown parameters $p_i.$ and $p_{.j}$ are estimated by their maximum-likelihood estimates, the chi-square distribution may still be used.

$$\text{Therefore } \Sigma \frac{\left(f - n \cdot \frac{n_i. \, n_{.j}}{n.n} \right)^2}{n \cdot \frac{n_i.}{n} \cdot \frac{n_{.j}}{n}}$$

is distributed as chi-square and $= \Sigma \dfrac{\left(f - \dfrac{n_i. \, n_{.j}}{n} \right)^2}{\dfrac{n_i. \, n_{.j}}{n}}$

$$= \Sigma \frac{(\text{Observed Frequency} - \text{Expected Value})^2}{\text{Expected Value}} \quad \text{where Expected Value}$$

$$= \frac{\text{Row Total} \times \text{Column Total}}{\text{Grand Total}} \cdot \text{The sum } \Sigma \frac{(O - E)^2}{E} \text{ is called } \chi^2$$

Therefore, on condition that f is binomially distributed, that the sample size is large enough to use the normal approximation to the binomial, and that the unknown parameters are replaced by their maximum-likelihood estimates, the statistic χ^2 has approximately the chi-square distribution.

Where np < 5 the second condition is not met and the test is not valid. In that case either categories must be combined or, in a 2×2 table, Fisher's test must be used. The effect of cluster-sampling on these conditions is now examined.

3. *Simple Random Sampling*: If the sample is a simple random sample the conditions are met. For the effect of cluster-sampling no exact solution is known. It is known that f is no longer binomially distributed. Its mean remains np, but its variance is now no longer npq, but a larger quantity. The relationship between the size of the binomial variance and the cluster-sampling variance depends on whether or not the clusters are equal in size. Whether or not the clusters are equal, the cluster-sampling variance always exceeds the binomial variance (11). It follows that, using np as the variance of f and estimating np by the expected value calculated as above, the denominator of each cell value is too small and consequently the value of χ^2 is too large. This means that the significance level is incorrect: the chance of finding a significant value is too great.

A further element of approximation is introduced by the fact that when $\dfrac{\text{Row} \times \text{Column}}{\text{Grand}}$ Total is used to estimate p_i. and $p_{\cdot j}$, the estimates when using a cluster-sample are no longer maximum-likelihood estimates but ratio estimates. However, the effect of this is small compared to that of the variance.

The only solution to the problem is to scale down the chi-square values calculated in the usual way by using a correcting factor. The factor is complex when cluster sizes are not equal. Although they were not equal in this sample, it was decided that using the correct factor would be too difficult and expensive, and that the simpler equal-cluster factor would be used, as this at least shows the order of magnitude of the reduction.

For clusters of equal size n the cluster variance = Binomial Variance $+ n(n-1)\sigma^2_p$ where σ^2_p = variance of the cluster proportions (12). The individual cell values of chi-square had been obtained as output from the programme for the chi-square test. Each value estimated a quantity $\dfrac{(f-np)^2}{np}$. These had to be corrected to take into account that the denominator should have approximated not to npq but to npq $+ n(n-1)\sigma^2_p$. A programme was written by Mr. D. Harrington which corrected the individual values and summed them to give a corrected chi-square sum.

To calculate σ^2_p it was necessary to have the P values for each firm (cluster). These were not in general available but, in the case of estimates for locations and membership of The Irish Management Institute, they had been obtained as output from the programme used for the calculations in Note 2.2. above.

Consequently it was possible to carry out the above adjustment only in the case of tests involving size, location, or membership of the Irish Management Institute. The results of the adjustments were used as an indication of the order of magnitude of the reduction of chi-square and the results of tests involving other factors were scrutinised in the light of these reductions.

The author is indebted to Mr. Alan Stuart of London University for indicating this method of dealing with chi-square tests in cluster-sampling.

In fact the adjustments made practically no difference to the values of χ^2 because the average size of cluster was small and because the values of P were not usually widely dispersed around their mean. The only cases in which the reduction was appreciable were those in which the three size-groups were being compared with one another. The fact that the top stratum was included in these comparisons meant that the average size of cluster was increased. However, even in such cases the reduction still left the values of χ^2 well above a significant level. As an example, in table 2.6.

stratum two, in contrasting the totals in each functional area to see if the proportions differed significantly between functions, the value of chi-square was reduced only from 321.52 to 316.18. In contrasting the three size-groups, chi-square was reduced from 232.18 to 136.21 with 10 degrees of freedom—still giving a highly significant result.

Before leaving this discussion two final points may be mentioned. The first is that in the top stratum the entire population was sampled. It was not necessary to carry out tests within that stratum as any differences observed were by definition significant statistically. The second point is that in 1×2 and 2×2 tables a continuity-correction was applied to the chi-square values to improve the normal approximation.

Statistical Note 2.4.

When dealing with attributes of managers the possibility arose that tests within the separate strata would give non-significant values but, the direction of differences in each stratum being the same, that it would be desirable to combine the results of the individual tests so as to obtain an overall test of greater power. When k independent samples are drawn and chi-square tests carried out on each, the exact probability of obtaining each of the observed chi-square values is $p_1, p_2 \ldots p_k$. (These may be obtained by interpolation in the chi-square tables). If these probabilities are not significant they may be combined into an overall test, because $-2\sum_{i=1}^{k}\log_e p_i$ follows the chi-square distribution with 2k degrees of freedom.

In dealing with manager attributes it was not possible to proceed as above because of the approximate nature of the correction to the chi-square values and the consequent impossibility of finding correct values of $p_1 \ldots p_k$.

When dealing with attributes of firms, as in chapter 10 onwards, the sample was selected at random within strata and the above procedure was followed where necessary.

It was mentioned in note 2.3. that a continuity correction was applied to the chi-square values where appropriate. In adding the results of separate chi-square tests the continuity correction over-corrects, and should not be used. Wherever test results were being added the chi-square values were first re-calculated without the correction.

Statistical Note 2.5

The theoretical objection to carrying out a series of tests such as this is that it may involve "capitalisation on chance". Snedecor (13) discusses this point in relation to testing several means. He points out that if a set of means is obtained it is not permissible, unless designed comparisons are being made, to test them one against the other without first carrying out an overall test on all n simultaneously.

It was felt, however, that this refers only to the case of sub-divisions of data within a particular test: in the chi-square test, for instance, it would certainly not be permissible to test the numbers in one functional area against the numbers in some other area without first testing for an overall difference. If, however, a difference is tested between one set of factors, for instance, locations, and afterwards between another set, for instance, type of ownership, it appears that while the basic data being used are the same nevertheless the different comparisons being made are independent of one another. It seemed, therefore, that the possibility of capitalising on chance did not arise.

Statistical Note 4.1.

It was mentioned in the discussion of the χ^2-test that a condition for its validity is that the expected values should not be less than 5 in more than 20 per cent of the cells.

When dealing with such cases, if the data can be put in the form of 2×2 table, Fisher's Exact Probability Test may be used.

The basis of the test is that, if the row and column totals are regarded as fixed, the exact probability of getting the observed division into classes may be calculated as $\dfrac{(A+B)! \ (C+D)! \ (A+C)! \ (B+D)!}{N! \ A! \ B! \ C! \ D!}$ where the data are arranged in the following

form:

	A	B	A+B
	C	D	C+D
	A+C	B+D	N

The probability of occurence of each value more extreme than that observed, but with the same row and column totals, is calculated in the same way. These probabilities are then added to give the required probability.

The condition that the marginal totals be regarded as fixed was not met by the data. It is pointed out in the Biometrika Tables (14) that the effect of introducing variation is to reduce the exact probability. That is, by calculating in the way outlined above, the correct probability is overestimated. There is therefore no danger of incorrectly rejecting the null hypothesis by using this calculation. Siegel (15) puts forward a modification to increase the power of the test, but this was not considered as a computer programme already existed for the more usual form.

It is worth pointing out that Fisher's test is in essence a "one-tail" test, that is, it takes account of the direction of differences in the table. If the null hypothesis is of the form $\dfrac{A}{A+B}$ is not less than $\dfrac{C}{C+D}$, Fisher's test shows the exact probability under this hypothesis of getting the observed or more extreme values. If, however, the hypothesis is of the form $\dfrac{A}{A+B}$ does not differ from $\dfrac{C}{C+D}$, Fisher's test understates the probability

In this case the observed probability must be doubled or, more correctly, the significance-level at which the null hypothesis may be rejected must be doubled. For example, suppose the probability obtained is 0.035. To reject the null hypothesis at the 5 per cent level, the observed probability must be compared not with 0.05 but with 0.025, and the decision in this case would be not to reject at the 5 per cent level. The null hypotheses tested in this book are all of the second form.

The programme used to compute the probabilities was that reported by Robertson (16).

It should be pointed out that in dealing with manager attributes it is not really justifiable to use Fisher's test to project the inferences to the population sampled. It was seldom used in this context and never reached a significant level where it was used. Its main use was in chapter 10 onwards in connection with attributes of firms, i.e., when dealing with a simple random sample within a stratum.

Statistical Note 6.1.

Although the conditions for analysis of variance were most nearly met by the data on ages of managers it was decided not to use the technique. The reasons were that the basic data were not reliable enough to justify their use: in many cases chief executives did not know the exact age of other executives, but gave indications within a range of years. Further, the standard programme which existed was for a completely random model and had facilities to print only the overall mean. In the present survey the strata were fixed and therefore a mixed model would have had to be used.

Having regard to the nature of the basic data, the further drawback imposed by the necessity to amend the standard programme tilted the balance against carrying out an analysis of variance.

Statistical Note 10.1.

From chapter 10 on the main concern was with the percentage of *firms* having various attributes and with carrying out tests on the relative numbers of different types of firms having those attributes.

When dealing with attributes of firms the sample was a simple stratified sample; within strata it was a simple random sample. The problem of confidence limits for percentages is dealt with first and then the problem of tests.

CONFIDENCE LIMITS FOR PERCENTAGES

(a)   Within individual strata: In this case there is a simple sample.

The usual approximate practice is to estimate the standard error of the observed percentage and to refer it to either the normal or the t-distribution. When sampling from a finite population a correction factor is applied to the standard error.

This practice is correct only under certain conditions (see Cochran (17)) relating to the size of the sample and to the smaller of the proportions under consideration. When these conditions are not met the approximation is not valid and the exact distribution of the proportion must be used. The exact distribution when the population is finite is the hypergeometric distribution, but the binomial distribution is close enough for most purposes. It was therefore decided, when the conditions mentioned were not met, that the binomial distribution would be used.

This is a tedious procedure, and fairly lengthy even on a computer. As the number of occasions on which it might be used was large, the conditions laid down by Cochran were relaxed and the normal approximation was used unless the smaller of the two percentages fell below 20 per cent.

Where this happened the binomial was used. Some trial comparisons showed little difference between the two results for $P > 20$ per cent, the main difference being a slight understatement of the upper limit.

Non-response to a question raises problems, even if it is not large. The problem is whether to express the "successes" as a proportion of those who replied or of the total in the sample. The answer basically depends on whether or not it is considered likely that those who did not reply resemble those who did. If it is assumed that they would have replied in the same way as the respondents, then P should be calculated as:

$\dfrac{100 \times \text{No. of successes}}{\text{No. of replies}}$ In this case there is a difficulty in calculating the standard

error when the population is finite. A correction factor must be applied. The factor ought to be:

$$\sqrt{\left(1 - \frac{\text{number of replies in sample}}{\text{number of replies in population}}\right)} = \sqrt{1 - \frac{n'}{N'}}$$

But N' is not known. However, $\dfrac{n}{N} = \dfrac{\text{Number of units in sample}}{\text{Number of units in population}}$ is known.

Cochran (18) points out that $\dfrac{n}{N}$ may be used to estimate $\dfrac{n'}{N'}$. The correction-factor then becomes

$$\sqrt{1-\dfrac{n}{N}}\left(\text{or, more exactly, }\sqrt{\dfrac{N-n}{N-1}}\right)$$

The practice throughout has been to calculate P as $\dfrac{100 \times \text{No. of successes}}{\text{No. of replies.}}$

The number of replies on which P was based are always quoted in any table where estimates are made. Non-response was always small.

Note that estimates have always been based on all the firms in the sample, whereas tests are carried out only on firms which did not change their size. It might have appeared better not to have included in a stratum firms which had since left it. The reason they were included was the necessity for calculating the correction-factor. If they had not been included the factor would be

$$\sqrt{1-\dfrac{\text{No. of replies from sampled firms not changed in size}}{\text{No. of replies from population of firms not changed in size}}} = \sqrt{1-\dfrac{n''}{N''}}$$

Again N″ is not known and as it was not known whether $\dfrac{n}{N}$ would be an unbiased estimate of $\dfrac{n''}{N''}$ it was decided to calculate P based on the entire sample, thus retaining a known correction-factor, $\sqrt{1-\dfrac{n}{N}}$ (But see the addendum to this appendix.)

(b) Overall Percentages: Any percentages quoted are, of course, always weighted to allow for the different sampling-fractions in each stratum.
The variance of the overall percentage is as usual a weighted sum of the individual strata variances. To get confidence limits, the standard-error was referred to the normal distribution.

(c) Multiple Percentages: Confidence limits are never quoted where a total is divided into more than two classes. It was considered that multiple classification is implied that the proportions were distributed multinominally and that the binomial variance formula was therefore inappropriate (but see Cochran (19)).

Tests of hypotheses:
Depending on the numbers, either the chi-square test or Fisher's test was used, within individual strata. When tests within the strata gave results which were not significant the results were sometimes combined into an overall test as described in note 2.4.

Statistical Note 11.1.
It will be remembered that, when discussing the conditions for validity of the chi-square test, it was mentioned that the observations must be independent. Siegel (20) points out that "one may not make several observations on the same person and count

each as independent". In the chapter to which this note refers, each interviewee was asked for his opinions about areas in which training needs were most important. Many individuals gave more than one reply, consequently there were more opinions than individuals.

It could be argued that, despite this fact, the opinions were independent of one another, essentially on the basis that the fact that an individual gave an opinion about one area did not necessarily influence his opinion about another. This argument was not accepted.

In case anyone should wish to know the result of a chi-square test on the data used to construct table 11.2, a test was carried out on the difference between the three size-groups, combining the categories "other" and "special training for own industry" in order to meet the conditions on expected values. The result showed the differences to be significant beyond $p = 0.001$.

Addendum to Appendix B

During the course of the project it was necessary to make point estimates of strata and population totals, averages and proportions, and to associate confidence intervals with each.

The sample was in three strata, while a further stratum of the population—firms employing under 20 people—was not sampled at all.

When firms were visited, it was found that some had changed from their original size-groups.

In making estimates, firms were regarded as being still in their original strata. It is now realised that this was unnecessary in the case of averages and of some proportions. For guidance in future surveys the point is discussed here.

TOTALS. In estimating strata manager-totals it is necessary to know the total number of firms in each stratum so as to multiply the sample number of managers by the reciprocal of the sampling fraction. In the present case it was necessary for this purpose to regard firms as being still in their original strata. The other possible ways of dealing with change could not be used. They are: (i) To omit all firms which changed in size. This would not help, as the population totals would still be unknown. (ii) To assign the firms to the strata in which they were at the time of the interview, and to make proportionate changes in the population totals on the basis that the changes in the sample were unbiased estimates of the changes in the population. Although this would not take into account the entry into the population of completely new firms, it would have been a reasonable procedure if all strata had been sampled. But the fact that the under 20-employee group had not been sampled meant that no estimate was available of entry from the under-20 group into the 20 to 99 group, and hence that the total of the latter group was unknowable.

AVERAGES. Inclusion in a stratum of firms no longer in the stratum undoubtedly introduced a bias into the estimates. Wherever this was sizeable, the fact has been pointed out in the text. From the point of view of estimating strata averages it would have been possible to exclude all changed firms or to assign them to new strata. From the point of view of associating confidence limits with the average and of estimating an overall average, the latter method would not suffice: to do either it would have been necessary to know the total number of firms in each stratum, and this could not be estimated, because no estimate could be made of changes from the under-20 stratum.

It would, however, have been possible to omit all firms changed in size and to regard the sample as a random sample from a population of firms unchanged in size. Suppose in any stratum that the original total of firms was N_i and that the original sample was n_i. Let n'_i be the number of sampled firms unchanged in size, and N'_i be the unknown number of firms unchanged in size in the population. In estimating the variance of the mean of firms unchanged in size a finite population correcting factor $1 - \dfrac{n'_i}{N'_i}$ would have to be applied. N'_i is unknown, but $\dfrac{n_i}{N_i}$ could be used instead of $\dfrac{n'_i}{N'_i}$ because it is an unbiased estimate. Similarly, instead of using the weights $\dfrac{N'_i}{N'}$ in calculating the overall average, the weights $\dfrac{N_i}{N}$ could be used.

There is, therefore, no reason, in calculating averages, why firms changed in size cannot be excluded from the sample and the result regarded as an estimate of the population figure for firms unchanged in size. This still does not provide an estimate of the population figure for all firms actually in each size-group, but it would probably be less biased than the estimate made by assigning firms to their original groups irrespective of their present size.

PROPORTIONS. The same applies to proportions as to averages, when dealing with random samples. It was stated in note 10.1. that it was not known whether $\dfrac{n_i}{N_i}$ was an unbiased estimate of $\dfrac{n''_i}{N''_i}$, but in fact it is. It would probably be better in future surveys to eliminate firms changed in size when making estimates, while using the original population and sample figures N, N_i and n_i to calculate correcting factors and strata weights.

The case of a ratio estimate is somewhat different. The weight used in estimating an overall ratio from a set of strata ratios is $\dfrac{X_i}{X}$ where X means the total number of managers possessing a particular attribute, and not the total number of firms. As X can be calculated only by assuming firms to be still in their original size-groups, it is probably best to calculate ratio estimates also by assigning firms to their original groups.

REFERENCES:

1. Yates, F. *Sampling Methods for Censuses and Surveys,* 3rd Ed. London: Griffin & Co., 1960. pp. 153, 187, 202.
2. Cochran, W. G. *Sampling Techniques,* 2nd Ed. New York: Wiley & Sons, 1963, page 94.
3. Sampford, W. R. *An Introduction to Sampling Theory.* Edinburgh: Oliver & Boyd, 1962, page 71.
4. Cochran. *ibid.,* page 146.
5. Yates. *ibid.,* page 202.
6. Yates. *ibid.,* page 188.
7. Snedecor, G. W. *Statistical Methods,* 5th Ed. Ames, Iowa: Iowa State University Press, 1962, page 99.
8. Yates. *ibid.,* pp. 212-217.
9. Cochran. *ibid.,* page 164.
10. Siegel, S. *Nonparametric Statistics.* New York: McGraw-Hill, 1956, pp. 110, 178.
11. Hansen, Hurwitz & Madow. *Sample Survey Methods and Theory,* Vol. 1. New York:

12. Kendall & Stuart. *The Advanced Theory of Statistics,* Vol. I. London: Griffin & Co., 1958, pp. 127, 128.

13. Snedecor, *ibid.,* pp. 251-256.

14. *Biometrika Tables for Statisticians* (Ed. Pearson & Hartley), Vol. I. Cambridge: Cambridge University Press, 1962, pp. 65-71.

15. Siegel, *ibid.,* page 101.

16. Robertson, H. W. *Technometrics,* Vol. 2, No. 1. February, 1960.

17. Cochran, *ibid.,* page 57.

18. Cochran, *ibid.,* page 60.

19. Cochran, *ibid.,* page 60.

20. Siegel, *ibid.,* page 44.

APPENDIX C
Questionnaire

Company Number

QUESTIONS TO BE ANSWERED FOR EACH EXECUTIVE EMPLOYED ON 1ST JANUARY, 1964

Job Title _____   Superior's Title _____

Functional Area		Level in Management		Age		Univ. Deg.		Other Qualification		Mgt. Course		Country of Birth	
	19		20	21	22						33		34
Ch. Exec.	1	Ch. Exec.	1			Commerce	23	Financial & Secretarial	28	Yes	1	Ireland	1
Gen. Mgt.	2	Top	2			Arts	24	Engineering, Science, etc.	29	No	2	Britain	2
Marketing	3	Middle	3			Eng.	25	Marketing	30			Other	3
Production	4	Junior	4			Science	26	Personnel	31				
Finance	5					Other	27	Other	32				
Personnel	6												

Job Title _____   Superior's Title _____

Functional Area		Level in Management		Age		Univ. Deg.		Other Qualification		Mgt. Course		Country of Birth	
	19		20	21	22						33		34
Ch. Exec.	1	Ch. Exec.	1			Commerce	23	Financial & Secretarial	28	Yes	1	Ireland	1
Gen. Mgt.	2	Top	2			Arts	24	Engineering, Science, etc.	29	No	2	Britain	2
Marketing	3	Middle	3			Eng.	25	Marketing	30			Other	3
Production	4	Junior	4			Science	26	Personnel	31				
Finance	5					Other	27	Other	32				
Personnel	6												

Job Title _____   Superior's Title _____

Functional Area		Level in Management		Age		Univ. Deg.		Other Qualification		Mgt. Course		Country of Birth	
	19		20	21	22						33		34
Ch. Exec.	1	Ch. Exec.	1			Commerce	23	Financial & Secretarial	28	Yes	1	Ireland	1
Gen. Mgt.	2	Top	2			Arts	24	Engineering, Science, etc.	29	No	2	Britain	2
Marketing	3	Middle	3			Eng.	25	Marketing	30			Other	3
Production	4	Junior	4			Science	26	Personnel	31				
Finance	5					Other	27	Other	32				
Personnel	6												

Name of Firm   _____

Address   _____

Name(s) of
Respondent(s) _____
               _____

Position(s)   _____
               _____
               _____

Questionnaire Number

Membership/Used Courses

Industry

Locality/Size

Number of Managers

Q. 1

Were there any changes in your management team between the beginning of 1960 and last January 1st, i.e. new positions created or old ones done away with?

yes	no	d.k.	n.r.	n.a.
—	—	—	—	—

Q. 2

Could you tell me the titles of the positions created or done away with and the title of the position immediately superior to each.

Created Title	Superior	*Abolished* Title	Superior

	Created				Abolished			
	Total	Top	Mid.	Jun.	Total	Top	Mid.	Jun.
Chief Exec.								
General Mgt.								
Marketing								
Production								
Finance								
Personnel								
Total								

Q. 3a
Did any of your executives die, while still working as an executive, during 1963.

yes	no	d.k.	n.r.	n.a.
—	—	—	—	—

Q. 3b
If yes, what age at death (with number).

30	30-44	45-54	55-64	65+
—	—	—	—	—

Q. 4
At what age do your executives have to retire?

55	60	65	Other fixed age	No fixed age
—	—	—	—	—

Q. 5
Do you expect any of your present executives to retire by the end of 1966 or have any retired since January 1st.

yes	no	d.k.	n.r.	n.a.
—	—	—	—	—

Q. 6
If yes: would you name the title of each, and the title of his immediate superior.

Title   *Superior*

	Total	Top	Middle	Junior
Chief Exec.				
General Mgt.				
Marketing				
Production				
Finance				
Personnel				
Total				

Q. 7

Which of these vacancies do you *not* expect to fill by promoting or transferring one of your other managers:

Title

_____

_____

	Total	Top	Middle	Junior
Chief Exec.				
General Mgt.				
Marketing				
Production				
Finance				
Personnel				
Total				

Q. 8

Do you expect to have created any new managerial positions by the end of 1966, or did you create any since January 1st.

yes	no	d.k.	n.r.	n.a.
—	—	—	—	—

Q. 9

If yes: could you name the title of each and his immediate superior.

Title   *Superior*

_____

_____

_____

	Total	Top	Middle	Junior
Chief Exec.				
General Mgt.				
Marketing				
Production				
Finance				
Personnel				
Total				

Q. 10

Which of these vacancies do you *not* expect to be able to fill by promoting or transferring one of your managers.

Title   *Superior*

	Total	Top	Middle	Junior
Chief Exec.				
General Mgt.				
Marketing				
Production				
Finance				
Personnel				
Total				

Q. 11

What you have told me Mr. .... means that over the next three years, you will have to look outside your existing managerial staff to fill vacancies caused by retirement, promotion and expansion. As I name each vacant job, can you tell me whether you expect to fill it from inside or outside the firm?

Job Titles: In   Out
To replace retirals

To fill new jobs

To replace promotions   In   Out

	Inside the Firm				Outside the Firm			
	Total	Top	Mid.	Jun.	Total	Top	Mid.	Jun.
Chief Exec.								
General Mgt.								
Marketing								
Production								
Finance								
Personnel								
Total								

Q. 12

You say you will have to look outside the firm to fill .... vacancies. For how many will you want men with

P.Q.	P.M.E.	Both	Neither	d.k.	n.r.	n.a.
—	—	—	—	—	—	—

Q. 13

Would you say there is a shortage in industry of people with managerial talent?

Q. 14a

Were there any particular jobs during the last three years for which you found it impossible to get men in Ireland with *all* the qualities you were looking for?

yes	no	d.k.	n.r.	n.a.
—	—	—	—	—

Q. 14b
If yes: name title of each and immediate superior.

Title   *Superior*

	Total	Top	Middle	Junior
Chief Exec.				
General Mgt.				
Marketing				
Production				
Finance				
Personnel				
Total				

Q. 15
Was this because the candidate lacked

(a) the necessary academic qualifications —

(b) the necessary experience   —

(c) some other qualifications (specify)   —

(d) or for some other reason (specify)   —

                 d.k.   n.r.   n.a.
                 —   —   —

Q. 16
Apart from anyone you expect to promote from below managerial level over the next three years, do you have any people working in your firm in non-managerial or non-professional positions who have university degrees or professional qualifications?

        yes   no   d.k.   n.r.   n.a.
        —   —   —   —   —

Q. 17
If yes: could you tell me what qualifications they have? How many?

      Comm.   Arts   Eng.   Science   other
      —   —   —   —   —

Q. 18
Have you ever worked with or employed people with university degrees? Do you have one yourself?

      yes   no   d.k.   n.r.   degree   no degree
      —   —   —   —   —   —

Q. 19
Do you feel that any of the following courses could be improved

	yes	no	d.k.
Engineering	—	—	—
Science	—	—	—
Commerce	—	—	—
Economics	—	—	—
Other	—	—	—
University degrees	—	—	—
generally	—	—	—

Q. 20
Could you give a very rough idea of the changes you would like to see made.

_____

_____

_____

_____

_____

_____

Q. 21a
Is there any professional qualification besides university degrees which you would like
to see altered or introduced?

yes	no	d.k.	n.r.	n.a.
—	—	—	—	—

Q. 21b
If yes: which, and give details

_____

_____

_____

_____

_____

_____

_____

Q. 22
Has this firm ever recruited graduates direct from university?

yes	no	d.k.	n.r.	n.a.
—	—	—	—	—

Q. 23
Will you do so over the next three years?

yes	no	d.k.	n.r.	n.a.
—	—	—	—	—

Q. 24

If yes: could you give me an idea of the degrees they must have, and the sort of jobs they will fill?

	Comm.	Arts	Eng.	Sc.	Other	Total
Mgt. Trainees						
Research						
Technical or professional						
Other						
Total						

Q. 25

Have you found it necessary so far to have a formal company programme to develop people for managerial jobs, for instance by employing management trainees ...... or by planning training courses for your executives ...... or by development through work ...... or any other means ......?

         yes   no   d.k.   n.r.   n.a.

Q. 26

If you were to leave this firm, is there anyone in the firm with the qualifications and experience to succeed you?

         yes   no   d.k.   n.r.   n.a.

Q. 27

You may have heard/you know, that I.M.I. and other bodies arrange courses on management techniques and so on. Do you think that such courses can help your firm?

         yes   no   d.k.   n.r.   n.a.

Q. 28

Would you be prepared to let executives or potential executives off work for management training, or to come yourself?

Dublin

         yes   no   d.k.   n.r.   n.a.

Locally

         yes   no   d.k.   n.r.   n.a.

Q. 29

There are many different ways in which courses can be organised, for instance we could have them:

Full time, lasting from a few days to months —

Part-time, for a few hours a day or for a few days a week —

Extended week-ends —

Spare time at night —

Which of these sorts would you prefer?

———
———
———

Q. 30

If full-time mentioned ask: what is the longest full-time course your firm would use?

<1w.	1w.	1-2w.	2w.	2w.-1m.	1m.	>1m.	d.k.	n.r.	n.a.
—	—	—	—	—	—	—	—	—	—

Q. 31

Could you give us a rough idea of the number of people you would send on courses in a year

Dublin: Full Time .... Other ....
Locally: Full Time .... Other ....

Q. 32

Having in mind seasonal peaks and holidays, what months of the year suit you best for courses?

No pref.	Jan./Feb.	March	April	May	June	July	Aug.	Sept.	Oct.	Nov.	Dec.
—	—	—	—	—	—	—	—	—	—	—	—

Q. 33

Both universities in Dublin are thinking of putting on courses in management subjects for fresh graduates or for people already in business. This would involve letting people off work. The course could be arranged in any of the following ways:

(a) Full time release, for at least 3 months
(b1) Sandwich-courses, some months on, some months off
(b2)   some weeks on, some week off
(c1) Part-release for some days each week
(c2)   for some hours each day

A. Would you be prepared to send any of your executives or potential executives on such a course? If yes, which?

yes	no	d.k.	n.r.	n.a.
—	—	—	—	—
a	b1	b2	c1	c2
—	—	—	—	—

B. How many?

———
———
———

C. If no: why would you not do so?

_____
_____
_____
_____
_____

Q. 34a
If the IMI were to introduce a spare-time diploma in management studies, is there anyone in your firm whom you would encourage to take it?

      yes   no   d.k.   n.r.   n.a.

      —   —   —   —   —

b. If yes: how many?

Q. 35
What would you say are the most important things that management training could cover for your firm?

_____
_____
_____
_____
_____
_____
_____
_____

Q. 36
Is the firm a member of I.M.I.   see front ....

Q. 37
Has it ever used I.M.I. courses   see front ....
If a member who never used courses ask

Q. 38
I've noticed from our records that no one from .... has ever come on one of our courses. Is there a particular reason for this?

_____
_____
_____

Q. 39
Can you suggest any changes we could make in our training efforts to make them more useful to your firm?

Content

_____

Location, Duration and Timing:

_____

Form:

_____

Lecturers:

_____

Other aspects:

_____

General Comment:

_____

Questionnaire Number
Now I'd like to ask some questions about ....

....

(*Name of Firm*)

Q. 40
How many people altogether are employed by your firm in the Republic of Ireland?
How many of these are supervisors as distinct from the managers whom we counted?

MANAGERS _____

SUPERVISORS _____

OTHERS _____

TOTAL

Q. 41
Would you describe it
as a family firm? ....

Q. 42
Is the chief executive one of the owners?

yes	no	d.k.	n.r.	n.a.
—	—	—	—	—

Q. 43
Is it a branch or subsidiary of another firm?

yes	no	d.k.	n.r.	n.a.
—	—	—	—	—

Q. 44
If yes, is the parent firm Irish, British or what?

Ir.	Br.	Other	d.k.	n.r.	n.a.
—	—	—	—	—	—

Q. 45
What products do you make? _____

_____

Interviewer classify:

mostly producer goods	mostly consumer goods	repair work
—	—	—
d.k.	n.r.	n.a.
—	—	—

Q. 46
Do you sell them:
—locally only
—outside this locality, but not over the whole Republic
—over the whole Republic, but not outside
—both inside and outside the Republic
—d.k.
—n.r.
—n.a.

Q. 47
Could you tell me what routine breakdowns of your sales figures you get?
—By each salesman
—by each product line
—by regional area
—by type of distributor
—by any other variable
—no breakdown
—d.k.
—n.r.
—n.a.

Q. 48
Do you get figures regularly to show the margin earned over cost?
—by each salesman
—by each product line
—by any other variable
—not at all
—d.k.
—n.r.
—n.a.

Q. 49
Have you ever made a formal study to discover the total market for each of your products

yes, some	yes, all	no	d.k.	n.r.	n.a.
—	—	—	—	—	—

Q. 50
And to discover your share of the total

yes, some	yes, all	no	d.k.	n.r.	n.a.
—	—	—	—	—	—

Q. 51
Have you broken down the total market by region or by any other factor (specify)

yes, some	yes, all	no	d.k.	n.r.	n.a.
—	—	—	—	—	—

Q. 52
And your market-share

yes, some	yes, all	no	d.k.	n.r.	n.a.
—	—	—	—	—	—

Q. 53
Have you ever made studies to find out anything else about your market, e.g.
Socio/economic class

Age structure

Motivation

Other (specify)

yes	no	d.k.	n.r.	n.a.
—	—	—	—	—

Q. 54
What means have you used to collect all this information?
Market Research survey   —
Desk research using official statistics   —
                    trade information —
                    internal reports —
                    other   —

Q. 55
Have you ever used market research surveys for any purpose?

yes	no	d.k.	n.r.	n.a.
—	—	—	—	—

Q. 56a
Have you forecast your total market and market share more than for 1 year ahead?

yes	no	d.k.	n.r.	n.a.
—	—	—	—	—

b. How?

Q. 57a
Do you make in advance firm sales plans for the year ahead?

yes	no	d.k.	n.r.	n.a.
—	—	—	—	—

b. Are they broken down by product, salesman, region, etc.?

Prod.	Salesmen	Region	Other	d.k.	n.r.	n.a.
—	—	—	—	—	—	—

If no to Q. 57a, ask

Q. 58
Do you set sales targets for salesmen?

yes	no	d.k.	n.r.	n.a.
—	—	—	—	—

Q. 59
Do you have a programme for training your salesmen in sales techniques, product and company knowledge, etc.?

Sales technique	Product knowledge	Company knowledge	Not at all
—	—	—	—

d.k.	n.r.	n.a.
—	—	—

Q. 60
Speaking of training, do you have a formal company programme of ensuring training for all staff?

yes	no	d.k.	n.r.	n.a.
—	—	—	—	—

Q. 61
Do you use regularly any way of selecting people other than by interview?

yes	no	d.k.	n.r.	n.a.
—	—	—	—	—

Q. 62
Do you have a formal scheme of performance appraisal for all staff?

yes	no	d.k.	n.r.	n.a.
—	—	—	—	—

Q. 63
Could you give me an outline of what your manufacturing processes involve — is it mainly:
—extraction
—repair work
—assembly only
—packaging only
—fabrication
—process
—d.k.
—n.r.
—n.a.

Q. 64a
Do they involve:
—making jobs specially to order
—making standard products in batches
—making standard products continuously
—repairs
—d.k.
—n.r.
—n.a.
—b.   Which accounts for most of your workers?

Q. 65
In your production ordering then, do you operate a stock replacement system or what?

Q. 66
If batch-production ask: do you order batches on an E.B.Q. basis, i.e. using formulae to determine size?

yes	no	d.k.	n.r.	n.a.
—	—	—	—	—

Q. 67
Do you use printed works orders, material requisitions, stock-cards, etc.?

w.o.	m.r.	s.c.	none	d.k.	n.r.	n.a.
—	—	—	—	—	—	—

Q. 68
Do you have a separate production planning and control department?

yes	no	d.k.	n.r.	n.a.
—	—	—	—	—

Q. 69a
Do you keep records of the load on your machines?

yes	no	d.k.	n.r.	n.a.
—	—	—	—	—

b.   Do you have standard methods and times for operations?

yes	no	d.k.	n.r.	n.a.
—	—	—	—	—

Q. 70
If yes: are these times and methods based on work study?

yes	no	d.k.	n.r.	n.a.
—	—	—	—	—

Q. 71
Have you ever used work study for any purpose?

yes	no	d.k.	n.r.	n.a.
—	—	—	—	—

Q. 72
Could you tell me what you do about quality control of your products?
a) Is inspection routine

yes	no	d.k.	n.r.	n.a.
—	—	—	—	—

b) based on specified standards?

yes	no	d.k.	n.r.	n.a.
—	—	—	—	—

c) Is it on finished products only, or all through process?
d) Is it 100%, statistical sample, neither

Finished product	Right through process	100%	Statistical sample	Neither
—	—		—	—

Q. 73
To switch over to the accounting side, do you have a formal system of cost-accounts?

yes	no	d.k.	n.r.	n.a.
—	—	—	—	—

Q. 74a
Has it been possible to introduce budgetary control?

yes	no	d.k.	n.r.	n.a.
—	—	—	—	—

b) or standard costing?

yes	no	d.k.	n.r.	n.a.
—	—	—	—	—

Q. 75
If no to budgetary control:
How often are trading and profit and loss accounts prepared?

Wkly.	1w-1m	mthly.	1-3 mths.	$\frac{1}{4}$-yrly.	$\frac{1}{2}$-yrly.	yrly.
—	—	—	—	—	—	—

Q. 76
What other financial or cost information do you get?

_____

_____

_____

b) How often?

Wkly.	1w-1m	mthly.	1-3 mths.	$\frac{1}{4}$-yrly.	$\frac{1}{2}$-yrly.	yrly.
		—	—	—	—	—

Q. 77
Do you prepare formal forecasts of your capital requirements?

yes	no	d.k.	n.r.	n.a.
—	—	—	—	—

b) If yes: how far ahead?

<1 yr.	1-2 yrs.	2-5 yrs.	5 yrs.	>5 yrs.
—	—	—	—	—

Q. 78

a) Do you prepare formal forecasts of your manpower requirements?

yes	no	d.k.	n.r.	n.a.
—	—	—	—	—

b) If yes: how far ahead?

<1 yr.	1-2 yrs.	2 yrs.	2-5 yrs.	5 yrs.	>5 yrs.

Q. 79

a) Are reports on the progress of individual depts. produced for the executive in charge?

yes	no	d.k.	n.r.	n.a.
—	—	—	—	—

Q. 79

b) If yes: how often?

wkly.	2 w.	mthly.	$\frac{1}{4}$ yr.	$\frac{1}{2}$ yr.
—	—	—	—	—

Q. 80

What regular reports or figures do you yourself get on the company's activities?

Sales	Prod.	Cost	Budgetary
d.w.m.	d.w.m.	w.4-w.m.	w.4-w.m.

Other

d.w.4-w.m. other

Q. 81

Has it been necessary yet to have statements of executive responsibility
—statements of current company policy
—statements of basic company objectives
—an organisation chart
—d.k.
—n.r.
—n.a.

Next Two Questions for Firms with <500 Employees Only

I'd like to ask a few questions which will help us compare Irish firms with firms
of the same size studied in the U.S. by the University of Minnesota.

Q. 82

Which of the following exist as separate units in your firm, i.e. as separate departments
with their own department heads:

PRODUCTION
—Overall only
—no separate department
—manufacturing
—prod. R & D inc. design
—industrial engineering
—prod. plan and control
—stores
—purchasing
—quality control

PERSONNEL
—Overall only
—no separate department

MARKETING
—Overall only
—no separate department
—selling
—market research
—advertising
—public relations
—transport

FINANCE AND OFFICE ADMINISTRATION
—Overall only
—no separate department
—accounting
—costing
—credits
—office administration
—legal and secretarial

Q. 83

Do you use outside agencies for any of the following services:
—auditing
—accounting
—legal
—production methods
—product research
—industrial design
—personnel
—employee selection and training
—labour relations and negotiations
—organisational planning
—marketing research
—advertising

Q. 84

a) In other words, you have/have not used industrial consultants?

used —   not used —   consultants

b) Have you put their recommendations into practice?

used —   not used —   recommendations

Q. 85

I have noticed from our records that your firm is not a member of IMI. Is there a reason for this?

_____
_____
_____
_____
_____
_____
_____

Q. 86   *Chief Executive*
Is there one?   Age
    yes   no   <30   30-44   45-54   55-64   65+
    —   —   —   —   —   —
             Nationality   Graduate
    Irish   Other   yes   no
    —   —   —   —
             Other Qualifications   Management Training
    yes   no   yes   no
                                                  —   —

Q. 87   *Marketing Manager*
Is there one?   Age
    yes   no   <30   30-44   45-54   55-64   65+
    —   —   —   —   —   —
             Nationality   Graduate
    Irish   Other   yes   no
    —   —   —   —
             Other Qualifications   Management Training
    yes   no   yes   no
    —   —   —   —

Q. 88   *Production Manager*
Is there one?   Age
    yes   no   <30   30-44   45-54   **55-64**   65+
    —   —   —   —   —
             Nationality   Graduate
    Irish   Other   yes   no
    —   —   —   —
             Other Qualifications   Management Training
    yes   no   yes   110
    —   —   —   —

Q. 89   *Finance Manager*
Is there one?   Age
    yes   no   <30   30-44   45-54   55-64   65+
    —   —   —   —   —   —
             Nationality   Graduate
    Irish   Other   yes   no
    —   —   —   —
             Other Qualifications   Management Training
    yes   no   yes   no
    —   —   —   —

Q. 90   *Personnel Manager*
Is there one?   Age
    yes   no   <30   30-44   45-54   55-64   65+
    —   —   —   —   —   —   —
             Nationality   Graduate
    Irish   Other   yes   no
    —   —   —   —
             Other Qualifications   Management Training
    yes   no   yes   no
    —   —   —   —

APPENDIX D

Branches of Economic Activity and Sources of Listings of Firms

The following associations were approached for lists in 1962-63 in order to cover the economic activity indicated. Their names and addresses were found in trade directories. Other associations have since been established.

1) *Activity covered by the Census of Industrial Production*

Industry	*Possible Sources of Lists*
Extraction	Central Statistics Office (CSO)
Manufacture	Central Statistics Office
Service:	
Building & Construction	Federation of Builders, Contractors and Allied Employers of Ireland
	Civil Engineering Contractors Association
	Federation of Master Painters
	Electrical Contractors Association (Incorp.)
	Flooring Specialists Association
	Master Glaziers Association
	Association of Master Plumbers, Heating and Ventilating Engineers of Ireland
Electricity	Electricity Supply Board
Gas	Irish Gas Association
Laundry	Trade Directories
Railway repairs	Coras Iompair Eireann

2) *Activity covered by the Census of Distribution*

Distribution: Retail	CSO, for firms with 50 or more employees
Grocery	Retail Grocery, Dairy & Allied Trades Association (RGDATA)
Grocery with Public House	RGDATA
	Irish County Vintners Association
Public Houses	Licensed Grocers and Vintners Association
Fresh Meat	Dublin Master Victuallers Association
Country General Shop	RGDATA
	Hardware & Allied Traders Association
Other Food, Drink & Tobacco	
Bread, Flour, Confectionery	Confectioners & Fruiterers Association
Dairy	Trade Directories
Fish & Poultry	National Retail Fish Merchants Association
Fruit & Vegetable	Trade Directories
Boots & Shoes	Trade Directories

415

Drapery & Apparel	National Federation of Drapers & Allied Traders Ltd.
	Drapers Chamber of Trade (Eire) Ltd.
Motor Vehicles & Cycles	Irish Motor Traders Association
	Irish Cycle Manufacturers Factors & Wholesale Traders
Garage & Filling Station	Trade Directories
Drugs	Irish Drug Association
Hardware	Hardware and Allied Traders Association of Ireland.
Other non-food	
Radio & Electrical	Electrical Federation of Ireland
	Society of Irish Electrical Traders
	Wireless Dealers Association
Jewellery, Watches, Clocks	Goldsmiths Corporation of Ireland
	Irish Jewellers Association
	Irish Watch & Clock Assemblers Association
Optical Goods	Trade Directories
Books, Stationery, not only newsagents	Irish Retail Newsagents, Booksellers and Stationers Association
	Irish Stationers Association
Furniture, carpets, etc.	Retail Association for the Furnishing Trade
Coal, Turf & other solid fuel	Irish Coal Importers Limited
	Eire Coal Importers Central Association
Leather, Sports & Fancy Goods	Toy and Fancy Goods Association
Dept. Stores, Variety, Chain	Trade Directories
Other non-food	Irish Seed & Nursery Trades Association
Distribution: *Wholesale*	CSO, for firms with 50 or more employees
Eggs & Poultry	Poultry Exporters Association
Groceries	Irish Wholesale Grocers Association
Tea, Coffee, Sugar	Tea Council of Ireland
	Wholesale Tea Association
Wines & Spirits	Wholesale Wine & Spirit Merchants Association
Fruit & Vegetables	Wholesale Fruit & Produce Merchants Association of Ireland Ltd.
	Wholesale Fruit Importers and Distributors Association
	Irish Potato Merchants Association
Other Food	Wholesale Confectioners (Sweets) Association
	Dublin Wholesale Confectioners Association
Boots & Shoes	Irish Wholesale Footwear Association
Other Clothing & Textiles	Irish Wholesale Drapers Association Ltd.
	Irish Wholesale Woollen Merchants Association
Motors & Accessories	Motor Traders (see Retail)
	Irish Cycle Manufacturers, Factors & Wholesale Traders Association
Petroleum	Trade Directories

Chemist & Photo	Wholesale Drug Federation of Ireland
Hardware & Electrical	Hardware and Allied Traders Association
	Wireless Dealers Association (see under retail)
	Electrical Contractors Association (see under service)
Builders' Suppliers	Irish Builders' Providers Association
	Association for Sub-contractors and Nominated Suppliers
Other:	Irish Wool Federation
Wool, skins, leather	Federation of Irish Fellmongers
	Irish Wholesale Woollen Merchants Association
	Irish Fellmongers Association
Grain & Forage	Irish Native Grain Traders Association
	Irish Wheat Association
Paper, Stationery & Books	Irish Stationers Association
Other non-food:	Irish Agrochemicals Association
	Irish Soft Drinks & Beer Bottlers Association
	Irish Fertilizer Importers Association
	Scrap Metal Merchants Association
	Native Timber Merchants Association
	Irish Timber Importers Association
	Irish Wholesale Tobacco & Match Traders Association
	Federated Association of Waste Material Dealers
Entertainment	
Cinema, Theatre	Irish Cinemas Association
	Theatre & Cinema Association of Ireland
Personal Service	
Hotels	Bord Failte
	Irish Hotels Federation
Catering	Trade Directories
Hairdressing, Bookmakers, Pawnshops	Trade Directories

3) *Activities not covered by Central Statistics Office Business Censuses.*

Insurance and Banks	Trade Directories
Transport	
Rail	Coras Iompair Eireann
Bus	Coras Iompair Eireann
Other Road	Licensed Road Transport Association
Sea	Irish Shipowners Association
Air	Aer Lingus. Others from trade directories
Cartage & Hauling	Licensed Road Transport Association
Canal	Coras Iompair Eireann
Loading Vessels	Trade Directories
Incidental	,,
Storage & Warehousing	,,
Professions	
Accountancy	Professional Institutes concerned
Engineers & Architects	Cumann na nInnealtoiri
Auctioneers	Irish Auctioneers Association
Advertising Agencies	Irish Association of Advertising Agencies
Sweepstakes	Trade Directories

APPENDIX E

Total Employed and Total Managers in Each Individual Firm Included in the Sample and Which Had Not Left its Assigned Size-Group

Total Employed (Managers & Others)	23	23	24	25	27	29	30	30	30	33	38	
Number of Managers	1	2	1	4	1	1	1	1	2	3	1	
Total Employed	40	40	40	40	42	45	47	47	48	48	50	50
Number of Managers	3	2	2	6	2	4	1	1	3	4	4	2
Total Employed	53	55	56	59	62	62	66	70	70	70	75	82
Number of Managers	3	12	4	4	4	2	3	2	4	3	3	4
Total Employed	86	90	90	90	92	95	97					
Number of Managers	5	1	3	6	6	5	4					

Total Employed	101	110	112	119	125	130	145	160	160	166
Number of Managers	7	12	2	5	5	2	8	7	9	6
Total Employed	180	184	200	200	203	203	207	210	220	222
Number of Managers	8	3	5	6	5	13	27	10	6	6
Total Employed	223	250	250	268	270	270	273	280	297	298
Number of Managers	11	10	14	6	6	8	8	10	4	6
Total Employed	298	298	300	300	320	350	351	351	372	395
Number of Managers	8	8	9	6	13	15	7	15	8	5
Total Employed	450	452	460	466						
Number of Managers	12	13	9	6						

Total Employed	550	564	650	650	652	653	654	658	673
Number of Managers	11	15	9	5	12	28	21	11	11
Total Employed	682	688	700	741	750	750	750	794	800
Number of Managers	15	20	16	23	13	19	29	19	15
Total Employed	800	858	900	906	913	941	950	968	986
Number of Managers	23	38	23	46	13	21	26	17	26
Total Employed	1111	1184	1217	1269	1269	1300	1409	1437	1547
Number of Managers	21	10	17	19	25	24	30	37	38
Total Employed	1599	1674	1718	1859	2221	3320	3998	3999	4257
Number of Managers	31	19	18	59	21	40	58	99	82

APPENDIX F

BIBLIOGRAPHY

The following books were consulted during the project. It was decided to classify them, but only very broadly. Books written for a specific area are classified accordingly. Those not so written are categorised under the heading "general".

MARKETING

Alexander, R. W., Cross, J. S. and Cunningham, R.M. *Industrial marketing.* Homewood (Ill.): Irwin, 1961, 658 p. *case studies.*

Crisp, R. D. *Marketing research.* New York: McGraw-Hill, 1957, 798 p. *bibliography.*

Ferber, R. and Verdoorn, P. J. *Research methods in economics and business.* New York: MacMillan, 1962, 573 p.

Lazo, H. and Corbin, A. *Management in marketing: text and cases.* New York: McGraw-Hill, 1961, 657 p.

Luck, D. J., Wales, H. G. and Taylor, D. A. *Marketing research: a comprehensive guide to modern techniques and applications with case problems.* 2nd edition. New Jersey: Prentice-Hall, 1961, 541 p.

The Market Research Society. *Marketing.* London: The Society, 1961, 74 p.

Newman, J. W. *Motivation research and marketing managment.* Boston: Harvard University Press, 1957.

Stacey, N. A. H. and Wilson, A. *Industrial marketing research: management and technique.* London: Hutchinson, 1958, 283 p.

PRODUCTION

Amber, G. H. and Amber, P. S. *Anatomy of automation.* New Jersey: Prentice-Hall, 1962, 245 p.

Burbidge, J. L. *The principles of production control.* London: MacDonald and Evans, 1962, 473 p. *glossary; tables; charts.*

Currie, R. M. *Work study.* London: Pitman, 1963, 251 p.

Eilon, Samuel. *Elements of production planning and control.* New York: MacMillan, 1962, 585 p.

International Labour Office. *Introduction to work study.* Geneva: ILO, 1959, 355 p.

Lockyer, K. G. *Factory management.* London: Pitman, 1962, 232 p.

MacNiece, E. H. *Production forecasting planning and control.* 3rd edition. New York: Wiley, 1961, 402 p.

Moore, F. G. *Production control.* New York: McGraw-Hill, 1959, 655 p.

Willsmore, A. W. *Modern production control.* London: Pitman, 1951, 185 p.

FINANCE AND OFFICE ADMINISTRATION

Broad, H. W. and Carmichael, K. S. *A guide to management accounting.* 2nd edition. London: H.F.L. (Publishers) Limited, 1960, 173 p.

Cave, S. R. *Budgetary control, standard costing and factory administration.* London: Gee, 1960, 211 p.

Goetz, B. E. *Management planning and control: a managerial approach to industrial accounting.* New York: McGraw-Hill, 1949, 295 p. *bibliography.*

Grillo, E. G. and Berg, C. J. *Work measurement in the office: a guide to clerical cost control.* New York: McGraw-Hill, 1959, 186 p.

The Institute of Cost and Works Accountants. *An introduction to budgetary control, standard costing, material control and production control.* London: The Institute, 1950, 55 p. *tables.*

Office Management Association. *Management of the smaller office by the Joint Office Management Committee of the Institute and Association.* London: British Institute of Management, 1951, 91 p. *tables; diagrams; bibliography.*

Rose, T. G. *Higher control in management.* London: Pitman, 1957, 303 p. *tables; charts.*

PERSONNEL MANAGEMENT

Jucius, M. J. *Personnel management.* 4th edition. Homewood (III.): Irwin, 1959, 763 p.

Northcott, C. H. *Personnel management: principles and practices.* London: Pitman, 1960, 417 p.

GENERAL

Argyris, Chris. *Integrating the individual and the organization.* New York: Wiley, 1964, 330 p.

Argyris, Chris. *Personality and organization: the conflict between system and the individual.* New York: Harper & Row, 1957, 291 p.

Argyris, Chris. *Understanding organizational behavior.* Homewood (Ill.): The Dorsey Press, 1960, 179 p.

Barnard, Chester I. *The functions of the executive.* Cambridge (Mass.): Harvard University Press, 1954, 334 p.

Bennet, C. L. *Defining the manager's job*: *the AMA manual of position descriptions*. New York: American Management Association, 1958, 446 p.

Beer, Stafford. *Cybernetics and management*. London: English Universities Press, 1959, 214 p.

Blau, R. M. and Scott, W. R. *Formal organizations*: *a comparative approach*. London: Routledge & Kegan Paul, 1963, 130 p.

Bonini, C. P., Jaedicke, R. K. and Wagner, H. M. *Management controls*: *new directions in basic research*. New York: McGraw-Hill, 1964, 341 p.

Boulding, K. E. and Spivey, W. A. *Linear programming and the theory of the firm*. New York: MacMillan, 1960, 227 p. *bibliography*.

Brech, E. F. L. *Organisation the framework of management*. London: Longmans Green, 1957, 424 p.

Brech, E. F. L. ed. *The principles and practice of management* by R. M. Aldrich, A. W. Field, J. Maddock and F. L. Woodroffe. London: Longmans, 1953, 752 p. *tables; diagrams; bibliography*.

British Institute of Management. *Information for decision-making; the statistics required by general management in different types of company*. Paper read by H. C. Rutherford, Scottish Management Conference, Gleneagles, May 3-5, 1957, 13 p. typescript.

British Institute of Management. *Management Techniques in the Smaller Enterprise*. London: The Institute, 1954, 36p.

Brown, Wilfred. *Exploration in management*. London: Heinemann, 1960, 326 p.

Brown, Wilfred. *Piecework abandoned*. London: Heinemann, 1962, 119 p.

Carlson, D. *Modern management principles and practice*. Paris: Organisation for Economic Co-operation and Development, 1962, 183 p.

Cartwright, D. and Zander, A. eds. *Group dynamics*: *research and theory*. 2nd edition. New York: Harper & Row, 1953, 809 p.

Chapple, E. D. and Sayles, L. R. *The measure of management; designing organizations for human effectiveness*. New York: MacMillan, 1961, 218 p.

Churchman, C. W., Ackoff, R. L. and Arnoff, E. L. *Introduction to operations research*. New York: Wiley, 645 p. *bibliography*.

Cooper, J. D. *The art of decision making*. New York: Doubleday, 1961, 394 p.

Dale, E. and Urwick, L. F. *Staff in organization*. New York: McGraw-Hill, 1960, 241 p.

Dalton, M. *Men who manage*. New York: Wiley, 1959, 318 p. *bibliography*.

Dean, Joel. *Managerial economics*. Englewood Cliffs (N.J.): Prentice-Hall, 1951, 621 p.

Drucker, P. F. *The practice of management*. London: Heinemann, 1955, 355 p.

Fayol, H. *General and industrial management*. London: Pitman, 1955, 110 p.

Follett, Mary P. *Dynamic administration*: *the collected papers of Mary Parker Follett*, edited by H. C. Metcalf and L. Urwick. New York: Harper, 1940, 320 p. *bibliography*.

Forrester, Jay W. *Industrial dynamics*. Published jointly by the Massachusetts Institute of Technology and John Wiley, New York, 1961, 464 p.

Fraser, J. M. *Psychology*: *general, industrial, social*. 2nd edition. London: Pitman, 1963, 336 p.

Granick, David. *The European executive*. London: Weidenfeld and Nicolson, 1962, 384 p.

Guilbaud, G. T. *What is cybernetics?* London: Heinemann, 1959, 126 p. *bibliography*.

Gulick, N. and Urwick, L. *Papers in the science of administration*. New York: Institute of of Public Administration, Columbia University, 1937.

Haire, Mason, ed. *Modern organization theory*: *a symposium of the Foundation for Research on Human Behavior*. New York: Wiley, 1959, 324 p.

Haire, Mason, ed. *Organization theory in industrial practice*: *a symposium of the Foundation for Research on Human Behavior*. New York: Wiley, 1962, 173 p.

Haire, Mason. *Psychology in management*. New York: McGraw-Hill, 1956, 212 p.

Jaques, Elliott. *The changing culture of a factory*: *a study of authority and participation in an industrial setting*. London: Tavistock, 1951, 341 p.

Jaques, Elliott. *Equitable payment*: *a general theory of work differential payment and individual progress*. London: Heinemann, 1961, 336 p. *bibliography*.

Jaques, Elliott. *Measurement of responsibility*: *a study of work, payment and individual capacity*. London: Tavistock, 1956, 139 p.

Jaques, Elliott. *Time-span handbook*: *how to use time-span of discretion to measure the level of work in employment roles and to arrange an equitable payment structure*. London: Heinemann, 1964, 133 p.

Landsberger, H. A. *Hawthorne revisted*: '*Management and the worker*' *its critics and developments in human relations in industry*. New York: Cornell University, 1958, 119 p.

Leavitt, H. J. ed. *The social science of organizations*: *four perspectives*. New Jersey: Prentice-Hall, 1963, 182 p.

Likert, Rensis. *New patterns of management*. New York: McGraw-Hill, 1961, 279 p.

Litterer, J. A. *Organizations*: *structure and behavior*. New York: Wiley, 1963, 415 p.

Lupton, T. *On the shop floor. Two studies of workshop organisation and output*. London: Pergamon Press, 1963, 208 p.

McGregor, Douglas. *The human side of enterprise*. New York: McGraw-Hill, 1960, 246 p.

Maier, N. R. F. *Problem-solving discussions and conferences: leadership methods and skills.* New York: McGraw-Hill, 1963, 261 p.

Maier, N. R. F. *Psychology in industry: a psychological approach to industrial problems.* 2nd edition. London: Harrap, 1955, 678 p.

March, J. G. and Simon, H. A. *Organizations.* New York: Wiley, 1958, 262 p. *bibliography.*

Mayo, Elton. *The human problems of an industrial civilization.* Boston (Mass.): Harvard University, 1933, 130 p.

Mayo, Elton. *The social problems of an industrial civilization.* London: Routledge & Keegan Paul, 1949, 148 p.

Newman, W. H. and Summer, C. E. Jnr. *The process of management: concepts, behavior and practice.* New Jersey: Prentice-Hall, 1961, 675 p.

Pfiffner, J. M. and Sherwood, F. P. *Administrative organization.* New Jersey: Prentice-Hall, 1960, 481 p.

Putnam, A. O., Barlow, E. R. and Stilian, G. N. *Unified operations management. A practical approach to the total systems concept.* New York: McGraw-Hill, 1963, 328 p.

Rice, A. K. *Productivity and social organization: the Ahmedabad experiment.* London: Tavistock, 1958, 298 p.

Rivett, P. and Ackoff, R. L. *A manager's guide to operational research.* New York: Wiley, 1963, 107 p.

Roethlisberger, F. J. and Dickson, W. J. *Management and the worker: an account of a research program conducted by the Western Electric Company, Hawthorne Works, Chicago.* Cambridge (Mass.): Harvard University Press, 1950, 615 p.

Shartle, C. L. *Executive performance and leadership.* London: Staples Press, 1957, 302 p.

Simon, H. A. *The new science of management decision.* New York: Harper, 1960, 50 p.

Simon, H. A. *Administrative behavior: a study of decision-making processes in administrative organization.* New York: MacMillan, 1955, 259 p.

Strother, G. B., Argyris, C., Dubin, R., Haire, M. and others. eds. *Social science approaches to business behavior.* London: Tavistock, 1962, 183 p.

Tannenbaum, R., Weschler, I. R. and Massarik, F. *Leadership and organization: a behavioral science approach.* New York: McGraw-Hill, 1961, 455 p. *bibliography.*

Taylor, F. W. *Scientific management.* New York: Harper & Bros., 1911, 287 p.

Urwick, L. *The elements of administration.* London: Pitman, 1947, 132 p. *diags.; tables.*

Urwick, L. and Brech, E. F. L. *The making of scientific management.* 3 vols. London: Pitman. *Vol.* 1. Thirteen pioneers, reprinted 1951, 196 p. *Vol.* 2. Management in British industry, reprinted 1953, 241 p. *Vol.* 3. The Hawthorne investigations, reprinted 1952, 225 p.

Walker, C. R. and Guest, R. H. *The man on the assembly line.* Boston (Mass.): Harvard University Press, 1952, 180 p. *tables; diags.*

MANAGEMENT DEVELOPMENT

The Acton Society Trust. *The Arts graduate in industry.* London: Acton Society Trust, 1962, 103 p.

Edwards, Sir Ronald. *Universities and the world of business.* London: British Institute of Management, March, 1965, 19 p. (First Urwick Lecture, Brighton, March, 1965.).

Koontz, H. *Requirements for basic and professional education for scientific management.* London: British Institute of Management, 1964, 32 p.

Organisation for Economic Co-Operation and Development. *Development of a body of management teachers.* Paris: OECD, 1962, 45 p.

Organisation for Economic Co-Operation and Development. *Issues in management education.* Paris: OECD, 1963, 92 p.

Organisation for Economic Co-Operation and Development. *Training of technicians in Ireland.* Paris: OECD, 1964, 112 p.

Silberston, A. *Education and training for industrial management.* London: Management Publications, 1955, 101 p.

RESEARCH BACKGROUND

Ackoff, R. L., Gupta, S. K. and Minas, J. S. *Scientific method: optimizing applied research decisions.* New York, Wiley, 1962, 464 p.

Committee on Industrial Organisation. *Reports of the Committee 1962-65.* Dublin: The Stationery Office.

Copeman, G., Luijk, H. and Hanika, F. de P. *How the executive spends his time.* London: Business Publications, 1963, 149 p.

Ingham, H. and Harrington, L. T. *Interfirm comparison for management.* London: British Institute of Management, 1958, 70 p.

International Labour Office. *International standard classification of occupations.* Geneva: ILO, 1962, 235 p.

Universite Catholique De Louvain. *Centre de Perfectionnement dans la direction des entreprises.* Les dirigeants d'entreprise de l'economie Belge by M. Woitrin, P. L. Mandy, G. de Ghellinck and P. Duvieusart. Bruxelles: Office Belge Pour L'Accroissement de la Productivite, 1960, 367 p.

Woodward, Joan. *Management and technology.* London: Her Majesty's Stationery Office, 1958, 40 p. (Problems of Progress in Industry—3).

The references to works on statistical method are at the end of Appendix B.

THE CONSULTATIVE BOARD OF THE IRISH MANAGEMENT INSTITUTE